Modern Database Systems

The Object Model, Interoperability, and Beyond

WON KIM, *Editor*

ACM Press
New York, New York

Addison-Wesley Publishing Company

Reading, Massachusetts • Menlo Park, California • New York
Don Mills, Ontario • Wokingham, England • Amsterdam • Bonn
Sydney • Singapore • Tokyo • Madrid • San Juan • Milan • Paris

Publishing Partner: Peter S. Gordon
Associate Editor: Helen M. Goldstein
Associate Production Supervisor: Amy Willcutt
Copyeditor: Karen Stone
Proofreaders: Cheryl Metzger, Teresa Robeck
Manufacturing Manager: Roy Logan

Library of Congress Cataloging-in-Publication Data

Modern database systems : the object model, interoperability, and beyond / Won Kim, editor.
p. cm.
Includes bibliographical references and index.
ISBN 0–201–59098–0
1. Object-oriented data bases. 2. Relational data bases.
I. Kim, Won.
QA76.9.D3M643 1995
005.75—dc20 93-36405
CIP

1 2 3 4 5 6 7 8 9 10-MA-9897969594

Preface

This book brings together in a single volume a discussion of many of the issues that must be addressed in order to solve two technical challenges facing database system users (end users and application developers) in the 1990s:

- The transition from relational database technology to postrelational technology
- Provision for the coexistence and interoperability of old and new database technologies.

Since the 1960s, the technology for managing data has evolved from file systems to hierarchical, to network, to relational. The 1980s were a gestation period for the new-generation technology. There was a flurry of activity to develop database systems that could meet the following requirements:

- Support an object-oriented data model
- Provide an architecture that easily can accommodate various functional extensions
- Support the management of, among others, temporal data (history and versioning), spatial data, multimedia data, long-duration transactions, imprecise data, and rules

This activity was fueled by the emergence of database applications that today's commercial relational database systems cannot support to the desired level of productivity in application development and run-time performance. Today, however, there is almost enough knowledge to develop commercially viable next-generation systems. Thus, the first challenge to meet in the 1990s is the transition from relational database technology to postrelational database technology.

However, next-generation systems so far have not replaced older-generation systems. This has led to the coexistence of database systems of all generations. Therefore, the second database challenge of the 1990s is to bring about interoperability of the database and file systems installed worldwide during the past three decades.

In the 1980s, database vendors began offering gateways that allowed relational database applications to retrieve data from nonrelational database systems or file systems. At the same time, database researchers worked to lay a foundation for building multidatabase systems—systems providing a single database view over various independently developed database and file systems. Such systems will allow users to access various databases and files in one, uniform database language without the users' being aware of the heterogeneity of the underlying systems. Here, too, there is almost enough knowledge to develop commercially viable systems.

This book, rather than being a mere collection of already published papers, is a compendium of contributions that are largely original. I specifically solicited the chapters from leading database researchers, database developers, and industry experts, and edited each chapter for technical accuracy and uniform style of presentation. Space limitations prevented me from giving a more in-depth treatment to each topic, but I believe each has been covered sufficiently to give the reader a good grounding on the subject. Each chapter includes a comprehensive overview of the issue covered, proposed solutions to problems, and directions for further research and development. I hope this book will help readers understand the current status of the database field and where it should go.

I enjoyed working with the expert contributors, and thank them for their submissions. I also want to thank Helen Goldstein of Addison-Wesley Publishing Company, Inc., and Nhora Cortes-Comerer of ACM Press Books, both of whom worked with me from conception through final production of this book. Finally, I want to thank Janelle Larson and Catherine Richardson for painstakingly converting the chapters, which were received from the contributors in many different formats, into a single uniform style in Framemaker. Their work reduced the production schedule by as much as six months.

W.K.

Contributing Authors and Their Addresses (in alphabetical order)

Rafiul Ahad
Hewlett-Packard Laboratory
1501 Page Mill Road
Palo Alto, CA 94304-1181

Timothy Andrews
Ontos
3 Burlington Woods
Burlington, MA 01803

Jurgen Annevelink
Hewlett-Packard Laboratory
1501 Page Mill Road
Palo Alto, CA 94304-1181

Walid G. Aref
Dept. of Computer Science
University of Maryland
College Park, MD 20742-3411

Jose A. Blakeley
Computer Science Center
Texas Instruments
P.O. Box 655474
Dallas, TX 75265

Yuri Breitbart
Computer Science Department
University of Kentucky
Lexington, KY 40506

Amelia Carlson
Hewlett-Packard Laboratory
1501 Page Mill Road
Palo Alto, CA 94304-1181

Injun Choi
Department of Industrial Engineering
Pohang Institute of Technology
Pohang, S. Korea

Stavros Christodoulakis
Electronic and Computer Engineering Department
Technical University of Crete
73100 Chania
Crete, Greece

Jim Davis
Hewlett-Packard Laboratory
1501 Page Mill Road
Palo Alto, CA 94304-1181

Umeshwar Dayal
Hewlett-Packard Laboratory
1501 Page Mill Road
Palo Alto, CA 94304-1181

Klaus Dittrich
Universität Zürich
Institut für Informatik
Winterthürstrasse 190
CH-8057 Zürich
Switzerland

Weimin Du
Hewlett-Packard Laboratory
1501 Page Mill Road
Palo Alto, CA 94304-1181

Daniel Fishman
Hewlett-Packard Laboratory
1501 Page Mill Road
Palo Alto, CA 94304-1181

Sunit Gala
UniSQL, Inc.
9390 Research Blvd.
Austin, TX 78759

Hector Garcia-Molina
Department of Computer Science
Stanford University
Stanford, CA 94305

Jorge F. Garza
UniSQL, Inc.
9390 Research Blvd.
Austin, TX 78759

Nathan Goodman
The Whitehead Institute
9 Cambridge Center
Cambridge, MA 02142

Bruce Graham
UniSQL, Inc.
9390 Research Blvd.
Austin, TX 78759

Eric Hanson
Department of Computer and Information Sciences
University of Florida
Gainesville, FL 32611

Mike Heytens
Hewlett-Packard Laboratory
1501 Page Mill Road
Palo Alto, CA 94304-1181

Mei Hsu
Digital Equipment Corporation
529 Bryant Street
Palo Alto, CA 94301

Gail E. Kaiser
Department of Computer Science
Columbia University
New York, NY 10027

William Kelley
UniSQL, Inc.
9390 Research Blvd.
Austin, TX 78759

Alfons Kemper
Lehrstuhl für Informatik III
Rhein-Wesff. Technical Hochschule
Ahornstrasse 55
D-5100 Aachen, Germany

William Kent
Hewlett-Packard Laboratory
1501 Page Mill Road
Palo Alto, CA 94304-1181

Won Kim
UniSQL, Inc.
9390 Research Blvd.
Austin, TX 78759

Angelika Kotz-Dittrich
Union Bank of Switzerland
Zürich, Switzerland

Leonidas Koveos
Electronic and Computer Engineering Department
Technical University of Crete
73100 Chania
Crete, Greece

Vincent J. Kowalski
Petrotechnical Open Software Corporation
10777 Westheimer, Suite 275
Houston, TX 78042

David Krieger
Ontos
3 Burlington Woods
Burlington, MA 01803

Teresa F. Lunt
Computer Science Laboratory
Stanford Research International
333 Ravenwood Ave.
Menlo Park, CA 94025

Weiyi Meng
Department of Computer Science
State University of New York
Binghamton, NY 13902

Guido Moerkotte
Fakultat für Informatik
Universitat Karlsruhe
D-76128 Karlsruhe, Germany

Amihai Motro
Department of Information Systems and Systems Engineering
George Mason University
4400 University Drive
Fairfax, VA 22030

Edward Omiecinski
College of Computing
Georgia Institute of Technology
Atlanta, GA 30332-0280

M. Tamer Ozsu
Department of Computing Science
University of Alberta
Edmonton, Alberta, Canada T6G2H1

Tom Reyes
UniSQL, Inc.
9390 Research Blvd.
Austin, TX 78759

Marek Rusinkiewicz
Computer Science Department
University of Houston
Houston, TX 77204-3475

Hanan Samet
Department of Computer Science
University of Maryland
College Park, MD 20742-3411

Mark Scheevel
UniSQL, Inc.
9390 Research Blvd.
Austin, TX 78759

Ming-Chien Shan
Hewlett-Packard Laboratory
1501 Page Mill Road
Palo Alto, CA 94304-1181

Amit Sheth
Bell Communications Research
444 Hoes Lane
Piscataway, NJ 08854

Avi Silberschatz
AT&T Bell Laboratories
600 Mountain Ave.
Murray Hill, NJ 07974

Richard Snodgrass
Department of Computer Science
University of Arizona
Tucson, AZ 85721

Richard Mark Soley
Object Management Group
492 Old Connecticut Path
Framingham, MA 01701

Ralph L. Stout
Information Builders, Inc.
1250 Broadway
New York, NY 10001

Craig Thompson
Computer Science Center
Texas Instruments
P.O. Box 655474
Dallas, TX 75265

Jennifer Widom
Department of Computer Science
Stanford University
Stanford, CA 94305

Clement Yu
Department of Electrical
Engineering and Computer
Science
University of Illinois
Chicago, IL 60680

Contents

PART I

Next-Generation Database Technology

PART Ia

Object-Oriented Database

1

Introduction to Part 1: Next-Generation Database Technology

1.1 Overview

1.1.1 Object-Oriented Database Systems

During the past decade, the nature of database applications has rapidly undergone changes from simple applications to complex applications. Simple applications retrieve a small number of flat records that contain numeric and short symbolic data. Besides the numeric and short symbolic data that simple applications have dealt with, complex applications store and retrieve complex nested data (e.g., bills of materials), compound data (e.g., sets, arrays, structures), and multimedia data (e.g., images, audios, texts). Today's best relational database systems can support neither the productivity requirement in developing complex applications nor the performance requirement in running such applications.

During the past several years, two generations of object-oriented database systems (OODBs) and associated tools have been introduced to the market, partly in response to the anticipated growth in the use of object-oriented programming languages and partly as an attempt to address some of the key deficiencies of relational database systems that are due to the inherent restrictions in the relational model of data. The first- and second-generation object-oriented database systems available today are, more accurately, persistent storage managers for object-oriented programming languages (OOPLs) and object-oriented databases with full support for ANSI SQL (or a unified relational and object-oriented system), respectively. The emerging consensus in the field is that the latter is the basis of the mainstream post-relational database technology.

A persistent storage manager for an OOPL is a file system that automatically stores on disk each object created in an object-oriented program and, after the program terminates, automatically fetches any stored object on demand by another program. This type of OODB includes almost all of the first crop of OODBs. OODBs of this type also include various database features, such as a simple query language, access methods such as hashing and clustering, transaction management, and concurrency control and recovery.

These systems are not compatible with relational database systems (RDBs) and lack many of the major database features polished in RDBs, such as a full nonprocedural query language, meta data management, views, and authorization. One benefit of this type of system initially perceived is the seamless interface between an OOPL and a database system; that is, OOPL programmers would not need to learn a separate database language. As long as persistent storage management is the only objective of such a system, the benefit is more or less achievable. However, if all or most of the database features that match the mission-critical database features that have been incorporated into RDBs during the past decade are to be added, seamlessness is no longer feasible.

A unified relational and object-oriented system extends the relational model with core object-oriented concepts found in OOPLs. Core object-oriented concepts include encapsulation of data and programs into an object, object identity, multiple inheritance, arbitrary data types, and nested objects. An OODB of this type extends the ANSI SQL relational language and corresponding call-level interface into an object-oriented SQL and corresponding call-level interface. Application developers use the object-oriented SQL and call-level interface within any host programming language (such as C). This type of OODB brings the benefits of an object-oriented technology to non-object-oriented programming languages in the management of a database. Further, although this type of OODB is not wedded to any specific OOPL, it is not difficult to develop an OOPL interface layer on top of the database system. The combination of an OOPL interface layer and a unified relational and object-oriented database system running underneath it is essentially a persistent storage manager, with full database features, for the OOPL.

Now relational database vendors are planning to augment their database systems and tools with object-oriented database design and management facilities. At the same time, first-generation object-oriented database vendors are planning to augment their systems with a query language that is compatible with ANSI SQL. The ANSI SQL-3 standards committee is attempting to extend ANSI SQL-2 with object-oriented data modeling and query facilities, while the Object Data Management Group, a loose consortium of five object-oriented database vendors, is actively working to forge a base proposal for an object-oriented database language.

There is a general agreement in the database market today that the foundation of the post-relational database technology is a unified relational and object-oriented database system; that is, a relational database system extended with the concepts of encapsulation (methods), arbitrary data types, nested objects, and inheritance; or an object-oriented database system extended with ANSI-SQL-compatible non-procedural query language and all major database features found in today's relational database systems (such as automatic query optimization, views, constraints, meta data management, authorization, triggers, transaction management, two-phase commit, parameterized performance tuning, etc.).

Database systems are tools that application developers use to develop applications, and database run-times are embedded in such applications. As such, if a database system lacks an important facility, application developers must implement the facility within the application. Today's database systems, both relational and object-oriented systems, lack some major facilities that are often required in application development or in supporting application executions, including, for example, facilities for multimedia data management, long-duration transaction management, spatial data management, temporal data management (history data and versioning). These have been subjects of extensive research for 10 to 20 years, but there are very few commercial database systems that support these facilities.

I believe that next-generation database systems will be built on a unified relational and object-oriented data model with support for management of multimedia data, long-duration transactions, spatial data, temporal data, and the like. In other words, even second-generation OODBs are not the ultimate database technology, and they must be augmented with the additional facilities that are orthogonal to object-oriented concepts. I will review these issues and offer my own views on the directions of research and development, to complement the views that invited authors offer and amplify in their respective chapters.

1.1.2 Beyond Objects

Multimedia Data Management

There is a growing trend in the computer industry to provide support for nonnumeric data. The availability of low-cost data capture devices (digital cameras, digital scanners, digital audio, etc.), combined with low-cost mass storage (digital audio tape, optical disk media) and high-resolution display devices, has ushered in new classes of computer applications that manage multimedia data. Multimedia applications extend and apply the hypertext concept to a wide variety of data types beyond textual data to audio data, image data, video data, and animation.

Most of the current commercial database systems suffer from an inability to manage arbitrary types of data, arbitrarily large data, and data stored on devices other than magnetic disks. They understand a relatively limited set of data types, such as integer, real, date, monetary unit, short strings, and BLOBs (binary large objects). Further, they are not designed to manage data stored on such increasingly important storage devices as CD-ROMs and video disks.

Broadly, *multimedia data* means arbitrary data types and data from arbitrary data sources. Arbitrary data types include the numeric data and short string data supported in conventional database systems; large unstructured data such as text, image, audio, graphics, video, animation, and so on; complex structured data, such as charts, graphs, tables, and arrays; and compound documents that are comprised of such data. Arbitrary data sources include a native database; external (remote) databases; host file base; data input, storage, and presentation (output) devices; and even data-generating and data-consuming programs (such as a text processing system).

The above definition of multimedia data leads to an enumeration of the requirements for multimedia data management, as follows:

1. The ability to represent arbitrary data types (including compound documents) and specification of procedures (programs) that interact with arbitrary data sources.
2. The ability to query, update, insert, and delete multimedia data (including retrieval of multimedia data via associative search within multimedia data: minimally, text).
3. The ability to specify and execute abstract operations on multimedia data; for example, to play, fast forward, pause, and rewind such one-dimensional data as audio and text; to display, expand, and condense such two-dimensional data as a bit-mapped image.
4. The ability to deal with heterogeneous data sources in a uniform manner; this includes access to data in these sources and migration of data from one data source to another.

The fact that multimedia data management requires dealing with large unstructured data, besides the conventional small data, implies changes in the unit of concurrency control and authorization. The unit of concurrency control in conventional database systems is often a page or even a table rather than a single record. The unit of authorization in conventional database systems is usually an entire table or a column of a table but never a single record. In a multimedia environment, a single object, such as a single compound document, is the logical unit of access, and as such the unit of concurrency control and authorization in database systems that support multimedia data should really be a single object (comparable to a single record in a relational database).

Multimedia data sources, such as a satellite feed, often produce data at a rate that a database system cannot process in real-time. The relationship between a database system and multimedia data sources needs a closer examination, so that perhaps to some extent real-time data input and output may be combined with database processing (queries and updates).

There are situations when it becomes desirable to synchronize the presentation of data to the user. One example of this is the synchronization of audio data with visual data in a multimedia display. The need for synchronization creates a time-line dependency between the data and the actual presentation of the data. This implies a level of cooperation between the different presentation mechanisms for the different types of data. To some degree, this is an application-specific problem because each multimedia application will have different synchronization requirements.

Long-Duration Transactions

The objective of long-duration transactions is to model long-duration, interactive database access sessions in application environments. The fundamental assumption about short duration of transactions that underlies the traditional model of transactions is inappropriate for long-duration transactions. The implementation of the traditional model of transactions may cause intolerably long waits when transactions attempt to acquire locks before accessing data and may also cause a large amount of work to be lost when transactions are backed out in response to user-initiated aborts or system failure situations.

The literature is rich with proposals for long-duration transaction management. However, there exists confusion about long-duration transactions. There are two reasons for this. First, there is a variety of flavors of long-duration transactions, including transactions by interactive users, transactions among cooperating users, just plain long transactions, transactions that are really sequences of well-defined subtransactions, transactions that correspond to a hierarchical organization of users in terms of their roles, and so on. Second, proposed models of long-duration transactions have largely been developed to allow flexibility of interaction among users, without consideration of any consistency criterion that they may have to satisfy.

The objective of a transaction model is to provide a rigorous basis for automatically enforcing a criterion for database consistency for a set of multiple concurrent read and write accesses to the database in the presence of potential system failure situations. The consistency criterion adopted for traditional transactions is the notion of serializability. Serializability is enforced in conventional database systems through the use of locking for automatic concurrency control and logging for automatic recovery from system failure situations. A "transaction" that does not provide a basis for automatically enforcing database consistency is not really a transaction. To be sure, a long-duration transaction need not adopt serializability as its consistency criterion; however, there must be some consistency criterion.

There are two fundamentally different models of long-duration, interactive database access sessions: single-database model and multiple-database model. The single-database model captures the situations where multiple transactions should share a single common database. The multiple-database model addresses situations where multiple transactions should operate with multiple databases.

The single-database model has received considerably more attention than the multiple-database model. The focus of research into the single-database model has been on addressing the twin problems of long waits and loss of work that the long duration of transactions brings about.

The multiple-database model is represented by proposals for shared and private database architectures, checkout and checkin of data to and from shared and private databases. Each user may populate his or her private database with data checked out of the shared database, perform updates against the data, and check them back into the shared database.

The single-database model requires the introduction of a notion of database consistency, and protocols for concurrency control and recovery, that are different from those supported in traditional database systems. If a reasonable notion of database consistency is to be supported (i.e., the database system is to enforce it automatically), there are bound to be conflict situations where one transaction comes into an access conflict against some other transaction. If a wait is to be avoided, some means of a negotiated settlement of the conflict must be provided, thereby dragging the users into the details of concurrency control. The single-database model is more appropriate than the multiple-database model in an environment where it is difficult to determine in advance logical partitions of the database that correspond to work to be performed and where the users closely cooperate.

The multiple-database model can be used to work around the conflict situations inherent in long-duration database sessions. Since each user may copy data from the shared database and work against his or her private database, "disconnected" from the shared database (at least on the surface), the users can avoid the conflict situations. In particular, multiple users may be simultaneously updating the "same" data, without having to wait for other users to complete their updates. However, when updated data is to be checked into the shared database, it may have to be checked in as a new version, necessitating version management. Further, when data in a private database reference data in the shared data, or vice versa, a private database is not really disconnected from the shared database. For example, the evaluation of a query in general will require the database system to access both a private database and the shared database, even if the query may have been formulated against a private database. The multiple-database model is more appropriate than the single-database model in an environment where it is easy to determine in advance logical partitions of the database that correspond to work to be performed and where the users do not or cannot cooperate.

The two models of long-duration transactions are both valid; one is more appropriate than the other in different situations. As such, in a general-purpose database system, both models should be supported. The single-database and multiple-database dichotomy is analogous to the single-version and multi-version approaches in database concurrency control.

There have been various proposals for nested transactions. A nested transaction is the transaction equivalent of a nested complex object in data modeling. A transaction may recursively spawn (fork) one or more subtransactions, and the subtransactions may execute in parallel and commit/abort independently of one another. Nested transactions are primarily mechanisms for exploiting parallelism inherent in computations; they were not originally proposed as a means of addressing the requirements of long-duration transactions. However, the possibility of mapping the hierarchical structure of a group of interactive database users (e.g., the organizational structure of a company, contractor and subcontractors, etc.) to a nested transaction motivated various proposals of nested transactions in the context of long-duration, interactive database sessions. These proposals all presume a single database and may be regarded as a variation of the single-database model that maps individual transactions to users in a hierarchical structure in terms of the roles they play within a cooperative project involving database accesses. The nesting of transactions, although clearly useful, adds another dimension of difficulty, in terms of both semantics and implementation.

The most urgent research issue in long-duration transactions is to establish a taxonomy of cooperating transactions (including hierarchical organizations of transactions). The resulting taxonomy, along with the models of database consistency, can then be used to guide the design and implementation of one or more worthy models of cooperating transactions. The taxonomy should be based on a careful consideration of the type and importance of the application environment for which a particular proposal has been designed and the model of database consistency the proposal implies. If a particular proposal implies no consistency, it should be discarded. If a proposal aims at a narrow area of application, it too should be discarded.

Spatial Data Management

Spatial data management has been an active area of research in the database field for two decades, with much of the research being focused on developing data structures for storing and indexing spatial data. However, very few commercial database systems provide facilities for directly defining and storing spatial data and for formulating queries based on search conditions on spatial data. I believe the following are the relevant issues on which near-term research should be focused (in the order of decreasing importance and urgency).

First, relational query optimization techniques need to be extended to deal with spatial queries, that is, queries that contain search conditions on spatial data. In particular, a reasonable cost model for computing the selectivity of spatial predicates needs to be developed.

Second, more work needs to be done on data structures and algorithms for performing a much broader set of operations (e.g., intersection, neighbor search) than just a few operations (e.g., exact match) that have typically been used to guide development of spatial index structures.

Third, it is difficult to build into a single database system multiple data structures for spatial indexing and all spatial operators that are useful for a wide variety of spatial applications; as such, it is desirable to build a database system so that it will be as easy as possible to extend the system with additional data structures and spatial operators.

Temporal Data Management

There are two components to temporal data management: history data management and version management. Both have been the subjects of research for over a decade. The troublesome aspect of temporal data management is that the boundary between applications and database systems has not been clearly drawn. Specifically, it is not clear how much of the typical semantics and facilities of temporal data management can and should be directly incorporated in a database system and how much should be left to applications and users. In the following, I will provide a list of short-term research issues that should be examined to shed light on this fundamental question.

The focus of research into history data management has been on defining the semantics of time and time interval and on issues related to understanding the semantics of queries and updates against history data stored in an attribute of a record. Typically, in the context of relational databases, a temporal attribute is defined to hold a sequence of history data for the attribute. A piece of history data consists of a data item and a time interval for which the data item is valid. A query may then be issued to retrieve history data for a specified time interval for the temporal attribute.

In the absence of a support for temporal attributes, application developers who need to model and manage history data have simply simulated temporal attributes by creating attribute(s) for the time interval, along with the "temporal" attribute. This of course may result in duplication of records in a table and more complicated search predicates in queries. The one necessary topic of research in history data management is to quantitatively establish the performance (and even productivity) differences between using a database system that directly supports temporal attributes and using a conventional database system that does not support either the set-valued attributes or temporal attributes. If it can be convincingly established that the benefits of a database system that supports temporal attributes are substantial, database vendors will be strongly motivated to augment their systems with history data management.

Despite a large number of proposals on version support in the context of computer-aided design and software engineering, the absence of a consensus on version semantics has been a key impediment to version support in database systems. Because of the differences between files and databases, it is intuitively clear that the model of versions in database systems cannot be as simple as that adopted in file systems to support software engineering. For databases, it may be necessary to manage not only versions of single objects (e.g., a software module, a document, etc.) but also versions of a collection of objects (e.g., a compound document, a user manual, etc.) and perhaps even versions of the schema of a database (e.g., a table or a class, a collection of tables or classes).

Broadly, there are three directions of research and development in versioning. First is the notion of a parameterized versioning, that is, designing and implementing a versioning system whose behavior may be tailored by adjusting system parameters. This may be the only viable approach, in view of the fact that there are various plausible choices for virtually every single aspect of versioning (e.g., updatability and deletability of versions, version identifier, version timestamp, version-derivation hierarchy). The second is to revisit these plausible choices for every aspect of versioning, with the view to discarding some of them as either impractical or flawed. The third is the investigation into the semantics and implementation of versioning collections of objects and versioning the database schema.

1.2 Organization of Part 1

Part 1 of this book consists of two major subparts, Part 1a and Part 1b. Part 1a focuses on the current status and research and development agenda for object-oriented database technology. In my view, object-oriented database technology, in combination with the relational database technology, is the basis of the next-generation database technology. As such, a critical examination of the current technological status, experiences, and clearly emerging trends in object-oriented database technology is provided first. I have purposely omitted any chapters that describe first-generation commercial OODBs, since they are being supplanted by second-generation OODBs. Part1b deals with the research and development agenda for the next-generation database technology beyond unification of relational and object-oriented database technologies. The agenda includes several subjects of longstanding research and prototyping whose results have not been widely incorporated into commercial database products, including management of multimedia data, spatial data, temporal data, active data, and long-duration transactions. It also includes issues of database management in a distributed and parallel architecture, whose importance is expected to grow in the foreseeable future.

Part 1a consists of four subparts: object data model, database languages, architectural issues impacted by the object model, and experiences with early object-oriented database systems and clearly emerging trends for the next wave of systems. The first subpart, Chapter 2, provides a description of the core object-oriented data model developed by member companies that form the Object Management Group consortium. The core object-oriented data model consists of concepts found in object-oriented programming languages, such as encapsulation, arbitrary data types, and multiple inheritance. The model serves as the core of the full data model that needs to be supported in next-generation database systems. The full data model should augment the core data model with considerations of temporal and spatial dimensions to data.

The second subpart of Part 1a, Chapters 3 through 6, deals with nonprocedural query languages that capture the core object data model. A database language represents a concrete embodiment of the concepts included in a data model. The chapters in this subpart show how many of the concepts included in the core object-oriented data model described in Chapter 2 may interact and be embodied in a database query language and how a database language may be integrated into an object-oriented programming language. Chapter 3, titled "Object SQL—A Language for the Design and Implementation of Object Databases," discusses the principles underlying the SQL-like object-oriented query language supported in the OpenODB object-oriented database product from Hewlett-Packard. Chapter 4, titled "OQL[C++]: Extending C++ with an Object Query Capability," discusses issues in designing a SQL-like query language as an extension to the C++ programming language; the issues arise from the mismatch between a programming language in general and a database query language—in particular, the nonprocedural nature of a database query language and the procedural nature of a programming language as well as the need to deal with a set of objects in the result of a query and the inability of a programming language to accommodate it. Chapter 5, titled "C++ Bindings to an Object Database," discusses how persistent storage facilities may be integrated with the C++ object-oriented programming language to provide the basis of a seamless interaction between a programming language and a database language. Chapter 6, titled "On View Support in Object-Oriented Database Systems," explores key semantic and implementation issues that arise in supporting views in object-oriented database systems—issues include whether views should form an inheritance hierarchy, whether such an inheritance hierarchy should be separate from an inheritance hierarchy of classes, and whether a view may be used as the domain of an attribute of a view or a class. A view may be used as a unit of authorization in object-oriented database systems just as in relational database systems. Further, views constitute the external schema in a three-schema architecture for object-oriented database systems, comparable to that for relational database systems.

The third subpart of Part 1a, Chapters 7 through 10, explores architectural aspects of a database system that require changes due to the data modeling concepts that an object-oriented data model introduces, such as multiple inheritance, methods, arbitrary data types, and nested objects. These concepts impact various aspects of a database system architecture, including authorization, concurrency control, query optimization and processing, physical data structures for storing and accessing a database, and so on. Further, an object-oriented database system requires a new performance benchmark that reflects its new capabilities. Such widely used benchmarks as the TPC benchmark and the Wisconsin benchmark are applicable to online transaction processing systems and relational database systems, respectively. The Cattell benchmark and Wisconsin OO7 benchmark have been proposed for object-oriented database systems. Chapter 7, titled "Authorization in Object-Oriented Databases," examines security and authorization issues. The chapter deals with both discretionary authorization (i.e., the traditional authorization on database contents) and mandatory multilevel authorization. Chapter 8, titled "Query Processing in Object-Oriented Database Systems," examines query optimization (i.e., determining the best way to process a given query) and query processing techniques (i.e., access methods, sorting, etc.). Chapter 9, titled "Physical Object Management," discusses such physical data access issues as object storage format, clustering, and indexing. Chapter 10, titled "Requirements for a Performance Benchmark for Object-Oriented Database Systems," summarizes requirements for a new performance benchmark with the view to defining a benchmark that may be used not only for comparing the performance of object-oriented database systems but also for comparing the performance of object-oriented database systems against relational database systems.

The fourth subpart of Part 1a, Chapters 11 through 15, covers experiences with the early object-oriented database systems and the current trends toward unification of relational and object-oriented database technologies. Chapter 11, titled "An Object-Oriented DBMS War Story: Developing a Genome Mapping Database in C++," relates experiences in developing a complex application in C++ using a first-generation OODB. Chapter 12, titled "Where Object-Oriented DBMSs Should Do Better: A Critique Based on Early Experiences," summarizes the achievements and deficiencies found in an early crop of object-oriented database systems (largely persistent storage systems rather than full-blown database systems).

Chapter 13, titled "Object-Oriented Database Systems: Promises, Reality, and Future," discusses how the relational data model may be generalized into a core object-oriented data model, and therefore how a relational database system may be extended into an object-oriented database system as a way to provide a natural migration path from relational technology to object-oriented technology. Chapter 14, titled "The POSC Solution to Managing E&P Data," offers a concrete set of data management requirements for a major next-generation database application—namely, exploration and production of oil and gas. It also discusses how a number of database-related standards are being adopted as the basis of database access technology for this application area. Chapter 15, titled "The Changing Database Standards Landscape," provides a snapshot summary of a few key standards activities on database languages, including ANSI SQL-3 and Object Data Management Group, and observes the current trend towards segmentation of database standards.

I note that although I did not invite papers that describe specific commercial or research prototype OODBs, five of the chapters in Part 1a describe salient aspects of four real OODBs. Chapter 3 describes the ObjectSQL language supported in the OpenODB product from Hewlett-Packard. Chapter 4 is a database-language-centric description of the Zeitgeist prototype OODB developed at Texas Instruments. Chapter 5 highlights the C++ support in the Ontos commercial OODB. Chapters 6 and 13 describe the view support, data model, query support, and navigational access support in the UniSQL/X product from UniSQL, Inc.

Part 1b of the book consists of 10 chapters on 8 different topics that require further research and development as components of a next-generation database system beyond unification of relational and object-oriented data models. Chapter 16, titled "Multimedia Information Systems: Issues and Approaches," sets forth multimedia data management requirements and surveys various approaches to developing multimedia information management systems, including multimedia document systems, multimedia database systems, multimedia information retrieval systems, and hypermedia systems. Chapter 17, titled "Spatial Data Models and Query Processing," outlines an approach to modeling spatial data and also an approach to processing queries against spatial data. Chapter 18, titled "Spatial Data Structures," reviews data structures for storing and accessing spatial data. Chapter 19, titled "Temporal Object-Oriented Databases: A Critical Comparison," surveys a variety of approaches to adding a temporal dimension to an OODB. Chapter 20, titled "Cooperative Transactions for Multiuser Environments," provides a survey of transaction models proposed for long-duration cooperative activities. Chapter 21, titled "Active Database Systems," surveys the models and semantics of production rules and implementation issues in database systems augmented with production rules. Chapter 22, titled "Management of Uncertainty in

Database Systems," classifies types of uncertainty in databases (e.g., imprecision, incompleteness, vagueness, inconsistency) and provides a survey of solutions that have been proposed to address the issues that arise due to uncertainty in databases. Chapter 23, titled "Distributed Databases," examines distributed database support in current commercial database systems and outlines directions for future research and development. Chapter 24, titled "Parallel Relational Database Systems," surveys parallel database architectures and reviews query processing techniques in parallel database systems.

I should note that this book is missing chapters on a few important subject areas relevant to the research and development agenda for the next-generation database technology—namely, database design and database interface and application development tools. Methodologies and tools that aid the conceptual design (classes, attributes, methods, inheritance hierarchy, and composition hierarchy) and the physical design (indexes, sorting, clustering) of an object-oriented database are badly needed. Further, application developers need not only a database management system but also assorted database interface tools, such as a database browser and a report writer, and database application development tools, typically a fourth-generation language for automatically generating a graphical-user-interface front end for applications. As such, database vendors offer a variety of database interface tools and application development tools. I simply was not able to find or sign up industry experts to contribute chapters to this book on database design, database interface tools, or database application development tools. The reader should not mistake the absence of chapters on these subjects in this book to mean that these subjects are less than important.

Further, in addition to the genetics mapping application and the oil and gas exploration and production described in Chapters 11 and 14, respectively, I had envisioned including several chapters on significant and well-matching applications for post-relational database systems, such as geographical information systems, computer network domain management, CASE repository, and the like. However, I again was unable to recruit authors to contribute chapters on these topics. The reader should not infer from the small number of chapters on applications in Part 1 of this book that post-relational database systems have few applications. The trend toward complex applications is very real, and the call for more powerful database systems and corresponding tools than are available today is very real.

2

The OMG Object Model

RICHARD MARK SOLEY
WILLIAM KENT

Heterogeneity is an unavoidable consequence of the way in which computer hardware and software systems are designed, built, and acquired today. Multiple vendors and standards contribute to a profusion of approaches in the marketplace. The Object Management Group (OMG), an industry consortium seeking to define consensus standards for interoperability in heterogeneous distributed systems, has taken as a first step an agreement on an *object model* for consistent interaction models across OMG standards specifications. The OMG Core Object Model and its application to a cross-platform integration standard (the Common Object Request Broker Architecture, or *CORBA*) are presented in detail.

2.1 Introduction

Heterogeneity is becoming the way of life in computational systems. Applications autonomously developed at diverse sites in diverse languages on diverse hardware and software platforms increasingly need to share information and to invoke each other's services. Object technology facilitates such interoperation by providing a common framework in which to represent complex data structures as well as behavioral specifications.

Ironically, though, the current state of object technology is itself contributing to the problem via the diversity of object models. Various object-oriented models of interface can be found in different user interfaces, spreadsheets, project managers, plant floor automation systems, and so forth. What is lost is portability—not of programs, but of *programmers*.

For an example, think of a programmer who must write code for both an X-Windows based user interface and a project management tool. This programmer understands that X-Windows "classes" (widgets) have a certain model of interaction (attributes, operations, etc.) while the projects portrayed by the project management tool have another model of interaction (attributes, operations, some limited inheritance).

It surely would be valuable if both of these tools, different though they are, had the *same* model of interaction. For a programmer, or *even a user*, the ability to reliably understand how "objects" and "classes" are related in a consistent way would be of great value.

2.2 The Object Management Group

This is one of the root problems with which the Object Management Group (OMG) has been struggling since its inception in 1989. The OMG is an international software industry consortium with two primary aims:

- promotion of the object-oriented approach to software engineering in general
- development of command models and a common interface for the development and use of large-scale distributed applications (open distributed processing) using object-oriented methodology

Although the OMG is not a recognized standards group (like ISO or national bodies such as ANSI and AFNOR), OMG is developing standards in the form of wholesale agreements among member companies leading to a single architecture and interface specification for application and enterprise integration on both small and large scales.

Now comprising about 340 companies, the OMG membership is composed of large and small hardware and software vendors (IBM, Canon, DEC, Philips, Olivetti, AT&T, Groupe Bull, Sun Microsystems, Informix, ICL, Enfin Systems, Architecture Projects Management, Apple Computer, O2 Technology, etc.) as well as end-user companies (Citicorp, British Telecom, American Airlines, Royal Bank of Canada, John Deere, etc.) with a common goal: the promotion of open standards for interoperability of applications using an object-oriented framework. A key differentiation of the OMG standards approach is that such standards are and will be based, as far as possible, on existing commercially available products.

One of the major OMG working groups, the Object Model Subcommittee, has worked since its inception in December 1990 specifically on the problem of defining a portability model. Certainly OMG's main standards mission of developing a set of tools and interoperability standards for distributed application integration requires a particular model of interface (or *object model*). This is a snapshot of the current status, phrased primarily around a consensus-based *object model* that forms a common framework for OMG-adopted technology.

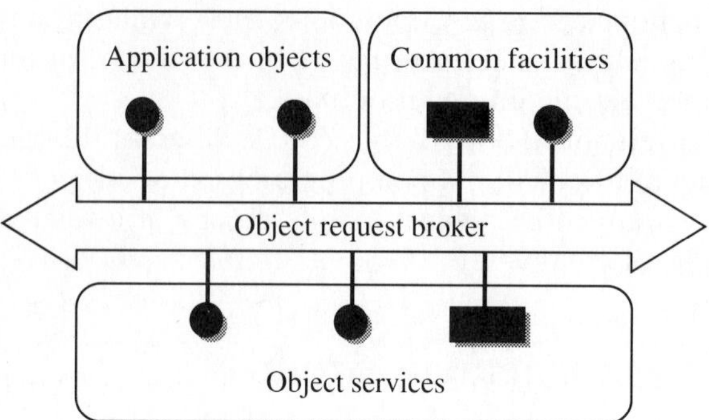

FIGURE 2–1
The Object Management Architecture (OMA)

2.3 Context

The primary direction and requirements of the OMG are set forth in the *Object Management Architecture Guide, Second Edition* [Soley 1992]. In general, OMG technology adoption (standardization) is performed around the general reference model (or architecture) called the Object Management Architecture (OMA), which is outlined in Figure 2–1.

An application that is OMA compliant consists of a set of interworking classes and instances that interact via the Object Request Broker (ORB), a distributed "software bus" that enables objects to make and receive requests and responses. Every application or service in a distributed system is modeled as an object; objects are categorized loosely as follows:

- Object Services (OS) objects are collections of services with object interfaces that provide basic functions for realizing and maintaining objects of any category
- Common Facilities (CF) objects are collections of classes and objects that provide general-purpose capabilities useful in many applications
- Application Objects (AO) are specific to particular end-user applications

In general terms, the application objects and common facilities have an application orientation, while the object request broker and object services are concerned more with the system or infrastructure aspects of distributed object management. Common facilities may, however, provide higher-level services, such as transactions and versioning, that make use of primitives provided within object services.

The three categories (object services, common facilities and application objects) reflect a partitioning in terms of functions, from those basic to most applications or common enough to broad classes of applications to standardize, to those too application specific or special purpose to standardize at this time. Thus, the object request broker, object services, and common facilities will be the focus of OMG standardization efforts.

In general, object services, common facilities, and application objects all intercommunicate using the object request broker. Objects may also use non-object interfaces to external services, but these are outside the scope of the OMA. Although not explicit in the reference model, objects may (or may not) communicate with the object services via object interfaces. For example, the addition of a new class may be cast as a request to an object that provides this service, but equivalently, it could be performed by editing a class definition script or a C++ include file.

The application objects and common facilities use and provide functions and services via object interfaces. In general, objects can issue as well as process requests. Thus, objects categorized as application objects can provide services for other applications or facilities. For example, an application-specific service such as printer rendering could be cast as an application object that is invoked by a common facility such as a print queue. Similarly, objects categorized as common facilities may use services provided elsewhere.

2.3.1 Current Work

The current work of the OMG is along four major lines:

- definition of object request broker (ORB) and extensions
- definition of object services and common facilities
- definition and extension of a common core object model
- consensus building among subgroups of OMG membership in such areas as analysis and design methodologies

The current published level of consensus is reflected in Soley 1992 and OMG 1991, both subject to further revision.

The OMG object model is organized as a menu of features, structured as a core object model and an extensible set of components. A profile consists of the core object model and a specified set of components appropriate for a given domain.

The core object model defines features required in all conforming facilities and on which consensus has been reached. The core object model may be extended with additional features as consensus develops, provided that no profile has been adopted excluding such features. Conformance to OMG guidelines is assessed with respect to a complete profile.

This chapter describes the OMG core object model and briefly covers the extensions implicit in the CORBA specifications outlined in OMG 1991. The components that will be combined to form the profile for the

CORBA model described in OMG 1991 are currently under development in OMG.

2.4 The OMG Core Object Model

This section describes the core object model, which specifies the common features that all compliant object systems should support. It includes a formal model of types, operations, and subtyping. In the core object model, the user can manipulate instances but not types or operations as first-class objects.

2.4.1 Basic Concepts

The OMG core object model is based on a small number of basic concepts: objects, operations, types, and subtyping. An object can model any kind of entity—for example, a person, a ship, a document, a department, a tuple, a file, a window manager, or a lexical scanner. A basic characteristic of an object is its distinct identity, which is immutable, persists for as long as the object exists, and is independent of the object's properties or behavior.

Operations are applied to objects.[1] Thus, to determine a person's date of birth, the **date_of_birth** operation is applied to the appropriate **person** object. The relationship between a person and his or her spouse may be modeled as an operation **spouse** on one person object that returns another person object. The operations associated with an object collectively characterize its behavior.

Objects are created as instances of types[2] (e.g., **integer, person, ship, stack**). A type characterizes the behavior of its instances by describing the operations that can be applied to those objects. Types can be related to one another through supertype/subtype relationships.

State is required in an object system because it captures the information needed to affect operations. For example, the operation **marry** takes two **person** objects as input arguments and produces side effects on these two objects. State captures these side effects, and, presumably, a subsequent application of the **spouse** function to either object will now yield a different result from what it did before. In the core object model, operations are used to model the external interface to state. *Attributes* and *relationships*, which

1. This chapter speaks in terms of *operations being applied to objects*. This same concept can be described as *sending requests to objects*. For the purposes of the core object model, the two phrases mean the same thing.

2. Saying that an object is *an instance of type T* is the same as saying that an object is *of type T* in this model.

can be used to model the externally visible declarations of state more succinctly, are currently defined in the OMG OM Components Guide.

2.4.2 Object Identity and Object Identifiers

Each object has a unique *identity* that is distinct from and independent of any of its characteristics. Characteristics can vary over time, whereas identity is constant.

In the core object model, each object has an *identifier* that provides a means to denote or refer to the object. This identifier is called an OID[3]. OIDs label (or refer to) objects. The set of all OIDs is denoted as *Obj*.

The core object model does not require systems to support a comparison operation for OIDs, since it is not reasonable to require that all services support this capability in a distributed environment. In other words, you may not be able to ask if two OIDs refer to the same object. However, if two OIDs, A and B, refer to the same object, then invoking an operation with A as an argument is the same as invoking that operation with B in place of A.

The implementation of OIDs is not within the realm of the core object model. The core object model does not specify if OIDs are fixed length or varying in size. For example, there is no assumption that OIDs are 32-, 64-, or 128-bit strings. Furthermore, the core object model does not care about the internal structure of an OID. For example, it does not state that the location of the object is encoded within an OID in some way known to the system or its users. OIDs are opaque as far as the core object model is concerned.

2.4.3 Object Types

Objects support only certain operations. The operations applicable to an object collectively characterize its behavior. Types describe these operations and thus characterize the behavior of objects. Objects are created as instances of their types, and in the core object model, objects do not change their types.

Each operation has a signature, which consists of a name, set of parameters[4], and set of results (see section 2.4.5). The set of operation signatures defined on a type is called the type's *interface*. A type's interface includes signatures that are inherited from supertypes (see section 2.4.6). Every instance of a type satisfies the interface of that type.

3. OIDs in the core object model denote the same concept as *object references* in CORBA.

4. In the core object model, the term *parameter* is used when referring to the declaration of an operation's interface. *Argument* is used when referring to an operation invocation.

As an example, suppose **sam** denotes some object. If the operations *name, address,* and *move* can be applied to **sam** without causing an error, then these operations characterize the behavior of **sam**. Trying to apply other operations to **sam**, such as *Print,* will fail, resulting in an error.

The type `Person` can be defined as supporting operations whose signatures are:

```
String name (P: Person)
String address (P: Person)
move (P: Person, A: String)
```

These three operations constitute the interface of the type `Person`. The fact that **sam** is an instance of the type `Person` implies that these operations may be applied without error to **sam**.

Types are arranged into a type hierarchy that forms a directed acyclic graph. The root of this type hierarchy is the type *Object.* Applications introduce new types by subtyping from *Object.* Having a single root allows programs to specify that a parameter can take an object of any type. The set of all object types is referred to as *OTypes.*

To extend our example, suppose the type `Employee` is defined as supporting an operation whose signature is as follows:

```
Real salary (E: Employee)
```

If **sally** is an instance of `Employee`, then the operation *salary* is applicable to **sally**. If `Employee` is a subtype of Person (i.e., below `Person` in the type hierarchy), then the other three operations above (*name, address,* and *move*) are also applicable to **sally**. The interface of `Employee` includes all four operations.

A type is distinct from its interface and its set of instances (extension). Both its interface and its extension can change over time without changing the identity of the type. Although the core object model defines types and operations as concepts, systems that comply with the model need not provide objects that correspond to these concepts. Types and operations as objects will be considered for inclusion in the Meta_data component of the OMG OM Components Guide.

2.4.4 Non-Object Types

Many object systems, for example C++ and CORBA, explicitly distinguish between objects and things that are not objects[5]. The core object model has chosen to recognize that this distinction exists. Things that are not objects

5. In the sense that objects have been defined in the core object model.

are called *non-objects*[6]. Objects and non-objects collectively represent the set of denotable values in the core object model.

In the core object model, non-objects are not labeled by an object reference, and therefore cannot be the controlling parameter for an operation request. Each non-object can be considered to belong to a type of value, called a *Non-object type*. This is analogous to objects being instances of types. Non-object types, however, do not belong to the Object type hierarchy. Thus non-object types are not subtypes of *Object*. Moreover, the rules for subtyping and inheritance defined later in this section do not apply to non-object types. Components can add more structure to the non-object types; for example, a component could define subtyping and inheritance rules for non-object types.

The core object model does not specify a set of non-object types; these types are defined in a component and chosen for inclusion in a profile. For example, CORBA would define in its profile that the non-object types would include Short, Long, UShort, Ulong, Float, Double, Char, String, Boolean, Octet, Enum, Struct, Sequence, Union, and Array. The set of non-object types can be extended by adding new types to the Non-object component.

Profiles can choose which non-object types to support. In a pure object system, such as Smalltalk, all denotable values are expressed as objects, and so the set of non-object types may be empty. Thus, profiles are allowed to make the difference between the set of objects and the set of non-objects that they recognize as wide or as narrow as needed.

The set of all non-object types is called *NTypes*. The set of all non-objects is called *Nobj*. The complete set of values that may be manipulated in the core object model is described as *DVal* = *Obj* U *Nobj*. *DVal* can be thought of as the denotable values in the core object model. The elements of *DVal* are called *dvals*. *DVal* is not a type in the core object model. It does not exist as a supertype of *Object* and the types in *NTypes*. Therefore, you cannot specify, for example, an operation parameter that may be either an object or a non-object. This eliminates the difficulty of systems having to provide run-time discrimination of objects and non-objects.

The remainder of this section deals primarily with objects. Unless otherwise noted, when this chapter refers to type, it means object type.

2.4.5 Operations

An operation describes an action that can be applied to parameters. An operation invocation, called a *request*, is an event (like a procedure invocation or function call) that indicates an operation and possibly lists some

6. Examples of non-objects are the basic and constructed values as defined in the CORBA specification, which will be outlined later.

parameters on behalf of a requester (client), possibly causing results to be returned. The consequences of a request can include:

1. An immediate set of results.
2. Side effects, manifested in changes of state.
3. Exceptions (currently not part of the core object model). An exception packages information indicating that some unusual event has occurred and passes that information to an exception handler.

Each operation has a signature. The signature includes the operation's name, list of parameters, and list of return values, if any. For example,

```
operation_name (param-1, ..., param-n)
     returns (res-1, ..., res-m)
param-i ::= parameter_name: parameter_type
res-i ::= result_name: result_type
```

The core object model does not describe the syntax of operation specification. For example, it does not specify how results are to be associated with variables. The above syntax is simply for illustrative purposes.

Formally, an operation Ω has the signature:

$$\omega:(x_1:\sigma_1, x_2:\sigma_2, \ldots, x_n:\sigma_n) \rightarrow (y_1:\rho_1, y_2:\rho_2, \ldots, y_m:\rho_m)$$

ω is the name of the operation. The operation signature specifies $n \geq 1$ parameters with names x_i and types σ_i, and $m \geq 0$ results with names y_i and types ρ_i.

In the core object model, operations are always specified with a *controlling parameter.* For discussion purposes, this section will assume that the first parameter (x_1) is the controlling parameter, although the core object model does not require this. Each object type $T \in$ *OTypes* has a set of operations *Ops(T)* = { Ω_1^T, Ω_2^T,... }.

An operation is part of the interface of its controlling parameter's type and the interface of all subtypes of that type (see section 2.4.6). An operation is *defined on* the type of its controlling parameter; for example, Ω is defined on σ_1[7]. All operations defined on a type have distinct names. In the core object model, an operation is defined on a single type (the type of the controlling parameter), so there is no notion of an operation independent of a type or of an operation defined on two or more types[8].

In the core object model, operations can only be defined on object

---

7. Note that *defined on* does not refer to a lexical scope or context where the operation is syntactically specified.

8. Requiring operations to be defined on a single type is sometimes referred to as the *classical* object model. Relaxing this constraint to allow operations to be defined on zero or more types is called the *generalized* object model. The core object model is a classical model.

types, not on non-object types. The controlling parameter type may only be an element of *OTypes*. However, with the exception of the controlling parameter type σ_1, σ_i and ρ_i can be elements of *OTypes* ∪ *NTypes*.

An operation may have side effects—updates—that are reflected in the altered result of one or more operations. For example, applying the *move* operation in the example types above may change result of a future *address* request. The core object model does not distinguish a subcategory of operations that are side-effect free.

The core object model does not address exception handling. Exceptions are intended to be introduced as a component and can therefore be included in profiles.

The core object model does not specify anything about the execution order for operations. For example, whether clients issue requests sequentially or concurrently is not part of the core object model. Furthermore, whether requests get serviced sequentially or concurrently is also not part of the core object model. Although the core does not specify support for sequential or concurrent operations, it does not preclude an implementation from providing such support.

The core object model does not require support for atomic operation execution, nor does it preclude it. An implementation might choose to provide atomic operations in lieu of separate transaction_begin, transaction_commit, and transaction_abort operations.

In the core object model, operations (definitions of signatures) are not objects. Requests (operation invocations) are also not defined to be objects.

The core object model does not require a formal specification of the semantics of an operation, although it is good practice to include a comment that specifies the purpose of the operation, any side effects it has, and any invariants it is intended to preserve.

2.4.6 Subtyping and Inheritance

Subtyping is a relationship between types based on their interfaces. It defines the rules by which objects of one type are determined to be acceptable in contexts expecting another type. *Inheritance* is a mechanism for reuse. It allows a type to be defined in terms of another type. Many object systems do not distinguish between subtyping and inheritance. This section defines the two concepts separately but then explicitly states how they are related in the core object model.

Subtyping

The core object model supports subtyping for Object types. Intuitively, one type is a subtype of another if the first is a specialization or a refinement of the second. Operationally, this means that any object of the first type can be used in any context that expects an object of the second type; that is, if *S* is a subtype of *T*, an object of type *S* may be used wherever an object of type *T* may be used. In other words, objects of type *S* are also of type *T*. Subtypes can have multiple parent types, with the implication that an object that is an instance of a type *S* is also an instance of all supertypes of type *S*. The relationships between types define a type hierarchy, which can be drawn as a directed acyclic graph.

An object is a direct instance of a type if it is an instance of that type and not an instance of any subtype of that type. The core object model restricts objects to be direct instances of exactly one type. That one type is the object's *immediate* type. The core object model has no mechanism for an object to change its immediate type.

In the core object model, the type designer is required to declare the intent that a type *S* is a subtype of *T*. Formally, if *S* is declared to be a subtype of *T* (and conversely, *T* is a supertype of *S*), then for each operation $\Omega_1^T \in Ops(T)$, there exists a corresponding operation $\Omega_j^S \in Ops(S)$ such that the following conditions hold:

1. The names of the operations match.
2. The number and types of the parameters are the same (except that the controlling parameter types may differ).
3. The number and types of the results are the same.

Thus, for every operation in *T* there must be a corresponding operation in *S*, though there may be more operations in *Ops(S)* than *Ops(T)*. The specifications of corresponding operations must match precisely (with the exception of the controlling parameter).

The core object model presents very strict typing rules that ensure that substitutability[9] can be guaranteed using the information in the specifications. These rules can be relaxed somewhat and still guarantee substitutability. One of the components defined in the OMG OM Components Guide describes a modified set of rules that loosen the above conditions to allow parameter and result types to differ but still preserve substitutability.

A single type can have multiple supertypes in the core object model. The above typing rules, however, prevent two types that have an operation with the same name but different signatures from having a common subtype.

Supertypes are used to characterize functionality that is common to their subtypes. Often a supertype's interface is incomplete as a stand-alone type. It relies on its subtypes to extend the interface. Other times, a super-

9. *Substitutability* means being able to substitute an object of some type *S* when an object of type *T* is expected, where *T* is a supertype of *S*, while guaranteeing that the substituted object will support the same operations as specified by the supertype *T*.

type specifies a complete definition of some type, but the type is useful only when it is combined with other types in a new subtype. In both cases, the supertype does not have any direct instances of its own. Only subtypes of this supertype can have direct instances. The core object model refers to these types as *Abstract* types.

Inheritance

Inheritance is a notational mechanism for defining a type *S* in terms of another type *T*. The definition of *S* inherits all the operations of *T* and may provide other operations. Intuitively, *inherit* means that the operations defined for *T* are also defined for or can be used by *S*[10].

Subtyping is a relationship between interfaces (types). Inheritance can apply to both interfaces and implementations; that is, both interfaces and implementations can be inherited. The core object model is concerned with inheritance of interfaces. It does not specify what can happen with implementations of inherited operations (e.g., whether they may be changed or overridden by a subtype).

The core object model relates subtyping and inheritance. If *S* is declared to be a subtype of *T*, then *S* also inherits from *T*. The core object model supports multiple inheritance, which allows a subtype to have multiple supertypes. The core does not provide a name conflict resolution mechanism, nor does it allow subtypes to redefine inherited operation signatures. These two constraints are relaxed in a component defined in the OMG OM Components Guide.

Consider the following type definitions:

```
type Person
  abstract
  supertypes: Object

  operations:
    String social_security (P: Person)
    String name (P: Person)

end type

type Employee
  supertypes: Person
  operations:
    Department dept (E: Employee)
    Money salary (E: Employee)

end type
```

10. Whether *Ops(S)* is a superset of *Ops(T)* or the two are disjoint sets is an implementation issue and does not affect the core object model semantics.

In this example, type Employee is declared to be a subtype of type Person. In the core object model, this implies that

1. All instances of type Employee are also instances of type Person, and so an Employee object can be used wherever a Person object is expected.
2. Employee inherits the name and social_security operations from Person.

Furthermore, Person is declared to be an abstract type, and so it cannot have any direct instances.

Operation Dispatching

When an operation request is issued, a specific operation implementation (method) is selected for execution. This selection process is called *operation dispatching.* In the core object model, the process of selecting an implementation to invoke is based on the type of the object supplied as the controlling argument of the actual call[11]. The operation of the given name defined on the immediate type of the controlling argument is chosen for invocation. In some cases, this can be done at compile time with no loss of flexibility; in others, it must be delayed to execution time.

2.4.7 Argument Passing and Results

Consider an operation Ω with the signature

$$\omega{:}(x_1{:}\sigma_1, x_2{:}\sigma_2, \ldots, x_n{:}\sigma_n) \rightarrow (y_1{:}\rho_1, y_2{:}\rho_2, \ldots, y_m{:}\rho_m)$$

An invocation (request) of Ω might be written as:

$$r_1, \ldots, r_m \leftarrow \omega(E_1, \ldots, E_n)$$

where ω is the name of Ω, E_i are expressions providing the input arguments, and r_i accept the return results.

The request is legal if the expressions $E_1, \ldots, E_n$ evaluate to $\alpha_1, \ldots, \alpha_n$ and the immediate type of $\alpha_i \leq \sigma_i$ ($\leq$ is the subtype relationship). The signature guarantees that the request returns a set of results, $\beta_1, \ldots, \beta_m$, and the immediate type of $\beta_i \leq \rho_i$.

Note that if the types of the parameters or results of Ω belong to *NTypes,* then the subtype check is defined by the component that defined the non-object types. In most cases, this is likely to be type equality.

11. The single controlling argument restriction can be relaxed in a component and generalized to multiple argument dispatching.

The execution semantics consist of binding arguments and return values to formal parameters. The expressions E_i result in either non-objects or OIDs (collectively DVals). Operationally, these DVals are copied into the formal parameters. How the effect of copying is accomplished is not specified, nor is it required that the OIDs be the same, only that the object they refer to be the same. The objects that the OIDs refer to are *not* copied. For example, consider the following operation specification and invocation:

operation X defined in Type T

```
...
X (x: T)
```

X being invoked in some code

```
...
X (a_T)
```

Following the invocation, *x* refers to the same object as *a_T*. Operation requests made to the OID in *x* will function exactly as if they had been made to the OID in *a_T*. It is not the case, however, that an assignment to *x* will change *a_T* (or even the object *x* refers to). In this sense, the core object model defines a pass-by-value argument passing semantics.

2.4.8 Interfaces of a Type

In the core object model, a type exports all the operations that are defined on it. There is no notion of multiple named interfaces defined on a type that export less than the full type specification. Visibility attributes such as private, public, subtype_visible, and friends are not supported either. These may be defined by components.

There is also no notion of a program binding to a subschema that restricts a program's access to some subset of the types defined in the system, and for any type within this subset, further restricts access to some subset of the characteristics defined by the type. Subschemas and subschema-specific interfaces to types may also be defined in a component.

Example Type Interface

A type's interface defines the externally visible state and behavior of instances of the type. Behavior is defined as a set of operation signatures. The following example shows the interface portion of an object type definition that illustrates these concepts. The syntax is illustrative only.

```
type IMAGE
  supertypes: OBJECT
  operations:
```

```
    INTEGER get_length (i: IMAGE)
    set_length (i: IMAGE, length: INTEGER)
    INTEGER get_width (i: IMAGE)
    set_width (i: IMAGE, width: INTEGER)
    scale (i: IMAGE, by: FACTOR)
    rotate (i: IMAGE, by: DEGREES)
    IMAGE crop (i: IMAGE, to: SIZE)
end_type
```

The core object model does not formally define state but acknowledges that the execution of some operations may affect the way the same operation or other operations behave in the future.

2.4.9 Implementation

As noted earlier, the core object model formally specifies only the semantics of objects. It has nothing to say about their implementation. It neither requires nor excludes systems in which there is more than one implementation for a given type. It permits systems in which each object type has a separate implementation or in which clusters of related types share an implementation.

The combination of a type specification and one of the implementations defined for that type is termed a *class*. An individual object, at any given point in time, is an instance of one class. The core object model makes no statement about whether an object must retain the implementation chosen for it at the time it was created or whether an object can change implementations over its lifetime. Moreover, implementations may vary among different instances of a type and even for the same instance over time. As an example, consider the following scenario of a type with two implementation classes:

```
type Disk
    Real Radius (D: Disk)
    Real Diameter (D: Disk)
end type

class Disk-1 implements Disk
    Radius stored;
    Diameter := Radius * 2;
end class

class Disk-2 implements Disk
    Diameter stored;
    Radius := Diameter / 2;
end class
```

Allowing multiple implementations for a given type specification seems necessary to support several domains, including databases that

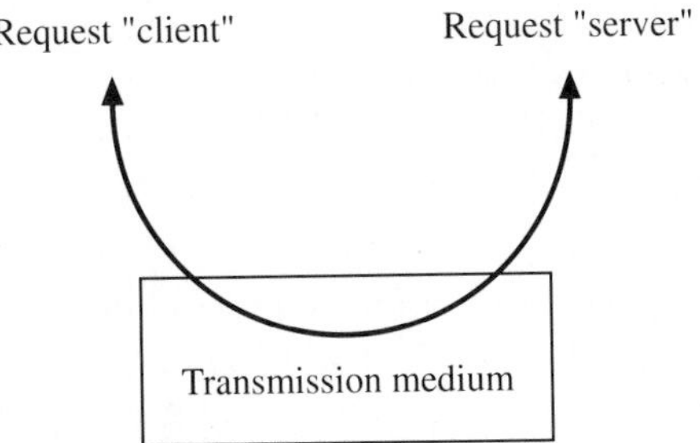

FIGURE 2–2
Simple Model of Client/Server Interaction

span networks that include machines with different architectures, and mixed-language environments. But even in a single-machine, single-language environment, there are cases where the programmer wants to have available different implementations of a type based on different data structures or algorithms. In the absence of multiple implementations for a single type, the type programmer would be forced to abuse the subtype mechanism to achieve this differentiation—for instance, by defining a distinct subtype for each distinct implementation of a type. **Set_as_Btree** and **Set_as_Linked_List** would be introduced, for example, as subtypes of the type **Set**, rather than as alternate implementations for the type **Set.**

2.5 The Object Model for CORBA

The current CORBA documentation [OMG 1991] includes a general object model description based on an earlier version of Soley 1992. Future versions of OMG 1991 will be aligned with the core object model in Soley 1992.

The principal content of OMG 1991 is a set of detailed specifications, implicitly containing the refined object model for CORBA. Definition of object model components to constitute the profile for CORBA is currently under way in OMG. In this section, we give a brief overview of how the CORBA object model's extensions beyond the core object model could be modeled, without decomposition into components.

2.5.1 CORBA Architecture

The basic service provided by CORBA (or any calling distribution service) is delivery of messages (requests) from one piece of code to another and delivery of a response (return or exception) to the caller (as in Figure 2–2). It is convenient to call these two objects the *client* and the *server* in such a transaction, although in the CORBA structure any object can be a client, a server, or both. In fact, it is expected that most objects (i.e., applications) will be both clients and servers of requests over their lifetimes.

To implement this basic service, the CORBA includes several major architectural parts:

- A single specification language, called *OMG IDL* (for OMG Interface Definition Language), is used to specify interface independent of execution (programming) language. While IDL is not itself a programming language, it provides language independence for programmers who do not know a priori the likely user language of callers. The IDL is also *object oriented*, allowing abstraction of interface representation (encapsulation), polymorphic messaging (function calls), and inheritance of interface. The IDL can be thought of as a concrete syntax for the expression of the object model extended from the OMG core object model.
- A fully dynamic representation of available interfaces in an *interface repository* (IR) representing the interfaces (or classes) of all objects available in the distributed computing system.
- A fully dynamic calling extension allowing run-time discovery of objects, discovery of available interface from an IR, construction of message requests, and sending of those requests.
- A *context* extension allowing passing of optional named (rather than order-based) parameters, for explicit control over execution.
- An abstraction mechanism (*object adapter*) for removing the details of object implementation from the messaging substrate.

This chapter will concentrate primarily on the model implied in IDL. As in any remote procedure call system, the IDL is used to automatically generate code to perform procedure calls across a network interface (so-called *stubs* and *skeletons*; see Fig. 2–3); in the CORBA, IDL specifications also are available to the run-time system to support dynamic request generation (see Fig. 2–4).

2.5.2 CORBA Interfaces

Object specifications are divided into object interfaces and object implementations.

The essential CORBA object model is expressed in IDL, governing the syntax and semantics of requests issued to the ORB via a stub or the dynamic invocation interface and interpreted via an object adapter, a skeleton, and an implementation. The *object adapter* adapts to the local definition of objects (be they stored in a database, defined by an object-oriented language, or represented by operating system processes). Although IDL has a precisely defined readable syntax, it is intended to be used only as a

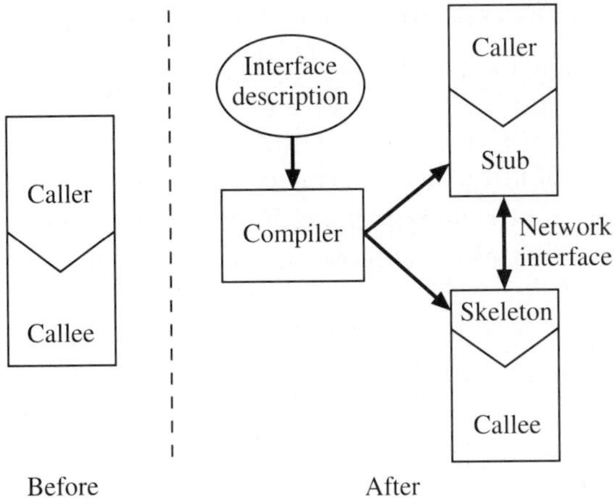

FIGURE 2–3
Remote Procedure Calls

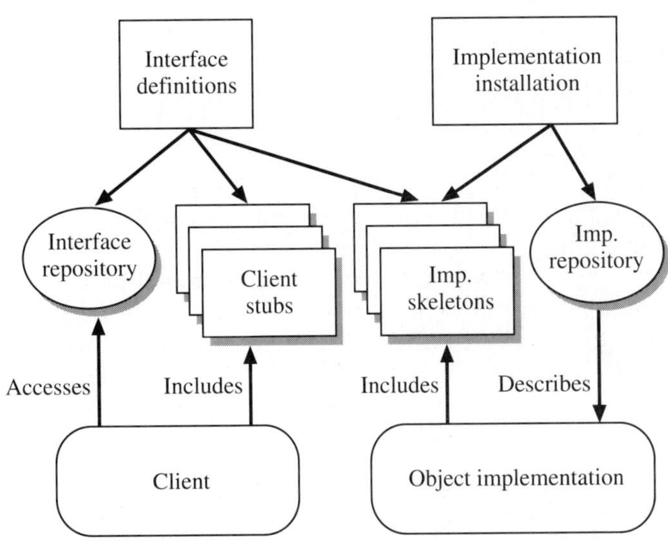

FIGURE 2–4
CORBA Interfaces

specification language. Language mappings will be defined for various application languages. Clients generally see objects and ORB interfaces through the perspective of a language mapping, bringing the ORB right up to the programmer's level. A representative mapping to C is described in OMG 1991; further standardization of language mappings is underway in OMG.

Further mapping of model constructs is possible on two sides:

- Applications are expected to invoke local routines to generate ORB requests in IDL. Such routines could map various capabilities into IDL form, supported by appropriate interpretations in the adapter, skeleton, and implementation to which the requests are routed.
- Specific mechanisms of how an implementation is chosen and activated are determined by specific implementations of ORBs, adapters, and skeletons.

2.5.3 Types and Object Interfaces

Type in general refers to things that may be specified as arguments or results in the signatures of operations.

Object Interfaces

In IDL, an interface name is a legal type name.

IDL Data Types

Interface Definition Language also defines the following types (see OMG 1991 for details):

- Basic Types
  — Integer types (long and short signed and unsigned)
  — Floating point types (float and double)
  — Char
  — Boolean
  — Octet
- Constructed Types
  — Struct
  — Union
  — Enum
- Template Types
  — Sequence
  — String
- Array

Pseudo-Objects

Strictly speaking, the term *object* is reserved in CORBA for things whose implementations are outside the ORB but accessed via the ORB. It is, however, convenient to be able to treat certain internal ORB command and control mechanisms as objects themselves (i.e., perform requests on the ORB itself or other control functions using the same style of interface as the programmer would use for objects outside the ORB). Implementations of a class of ORB-support mechanisms called *pseudo-objects* (because they are generally accessed as objects) are provided within the ORB itself. These include:

- Requests [OMG 1991], for managing requests on objects (that is, ORB requests may be represented as objects and treated as first-class objects within certain boundaries)
- Named-Value Lists [OMG 1991], for managing memory
- Contexts [OMG 1991], for managing special request-property control lists
- Interface definition objects [OMG 1991] in the Interface Repository, for managing the dynamic representation of IDL interface definitions available to objects at run-time
- Implementation definition objects [OMG 1991] in an Implementation Repository, for managing run-time information mapping interfaces to implementations

Other Built-In Objects and Interfaces

In addition to the pseudo-objects mentioned above, certain other interfaces and objects are defined in CORBA.

The Object Interface

An interface named *Object* [OMG 1991] defines operations that may be applied to all objects, including:

- get_implementation, for retrieving the implementation for an object
- create_request, for creating a request pseudo-object on an object
- get_interface, to determine the interface type of an object (from the Interface Repository)
- duplicate, to create a duplicate object reference for an object
- release, to destroy an object reference
- is_nil, to determine if an object reference is to the distinguished object NIL

The ORB Interface

An interface for creating persistent, storable object references also is included with the ORB [OMG 1991]:

- object_to_string, which generates a unique ASCII string for a given object reference that the generating ORB guarantees may be mapped back to the original object reference

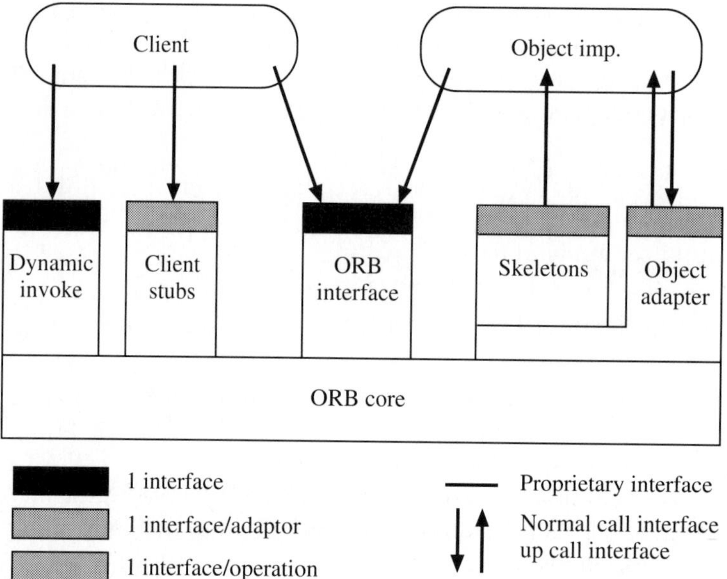

FIGURE 2–5
CORBA Internal Architecture

- string_to_object, which generates a (duplicate) object reference given the storable ASCII string as input

2.5.4 Operations and Requests

A client performs a request by having access to an object reference for an object and knowing the immediate type of the object and the desired operation to be performed. The client initiates the request by calling a stub routine specific to the object type or by constructing the request dynamically via the Dynamic Invocation Interface. This allows access to objects via remote-procedure-call methods (the so-called *static* approach), or to dynamically discover objects, ascertain their types, construct and send requests, and receive responses. These interfaces are depicted graphically in Figure 2–5.

The following sections describe the features of operations that can be specified in IDL beyond those described in the core object model.

Invocation Semantics

When an operation defined as *one way* is invoked, the invocation semantics are best effort, which does not guarantee delivery of the call; *best effort* implies that the operation will be invoked at most once. For other operations, the invocation semantics is at most once if an exception is raised, and exactly once if the invocation returns successfully.

Parameter Directions

Parameters are declared to be in, out, or inout. Out and inout parameters return values in addition to the operation's return result.

Exceptions Raised

An operation signature may specify the exceptions that may be raised by the operation.

Context

In order to control method selection and execution with varying execution environments, CORBA includes a concept of a *context object* that contains a list of properties [OMG 1991]. Each of these properties consists of a name and a string value associated with that name. Implementations may use these pairs in any way they see fit; there is no standardization of context-defined properties at this time. However, operations may define any number of operation-specific properties in addition to a set of standard default system properties to help control request execution.

2.5.5 Attributes

Interface Definition Language supports the specification of attributes. An attribute definition is logically equivalent to declaring a pair of accessor functions, one to retrieve the value of the attribute and one to set the value of the attribute. In IDL, declaring an attribute named x implies the existence of operations named_get_x and _set_x. The actual accessor function names are language-mapping specific.

Attributes may be read only, indicating that only the retrieval function exists.

2.5.6 Exceptions

Interface Definition Language supports the specification of exceptions [OMG 1991], which declare structures much like a *struct*, but which may be used on return from a request to indicate an exceptional (e.g., error) condition during performance of the request. Exceptions comprise an IDL identifier, an exception type, and a return value type. The exception identifier is available to the user on an exception return from a request execution.

2.5.7 Naming Scopes

Interface Definition Language supports a rich syntactic (i.e., lexical) name scoping scheme [OMG 1991]. Besides the implicit name scopes that arise from programming-language-like structures in the IDL (e.g., *interfaces, operations,* and *exceptions*), IDL includes a *module* directive to identify a new lexical name scope.

The multiple-inheritance nature of IDL complicates this simple lexical structure by requiring the "importing" of names into specialized (derived) interfaces. IDL allows disambiguation between collisions that arise because of multiple inheritance using a simple syntactic structure.

2.5.8 Object Implementations

Interface Definition Language describes interfaces, not implementations. However, CORBA defines certain objects related to implementations.

The ORB routes a request to an object implementation. The ORB is responsible for all the mechanisms required to find the implementation for the request, to prepare the object implementation to receive the request, and to communicate the data making up the request.

Nothing is architected about the criteria by which an implementation is selected, nor about how implementations are established, nor about the correspondences between interfaces and implementations. A variety of object implementations can be supported, including separate servers, libraries, a program per method, an encapsulated application, an object-oriented database, and the like. It is possible to support virtually any style of object implementation. The architecture does not require all methods for a given object be implemented at the same location. When a new object is created, the ORB may be notified so that it knows where to find the implementation for that object. Usually, the implementation also registers itself as implementing objects of a particular interface. However, such registrations are optional (e.g., for objects accessed via an object-oriented database object adapter, or some other object adapter, responsible for adapting to the implementation details of objects within a specific regime).

2.6 Conclusions

This chapter presented in detail the core object model adopted as a baseline by the Object Management Group in its quest to develop a suite of standard interfaces to support an interoperable, distributed, heterogeneous computing model. To show how the model can be extended, a brief exposition of implied extensions of that model to support the concepts of the OMG-standard CORBA Object Request Broker is presented. This overview of an extension is not intended to be exhaustive, but instructive. Further review of both Soley 1992 and OMG 1991 is urged to get a complete picture of how the core object model and CORBA standard figure in the goals and plans of the OMG.

It is important to note what the core object model is *not:* The core object model does not intend to prescribe a concrete syntax for modeling object systems (though the CORBA standard does), and it does not intend to prescribe a *complete* object model. Both of these decisions were taken to support the needs of the many computing communities that are beginning to use the object-oriented approach. Prescription of a concrete syntax, while necessary for any integration architecture (such as CORBA), is impractical in a world with object-oriented databases, user interfaces, and languages that use very different metaphors of interaction. Further, a complete object model that attempted to prescribe all object-based interactions would ignore the needs of the various communities, especially those intending to extend the model in future research. The core object model thus provides a baseline to support a meaningful concept of conformance, which can be extended into conformance profiles as needed; the overview draft CORBA profile given above represents such an extension.

ACKNOWLEDGEMENTS

The core object model presented here was the work of a subcommittee of the Object Management Group Technical Committee, under the leadership of John Schwartz (then of Mentor Graphics Corp.), of which the authors were but two members.

REFERENCES

Object Management Group. 1991. The Common Object Request Broker: Architecture and Specification, Revision 1.1, OMG Document No. 91.12.1.

Soley, R., ed. 1992. *Object Management Architecture Guide,* 2d Edition. Object Management Group.

3

Object SQL—A Language for the Design and Implementation of Object Databases

JURGEN ANNEVELINK
RAFIUL AHAD
AMELIA CARLSON
DAN FISHMAN
MIKE HEYTENS
WILLIAM KENT

Object SQL (OSQL) is a language for the design and implementation of object databases. The OSQL language is computationally complete and provides a rich set of constructs that allow definition, implementation, and integration of information services in a distributed environment. It also provides a declarative query capability similar to that provided by SQL for relational databases. This chapter includes examples of OSQL types and functions used in actual distributed applications, based on Hewlett-Packard's OpenODB implementation of OSQL.

3.1 Introduction

Object SQL (OSQL) is a database (programming) language that combines an expression-oriented procedural language with a high-level, declarative, and optimizable query language. The OSQL language combines the object-oriented features found in such languages as C++ [Ellis and Stroustrup 1990] and Smalltalk [Goldberg and Robson 1983] with a query capability that is a superset of the familiar SQL relational query language. Consequently, OSQL provides many of the advantages of object orientation, including a more intuitive model, improved productivity, code reuse, and extensibility, together with all the features of current database technology, such as query optimization, integrity constraints, multiuser access, authorization, and security. The OSQL language was developed as part of the Iris project at Hewlett-Packard Laboratories [Fishman et al. 1989; Lyngbaek 1991; Wilkinson, Lyngbaek, and Hasan 1990]. It has evolved to include general computational primitives [Annevelink 1991] and is now a computationally complete, extensible database language. The design of OSQL was influenced by pioneering work on semantic and functional database models, notably the functional language Daplex [Shipman 1981] and the language Taxis [Mylopoulos, Bernstein, and Wong 1980].

The design goals for OSQL are that it should

- be based on a simple orthogonal object-oriented model and type system
- be computationally complete and independent of specific application programming languages
- provide constructs for specifying declarative queries and allow such queries to be compiled and optimized, similar to the capabilities offered by relational query languages
- be extensible—that is, allow the user to (dynamically) define new types and operations
- create no artificial distinctions between meta-data objects and user-defined objects
- allow separate definition of the interface of an object (type) and the corresponding implementation(s)

OSQL is object oriented in that it provides object identity, a type system with multiple inheritance, polymorphic functions, and built-in aggregate object types such as sets and lists. It differs from other object-oriented languages, in particular C++, in that it does not mix the definition of the interface of an object type with a particular representation of the instances of the type. OSQL allows the interface of an object type to be defined independent of a specific choice for implementing the interface and allows the implementation to change over time.[1] In OSQL, the state of an object is not an intrinsic part of the object itself; rather, it is defined by functions that model attributes of the object, interobject relationships, and arbitrary computations. By disassociating the interface of an object type from any specific representation of the instances of the type, one can allow objects to dynamically acquire and lose types, thus enabling one to model the evolution of objects over their lifetimes in a natural way. The OSQL type system allows the OSQL compiler to do compile-time type checking. However, since OSQL allows objects, including types and functions, to be created dynamically, compile-time type checking has to be supplemented by run-time type checks.

Functions are major modeling constructs of OSQL and are used to model attributes of the object, interobject relationships, and arbitrary com-

1. Future versions of the language may include additional constructs to allow the specification of multiple implementations of a given interface.

putations. Functions can be implemented as stored functions (e.g., by storing a direct representation of the relationship in the form of a table in the database), or they can be computed. The implementation of a computed function is specified by an expression, the *body* of the function; the free identifiers in this expression are the formal parameters of the function, and the value computed by the expression is the value returned by the function. The body of a computed function may include query expressions. In addition to stored and computed functions, OSQL also supports external functions. External functions provide a crucial measure of extensibility because they allow a function to be implemented by a routine written in an external programming language (e.g., C, C++, or COBOL).

The OSQL authorization mechanism is also designed around functions [Ahad et al. 1992]. Users are members of UserGroups that are assigned call and/or update privileges to functions. The OSQL authorization mechanism is not further discussed in this chapter.

The OSQL language is independent of specific application programming languages (e.g., C, C++, Smalltalk, COBOL) and specific implementations. The examples used in this chapter are slightly stylized versions of actual OSQL functions used by applications running on top of OpenODB, Hewlett-Packard's object-oriented database management system and implementation of OSQL [Ahad and Dedo 1992; Ahad and Cheng 1993; Hewlett-Packard 1992]. The programmatic interface provided by OpenODB allows client applications to call any OSQL function and map the results returned by OSQL functions to the data-types provided by the programming interface.

In this chapter we will give an outline of the OSQL model (section 3.2), followed by a discussion of the major constructs found in the OSQL language (section 3.3), with special attention to the *select* construct (section 3.4). In section 3.5, we will give a number of examples highlighting some of the more advanced applications made possible by OSQL.

3.2 OSQL Object Model

The OSQL language is centered around three basic concepts: objects, types, and functions. Objects, types, and functions are related as shown in Figure 3–1.

3.2.1 Objects

Objects represent the real-world entities and concepts from the application domain that the database is storing information about. For example, in a clinical database, objects may represent clinics, physicians, nurses, patients, problem lists, and so on. In OSQL, objects can be classified in one of three categories:

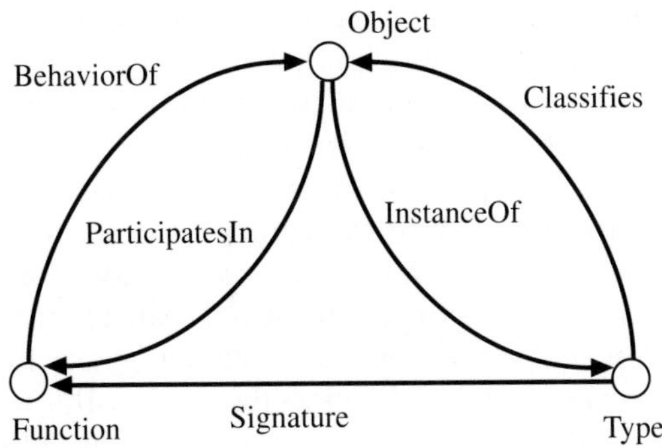

FIGURE 3–1
OSQL—Basic Data Model Elements and Relationships

- literals—for example, integers, character strings, and binary objects
- aggregates—for example, a problem list or a tuple containing demographic data for a patient, such as name, age, and Social Security number
- surrogates—for example, patients and clinics

Surrogate objects are characterized by a system-generated unique object identifier (OID). Surrogate objects also represent entities used to implement OSQL—for example, system types and functions. Surrogate objects are explicitly created and deleted.

3.2.2 Types

The second major concept in OSQL is that of a type. Types are used to classify objects on the basis of shared properties and/or behavior. For example, it is natural to group together all patient objects and similarly group all physician objects, all nurse objects, and all clinic objects. Types are also used to define the signature of functions (i.e, their argument and result type). The extension of a type is the set of objects that are instances of the type. Some types, for example Integer, have predefined extensions. Surrogate types have dynamic extensions that change depending on the type(s) and order in which objects are created and deleted. Aggregate types and aggregate objects can be constructed from other types and objects, respectively, using system-defined aggregate type and object constructors[2]. For example, an instance of the type `SetType(SmallInteger)` is denoted by the expression: `Set(1,2,3)`. Note that this does not construct a new object but rather returns a specific object from the extent of the type `SetType`

2. OpenODB supports four aggregate type and object constructors, BagType, SetType, ListType and TupleType to construct aggregate types and Bag, Set, List and Tuple to construct the corresponding objects.

(SmallInteger), in the same way that the expression 1 does not return a new object but returns an instance of the type SmallInteger.

Types are related in a subtype/supertype hierarchy that supports multiple inheritance. The type hierarchy enforces type containment—that is, if an object is an instance of a given type *T*, it must also be an instance of all supertypes of the type *T*. An overview of the (predefined) system type hierarchy is shown in Figure 3–2. User-defined types can be added as subtypes of the type UserSurrogate[3]. OSQL surrogate objects can be instances of any number of types, even if the types are not related by a subtype/supertype relationship. This is obviously required in the real world, where, say, a person may belong to many different groups and assume different roles depending on the context. For example, the group of cancer patients can be distinguished from the group of diabetics; different types of properties are applicable and relevant to each of the members of the two. Moreover, people can change their memberships in groups and thus change what roles and what properties and behavior are applicable. For example, a person can be cured and thus no longer be a cancer patient, or he can get sick and be diagnosed with diabetes.

3.2.3 Functions

The third concept, functions, is used to model attributes of the object, inter-object relationships, and arbitrary computations. One of the key distinctions of OSQL as compared to other models (e.g., those inspired by object-oriented programming languages) is this unifying notion of a function to model stored and derived attributes, stored and derived relationships, and arbitrary computations (behavior). In OSQL, the distinction between these is relegated t the implementation domain, thus making the actual modeling more independent of implementation tradeoffs and allowing a greater freedom in choosing an implementation, including the possibility of evolving an implementation (e.g., choosing to reimplement something that was a stored attribute as a derived or computed attribute).

An OSQL function takes an object as an argument and may return an object as a result[4]. OSQL functions can be overloaded—that is, there can be multiple functions with the same name but different argument types. OSQL does not currently allow overloaded functions to have different result types.

3. The version of OSQL implemented by OpenODB currently does not allow the creation of user-defined subtypes of predefined system types.

4. OSQL functions can take aggregate objects as argument and/or return them as results. Functions with multiple arguments are implemented by combining the arguments into a single tuple value and applying the function to the tuple. The argument type of function with multiple arguments is the tupletype corresponding to the types of the arguments.

OSQL refers to an overloaded function as a *generic function*. The resolvents of a generic function are called *specific functions*. For a given function *f*, the argument object must be an instance of the argument type specified for one of the specific functions that resolve the function *f*. A function can only return an object that is an instance of the result type of the function. The result type of functions that never return a value is `Void`. Functions may change the state of the database as a side effect of their application by updating other functions. Functions that perform updates are said to have side effects and cannot be called as part of a query. Similar to types, functions have extensions. The extension of a function is the mapping from its arguments to its results. Function extensions can be explicitly stored, or they can be computed. Functions whose extent is computed can be implemented either as an OSQL expression or as a program (subroutine, procedure) written in a general-purpose programming language. These latter are called *external functions* and give OSQL a unique form of extensibility by allowing the encapsulation of (entry points in) external libraries.

An important property of functions is their updatability. A function *f* that is updatable has a companion function, say `set_f`, that will set the value to be returned by *f* for a given argument, when called. If a function *f* returns an aggregate type, then it will have three such companion functions: one to set the value as before, the other two to add or remove a value in the aggregate. The set, add, and remove functions can be specified explicitly, or they can be generated automatically by the system (e.g., when the extent of the function *f* is explicitly stored). For example, a stored function `translate` can be defined as follows:

```
create function translate(Char english) -> Char /*french */;
```

Since this is an atomic valued stored function, the system will automatically create a second function to allow it to be updated. This function has no name and can be found by evaluating the (system-defined) function `FunAssign`. The latter function will be invoked when the function `translate` is to be updated; for example,

```
translate('one') := 'un';
```

3.2.4 OSQL System Types

To make an OSQL system work, a great many built-in objects, types, and functions need to be defined. The basic type hierarchy is shown in Fig. 3–2. The root object type is called *Object* and is the supertype of all other object types. Subtypes of object are:

- TypeRef—the type whose extension is the set of all type objects, including aggregate types; for example, SetType(Integer) and surrogate types (all the instances of type Type)

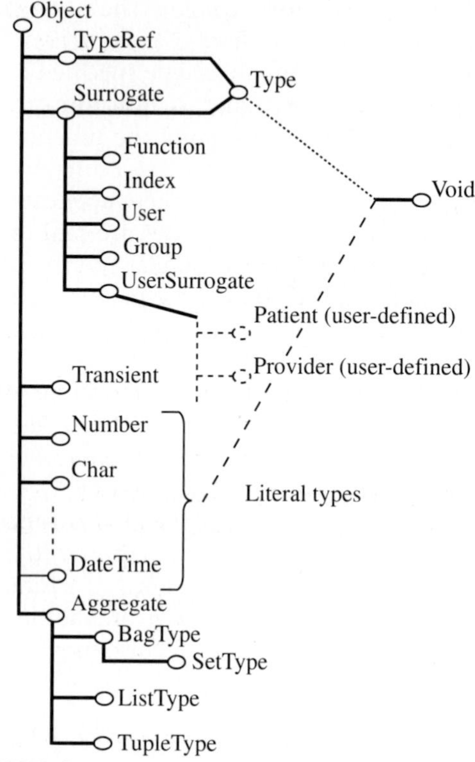

FIGURE 3–2
OSQL System Type Hierarchy (Simplified)

- Surrogate—the supertype of all types whose instances have OIDs, including Function, Type, Index, User, UserGroup, and UserSurrogate
- UserSurrogate—supertype of all user-defined types; for example, Patient, Provider, and so on
- Type—the type whose extension is the set of all surrogate types (i.e., all types other than aggregate types)
- Transient—the supertype of all transient object types (i.e., the types whose instances are transient—for example, Transaction, Savepoint, Session, and Cursor)
- Aggregate—the supertype of all aggregate types. Aggregate types supported include BagType, SetType, ListType, and TupleType. Instances of Bag, Set, and List types can have any number of components that must all be instances of the component type of the Bag, Set, or List. A tuple object, on the other hand, has a fixed number of components, each with its own type

- Literal Types—The literal types supported by OSQL include Number (Integer, SmallInteger, Double, Real), Char, Binary, Date, Time, DateTime, and Interval
- Void—Void is a subtype of all types except aggregate types; its extension is the empty set

3.2.5 OSQL System Functions

There is also a large number of system-defined functions that provide the functionality necessary to implement a full-fledged object-oriented data manager. Some of the more important functions provided are the following:

- CreateType—create a new (user-defined) type and (optionally) create one or more functions that have the new type as their argument type
- CreateFunction—create a new (user-defined) function
- ImplStored—implement a function or set of functions as a stored function (i.e., a function whose extent is explicitly stored in the database)
- ImplOSQL—implement a function as an OSQL expression, either as a procedural language expression (section 3.3) or as a query expression (section 3.4)
- ImplExternal—implement a function as an arbitrary program, written in an external programming language
- CreateObj—create a new object, an instance of a user-defined type, optionally initializing one or more functions for the new object

The OSQL language implemented by OpenODB provides convenient syntactic sugaring to invoke the above and other functions. For example, to create a new type and a set of associated functions, one can submit an OSQL statement, as follows:

```
create type Patient subtype of Person functions (
     patId Char (var 32)
);
```

A statement such as the one above will be parsed into a call to the function CreateType as follows:

```
CreateType('Patient',Set(type Person),
             List(Tuple('patId',type Char (var 32))))
```

It is also important to note that users can define their own functions that involve system objects such as types and functions. For example, to allow type objects to be annotated, one can define and use a stored function, help, as follows:

```
create function help(Type t) -> Char as stored;
help(Type Patient):= 'Patient object type help descriptor';
```

```
Expr          := Constant                                         (1)
               | Identifier                                       (2)
               | FuncAppl                                         (3)
               | Assign                                           (4)
               | Conditional                                      (5)
               | BlockExpr                                        (6)
               | ForLoop                                          (7)
               | WhileLoop                                        (8)
               | Quote                                            (9)
               | Select                                          (10)
               ;                                                 (11)
FuncAppl      := func_ref: Expr arg: Expr;                       (12)
Conditional   := pred: Expr then: Expr else: Expr;               (13)
Assign        := id: Identifierval: Expr                         (14)
BlockExpr     := declare: Declaration+ exprs: Expr+;             (15)
ForLoop       := id: Identifier domain: Expr loop: Expr;         (16)
WhileLoop     := pred: Expr loop: Expr;                          (17)
Quote         := Expr;                                           (18)
Declaration   := t: TypeRefid: Identifier;                       (19)
```

FIGURE 3–3
OSQL Abstract Syntax

3.3 Expression Language (DML)

In the previous section, we described the computational model of OSQL as being one of expression evaluation. In this section, we will discuss the various types of expressions allowed and the means provided to compose expressions.

In addition to the function application expression as described above, there is a number of special forms, including if-then-else, quote, and a number of iterative constructs. An abstract syntax[5] that defines the types of expressions is shown in Figure 3–3:

The first rule defines an expression to be a constant, an identifier, a function application, an assignment, a conditional, a block expression, a for loop, a while loop, a quoted expression, or a select expression (discussed separately in section 3.4).

Constants and identifiers are defined as usual, except that OSQL also supports aggregate constants that can be specified using the tuple, set, bag

5. The notation used to define the abstract syntax uses three constructs, respectively: choice, denoted by |, aggregation, denoted by a tuplelike notation that labels the components of the syntactic construct, and repetition, denoted by +, to mean one or more, or *, to mean zero or more. Note that the labels used to identify the components of an aggregate construct resemble but are not the same as the keywords used in specifying a concrete syntax.

(multiset), and list constructors. For example, a set constant can be specified as `Set(1, 2, 3 + 4)`. The elements of the set can be specified as expressions themselves. An aggregate object will in general have many types that can be inferred from the types of their elements. The OSQL language as implemented by OpenODB also supports a special notation to denote type and function constants. For example, the generic function `name` is denoted by the constant expression: `function name`. Similarly, the specific `name` function whose argument type is `Person` is denoted by: `function name. Person`, and the type *T* is denoted by the expression: `type T`.

The most frequently used kind of expression is the function application. Abstractly, a function application expression consists of two expressions: a function reference (labeled func_ref in Figure 3–3 line 12) and an argument (labeled arg). The func_ref expression evaluates to a (generic or specific) function identifier, which may be the same as the function the expression is a part of, thus allowing recursive function invocations. The expression labeled *arg* evaluates to an arbitrary object or aggregate object. The semantics of evaluating function applications were discussed in detail in section 3.2. For example, to set the name of a person, we evaluate the following expression:

```
FunAssign(function name.person) (p1,'John')
```

In this example, the first expression is itself a function call, applying the function `FunAssign` to the function `name.person` (an example of a specific function reference). This returns the OID of the function that sets a person's name, which is subsequently applied to a tuple of two elements, the OID of the person and the new name (a string object), and sets the name of the person accordingly. The parentheses and ',' are used here to denote an operator that creates a tuple. The OSQL language as implemented by OpenODB provides a convenient syntactic shorthand for the above expression, as shown below:

```
name.person(p1) := 'John'
```

OSQL provides an imperative model of variables and assignment similar to C. Variables can be declared and have scope equal to the block expression in which they are declared. Within such scope, one can assign a value to the variable using an assignment, similar to what one would do in a language like C. The introduction of assignment in OSQL is not strictly necessary but is needed to support such imperative constructs as while loops. Alternatively, one can use recursion and recursive functions to avoid the need for assignment. The OSQL language as implemented by OpenODB provides the following concrete syntax for variable assignment:

```
i := 2
```

The conditional or if-then-else expression consists of three subexpressions: a predicate expression, a then expression, and an else expression. A specific example using the concrete syntax implemented by OpenODB is shown below:

```
ticketPrice := if age(p1) >= 60 then 27 else 40
```

The semantics of its evaluation is to first evaluate the predicate expression; for example, `age(p1) >= 60`. If it returns true, we evaluate the then expression; if it returns false, we evaluate the else expression. The if-then-else expression returns the value of the then or else expression.

The next expression is the block expression or begin-end expression. It consists of a list of (local) variable declarations and a list of expressions. Its semantics is to evaluate the expressions in the list in order, in the environment created by extending the environment of the block expression with bindings for the local variable identifiers. The value returned by the block expression is the value returned by the last evaluated expression in the list. For example, a simple block returning 5 is defined as follows:

```
begin declare Integer i, j; i := 1; j := 4; i + j; end
```

Next there are two types of iterative expression: a for loop expression and a while expression. The for loop provides iteration over the elements of an aggregate. It returns no value (i.e., its return type is Void) and is thus evaluated only for its side effects. For example, to set the primary provider for a set of patients to a given provider, `prov`, one could evaluate the following expression:

```
for p in Set(p1, p2, p3, p4) do primProvOf(p) := prov
```

The while expression allows one to iteratively evaluate an expression (the loop expression) until another expression (the pred expression) returns true. The while loop also returns no value, similar to the for loop.

The next expression type is the so-called quote special form. A quoted expression returns its arguments unevaluated. A variation of the quote is the so-called backquote expression. This also returns its argument expression unevaluated, except for those parts that are wrapped in a call to the unquote function. The quote function is required to allow functions to evaluate their own arguments. This is often useful—for example, when defining functions that create and implement other functions.

The last construct shown in the abstract syntax is a type declaration. This is not an expression but rather is required to be able to define variables. A type declaration defines a binding between an identifier and a variable (i.e., a storage location used for storing the value). The identifier serves as the name of the variable. Declarations can only be specified as part of a block expression, which is the scope of the declaration.

```
create function filter(Function f, SetType(Object) arg) ->
                SetType(Object) as osql
begin
   declare SetType(Object) r;
   declare Object e;

   for e in arg do
         if(f(e)) then r := r + e; endif;
   return r;
end;
```

FIGURE 3–4
Example OSQL Function—Filter

In addition to the special forms discussed above, there is a number of system functions that provide a degree of nonlocal control that is often convenient when defining a function. The first such function is the `return` function. The effect of calling the `return` function is that the function containing it immediately returns the value of the only argument of the `return` function. Another function is the `raise-error` function. This function raises an exception that will transfer control back to the client application, undoing any changes the function containing the call made.

An example highlighting a number of these constructs is shown in Fig. 3–4. Given a tuple consisting of a function `f` and a set of objects `arg`, the `filter` function will return the set of objects `e` in `arg` for which `f(e)` returns `true`. Note that the parameter `f` is function valued and that the function application `f(e)` in the filter function above will not be resolved until run-time.

3.4 Query Language

OSQL supports a query language whose semantics are based on domain calculus, with support for aggregate domains, functions, and multisets (bags). The OSQL SELECT function provides the basic query facilities of OSQL and closely resembles the Select statement of SQL. The abstract syntax of a select expression shows that it consists of six parts:

```
Select: = resStruct: ResStruct
            resList: Expr+
            forEach: Declaration*
            where: Expr
            groupBy: Group*
```

```
having: Expr
orderBy: orderSpec*;
```

All the parts of the select expression shown above, except for the resList, are optional. For example, using the concrete syntax used by OpenODB to retrieve the name of a person, we evaluate the following expression[6]:

```
select name(p)
```

The query compiler will infer that the type of this expression is BagType(TupleType(Char)). We can use the resStruct options of the select expression to change the result type. For example, to have the select expression return a bag of strings, we add the keyword *atomic*. Similarly, to have the query return just a single name, we add the keyword *single*. A query that returns the name of a person (or null) can be defined as follows:

```
select single atomic name(p)
```

Select expressions are evaluated by parsing them into a call to the (system-defined) select function and passing the select function its arguments—that is, the parts of the select expression as indicated by the abstract syntax above—without evaluating them. The select function compiles the query by creating an unnamed function with no arguments, whose body is the compiled and optimized query expression. The query is evaluated by calling this function without any arguments. In the case of a stand-alone query expression, the unnamed function is transient and deleted after the function is evaluated. If the query expression is part of the body of a function, the compiled and optimized expression becomes part of the body of that function.

More complicated query expressions than the ones shown above can be easily expressed as well. For example, to return the set of names of all persons living in San Jose, California, we evaluate the following expression:

```
select distinct atomic name(p) for each Person p where
    City(p) = 'San Jose' and State(p) = 'CA'
```

The type of this expression is SetType(Char). The reason this query returns a set instead of a bag is that we included the keyword *distinct* as part of the resStruct clause. Similarly, a query that includes an orderBy clause will return a list object instead of a bag. For example, to return a list of the names and OIDs of the next *n* persons whose names are lexically greater than a given prefix string *fr*, we can define a function PersonsByName as follows:

```
create function PersonsByName(Char fr, Integer n) ->
        ListType(TupleType(Char, Person)) as osql
```

6. Note: We assume that the identifier p is bound to the OID of a person object.

```
begin
    declare Cursor c;
    declare ListType(TupleType(Char, Person)) r;
    if( n > 0) then
     open cursor c for
        select name(p), p for each Person p where
           name(p) >= fr order by name(p);
    else begin
     open cursor c for
        select name(p), p for each Person p where
           name(p) <= fr order by name(p) desc;
     n := n * -1;
    end; endif;
    r := fetch(c,n); / * fetch first n elements of
         cursor c*/
    close(c);
    return r;
end
```

The function above can be called directly by an application or via another function. When called by an application, it can, for example, be used to fill in the elements of a menu used to select a person from among all the persons in the database. The second argument of the function PersonsByName is used to specify the number of persons to return as well as to control the direction of the scan—for example, allowing a client application to use this function to scroll up and/or down a list of persons. Note also that the efficient evaluation of the function PersonsByName is dependent on both the presence of an index on the result of the name function and the query optimizer choosing this index to access the corresponding storage structure. OSQL provides the necessary system functions to define such an index, and the query optimizer will select it when compiling a query such as the one above.

The forEach clause[7] defines the search domain of the query by declaring a list of identifiers and their types. The domain of the query is formed by taking the cartesian product of the domain of each of the identifiers in the forEach clause. Doing so will generate a set of bindings for the identifiers, one binding per element of the domain. From the examples shown so far, it can be inferred that the where clause of the select is a functional expression that returns a boolean value. In fact, in OSQL, the where clause can return any natural number. In case the expression actually returns boolean TRUE, the value returned is 1; similarly, in case the expression actually returns boolean FALSE, the value returned is 0. The counter value returned by the

7. Note: The concrete syntax for the forEach clause as implemented by OpenODB allows the keyword *from* to be used instead of *for each* for reasons of compatibility with SQL.

where clause determines the number of times the result clause of the query should be evaluated for a given binding in the search domain of the query. A full treatment of the semantics of OSQL queries is beyond the scope of this chapter but can be found in Kent 1993.

The groupBy and having clauses of a query are similar to those found in SQL and will not be further explained here.

OSQL does not restrict the kinds of functions allowed in the expressions associated with the resList and where clause of a query expression, other than that functions cannot have side effects. A function has a side effect[8] when it updates another function, either directly or indirectly. To be able to include external functions in query expressions, the query compiler has to ensure that their arguments are bound before they are called.

OSQL query expressions support late binding semantics of functions—that is, function resolution is postponed until the query is actually evaluated, unless the query compiler can determine a unique resolvent at query compile time. For example, suppose that we have a function named area defined on Circle, Rectangle, and Polygon, all subtypes of type Shape; the following query will return the area of all shape objects found in the database, using the appropriate specific function for each:

```
select area(s) for each Shape s
```

3.5 Annotated Examples

In this section, we give examples of OSQL functions that are intended to highlight the various capabilities of OSQL. These examples are all derived from actual OpenODB applications and reflect the capabilities of OSQL as it stands today. We hope to evolve these capabilities by increasing our understanding of applications and extending the language to provide more and higher-level constructs aimed at simplifying the development of applications such as these to increase programmer productivity and to simplify maintenance of the resulting systems.

3.5.1 Queries

The first set of examples shows OSQL's query capabilities and illustrates the modeling of objects with nested structure, the use of function overloading, and the use of recursion in queries.

8. The OpenODB OSQL function compiler determines whether a function has a side effect automatically and marks the function as such in the system dictionary.

```
create type part functions (
    name Char (var 128)
);
create type complexPart subtype of part;
create function subparts(complexPart) -> bagtype(part);

create function price(part) -> Real;
create function price(complexPart p) -> Real as osql
 sum(select atomic price(q) for each part q
          where q occurs in subparts(p));
```

The first two statements above define type part and a subtype complex-Part. The definition of type part is combined with the definition of a function, name, that returns the name of a part. A complex part is distinguished from a part in that it has subparts. The function subparts, defined in the third statement above, return a bag of parts, thus allowing a complex part to include a given part multiple times. Function price illustrates how easily a transitive closure operation can be expressed as an OSQL query, mostly because the price function can be overloaded on the types part and complexPart and will be dynamically resolved as part of the query to compute the price of a complex part p. Note that the occurs in clause in the where clause of the query serves as a multiplier—that is, the price of a given part will be duplicated in the result of the query as many times as the part is included as a subpart of a complex part, so that the summation of the elements of the bag returned by the query returns the intended result. The function to compute the price of a complex part could also have been implemented procedurally, as follows:

```
create function price(complexPart p) -> Real as osql
   begin
         declare Real pPrice;
         declare part sp;
         pPrice := 0;
         for sp in subparts(p) do pPrice := pPrice +
              price(sp);
         return pPrice;
   end;
```

The implementation as a procedure is semantically equivalent to the implementation as a (declarative) query, but the query form is more amenable to optimization.

Another example, showing transitive closure for a parts explosion, is the following:

```
create type material functions (name char(64));
create type simplePart subtype of part functions (
   mat material
);
```

```
create function partExplode(part p) -> bagtype(simplePart)
   as osql bag(p);
create function partExplode(complexPart p) -> bagtype
     (simplePart)
   as osql select atomic sp
   for each simplePart sp, part q where q occurs in
       subparts(p) and sp occurs in partExplode(q);
```

The function partExplode defined above can be used in queries, as follows:

```
select name(sp) for each part p, simplePart sp
where sp occurs in partExplode(p) and name(p) = 'mercedes'
    and name(mat(sp)) = 'asbestos';
```

This query will find the names of all components of parts whose name is ‘mercedes’ that are made of ‘asbestos’.

3.5.2 Distributed Application Integration example

In a distributed environment, the database system or, more precisely, the database server processes must be able both to receive messages from other applications and to send messages to other applications, including other database servers. In general, it is easy to provide a customized interface (client front end) to a database that enables it to receive messages from other applications and to respond to these messages. The other way around is more difficult and will require that the database system provide the ability for users (developers) to invoke their own code, both inside the database server process or a specialized external server process and as part of the client application. Such a capability can then be used to notify other applications of events in the database, such as a change in state in the database as a result of an update, thus implementing a basic active database capability, or to request from other applications (services) information that is needed inside the database.

For example, a slightly stylized function that can be used to send messages to objects residing in other applications can be defined as follows:

```
create function genEvent(Object sender, Object rec,
    Object msg,
               Object msgArgs) -> Object as
        simpleextfun 'gen_event';
```

The function genEvent sends an event or message msg with arguments msgArgs to an Object rec from an Object sender. Note that the sender and receiver objects may be instances of subtypes that have properties that will enable the actual message sending code to retrieve their external identifiers—for example, some kind of globally unique object identifier that enables identification of sender and receiver objects. The `genEvent` function is implemented as a simple external function, meaning that when it is called the C routine registered as gen_event is called. OpenODB allows such C routines to be called in the context of the client application, thus allowing the database server to have access to the state of the client application and providing a degree of isolation between application code and database code[9]. The gen_event routine will format the actual message and forward it to the receiver object. The reason we call this capability *active database* is because it allows the database to affect the state of an object outside the database itself. The actual capabilities are to a large extent determined by the external environment. For example, in a CORBA [Object Management Group 1991] environment, the routine `genEvent` could format and send a message to a remote object, according to the actual arguments supplied as part of the `genEvent` function invocation.

Functions like genEvent can be used as building blocks in other functions, to be called whenever an action is required outside of the database. An example of an actual invocation is as follows:

```
genEvent(LabTechNamed('John'),ProviderNamed('Dr.Heartdoc'),
         'send_email',
         'call 415-123-4567, regarding your patient:
             John - critical high K+ 14.5');
```

This call shows how, in a hospital environment, a lab tech object can notify a provider object about a critically high lab value. In this case, notification involves sending a relevant message, via e-mail, to the receiver.

Another example, along the same lines, shows how we can create functions that spawn and control other processes.

```
create function sendMail(Char to, Char subject, Char msg)
     -> Void as osql
begin
 declare TupleType(Integer,Integer) pty;

 pty := PtySpawn('/usr/bin/mailx',List('-s',subject,to));
 PtySend(pty,StrAppend(msg,'\n.\n'));
end;
```

This function shows the use of some system-defined process control functions (`PtySpawn`, `PtySend`) that allow programs to be executed in a terminal emulator (pseudo-terminal device) and control the program by sending it data or reading back data generated by the program. In this case, we create an external process, using the function `PtySpawn`, and then send that process some data (i.e., the contents of the mail message) using the

9. Future releases will also allow such routines to be made part of so-called external server processes that are independent of any specific applications.

function PtySend. The mailx process sends the mail message when it receives a terminating '.' on a line by itself and then terminates, as if it was invoked interactively from a terminal and the mail message had been typed in directly.

```
create function dhcp_eval(Char cmd) -> ListType(Char) as osql
begin
   declare TupleType(Integer,Integer) pty;
   declare TupleType(Integer,Char) ans;

   /* lookup or establish connection with msm interpreter */
   pty := LookupMsmPty();
   if(NotExists(pty)) then begin
         pty := PtySpawn('/mumps/msm',List());
         LookupMsmPty() := pty;
   end;
   else if (not(PtyAlive(pty))) then begin
         pty := PtySpawn('/mumps/msm',List());
         LookupMsmPty() := pty;
   end; endif; endif;

   /* send command to interpreter and receive echo back */
   PtySend(pty,cmd);
   PtyReceive(pty,List(Tuple(0,MkRegExprToMatch(cmd))));

    /* receive, parse (split in lines) and return answer */
    ans := PtyReceive(pty,List(Tuple(0,'\r> ')));
    return SplitLines(ans[1]);
end;
```

The function dhcp_eval above is similar to the sendMail function but shows an example of the type of processing required to establish a connection with another process and then repeatedly send commands and receive replies. Note the use of LookupMsmPty(), a stored function used to store the values of the external process id and file descriptor. The function PtyAlive is called to check that the process whose process identifier is in the variable pty is still present and responding; if not, a new process will be spawned. The function PtyReceive provides capability to do pattern matching on the output stream sent back by the external process, allowing the function dhcp_eval to recognize the end of a reply. The function MkRegExprToMatch takes a string as an argument and returns a string that is a regular expression that matches the argument. The newline characters in the result returned by the second call to PtyReceive are used to split the answer into a list of strings, which is returned as the result of the function dhcp_eval.

The program started by the function dhcp_eval is a stand-alone interactive interpreter for the MUMPS language. This language is used extensively in hospitals to implement information systems that manage all kinds of data associated with patients—for example, laboratory test results, prescription records, demographic information, and so on [Dept. of Veterans Affairs 1990]. The details are outside the scope of this chapter, but the important thing to note is that the msm program provides us access to all this information by evaluating specific commands. For example, using MUMPS interface routines that we developed [Annevelink, Young, and Tang 1991], we can request a list of the next *n* names and identifiers for patients, starting from a given prefix. Given the identifier of a patient, we can then request values of attributes for these patients and so on, thus enabling us to access the external database.

3.5.3 Constraints, Rules, and Triggers

The next example utilizes genEvent and shows how OSQL procedures can be used to encode rules, constraints, and triggers. In this case, we want to create a function to update a patient's lab values that generates a message when the lab value is abnormal.

```
create function newLabResult(LabTech lt, Patient p, TestOrder t,
           Char value) -> Boolean as osql

begin
   declare isAbnormal;
   LabtestResults(LabTestOf(t),p,CurrentDate()) :=
        Tuple(value,lt);
   isAbnormal := CheckCriticalRange(LabTestOf(t),value);
   if(isAbnormal) then
    genEvent(lt,PrimaryPhys(p),'send-email',
         StringAppend('call ',
          ToChar(work_phone(lt)),
          'regarding your patient: '
          name(p),
          ' critical value of lab test: ',
          name(LabTestOf(t)),
          'value: ',
          value);
   endif;
   return isAbnormal;
end;
```

The function shown above will update the LabTestResults function to reflect that a lab test result has come in. It will then compare the value of the lab test with the critical range defined for it and determine whether it is abnormal. If so, the function will format a message using information stored in the database and send that to the patient's primary physician.

This example is not intended to show the utility of OSQL as a language for defining rules or constraints. Rather, it intends to show how one can enforce arbitrarily complex rules or constraints by "programming" them by hand. Future versions of OSQL may include more specialized rule and constraint subsystems that can be invoked directly or used to compile functions similar to this one automatically, from a more declarative specification.

3.5.4 Integration of Legacy Applications (External Data Sources)

In many situations, there is a need to integrate existing so-called *legacy* systems and applications to simplify access to these systems and to provide a capability to formulate queries that range over data included in several such systems or applications.

The types and functions below are prototypical for the situation in which one wants to integrate an external system with an OSQL database. The type ExtObject provides the capability to define an external key for an object. The external key must provide the ability to uniquely identify the object in the external system, in the same way that its object id allows that inside the OSQL database.

The function CrExtObject provides the capability to create instances of local objects that represent external objects. It provides an example of the capability to call system functions such as CreateObj with arbitrary parameters. CreateObj is a system function that provides the capability to create objects and initialize one or more functions that have the newly created objects as their argument. CrExtObj also shows the capability of OSQL functions to contain arbitrary OSQL queries. The object created by the function CrExtObject is an instance of the type *t*, which must be a subtype of the type ExtObject. The latter constraint is enforced by a run-time typecheck on the value returned by the function CreateObj, added by the OSQL compiler.

```
create type ExtObject functions (xkey Char);

create function CrExtObj(Type t, Char key) -> ExtObject
    as osql
begin
   declare ExtObject eObj;
   declare ListType(ExtObject) eObjs;
   eObj := select single atomic o for each ExtObject o
             where xkey(o) = key;
   if(isNull(eObj)) then
         eObj := CreateObj(t,List(FUNCTION xkey),
               List(Tuple(key));
   endif;
   return eObj;
end;
```

Using the functions described so far, it is now relatively straightforward to define the function ReadExtSurrAttr, which returns the value of an attribute of an object stored in an external MUMPS database. The external database is accessed through the dhcp_eval function defined before. The argument of the function dhcp_eval is an example of a MUMPS expression used to retrieve the value of the attribute.

```
create function ReadExtSurrAttr(Char id, Type objType,
    Char attrName) -> Object as osql
begin
   declare ListType(Char) ans;
   ans := dhcp_eval(strAppend(
             'S DR=',attrName,',OID=',id,' D EN^HPRD\r'));
   return CrExtObj(objType,ans[0]);
end;
```

The function above returns the value of a surrogate-valued attribute of an external object. For example, the following call will return the OID of the spouse of the patient whose id is '^DPT(^2301^2'[10]:

```
ReadExtSurrAttr('^DPT(^2301^2',type patient, 'SPOUSE')
```

The arguments are the external key (id) of the external object, the type of the surrogate object, and the name of the external attribute. The function ReadExtSurrAttr invokes the function dhcp_eval to retrieve the value of the external key of the surrogate attribute from the MUMPS database and calls the function CrExtObj to convert the external key into a corresponding OID, which is then returned.

The next two functions show how OSQL system functions can be used to dynamically create types and functions. In this example, the function ImpExtType creates a type whose extension maps to a set of objects residing in an external system. It also creates, by calling the function CrAttrF, a set of attribute functions that can be used to access the attributes of the objects that reside in the external database. The functions ImpExtType and CrAttrF access the data dictionary of the external system to determine different properties of the attributes—for example, what type of value they return and what indexes, if any, are defined to access the data in the external system. The functions ImpExtType and CrAttrF in effect map the schema specified by the external data dictionary into an OSQL schema. Similar functions can be defined to import other data sources and/or applications.

10. This string is an example of an external id. It contains the information necessary to uniquely identify an object in an external database, in this case a record that contains a.o. a reference to the spouse.

```
create function ImpExtType(Char tName, Char extTypeName,
    ListType(TupleType(Char /* fname */, Char /* attrName */,
                      Integer /* attrMod */)) attrs)
    -> TupleType(Type, ListType(Function)) as osql
begin
 declare Function f;
 declare ListType(Function) attrFncs;
 declare Type extType;
 declare TupleType(Char, Char, Integer) attr;

 extType := MkExtType(tName, extTypeName);
 attrFncs := List();
 for attr in attrs do begin
   f :=CrAttrF(attr[0],extType,attr[1],attr[2]);
   attrFuncs := attrFuncs + f;
 end;
 return Tuple(extType,attrFncs);
end;

create function CrAttrF(Char fname, Type argtype, Char attrName,
   Integer attrMod) -> Function as osql
begin
   declare ExtAttr attr;
   declare Type resType;
   declare Function f;

   attr := FindExtAttrByName(argtype,attrName);
   if(isNull(attr)) then
         raise error StrAppend('Attribute does not exist: ',
                  attrName);

   endif;
   resType := TypeOfExtAttr(attr);
   f := CreateFun(fname,argtype,resType,List());
   if(SurCategory(resType) = 0) then
         ImplOsql(f,List('ARG'), BACKQUOTE(ReadExtCharAttr(
                  xkey(ARG), UNQUOTE(attrName))));
   else
         ImplOsql(f,List('ARG'),BACKQUOTE(ReadExtSurrAttr(
              xkey(ARG), UNQUOTE(resType),
                  UNQUOTE(attrName))));
   endif;
   return f;
end;
```

The function ImpExtType creates a new type by calling the function MkExtType. This function is not shown here, but it will ultimately create the new type by calling the system function CreateType. After creating the new type, the function CrAttrF is called repeatedly to create the functions that will allow us to access the attributes of the objects residing in the external system.

The function CrAttrF creates a surrogate or character-valued attribute function for an external attribute. CrAttrF is implemented as a procedure that first checks the existence of the attribute. If the attribute does not exist, an error will be raised. Next the function TypeOfExtAttr is called to determine the type of the attribute. This information can be found by accessing the data dictionary of the external database. Given the type, we can create the attribute function by calling the system function CreateFun. This function takes the name of the function to be created, its argument and result type, and a list of constraints and returns the OID of the newly created function. The next step is to implement the just-created function. Essentially, the body of the function will be a call to either of the functions ReadExtCharAttr or ReadExtSurAttr, depending on whether the attribute's type is a string or a surrogate type. The body of the function is specified as a backquoted expression, to allow us to substitute the attribute name and possibly the attrType into the function body. The function ReadExtSurAttr is the one defined earlier. The function ReadExtCharAttr is similar to ReadExtSurAttr, except that it returns a string object instead of a surrogate object.

The examples shown here are in many ways simplifications of the ones we have actually implemented. Due to the fact that OSQL is computationally complete and all of the system functionality is accessible by calling the appropriate system functions, there are few limits on what can be done. Other examples of extensions we have implemented include functions to control caching of data residing in external systems. This is often necessary to overcome performance limitations inherent in accessing the external system—for example, when the external system does not provide the indexes needed to efficiently evaluate queries posed by the applications running on top of our system.

3.6 Alternative Approaches

In this section, we want to compare the approach we have taken with OSQL to that of extending the C++ programming language with persistence mechanisms. The first observation that we make is that, due to the fact that extension constructs provided by C++ are limited, approaches that provide a seamless integration between programming language constructs and query constructs and that allow for the compilation and optimization of queries (e.g., those described in Agrawal and Gehani 1989, and Blakeley 1994) require the use of a language preprocessor. In effect, one defines a new and extended language. Secondly, the C++ object model is at the same time more complex and less flexible than the OSQL object model. As alluded to before, the C++ object model mixes the representation of an object with its interface definition. Also, the C++ model does not provide support for adding or removing types from objects, a requirement if one wants to realistically model persistent objects. Third, the C++ language provides only very limited mechanisms for function polymorphism, and the type system requires that the types of the identifiers in an expression be known at compile time. These restrictions, while useful at times, also prevent the definition of functions like those discussed in section 3.5, where we pass types and functions as arguments.

In our view, C++ is not a suitable basis for defining a database programming language because it falls short of meeting some of our essential design goals as summarized in the introduction. That notwithstanding, C++ can be an excellent choice as an applications programming language. By carefully designing and implementing the C++ application programming interface, taking advantage of the data abstraction capabilities offered by C++, one can easily create a set of classes to provide a seamless interface to the OSQL data model.

3.7 Conclusions

We have presented OSQL, a language developed to facilitate the design and implementation of object databases. OSQL is a computationally complete language that combines the power of relational query languages with the expressiveness and extensibility characteristic of a functional programming language. OSQL provides a type system that allows objects to evolve over time, acquiring new types and losing old ones as their roles change. OSQL provides support for aggregate types and avoids the impedance mismatch problem between programming language and query language by tightly integrating the two. OSQL is very well suited to developing applications in a distributed world. By providing the capability to evaluate (user-defined) functions in the database server, the application developer can implement functions and then share these across a large number of applications. In addition, as shown by the examples in this chapter, database functions can interact with other application services, providing the capability to integrate data residing in external applications and/or databases and building integrated information management systems that preserve the integrity and autonomy of legacy applications. Moreover, by providing this capability as an orthogonal extension to the base language, one can use OSQL's declarative query processor to transparently query data residing either in the object database or in one or more external databases.

The OSQL language is characterized by the fact that it can evolve by extending the set of (system) types and functions provided. As a result, a lot of our development effort is directed toward building libraries of functions and types that facilitate the rapid development of applications in specific application domains and that provide the constructs needed to integrate information available in existing databases and other types of legacy applications. This is a first step toward an approach that would allow application developers to quickly construct information services by picking from an existing set of type and function definitions, refining them as needed, and interfacing them with their (application-specific) user interfaces using the communications facilities and application development tools provided in a distributed computing environment.

ACKNOWLEDGMENTS

We would like to acknowledge the many contributions made by our colleagues in the database department of Hewlett-Packard Laboratories, where most of the early work on OSQL was done and where the Iris prototype was developed, as well as the Commercial Systems Division of Hewlett-Packard, where OpenODB was designed and implemented.

REFERENCES

Agrawal, R., and Gehani, N.H. 1989. ODE (Object Database and Environment): The Language and Data Model. *Proceedings of ACM SIGMOD International Conference on Management of Data 1989,* May 1989, Portland, 36–45.

Ahad, R., and Cheng, T. 1993. OpenODB—An Object-Oriented Database Management System for Commercial Applications. *HP Journal,* Vol. 44, No. 3, 20–30.

Ahad, R., and Dedo, D. 1992. OpenODB from Hewlett-Packard: A Commercial OODBMS. *Journal of Object Oriented Programming,* Vol. 4, No. 9.

Ahad, R., et al. 1992. Supporting Access Control in an Object-Oriented Database Language. *Proceedings of International Conference on Extending Database Technology,* Vienna, Austria, March 1992.

Annevelink, J. 1991. Database Programming Languages: A Functional Approach. *Proceedings of ACM SIGMOD International Conference on Management of Data 1991,* May 1991, Denver, 318–327.

Annevelink, J., Young, C.Y., and Tang, P.C. 1991. Heterogeneous Database Integration in a Physician's Workstation. *Proceedings of 15th Annual Symposium on Computer Applications in Medical Care,* McGraw-Hill, New York, 1991, 368–372.

Blakeley, J. A. 1994. ZQL[C++]: Extending the C++ Language with an Object Query Capability. In: *Modern Database Systems.* W. Kim, ed. Addison-Wesley, Reading Mass.

Department of Veterans Affairs. 1990. *VA Fileman User's Manual,* Version 18.

Ellis, M.A., and Stroustrup, B. 1990. *The Annotated C++ Reference Manual.* Addison-Wesley, Reading, Mass.

Fishman, D.H., et al. 1989. Overview of the Iris DBMS. In: *Object Oriented Concepts, Databases and Applications.* W. Kim and F.H. Lochovsky, eds. ACM, New York.

Goldberg, A., and Robson, D. 1983. *SMALLTALK-80: The Language and Its Implementation.* Addison-Wesley, Reading, Mass.

Hewlett-Packard. 1992. *OpenODB Reference Manual* B3185A.

Kent, W. 1993. A Model-Independent Query Paradigm Founded on Arithmetic. In preparation.

Lyngbaek, P. 1991. OSQL: A Language for Object Databases. Hewlett-Packard Laboratories technical report HPL-DTD-91-4.

Mylopoulos, J., Bernstein, P.A., and Wong, H.K.T. 1980. A Language Facility for Designing Database-Intensive Applications. *Proceedings of ACM Transactions on Database Systems,* Vol. 5, No. 2.

Object Management Group. 1991. The Common Object Request Broker: Architecture and Specification. Document No. 91.12.1.

Shipman, D. 1981. The Functional Data Model and the Data Language DAPLEX. *ACM Trans. on Database Systems,* Vol. 6, No. 1.

Wilkinson, K., Lyngbaek, P., and Hasan, W. 1990. The Iris Architecture and Implementation. *IEEE Transactions on Knowledge and Data Engineering,* Vol. 2, No. 1.

4

OQL[C++]: Extending C++ with an Object Query Capability

JOSÉ A. BLAKELEY

This chapter presents an approach to extending C++ with an object query capability. The result is a language called OQL[C++] that uses the C++ type system as an object data model, extends C++ with a query statement based on the standard SELECT-FROM-WHERE structure of SQL, and allows certain C++ expressions to be used in the formulation of queries. OQL[C++] allows queries on transient or persistent data and permits user-defined functions in the formulation of queries including collection-valued and Boolean-valued functions. OQL[C++] supports queries on semantically different collection types, data abstraction, inheritance, and complex objects. It also supports uniform type checking of the entire application, including queries and programming language expressions. In OQL[C++], the notions of type and type extent are distinguished, thus allowing multiple sets of a type in an application. These features of OQL[C++] yield a unique integration between C++ and a query language.

4.1 Introduction

Object query language design is one of the most important challenges to designers of object-oriented database systems (OODBs). This chapter addresses the problem of integrating query and programming languages.

Given the lack of a standard data model, a common approach to building OODBs consists of adopting the type system of an existing object-oriented programming language and extending it to support database capabilities such as persistence, transactions, and queries. Several commercial products following this approach are currently available for languages such as C++ (e.g., Objectivity, ObjectStore [Lamb et al. 1991], Versant [Versant 1991]) and Smalltalk (e.g., GemStone [Maier and Stein 1987], Versant). Since programming languages (PLs) do not incorporate non-procedural query statements, designers of OODBs need to devise ways to add query support to their systems.

With traditional database management systems (DBMSs) (e.g., relational, hierarchical), database applications are written using query statements embedded in a general purpose PL. The embedding of query statements has five serious problems and limitations. First, the data model of the database and the type system of the PL do not match [Copeland and Maier 1984]. For example, programming languages for which query embedding is available (e.g., C, FORTRAN, COBOL) do not provide a set type among their basic types; consequently, sets of objects returned by a query cannot be manipulated as a unit by programming language constructs. Second, the lack of type checking spanning both the application and the query code creates the opportunity for inconsistencies to be introduced in the database. For example, application program variables representing database objects could be assigned illegal values or values of the wrong type, and this problem may pass undetected even after the transaction commits. Third, queries can only be formulated on persistent database objects (e.g., relations); they cannot be formulated against transient objects or against persistent objects after they enter the application address space. Fourth, query and PL statements cannot be freely combined. For example, it is impossible to pose a query on the values returned by a set-valued function in the program or to use a query as a parameter to a function expecting a set-valued parameter. Finally, the syntax and semantics of the two languages are completely different and the programmer needs to learn the differences.

Research into persistent database programming languages addresses some but not all of the above query-PL integration issues. Most database programming languages proposed offer some form of query capability, but their designs emphasize different concerns, such as support for semantic data modeling abstractions (e.g., aggregation, generalization), transactions, type checking, and exception handling [Albano et al. 1985], rather than the query-PL integration aspects. Indeed, reducing the stylistic and computational mismatch between set-oriented and object-at-a-time processing continues to be an important challenge faced by designers of persistent PLs, database PLs, and OODBs [Hull et al. 1990].

Even though we address the query-PL integration problem in the context of an OODB that uses the type system of an existing PL as an object data model, we believe that many of the ideas presented apply to the design of new database PLs or OODBs attempting to incorporate query capabilities.

The following is an example of a OQL[C++] query in a C++ program that obtains the employee name and department of all employees who are at least 32 years old, work in a department on the third floor, and have received a salary increase after January 1, 1993. The query includes the use of a set-valued program variable (i.e., `aResult`) to hold the result of the query, abstract data type operators (e.g., > for `Date`), join and projection (i.e., generation of objects of type `Newobject` with new identity), and data abstraction (i.e., all predicates expressed in terms of the objects' public interface).

```
Set<Newobject> *aResult;
Date aDate(01,01,1993);
aResult = SELECT Newobject( e->name(), d )
          FROM Employee *e IN Employees, Department *d IN
               Departments
          WHERE e->department() == d && e->age() >=32
             && e->last_raise() > aDate && d->floor() == 3;
```

By using the C++ type system as an object data model instead of inventing yet another object model, we are able to benefit directly from the support for complex objects, inheritance, data abstraction, polymorphism, parameterized types, and computational completeness already available in C++. OQL[C++] supports queries on semantically different collection types, data abstraction, inheritance, and complex objects. It also supports uniform type checking of the entire application, including queries and PL expressions. OQL[C++] allows queries on transient or persistent data. Future database query capabilities should be orthogonal to semantic and physical characteristics of data, such as persistence, distribution, versioning, and time. OQL[C++] permits PL expressions in the formulation of queries including collection-valued, Boolean-valued, and constructor expressions. OQL[C++] query expressions can operate on semantically different collection types. Also, the notions of type and type extent are separated, enabling the creation and querying of multiple collections of a type in an application. All the above features of OQL[C++] yield a *unique integration* between C++ and a query language. An early description of this work is presented in Blakeley et al. 1991.

An initial prototype of OQL[C++] was built as part of the Zeitgeist OODB project at Texas Instruments [Ford et al. 1988], and development has continued with the Open OODB system [Wells et al. 1992; Blakeley et al. 1993].

The rest of this chapter is organized as follows: Section 4.2 describes important requirements in the integration between query and programming languages. Section 4.3 is a brief introduction to the basic C++ terminology used throughout the chapter. Readers familiar with C++ may skip this section entirely. Section 4.4 presents an overview of the OQL[C++] language, using examples. Section 4.5 presents our conclusions and directions for future work.

4.2 Query and Programming Language Integration

What does it mean for a query language to be well integrated with a programming language? There are currently no criteria or formalism to help answer this question. This section proposes some requirements that contribute to defining a good query-PL integration. These requirements are derived largely from our observation of the deficiencies in the embedding of existing query languages in PLs. Not all these requirements are mutually exclusive. It is not clear whether all requirements can be met at once, so some compromises may be necessary.

4.2.1 Language Type System = Object Data Model

Unifying the PL's type system and the data model supported by the database system substantially reduces the impedance mismatch problem. This approach, pioneered by PS-Algol [Atkinson et al. 1983] and used by existing C/C++-based OODBs, attempts to increase software development productivity by eliminating the need for programmers to code the mapping between the data structures of the PL in which applications are written and the database. This approach also facilitates type checking of the entire application including query and PL code.

There are two other approaches to reconciling the programming language and the database model. *Programming language independent* data models (e.g., relational [Codd 1979], Iris [Fishman et al. 1987], UniSQL [Kifer at al. 1992]) have been designed to increase the degree of sharability of data across applications written in different programming languages at the expense of perpetuating the impedance mismatch problem. *Database programming languages* (DPLs) (e.g., Taxis [Mylopoulos et al. 1980]) are programming languages designed from the ground up to provide the highest integration and transparency of database access from applications. But query and PL integration has not been a central issue in the design of DPLs.

4.2.2 Type-Checking

A good query-PL integration should support strong typing of the entire application, including PL and query statements. Type-checking is desirable in database applications to ensure that objects transferred between the application space and the database are consistent and that any operation performed by the application, including queries, operates on objects of the right type. Type-checking can be done at compile-time (static), at run-time (dynamic), or at a combination of compile-time and run-time. Lack of (or deficient) type checking may allow expensive application run-time errors caused by applying an operation to an operand of the wrong type, which may compromise the integrity of the database. Languages that prevent this kind of error are called *strongly typed* and are generally viewed as safer and more efficient than languages that do not.

OQL[C++] performs a combination of static and dynamic type-checking. The OQL[C++] compiler translates queries into a sequence of equivalent C++ statements that are statically type-checked by a C++ compiler. Run-time type-checking ensures that only type-correct objects are transferred between the persistent object base and the application's address space. Compile-time type-checking ensures that once the objects enter the application space, they are manipulated consistently.

4.2.3 Queries Orthogonal to Persistence

Today's commercial query languages allow only queries on persistent data. From a programmer's point of view, it is desirable to be able to query transient and persistent data in a uniform way. Orthogonality of queries with respect to persistence can be extended to other database functionality dimensions. That is, the ability to query objects should be independent of the physical or logical properties associated with the objects manipulated by an application. It should be possible to query objects regardless of whether they are transient, persistent, distributed, replicated, versioned, or time-varying. Furthermore, it is desirable to be able to pose a query on the result of another query. Full orthogonality of queries with respect to other database functionality is a long-term goal in the design of OQL[C++]. Currently, OQL[C++] supports queries on *transient and persistent* data.

4.2.4 Separation of Types and Type Extents

An object query language should be able to operate on semantically different collection types (e.g., set, bag, array). Furthermore, queries should be allowed on any collection-valued expression defined by an application. A corollary to this requirement is the separation of the concepts of type and type extent in the data model.

A *type extent* (also called *implicit* collection) is a collection maintaining all instances of a particular type. In systems supporting type extents (e.g., Iris, UniSQL, Versant) a newly created instance immediately becomes a member of its type extent. An *explicit* collection is a collection defined and maintained explicitly by an application. The support of explicit collections makes types orthogonal to type extents and provides more flexibility to the programmer by allowing the definition of multiple collections of a type and sharing of member objects among multiple collections. Explicit collections appear to be a more natural choice to programmers of conventional PLs.

Support for implicit and explicit collections is not mutually exclusive. A system capable of supporting explicit collections can also support implicit ones as a special case. That is, at object creation time, an object could be inserted into a special collection designated as a type extent. Membership in type extents can be enforced as part of the constructor function of a type.

4.2.5 Combining Query and Programming Language Statements

A well-integrated query language should allow the specification of PL expressions within a query where it makes sense; conversely, query expressions should be allowed as arguments to any PL expression. Examples include allowing (Boolean) user-defined expressions (e.g., functions) as query predicates; collection-valued expressions, objects, and variables as targets for queries; constructor function calls to create objects of a new type, possibly with new identity (e.g., to support projection and join); and a query expression to be used in a PL expression expecting a collection-valued argument.

OQL[C++] allows (Boolean) user-defined expressions to be used as predicates in the `WHERE` clause and collection-valued expressions, objects, and variables as targets for queries in the `FROM` clause. The declaration of range variables in the `FROM` clause is identical to the declaration of variables in C++. OQL[C++] allows the creation of new objects as a result of a query (e.g., projection and join) through type constructors in C++. Extended relational DBMSs such as Postgres [Stonebraker and Kemnitz 1991] allow C functions, operators, and Postquel functions in queries.

4.2.6 Data Abstraction

An abstract data type specification describes a class of data structures not by an implementation but by a public interface (i.e., operations and properties) available on the data structures [Meyer 1988]. Manipulation of an ADT is done only through this public interface. This subsection briefly addresses two issues in the support of data abstraction by a query language—namely, determining the degree to which data abstraction should be enforced by the query language and the consequences that such an enforcement may have on query processing.

The degree of support of data abstraction in a query language goes hand in hand with the degree of support of data abstraction in a data model. While some data models provide no support for data abstraction (e.g., C), others provide strict enforcement of it (e.g., Smalltalk). Yet other data models like C++ allow implementation details to be exposed in the public interface. Although the support of data abstraction is desirable, it is arguable whether the query language should enforce it more strictly than the underlying data model. We propose that a good query-PL integration should enforce data abstraction only to the extent the underlying data model enforces it. Specifically, OQL[C++] allows predicates on any public member (state or methods).

The enforcement of data abstraction by a query language raises some issues regarding query optimization [Graefe and Maier 1988]. In addition to using knowledge about value distribution and predicate selectivity, query optimization may require knowledge about structural properties (e.g., object size, index availability, dependencies of methods on state) of objects for cost estimation purposes. Thus, while it is important to enforce data abstraction from the point of view of the applications, the query optimizer needs a way to access structural information about objects.

4.2.7 Uniform Syntax and Semantics of Query and PL Statements

Ideally, the syntax and semantics of the query extension should be compatible with those of the programming language being extended. Currently, there is no metric to measure such a degree of compatibility. Some query languages generalize the syntax of relational query languages SQL (e.g., O_2 [Bancilhon et al. 1989], OQL[C++], UniSQL) or QUEL (e.g., Postquel) to support objects. Some database programming languages (e.g., Taxis) and persistent programming languages (e.g., E [Richardson and Carey 1987], O++ [Agrawal and Gehani 1989]) generalize the syntax of iterative statements to accommodate predicates. Finally, languages like ObjectStore's query language have a completely new syntax. Which syntactic approach is better is typically subjective and depends on the query language designer's and programmer's taste.

4.3 The Data Model

The object data model of OQL[C++] is the type system of the C++ programming language [Ellis and Stroustrup 1990]. This section briefly summarizes some of the C++ terms and concepts used throughout the chapter.

The C++ data model includes a set of *fundamental* (built-in or primitive) data types: character, integer, long, short, float, and double. They can be used to build more complex (or derived) types by means of array, class, union, and struct constructors. A *class* is a user-defined type that determines the *structure* and *behavior* of the instance objects of a class. Throughout this chapter, we use synonymously each pair of terms class/type and object/instance. We refer to the set of all instances of a class as a *class extent*. The declaration of a class involves defining a set of *data members* (attributes or slots) and a set of *member functions* (operations or methods) describing the structure and behavior, respectively. A *class member* (a member function or a data member) can be declared as public, private, or protected. A public

```
class Person {
public:
 Person( Name&, Birthdate& );
 int age();
 Name name();
 virtual void print();
 void set_name( Name& );
private:
 Name n;
 Birthdate b;
};
```

FIGURE 4–1
Example of a C++ Class Definition

member can be accessed from anywhere in a program. A private member can be accessed only by the member functions of its class. A protected member can be accessed by the member functions of its class as well as the member functions of the classes derived from it. An *abstract data type* is simulated by a class that has a set of public member functions and no public data members (all its data members are declared as private or protected). For example, Fig. 4–1 illustrates the definition of a class `Person`.

The data members of the class `Person`, declared as private, represent the name and birthday of a person. The member functions of `Person`, declared as public, are `age()`, `name()`, `print()`, and `set_name()`; they are the operations that may be invoked on `Person` objects. The member function `age()` computes its value using the person's birthday and the system date. A constructor for `Person` objects that takes references to name and birthday arguments is shown after the keyword `public`.

The type of a data member in a class can be one of the fundamental data types or it can be a user-defined class. This C++ capability allows for building aggregation (i.e., composition) graphs to represent *complex objects*, which may be defined in terms of other classes. A class can be *derived* (specialized) from one (*single inheritance*) or more (*multiple inheritance*) classes. A derived class can itself serve as the parent class for further derivations.

OQL[C++] supports explicit sets (see subsection 4.2.4 above). OQL[C++] collection types are defined using C++'s parameterized classes [Ellis and Stroustrup 1990]. A portion of the template used to generate the set declaration is illustrated in Fig. 4–2. For brevity, we omit details of the implementation of the set member functions.

4.4 The Query Language

An OQL[C++] query statement is an extension of the SQL query block [Chamberlin et al. 1976] represented as follows:

```
<result> = SELECT<objects>
           FROM  <range variable> IN <collection>
           WHERE <predicate>;
```

We adopted the basic structure of SQL because it has the potential of providing C++ with a well-known model for the formulation of queries that currently enjoys wide use in relational database applications. Also, any syntax of an associative query statement needs to provide a way of specifying the three basic components of the query block above. Therefore, we decided not to design yet another completely new query syntax that would achieve the same purpose and instead chose to evolve the SQL SELECT statement to an "Object SQL." Clearly, other syntactic approaches are possible (e.g., O++, ObjectStore).

The SELECT clause identifies the type of the objects in the collection to be returned by the query. The FROM clause declares the range variables and the target collection to be queried. Several variables ranging over several collections may be declared in this clause (e.g., in the case of joins). The WHERE clause specifies the predicate that defines the properties to be satis-

```
template <class Type>
class Set<Type> {
public:
   Set<Type>();                              // Set constructor.
   Set<Type>(Set<Type>&);                    // Copy initialization constructor.
   ~Set<Type>();                             // Destructor.
   int Is_Empty ();                          // Test for empty set.
   int Is_Persistent();                      // Test persistence status of the set.
   int Contains_Member (Type&);              // Test for membership in set.
   int Is_Equal_To (Set<Type>&);             // Test for equality between sets.
   int Is_Subset_Of (Set<Type>&);            // Test for set containment.
   int Cardinality ();                       // Cardinality of the set.
   int Insert_Member (Type&);                //     insert,
   int Remove_Member (Type&);                //     remove, and
   int Delete_Member (Type&);                //     remove and delete a member.
                                             // Set operators:
   Set<Type>& Union (Set<Type>&);            //     union,
   Set<Type>& Intersection (Set<Type>&);//     intersection, and
   Set<Type>& Difference (Set<Type>&);       //     difference.
                                             // Set iteration operators:
   Type& Get_Member (Iterator&);             //     get member pointed to by iterator,
   void First_Member (Iterator&);            //     set iterator to first member,
   void Last_Member (Iterator&);             //     set iterator to last member,
   void Next_Member (Iterator&);             //     set iterator to next member,
   void Prev_Member (Iterator&);             //     set iterator to previous member,
   int Is_End_Of_Set (Iterator&);            //     test if iteration is complete.
protected:
   ...
};
```

FIGURE 4–2
Fragment of the Set Template

```
class Person {
public:
Person( Name&, Address&, Birthdate& );
 int age ();
 String sex();
 Name name();
 Address home_address();
 virtual void print();
 void set_name( Name& );
 void set_address( Address& );
...
};
class Physician : public Person {
public:
 String specialty();
 Address office_address();
 String phone();
 virtual void print();
...
};
```

```
class Medical_Record {
public:
 int patient_no();
 Date date();
 String diagnosis();
 List< Lab_Test > lab_tests();
 List< X_Ray > x_ray_tests();
...
};
class Patient : public Person {
public:
 int indent();
 Physician family_doctor();
 Set< Medical_Record > records();
 virtual void print();
...
};
```

FIGURE 4–3
Types for a Clinical Database

fied by the objects to be retrieved. The result of the query is assigned to a collection-valued variable in the program.

In addition to adopting the basic SELECT-FROM-WHERE structure of SQL, OQL[C++] accepts certain C++ expressions when it makes sense within a query. In particular, <objects> specifies objects of the same type as a range variable declared in the FROM clause or the creation of new objects via C++ class constructors whose type is different from any range variable declared in the query; <range variable> declares a range variable using the same syntax as C++ variable declarations; <collection> can be a named collection-valued object stored in the database or a collection-valued function or variable defined in the program; <predicate> includes any conditional expression that can be used in a C++ if statement. Such a conditional expression may involve arbitrary user-defined (Boolean) functions or C++ path expressions. In addition, predicates may be formed by composing conditional C++ expressions via the logical operators AND, OR, and NOT and by including nested subqueries, as in SQL. Predicates are defined more formally below. We hope that by combining aspects of SQL and C++ syntaxes, we will provide an object query capability that will appeal to both database and C++ programmers.

We present an overview of OQL[C++] using example queries on the database schema of Fig. 4–3, which includes the types Person, Physician, Patient, and Medical_Record. The types show only relevant member functions used in the examples. Other public member functions, including constructors and functions that modify the values of data members, as well as private and protected data, are omitted. Sets Patients and Physicians, with the obvious associated types, will be used for the queries.

4.4.1 A Simple Example

This query illustrates the role of range variables, inheritance of member functions, and object composition in OQL[C++].

EXAMPLE 1 Retrieve the patients who are treated by Dr. J. Smith.

```
Set<Patient> result;
result = SELECT p FROM Patient p IN Patients
         WHERE p.family_doctor().name() == "J. Smith";
```

In the query, p is declared in the FROM clause as a *range variable* over member objects of the set named Patients of type Set<Patient> stored in the database. The need for declaring the type of range variables in the FROM clause may seem superfluous since it is possible for the query parser to infer the type that p must have from the Patients set. However, for compatibility with the way variables are declared in C++, we decided to use the same C++ syntax for range variable declaration. The function name() used in the WHERE clause is a public member function of Person *inherited* by Patient and Physician. Inheritance of member functions comes at no cost because the OQL[C++] object data model is the C++ type system. The SELECT clause indicates that the objects returned by the query are Patient objects. The expression p.family_doctor().name(), called a *path expression,* allows navigation through the *object composition graph,* which enables the formulation of predicates on values deeply nested in the structure of an object. The function family_doctor() is of type Physician; therefore, we use the dot notation (following C++ convention) to invoke the function name() of physician. The result of the query is an object of type Set<Patient>, which is assigned to the variable result of the same type. As expected in C++, result needs to be declared before it is used. In this example, the variable result is a transient set instance. A programmer may decide to make this transient set persistent at a later time, using the specific protocol provided by the target persistent language. Subsequent queries can be posed against the variable result within the same program.

The path expression p.family_doctor().name() returns an object of type Name. The operator== for the Name class is overloaded by the definer of this class to allow comparison with explicit strings (e.g., "J. Smith") within a query predicate. More sophisticated overloadings of operator== are possible to include—for example, approximate string matching.

More generally, predicates in the WHERE clause can be defined using *comparison* operator $\theta \in$ {==,<,<=,>,>=,!=}, and *logical* operators && (AND), || (OR), and ! (NOT). The syntax of comparison and logical operators is the same as in C++. *Atomic terms* are t_1 θ t_2, t_1 IN s_1, s_1 CONTAINS s_2, t_1 θ ALL s_1, t_1 θ ANY s_1, and EXISTS s_1; where t_1 and t_2 are single-valued path expressions or constants, s_1 and s_2 are sets or set-valued path expressions, and θ is a comparison operator. The atomic terms involving ANY and ALL are used for existential and universal quantification, respectively. A *predicate* is a Boolean combination of atomic terms.

4.4.2 Pointer Range Values

OQL[C++] allows the use of pointer range variables in the FROM clause. The following query is equivalent to the query in Example 1.

```
result = SELECT p FROM Patient *p IN Patients
         WHERE p->family_doctor().name() == "J. Smith";
```

In this query, the range variable p is declared as a pointer to Patient objects. Since the function family_doctor() is of type Physician, we still need to use dot notation to invoke the name() function of class Physician. The declaration of pointer range variables in the FROM clause — another aspect of orthogonality between OQL[C++] and C++—is introduced for convenience to C++ programmers. Hereafter, even though the rest of the examples do not use pointer range variables, it should be clear to the reader that they are supported.

4.4.3 Path Expressions

Path expressions may be *single valued* or *set valued* [Zaniolo 1983]. In Example 1, p.family_doctor().name() is single valued. The next example shows how set-valued path expressions are handled. This query also illustrates the use of set-valued functions in the FROM clause.

EXAMPLE 2 Retrieve male patients who have been diagnosed with flu prior to June 5, 1993.

```
result = SELECT * FROM Patient p IN Patients
         WHERE p.sex() == "male" &&
         EXISTS ( SELECT r FROM Medical_Record r IN
              p.records()
                   WHERE r.date() < Date(06,05,93) &&
                         r.diagnosis() == "flu" );
```

In this query, the path expression p.records() returns an object of type Set <Medical_Record>. OQL[C++] requires the programmer to write the query by defining a variable (e.g., r) to range over the members of this set. This introduces the use of nested subqueries. The `EXISTS` keyword in OQL[C++] has the same semantics as in SQL. The expressions `r.date()` and `Date(06,05,93)` are of type Date. The evaluation of the condition involving dates uses the comparison operator < overloaded for `Date` instances.

Path expressions provide a uniform mechanism for the formulation of queries that involve object composition and inherited member functions. Let $p.m_1(\alpha_1).m_2(\alpha_2).\cdots.m_n(\alpha_n)$ be a path expression, where each α_i, $1 \leq i \leq n$, represents a (possibly empty) list of arguments to the corresponding function m_i. To use this path expression in a query, every $m_i(\alpha_i)$ must be single valued (enforced during query parsing). If a function $m_k(\alpha_k)$, $1 \leq k \leq n$ is set valued, then the programmer must break the path expression by defining a subquery on the set $p.m_1(\alpha_1).m_2(\alpha_2).\cdots.m_k(\alpha_k)$. Alternatively, OQL[C++] could have performed the iteration over $m_k(\alpha_k)$ transparently to the programmer, but this would have made the semantics of queries more difficult to understand. For now, we opt for a simpler design that requires querying set-valued expressions explicitly. We may revisit this design decision in the future.

Query blocks involving a single range variable in the `FROM` clause may use unambiguously the form `SELECT *` of SQL to indicate that the objects in the result are of the same type as the objects in the set being queried. The query language supports *data abstraction* by requiring that all predicates be expressed in terms of the object's public class members. Queries on the private or protected class members are not allowed. Support for data abstraction represents one of the main advantages of OQL[C++].

4.4.4 Type of Results

The type of the objects in the result of a OQL[C++] query may be the same as the type of the objects in the set being queried (as illustrated in the examples presented so far), a type that is an ancestor of the type of the objects being queried, or a new type.

To obtain objects whose type is a supertype of the type of the objects being queried, OQL[C++] uses a notation similar to a C++ cast. For example, the following query extracts a subset of objects from the `Patients` set. The `Person` objects produced by the query have the same identity as the `Patient` objects in the set being queried. Only `Person` member functions can be invoked on objects in the answer set.

```
Set<Person> result;
result = SELECT (Person) p FROM Patient p IN Patients
         WHERE p.family_doctor().name() == "J. Smith";
```

A query may also return objects of a type that is unrelated to the type hierarchy of the objects being queried. This is necessary to support queries involving *projection* and *join*. The following query illustrates the use of projection.

EXAMPLE 3 Retrieve only the name and age information of patients less than 10 years old.

```
class New_Object {
public:
  New_Object( Name&, int& );
  ...
};
Set<New_Object> result;
result = SELECT New_Object (p.name(), p.age())
         FROM Patient p IN Patients WHERE p.age() < 10;
```

The query illustrates a natural use of the C++ class constructor as part of the `SELECT` clause to create a set of objects (i.e., with their own new identity) of a new type. In this query, the class `New_Object` needs to be defined before issuing the query that uses the `New_Object` constructor. The results produced by OQL[C++] queries are always collections of objects. The following query illustrates the use of join.

EXAMPLE 4 Retrieve all doctors and patients who live on the same street within the same city.

```
class Dr_Patient {
public:
  Dr_Patient( Physician&, Patient& );
...
};
Set<Dr_Patient> result;
result = SELECT Dr_Patient( d, p )
         FROM Physician d IN Physicians, Patient p IN
              Patients
         WHERE d.office_address().street() ==
              p.home_address().street()
              && d.office_address().city() ==
              p.home_address().city();
```

Again, the query will return a new set of `Dr_Patient` objects, each of which has new identity. It is up to the user defining the `Dr_Patient` class to determine whether the object in that class will point to the original patient and physician objects or to new copies of these objects. The support of joins is important in a query language to derive relationships among objects based on the values of their properties. The programmer is responsible for defining the types associated with new objects generated by a query.

4.4.5 User-Defined Functions

The next example illustrates the use of user-defined functions in the FROM and WHERE clauses of a query statement.

EXAMPLE 5 Retrieve patients who have X-ray exams that match a tuberculosis of the lungs pattern.

```
Set<Patient> result;
result = SELECT p FROM Patient p IN Patients
         WHERE EXISTS ( SELECT * FROM Medical_Record r
              IN p.records()
                WHERE EXISTS ( SELECT * FROM X_Ray x IN
                     r.x_ray_tests()
                               WHERE x_ray_match
                                    (x.picture(), pattern)));
```

Every medical record of a patient contains a list of X-ray exams for the patient. OQL[C++] allows queries on sets (e.g., Patients, p.records()) and on lists (e.g., r.x_ray_tests()). The user-defined (Boolean) function x_ray_match compares a digital representation x.picture() of an X ray with the program variable pattern of type Bitmap* holding a typical tuberculosis pattern.

4.4.6 Heterogeneous Collections

OQL[C++] sets and lists support a restricted form of heterogeneity—namely, member objects of different types related through inheritance via a common ancestor type. When querying these collections, the query predicate must refer only to member functions of the common supertype. More general forms of heterogeneity that support member objects of totally unrelated types require the ability of the system to invoke arbitrary methods on any object. This requires, in general, dynamic method dispatching and exception handling mechanisms. In the current C++ language specification, dynamic method dispatch is limited to the use of virtual functions. OQL[C++] inherits this current C++ limitation.

4.4.7 Updates

As in SQL, OQL[C++] also supports the update statements UPDATE, DELETE, and INSERT. UPDATE applies functions to modify the state of a subset of objects specified by a predicate. The public interface to parameterized sets (see Fig. 4–2) includes member functions Insert_Member and Remove_Member, which provide insertion and deletion of single member objects into and from a set, respectively. However, sometimes it is convenient for a programmer to have the capability to perform bulk insertions and deletions of objects in a set. The DELETE and INSERT statements provide such a capability. The following examples illustrate the use of set-oriented update operations in OQL[C++].

EXAMPLE 6 Change the phone number of all physicians whose offices are located in 453 First St., Dallas, Texas, to (214) 444-9999.

```
UPDATE SET p.set_phone("214-444-9999")
FROM Physician p IN Physicians
WHERE p.address().street() == "453 First St." &&
     p.address().city() == "Dallas"
     && p.address().state() == "Texas";
```

In this query, we assume that set_phone() is a member function of the Physician class.

EXAMPLE 7 Delete all patients of Dr. Smith from the set Patients.

```
DELETE FROM Patient p IN Patients
WHERE p.family_doctor().name() == "J. Smith"
```

EXAMPLE 8 Transfer all patients of Dr. Smith in the Patients set suffering from tuberculosis to the new Tuberculosis_Patients set.

```
Set<Patient> Tuberculosis_Patients;
INSERT INTO Tuberculosis_Patients
SELECT * FROM Patient p IN Patients
WHERE p.family_doctor().name() == "J. Smith"
    && EXISTS ( SELECT r FROM Medical_Record r IN p.records()
                WHERE r.diagnosis() == "Tuberculosis" );
```

4.4.8 Queries in C++ Programs

Figure 4–4 illustrates the use of queries within C++ programs. In the example, statements 5 and 6 show the way to declare and define a parameterized set and list. Statement 9 declares the variable aResult of type Set<Patient>. Statement 10 declares the variable aPattern of type Bitmap*. Statement 11 declares the (Open OODB) variable sys through which naming and transaction services are invoked. Statements 12 and 19 establish the transaction boundaries. Statement 13 fetches the object named "Tuberculosis-pattern" from the database. Statement 14 shows the query of Example 5 on the set Patients. Statements 16–18 show a way to iterate through the aResult set to print the result of the query. Statement 21 represents the definition of the function x_ray_match().

```
#include "Patient.h"          // Patient class declaration
#include "X_Ray.h"            // X_Ray class declaration
#include <Set.h>              // File containing the parameterized
                                 set template
#include <List.h>             // File containing the parameterized
                                 list template
DECLARE  Set<Patient>;        // Expands the declaration of a set
DECLARE  List<X_Ray>;         // Expands the declaration of a list
main()
{
  Set<Patient> aResult;
  Bitmap *aPattern;
  OODB sys("hospital");
  sys.beginTransaction(); // Begin the transaction
  aPattern = sys.fetch( "Tuberculosis-pattern" );
  aResult = SELECT p FROM Patient p IN Patients
  WHERE EXISTS ( SELECT * FROM Medical_Record r IN p.records()
        WHERE EXISTS ( SELECT * FROM X_Ray x IN r.x_ray_tests()
              WHERE x_ray_match(x.picture(), *aPattern)));
  Patient *pat;               // Iterate through the set and print
                                 the result
  for(aResult->First_Member(i); !aResult->Is_End_Of_Set(i);
       aResult->Next_Member(i)) {
  pat = &s->Get_Member(i); pat->print();
  }
  sys.commitTransaction();// Commit the transaction
};                            // End main()
Boolean x_ray_match( Bitmap&, Bitmap& ) { // User-defined function
...
}
```

FIGURE 4–4
Example of a Query within a C++ Program

4.5 Conclusions and Future Work

This chapter presented a query extension to C++ and its integration with a persistent C++ language. We began our presentation by establishing the need for defining better integration between query and PLs and summarized five limitations in existing query-PL embeddings. To overcome these limitations, we proposed a set of requirements to obtain better query-PL integration in future query language designs. We then introduced OQL[C++], a query extension to C++ that satisfies most of the proposed requirements. The OQL[C++] approach contributes to solving the first four query-PL limitations as follows: (1) it solves the *impedance mismatch* problem by unifying the type system of the programming language with the data model of the database; (2) it solves the *type-checking* problem by compiling queries into equivalent C++ statements in a persistent C++ abstraction that are statically type-checked by a C++ compiler; (3) it solves the problem of querying on *transient and persistent* collections by allowing queries on any collection type regardless of their persistence status; and (4) it increases the degree of *integration* between the query and PL by allowing the use of collection-valued functions as targets for queries, user-defined (Boolean) functions on predicates, and constructor expressions to build new objects resulting from the evaluation of queries. OQL[C++] substantially solves the fifth limitation by defining a query statement extension to C++ that provides a reasonable combination between the SELECT-FROM-WHERE query structure of SQL and C++ expressions. Although a programmer in our environment has to be aware of C++ and OQL[C++] syntax and semantics, we believe this deficiency will be present in any query extension to an imperative programming language not originally designed to support queries. Although the work presented in this chapter concentrates on a particular integration of C++ with SQL, we believe our approach can also be applied to extending other programming languages or data models with a query capability. Future research will address issues in the design of query extensions to other data models, development of an interactive OQL[C++] facility, refinements to the existing query optimizer, and development of a high-performance query execution engine.

ACKNOWLEDGMENTS

This research is sponsored by the Advanced Research Projects Agency under ARPA Order No.~A016 and managed by the U.S. Army Research Laboratory under contract DAAB07-90-C-B920. The views and conclusions contained in this document are those of the author and should not be interpreted as necessarily representing the official policies, either expressed or implied, of the Advanced Research Projects Agency or the United States Government.

REFERENCES

Agrawal, R., and Gehani, N.H. 1989. ODE (Object Database and Environment): The Language and the Data Model. *Proceedings of ACM SIGMOD International Conference on the Management of Data 1989*, May 1989, Portland, 36–45.

Albano, A., Cardelli, L., and Orsini, R. 1985. Galileo: A Strongly-Typed, Interactive Conceptual Language. *ACM Transactions on Database Systems*, Vol. 10, No. 2, 230–260.

Atkinson, M., Bailey, P., Chisholm, K., Cockshott, P., and Morrison, R. 1983. An Approach to Persistent Programming. *The Computer Journal*, Vol. 26, No. 4.

Bancilhon, F., Cluet, S., and Delobel, C. 1989. A Query Language for the O_2 Object-Oriented Database System. *Database Programming Languages II*, Salishan, Ore., June 1989.

Blakeley, J.A., McKenna, W.J., and Graefe, G. 1993. Experiences Building the Open OODB Query Optimizer. *Proceedings of ACM SIGMOD International Conference on the Management of Data 1993,* May 1993, Washington, D.C., 287–296.

Blakeley, J.A., Thompson, C.W., and Alashqur, A. 1991. A Strawman Reference Model for Object Query Languages. *Computer Standards & Interfaces,* Vol. 13, 185–199.

Chamberlin, D., et al. 1976. SEQUEL 2: A Unified Approach to Data Definition, Manipulation and Control. *IBM Journal of Research and Development,* November.

Codd, E. 1979. Extending the Database Relational Model to Capture More Meaning. *ACM Transactions on Database Systems,* Vol. 4, No. 4, 397–434.

Copeland, G., and Maier, D. 1984. Making Smalltalk a Database System. *Proceedings of ACM-SIGMOD International Conference on Management of Data 1984,* June 1984, Boston, 316–325.

Ellis, M.A., and Stroustrup, B. 1990. *The Annotated C++ Reference Manual.* Addison-Wesley, Reading, Mass.

Fishman, D.H., et al. 1987. IRIS: An Object-Oriented Database Management System. *ACM Transactions on Information Systems,* Vol. 5, No. 1, 48–69.

Ford, S., et al. 1988. ZEITGEIST: Database Support for Object-Oriented Programming. *Advances in Object-Oriented Database Systems, 2nd International Workshop on Object-Oriented Database Systems,* September 1988, Bad Munster am Stein-Ebernburg, FRG. Springer-Verlag, 23–42.

Graefe, G., and Maier, D. 1988. Query Optimization in Object-Oriented Database Systems: A Prospectus. *Advances in Object-Oriented Database Systems, 2nd International Workshop on Object-Oriented Database Systems,* September 1988, Bad Munster am Stein-Ebernburg, FRG. Springer-Verlag, 359–363.

Hull, R., Morrison, R., and Stemple, D. 1990. *Proceedings of the 2nd International Workshop on Database Programming Languages.* Morgan Kaufmann, Gleneden, Ore.

Kifer, M., Kim, W., and Sagiv, Y. 1992. Querying Object-Oriented Databases. *Proceedings of ACM SIGMOD International Conference on the Management of Data,* 1992, San Diego, 393–402.

Lamb, C., Landis, G., Orenstein, J., and Weinreb, D. 1991. The ObjectStore Database System. *Communications of the ACM,* Vol. 34, No. 10, 34–49.

Maier, D., and Stein, J. 1987. Development and Implementation of an Object-Oriented DBMS. *Research Directions in Object-Oriented Programming.* MIT Press, Cambridge, Mass., 355–392.

Meyer, B. 1988. *Object-Oriented Software Construction.* Prentice-Hall, Englewood Cliffs, N.J.

Mylopoulos, J., Bernstein, P., and Wong, H. 1980. A Language Facility for Designing Database Intensive Applications. *ACM Transactions on Database Systems,* Vol. 5, No. 2.

Richardson, J.E., and Carey, M.J. 1987. Programming Constructs for Database System Implementation in EXODUS. *Proceedings of ACM-SIGMOD Annual Conference 1987,* San Francisco, 208–219.

Stonebraker, M., and Kemnitz, G. 1991. The POSTGRES Next-Generation Database Management System. *Communications of the ACM,* Vol. 34, No. 10, 78–93.

Versant Object Technology. 1991. *VERSANT Language Interfaces Manual.* Release 1.6.

Wells, D.L., Blakeley, J.A., and Thompson, C.W. 1992. Architecture of an Open Object-Oriented Database Management System. *Computer,* Vol. 25, No. 10, 74–82.

Zaniolo, C. 1983. The Database Language GEM. *Proceedings of ACM-SIGMOD Annual Conference 1983,* San Jose, CA, 207–218.

5

C++ Bindings to an Object Database

DAVID KRIEGER
TIM ANDREWS

Object databases provide a unified development and run-time environment for database applications by tightly integrating the application language and the database language. This integration is achieved by extending the application language, in this case C++, with database language constructs, including constructs for data manipulation (DML), data definition (DDL), and concurrency control. The two most common approaches to extending C++ are registration, where persistence constructs are added as primitives to the language, and inheritance, where a protocol for achieving database functionality is inherited from a base persistent object. Registration-based environments provide a more transparent integration for the C++ programmer, requiring little or no change to the existing source code. Inheritance-based environments require more from the C++ developer, but by utilizing C++'s built-in mechanism for extensibility, they provide a uniform protocol and a sound architectural foundation for more powerful database applications.

5.1 Introduction

Object databases (ODBs) represent the convergence of two major technology streams—databases and object oriented programming. On the one hand, C++ applications needed a means of providing persistence for their objects. On the other hand, modern applications have levied requirements on their database management systems (DBMS) that the traditional DBMS have difficulty satisfying. One of these requirements has been to remove the barrier between the application language and the database language by incorporating database functionality into the application language, in this case C++. Applications are written, compiled, debugged, and run in a single environment, that of the C++ programmer.[1] There is no need to copy and

1. Leading from a database-centric point of view as opposed to a language-centric point of view leads to the current crop of "extended relational" approaches in which traditional relational DBMS is extended to incorporate OO application language constructs.

transform the data between database and application language representations. In addition, the need for the application programmer to learn a separate data manipulation language (DML) has been eliminated.

Database language issues are covered elsewhere in this book. At the very least, any database language includes constructs for opening and closing a database; starting, ending, committing, and aborting transactions; defining the database schema; and creating, updating, retrieving, and deleting instances from a subset of that schema. In some database languages, updating is divided into modifying simple attributes of a base schema object versus modifying relationships between a base schema object and one of its partners. For instance, since the relational model represents relationships as foreign key columns[2], the SET clause in an SQL UPDATE statement makes no syntactic distinction between removing an association between sets of data and changing a simple value for a single data item.

This chapter surveys the issues and approaches involved in adding database functionality to C++. While we speak generally about extending the application language to support database functionality, it must be emphasized that this does not necessarily imply changes or additions to the base syntax of the language. One of the great things about object-oriented languages in general, and C++ in particular, is the built-in mechanisms for extending the language through inheritance and operator overloading. In fact, some ODB vendors have taken this approach, providing database functionality through inheritance from a persistent base class. Others have modified C++ itself and require a preprocessing step to deal with these modifications. Both of these approaches are subsequently referred to as *extending the language*.

Note also that the chosen means of providing the binding may reflect a bias towards either persistent language extensions or more explicit support for database applications. These choices are sometimes orthogonal to the means chosen to extend the language but will also be highlighted throughout this chapter.

5.2 The Scope and the Lifetime of Variables and Objects

All computer languages have precise rules for defining the scope and the lifetime of variables. In standard C, a variable declared as **automatic** in a function exists only as long as the function in which it was declared and is

2. A long-standing irony, especially popular among IDMS enthusiasts, observes that the relational model has no explicit representation for relationships. The notion of a join is dynamically created by the DML Select statement. Both the hierarchical and network models have included relationship declarations in their schema definition facility (DDL), acknowledging that these relationships represent joins of enduring interest.

coterminal with the procedure. The lifetime of variables declared as **static** or **extern** is bound to the entire program and is coterminal with the process. C++ basically uses the same rules for objects as for variables. Extending the language to account for persistence is the equivalent of introducing an additional storage class that specifies that an object persists beyond the lifetime of either its originative procedure or process. At the very least, the binding must provide for one program to store an object out to nonvolatile memory and for another program, or a different execution of the same program, to retrieve that object and its associated values.

5.3 Goals and Implications

What exactly does it mean to provide a unified application and database language? What are the goals for providing database language extensions to C++? Broadly speaking, the language should maintain a syntactic compatibility with C++, providing the developer with a single language, not two separate languages.[3] More specifically:

- The developer should perceive a unified type system across both C++ and the database.
- The C++ binding to the database should respect the syntax of C++. Differences between a program using standard C++ and one using the bound database language constructs should, as much as possible, consist of natural extensions to C++ such as class definitions and operator overloads rather than changes to the existing syntax.
- The bindings should be a well-structured small set of additions to the base programming language. They should not introduce sublanguage-specific constructs that duplicate functionality already present in C++.
- Expressions using the database language extensions should combine freely with expressions from C++ and vice-versa.

5.4 A Comparative Example

An application with embedded database language calls follows a general pattern, shown below:

```
Declare the query in the embedded database language.
Declare a cursor to hold one instance of the result
      set from that query.
Declare a structure in the host 3GL to hold the
      results for 3GL processing.
```

3. This list is derived from work done by the Object Database Management Group (ODMG).

```
Open the database.
Start a transaction.
      Set up the cursor.
      Execute the database query.
      Loop through each instance.
           Copy the values into the host language
               structure.
           Process those values. This is the real meat of
               the application.
           Write the results out to the database, copying
               the values held by the host structure to
               the database language variables.
Close the transaction.
```

For an SQL application, one of the causes of the impedance mismatch between the host language and the query language is their different processing paradigms. One of the nice things about the relational model is that queries always return tables. SQL, the dominant language interface to relational systems, is essentially a set processing language. However, most 3GL database applications process the tuples an instance at a time. A cumbersome cursor/looping mechanism is required to map SQL's set-at-a-time processing to the host 3GL's instance-at-a-time processing.

In addition to the design and programming burdens placed on the application developer, there is the additional complication and overhead imposed by the incompatible development environments of the 3GL and the database language. This greatly complicates and lengthens the code-test-debug cycle.

A single language environment removes these problems, greatly simplifying the code-test-debug activity. Furthermore, there is no need to set up a cumbersome transduction mechanism, like a cursor, to link two different processing models.

An application where the database language is seamlessly integrated with the application language has the following pattern:

```
Open the database
Start the transaction
      Retrieve the objects from the database
      Process the objects
      Write the objects back out to the database
Commit the transaction
```

At all times, the programmer is dealing with C++ objects under a single environment, using a single computation model. This is one of the goals and one of the major benefits derived from an integrated, as opposed to an embedded, database language binding. In essence, a well-defined database binding to C++ can be thought of as the ultimate 4GL. 4GLs provide a more integrated database programming environment but have suffered because of the balkanization of many competing languages and their generally haphazard grammars. C++ has rich expression processing and a relatively orthogonal grammar, is standardized by ANSI, and can be tightly bound to an object DBMS through its built-in extensibility.

5.5 Mechanisms for Binding C++ to an ODB

There are many ways to extend C++ to achieve this seamless binding with a database language. Two in use today are the following:

1. A class library approach, in which objects inherit persistent behavior. This approach enables binding to standard C++; there is no need for syntactic extensions to the base language. User-class definitions are altered to inherit from a persistent object class that provides the necessary member functions to make objects of those classes persistent.
2. A procedural approach, in which objects are registered into a persistent space at instantiation. A specific set of procedure calls is used instead of a set of inherited member functions. User-class definitions are not altered. A preprocessor is often used in conjunction with this approach, and syntactic changes are made to the base language to aid in the appearance of tight integration. The preprocessor generates a C++ program with appropriate calls to the ODB runtime.

All the products in use today use a preprocessor for the schema definition to generate the appropriate type information in the ODB from C++ class definitions as well as the calls to the ODB. The semantic richness required to fully declare an object schema is more conveniently expressed using small additions to the base language, requiring a preprocessing step.

There are two primary distinctions between the inheritance-based and the procedure-based models. First, the inheritance-based model enforces a standard protocol for persistence of objects that can be tailored within subclasses. Second, the inheritance-based model distinguishes between objects in program, or transient, memory, and those in the persistent memory of the ODB. This makes the inheritance-based model more complex, especially for the initial applications developed. The primary tradeoff is one of scale. The procedure-based model, when combined with base syntax extensions, works well and is less complex for small applications. While this mechanism, in and of itself, does not inherently limit the number of concurrent users, its overall goal of transparency from database considerations for the programmer results in applications that do not scale to support large numbers of concurrent users. The inheritance-based model adds complexity but also the flexibility to enable the development of larger, more concurrent applications. These distinctions will be examined further in the following sections.

5.6 To Subclass or Not to Subclass

The procedure-based approach does not alter existing class definitions. At object declaration time or at variable creation time, additional constructs (recognized by the preprocessor) added to the language specify the lifetime of the object that persist beyond its defining process in nonvolatile memory.

For example, in ODE [Agrawal and Gehani; 1989], a new storage class specifier was added to the language, in addition to *static* and *extern*, so that the user can specify the lifetime properties of the object. Programs using these constructs require precompilation since the C++ language has been extended in a nonstandard way. While simplifying the programming task in certain situations, this raises all the well-known problems with preprocessors—particularly the difficulty in providing standard development and debugging tools that work effectively with preprocessed source code.

As noted above, the major difference between the inheritance-based and procedure-based approaches arises not so much as a result of the use of a preprocessor but rather from the absence of a common base class of persistent object. The use of a base class enforces a standard uniform protocol for dealing with persistent objects. This enables integrity constraints to be programmed directly in C++ by overriding the member functions in subclasses and encapsulates these constraints within class definitions for organization. It is the authors' opinion that this is one of the most significant advantages of inheritance-based ODBs in general over procedure-based ODBs or trigger-based or 4GL-based approaches. These other approaches allow integrity constraints to be programmed but only on system-defined events (Insert, Update, Delete, Select) and with no organization. Large-scale systems with possibly thousands of integrity constraints become very difficult to write or maintain, as each application is forced to be cognizant of the data integrity rules to insure that modifications to the database don't introduce inconsistencies. In a sense, the procedure-based approach masks one form of complexity from the user but creates another by debasing many of the benefits of object-oriented development—namely, uniform interface, standard protocols, and reusable behaviors.

The major benefit of the procedure-based approach is that C++ programmers can add persistence to existing off-the-shelf class libraries since the existing class definitions need to change little if at all. This has great appeal since more and more class libraries are being shipped in binary form, and one of the promises of objects is the ability to combine prefabricated classes for greater reuse. However, in practice this has proven to be less useful than at first it would appear. For example, whenever an application requires some form of composite behavior (which is almost always), related class *implementations* need to be altered to add persistence, even if the class *definitions* can remain unchanged. This requires access to the source code of the class library, negating the supposed advantage.

For example, consider a graphics class library with primitives such as points and lines and composite shapes such as squares, pentagons, and the like. While it would appear that such a library could be used without modification with an ODB supporting the procedure-based approach, such is not the case in practice. For instance, the implementation of the constructor for the Square class will call the Line class constructor four times[4]:

```
Square::Square () {
  Line *side1 = new Line (topRight, topLeft);
  ...   // three more times
  }
```

The square object can be made persistent using the procedure-based approach, but the embedded line objects cannot. Source code is required to modify the internal construction of objects to add persistence even with a procedure-based approach to the ODB. Serious C++ practitioners are discovering that the siren song of seamless integration between one's own application and vendor-supplied class libraries, without access to those libraries' implementation, is more difficult than would at first appear. One must look very carefully at the specifics of both the application and prospective class libraries before determining that they can be joined into a single application.

5.7 The Illusion of the Single-Level Store

Another important distinction between these approaches to the database binding is the abstract memory model provided to the programmer. The procedure-based approach combined with a preprocessor can be used to eliminate the distinction between the program's working memory and persistent storage. This provides a single-level storage model for the programmer, much like the virtual memory model for modern operating systems. The developer does not have to write any special code to save or retrieve an object from the persistent store. Objects are automatically saved and read into working memory when referenced via a pointer. This memory model substantially simplifies the programming task, eliminating many common errors (such as forgetting to save an object). However, it has two basic problems. The first is the lack of access to the database storage interface, thus eliminating the capability for the programmer to use member functions to

4. Actually, any decent implementation would not construct four lines but probably store a corner and one line as an optimization, or perhaps a corner and a height. Eventually, however, if the square is to be displayed or used in a calculation, the actual line objects must be created, and this creation occurs within the "sealed" class library, leading to the same issue.

encapsulate complex logical relationships and integrity constraints—one of the major advantages of object-oriented programming. Second, it removes the ability to tune the way objects are moved from persistent storage to memory. While this has the advantage of simplicity, it must be remembered that the single-level store is an illusion. In reality, access to persistent store can be a thousand times slower than access to memory. Thus, having explicit control over the interface between persistent storage and program memory is crucial to support high-performance database applications.

A more troublesome problem for modern database applications is the incompatibility between the single-level storage model and a transaction model. A transaction groups a set of operations into a logical unit of work. In order to take effect, the objects that were modified within the scope of the transaction must be written from program memory to persistent memory, and program memory must be recovered so that a new transaction can begin. Since the programmer has no direct control over the writing of objects to persistent storage separate from the clearing of them from program memory, the only recourse is to use the transaction boundaries to manage the program's working memory. Specifically, in a single-level storage model, there is no way to remove an object from working memory without also removing it from persistent memory. This (mis)use of the transaction constructs to manage the program's working memory obfuscates the program, offsetting any complexity reduction provided by the illusion of a single-level store.

5.8 Schema Definition and an Object Definition Language

Broadly speaking, database languages are typically divided into a data definition language (DDL) and a data manipulation language (DML). By simple extension, we can think in terms of object definition language (ODL) and object manipulation language (OML) to emphasize the fact that we are dealing with objects that include the encapsulation of both data and behavior in objects.

The ODL binding to C++ must provide the means for defining a schema in a simple, declarative manner that is familiar to C++ programmers. It should require minimum extensions to the base language that necessitate proprietary preprocessing and/or a proprietary compiler.

The Object Management Group (OMG) has defined an object interface description language (IDL [OMG 1991]) that provides a protocol for the specification of an object interface in terms of named operations and parameters to those operations. This could provide a basis for defining an ODL. The IDL defines an abstract modeling construct, the **attribute**, that represents an object property and automatically provides the simple **get** and **set** accessor functions with a single declaration.

```
interface order
      {
            attribute int order_number;
            attribute char *description;
            attribute item *OrderItem
}
```

Notice that the OrderItem attribute is really a reference to another class—that is, it is a relationship. Here the IDL lacks expressiveness in that the **attribute** specified can only specify a unidirectional one-to-one relationship. Most of the ODB vendors have found it necessary to explicitly represent relationships in their ODL to capture binary and even ternary relationships between objects. A possible extension to the IDL that accommodates explicit declaration of relationships might look as follows:

```
// an n-to-one relationship
relationship target_type relname(specifier) inverse irelname;

// an n-to-many relationship
relationship collection{target_type} relname(specifier)
    inverse irelname
```

Target_type specifies the object type at the other end of the relationship. Relname is the name of the relationship. The *inverse* keyword specifies a bidirectional relationship—that is, a relationship that can be traversed in both directions—and the irelname is the name of the relationship from the target object's perspective. Optional specifier keywords could further qualify the relationship with such properties as optional/mandatory, minimum and maximum cardinality, default values, and sort order.

Using this syntax, an Order with many OrderItems could be specified as follows:

```
interface Order
      {
            attribute int order_number;
            attribute char *description;
            relationship list{OrderItem} contains inverse
                  contained_by;
      }
interface OrderItem
      {
            attribute....;
            relationship order contained_by inversecontains;

}5
```

5. This suggested extension actually comes from early work done by the Object Database Management Group, a set of OMG members, mostly from ODB companies, who are working on object database standards. They have subsequently withdrawn this suggestion. We use it here for illustrative purposes only.

While this abstraction would seem very natural to data modelers or database designers, it requires the average C++ programmer to learn a new set of nonstandard keywords to accomplish what in his or her mind is essentially the same thing as is done with vanilla class member specification, as is shown below.

```
class Order
      {
            int id;
            char *description;
            class OrderItem *Contains;
            Order();
            ~Order();
      };

class OrderItem
      {
            Order *ContainedBy;
            char *name;
            OrderItem();
            ~OrderItem();
      };
```

In addition, it introduces the equivalent of an embedded database sublanguage—something the binding seeks to avoid.

An ODL that somehow describes the schema using the simple standard C++ constructs as shown above would be completely transparent to the programmer. While one can use pointers to specify a two-way navigation between the objects, they do not express cardinality or referential integrity constraints that belong in a schema relationship declaration.

A middle ground might utilize existing C++ data member declaration syntax for simple object properties—that is, those that resolve to a literal and add a modest set of extensions to explicitly model relationships. Below is an example of such a schema declaration. Modeling relationships as objects themselves, using either a specially designated **reference** class or a template class, as shown below, allows the schema declaration to express logical, referential, and cardinality constraints as well as modeling binary, ternary—essentially n-ary—relationships between objects.

```
class Order
      {
            public:
                  int id;
                  char *description;
                  set<reference<OrderItem>>Contains
                  inverse ContainedBy;
                  Order();
                  ~Order();
      };
```

```
class OrderItem
      {
              public:
                      reference<Order> ContainedBy inverse
                      Contains;
                      char *name;
                      OrderItem();
                      ~OrderItem();
      };
```

In this example, the inverse is defined right in the body of the reference clause. It would be just as easy to create a separate reference descriptor that is preprocessed along with the schema definition, to express all the relationship properties, including cardinality, optionality, and so on.

5.9 Keys

Property-based keys, serving as object identifiers, play a prominent role in relational database systems. A key is defined as one or more properties that uniquely identify an instance of a type. Object-oriented languages have focused on the notion of object identity independent of any of the object's semantic properties. The notion that an object's identity is independent of any of its physical characteristics stems from both pragmatic and philosophical considerations in which object identity is considered part of the very foundation of cognitive processes. Leaving aside the philosophic argument, let's consider the pragmatics.

In relational systems, a relation may have a primary key composed of one or more columns that guarantee to uniquely identify an instance of that relation. For many applications involving thousands or even millions of components, having to artificially create and manage a unique identifier for each of those components increases the complexity of the programmer's task by several orders of magnitude. For example, imagine a geographic drawing application managing millions of points and route segments. Perhaps there is some combination of properties that uniquely identifies each one of these objects. However, no designer would use this set of properties to identify each individual for retrieval and processing. Instead, he or she would create a program to generate a unique identifier for each of the objects, create a lookup scheme perhaps based on physical proximity, and access instances through that identifier or via its connection to some previously accessed object. Without OIDs, the programmer must absorb the complexity and overhead of managing the references to these objects. In ODBs, this complexity is managed for the programmer by the OID infrastructure.

However, even though value-based lookup has traditionally not been as common in OO systems as it is in relational database systems, the notion of a key based on one or more properties of the object has migrated to ODBs and is often defined in the ODL. Since objects are almost always indexed on their key for fast lookup, many people in the ODB community feel that keys should be defined dynamically at run-time rather than statically in the ODL. Nonetheless, a complete ODL should allow the static definition of the object's key, although it should not be required.

We have briefly covered some of the issues involved in specifying a database schema using extensions to the C++ language. Different ODB vendors realize this binding in different ways, trading off ease of use for the C++ programmer against more powerful schemes that enable the programmer to control the mechanics of the storage and retrieval. The major differences in terms of ODL are especially apparent in the way ODLs deal with relationships. The extremes vary from providing a templated class for references to overloading the standard dereference operator(s) to account for objects not yet in memory. These differences become even more apparent when we deal with the object manipulation constructs in the next section.

5.10 Object Manipulation Language (OML)

All DMLs (and OMLs) have a set of primitive constructs that account for the manipulation of persistent data. A program must be able to create an object and write it out to nonvolatile storage, to retrieve a specified object for viewing or processing, to change some of the characteristics of that object, to delete an object, and to relate that object to other objects and/or remove that object from an existing relationship—that is, to unrelate it. In short, the OML must be able to manipulate instantiations of all the constructs defined in the ODL.

5.11 Object Creation

The differences between the inheritance-based approach and the procedure-based approach to language extension are apparent when dealing with object creation. In the inheritance-based approach, persistence is specified using member functions defined on a base class and inherited by a subclass, in which case all the instances of that subclass have the *potential* to exhibit persistent behavior. Alternative schemes specify persistence when the object is created. Both schemes have advantages and disadvantages.

The inheritance-based approach is conceptually very simple. The programmer knows immediately if the objects of a given class can exhibit persistent behavior. Note that this does not force all the objects of a given class to persist. Rather, it enforces that persistence appears via a uniform, polymorphic protocol. In C++ terms, a virtual member function must be invoked on an object for it to become persistent. This approach fully exploits object-oriented techniques for encapsulation and reuse of complex behavior. Any class can implement its own specialized member functions, insuring that objects of that class and all its subclasses will perform those functions. This is especially important for enforcing logical integrity constraints. For instance, a Circuit object class might specialize its "store" member function to check design constraints on objects contained in the circuit, preventing circuits that fail the check from ever getting into the ODB. The alternative is to have every application that stores circuits enforce those constraints.

The procedure-based approach leaves existing class definitions unchanged and specifies object persistence when the object is created. In standard C++, objects are implicitly created when the thread of execution enters the function in which the object has been declared. They are created explicitly using a call to **new.** The preprocessor approach essentially extends the standard language in order to specify persistence for the object. For instance, one could add a new storage class specifier, **persistent,** to the language in addition to **extern** and **static**. In standard C++, an object declared *extern* or *static* is coterminal with the process. One declared automatic (the default) is coterminal with the procedure. This extension allows an object to be declared persistent, with a lifetime that extends beyond the process that created it.

Explicit creation of persistent objects is accomplished by overloading the **new** operator, allowing it to accept additional arguments specifying the lifetime of the object and some optional storage directives.

5.12 Object Deletion

Object deletion shares many of the same issues with object creation as described above. The inheritance-based approach provides the benefits of reuse and encapsulation of complex integrity constraints between objects, such as cascading deletes and referential integrity checks. It is also possible to control the synchronization between working storage and persistent storage such that an object may be deleted from the database but still exist in the program's working storage. This is useful, for instance, in a journalling application where an object may be removed from one database but still require subsequent processing such as archiving. This flexibility is only possible by providing an additional member function to persistent objects for their removal from the database, separating the management of an object's process memory representation from the management of its persistent memory representation.

The alternative preprocessor approach would overload the delete operator to handle persistent as well as transient objects. However, since the C++ **delete** operator requires a pointer to an object rather than a surrogate or some kind of handle, the object cannot persist in working storage beyond its life in the database. While maintaining tight synchronization between program working memory and the database image is often desirable, a price is paid in terms of reduced functionality and lack of flexibility. The section above on abstract memory models and single-level storage discusses some of these issues in detail.

5.13 Object Modification

Objects are updated by modifying members or running member functions against them. If the object is persistent, these changes are reflected in the database when the transaction is committed. At that time, the updated object is visible to other applications transacting against the database. When an object has been modified, the ODB run-time process must be notified that its state has changed. The ODB can then reflect these changes to the database, making them available to other processes transacting against the same data. One could imagine that the ODB infrastructure could automatically register that the object has changed, setting the equivalent of a dirty field automatically to save the programmer from having to do this. Nonetheless, most ODBs have exported this capability, providing an explicit member function, for example, **::MarkAsModified**, for this purpose. This enables the system to sweep through all the objects within a transaction boundary and only write to persistent storage those objects so marked. An equivalent scheme maintains a specially defined list of all the modified objects and writes out the members of that list when the transaction is committed.

While this may be unnecessary for small, tightly controlled, atomic transactions, it is very useful in supporting the long non-OLTP type applications for which ODBs are often employed. For instance, in a single-user ECAD application, a session may last hours or even days. Rather than wrap every modification in a transaction, doing multiple writes every time an object is modified, the programmer merely has to mark an object as having been modified and periodically allow the system to save the modifications to persistent store. This illustrates the balance that ODBs have to sustain in supporting both the database transaction model and the language persistence model.

5.14 Object Retrieval

Simply stated, there are two ways in which an object is retrieved from persistent memory: explicitly by name and implicitly by traversing a reference. Issues of object identity and object referencing naturally arise when discussing a database retrieval binding for C++.

5.14.1 Object Identifiers and References

As mentioned earlier in the section on keys, one of the fundamental advances provided by ODBs is the system creation and maintenance of an object identity for each object that is independent of any of the object's semantic properties or features. Usually referred to as *object identifiers* (OIDs), these references are assigned and managed by the ODB and are crucial for program performance and language usability for the programmer. Object identity has a profound impact on the means by which objects are accessed, providing a flexibility not found in relational systems.

On the other hand, for some applications, retrieval based on some set of the object's semantic properties is very useful—for example, ad hoc queries for decision support. Most ODBs have found it necessary to extend the language to support this kind of access as well. Many authors distinguish these two types of retrieval, designating them as reference-based versus value-based lookup. We now discuss the C++ bindings that respectively support these retrieval modes.

5.14.2 Reference-Based Retrieval

In a typical C++ program, references to objects are via a pointer to some location in memory. This has no meaning for objects in persistent storage since their resultant in-memory locations cannot be determined before they are actually read into working memory. A major challenge for the binding is to provide a mechanism to insure that object references are properly resolved when the objects referred to are moved from persistent storage to program memory.

Most ODBs provide the programmer with two ways to reference objects. For instance, ONTOS DB [ONTOS 1993] provides direct references to objects, which are simply C++ pointers, and more powerful abstract references. Direct references must be created and maintained by the programmer within the application program, whereas abstract references are created and maintained automatically by the ODB. Using the direct references adds no overhead to a standard C++ pointer dereference but requires the programmer to exercise extreme care to insure that the pointer is still valid and that the object being referenced has not been deleted. Dereferencing stale pointers accounts for many of the critical defects and system crashes all too common in C and C++ programs.

Notice also that with addition of persistence, it now becomes *more* likely that an object of one lifetime specification will refer to an object with a different lifetime specification—for example, a persistent object references an object that is coterminal with a procedure. The rules for an object of one lifetime referring to an object of a different lifetime are straightforward extensions of existing C++ rules. Objects of one lifetime may always reference objects of a longer lifetime. However, an object may only refer to an object of shorter lifetime as long as that object exists. If the persistent object references an object coterminal with a procedure, when that procedure terminates, its memory resources are returned to the global heap and may subsequently be reallocated by the program. The reference is now meaningless. Therefore, an OML must provide a safe way to reference objects and insure that a reference either returns an object or raises an exception that can be handled by the application.

A common approach taken by some ODB vendors is to have the reference operator refer to a logical address, which may ultimately return a pointer, rather than a physical address in memory. The most natural way for C++ programmers to refer to an object is through a pointer, so one binding that naturally suggests itself is to overload the dereference operators, arrow (->) or dot (.) to actually refer to a logical address. The current language definition, unfortunately, does not allow overloading the "." operator, so this solution requires nonstandard language extensions.

The OID of the referent object is either in working memory or transparently loaded into working memory and the reference converted into a physical pointer. However, there is overhead involved in maintaining the logical pointers and in converting OIDs to pointers and back again each time an object is referenced.

As mentioned earlier, the C++ binding must insure that every persistent object is guaranteed to have a unique object identity that is somehow mapped to its in-memory address. For instance, ONTOS provides a function, **OC_lookup**, which retrieves an object by name, with the following signature:

```
Object * OC_lookup(char * ObjectName, ...);
```

This function is used as follows:

```
char * ItemName;
ItemName = new char*;

cout << "\nEnter item name\n";
cin >> ItemName;
OrderItem *Item =  (OrderItem *)OC_Lookup(ItemName);
```

Abstract references are used to retrieve associated objects and to instantiate new relationships. In most products, this is achieved by creating a relationship object rather than using pointers to represent a relationship. Again, using ONTOS as an example, a relationship is created on the Order object to the OrderItem Object.

The declaration for the Order object is as follows:

```
class Order : public PersistentObject
{
    private:
        int OrderNumber;
        Reference Contains;
    public:
        ...
        OrderItem *getOrderItem()
            {return (OrderItem*)Contains.Binding (this);}
        void setOrderItem(OrderItem *Item)
            {Contains.Reset(Item.this);}
};
...
main()
{
    Order *MyOrder, NewOrder;
    OrderItem *MyItem, *NewItem;
    char *OrdName;

    Ordname = new char*;


    cout <<"\nEnter Order Name\n";
    cin >> OrdName;
    Order *MyOrder=  (Order *)OC_Lookup(OrdName);//get the
order
    MyItem = MyOrder->getOrderItem(); // get the connected
        item.

    NewItem = new(OrderItem);//create a new order
    NewOrder = new(Order);//create an item

    NewOrder->setOrderItem(OrderItem);// connect the new item
        to the new order
}
```

5.14.3 An SQL Binding for Value-Based Lookup

While reference-based access is very powerful and natural for C++ programmers, the relational approach to querying, based on one or more properties of one or more classes is very useful for a whole host of applications or as a stand-alone facility for ad hoc querying of the ODB. Many ODBs provide a declarative, SQL-like query engine with an SQL-like syntax. In most cases, this query facility provides ease of use at the expense of computational completeness. Additionally, when used in an application, it is an embedded language working within a C++ host language and suffers the same problems as traditional embedded database language. Nonetheless, this capability has proven to be useful, providing users unfamiliar with C++ access to the information stored in the object base.

5.15 Transactions

Object databases have evolved capabilities beyond persistent storage to support traditional database functionality. Among the most important is the ability to wrap database operations into atomic units of work called *transactions*. Enforcing a discipline of transaction processing means the ODB is moved from one consistent state to another. This prevents violation of object integrity constraints that could otherwise lead to catastrophic data corruption.

The C++ bindings for transaction management are straightforward. Functions for starting, committing, and aborting transactions must be provided. Additionally, a means to specify a conflict resolution/concurrency control must be available.

5.16 Conclusion

As stated originally, the emergence of ODBs represents a convergence of two mature technology streams. The origins of these two technologies and their subsequent evolutions reflect very different orientations. The manner in which various issues are negotiated in some cases reflects a bias towards the database mindset, sometimes a bias toward the OO language mindset. The inheritance-based approach accounts for the fact that in real high-performance production database applications, the system must provide a mechanism that allows the developer the flexibility to manage both persistent and transient memory, tuning both to support its applications. There is more for the C++ programmer to think about. This approach explicitly accounts for the fact that he or she is designing and building a database application and provides the tools to successfully accomplish this. Alternate approaches let the C++ programmer develop applications as always, managing many of the issues concerning persistence and referential integrity. While this provides a shorter learning curve for the C++ programmer and works well for applications in which the only issue is persistence, it often does not scale up to real database requirements.

REFERENCES

Agrawal, R., and Gehani, N.H. 1989. ODE (Object Database and Environment): The Language and the Data Model. *Proceedings of ACM-SIGMOD International Conference on the Management of Data 1989*, Sigmod Record Vol. 18, No. 2, June 1989.

Atkinson, M., Bancilhon, F., Dewitt, D.J., Dittrich, K.R., Maier, D. and Zdonik, S. 1989. The Object-Oriented Database System Manifesto. *Proceedings of the DOOD Conference*, Kyoto, Japan, December 1989 40–57.

Date, C.J. 1986. *An Introduction to Database Systems*, 4th Ed. Addison Wesley, Reading, Mass.

Fishman, D.H., Beech, D., Cate, H.P., et al. 1987. Iris: An Object-Oriented Database Management System. *ACM Trans. on Office Information Systems*, Vol. 5, No. 1, 48–69.

Kim, W. and Lochovsky, F., eds. 1989. *Object-Oriented Concepts, Databases, and Applications*. Addison Wesley, Reading, Mass.

Object Management Group. 1991. The Common Object Request Broker: Architecture and Specification. OMG Document No. 91.12.1, Revision 1.1.

1993 *ONTOS DB2.2 Reference Manual*. Vol. 1, Class and Function Libraries.

Taylor, D.A. 1990. *Object-Oriented Technology: A Manager's Guide*. Servio Corp., Alameda, Cal.

Wiederhold, G. 1993. *Database Design*. McGraw-Hill, New York.

Zdonik, S.B. and David, M., eds. 1990. *Readings in Object-Oriented Database Systems*. Morgan Kaufmann Publishers, San Mateo, Cal.

6

On View Support in Object-Oriented Database Systems

WON KIM
WILLIAM KELLEY

The three-level schema architecture consisting of a storage schema, a conceptual schema, and an external schema has been used as a guide for an abstract architecture of relational database systems. During the past several years, research has resulted in good understanding of the conceptual and storage schemas for object-oriented database systems. However, to date, the external schema—namely, views—has received inadequate attention. In this chapter, we define the semantics of views in object-oriented database systems by augmenting the semantics of relational views with the semantics of such key object-oriented concepts as nested objects, methods, inheritance, and object identity. Further, we extend the utility of views from merely a dynamic window into a stored database to a dynamic window into the schema (metadata) of a stored database. This allows the simulation of many types of schema change without causing the changes to propagate to the database.

6.1 Introduction

During the past several years, a reexamination of various aspects of relational database systems under the richer object-oriented data model [Kim 1990; Object Management Group 1991] has established that the paradigm shift from the relational model of data to an object-oriented model requires significant changes to the semantics and implementation of schema evolution [Banerjee et al. 1987; Penney and Stein 1987], queries [Carey et al. 1988; Cluet et al. 1989; Kifer et al. 1992; Kim 1989], authorization [Rabitti et al. 1991; Thuraisingham 1989], indexing [Kim et al. 1989; Maier and Stein 1986], concurrency control [Garza and Kim 1988], and the like. One of the features of relational database systems that has not been reexamined for applicability to object-oriented database systems is view support.

Views are integral parts of the ANSI three-level schema architecture standard that has guided the construction and use of relational database systems. The schema architecture consists of the storage schema that describes the storage structures for a database, the conceptual schema that describes the logical model of the integrated database, and the external schema for describing the derived views of the conceptual schema for particular users or groups of users. A foundation for the external schema will complete the development of a three-level schema architecture for object-oriented database systems, comparable to that for relational database systems.

In relational databases, a view is defined as a *virtual relation* derived by a query on one or more stored relations and/or other views. Views have been used for data protection and as a shorthand for queries. That is, authorizations may be granted and revoked on views, and queries (and sometimes updates) may be issued against views. Views are useful for object-oriented databases for similar reasons. Views may be used to specify logical partitioning of the instances of a class. Views may be used to define a content-based authorization in object-oriented databases.

The subject of view support for object-oriented database systems is only beginning to receive attention. Abiteboul and Bonner 1991 and Scholl et al. 1992 explore the use of views as virtual classes to augment the class hierarchy to enhance the modeling and schema restructuring capabilities in object-oriented database systems. An area of research related to views for object-oriented database systems is schema integration in heterogeneous distributed database systems using a functional (or comparable) data model [Dayal and Hwang 1984; Motro 1987]. The approach explored was largely the construction of global entities (views) that generalize entities in local databases. The introduction of an object-oriented data model necessitates significant extensions to this line of earlier research to more fully account for such concepts as methods, object identity, and aggregation.

The objectives and contributions of this chapter are twofold. One is to define the semantics of views under an object-oriented data model by extending the semantics of views in relational database systems with considerations of such object-oriented concepts as methods, object identity, inheritance, and nested attributes (aggregation). The semantics include view definition, view update, and changes to a view definition. Another objective of this chapter is to explore the applicability of views to schema integration of heterogeneous databases and to a simulation of schema evolution to allow the users of a database to experiment with schema changes without causing permanent changes to the database.

We note that most of the observations about the impact of object-oriented concepts on views presented in this chapter, taken separately, may appear to be relatively small ideas; however, collectively they form a complete basis for defining the extended semantics of views for object-oriented database systems. Further, the semantics of views explored in this chapter, with certain pragmatic compromises, have been implemented in UniSQL/X, a commercial unified relational and object-oriented database system from UniSQL, Inc. In particular, UniSQL/X supports view definition, queries and updates through views, granting and revoking of authorizations on views, and schema changes involving views. To the best of our knowledge, UniSQL/X is the only database system with an object-oriented foundation that supports views with extended semantics consistent with object-oriented concepts. Further, an extended version of the view mechanism supported in UniSQL/X has also been implemented in UniSQL/M, a commercial multidatabase system that supports schema integration for SQL-based relational database systems and UniSQL/X. The extended view mechanism in UniSQL/M allows the integration of heterogeneous database schemas using the UniSQL/X unified relational and object-oriented data model as the global data model.

The remainder of the chapter is organized as follows. Section 6.2 defines views in object-oriented database systems and explores the implications of the object-oriented concepts of inheritance, methods, object identity, and nested attributes on the semantics of views. Section 6.3 explores schema changes that affect view definitions. Section 6.4 examines uses of views in integrating heterogeneous database schemas and simulating schema changes. Section 6.5 concludes the chapter.

6.2 Views in Object-Oriented Databases

In relational databases, the definition of a view consists of the view name, a list of attributes (and their domains), and a query that defines how the view will be materialized from one or more stored relations and/or other views [Date 1986]. A view is used almost like a stored relation: It may be dynamically created and dropped, queries may be issued against it, updates may sometimes be issued against it, and additional views may be defined on it. In other words, the goal is to define and use a view as a virtual relation, which differs from a stored relation only in that it draws tuples from some stored relations rather than having its own stored tuples.

The goal of a view in object-oriented database systems is similarly to define and use a view as a virtual class. This means that the definition of a view should consist of all schema elements that can be included in a class and a query that defines how the view will draw instances from one or more stored classes (and/or other views). The definition of a class includes a list of attributes (and their domains), a list of methods, and a list of superclasses [Kifer and Lausen 1989; Kim 1990; OMG 1991]. Therefore, the definition of a view should include a list of attributes (and their domains), a list of methods, and a list of superclasses, as well as a query specification.

Abiteboul and Bonner 1991 and Scholl et al. 1992 assume that views and classes are largely interchangeable; for example, views and classes coexist in a single class hierarchy, and the same inheritance rule applies between a class and a view and between views. Unhappily, a closer look at the object-oriented concepts has revealed significant problems that must be considered and overcome before views and classes can be used interchangeably in object-oriented databases. In the remainder of this section, we discuss these problems in turn.

The following summarizes the differences between a class and a relation (under the normalized relational model of data). Insofar as a view is to be a virtual class, these differences must be taken into account in defining the semantics of a view in object-oriented databases.

1. A class has associated with it attributes and methods rather than just attributes, as is the case with a relation. Further, an attribute of a class may be set valued, whereas an attribute of a relation is scalar valued.
2. A class can inherit properties (attributes and methods) from its superclasses and can have properties newly defined for it, while a relation does not inherit anything from any other relation.
3. A class carries the specialization semantics with respect to its superclasses, which means that all instances of a class are also instances of its superclasses; a relation is not a specialization of any other relation.
4. A class can have nested attributes—that is, attributes whose domains are other classes—whereas a relation does not have nested attributes, since an attribute of a relation has only a primitive type.

The following will summarize the properties of views in object-oriented database systems; we will explore and elaborate on salient aspects of these in the remainder of this chapter.

PROPERTY 1 The definition of a view consists of the name of the view, the list of attribute specifications (attribute name and data type for the attribute) and method specifications (method name, parameter list, and method body) for the view, and a query against the stored database.

PROPERTY 2 The query part of a view definition may be a method or an arbitrary query against stored classes and/or other views and may involve projection and selection operations or methods on a single class or projection, selection, join, and methods on two or more classes.

PROPERTY 3 An attribute specification for a view may be identical to that of a corresponding attribute in a stored class, or it may be a new computed attribute that is not defined in the stored class.

PROPERTY 4 The data type of an attribute or a method in the view with a corresponding attribute or method of a stored class is the same as that of the attribute or method of the stored class, or a specialization of it, or a generalization of it.

PROPERTY 5 A newly defined attribute is an attribute that is derived from one or more of the attributes in stored classes.

PROPERTY 6 A method specification may be the same as that defined in a corresponding stored class or may be newly defined for the view.

PROPERTY 7 Only the definition of a view is stored, and the contents of the view materialize only upon evaluation of the query part of the view definition.

PROPERTY 8 A view may be used just like a class for the purpose of a retrieval query; in particular, views may be defined on a view.

PROPERTY 9 There are certain restrictions on the types of updates to the database through a view—in particular, views involving derived attributes and joins.

The following examples define two stored classes, `Employee` and `Vehicle`, and two views, `EmpPay` and `OldVehicle`, defined on the stored classes, `Employee` and `Vehicle`, respectively. (In the remainder of this chapter, we will use a simplified version of SQL/X [Kifer et al. 1992], the database language supported in UniSQL/X.)

```
Create Class Employee
      (SSN: char(11), Name: char(20), Age: integer, Salary:
          real, Commission: real,
      Department: char(20), Hobby: char(50));

Create Class Vehicle
      (VehicleID: char(20), Color: char(20), Manufacturer:
          Company, Year: integer)
      methods (Weight (): integer);

Create View EmpPay
      (SSN, Total-Pay: real, Department) AS
      Select   SSN, Salary + Commission, Department
      From Employee;

Create View OldVehicle
      (ID, Manufacturer, Year)
      methods (Weight) As
      Select VehicleID, Manufacturer, Year
      From    Vehicle
      Where   Year < 1981;
```

Note that the definition of `OldVehicle` has an attribute, `Manufacturer`, whose domain is the class `Company`; and it also includes a method, `Weight`, that computes the weight of each materialized instance of `OldVehicle`.

6.2.1 Inheritance

The schema of an object-oriented database consists of classes and views, just as the schema of a relational database consists of relations and views. The schema of an object-oriented database, without views, is a class hierarchy formed by the generalization/specialization and aggregation relationships among all the classes in the database. If views are to be admitted to the schema of an object-oriented database, the critical issue that must be addressed is the placement of views in the schema. Our conclusion is that it is very difficult to support the commingling of classes and views in a single inheritance hierarchy. In UniSQL/X, the schema consists of two separate structures; one for the classes (i.e., the class hierarchy), and one for the views. The structure for the views is a structure analogous to the class hierarchy—that is, a view hierarchy in which subviews inherit attributes and methods from superviews.

It is intuitively more appealing to regard the schema as being a single inheritance hierarchy that includes both classes and views. However, this approach, assumed in Abitebould and Bonner 1991 and Scholl et al. 1992, has a few serious problems. Let us examine these problems.

First, allowing views in an inheritance hierarchy along with classes will expose views to the effects of schema changes involving classes. If an attribute is added to a class, or an attribute is dropped from a class, or a new superclass link to a class is established, the addition or dropping of an attribute is propagated to all subclasses of the class [Banerjee et al. 1987; Penney and Stein 1987]. If one of the subclasses is a view, the query specification in the definition of the view must in general be modified to reflect the change in the list of attributes in the view definition. It is in general impossible for a database system to automatically change the query specification in a view definition (this will be further discussed in section 6.3.1). In an inheritance hierarchy of only classes, the effects of most schema changes propagate down the hierarchy automatically.

Next, the semantics of the inheritance hierarchy may be violated (i.e., incorrect schema may result) unless the placement of a view on the inheritance hierarchy is made by considering the two aspects of a view definition: the *signature* (list of attributes and methods, along with their domains) and the *extent* of the view (the set of instances that will be materialized when the query part of the view is evaluated). The set of attributes and methods and their domains in the signature of a view will determine whether the view may be placed as a subclass or a superclass of an existing class or a view that the definer of the view may select. A careless placement of a view may result in the overlapping of the extents of the view and a superclass or subclass of the view. In a class hierarchy, each class has its own extent, and there is no overlapping of the extents of any pair of classes. As an example, suppose that one defines a view `BigCompany` on a stored class Company as follows, and places it as a virtual subclass of the class Company.

```
Create Class Company
     (Name: char(20), Location: char(20), Manager:
          set-of Employee, Budget: real);

Create View BigCompany (Name, Location, Manager, Budget,
     MonthlyBudget)) AS
     Select Name, Location, Manager, Budget, Budget/12
     From Company
     Where Budget > 20,000,000;
```

The extent of this view will include some of the instances of the class Company. If we are to preserve the disjointedness of the extents in the inheritance hierarchy, we must disallow the placement of a view along the same superclass chain that includes a class from which the extent of the view will be materialized. This means that in the above example, the view BigCompany cannot be a direct or indirect superclass or subclass of the class Company. Unhappily, it is very difficult to have the database system automatically detect and reject attempts to include a new view or modify the definition of an existing view in an inheritance hierarchy in a way that violates the disjointedness of the extents. So the burden of ensuring the disjointedness of the extents will fall on the users who define or modify views and classes. For example, consider two views, V1 and V2, with an identical signature, where V1 is defined on the class Employee with a query predicate "Age > 25" and V2 is defined on the class Employee with a query predicate "Salary < 20000". It is not possible for the database system to determine at compile time whether the extents of these views will overlap.

If we are to allow the extents of views and/or classes to overlap (although we believe it is a bad practice in designing a database), then we must be prepared to detect the overlap during the processing of queries that retrieve from more than one class/view or from an inheritance subhierarchy (i.e., a class/view and its subclass/subviews). The overlapping of the extents does not cause any difficulty for queries involving a single class or a single view defined on a single class. However, even a query involving a single view may cause difficulty if the view is defined on more than one stored class, and the extents of the classes overlap.

We decided that there is sufficient practical value to empowering views with inheritance, despite the fact that the burden of ensuring the correctness of the view hierarchy falls on the users. However, we also decided that we should not at this time muddy the semantics of the class hierarchy with views. Therefore, in UniSQL/X, we made a pragmatic compromise and decided to support one inheritance hierarchy for classes and a separate inheritance hierarchy for views, although the problems mentioned above for a single inheritance hierarchy for both classes and views still exist for the view hierarchy.

Finally, we note that since views may be defined on one or more views and/or classes, we may define a hierarchy (directed graph) of views, which we may call a *view-derivation hierarchy*. The "derived-from" relationship is clearly not the generalization (specialization) and inheritance relationship between a class and its superclass (subclass). It may be useful to maintain the view-derivation hierarchy as a separate structure from the class/view hierarchy; however, the derived-from relationship is not a part of the object-oriented paradigm, and we will not discuss it further.

6.2.2 Nested Attributes

In relational databases, the domain (data type) of an attribute is strictly limited to a primitive type, such as integer, real, string, date, and the like. In object-oriented databases, the domain of an attribute is an arbitrary type, including a primitive type, an arbitrary user-defined class, or even a set of heterogeneous types. Relational systems do not admit a view or a relation as the domain of any attribute. In this section, we will address the issue of whether a view may also be used as the domain of an attribute and explore the properties of the domain of an attribute in a view definition.

View as the Domain of an Attribute

Let us consider classes `Vehicle` and `Company` and a view `GiantCompany` defined on the class `Company`. Note that the domain of the `Manufacturer` attribute of the class `Vehicle` is the view `GiantCompany`.

```
Create Class Company
   (Name: char(20), Location: char(20), Managers: set-of
       Employee, Budget: real);

Create View GiantCompany (Name, Location) AS
   Select Name, Location
   From Company
   Where Budget > $100,000,000;

Create Class Vehicle
   (VehicleID: char(20), Color: char(20), Manufacturer:
       GiantCompany, Year: integer)
   methods (Weight (): integer);
```

The value of the `Manufacturer` attribute in an instance of the class `Vehicle` should be an instance of the view `GiantCompany`; however, the instances of `GiantCompany` need to be materialized by evaluating the query in the view definition for `GiantCompany`. The materialized instances of a view should really be regarded as objects, especially when they are used as values of an attribute. After all, if `GiantCompany` is a class rather than a view, the value of the `Manufacturer` attribute would be an instance of `GiantCompany`.

Conceptually, if the domain of an attribute is a view, the value of the attribute should be an object identifier (OID). But should the OID identify the materialized instance of the view or an instance of a stored class on which the view is defined? If the OID is to merely identify an instance of a stored class, there are two difficulties. First, if the view is defined by joining two or more stored classes or views, it is not possible for a single OID to identify multiple stored instances. Second, if the OID identifies an instance of a stored class, the domain of the attribute is really not the view but a stored class on which the view is defined.

Therefore, the correct thing to do is to have the value of an attribute whose domain is a view identify the materialized instance of a view. However, its implementation will incur serious overheads. First, the database system must generate the OID when the instance is materialized from stored instances, and it must maintain the OID until the materialized instance can be dropped (i.e., at the end of a transaction). Second, for updatable views, the system must also create a hash table of the OIDs of the materialized instances and the OIDs of the corresponding stored instances of the class(es) on which the view is defined.

For an instance of a class, what is stored as the value of an attribute whose domain is a user-defined class is the OID (or a set of OIDs) of the instance(s) of the domain. However, if the domain of an attribute is a view, the value of the attribute is a query that is defined against a class that will materialize instances of the view. This leads to fairly serious complications in the processing of queries that involve path expressions—that is, queries that state search conditions on a chain of nested attributes (e.g., `Vehicle.Manufacturer.Location = "Detroit"`) [Kifer et al. 1992]. If the domain of an attribute of a class C is another class D, the values stored for the attribute of C are the OIDs of instances of the class D. Therefore, in processing a path expression involving the classes C and D, the OIDs stored as the values of C's attribute are retrieved, and the instances of D that are associated with the OIDs are then fetched via hash-table lookups. However, if the domain of an attribute of a class C is a view V, the values stored for the attribute of C need to be references (pointers) to the query specification in the definition of V. In processing a path expression involving the class C and the view V, then the view-defining query must first be retrieved from an attribute, and the query must be executed dynamically in order to yield OIDs, which are then used to fetch associated stored instances of the class on which the view is defined.

Because of the performance problem anticipated, in UniSQL/X we again settled for a pragmatic compromise solution. In particular, the domain of an attribute of a view may be another view or a stored class; however, the domain of an attribute of a stored class may not be a view (i.e., the example class `Vehicle` above is not allowed, since it contains an attribute whose domain is a view). Further, UniSQL/X does not generate

OIDs of the materialized instances of a view; instead, it uses the OIDs of the instances of the stored class on which the view is defined. As discussed earlier, because UniSQL/X uses the OIDs of a stored class on which a view is defined, it places the restriction that if a view is to be used as the domain of an attribute of another view, the view must be defined on a single stored class (i.e., the view must not be defined as the join of two or more classes).

Let us consider an example. The class `Vehicle` is redefined so that the domain of the attribute `Manufacturer` is the class `Company`. Further, a view named `NewVehicle` is defined on the class `Vehicle` such that the domain of the attribute `Manufacturer` is the view `GiantCompany`, which, as before, is defined on the class `Company`. When an instance of the view `NewVehicle` is materialized, the value found for the attribute `Manufacturer` is the OID of the class `Company` on which the view `GiantCompany` is defined.

```
Create Class Company
   (Name: char(20), Location: char(20), Managers:
         set-of Employee, Budget: real);

Create View GiantCompany (Name, Location) AS
   Select Name, Location
   From Company
    Where Budget > $100,000,000;

Create Class Vehicle
   (VehicleID: char(20), Color: char(20), Manufacturer:
         Company, Year: integer)
   methods (Weight (): integer);

Create View NewVehicle (ID,
   Manufacturer: GiantCompany, Year) As
   Select VehicleID, Manufacturer, Year
   From     Vehicle
   Where    Year > 1991;
```

Domain of an Attribute of a View

In object-oriented databases, it should be possible to define the domain of an attribute or method as a specialization of that of the attribute specification of the stored class or view on which the view is defined. If the domain of an attribute in a stored class is a class D, then the domain of the corresponding attribute in a view may be either D or any subclass of D. On the other hand, if the domain of an attribute in a stored class is a heterogeneous set S of types Ti, the domain of the corresponding attribute in a view may be either S or a subset of S, such that every type Ti of S in the view is a subclass of some Ti of S in the stored class.

For example, let us redefine a view OldVehicle, such that the domain of the attribute Manufacturer is VehicleCompany, a subclass of Company.

```
Create View OldVehicle (ID, Manufacturer: VehicleCompany,
     Year) methods (Weight) As
     Select VehicleID, Manufacturer, Year
     From    Vehicle
     Where   Year < 1981;
```

The domain of an attribute in a view may be a specialization (subclass) of that of the corresponding attribute of a stored class or view, if the view is defined on a single stored class or view. However, when a view is defined on more than one stored class or view, the domain of its attribute may be a generalization (superclass) of the corresponding attributes of the stored classes or views. To illustrate this, let us consider an example. Suppose that DomesticCompany and ForeignCompany are defined as subclasses of the Company class. Further, SmallVehicle and LargeVehicle are subclasses of the class Vehicle; the domain of the Manufacturer attribute they inherit from Vehicle is modified to ForeignCompany and DomesticCompany, respectively, as shown below.

```
Create Class DomesticCompany
     AS Subclass of Company;

Create Class ForeignCompany
     AS Subclass of Company;

Create Class SmallVehicle
     (Manufacturer: ForeignCompany)
     As Subclass of Vehicle;

Create Class LargeVehicle
     (Manufacturer: DomesticCompany)
     As Subclass of Vehicle;
```

It may be desirable to define a view AllVehicle as a union of DomesticVehicle and ForeignVehicle, as shown below. Note that the view is defined on two stored classes, and the domain of its attribute Manufacturer is the class Company—that is, the superclass of the domains of the corresponding attributes in the stored classes—that is, ForeignCompany and DomesticCompany.

```
Create View AllVehicle (ID, Manufacturer:
     Company, Year) methods (Weight) As
     (Select VehicleID, Manufacturer, Year
     From SmallVehicle) union
     (Select VehicleID, Manufacturer, Year
     From LargeVehicle);
```

6.2.3 Methods

A method, when included in the definition of a view, is to be used to perform computations on the materialized instances of the view. A method may be regarded as a generalization of a derived attribute that is allowed in the definition of a view in relational databases.

There is one difference between methods specified in a view and those defined in a class. Since methods specified in a class may operate against object identifiers of the instances of the class, if methods specified in a view are to operate on the identifiers of the virtual instances of the view, the database system must generate the identifiers for the virtual instances of the view. Further, methods that operate on virtual instances should not assume persistence of the OIDs of the virtual instances. In UniSQL/X, since virtual OIDs of the materialized instances of a view are not generated, methods specified in a view must be written to operate against either the values of the materialized instances of the view or the OIDs of the stored class on which the view is defined.

6.2.4 View Update

It is well known that there are restrictions on the types of relational views that permit updates to the stored database through views [Bancilhon and Spyratos 1981; Dayal and Bernstein 1982]. It is not possible to update stored relations through a relational view if a unique one-to-one mapping of the update cannot be established between each tuple of the view and a corresponding tuple of a stored relation on which the view is defined. For example, if the `Total-Pay` attribute of the view `EmpPay` introduced earlier is updated, the update cannot really be propagated to the stored relation `Employee` since there is no guideline for distributing the change in `Total-Pay` to its `Salary` and `Commission` components in `Employee`.

The same difficulty remains for updating an object-oriented database through views. However, two aspects of object-oriented databases—namely, object identity and nested attributes—necessitate a reexamination of the problems of update through views.

Object Identity

Object identity makes it possible to establish a one-to-one mapping between instances of a view and instances of a stored class on which the view is defined. In other words, object identity can be used to admit a class (category) of updates through views that are not possible in relational databases (this is observed in Kifer et al. 1992). In principle, if a one-to-one correspondence can be established between a materialized instance of a view and an instance of a stored class on which the view is defined, it becomes possible to propagate updates through the view. For example, let us consider a view EmpSal defined on the stored class Employee as follows:

```
Create View EmpSal (Salary) AS
     Select     Salary
     From Employee;
```

The result of materializing the view EmpSal is a unary relation of employee salary. As is, there is no correspondence between an instance of the EmpSal view (i.e., a salary value) and an instance of the class Employee. However, a unique one-to-one correspondence can be established if we introduce a mechanism that assigns an OID to each materialized instance of a view and that maps the OID to the OID of the instance of the stored class from which the instance of the view originates. In the above example, assuming that duplicates are not removed from the materialization of the view EmpSal, the identifier assigning and mapping mechanism will establish a one-to-one correspondence between the instances of EmpSal and the instances of the stored class Employee. An update of an instance of EmpSal can straightforwardly be propagated to a corresponding instance of Employee.

We note that, although the OID-mapping mechanism certainly makes it possible to update the database through views to a greater extent than is possible without it, it does not address other situations that preclude a unique one-to-one mapping between an instance of a view and an instance of a stored class; for example, the mechanism does not make it possible for an update to the Total-Pay attribute of the view EmpPay to propagate to a corresponding instance of the stored class Employee.

Nested Attribute

Let us now consider the impact of nested attributes on the semantics of updates through views. Consider the Book, BookCompany, and BookCompanyEmployee classes and the view BookEditors defined below. The correspondence between an instance of the view BookEditors and an instance of each of the classes Book, BookCompany, and BookCompanyEmployee can be illustrated using the example nested object in Fig. 6–1. An instance of BookEditors is derived from two of the three instances that constitute a nested object involving an instance of Book, an instance of BookCompany, and an instance of BookCompanyEmployee.

```
Create Class Book
     (Title: char(40), Author: set-of Person, Publisher:
          BookCompany, Year: integer) methods (Price ():
               integer);

Create Class BookCompany
     (Name: char(20), Location: char(20), Editors:set-of
          BookCompanyEmployee,Budget:real);
```

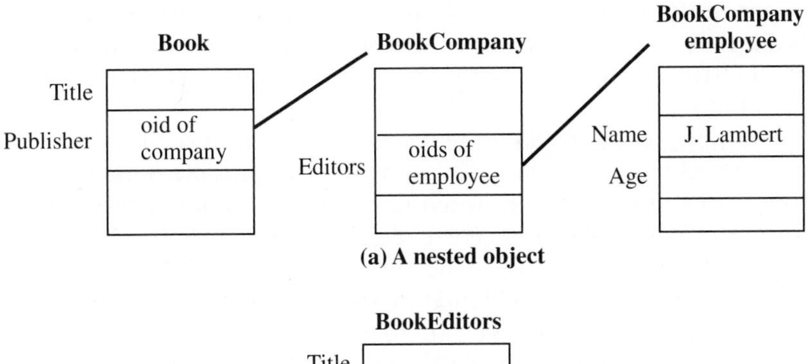

(b) An instance of a view derived from a nested object

FIGURE 6–1
A Stored Nested Object and an Instance of a View Defined on It

```
Create Class Person
     (SSN: char(11), Name: char(20), Age: integer);

Create Class BookCompanyEmployee
     (Salary: real, Commission: real)
     As Subclass of Person;

Create View BookEditors (Title: char(40),
     Editor-Name: set of char(20)) AS
     Select    Title, Publisher.Editors.Name
     From      Book
     Where     Book.Publisher.Editors.Age all> 45;
```

Before a database can be updated through a view, two conditions must be satisfied. First, there must be a unique one-to-one correspondence between an instance of a view and an instance of a corresponding stored class; that is, given a materialized instance of a view, a unique instance of the stored class on which the view is defined can be identified. Second, the attribute of the view being updated must not be a derived attribute. The one-to-one correspondence between an instance of a view and an instance of a corresponding class may be maintained in one of two ways. The system may maintain a hash table of the OIDs of the materialized instances of the view and the OIDs of the corresponding instances of a stored class. Or the attributes in the view signature may include a key of the corresponding stored class.

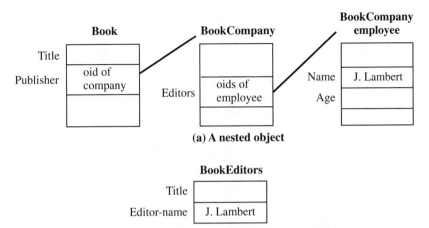

These two conditions, however, are not sufficient to determine updatability of views in object-oriented databases because of ambiguities that may be introduced in views on nested objects. A rule, which we will call the *materializability rule,* is necessary. The rule stipulates that the update be reflected in the view when the view is materialized after the update. (We will illustrate the utility of this rule shortly.) We note that UniSQL/X supports updates through views; however, it does not currently support the materialization rule.

For now, let us consider the deletion of an instance of a view derived from a stored nested object. One can define two possible semantics. One is to delete all instances of the stored nested object from which the instance of the view takes its values. For example, in Fig. 6–1, if the instance of the view `BookEditors` is to be deleted, the `Book` instance and the `BookCompanyEmployee` instance in the nested object from which the instance of the view was derived are to be deleted.

Another option, which we adopt, is to delete only the root of the stored nested object. This means, in our current example, that only the `Book` instance of the stored nested object is to be deleted. This option satisfies the materialization rule. Deleting the root of the nested object is sufficient to prevent subsequent rematerialization of the instance of the view; that is, if the root object does not exist, the instance of the view that was previously materialized cannot be materialized again.

Next, let us consider the insertion of an instance through a view. In order to satisfy the materializability rule, an instance to be inserted must include values for all the attributes in the WHERE clause of the query part of the view definition. For example, it is inherently impossible to insert an instance of the view `BookEditors` since it does not include a value for the attribute `Age`. If an instance of the view (without the value of `Age`) is inserted, by creating a new instance of `Book` and a new instance of `BookCompanyEmployee`, the instance of the view is unobtainable through materialization of the view since the two newly created stored instances will not satisfy the query part of the view definition.

Consider a different view, `BookEditorsAge`, defined as follows:

```
Create View BookEditors (Title,Employee-Name:set-of
     char(20), Age:set-of integer) AS
     Select   Title, Publisher.Editors.Name, Age
     From     Book
     Where    Book.Publisher.Editors.Age all> 45;
```

Insertion of an instance of this view, provided that the value of `Age` is > 45, results in the creation of a new stored nested object. The new nested object consists of an instance of the class `Book`, an instance of the class `BookCompany`, and an instance of the class `BookCompany-Employee`. We note that each new instance of the stored classes will contain values only for the attributes with corresponding attributes in the view; those attributes of the classes without corresponding attributes in the view will have null values. In particular, all but one attribute of the new instance of the class `BookCompany` will have null values; only the

Editors attribute will contain a reference to the new instance of the BookCompanyEmployee class.

Next, we consider update of an instance of a view. Once again, the materialization rule dictates the semantics. If there is a unique one-to-one correspondence between an instance of a view and a stored nested object, and if the attribute of the view being updated is not a derived attribute, update through a view is straightforward: The new value of an attribute of the instance of a view simply propagates to the attribute of the corresponding stored object. For example, if the Editor-Name of the instance of the view BookEditors in Fig. 6–1 is changed from "J. Lambert" to "J. Greene," the Name attribute of the stored instance of Book-Company-Employee for "J. Lambert" is changed to "J. Greene."

We note that an update of an instance of a view may result in removal of the instance from the view, if the attribute is involved in the WHERE clause of the query part of the view definition. For example, in the view BookEditorsAge, if the age value of an instance of a view is changed from 46 to 26, the instance will not be materialized again, since it will no longer satisfy the WHERE clause of the query part of the view definition.

6.3 Schema Changes

Banerjee et al. 1987 and Penney and Stein 1987 have shown that an object-oriented data model leads to a fairly large number of schema changes, and the effects of a schema change can be rather involved. The definition of a view may be affected by a change in the definition of a view or stored class on which the view is based. In this section, we will examine the effects of schema changes on view definitions.

The effects of a schema change on a view definition are considerably more involved in object-oriented databases than in relational databases. The following is a set of schema changes, adapted from Banerjee et al. 1987, that can affect existing view definitions:

1. Change the definition of a class (view) on which a view is defined
   - 1.1 add a new attribute
   - 1.2 add a new method
   - 1.3 drop an attribute
   - 1.4 drop a method
   - 1.5 change the domain of an attribute
2. Change the structure of the class hierarchy or view hierarchy
   - 2.1 add a new class (view)
   - 2.2 drop a class (view)
   - 2.3 make a class (view) S a new superclass of a class (view) C
   - 2.4 remove a class (view) S as a superclass of a class (view) C

Due to space limitations, we will discuss only the adding and dropping of an attribute in a class here. Adding and dropping an attribute in a view are similar. The adding and dropping of a method are also similar to the adding and dropping of an attribute. Further, the adding or dropping of a class or superclass are reduced to the adding or dropping of attributes and methods in the class.

First, let us take the dropping of an attribute. If an attribute is dropped from a stored class, the definition of any view whose query specification references the attribute becomes invalid, and either the view should be dropped or its definition needs to be modified. The dropping or modification of the view in turn may make invalid other views whose query specifications reference the view or the dropped attribute. If a view is placed in an inheritance hierarchy, subviews in the hierarchy may similarly become invalid and may need to be dropped or modified, again affecting other views that are defined on them.

Next, let us consider the adding of a new attribute to a stored class. Adding a new attribute to a stored class has no effect on views defined on it unless the query specifications include the "*" designation in the SELECT clause (i.e., to always retrieve all attributes of the stored class). If the query specification uses the "*" designation in the SELECT clause, either all current attributes of the class should be explicitly listed (if the new attribute is not desired in the view) or the signature of the view should be modified to include the new attribute. Once again, if a view is placed in an inheritance hierarchy, the change in the view thus affected may necessitate further changes on subviews in the hierarchy.

The above two cases make it clear that it is in general impossible for a database system to automatically make changes to the definitions of existing views in response to changes to the definitions of stored classes and other views. However, at the minimum, the database system should maintain dependency relations between a view and other view(s) or classes on which it is defined, so that it may issue warnings to the users about the existence of potentially invalid views. Or a utility program may be run periodically to verify the validity of view definitions.

6.4 Extending Views

In relational database systems, the use of views has been as a dynamic window into a stored database. Views can, of course, be used in this way for object-oriented database systems, as has been discussed thus far. However, there are two additional ways in which views may be used. One is in integrating heterogeneous database schemas into a single global database schema (this is well known). Another is a dynamic window into the metadata (schema) of a stored database—that is, to simulate schema changes without committing the changes to the database.

6.4.1 Heterogeneous Schema Integration

(This subsection is included here only for completeness. A detailed treatment of this subject is beyond the scope of this chapter and is deferred to Chapter 30, which describes the schema architecture of the UniSQL/M multidatabase product.) The view definition, as discussed so far, includes only a single query specification (even if the query may involve more than one stored class and/or other view). For use in integrating heterogeneous database schemas, the view definition needs to be extended by allowing a list of query specifications—one for each local database involved in the integration. As a simple example, let us assume that there are two relational local databases, LDB-1 and LDB-2, each with a Vehicle relation defined as follows:

```
Create Table Vehicle
   (VehicleID: char(20), Color: char(20), Manufacturer:
       char(20), Year: integer);
```

The following multidatabase view may be defined over the two independent `Vehicle` relations. (We note that this is not quite the way it is done in UniSQL/M, but for the limited illustrative purposes here it should suffice.) Note that the multidatabase view consists of two query specifications, one for each local database.

```
Create View Vehicle
   (VehicleID, Manufacturer, Year) AS
    SELECT VehicleID, Manufacturer, Year
    FROM LDB-1.Vehicle,

    SELECT VehicleID, Manufacturer, Year
    FROM LDB-2.Vehicle ;
```

6.4.2 Simulating Schema Evolution

It is possible to extend the traditional concept of a view to a dynamic window into the schema of a database, so that a view of a schema may be used to simulate changes to the database schema—that is, make virtual changes to the database schema without having the changes propagate to the stored database. We note that this use of views has not been implemented in UniSQL/X.

The following is a simplified list from Banerjee et al. 1987 of schema changes meaningful under an object-oriented data model:

1. Change the definition of a class
   - 1.1 add a new attribute
   - 1.2 add a new method

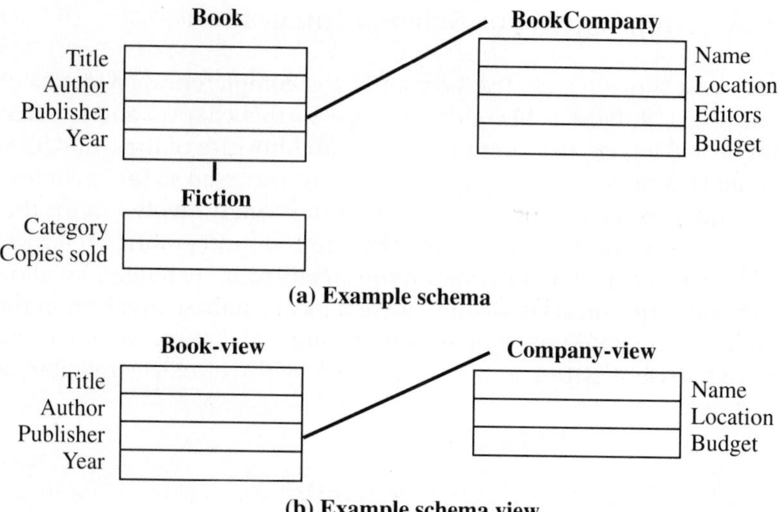

FIGURE 6–2
Schema and View of Schema

   1.3 drop an attribute
   1.4 drop a method
   1.5 change the domain of an attribute
2. Change the structure of the class hierarchy
   2.1 add a new class
   2.2 drop a class
   2.3 make a class S a new superclass of a class C
   2.4 remove a class S as a superclass of a class C

Let us explore the characteristics of schema changes that are meaningful for a view of a schema. Figure 6–2 shows a very simple schema and a view defined on it. First of all, insofar as a view is a dynamic window of the stored database, it should be possible to define a view that exposes an arbitrary subset of the stored database. Similarly, it should be possible to define a view of a schema to expose an arbitrary subset of the schema of the stored database; that is, it should be possible to define a view of a schema in which classes, attributes, and methods defined in the underlying schema are removed (changes 1.3, 1.4, and 2.2). The view of schema in Fig. 6–2b is defined on the schema of Fig. 6–2a by omitting the `Editors` attribute from the class `BookCompany` and also excluding the class `Fiction`.

Since views are defined on stored classes, a view cannot be used to simulate the adding of a new class (change 2.1). Further, a view is fundamentally a mechanism for deriving data from the stored database; as such, defining a view that includes a new attribute that is not a derived attribute (change 1.1) is troublesome indeed. A nonderived attribute defined in a view obviously has no corresponding attribute in a stored class. Therefore, values inserted into the attribute cannot be stored in any "corresponding" stored class, and also the attribute cannot be materialized. Abiteboul and Bonner 1991 propose the notion of "imaginary objects" to allow a view to include attributes with no corresponding attributes in stored classes.

It is possible to define a view that includes methods that are not defined in the corresponding stored class (change 1.2), so long as the methods will operate on data derived from the class. Further, changes to the superclass/subclass relationship between classes can be accommodated in views (changes 2.3 and 2.4). Although these changes require only modifications to the definitions of affected views, these modifications do not propagate to the stored database. Let us see how changes in the superclass/subclass structure translate to changes in view definitions.

Information about superclasses and subclasses of a class (view) is defined within the class (view). Therefore, each of the schema changes listed above, except for 2.1 and 2.2, may be specified as a change to the definitions of classes (views) affected by the schema change. For example, the schema change 2.3 may be specified as a redefinition of the superclass (superview) list in the definition of the class (view) C. That is, a class (view) C that may have been defined as

```
Create View C attributes (A1, A2, ....)
    methods (M1, M2, ....) As Subview Of  X, Y;
```

may be redefined as

```
Create View  C  attributes (A1, A2, ....)
    methods (M1, M2, ....) As Subview Of  X, Y, S;
```

6.5 Summary and Conclusion

In this chapter, we defined the semantics of views in object-oriented database systems. The approach we took was to extend the semantics of relational views by reflecting the semantic changes necessitated by the object-oriented concepts, such as methods, inheritance, nested objects, and object identity. The semantics of views we defined include not only the use of views for dynamically materializing objects from the stored database but also updating the database through views.

Just as there are similarities and differences between a relation and a view defined on the relation, there are similarities and differences between a class and a view defined on the class. One particular issue that we explored was whether views may be accorded a status equal to classes in the schema of an object-oriented database. If we may apply typing and inheritance uniformly to views and classes, then the schema of an object-oriented database may be regarded as a single hierarchy of classes and views; views may be used not only as targets of queries but also as domains of attributes of classes and other views. Unfortunately, there are many problems that make this nice unification of classes and views impractical. We brought out these problems.

We also explored an entirely new use of views—namely, as a dynamic window into the schema (metadata) of a stored database, rather than merely as dynamic windows into a stored database. To this end, we explored how a range of changes to a database schema may be simulated by creating and modifying views of the schema—that is, without causing any schema changes to propagate to the stored schema or the stored database.

The semantics of views defined in this chapter have largely been implemented, with certain pragmatic compromises, in the UniSQL/X unified relational and object-oriented database system commercially available from UniSQL, Inc. In particular, UniSQL/X supports view definition, queries and updates through views, granting and revoking authorizations on views, and schema changes involving views. Further, an extended version of the same view mechanism has been implemented in the UniSQL/M commercial multidatabase system that supports the integration of SQL-based relational database systems and UniSQL/X.

ACKNOWLEDGMENTS

Injun Choi, Sunit Gala, Michael Kifer, and Mark Scheevel offered helpful suggestions and raised various important issues that are addressed in the current version of this chapter.

REFERENCES

Abiteboul, S., and Bonner, A. 1991. Objects and Views. *Proceedings of ACM-SIGMOD International Conference on Management of Data 1991*, May 1991, Denver.

Bancilhon, F., and Spyratos, N. 1981. Update Semantics of Relational Views. *ACM Trans. on Database Systems*, Vol. 6, No. 4, 557–575.

Banerjee, J., Kim, W., Kim, H.J., and Korth, H.F. 1987. Semantics and Implementation of Schema Evolution in Object-Oriented Databases. *Proceedings of ACM-SIGMOD International Conference on Management of Data 1987*, May 1987, San Francisco.

Carey, M., DeWitt, D., and Vandenberg, S. 1988. A Data Model and Query Language for EXODUS. *Proceedings of ACM-SIGMOD International Conference on Management of Data 1988*, June 1988, Chicago, 413–423.

Cluet, S., Delobel, C., Lecluse, C., and Richard, P. 1989. Reloop: An Algebra-Based Query Language for an Object-Oriented Database System. *Proceedings of First International Conference on Deductive and Object-Oriented Databases*, Kyoto, Japan, December 1989.

Date, C. 1986. *An Introduction to Database Systems,* Addison-Wesley, Reading, Mass.

Dayal, U., and Bernstein, P. 1982. On the Correct Translation of Update Operations on Relational Views. *ACM Trans. on Database Systems,* Vol. 8, No. 2, 381–416.

Dayal, U., and Hwang, H. 1984. View Definition and Generalization for Database Integration in a Multidatabase System. *IEEE Trans. on Software Engineering,* Vol. SE-10, No. 6, 628–645.

Garza, J., and Kim, W. 1988. Transaction Management in an Object-Oriented Database System. *Proceedings of ACM-SIGMOD International Conference on Management of Data 1988,* June 1988, Chicago.

Kifer, M., Kim, W., and Sagiv, Y. 1992. Querying Object-Oriented Databases. *Proceedings of ACM-SIGMOD International Conference on Management of Data 1992,* June 1992, San Diego.

Kifer, M., and Lausen, G. 1989. F-Logic: A Higher-Order Language for Reasoning about Objects, Inheritance, and Scheme. *Proceedings of ACM-SIGMOD International Conference on Management of Data 1989,* May 1989, Portland.

Kim, W. 1989. A Model of Queries for Object-Oriented Databases. *Proceedings of International Conference on Very Large Data Bases,* August 1989, Amsterdam.

Kim, W. 1990. *Introduction to Object-Oriented Databases,* MIT Press, Cambridge, Mass.

Kim, W., Kim, K.C., and Dale, A. 1989. Indexing Techniques for Object-Oriented Databases. In: *Object-Oriented Concepts, Applications, and Databases.* W. Kim and F. Lochovsky, eds. Addison-Wesley, Reading, Mass.

Maier, D., and Stein, J. 1986. Indexing in an Object-Oriented DBMS. *Proceedings of International Workshop on Object-Oriented Database Systems, Languages,* Pacific Grove, Calif., September 1986.

Motro, A. 1987. Superviews: Virtual Integration of Multiple Databases. *IEEE Trans. on Software Engineering,* Vol. 13, No. 7, 303–319.

Object Management Group. 1991. Common Object Request Broker: Architecture Specification. Document No. 91.12.1.

Penney, J., and Stein, J. 1987. Class Modification in the GemStone Object-Oriented DBMS. *Proceedings of Second International Conference on Object-Oriented Programming Systems, Languages, and Applications,* Orlando, Fl., October 1987.

Pernici, B. 1990. Objects with Roles. *Proceedings of ACM Conference on Office Information Systems,* Cambridge, Mass., April 1990.

Rabitti, F., Bertino, E., Kim, W., and Woelk, D. 1991. A Model of Authorization for Next-Generation Database Systems. *ACM Trans. on Database Systems,* Vol. 16, No. 1, March 1991, 88–131.

Scholl, M., Schek, H., and Tresch, M. 1992. Object Algebra and Views for Multi-Objectbases. *Proceedings of Workshop on Distributed Object Management,* Edmonton, Alberta, August 1992.

Thuraisingham, M.B. 1989. Mandatory and Discretionary Security Issues in Object-Oriented Database Systems. *Proceedings of Object-Oriented Programming Systems, Languages, and Applications,* New Orleans, October 1989.

7

Authorization in Object-Oriented Databases

TERESA F. LUNT

Object-oriented systems are emerging technologies of great import for applications in business, industry, and the military. Many of these applications must share information among users with different needs and authorizations. The specific access rules desired will vary from application to application. Thus, a flexible approach to discretionary access control is called for. We describe such an approach. We also describe a model of multilevel security for an object-oriented database. In the model, each object has a single uniform security classification. Typical military database security policies can be supported by this model.

7.1 Introduction

The Department of Defense (DoD) policies restricting access to classified information to cleared personnel are called *mandatory security*. In addition, the more familiar identity-based access control policies are known as *discretionary security*. The access controls commonly found in most commercial database systems are examples of discretionary access controls. In this chapter, we discuss both mandatory and discretionary access control for object-oriented databases. We first give a brief description of the object-oriented constructs we will be using later. Then, in section 7.2, we discuss discretionary security issues for object-oriented databases. Section 7.3 discusses mandatory security for object-oriented databases. Section 7.4 contains our conclusions.

For security, it suffices to consider the following description of object-oriented databases. All conceptual entities are modeled as *objects*. Each object has some *state* and a defined set of operations that can be performed on it. An object's state is represented by a set of *instance variables* that are part of the definition of the object's *class*. Each object has a unique object identifier.

Operations on objects are handled by *methods*, which are executed in the context of the object's state upon the receipt of *messages*. Methods encapsulate the behavior of an object, in that an object can be acted upon only through executing the methods defined for the object. A method may read and write the variables of the object where it resides; it may send messages to other objects, to invoke methods there; and it may, when it terminates, return a value to the sender of the message that invoked it.

A group of objects with similar properties forms a class, which is also an object. Thus, an object represents either a class or an individual instance. Inheritance allows the object structure, names and default values of instance variables, and methods to be inherited from the object's parent or class object. The distinction between classes and their ground instances is not relevant for a discussion of security. Thus, here we do not distinguish between objects representing ground instances and objects representing classes. Thus, we use the terms *instance* and *subclass* interchangeably, and we use the terms *object* and *class* interchangeably.

7.2 Discretionary Access Control

Here we address some aspects of discretionary access control for object-oriented databases. We will discuss inheritance of authorizations, negative and positive authorizations (i.e., explicit denials of authorization), overriding authorizations, modes of access, least privilege, and roles.

Discretionary authorizations can be attached to objects or stored in separate authorization structures. Most relational database systems use separate authorization structures. In an object model, such separate authorization structures could be represented as a set of objects. This approach would represent authorizations as attributes of users and groups, and a user would inherit the authorizations of all the groups he or she belongs to. In addition, subgroups would inherit the authorizations of their parent groups. This approach has the drawback that it would be difficult to implement a least-privilege policy. An alternate approach is to attach authorization lists to the objects they refer to. An *authorization list* is a list of individuals and groups. (For convenience, we will consider an individual to be a group of one.) Attached to objects, authorization lists are inherited, which seems a more natural approach for the object model. We assume this approach for the remainder of the chapter.

There is not enough room here to fully describe all aspects of the discretionary security problem—for example, administrative aspects, object ownership, control of propagation of authorizations and of revocations, and controlling access to an object's transitive closure. Several research groups have been studying discretionary security for object-oriented databases; some of these issues are addressed in the work of others.

A formal model of discretionary security for object-oriented databases was developed by Rabitti et al. using ORION as an illustration [Rabitti et al. 1988, 1991]. In that model, implied authorizations are inherited through the object hierarchy. They introduce the notion of weak and strong authorizations, where strong authorizations can override weak authorizations. Their model also includes positive and negative authorizations, where negative authorizations are used to represent explicit denial of authorization. The approach proposes algorithms for reconciling negative and positive authorizations through the use of strong and weak authorizations.

Kelter is developing models for distributed structurally object-oriented database systems [Kelter 1990]. A similar model was developed by Dittrich et al. for DAMOKLES [Dittrich et al. 1988]. The model defines *complex objects*, which are composed of sets of other objects as component parts. In Kelter's model, complex objects are the units of access control. Authorization conflicts may arise if complex objects share components. The model also includes a hierarchy of user groups, and subgroups inherit authorizations from supergroups.

Larrondo-Petrie et al. have developed an authorization model for object-oriented semantic databases specially tailored to OSAM*, a CAD/CAM database system being implemented at the University of Florida [Larrondo-Petrie et al. 1990; Song et al. 1990]. The approach divides up the network of objects into administrative domains. The intent of this approach is to make the database suitable for large financial applications. The model defines authorization inheritance through the object hierarchy. Recent work also considers how to handle negative authorizations and the use of predicates [Gudes et al. 1990].

Moffet and Sloman use a model that treats administrative users differently from ordinary users of the data [Moffet and Sloman 1988; Moffet and Sloman 1990]. Their model also includes the notion of object ownership; owners can grant administrative authorizations.

7.2.1 Inheritance of Discretionary Authorizations

With discretionary authorizations attached to objects, an object inherits the authorizations of its parents. This means that if a user is authorized for an object, then the user is also authorized for the descendants, or instances, of the object. This approach has the convenience that a user can be authorized for an entire set of objects simply by authorizing the user for an appropriate class.

An object inherits the discretionary access control attributes not only of its immediate parent but also of its parent's parents, and so on up the object hierarchy. Additional discretionary access control attributes can be defined for an object and be applied in addition to those that are inherited.

In the case of multiple inheritance, an object inherits the discretionary authorization attributes of each of its parents.

However, intuitively it seems that the type of policy that many applications require would be one in which more and more privilege is needed in order to access objects further down in the class hierarchy. Thus, in addition to the convenience of inherited authorizations, we need a way to restrict or override the inherited authorizations so that users can assign the precise authorizations desired for an object. We discuss a means of doing this in the next section.

7.2.2 Negative and Positive Authorizations

One of the requirements in the *DoD Trusted Computer System Evaluation Criteria* [DoD 1985] that appears at Class B3 for discretionary access control is that users be able to specify which users and groups are authorized for specific modes of access to named objects, as well as which users and groups are explicitly *denied* authorization for particular named objects. Following the work of Rabitti et al. [Rabitti et al. 1991; Rabitti et al. 1988], we will call the explicit discretionary authorizations *positive authorizations* and the explicit denials of authorization *negative authorizations*.

Just as an object's positive authorizations are attached to the object, we also attach the object's negative authorizations to the object. A negative authorization list is a list of groups (an individual is considered a group of one). The positive authorizations are interpreted as "must belong to." That is, in order to be authorized for the object, a user must belong to one of the groups in the positive authorization list. The negative authorizations are interpreted as "must not belong to." That is, if a user belongs to one of the groups on this list, the user cannot access the object.

Negative authorizations can be used to nullify the effects of positive authorizations. For example, if the group Astronauts is authorized for class Spaceship, since authorizations are inherited, this would imply that the members of the astronaut group are also authorized for all spaceships. However, we can restrict access so that user Glenn of the Astronauts group is not authorized for the Hubble spaceship by putting Glenn on the negative authorization list for the Hubble spaceship.

The use of negative authorizations in conjunction with positive authorizations allows users to implement policies in which more privilege is needed in order to access objects further down in the class hierarchy. Negative authorizations provide a way to restrict the inherited authorizations so that users can assign the precise authorizations desired for an object.

There can be difficulties in reconciling conflicting negative and positive authorizations. In Rabitti et al. 1988, 1991, the concept of strong and weak authorizations is introduced to deal with this problem. We describe this approach in the next section.

7.2.3 Strong and Weak Authorizations

A *strong authorization* is one that cannot be overridden by another authorization; a *weak authorization* can be overridden by a strong authorization [Rabitti et al. 1991; Rabitti et al. 1988].

In Lunt 1989, various means of reconciling positive and negative authorizations are discussed. One of these is the *most-specific rule,* which requires that if an individual user is specifically granted or denied authorization for an object, this takes precedence over any authorizations for the object that are granted or denied to groups to which the user belongs. With the most-specific rule, negative authorizations are simply a convenience in forming the access control lists. They can be used as follows: If user *A* wants to make object *O* available to everyone in group *G* except user *B,* then instead of enumerating everyone except *B* in the access control list, *A* could grant authorization to *G* and explicitly deny authorization to *B*. The most-specific rule can be implemented by making individual authorizations strong and group authorizations weak.

Another approach discussed in Lunt 1989 is *denials take precedence.* With this approach, a user or group's denial of authorization for an object takes precedence over any authorizations that the user or group may have been granted for the object. Under the interpretation that denials take precedence, if a user *A* explicitly denies user *U* authorization for object *O* (by granting a negative authorization), and a user *B* later grants a positive authorization for *O* to *U*, then *U* will not become authorized. Thus, denial of authorization is a strong measure that can be taken to ensure that specific users and groups cannot obtain authorization to an object.

The denials-take-precedence rule can be implemented by making all negative authorizations strong and all positive authorizations weak. Thus, with inheritance of discretionary access control attributes, specifying a negative authorization for a group for a parent object ensures that no access is granted to members of the group to any of the object's offspring. On the other hand, specifying a positive authorization for a group for a parent object does not guarantee that the group will be authorized for the offspring; in fact, the group will be authorized for the offspring unless the child object contains a negative authorization for that group.

The denials-take-precedence and the most-specific policies are simply two possible policies out of very many possible ways of resolving conflicts among the positive and negative authorizations. To allow the application to specify how such conflicts are to be resolved, specific negative and positive authorizations can be individually labeled *strong* and *weak*, so that many more policy variations than these two are possible. Thus, four authorization lists can be attached to any object: strong positive authorizations, strong negative authorizations, weak positive authorizations, and weak negative authorizations.

It is still possible for negative and positive authorizations to conflict, if they are both weak or both strong. Ideally, a consistent assignment of weak and strong authorizations would be applied. However, it may not be obvious at the time that an authorization is granted or revoked that a conflict may result. Thus, it would be useful for the system to include a tool that would analyze an object's authorizations to detect conflicts. A user would be notified if the result of a grant or revoke operation would result in a conflict, so that either the grant/revoke operation would not take effect or the situation would be remedied. One mechanism for doing this would be to have integrity constraints on the authorization lists. These constraints would be part of the root object and inherited by every object in the system. Since it is possible for such a tool to detect and prevent such conflicts, we will assume that such conflicts do not exist.

Because authorizations are inherited, authorizations that are defined for the root object can be considered default access control rules. Weak and strong negative and positive authorizations assigned to the root object will be inherited by all other objects in the system. These default authorizations can be restricted or overridden by authorizations that are defined for objects lower in the object hierarchy. Similarly, different default access control rules can be specified for large portions of the object hierarchy simply by making entries in the authorization lists for objects sufficiently high up in the object hierarchy.

7.2.4 Access Modes

The discussion above was simplified, in that we assumed that the authorization lists are simply lists of users and groups. However, rather than assign blanket authorization for an object to a user or group, most security policies require the ability to assign specific modes of access for an object to users and groups. Thus, the authorization lists attached to objects must include an indication of which specific modes of access they authorized.

Thus, each of an object's authorization lists is actually a set of lists, each for a specific access mode, as shown below, where each list is a list of user and group identifiers.

strong positive authorizations
  method1: <list>
  method2: <list>
  etc.
weak positive authorizations
  method1: <list>
  method2: <list>
  etc.

strong negative authorizations
  method1: <list>
  method2: <list>
  etc.
weak negative authorizations
  method1: <list>
  method2: <list>
  etc.

Some access modes, such as create-instance, are relevant for all objects. Other access modes are relevant to a particular object class and its methods. The particular access modes may correspond one to one with the methods defined for the object. Alternatively, a smaller number of access modes could be defined, with each access mode relevant to a set of an object's methods.

Although the amount of information that must be stored with each object appears to be enormous, in practice the use of inheritance eliminates the need for storage of redundant data. Because most of the authorization information is inherited, only the additions to the lists need be actually attached to any instance.

7.2.5 Process Privileges

Given the set of strong and weak negative and positive authorizations for users and groups, some rule must be applied for deriving authorizations for *subjects*—that is, active processes. This is especially important when users may belong to several groups. A subject can

- assume the union of the user's individual authorization and those of all the groups to which the user belongs
- assume some subset of the union of the user's individual authorizations and those of all the groups to which the user belongs (this choice must be designated by the user or application at the time of subject invocation or must be predesignated by the application)
- assume the union of the user's individual authorizations and of a single group to which the user belongs (this group must be designated by the user or application at the time of subject invocation or must be predesignated by the application)
- assume either the user's individual authorizations or those of *one* of the user's groups (this choice must be designated by the user or application at the time of subject invocation or must be predesignated by the application)

The latter three options provide a means to support the concept of least privilege.

Note that unless the system can restrict a user to having a single subject active at a time, groups cannot be used to implement roles or separation of duty. To implement roles, an additional capability is needed. This is discussed in the next section.

7.2.6 Roles

Here we discuss the use of a roles mechanism such as that described by Baldwin [Baldwin 1990] for simplifying security management.

Some applications require that discretionary access controls be specified on the basis of user roles. Most systems have some built-in roles (e.g., system administrator, database administrator, system security officer). However, different users are likely to have different requirements and definitions for such roles. In addition, many applications require that arbitrary user job access control requirements be formalized in terms of roles (for example, the secure military message system [Landwehr et al. 1984]). Thus, a generic capability for application-defined roles is desirable.

Named protection domains (NPDs) [Baldwin 1990] can be used to provide a facility for specifying user roles. For example, a named protection domain can be defined for each application-specific role. The NPD would contain the strong and weak positive and negative authorizations that are required to define each role. The application designer would design each NPD so that it contains only those specific authorizations required by the role.

For example, the named protection domain Salary-Clerk could contain a weak positive authorization to invoke the increment-salary method on the salary object for the nonmanager instances of salary; it could contain strong negative authorizations for the increment-salary and review-salary methods on the manager instances of salary and for the increment-salary method on the clerk's own salary. The named protection domain Salary-Clerk could then be granted to the relevant individuals or groups. Thus, the authorizations associated with a salary clerk can be granted and revoked by a security administrator in a straightforward manner, without knowledge of the underlying object hierarchy and its authorization lists. If the system is designed so that only one NPD can be active at any one time for a user, it may be possible to enforce a separation-of-duties policy with this mechanism. Some have done extensive investigation into the design of a role facility for object-oriented databases [Ting et al. 1991].

7.3 Multilevel Security

The concern for multilevel security arises when a computer system contains information with a variety of classifications and has users who are not all cleared for the highest classification of data contained in the system. The *classification* of the information to be protected reflects the potential damage that could result from unauthorized disclosure of the information. The *clearance* assigned to a user reflects the user's trustworthiness not to disclose sensitive information to individuals not cleared to see it (and thus not so trusted). We use the term *access class* to apply to both users (i.e., clearances) and information (i.e., classification).

An access class consists of a *sensitivity level* (e.g., TOP SECRET, SECRET, CONFIDENTIAL, UNCLASSIFIED) and a set of *categories*. In order for a user to be granted access to classified information, the user must be cleared for the sensitivity level as well as for *each* of the categories in the information's access class. The sensitivity levels are linearly ordered. The categories do not have such a linear ordering. The set of access classes (<sensitivity level, category set> pairs) is partially ordered and forms a lattice [Denning 1982]. We call the partial ordering relation on the lattice of access classes the *dominance* relation. We say that one access class *A dominates* another access class *B* if the sensitivity level of *A* is greater than or equal to the sensitivity level of *B* and if the security categories of *A* include all those of *B*.

Mandatory security requires that classified data be protected not only from direct access by unauthorized users but also from disclosure through indirect means, such as covert signaling channels and inference. *Covert channels* are channels that were not designed to be used for information flow but that can nevertheless be exploited by malicious software to signal high data to low users.[1] For example, a high process (i.e., a program instance that has a high access class because it is acting on behalf of a high user) may use read and write locks observable to a low process over time to encode high information (e.g., locked = 1, unlocked = 0). *Inference* occurs when a low user can infer high information based on observable system behavior. For example, a low user attempting to access a high object can infer something depending upon whether the system responds with "object not found" or "permission denied."

Thus, mandatory security requires that no information can flow from high access classes to low. The mandatory access control requirements are formalized by two rules, the first of which protects data from unauthorized disclosure and the second of which protects low data objects from contamination by high data:

1. *Simple security property:* A subject *S* is not allowed to read data of access class *c* unless $classification(S) \geq c$, and
2. ★*-Property*: A subject *S* is not allowed to write data of access class *c* unless $classification(S) \leq c$.

---

1. We are using the terms *high* and *low* to refer to any two access classes when the second does not dominate the first in the lattice.

In the above rules, a *subject* is a process acting on a user's behalf; a process has a clearance, or access class, derived from the clearance of the user.

The simple security property and ★*-property* above are based on properties of the same names defined in the Bell and LaPadula security model [Bell and LaPadula 1976]. The ★*-property* is intended to prevent sensitive information from being transferred to an object whose access class is not dominated by that of the information, making the information accessible to users who are not cleared for it. This confinement property prevents subjects, represented by software acting on behalf of users, from *writing down* (including writing to noncomparable access classes). The motivation for the ★*-property* is that whereas cleared personnel can be trusted not to disclose classified information deliberately, computer programs, through errors of design or implementation, might move classified information to a location not protected at the required access class, or might contain *Trojan horses* that deliberately and maliciously violate security. A somewhat weaker property than the ★*-property* would allow a subject to write down when the subject does not have read access to information whose classification dominates the classification of the information being written. Although this weaker property would prevent malicious software from copying down, its enforcement would be more complicated than for the relatively simple ★*-property*.

Here we examine how to incorporate multilevel security properties into an object-oriented data model. We provide some background on multilevel security. We then present an informal model for extending the object model to include properties relating to multilevel security. Our presentation is based on the Lunt-Millen model [Millen and Lunt 1989; Millen and Lunt 1992]. That work was extended by Garvey and Lunt [Garvey and Lunt 1990a; Garvey and Lunt 1990b]. Examples of typical policies implementable using this approach are given in [Garvey and Lunt 1990a; Garvey and Lunt 1990b; Millen and Lunt 1989; Millen and Lunt 1992].

Another object-oriented multilevel security model has been suggested by Jajodia and Kogan [Jajodia and Kogan 1990]. Their model also takes a single-level-per-object approach but does not use subjects, and it expresses the security policy with a message filtering algorithm. The SODA model by Keefe takes a somewhat different approach, in which an object's variables and methods can have their own classifications [Keefe et al. 1989].

7.3.1 Access Rules

With our approach, each object has a single fixed access class that applies to everything within it. Portions of an object, such as its methods and variables, do not have access classes of their own. The access class of an object is constrained by the following rule:

- *Hierarchy property:* The access class of an object must dominate that of its parent class object.

This rule is needed to permit an object to inherit methods and variables from its parent. Any attempt to read an object by reading one of its variables, or execute it by sending a message to it, may implicitly read the object's parent class and perhaps the parent's parent class, and so on, until a default value or appropriate method is found.

A subject is an active entity that executes methods and sends messages. Each subject has a user associated with it, either derived from a login procedure or passed on from the invoking subject. A subject's access class will never be higher than the associated user's clearance or logon level. We can think of a subject as local to an object. When a message is received by an object, a subject is created to handle the message by executing an appropriate method; the subject is destroyed when the method terminates. A subject is given an access class when it is created, in accordance with the following rule:

- *Subject level property:* The access class of a subject created to handle a message dominates the access class of the invoking subject that sent the message, and it also dominates the access class of the object where the message is received.

This rule is needed so that the subject that is created to handle the message can read the message and can also read variables and methods in the object where it is located. Note that although a message does not have an explicit access class, we can informally treat a message as having the access class of the invoking (sending) subject.

The behavior of subjects is restricted in accordance with the following two rules:

- *Object locality property:* A subject can execute methods or read variables only in the object where it is located or in any superclass of that object; it can write variables only in that object.
- *★-Property:* A subject may write into the object where it is located only if its access class is equal to that of the object.

Writing up is not harmful from a security perspective, but it is generally not considered practical for multilevel database systems.

These rules allow a subject to send a message to an object at a higher access class. However, the invoking (sending) subject will not be able to receive a return value or message, as restricted by the following rule:

- *Return value property:* An invoking subject can receive a return value from a message only if the message handler subject is at the same access class as the invoking subject.

The invoking subject will receive a null message in return. The system, rather than the receiving subject, must determine the time it takes to deliver the null value; otherwise, a timing channel will exist.

A subject can cause an object to be created by sending a message to the class object. To avoid a covert channel, the new child object must be given an access class at least as high as that of the requesting subject, as required by the following rule:

- *Object creation property:* The access class of a newly created object dominates the access class of the subject that requested the creation.

A subject can create an object that has a higher access class than itself by specifying an access class for the new instance, and it can receive the object-id of the new instance (in this case, although the new object is classified high, the new object-id need not be, since the fact that the new object exists is known at the low level).

7.3.2 Classifying Object Existence

If an object was created by a high subject, its existence must be hidden from low subjects so as to avoid a covert channel through which a high subject could signal a low one by creating and deleting objects. The existence of an object can be inferred by the appearance of its object-id in the value of a variable in some other object. Thus, the existence of an object can be hidden from low subjects by preventing its object-id from being stored in low objects.

An object-id can appear in an object because it was copied from a variable in some other object or as a side effect of creating new objects. The access rules listed above will prevent an object-id from being copied from a high object to a low object. When an object is created, its object-id is normally appended to the list of instances in its parent object. However, if the access class of the creating subject is greater than that of the parent object, the new object-id cannot be stored in the parent object. The new object-id will be returned to the invoking (creating) subject, which can then store it in some object at its own access class.

The fact that object-ids must be unique can lead to a covert channel. When a low subject creates an object, the object-id must be different from any that are already in use, including those belonging to high objects. A low subject may be able to infer high information, depending on the mechanism used to assign object-ids to new objects. If subjects are free to ask for any object-id they wish, or if the system assigns object-ids sequentially, high subjects can maliciously transmit information to low subjects through the visible effects of creating high objects. The channel disappears entirely if object-ids are automatically concatenated with the access class of the requesting subject (or some encoding of it). This effectively assigns a fixed set of object-ids for use by each access class. An alternative is to use a pseudo-random number generator.

7.3.3 Polyinstantiation

The concept of *polyinstantiation* was introduced by SeaView for multilevel database systems [Denning et al. 1987b; Lunt et al. 1990]. Polyinstantiation arises when a person with a low clearance assigns what is intended to be a unique identifier (for example, employee-id) to a real-world entity (for example, a person) known to people with low clearances and is unaware that the identifier has already been assigned to some other real-world entity known only to persons with high clearances. This has been called *entity polyinstantiation* [Lunt 1990; Lunt 1991]. To preclude the possibility of an insecure information flow, the low person cannot be informed of the conflict.

Because we use globally unique object-ids instead of user-chosen object names to identify objects, entity polyinstantiation does not occur in our model. However, a similar effect may occur in the user-assigned object "names" or values of identifying instance variables. We call this *apparent polyinstantiation.* To illustrate, consider the Employee object and its instances C111, C112, and C113. Secret object C113 corresponds to the employee whose Employee-id (assigned by the employer) is E2345 and whose name is Susan Brown. Unclassified object C112 corresponds to the employee whose Employee-id is *also* E2345 but whose name is John Green. This apparent polyinstantiation can occur because the unclassified user who created the John Green instance does not see object C113 and thus does not know about employee Susan Brown with employee-id E2345.

One way of avoiding apparent polyinstantiation is through the use of classification constraints (see below). For example, in the above case, a classification constraint could be used that requires all instances of object Employee to be unclassified.

Note that if a subject modifies an attribute that was inherited from a lower-level ancestor object, the data in the lower-level object is not changed, but the overriding high data is stored in the higher-level object. This has been called *attribute polyinstantiation* [Lunt 1990; Lunt 1991].

7.3.4 Classification Constraints

Like integrity constraints, which are user-specifiable rules that restrict the values an object's variables may take, *classification constraints* restrict the classifications an object can have. They are user-specifiable rules that constrain the allowable classifications of the objects. They may be used to constrain all objects of a given class to have the same classification (these have been called *type-dependent* constraints [Denning et al. 1987a]). They may assign a classification to an object that depends on the value of one of its variables or on the value of a related object's variable. Or they may assign a classification to an object that depends on the classification of a related object (these latter two types have been called *value-dependent* constraints [Denning et al. 1987a]).

These constraints can be implemented as methods that are automatically invoked when any change is made to a relevant object. Applicable constraints may be found in the objects they reference or in ancestors of those objects. Methods implementing classification constraints, like other methods, are inherited.

7.4 Conclusion

We have presented approaches for both discretionary and mandatory security for object-oriented databases. The approach we have described for discretionary access control is flexible and sufficiently general to allow users to implement policies that are tailored to their application. Because each such specifiable policy is implemented with a common mechanism, each can be enforced with the same degree of assurance. Our approach for mandatory access control, which assigns a single access class for each object, is sufficient to support typical military database security policies. Classification policies for the existence of data and for the rules for classifying data can be supported. The approach allows an implementation that layers an untrusted object system on a conventional mandatory security kernel.

ACKNOWLEDGMENTS

This work was supported by the U.S. Air Force, Rome Laboratory, under contract F30602-89-C-0158 with SRI, subcontract C/UB-07 with CUBRC (U.S. Government contract F3002-88-D-0026), and subcontract R009406 with IITRI (U.S. Government contract F30602-87-D-0094).

REFERENCES

Baldwin, R. W. 1990. Naming and Grouping Privileges to Simplify Security Management in Large Databases. *Proceedings of the 1990 IEEE Symposium on Research in Security and Privacy,* May 1990.

Bell, D.E., and LaPadula, L.J. 1976. Secure Computer Systems: Unified Exposition and Multics Interpretation. Technical Report ESD-TR-75-306, The MITRE Corporation, Bedford, Mass., March 1976.

Denning, D.E., 1982. *Cryptography and Data Security.* Addison-Wesley, Reading, Mass.

Denning, D.E., Akl, S.G., Heckman, M., Lunt, T.F., Morgenstern, M., Neumann, P.G., and Schell, R.R. 1987a. Views for Multilevel Database Security. *IEEE Transactions on Software Engineering,* Vol. 13, No. 2.

Denning, D.E., Lunt, T.F., Schell, R.R., Heckman, M., and Shockley, W.R. 1987b. A Multilevel Relational Data Model. *Proceedings of the 1987 IEEE Symposium on Security and Privacy,* April 1987.

Department of Defense. 1985. *Department of Defense Trusted Computer System Evaluation Criteria, DOD 5200.28-STD.*

Dittrich, K.R., Hartig, M., and Pfefferle, H. 1988. Discretionary Access Control in Structurally Object-Oriented Database Systems. *Proceedings of the 2nd IFIP WG11.3 Workshop on Database Security,* October 1988.

Garvey, T.D., and Lunt, T.F. 1990a. Multilevel Security for Knowledge-Based Systems. Technical report, Computer Science Laboratory, SRI International, Menlo Park, Cal. 1990.

Garvey, T.D., and Lunt, T.F. 1990b. Multilevel Security for Knowledge-Based Systems. *Proceedings the Sixth Annual Computer Security Applications Conference,* December 1990.

Gudes, E., Song, H., and Fernandez, E.B. 1990. Evaluation of Negative and Predicate-Based Authorization in Object-Oriented Databases. *Proceedings of the 4th IFIP WG11.3 Workshop on Database Security,* September 1990.

Jajodia, S., and Kogan, B. 1990. Integrating an Object-Oriented Data Model with Multilevel Security. *Proceedings of the 1990 IEEE Symposium on Security and Privacy,* May 1990.

Keefe, T.F., Tsai, W.T., and Thuraisingham, M.B. 1989. SODA: A Secure Object-Oriented Database System. Technical report TR89-12, University of Minnesota, Computer Science Department.

Kelter, U. 1990. Group-Oriented Discretionary Access Controls for Distributed Structurally Object-Oriented Database Systems. Informatics Report N 93, Fern Universität Hagen, Hagen, Germany.

Landwehr, C.E., Heitmeyer, C.L., and McLean, J. 1984. A Security Model for Military Message Systems. *ACM Transactions on Computer Systems,* Vol. 2, No. 3.

Larrondo-Petrie, M.M., Gudes, E., Song, H., and Fernandez, E.B. 1990. Security Policies in Object-Oriented Databases. *Database Security III: Status and Prospects.* D.L. Spooner and C. Landwehr, eds. Elsevier.

Lunt, T.F. 1989. Access Control Policies: Some Unanswered Questions. *Computers and Security,* February 1989.

Lunt, T.F. 1990. The True Meaning of Polyinstantiation: Proposal for an Operational Semantics for a Multilevel Relational Database System. *Proceedings of the Third RADC Database Security Workshop,* June 1990.

Lunt, T.F. 1991. Polyinstantiation: An Inevitable Part of a Multilevel World. *Fourth IEEE Workshop on the Foundations of Computer Security,* June 1991.

Lunt, T.F., Denning, D.E., Schell, R.R., Shockley, W.R., and Heckman, M. 1990. The SeaView Security Model. *IEEE Transactions on Software Engineering,* June 1990.

Millen, J.K., and Lunt, T.F. 1989. Secure Knowledge-Based Systems. Technical Report SRI-CSL-90-04, Computer Science Laboratory, SRI International, Menlo Park, Cal.

Millen, J.K., and Lunt, T.F. 1992. Security for Object-Oriented Database Systems. *Proceedings of the 1992 IEEE Symposium on Research in Security and Privacy,* May 1992.

Moffet, J.D., and Sloman, M.S. 1988. The Source of Authority for Commercial Access Control. *Computer,* Vol. 21, No. 2.

Moffet, J.D., and Sloman, M.S. 1990. Delegation of Authority. Domino Report b1/ic/4, Dept. of Computing, Imperial College of Science and Technology, London.

Rabitti, F., Woelk, D., and Kim, W. 1988. A Model of Authorization for Object-Oriented and Semantic Databases. *Proceedings of the International Conference on Extending Database Technology,* 1988.

Rabitti, F., Bertino, E., Kim, W., and Woelk, D. 1991. A Model of Authorization for Next Generation Database Systems. *ACM Trans. on Database Systems,* Vol. 16, No. 1, March 1991, 88–131.

Song, H., Fernandez, E.B., and Gudes, E. 1990. Administrative Authorization in Object-Oriented Databases. *Proceedings of the EISS Workshop on Database Security,* European Institute for System Security, Karlsruhe, Germany, April 1990.

Ting, T.C., Demurjian, S.A., and Hu, M.-Y. 1991. Requirements, Capabilities, and Functionalities of User-Role Based Security for an Object-Oriented Design Model. *Proceedings of the Fifth IFIP Working Group 11.3 Workshop on Database Security,* November 1991.

8

Query Processing in Object-Oriented Database Systems

M. TAMER ÖZSU
JOSÉ A. BLAKELEY

One of the basic functionalities of database management systems (DBMSs) is to be able to process declarative user queries. The first generation of object-oriented DBMSs did not provide declarative query capabilities. However, the last decade has seen significant research in defining query models (including calculi, algebra, and user languages) and in techniques for processing and optimizing them. Many of the current commercial systems provide at least rudimentary query capabilities. In this chapter we discuss the techniques that have been developed for processing object-oriented queries. Our particular emphasis is on extensible query-processing architectures and techniques. The other chapters in this book on query languages and optimization techniques complement this chapter.

8.1 Introduction

One of the criticisms of first-generation object-oriented database management systems (OODBMSs) was their lack of declarative query capabilities. This led some researchers to brand first-generation (network and hierarchical) DBMSs as object oriented [Ullman 1988]. It was commonly believed that the application domains that OODBMS technology targets do not need querying capabilities. This belief no longer holds, and declarative query capability is accepted as one of the fundamental features of OODBMSs [Atkinson et al. 1989; Stonebraker et al. 1990]. Indeed, most of the current prototype systems experiment with powerful query languages and investigate their optimization. Commercial products have started to include such languages as well (e.g., O2 [Deux et al. 1991], ObjectStore [Lamb et al. 1991]).

In this chapter we discuss the issues related to the *optimization* and *execution* of OODBMS query languages (which we collectively call *query processing*). Query optimization techniques are dependent upon the query model and language. For example, a functional query language lends itself to functional optimization that is quite different from the algebraic, cost-based optimization techniques employed in relational as well as a number of object-oriented systems. The query model, in turn, is based on the data (or object) model since the latter defines the access primitives that are used by the query model. These primitives, at least partially, determine the power of the query model. Despite this close relationship, in this chapter we do not consider issues related to the design of object models, query models, or query languages in any detail. Language design issues are discussed elsewhere in this book. The interrelationship between object and query models is discussed in Blakeley 199; Özsu and Straube 1991; Özsu et al. 1993; and Yu and Osborn 1991.

Almost all object query processors proposed to date use optimization techniques developed for relational systems. However, there are a number of issues that make query processing more difficult in OODBMSs. The following are some of the more important issues:

1. *Type system.* Relational query languages operate on a simple type system consisting of a single aggregate type: *relation*. The closure property of relational languages implies that each relational operator takes one or more relations as operands and produces a relation as a result. In contrast, object systems have richer type systems. The results of object algebra operators are usually sets of objects (or collections) whose members may be of different types. If the object languages are closed under the algebra operators, these heterogeneous sets of objects can be operands to other operators. This requires the development of elaborate type inferencing schemes to determine which methods can be applied to *all* the objects in such a set. Furthermore, object algebras often operate on semantically different collection types (e.g., set, bag, list), which imposes additional requirements on the type inferencing schemes to determine the type of the results of operations on collections of different types.
2. *Encapsulation.* Relational query optimization depends on knowledge of the physical storage of data (access paths) that is readily available to the query optimizer. The encapsulation of methods with the data they operate on in OODBMSs raises (at least) two issues. First, estimating the cost of executing methods is considerably more difficult than estimating the cost of accessing an attribute according to an access path. In fact, optimizers have to worry about optimizing method execution, which is not an easy problem because methods may be written using a general-purpose programming language. Second, encapsulation raises issues related to the accessibility of storage information by the query optimizer. Some systems overcome this difficulty by treating the query optimizer as a special application that can break encapsulation and access information directly [Cluet and Delobel 1992]. Others propose a mechanism whereby objects "reveal" their costs as part of their interface [Graefe and Maier 1988].

3. *Complex objects and inheritance.* Objects usually have complex structures where the state of an object references other objects. Accessing such complex objects involves *path expressions*. The optimization of path expressions is a difficult and central issue in object query languages. We discuss this issue in some detail in this chapter. Furthermore, objects belong to types related through inheritance hierarchies. Efficient access to objects through their inheritance hierarchies is another problem that distinguishes object-oriented from relational query processing.

4. *Object models.* OODBMSs lack a universally accepted object model definition. Even though there is reasonable consensus on the basic features that need to be supported by any object model (e.g., object identity, encapsulation of state and behavior, type inheritance, and typed collections), how these features are supported differs among models and systems. As a result, the numerous projects that experiment with object query processing follow quite different paths and are, to a certain degree, incompatible, making it difficult to capitalize on the experiences of others. This diversity of approaches is likely to prevail for some time; therefore, it is important to develop extensible approaches to query processing that allow experimentation with new ideas as they evolve. We provide an overview of various extensible object query-processing approaches.

The organization of this chapter is as follows. In section 8.2 we present several representative query-processing architectures that have been developed and experimented with. These architectures, in one sense, define the query-processing methodology. In section 8.3, we discuss the various approaches to optimization of object queries. Section 8.4 is devoted to a discussion of query-execution strategies. We conclude, in section 8.5, with some comments on the state of the art in object query processing and optimization and the work that remains to be done.

8.2 Query-Processing Architecture

In this section we focus on two architectural issues: the query-processing methodology and the query-optimizer architecture.

8.2.1 Query-Processing Methodology

A query-processing methodology similar to relational DBMSs, but modified to deal with the difficulties discussed in the previous section, can be followed in OODBMSs. Figure 8–1 depicts such a methodology, proposed in Straube and Özsu 1990a.

The steps of the methodology are as follows. Queries are expressed in a declarative language that requires no user knowledge of object implementations, access paths, or processing strategies. The calculus expression is first

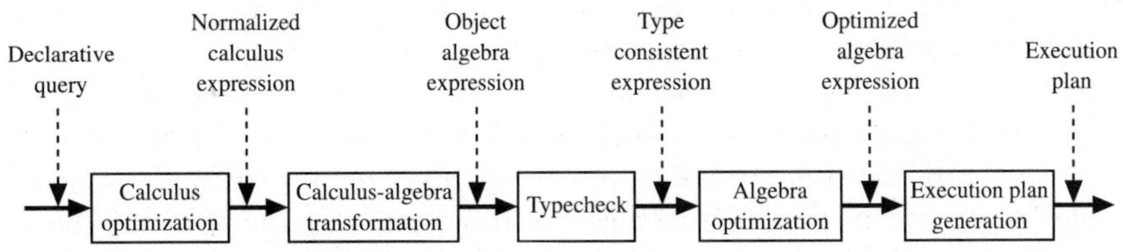

FIGURE 8–1
Object Query-Processing Methodology

reduced to a normalized form by eliminating duplicate predicates, applying identities, and rewriting. The normalized expression is then converted to an equivalent object algebra expression. This form of the query is a nested expression that can be viewed as a tree whose nodes are algebra operators and whose leaves represent extents of classes in the database. The algebra expression is next checked for type consistency to insure that predicates and methods are not applied to objects that do not support the requested functions. This is not as simple as type checking in general programming languages since intermediate results, which are sets of objects, may be composed of heterogeneous types. The next step in query processing is the application of equivalence-preserving rewrite rules [Freytag 1987] to the type consistent algebra expression. Lastly, an execution plan that takes into account object implementations is generated from the optimized algebra expression. The separation of the algebraic optimization step from the execution plan generation step follows the distinction that is made between "query rewrite" and "plan optimization" [Haas et al. 1989]. Query rewrite is a high-level process in which general-purpose heuristics drive the application of transformation rules. Plan optimization, on the other hand, is a lower-level process that transforms a query into the most cost-effective access plan, based on a specific cost model and knowledge of access paths and database statistics. This methodology clearly separates the various concerns and provides extensibility to the query processor. However, it faces one serious problem: the combinatorial cost of analyzing the large number of plans that are generated. The algebraic optimization step generates a family of equivalent query expressions based on the transformation rules defined for the algebra. The execution plan generation step creates a number of alternative mappings from each of these expressions to the object manager interface calls. Therefore, the number of alternatives that need to be considered may become quite high. One alternative followed in Starburst [Haas et al. 1989] is to use heuristic rules to control query rewrite so that a single query expression is generated as input to the plan optimization step. Cost-based optimization approaches, on the other hand, merge these two steps into one and consider the alternative execution algorithms as part of the search space.

This methodology assumes the existence of a fully specified calculus-based language and an object algebra. There are only a few calculi that have been defined for OODBMSs [Abiteboul and Beeri 1987; Peters et al. 1993; Straube and Özsu 1990a] and a few object logics with declarative query facilities [Kifer and Wu 1989; Maier 1986]. There is a large number of declarative user languages (e.g., Blakeley 1991; Carey et al. 1988; Kifer et al. 1992; Orenstein et al. 1992), but these generally do not have a formal calculus. Some of these languages are discussed elsewhere in this book. Work on object algebras has been more prevalent. Many algebras have been defined with varying operations (e.g., Alhajj and Arkun 1993; Beeri and Kornatzky 1990; Blakeley et al. 1993; Peters et al. 1993; Shaw and Zdonik 1990; Straube and Özsu 1990a; Vandenberg and DeWitt 1991).

8.2.2 Optimizer Architecture

Query optimization can be modeled as an optimization problem whose solution is the choice of the "optimum" *state* in a *state space* (also called *search space*). In query optimization, each state corresponds to an algebraic query indicating an execution schedule and represented as a processing tree. The state space is a family of equivalent (in the sense of generating the same result) algebraic queries. Query optimizers generate and search a state space using a *search strategy* applying a *cost function* to each state and finding one with minimal cost.[1] Thus, to characterize a query optimizer, three things need to be specified:

1. The search space and the transformation rules that generate the alternative query expressions that constitute the search space.
2. A search algorithm that allows one to move from one state to another in the search space.
3. The cost function that is applied to each state.

Many existing OODBMS optimizers either are implemented as part of the object manager on top of a storage system or are implemented as client modules in a client-server architecture. In most cases, the above-mentioned four aspects are hardwired into the query optimizer. Given that extensibility is a major goal of OODBMSs, one would hope to develop an extensible optimizer that accommodates different search strategies, different algebra specifications with their different transformation rules, and different cost functions. Rule-based query optimizers [Freytag 1987; Graefe and DeWitt 1987] provide a limited amount of extensibility by allowing the definition of new transformation rules. However, they do not allow extensibility in other dimensions. In this section we discuss some promising new proposals for extensibility in OODBMSs.

---

1. In this chapter we are mostly concerned with cost-based optimization, which is arguably the more interesting case.

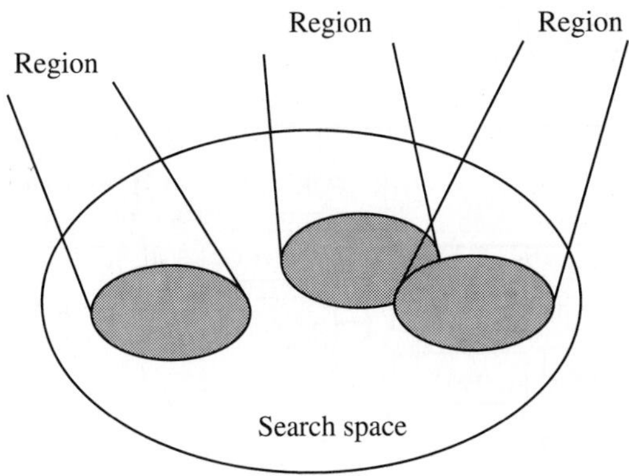

FIGURE 8–2
Partitioning the Search Space into Regions

The Open OODB project [Wells et al. 1992] at Texas Instruments[2] concentrates on the definition of an open architectural framework for OODBMSs and on the description of the design space for these systems. Query processing in Open OODB [Blakeley et al. 1993] follows steps similar to those in Fig. 8–1. The query module is an example of intramodule extensibility in Open OODB. The query optimizer, built using the Volcano optimizer generator [Graefe and McKenna 1993], is extensible with respect to algebraic operators, logical transformation rules, execution algorithms, implementation rules (i.e., logical operator to execution algorithm mappings), cost estimation functions, and physical property enforcement functions (e.g., presence of objects in memory). The clean separation between the user query language parsing structures and the operator graph on which the optimizer operates allows the replacement of the user language or optimizer. The separation between algebraic operators and execution algorithms allows exploration with alternative methods for implementing algebraic operators. Code generation is also a well-defined subcomponent of the query module that facilitates porting the query module to work on top of other OODBMSs. The Open OODB query processor includes a query-execution engine containing efficient implementations of scan, indexed scan, hybrid-hash join [Shapiro 1986], and complex object assembly [Keller et al. 1991].

The EPOQ project [Mitchell et al. 1993] is another approach to query-optimization extensibility, where the search space is divided into *regions*. Each region corresponds to an equivalent family of query expressions that are reachable from each other. The regions are not necessarily mutually exclusive (Fig. 8–2) and differ in the queries they manipulate, control (search) strategy they use, query transformation rules they incorporate, and optimization objectives they achieve. For example, one region

2. This is different from HP's Open ODB product.

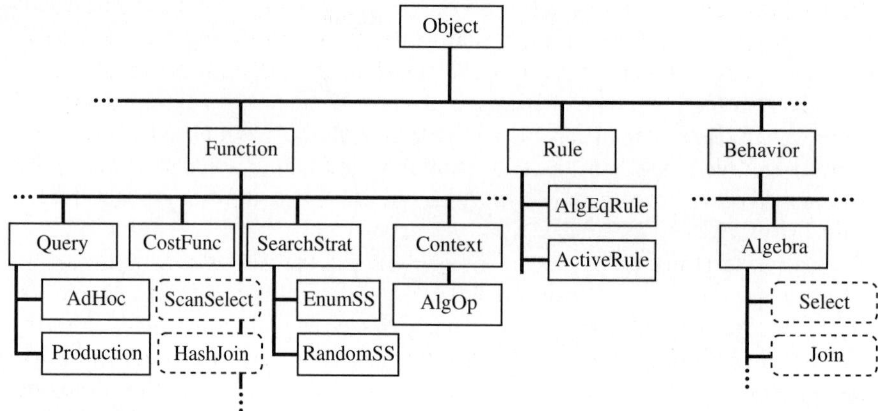

FIGURE 8–3
Optimizer as Part of the Type System

may cover transformation rules that deal with simple select queries, while another region may deal with transformations for nested queries. Similarly, one region may have the objective of minimizing a cost function, while another region may attempt to transform queries in some desirable form. Each region may be nested to a number of levels, allowing hierarchical search within a region. Since the regions do not represent equivalence classes, there is a need for a global control strategy to determine how the query optimizer moves from one region to another. The feasibility and effectiveness of this approach remains to be verified.

The TIGUKAT project [Peters et al. 1992] uses an object-oriented approach to query-processing extensibility. The TIGUKAT object model is an extensible uniform behavioral model characterized by a purely behavioral semantics and a uniform approach to objects. The model is behavioral in that the only way objects are accessed is by applying behaviors (which replace both the instance variables and the methods available in other object models) to objects. Behaviors are defined on types, and their implementations are modeled as functions. Every concept, including types, classes, collections, meta-information, and the like is a first-class object. The uniformity of the object model extends to the query model, treating queries as first-class objects [Peters et al. 1993]. A `Query` type is defined as a subtype of the `Function` type (Fig. 8–3). Thus, queries are specialized kinds of functions that can be compiled and executed. Furthermore, `Query` type can be specialized based on a classification scheme. Figure 8–3 shows, for example, specialization of ad hoc and production queries. The inputs and outputs of queries are collections (which are also objects), providing closure.

The TIGUKAT query optimizer [Muñoz 1994] follows the same philosophy of representing system concepts as objects and is along the lines of Lanzelotte and Valduriez 1991. The search space, the search strategy, and the cost function are modeled as objects (see Fig. 8–3). The incorporation of these components of the optimizer into the type system provide extensibility via the basic object-oriented principle of subtyping and specialization.

The states in the search space are modeled as processing trees (PT) whose leaf nodes are references to collections and whose nonleaf nodes denote behavior applications whose results are other objects. Those nodes that correspond to algebraic operator behaviors return temporary collections as result.

Algebraic operators (e.g., `Select`, `Join`) are defined as behaviors of the `Collection` type. They are modeled as instances (shown as dashed boxes in Fig. 8–3) of type `Algebra`, which is a subtype of type `Behavior`. The implementation (execution) algorithms for these algebraic operators are modeled as function objects (e.g., `HashJoin`, `ScanSelect`). These implementation functions cannot be used as nodes of a PT, since these nodes should represent execution functions all of whose arguments have been marshalled. Therefore, `AlgOp` type is defined whose instances are functions with marshalled arguments and represent nodes of a PT. In this fashion, each node of a PT represents a specific execution algorithm for an algebra expression.

Search strategies are similarly modeled as objects but separate from the search space. `SearchStrat` is defined as a subtype of type `Function`, and it can in turn be specialized. Figure 8–3 shows the specialization of `SearchStrat` into enumerated search strategies `EnumSS` and randomized search strategies `RandomSS`. The algebraic transformation rules that control the movement of the search strategy through the search space are implemented as instances of `AlgEqRule`, which is a subtype of `Rule`.

Cost functions (instances of `CostFunc`) are defined as special types of functions, making them first-class objects. Each function is associated a cost through the behavior *B_costFunction*. Application of this behavior to a function object *f* (i.e., *f.B_costFunction*) returns another function object *g* of type `CostFunc` that implements the computation of the cost of executing function *f*. This allows definition of parameterized cost functions whose values are dependent upon a number of factors.

Modeling the building blocks of a cost-based optimizer as objects provides the query optimizer the extensibility inherent in object models. The optimizer basically implements a control strategy that associates a search strategy and a cost function to each query.

8.3 Optimization Techniques

Our discussion of optimization techniques for object queries follows two fundamental directions. The first is the cost-based optimization of queries based on algebraic manipulations. Algebraic optimization techniques have been studied quite extensively within the context of the relational model. The work on relational DBMSs has benefited greatly from the availability of a universally accepted algebra definition. Despite over two dozen proposals, there is no universally accepted object algebra, making it very difficult to generalize research results. The second is the optimization of *path expressions*. Path expressions represent traversal paths between objects and are unique to OODBMSs. The optimization of path expressions is an important issue in OODBMSs and has been a subject of considerable investigation.

8.3.1 Algebraic Optimization

We previously identified the components of an algebraic optimizer. In this section, we discuss each of these components in some detail.

Search Space and Transformation Rules

A major advantage of algebraic optimization is that an algebraic query expression can be transformed using well-defined algebraic properties such as transitivity, commutativity, and distributivity. Therefore, each query has a (potentially large) number of equivalent expressions, which make up the *search space*. These expressions are equivalent in terms of the results they generate but may be widely different in terms of their costs. Thus, the query optimizers modify the query expressions, by means of algebraic transformation rules, in an attempt to obtain one that generates the same result with the lowest possible cost.

The transformation rules are very much dependent upon the specific object algebra since they are defined individually for each object algebra and for their combinations. The lack of a standard object algebra definition is particularly troubling since the community cannot benefit from generalizations of numerous object algebra studies. The general considerations for the definition of transformation rules and the manipulation of query expressions is quite similar to relational systems, with one particularly important difference. Relational query expressions are defined on flat relations, whereas object queries are defined on classes (or collections or sets of objects) that have inheritance relationships among them. It is, therefore, possible to use the semantics of these relationships in object-oriented query optimizers to achieve some additional transformations.

Consider, for example, the object algebra defined in Straube and Özsu 1990a whose operators work on and produce sets of objects. Consider three operators `union` ($\cup$), `intersection` ($\cap$), and parameterized `select` (denoted $P\sigma_F \langle Q_1 \dots Q_k \rangle$), where `union` and `intersection` have the usual set-theoretic semantics and `select` selects objects from one set P using the sets of objects $Q_1 \dots Q_k$ as parameters (in a sense a generalized form of semijoin). The following are some of the transformation rules that can be applied during optimization to get equivalent query expressions (for brevity we use *QSet* to denote $Q_1 \ldots Q_k$; *RSet* is defined similarly):

$$(P\,\sigma_{F_1}\langle QSet\rangle)\,\sigma_{F_2}\langle RSet\rangle \Leftrightarrow (P\,\sigma_{F_2}\langle RSet\rangle)\,\sigma_{F_1}\langle QSet\rangle \quad (1)$$

$$(P \cup Q)\,\sigma_F\langle RSet\rangle \Leftrightarrow (P\,\sigma_F\langle RSet\rangle) \cup (Q\,\sigma_F\langle RSet\rangle) \quad (2)$$

$$(P\,\sigma_{F_1}\langle QSet\rangle)\,\sigma_{F_2}\langle RSet\rangle \Leftrightarrow (P\,\sigma_{F_1}\langle QSet\rangle) \cap (P\,\sigma_{F_2}\langle RSet\rangle) \quad (3)$$

Rule 1 captures commutativity of `select`, while Rule 2 denotes that `select` distributes over `union`. Rule 3 is an identity that utilizes the fact that `select` merely restricts its input and returns a subset of its first argument. [3]

The first two rules are quite general in that they represent equivalences that are inherited from set theory. The third one is a special transformation rule for a specific object algebra operator defined with a specific semantics. All three, however, are syntactic in nature. Consider the following rules, on the other hand, in which C_i denotes the set of objects in the extent of class c_i and C_i^* denotes the deep extent of class c_j (i.e., the set of objects in the extent of c_j as well as in the extents of all those which are subclasses of c_j):

$$C_1 \cap C_2 \Leftrightarrow \phi \text{ if } c_1 \neq c_2 \quad (4)$$

$$C_1 \cup C_2^* \Leftrightarrow C_2^* \text{ if } c_1 \text{ is a subclass of } c_2 \quad (5)$$

$$(P\,\sigma_F\langle QSet\rangle) \cap R \overset{c}{\Leftrightarrow} (P\,\sigma_F\langle QSet\rangle) \cap (R\,\sigma_{F'}\langle QSet\rangle) \quad (6)$$

$$\overset{c}{\Leftrightarrow} P \cap (R\,\sigma_{F'}\langle QSet\rangle)$$

These transformation rules are semantic in nature since they depend on the object model and query model specifications. Rule 4, for example, is true because the object model restricts each object to belong to only one class. Rule 5 holds because the query model permits retrieval of objects in the deep extent of the target class. Finally, rule 6 relies on type consistency rules [Straube and Özsu 1990b] for its applicability as well as the condition that F' is identical to F except each occurrence of p is replaced by r (this last condition is denoted by the c over the $\Leftrightarrow$).

Since the idea of query transformation is well known, we do not elaborate on the techniques. The above discussion demonstrates the general idea and also highlights the unique aspects that need to be considered in object algebras. In section 8.3.2, we discuss the transformations for a new operator called `materialize`, recently proposed to optimize path expressions.

3. These rules make assumptions about the formulae (F_i) that we do not get into in this chapter.

Search Algorithm

Exhaustive search, whereby the entire search space is enumerated, is the most straightforward search strategy that can be used. A cost function can be applied to each equivalent expression to determine the cheapest. An improvement is to use a dynamic programming approach, whereby new expressions are constructed bottom-up using the previously determined optimal subexpressions [Lee et al. 1988; Selinger et al. 1979]. The Volcano optimizer generator uses a top-down, dynamic programming approach to search with branch-and-bound pruning [Graefe and McKenna 1993]. These are what we call *enumerative algorithms*.

Since the enumerative search algorithms are based on evaluating the cost of the entire search space, their overhead is quite high. In relational systems, the number of join operations typically determines the complexity of enumerative search. If there are N join operations and there are two choices for join ordering (for inner and outer relations), then there are $O(2^N)$ alternative query expressions to evaluate.[4] Heuristics such as performing selections and projections before joins (to reduce the sizes of the join operands) do not change the combinatorial nature of the problem. Therefore, the value of N and the threshold beyond which combinatorial nature of the problem makes enumerative solutions infeasible becomes an important issue. $N = 10$ has been suggested as an empirical threshold value [Ioannidis and Wong 1987].

This may be an important concern for object query optimization as well. First, a large number of the object algebras have join operators or operators with semantics similar to join. Second, it has been suggested [Ioannidis and Wong 1987] that even if it is not common to find many business data processing queries with more than 10 join operations, such queries are quite common in AI and decision support system applications. These are important applications that OODBMSs attempt to serve. Finally, as we will address in section 8.3.2, one method of executing path expressions is to represent them as explicit joins and then use the well-known join algorithms to optimize them. If this is the case, then the number of joins and other operations with join semantics in a query is quite likely to be higher than this empirical threshold of 10.

In these cases, *randomized search algorithms* have been suggested as one alternative to restrict the region of the search space that is analyzed. Randomized algorithms are well known in operations research, and two versions of these algorithms have been investigated within the context of relational query optimization: *simulated annealing* [Ioannidis and Wong

4. More accurate bounds for various types of join queries (linear and star) are given in Ono and Lohman 1990. However, the combinatorial nature of the problem remains.

1987] and *iterative improvement* [Swami 1989]. A combination of the two algorithms, called *two-phase optimization,* is proposed in Ioannidis and Cha Kang 1990. Without getting into the details of these algorithms, the general idea can be described as follows. The randomized algorithms start from a random state in the search space (i.e., an initial query expression that may be obtained as a result of query translation) and then walk through the search space, evaluating the cost of each state and stopping either when they estimate that they have found the optimum execution plan or when a predetermined optimization time expires. The walking between states is controlled by transformation rules such as the ones described in the previous section and a global control strategy. Iterative improvement accepts a move from one state to another only if the cost of the destination state is lower than the cost of the source state. Simulated annealing, on the other hand, allows a move to a higher-cost state with a certain probability that diminishes as optimization time moves along.

Since these are heuristic algorithms investigating only a portion of the search space, they cannot be guaranteed to be optimal. However, it has been shown that the randomized techniques converge to a state that is fairly close to the optimal state given sufficient time.

There has not been any study of randomized search algorithms within the context of OODBMSs. The general strategies are not likely to change, but the tuning of the parameters and the definition of the space of acceptable solutions should be expected to change. It is also interesting to note the surface similarity between randomized search algorithms and the regions approach proposed by Mitchell et al. 1993. Further studies are required to establish the relationship more firmly.

Cost Function

Typical cost functions used in query optimization take into account the various costs that are incurred in processing the query. In nondistributed systems, this is typically the I/O and CPU cost, while in distributed systems, the communication cost is also added.

The arguments to cost functions are based on information regarding the storage of the data. Typically, the optimizer considers the number of data items (cardinality), the size of each data item, its organization (e.g., whether there are indexes on it or not), and other issues. This information is readily available to the query optimizer in relational systems (through the system catalog) but may not be in OODBMSs. As indicated in the introduction, there is a controversy in the research community as to whether the query optimizer should be able to break the encapsulation of objects and look at the data structures used to implement them. If this is permitted, then the cost functions can be specified similarly to relational systems

[Blakeley et al. 1993; Cluet and Delobel 1992; Dogac et al. 1994; Orenstein et al. 1992]. Otherwise, an alternative specification must be considered.

The cost function can be defined recursively based on the algebraic processing tree. If the internal structure of objects is not visible to the query optimizer, the cost of each node (representing an algebraic operation) has to be defined. One way to define it is to have objects reveal their costs as part of their interface [Graefe and Maier 1988]. A similar approach is provided in the TIGUKAT project [Muñoz 1994]. Since the algebraic operations are behaviors defined on type `Collection`, the nodes of the algebraic processing tree are behavior applications. There may be various functions that implement each behavior (representing different execution algorithms), in which case the behaviors reveal their costs as a function of (1) the execution algorithm and (2) the collection over which they operate. The bottom line, in both cases, is the same: Let the type implementer specify a more abstract cost function for behaviors from which the query optimizer can calculate the cost of the entire processing tree. The definition of cost functions, especially in the approaches based on the objects revealing their costs, needs to be investigated further before satisfactory conclusions can be reached.

Parameterization

Compilation-time query optimization is a static process in the sense that the optimizer makes use of the database statistics at the time the query is compiled and optimized in selecting the optimal execution plan. This decision is independent of the execution-time statistics, such as the system load. Further, it does not take into account the changes to the database statistics as a result of updates that may occur between the time the query is optimized and the time it is executed. This is especially a problem in production-type queries that are optimized once (with considerable overhead) and executed a large number of times. This may be an even more serious issue in OODBMSs that may be used as repositories for design prototypes (software or otherwise). These databases are by definition more volatile, resulting in significant changes to the database (that is why dynamic schema evolution is so important in OODBMSs). The query optimization strategy has to be able to cope with these changes.

This issue can be handled in one of two ways. One alternative is to determine an optimization/reoptimization interval and reoptimize the query periodically. Even though this is a simple approach, it is based on a fixed time interval whose determination in general would be problematic. A slight variation may be to determine the reoptimization point based on the difference between the actual execution time, and the estimated execution time. Consequently, the run-time system can track the actual execution time, and whenever it deviates from the estimated time by more than a fixed threshold, the query is reoptimized. Again, the determination of this threshold would be a concern as well as the run-time overhead of tracking query execution.

An alternative that has been researched [Graefe and Ward 1989; Ioannidis et al. 1992] and implemented in ObjectStore [Orenstein et al. 1992] is *parametric query optimization*, which is also called *dynamic plan selection*. In this case, the optimizer maintains multiple execution strategies at compile-time and makes a final plan selection at run-time based on various system parameters and the current database statistics. This approach may also fit well with the methodology depicted in Fig. 8–1 using an optimizer that respects the encapsulation of objects. In this case, algebraic optimization can ignore all physical execution characteristics, instead generating a set of desirable (however defined) equivalent query expressions that are handed over to the object manager that is responsible for storing objects. The object manager can then compare the alternatives (at run-time) based on their execution characteristics. However, this approach also has the significant problem of potentially incurring high run-time overhead.

A problem with compile-time parametric optimization (and run-time resolution) is the potential exponential explosion of the dynamic plans as a function of the complexity of the query and the number of optimization parameters unknown at compile time. This problem, along with the problems of error propagation and inaccuracy of selectivity and cost estimation methods, makes run-time query optimization an attractive alternative.

8.3.2 Path Expressions

Most query languages allow queries whose predicates involve conditions on object access along reference chains. These reference chains are often called *path expressions* [Zaniolo 1983]; in the past they have also been called *complex predicates* or *implicit joins* [Kim 1989]. Optimizing the computation of path expressions is a problem that has received substantial attention in object-query processing.

Path expressions allow a succinct, high-level notation for expressing navigation through the *object composition graph* that enables the formulation of predicates on values deeply nested in the structure of an object. Path expressions provide a uniform mechanism for the formulation of queries that involve object composition and inherited member functions. Path expressions may be *single valued* or *set valued* and may appear in a query as part of a predicate, as a target to a query (when set valued), or as part of a projection list. Techniques to traverse path expressions forward and backward are presented by Jenq et al. 1990.

Let $p.m_1(\alpha_1).m_2(\alpha_2). \cdots .m_n(\alpha_n)$ be a path expression, where p is a variable representing an object instance; α_i, $1 \leq i \leq n$ represents a (possibly empty) list of arguments to the corresponding function m_i. If all are single-valued functions, then we call the path expression *single valued.* If at least one of the m_i is set valued, then the path expression is *set valued.*

The problem of optimizing path expressions spans the entire query-compilation process. During or after parsing of a user query but before algebraic optimization, the query compiler must recognize what path expressions can potentially be optimized. This is typically achieved through *rewriting* techniques that transform path expressions into equivalent logical algebra expressions [Cluet and Delobel 1992]. Once path expressions are represented in algebraic form, the query optimizer explores the space of *equivalent algebraic* and execution plans searching for one of minimal cost [Blakeley et al. 1993; Lanzelotte and Valduriez 1991]. Finally, the optimal execution plan may involve algorithms to efficiently compute path expressions including hash-join [Shapiro 1986], complex-object assembly [Keller et al. 1991], or indexed scan through path indexes [Kemper and Moerkotte 1994; Maier and Stein 1986; Valduriez 1987].

To illustrate this point, consider the query to retrieve all employee names, their departments, and job descriptions for employees working in a department located in a Dallas plant. We will use the OQL[C++] object query-language syntax as an example user query language [Blakeley 1994]. Figure 8–4 illustrates several key stages in processing this query.

Rewriting

Consider the path expression `e.dept().plant().location()`. Assume every employee instance has a reference to a department, each department has a reference to a plant, and each plant instance has a location field. Also assume that department and plant types have a corresponding type extent. The first two links of the above path may involve the retrieval of department and plant objects from disk. The third path involves only a lookup of a field within a plant object. Therefore, only the first two links present opportunities for query optimization in the computation of that path. An object-query compiler needs a mechanism to distinguish these links in a path representing possible optimizations. This is typically achieved through a *rewriting* phase.

Cluet and Delobel 1992 describe a type-based rewriting technique to be used as a basis for a new query optimizer being implemented in O_2 [Deux et al. 1991]. Their approach "unifies" algebraic and type-based rewriting techniques, permits factorization of common subexpressions, and supports heuristics to limit rewriting. They exploit type information to decompose initial complex arguments of a query into a set of simpler operators and to rewrite path expressions ("pointer chasing") into joins. Lanzelotte and Valduriez 1991 present a similar attempt to optimize path expressions within an algebraic framework using an operator called `implicit join`.

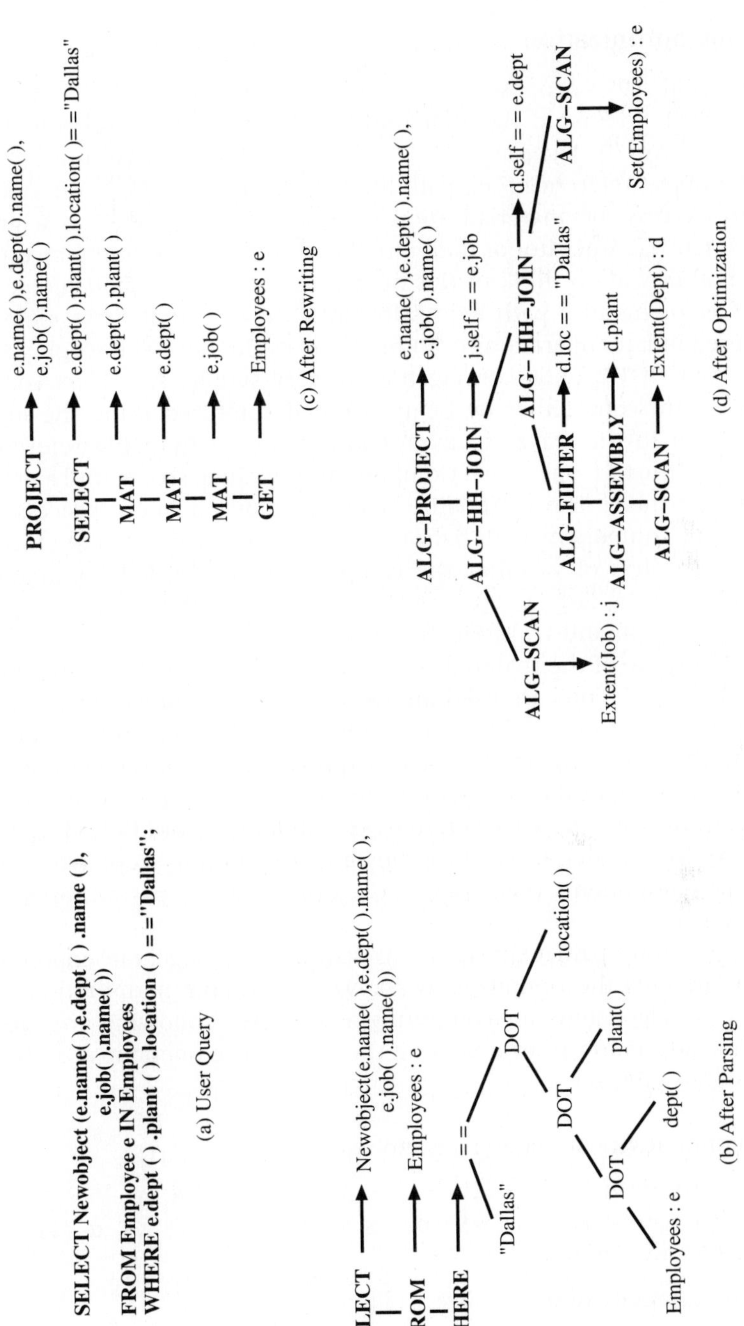

FIGURE 8–4
Optimization of Path Expressions

Algebraic optimization

Blakeley et al. 1993 proposed an object-algebra operator, called `materialize (Mat)`, to enable algebraic optimization of path expressions (e.g., `e.dept().plant()`). The purpose of `Mat` is to represent the computation of each interobject reference (i.e., path link) explicitly, allowing a query optimizer to express the materialization of multiple components as a group using a single `Mat` operator or individually using a `Mat` operator per component. Another way to think of this operator is as a *scope definition,* because it brings elements of a path expression into scope so that these elements can be used in later operations or in predicate evaluation. The scoping rules in TI's Open OODB optimizer algebra are very simple. An object component gets into scope either by being scanned (captured using the logical `Get` operator in the leaves of expressions trees) or by being referenced (captured in the `Mat` operator). Components remain in scope until a projection discards them. The materialize operator allows a query processor to aggregate all component materializations required for the computation of a query regardless of whether the components are needed for predicate evaluation (e.g., `e.dept().plant()`) or to produce the result of a query (e.g., `e.job()`) as shown in Fig. 8–4c.

The purpose of the materialize operator is to indicate to the optimizer where path expressions are used and where algebraic transformations can be applied. In the example illustrated in Fig. 8–4, the materialize operators can trade their positions in the query expression, with the condition that `plant` must be materialized before `department`. We presume that the `location` and `name` instance variables are similar to record fields that need not be explicitly materialized since they are brought into scope when their containing components (i.e., `employee`, `department`, `plant`, and `job`) are materialized.

Representing path expressions as sequences of algebraic materialize operators permits the optimizer to analyze all feasible permutations and cost-effective algorithms for computing a path. The following are sample logical transformation rules involving the materialize operator used in the Open OODB optimizer:

1. Commutativity of materialize and select.

MAT α_1 (SELECT α_2 (β_1)) $\rightarrow$ SELECT α_3 (MAT α_4 (β_1)).
SELECT α_1 (MAT α_2 (β_1)) $\rightarrow$ MAT α_3 (SELECT α_4 (β_1)); if α_1 is not dependent on α_2.

2. Commutativity of materialize and join.

MAT α_1 (JOIN α_2 ($\beta_1\beta_2$)) $\rightarrow$ JOIN α_3 ((MAT α_4 (β_1))β_2); if α_1 only depends on β_1.
JOIN α_1 (β_1(MAT α_2 (β_2))) $\rightarrow$ MAT α_3 (JOIN α_4 ($\beta_1\beta_2$)); if α_1 does not depend on α_2.

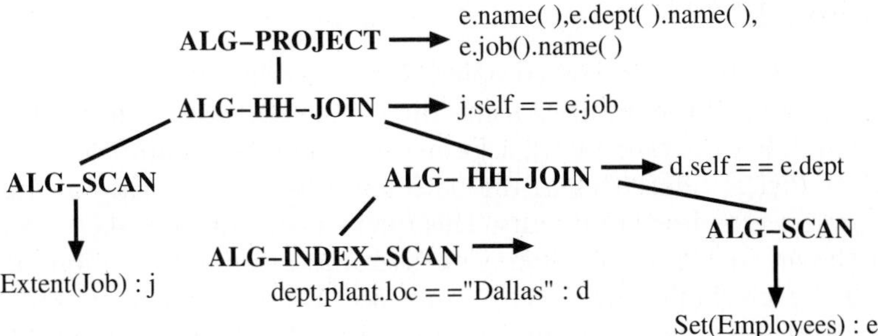

FIGURE 8–5
An Optimal Execution Plan Using a Path Index

3. Materialize to join.

MAT α_1 (β_1) $\rightarrow$ JOIN α_2 (β_1(GET α_3 ())); if β_1 is a scanable collection.

4. Commutativity of contiguous materialize operators.

MAT α_1 (MAT α_2 (β_1)) $\rightarrow$ MAT α_2 (MAT α_1 (β_1)); if α_1 does not depend on α_2.

5. Collapse contiguous materialize operators.

MAT α_1 (MAT α_2 (β_1)) $\rightarrow$ MAT α_3 (β_1).

In their work on the optimization of path expressions, Lanzelotte and Valduriez 1991 also present rules to transform a series of `implicit join` operators into an indexed scan using a path index when an index is available.

Path Indexes

Substantial research on object query optimization has been devoted to the design of index structures to speed up the computation of path expressions [Bertino and Kim 1989; Kemper and Moerkotte 1994; Maier and Stein 1986; Valduriez 1987]. Figure 8–5 shows an optimal execution plan equivalent to the execution plan in Fig. 8–4d for the case when the Department extent is indexed through the path `department.plant().location()`.

Computation of path expressions via indexes represents just one class of query-execution algorithms used in object-query optimization. In other words, efficient computation of path expressions through path indexes represents only one collection of implementation choices for algebraic operators, such as materialize and join, used to represent interobject references. Section 8.4 describes a representative collection of query-execution algorithms that promise to provide a major benefit on the efficient execution of object queries. We will defer a discussion of some representative path index techniques to that section. Bertino and Kim 1989 present a more comprehensive survey of index techniques for object query optimization.

An Example

We conclude this section by completing the description of the example presented in Fig. 8–4, optimized using the Open OODB optimizer. Recall that the materialize operators with arguments `job()`, `dept()`, and `plant()` represent the logical references in the path expressions appearing in the select and project operator arguments. This query results in the query execution plan shown in Fig. 8–4d. There are five interesting observations in comparing the algebraic query (Fig. 8–4c) and the optimal plan (Fig. 8–4d). First, two materialize operators are transformed to join operations and executed using hybrid-hash join. This transformation is possible because the materialize operators explicitly represent each of the path expressions' links that need to be traversed to establish the relationships between object components. Second, path expressions are computed in an order different than the one presented by the initial user query (compare where the employee-job relationship is established in Fig. 8–4c and 8–4d). Reversing the order in which the links are traversed is possible because the materialize operator represents links at the logical level and the equivalence rules allow the optimizer to choose the path-computation sequence with minimal cost. Third, the plan traverses some links in a direction opposite to that of the physical pointers between the objects. This interesting and initially counterintuitive choice stems from a small extent size for the `job` type and a small cardinality of filtered and assembled Department-Plant objects (used in this example), which permit very efficient executions of hybrid-hash join using only in-memory hash tables and no overflow files. Fourth, the placement of the assembly algorithm in Fig. 8–4d attempts to minimize the number of `plant` components that have to be assembled from disk. An unfortunate choice would be to assemble first departments and then plants—typically, the number of employees is much larger than the number of departments in an organization—although it might be considered the most natural execution of this example query. Finally, for the department and job components, there is an explicit extent and the optimizer can place an upper bound on the number of I/O operations needed to assemble the department and job components of an employee object. This example illustrates that naïve pointer chasing in object-query processing (i.e., gotos on disk) may be suboptimal in some cases. Therefore, value-based set-matching algorithms similar to those used in relational query optimization are also relevant in object-query optimization.

8.4 Query Execution

The relational DBMSs benefit from the close correspondence between the relational algebra operations and the access primitives of the storage system. Therefore, the generation of the execution plan for a query expression basically concerns the choice and implementation of the most efficient algorithms for executing individual algebra operators and their combinations. In OODBMSs, the issue is more complicated due to the difference in the abstraction levels of behaviorally defined objects and their storage. Encapsulation of objects, which hides their implementation details, and the storage of methods with objects pose a challenging design problem that can simply be stated as follows: At what point in query processing should the query optimizer access information regarding the storage of objects? In Straube and Özsu 1991, which follows the methodology depicted in Fig. 8–1, access to this information is left to an *object manager*. Consequently, the query-execution plan is generated from the query expression that is obtained at the end of the query-rewrite step by mapping the query expression to a well-defined set of object-manager interface calls. The object-manager interface consists of a set of execution algorithms. This section reviews some of the execution algorithms that are likely to be part of future high-performance object-query execution engines.

A query-execution engine requires three basic classes of algorithms on collections of objects: (collection) *scan, indexed scan,* and *collection matching.* Collection scan is a straightforward algorithm that sequentially accesses all objects in a collection. We do not discuss this algorithm further. Indexed scan allows efficient access to selected objects in a collection through an index. It is possible to use an object's field or the values returned by some method as a key to an index. Also, it is possible to define indexes on values deeply nested in the structure of an object (i.e., path indexes). In this section we mention a representative sample of path-index proposals. Set-matching algorithms take multiple collections of objects as input and produce aggregate objects related by some criteria. Join, set intersection, and assembly are examples of algorithms in this category.

8.4.1 Path Indexes

Indexes are essential components in database systems to speed up the evaluation of queries. Indexes enable fast computation of queries involving highly selective predicates and are useful access paths to accelerate the computation of set-matching operations (e.g., join).

Support for path expressions is a feature that distinguishes object-oriented from relational queries. Many indexing techniques designed to accelerate the computation of path expressions have been proposed [Bertino and Kim 1989; Maier and Stein 1986; Valduriez 1987]. *Access support relations* [Kemper and Moerkotte 1994] are general techniques to represent and compute path expressions. In their evaluation, Kemper and Moerkotte provide initial evidence that the performance of queries executed using access support relations improves by about two orders of magnitude over queries that do not use access support relations. A system using access support relations needs to also consider the cost of maintaining them in the presence of updates to the underlying base relations. For a detailed description of this topic, refer to Chapter 9, by Kemper and Moerkotte. Maier and Stein 1986 proposed a path indexing technique for the GemStone OODBMS that creates an index on each class traversed by a path. This technique was also proposed for the Orion OODBMS [Bertino and Kim 1989]. Access support relations generalize this indexing technique to allow set-valued path expressions. In addition to indexes on path expressions, it is possible to define indexes on objects across their type inheritance. Kim et al. 1989 provide a thorough discussion of such indexing techniques through inheritance.

8.4.2 Set Matching

In the subsequent discussion we assume that we have two sets of objects *R* and *S* that stand in a many-to-one relationship from *R* to *S*. We assume that *R* and *S* are stored as separate disk files and that the objects in *R* contain an OID to their related object in *S*.

Hybrid-Hash Join

An effective object-query execution engine needs a generic, value-based join algorithm for three reasons. First, naïve pointer traversal is not always the best algorithm to compute the join of *R* and *S* [Shekita and Carey 1990]. Second, if a query involving the join of *R* and *S* applies a highly selective predicate to the objects in *S*, then it is often more efficient to compute the join of *R* and *S* in the direction opposite to the direction of the pointers. Similarly, when interobject references do not include inverse relationships, a value-based join is an effective way to compute the interobject references between two related sets in the direction opposite to the pointers. Third, a slight modification of a generic join algorithm can be used to efficiently compute other set-matching operations (e.g., intersection) [Graefe 1993].

The hybrid-hash algorithm applies the divide-and-conquer principle to the problem of computing a join. The potentially large input sets are recursively partitioned into smaller subfiles (buckets), each of which may fit entirely in memory, using a hash function on the join attribute; at the end of this stage, each subfile contains objects from the input sets that may potentially join. Each pair of subfiles is joined to produce the result. The hybrid-hash join method takes advantage of the main memory available by performing the first subjoin while building the subfiles for subsequent manipulation. The standard hybrid-hash algorithm consists of $B+1$ steps where

$$B = \max(0, \left\lceil \frac{|R| * F - |M|}{|M| - 1} \right\rceil),$$

where $|R|$ and $|M|$ are the sizes of relation *R* and main memory available (in pages), respectively, and *F* is a space-overhead factor for hashing (typically,

1.2). During the first step, R and S are read into memory and partitioned into $B+1$ compatible subsets, R_i, S_i, $0 \leq i \leq B$, through a hash function on the joining attribute. In addition, the first subsets, R_0 and S_0 are joined at this time, while the remaining subsets are written to disk. The remaining B steps repeat the previous stage on subset pairs R_i, S_i, $1 \leq i \leq B$ by reading them into memory and joining them.

Pointer-Based Hybrid-Hash Join

The pointer-based hybrid-hash algorithm [Shekita and Carey 1990] is used in cases when each object in R contains a pointer (PID, physical identifier) to an S object. The algorithm is similar to standard hybrid-hash join and uses the following three steps. First, R is partitioned in the same way as in the hybrid hash algorithm, except that it is partitioned by PID values rather than by join attribute. The set of objects S is not partitioned. Second, each partition R_i of R is joined with S by taking R_i and building a hash table for it in memory. The table is built by hashing each object $r \in R$ on the value of its pointer (PID) to its corresponding object in S. As a result, all R objects that reference the same page in S are grouped together in the same hash-table entry. Third, after the hash table for R_i is built, each of its entries is scanned. For each hash entry, the corresponding page in S is read and all objects in R that reference that page are joined with the corresponding objects in S.

An important difference between this algorithm and standard hybrid-hash is that R is the only set that is partitioned, and as such it always plays the role of the *inner* set. This is necessary because the direction of the pointers is from R to S. Shekita and Carey 1990 showed that when R is significantly larger than S, standard hybrid-hash may outperform pointer-based hybrid-hash; therefore, an OODBMS can benefit by supporting both algorithms.

Assembly

The `assembly` operator [Keller et al. 1991] is a generalization of the pointer-based hash-join algorithm for the case when we need to compute a multiway join. There is a difference between assembly and n-way pointer joins in that assembly does not need the entire collection of root objects to be scanned before producing a single result. Assembling a complex object rooted at objects of type R containing object components of types S, U, and T is analogous to computing a four-way join of these sets.

Instead of assembling a single complex object at a time, the assembly operator assembles a *window*, of size W, of complex objects simultaneously. As soon as any of these complex objects becomes assembled and passed up the query-execution tree, the assembly operator retrieves another one to work on. Using a window of complex objects increases the pool size of unresolved references and results in more options for optimization of disk accesses. Due to the randomness with which references are resolved, the

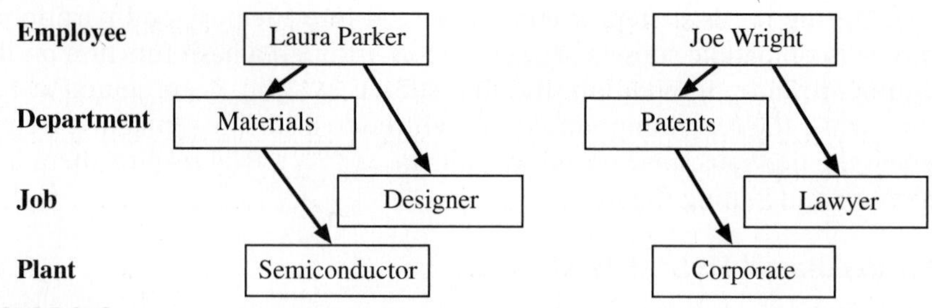

FIGURE 8–6
Two Assembled Complex Objects

assembly operator delivers assembled objects in random order up the query execution tree. This behavior is correct in set-oriented query processing but may not be for other collection types, such as lists.

To illustrate the behavior of assembly, consider the following example[5], which assembles a set of employee objects with the structure shown in Fig. 8–6. Suppose that assembly is using a window of size 2. The assembly operator begins by filling the window with two (since $W=2$) employee references from the set (Fig. 8–7a). The assembly operator begins by choosing among the current outstanding references, say *E1*. After resolving (fetching) *E1*, two new unresolved references are added to the list (Fig. 8–7b). Resolving *E2* results in two more references added to the list (Fig. 8–7c), and so on until the first complex object is assembled (Fig. 8–7g). At this point, the assembled object is passed up the query-execution tree, freeing some window space. A new employee reference, *E3*, is added to the list and then resolved, bringing two new references *D3*, *J3* (Fig. 8–7h).

The objective of the assembly algorithm is to simultaneously assemble a window of complex objects. At each point in the algorithm, the outstanding reference that optimizes disk accesses is chosen. There are different orders or schedules in which references may be resolved. Keller et al. 1991 study the performance of three reference resolution algorithms for assembly: depth first, breadth first, and elevator. The results indicate that elevator outperforms depth first and breadth first under several data-clustering situations.

8.5 Conclusions

This chapter reviewed some of the main contributions to object-database query processing to date. In the area of query-processing architectures, we expect future object-query architectures to continue to bear a strong similarity to relational and extended-relational query-processing architectures.

5. This example is taken from Keller et al. 1991, with slight modifications in notation.

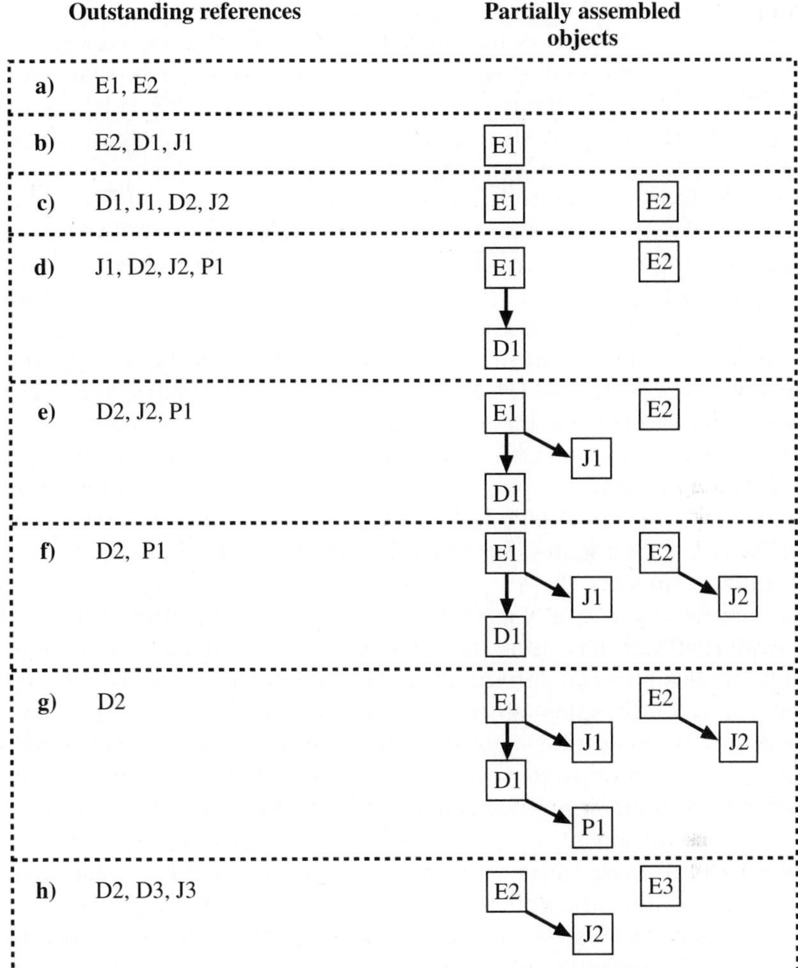

FIGURE 8–7
An Assembly Example

The refinement, design, and better understanding of internal interfaces among the modules that constitute a query-processing system will continue to be important research challenges. Building query processors under highly modular and extensible architectural frameworks will accelerate the technology transfer process of this rapidly evolving technology into working systems. The EREQ [Maier 1992], TI Open OODB [Wells et al. 1992], Volcano [Graefe and McKenna 1993], and TIGUKAT [Peters et al. 1992] are projects in this direction.

In the area of object-query optimization, some fairly comprehensive cost-based query optimizers have started to appear. Research into query-optimizer generator toolkits (e.g., Graefe and McKenna 1993), and rule-based query optimization has moved beyond the proof-of-concept stage. A few nonrelational query optimizers for object-oriented [Blakeley et al. 1993] and scientific databases [Wolniewicz and Graefe 1993] have been built with the help of such generators. Given that query optimizers are fairly complex software systems to build, we expect to see an increase in the use of optimizer generators to help build new query optimizers in the years to come. We also expect an increase in the scope of the optimization tasks for which optimizer generators are used. Cost-based query optimization has proven to be still an effective approach for the optimization of object queries. We believe that complexity and size of the search space are not immediate roadblocks in the effectiveness of cost-based query optimization for complex object queries. Rather, the deficiency of cost- and selectivity-estimation techniques and error propagation will be immediate concerns when scaling the cost-based query optimization approach to complex queries. The judicious incorporation of heuristic pruning, randomization techniques, and the combination of partial query execution (to obtain exact cost and selectivity estimates) with cost-based optimization are important areas of future research.

In the area of query execution, perhaps a main contribution by object-oriented DBMSs has been the development of indexing techniques over path expressions and inheritance type hierarchies to speed up access to collections of complex objects. It has also become clear that join and set-matching execution algorithms initially developed for relational databases will continue to play an important role in the development of high-performance object-query execution engines. Naïve pointer traversal (gotos on disk) is not always optimal when querying large collections of objects. New execution algorithms to efficiently access complex objects, such as object assembly and pointer-based joins, have been developed.

Future DBMSs will be hybrid open systems that combine the best capabilities of existing DBMSs. These future DBMSs will be as effective as existing relational DBMSs in the processing of queries and provide as rich data modeling and high-performance object-at-a-time access as existing OODBMS. In other words, relational DBMSs will try to provide better support for objects, and OODBMS will try to provide better support for queries. Database-query processing will continue to be an exciting and challenging research area.

ACKNOWLEDGMENTS

We would like to thank Goetz Graefe and Gail Mitchell for their careful reading and useful comments on the first version of this chapter. M. Tamer Özsu's research is supported by Natural Sciences and Engineering Research Council (NSERC) of Canada under the research grant OGP0951. José Blakeley's research is sponsored by the Advanced Research Projects Agency under ARPA Order No. A016 and managed by the U.S. Army Research Laboratory under contract DAAB07-90-C-B920.

REFERENCES

Abiteboul, S., and Beeri, C. 1987. On the Power of Languages for the Manipulation of Complex Objects. Technical Report 846, INRIA.

Alhajj, R., and Arkun, M.E. 1993. A Query Model for Object-Oriented Databases. *Proceedings of 9th International Conference on Data Engineering*, 163–172.

Atkinson, M., Bancilhon, F., DeWitt, D., Dittrich, K., Maier, D., and Zdonik, S. 1989. The Object-Oriented Database System Manifesto. *Proceedings of 1st International Conference on Deductive and Object-Oriented Databases*, 40–57.

Beeri, C., and Kornatzky, Y. 1990. Algebraic Optimization of Object-Oriented Query Languages. *Proceedings of 3rd International Conference on Database Theory*. Springer-Verlag, 72–88.

Bertino, E., and Kim, W. 1989. Indexing Techniques for Queries on Nested Objects. *IEEE Transactions on Knowledge and Data Engineering* 1, 2, (June), 196–214.

Blakeley, J. 1991. DARPA Open Object-Oriented Database Preliminary Module Specification: Object Query Module. Technical Report, Texas Instruments.

Blakeley, J. 1994. OQL[C++]: Extending C++ with an Object Query Capability. In *Modern Database Systems*. W. Kim, ed. Addision-Wesley, Reading, Mass.

Blakeley, J., McKenna, W., and Graefe, G. 1993. Experiences Building the Open OODB Query Optimizer. *Proceedings of ACM-SIGMOD International Conference on Management of Data*, 287–296.

Carey, M., DeWitt, D., and Vandenberg, S. 1988. A Data Model and Query Language for EXODUS. *Proceedings of ACM-SIGMOD International Conference on Management of Data*, 413–423.

Cluet, S., and Delobel, C. 1992. A General Framework for the Optimization of Object-Oriented Queries. *Proceedings of ACM-SIGMOD International Conference on Management of Data*, 383–392.

Deux, O., et al. 1991. The O_2 System. *Comm. of the ACM* Vol. 34, No. 10, 34–48.

Dogac, A., Ozkan, C, Arpinar, B., Okay, T., and Evrendilek, C. 1994. METU Object-Oriented DBMS. *Advances in Object-Oriented Database Systems*, A. Dogac, M.T. Özsu, A. Biliris, T. Sellis, Eds. Springer-Verlag.

Freytag, J. 1987. A Rule-Based View of Query Optimization. *Proceedings of ACM-SIGMOD International Conference on Management of Data*, 173–180.

Graefe, G. 1993. Query Evaluation Techniques for Large Databases. *ACM Computer Surveys* Vol. 25, No. 2, 73–170.

Graefe, G., and DeWitt, D. 1987. The EXODUS Optimizer Generator. *Proceedings of ACM-SIGMOD International Conference on Management of Data*, 160–172.

Graefe, G., and Maier, D. 1988. Query Optimization in Object-Oriented Database Systems: The Revelation Project. Technical Report CS/E 88-025, Oregon Graduate Center.

Graefe, G., and McKenna, W. 1993. The Volcano Optimizer Generator. *Proceedings of 9th International Conference on Data Engineering*, 209–218.

Graefe, G., and Ward, K. 1989. Dynamic Query Evaluation Plans. *Proceedings of ACM-SIGMOD International Conference on Management of Data*, 358–366.

Haas, L., Cody, W., Freytag, J., Lapis, G., Lindsay, B., Lohman, G., Ono, K., and Pirahesh, H. 1989. Extensible Query Processing in Starburst. *Proceedings of ACM-SIGMOD International Conference on Management of Data*, 377–388.

Ioannidis, Y., and Cha Kang, Y. 1990. Randomized Algorithms for Optimizing Large Join Queries. *Proceedings of ACM-SIGMOD International Conference on Management of Data*, 312–321.

Ioannidis, Y., Ng, R., Shim, K., and Sellis, T. 1992. Parametric Query Optimization. *Proceedings of 18th International Conference on Very Large Data Bases*, 103–114.

Ioannidis, Y., and Wong, E. 1987. Query Optimization by Simulated Annealing. *Proceedings of ACM-SIGMOD International Conference on Management of Data*, 9–22.

Jenq, B., Woelk, D., Kim, W., and Lee, W.-L. 1990. Query Processing in Distributed ORION. In *Advances in Database Technology—EDBT'90*. Springer-Verlag, 169–187.

Keller, T., Graefe, G., and Maier, D. 1991. Efficient Assembly of Complex Objects. *Proceedings of ACM-SIGMOD International Conference on Management of Data*, 148–157.

Kemper, A., and Moerkotte, G. 1994. Physical Object Management. In *Modern Database Systems*. W. Kim, ed. Addison-Wesley, Reading, Mass.

Kifer, M., Kim, W., and Sagiv, Y. 1992. Querying Object Oriented Databases. *Proceedings of ACM-SIGMOD International Conference on Management of Data*, 393–402.

Kifer, M., and Wu, J. 1989. A Logic for Object-Oriented Programming (Maier's O-Logic: Revisited). *Proceedings of ACM-SIGACT-SIGMOD Symposium on Principles of Database Systems*, 379–393.

Kim, W. 1989. A Model of Queries for Object-Oriented Databases. *Proceedings of 15th International Conference on Very Large Data Bases*, 423–432.

Kim, W., Kim, K., and Dale, A. 1989. Indexing Techniques for Object-Oriented Databases. In *Object-Oriented Concepts, Databases, and Applications*, W. Kim and F. Lochovshy, Eds. ACM/Addison-Wesley, Reading, Mass.

Lamb, C., Landis, G., Orenstein, J., and Weinreb, D. 1991. The Object-Store Database System. *Comm. of the ACM*, Vol. 34, No. 10, 50–63.

Lanzelotte, R., and Valduriez, P. 1991. Extending the Search Strategy in a Query Optimizer. *Proceedings of 17th International Conference on Very Large Databases*, 363–373.

Lee, M., Freytag, J., and Lohman, G. 1988. Implementing an Interpreter for Functional Rules in a Query Optimizer. *Proceedings of 14th International Conference on Very Large Databases*, 218–229.

Maier, D. 1986. A Logic of Objects. *Proceedings of Workshop on Foundations of Deductive Databases and Logic Programming*, 6–26.

Maier, D. 1992. Specifying a Database System to Itself. In *Specifications of Database Systems*, D. Harper and M. Norrie, Eds. Springer-Verlag.

Maier, D., and Stein, J. 1986. Indexing in an Object-Oriented DBMS. *Proceedings of 1st International Workshop on Object-Oriented Database Systems*, 171–182.

Mitchell, G., Dayal, U., and Zdonik, S. 1993. Control of an Extensible Query Optimizer: A Planning-Based Approach. *Proceedings of 19th International Conference on Very Large Databases*, 517–528.

Muñoz, A. 1994. An Extensible Query Optimizer for the TIGUKAT Object-Base Management System. Master's thesis, University of Alberta, Department of Computing Science, Edmonton, Alberta, 1994.

Ono, K., and Lohman, G. 1990. Measuring the Complexity of Join Enumeration in Query Optimization. *Proceedings of 16th International Conference on Very Large Databases*, 314–325.

Orenstein, J., Haradvala, S., Margulies, B., and Sakahara, D. 1992. Query Processing in the ObjectStore Database System. *Proceedings of ACM-SIGMOD International Conference on Management of Data*, 403–412.

Özsu, M., and Straube, D. 1991. Issues in Query Model Design in Object-Oriented Database Systems. *Computer Standards & Interfaces*, Vol. 13, 157–167.

Özsu, M., Straube, D., and Peters, R. 1993. Query Processing Issues in Object-Oriented Knowledge Base Systems. In *Emerging Landscape of Intelligence in Database and Information Systems*, F. Petry and L. Delcambre, Eds. JAI Press.

Peters, R., Lipka, A., Özsu, M., and Szafron, D. 1993. An Extensile Query Model and Its Languages for a Uniform Behavioral Object Management System. *Proceedings of 2nd International Conference on Information and Knowledge Management*, 403–412.

Peters, R., Özsu, M., and Szafron, D. 1992. TIGUKAT: An Object Model for Query and View Support in Object Database Systems. Tech. Rep. TR92-14, Department of Computing Science, University of Alberta.

Selinger, P., Astrahan, M., Chamberlin, D., Lorie, R., and Price, T. 1979. Access Path Selection in a Relational Database Management System. *Proceedings of ACM-SIGMOD International Conference on Management of Data*, 23–34.

Shapiro, L. 1986. Join Processing in Database Systems with Large Main Memories. *ACM Transactions on Database Systems* Vol. 11, No. 3, 239–264.

Shaw, G., and Zdonik, S. 1990. A Query Algebra for Object-Oriented Databases. *Proceedings of 6th International Conference on Data Engineering*, 154–162.

Shekita, E., and Carey, M. 1990. A Performance Evaluation of Pointer-Based Joins. *Proceedings of ACM-SIGMOD International Conference on Management of Data*, 300–311.

Stonebraker, M., Rowe, L., Lindsay, B., Gray, J., Carey, M., Brodie, M., Bernstein, P., and Beech, D. 1990. Third-Generation Data Base System Manifesto. *ACM-SIGMOD Record*, Vol. 19, No. 3, 31–44.

Straube, D., and Özsu, M. 1990a. Queries and Query Processing in Object-Oriented Database Systems. *ACM Transactions on Information Systems*, Vol. 8, No. 4, 387–430.

Straube, D., and Özsu, M. 1990b. Type Consistency of Queries in an Object-Oriented Database System. *Proceedings of ECOOP/OOPSLA '90 Conference*, 224–233.

Straube, D., and Özsu, M. 1991. Execution Plan Generation for an Object-Oriented Data Model. *Proceedings of 2nd International Conference on Deductive and Object-Oriented Databases*, C. Delobel, M. Kifer, and Y. Masunaga, Eds. Springer-

Verlag, 43–67. (A full version will appear in *IEEE Transactions on Knowledge and Data Engineering*.)

Swami, A. 1989. Optimization of Large Join Queries: Combining Heuristics and Combinatorial Techniques. *Proceedings of ACM-SIGMOD International Conference on Management of Data,* 367–376.

Ullman, J. 1988. *Principles of Database and Knowledge Base Systems.* Computer Science Press.

Valduriez, P. 1987. Join Indices. *ACM Transactions on Database Systems,* Vol. 12, No. 2, 218–246.

Vandenberg, S., and DeWitt, D. 1991. Algebraic Support for Complex Objects with Arrays, Identity, and Inheritance. *Proceedings of ACM-SIGMOD International Conference on Management of Data,* 158–167.

Wells, D., Blakeley, J., and Thompson, C. 1992. Architecture of an Open Object-Oriented Database Management System. *Computer,* Vol. 25, No. 10, 74–82.

Wolniewicz, R., and Graefe, G. 1993. Algebraic Optimization of Computations over Scientific Databases. *Proceedings of 19th International Conference on Very Large Databases,* 13–24.

Yu, L., and Osborn, S. 1991. An Evaluation Framework for Algebraic Object-Oriented Query Models. *Proceedings of 7th International Conference on Data Engineering,* 670–677.

Zaniolo, C. 1983. The Database Language GEM. *Proceedings of ACM-SIGMOD International Conference on Management of Data,* 207–218.

9

Physical Object Management

ALFONS KEMPER
GUIDO MOERKOTTE

In this chapter we will discuss a few physical object management techniques that are rooted in the relational context but were thoroughly adapted to the needs and requirements of the object-oriented model(s). After introducing a sample object-oriented database schema (and an extension thereof) we discuss *Access Support Relations*, an indexing technique for path expressions. Then we overview techniques for indexing within type hierarchies and describe the materialization of functions in an object-oriented context. We also provide an overview of techniques for deriving good object clustering and finally sketch a few proposals for storage models for objects.

9.1 The Running Example

The discussion of this chapter is based on an object-oriented data model called GOM (Generic Object Model) that unites the most salient features of many recently proposed models in one coherent framework, as described in Kemper and Moerkotte 1994. In this respect, the objective of GOM can be seen as providing a syntactical framework of the essential object-oriented features. Independently, but with the same intention, Zdonik and Maier 1989 proposed the so-called Reference Model. The features that GOM provides are relatively *generic* (and basic) such that the results derived for this particular data model can be applied to a variety of other object-oriented models.

Let us now introduce an example object base called `Company`. This database will be used throughout the chapter to illustrate the physical object management techniques. The (mostly self-explanatory) type definitions are shown in Fig. 9–1. The type `Manager` is defined as a subtype of `Emp`, which has two consequences: (1) `Manager` instances inherit the structural and behavioral specification of `Emp` instances, and (2) a `Manager`

```
type Emp is
  body
    [name: string;
    worksIn: Dept;
    salary: int;
    sex: char;
    jobHistory: {Task};]
  operations
    declare skill: → int;
  implementation
    define skill is !! derived from the jobHistory
      begin
      var totalC, totalD: float := 0.0;
      foreach (t in self.jobHistory)
          begin
          totalC := totalC + t.competence *t.duration;
          totalD := totalD + t.duration;
          end foreach
      return round(totalC/totalD);
    end define skill;
end type Emp;
```

```
type Task is
  body
    [competence:int;
    duration: float;
end type Task

type Dept is
  body
    [name: string;
    secretary: Emp;
    mgr: Manager;]
end type Dept;

type Manager
  supertype Emp is
  body
    [backUp; Emp;]
end type Manager;
```

FIGURE 9–1
Type Definitions of the Running Example *Company*

instance can occur wherever an Emp object is required. The latter is a consequence of the *substitutability* property. The type Emp (and also Manager) contains a set-valued[1] attribute jobHistory referring to an arbitrary number of Task instances.

A (small) object base extension for this schema is shown in Fig. 9–2. An object may be viewed as a triple (*OID, Type, rep*), where *rep* corresponds to the internal state (i.e., everything within the box). The labels id_i for $i \in \{1, 2, 3, \ldots\}$ denote the systemwide unique object identifiers (*OIDs*). References via attributes are maintained unidirectionally in GOM—as in almost all other object models. For example, in an extension of the above schema there exists a reference in the form of a stored *OID* from an Employee to his or her Dept via the worksIn attribute, but not vice versa. These references are maintained by storing the unique *OID* of the referenced object in the referencing attribute or variable.

Let us sketch a few example queries based on the Company object base—formulated in the query language GOMql of Kemper, Moerkotte, and Peithner 1993:

Q_1: **range** *e* : Emp
retrieve *e*
where *e*.worksIn.mgr.salary < 200000

1. Note that there is a major difference between a (nonsharable) set value and a set object.

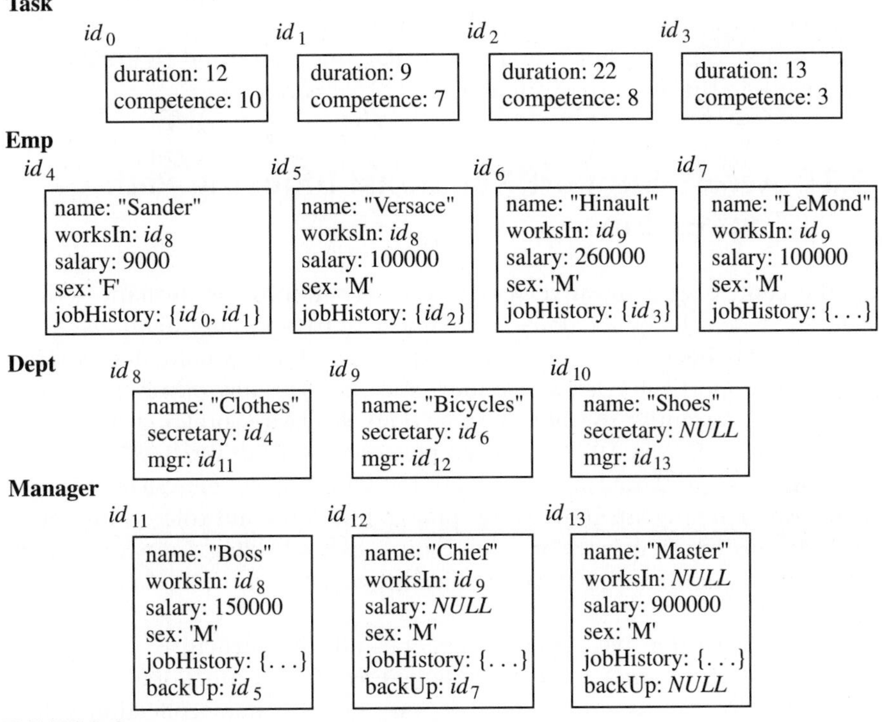

FIGURE 9–2
Example Extension of the Object Base *Company*

Q_2: **range** *e* : Emp
retrieve *e*.worksIn.mgr.salary
where *e*.name = "Sander"

Q_3: **range** *e* : Emp
retrieve *e*
where *e*.skill = 10

In query Q_1 those `Employees` are retrieved whose `Manager` earns less than 200000. This query involves a path expression (i.e., `e.worksIn.mgr.salary`), which is supported by the indexing structure discussed in section 9.2. With respect to this particular path expression, the query Q_1 is called a *backward query* because it logically involves traversing the path backwards from the qualifying `Manager` instances—that is, those earning less than 200000—to the `Emp` instances. Query Q_2, on the other hand, is a *forward query* since it involves traversing the same path expression in forward direction. The query Q_3 contains a user-defined function in the selection predicate. This query requires the evaluation of the function `skill` for all `Emp` instances. Section 9.4 describes an optimization technique for expediting the evaluation of such a query.

It should be obvious that, in particular, queries Q_1 and Q_3 are costly to evaluate—in the absence of suitable index structures.

9.2 Access Support Relations: Indexing Path Expressions

In the context of associative search, one of the most performance-critical operations in relational databases is the *join* of two or more relations. Much research has been done into expediting joins—for example, access structures to support join, *sort-merge* join, and *hash-join* algorithms have been developed. Recently, the binary join index structure, building on the so-called links of Härder 1978, has been proposed by Valduriez 1987.

In object-oriented database systems with object references, the join based on matching attribute values plays a less dominant role. More important are object accesses along reference chains leading from one object instance to another. This kind of object traversal is also called *functional* or *implicit join*.

In this section we present a general indexing structure, called *Access Support Relations (ASRs)*, which is designed to support functional join along arbitrarily long attribute chains that may even contain collection-valued attributes. In this respect, access support relations constitute materializations of frequently traversed reference chains.

9.2.1 Definitions

According to Kifer, Kim, and Sagiv 1992, a path expression has the form

$$o.A_1. \ldots .A_n$$

where o is a tuple structured object containing the attribute A_1 and $o.A_1. \ldots .A_i$ refers to an object or a set of objects, all of which have an attribute A_{i+1}. The result of the path expression is the set of objects (or values) of type t_n that can be reached from o via the specified attribute chain. Formally, a path expression or attribute chain is defined as follows:

DEFINITION 2.1 (Path Expression) Let $t_0, \ldots, t_n$ be (not necessarily distinct) types. A path expression on t_0 is an expression $t_0.A_1. \ldots .A_n$ if for each $1 \leq i \leq$ n one of the following conditions holds:

- The type t_{i-1} is defined as **type** t_{i-1} **is** $[\ldots, A_i : t_i, \ldots]$, that is, t_{i-1} is a tuple with an attribute Ai of type t_i[2].

- The type t_{i-1} is defined as **type** t_{i-1} **is** [..., A_i : $\{t_i\}$ ...], that is, the attribute A_i is set structured. In this case we speak of a set occurrence at A_i in the path $t_0.A_i. \ldots .A_n$.

For simplicity of presentation we assume that the types involved are not being defined as subtypes of some other type. This, of course, is generally possible; it would only make the definition a bit more complex.

The second part of the definition is useful to support access paths through sets. If it does not apply for a given path, the path is called *linear*. A path expression that contains at least one set-valued attribute is called *set valued.*

Since an access path can be seen as a relation, we will use relation extensions to represent materialized path expressions. The next definition maps a given path expression to the underlying access support relation declaration.

DEFINITION 2.2 (Access Support Relation [ASR]) Let $t_0, \ldots, t_n$ be types, $t_0. A_1. \ldots .A_n$ be a path expression. Then the access support relation $[t_0. A_1. \ldots .A_n]$ is of arity n+1 and its tuples have the following form:

$[S_0, \ldots, S_n]$

The domain of the attribute S_i is the set of identifiers (OIDs) of objects of type t_i for $(0 \le i \le n)$. If t_n is an atomic type then the domain of S_n is t_n, that is, values are directly stored in the access support relation.

We distinguish several possibilities for the extension of such relations. To define them for a path expression $t_0. A_1. \ldots .A_n$ we need n temporary relations $[t_0. A_1], \ldots, [t_{n-1}. A_n]$.

DEFINITION 2.3 (Temporary Binary Relations) For each i $(1 \le i \le n)$ —that is, for each attribute in the path expression—we construct the temporary binary relation $[t_{i-1}.A_i]$. The relation $[t_{i-1}.A_i]$ contains the tuples $(id(o_{i-1}), id(o_i))$ for every object o_{i-1} of type t_{i-1} and o_i of type t_i such that

- $o_{i-1}.A_i = o_i$ if A_i is a single-valued attribute.
- $o_i \in o_{i-1}.A_i$ if A_i is a set-valued attribute.

If t_n is an atomic type, then $id(o_n)$ corresponds to the value $o_{n-1}.A_n$. Note, however, that only the last type t_n in a path expression can possibly be an atomic type.

Let us reconsider the path expression of our schema *Company*, for which we now indicate the type constraints with the underbraces:

2. This means that the attribute A_i can be associated with objects of type t_i or any subtype thereof.

$$P \equiv \underbrace{\underbrace{\underbrace{Emp.worksIn}_{Dept}.mgr}_{Manager}.salary}_{int}$$

When considering the update problem, it should be obvious that strong typing is vital to indexing over path expressions. Therefore, models with a more relaxed typing paradigm have to impose user-specified and dynamically controlled type constraints on attributes and/or paths that are indexed.

For the path expression specified above, the temporary binary relations have the following extensions:

[Emp. worksIn]

OID_{Emp}	OID_{Dept}
id_4	id_8
id_5	id_8
id_6	id_9
id_7	id_9
id_{11}	id_8
...	...

[Dept. mgr]

OID_{Dept}	$OID_{Manager}$
id_8	id_{11}
id_9	id_{12}
id_{10}	id_{13}

[Manager. salary]

$OID_{Manager}$	*int*
id_{11}	150000
id_{13}	900000

9.2.2 Extensions of Access Support Relations

We now introduce different possible extensions of the ASR $[t_0. A_1. \dots .A_n]$. We distinguish four extensions:

1. The *canonical* extension, denoted $[t_0. A_1. \dots .A_n]_{can}$ contains only information about complete paths—that is, paths originating in t_0 and leading (all the way) to t_n. Therefore, it can only be used to evaluate queries that originate in an object of type t_0 and go all the way to t_n.
2. The *left-complete* extension $[t_0. A_1. \dots .A_n]_{left}$ contains all paths originating in t_0 but not necessarily leading to t_n but possibly ending in a NULL.
3. The *right-complete* extension $[t_0. A_1. \dots .A_n]_{right}$, analogously, contains paths leading to t_n but possibly originating in some object o_j of type t_j that is not referenced by any object of type t_{j-1} via the A_j attribute.
4. Finally, the *full* extension $[t_0. A_1. \dots .A_n]_{full}$ contains all partial paths, even if they do not originate in t_0 or do end in a NULL.

DEFINITION 2.4 (Extensions) Let |X| ( ]X[,]X| , |X[ ) denote the natural (outer, left outer, right outer) join on the last column of the first relation and the first column of the second relation. Then the different extensions are obtained as follows:

$$[t_0.A_1.\cdots.A_n]_{can} := [t_0.A_1] \bowtie \cdots \bowtie [t_{n\text{-}1}.A_n]$$

$$[t_0.A_1.\cdots.A_n]_{full} := [t_0.A_1] ⟗ \cdots ⟗ [t_{n\text{-}1}.A_n]$$

$$[t_0.A_1.\cdots.A_n]_{left} := (\cdots([t_0.A_1] ⟕ \cdots [t_1.A_2])\cdots ⟕ [t_{n\text{-}1}.A_n])$$

$$[t_0.A_1.\cdots.A_n]_{right} := ([t_0.A_1] ⟖ \cdots([t_{n\text{-}2}.A_{n\text{-}1}] ⟖ [t_{n\text{-}1}.A_n])\cdots)$$

For our example path expression, the full extension [Emp.worksIn.-mgr.salary]$_{full}$ looks as follows:

[Emp.worksIn.mgr.salary]$_{\mathbf{full}}$			
$S_0 : OID_{Emp}$	$S_1 : OID_{Dept}$	$S_2 : OID_{Manager}$	$S_3 : int$
id_4	id_8	id_{11}	150000
id_5	id_8	id_{11}	150000
id_{11}	id_8	id_{11}	150000
id_6	id_9	id_{12}	—
—	id_{10}	id_{13}	900000
...	...	...	...

This extension contains all paths and subpaths corresponding to the underlying path expression. The first three tuples actually constitute complete paths that would be present in the canonical extension as well; however, the fourth and the fifth paths would be omitted in the canonical extension. In the left-complete extension, the first four tuples would be present, whereas the fifth one would be omitted since it does not originate in Emp. Analogously, the right-complete extension, would contain the first three and the fifth tuple and omit the fourth tuple since it does not end in an *int* value representing the salary of some Manager.

It should be obvious that the full extension of an ASR contains more information than the left- or right-complete extensions, which, in turn, contain more information than the canonical extension. The right- and left-complete extensions are incomparable.

The difference in information contents has implications for the applicability of an ASR in evaluating a path expression originating in an object of type *s*:

DEFINITION 2.5 (Applicability) An access support relation $[t_0.A_1.\ \ldots\ .A_n]_X$ under extension X is applicable for a path $s.A_i.\ \ldots\ .A_j$ where s is a subtype[3] of $t_{i\text{-}1}$ under the following condition, depending on the extension X:

3. Note that every type is a subtype of itself.

$$Applicable\ ([t_0.A_1.\cdots.A_n]_X, s.A_i.\cdots.A_j) = \begin{cases} X = full & \wedge\ 1 \le i \le j \le n \\ X = left & \wedge\ 1 = i \le j \le n \\ X = right & \wedge\ 1 \le i \le j = n \\ X = can & \wedge\ 1 = i \le j = n \end{cases}$$

The *full* extension can be utilized to evaluate any subpath; the *left*- and *right-complete* extensions can only be applied to evaluate prefix- and suffix-paths, respectively. The *canonical* extension can only be applied to evaluate a complete path expression (i.e., one that spans the entire access support relation).

9.2.3 Storage Structure

The storage structure of access support relations is borrowed from the binary join index proposal of Valduriez 1987. Each ASR is redundantly stored in two index structures, the first being keyed on the leftmost attribute and the second on the rightmost attribute. Suitable index structures are hash tables or B^+-trees. The hash table is particularly suitable for keys consisting of OID attributes since only exact match queries have to be supported. On the other hand, B^+-trees are advantageous for attributes that allow range queries—for example, int and float values. Note that these attributes can only occur at the rightmost column of an ASR; an example is the rightmost column of the ASR `[Emp.worksIn.mgr.salary]`, which represents the salary attribute of `Manager` instances. The following discussion is solely based on B^+-trees; however, it can easily be adapted to hash tables.

Graphically, the redundant storage scheme consisting of two B^+-trees for each ASR is visualized for the canonical ASR `[Emp.worksIn.mgr.salary]`$_{can}$ as follows:

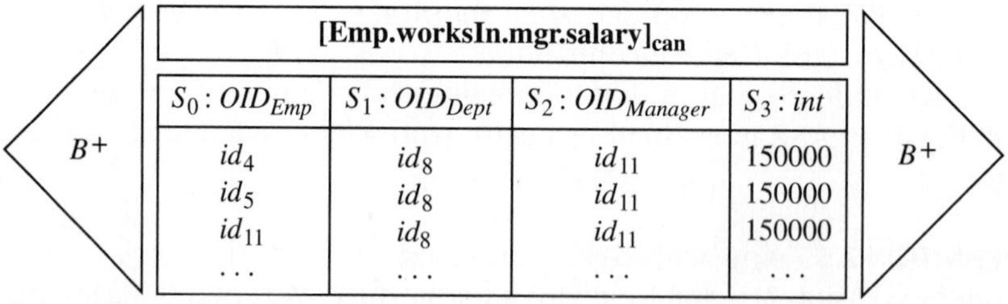

[Emp.worksIn.mgr.salary]$_{can}$

B^+	$S_0 : OID_{Emp}$	$S_1 : OID_{Dept}$	$S_2 : OID_{Manager}$	$S_3 : int$	B^+
	id_4	id_8	id_{11}	150000	
	id_5	id_8	id_{11}	150000	
	id_{11}	id_8	id_{11}	150000	
	...	...	...	...	

We will call the left B^+-tree the *forward clustered* tree and, analogously, the right one the *backward clustered* tree. The left B^+-tree supports the evaluation of a forward query (e.g., retrieving the salary of id_4's `Manager`). The right B^+-tree supports the evaluation of backward queries—with respect to the underlying path expression. For our example, an entry point for finding the `Emp` instances whose `Manager's salary` is below 200000 is provided by the backward clustered B^+-tree.

This storage scheme is also well suited for traversing paths from left to right (forward) as well as from right to left (backward) even if they span over several access support relations. Again, let us graphically visualize the situation:

[Emp.worksIn.mgr.]$_{can}$

B+ (left) / B+ (right)

$S_0 : OID_{Emp}$	$S_1 : OID_{Dept}$	$S_2 : OID_{Manager}$
id_4	id_8	id_{11}
id_5	id_8	id_{11}
id_{11}	id_8	id_{11}
...	...	...

[Manager.salary]$_{can}$

B+ (left) / B+ (right)

$S_0 : OID_{Manager}$	$S_1 : int$
id_{11}	150000
id_{13}	900000
...	...

The above example illustrates the virtues of the redundant storage model for ASRs. The right B$^+$-tree of the ASR [Manager.salary]$_{can}$ directly supports the lookup of those Manager instances whose salary is below 200000 (i.e., the Manager with OID id_{11} in our example). Then, the right B$^+$-tree of the ASR [Emp.worksIn.mgr]$_{can}$ supports the traversal to the corresponding *Emp* instances to obtain the result $\{id_4, id_5, id_{11}\}$. Thus, the backward traversal constitutes a right-to-left semijoin across ASRs:

$$\pi_{S_0}\ ([Emp.worksIn.mgr]_{can} \ltimes (\sigma_{S_1<200000}[Manager.salary]_{can}))$$

Analogously, the forward clustered B$^+$-tree supports the semijoin from left to right, such that, for instance, the salary of id_4's Manager can be retrieved efficiently. This corresponds to the left-to-right semijoin across ASRs:

$$\pi_{S_3}\ ((\sigma_{S_0=id_4}[Emp.worksIn.mgr]_{can}) \rtimes [Manager.salary]_{can})$$

9.2.4 Related Work

Access support relations were first proposed by Kemper and Moerkotte 1990. A more detailed description including a comprehensive quantitative evaluation can be found in Kemper and Moerkotte 1992. Access support relations constitute a generalization of two relational techniques: the *links* developed by Härder 1978 and the binary *join indices* proposed by Valduriez 1987. Rather than relating only two relations (or object types), the ASR

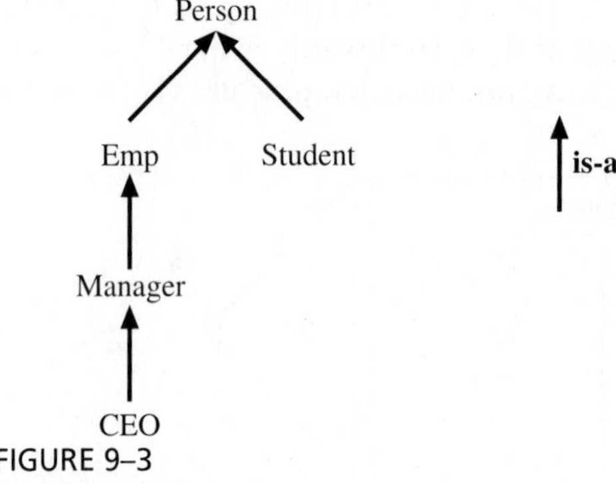

FIGURE 9–3
Sample Type Hierarchy

technique allows support of access paths ranging over many types. The ASR scheme subsumes and extends several previously proposed strategies for access optimization in object bases. The index paths of Maier and Stein 1986 are restricted to chains that contain only single-valued attributes, and their representation is limited to binary partitions of the access path. Similarly, the object-oriented access techniques described for the Orion model by Bertino and Kim 1989 are contained as a special case in the ASR framework.

ASRs differ in three major aspects from the aforementioned approaches:

- Access support relations allow collection-valued attributes within the attribute chain.
- Access support relations may be maintained in four different *extensions*. The extension determines the amount of (reference) information that is kept in the index structure.
- The paths over which ASRs are defined may be decomposed into partitions (subpaths) of arbitrary lengths. This allows the database designer to choose the best extension and path partitioning according to the particular application characteristics.

Also the (separate) replications of object values as proposed for the Extra object model by Shekita and Carey 1989 and for the Postgres model (see Stonebraker, Anton, and Hanson 1987 and Sellis 1988) are largely subsumed by ASRs.

9.3 Indexing over Type Hierarchies

For the discussion of this section, consider the type hierarchy shown in Fig. 9–3. Based on this type hierarchy, we can phrase the following three queries, the meaning of which should be obvious:

Q_4: **range** *e* : Emp
retrieve *e*
where *e*.salary > 200000

Q_5: **range** *c* : CEO
retrieve *c*
where *c*.salary = > 200000

Q_6: **range** *p* : Person
retrieve *p*
where *p*.age > 60

In query Q_4 we want to retrieve `Emp` instances (including `Manager` and `CEO` instances) whose `salary` exceeds 200000. In query Q_5, on the other hand, we are only interested in the `CEO` instances with such a high `salary`; because of substitutability, the result of Q_5 is a subset of the result obtained in query Q_4. In query Q_6 all `Person` instances whose `age` exceeds 60 are retrieved (i.e., including all `Emp`, `Manager`, `CEO`, and `Student` instances).

The evaluation of such queries can (and should) be supported by indexing. Indexing can be viewed as a special case of access support relations, except that mostly the backward clustered B$^+$-tree is relevant and, therefore, the forward clustered tree may be omitted. Consider, for example, the index for `Emp.salary` that is represented as the ASR [`Emp.salary`] as follows—assuming that id_{77} and id_{88} identify `CEO` instances:

[Emp.salary]

$S_0 : OID_{Emp}$	$S_1 : int$
id_4	90000
id_5	100000
id_7	100000
id_{11}	150000
id_6	260000
id_{13}	900000
id_{77}	1500000
id_{88}	2000000
...	...

B^+

Note that this index, because of substitutability, implicitly includes all `Manager` and `CEO` instances for which the `salary` is known. Therefore, the evaluation of query Q_4 is well supported since it involves a lookup in a single B$^+$-tree only. However, query Q_5 is not as well supported since it involves retrieving the OIDs from the index [`Emp.salary`] for which the salary attribute exceeds 200000. The resulting set, however, contains `Emp` and `Manager` instances as well. So, in a (costly) second phase, the `CEO` instances have to be extracted from this set.

9.3.1 Single Type Indexing

The idea of single type indexing is to incorporate only the *direct* instances of a particular type in the index. Let us denote the set of direct instances of a type T as $\underline{T}$. Then, for our example we could create three separate indexes: [Emp.salary], [Manager.salary], and [CEO.salary].

These indexes have the following form:

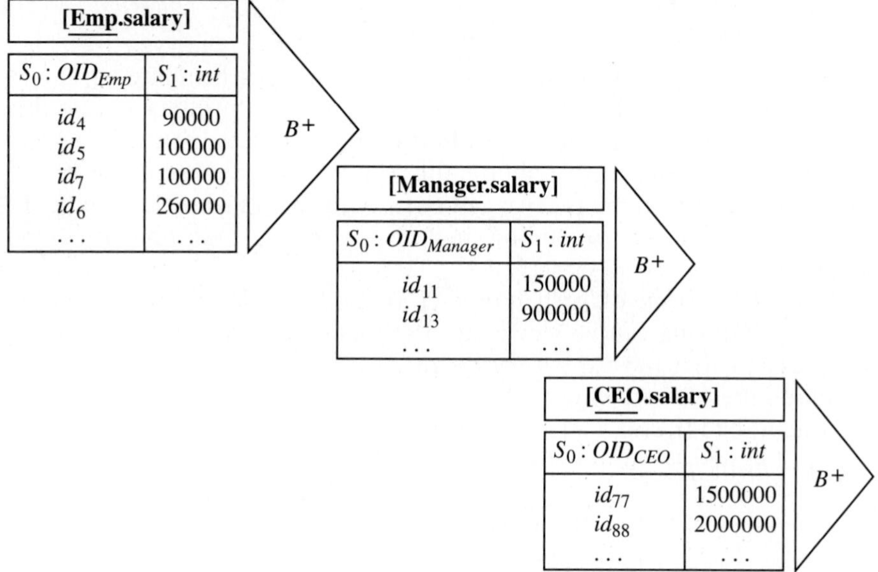

[Emp.salary] (B^+)

$S_0 : OID_{Emp}$	$S_1 : int$
id_4	90000
id_5	100000
id_7	100000
id_6	260000
...	...

[Manager.salary] (B^+)

$S_0 : OID_{Manager}$	$S_1 : int$
id_{11}	150000
id_{13}	900000
...	...

[CEO.salary] (B^+)

$S_0 : OID_{CEO}$	$S_1 : int$
id_{77}	1500000
id_{88}	2000000
...	...

Now evaluating query Q_5 is well supported because it involves only a lookup in the index [CEO.salary]. However, the evaluation of query Q_4 now involves a lookup in three separate B$^+$-trees and unioning the results:

$$(\sigma_{S_1>200000}\,[\underline{Emp}.salary] \cup \sigma_{S_1>200000}\,[\underline{Manager}.salary] \cup \sigma_{S_1>200000}\,[\underline{CEO}.salary]$$

This problem appears even more severe when considering query Q_6 under the assumption of separate single type indexing on the age attribute.

9.3.2 Type Hierarchy Indexing

Because of the above-discussed disadvantages of separate single type indexing, Kim, Kim, and Dale 1989 proposed the use of a type hierarchy index. The type hierarchy index consists of a single B^{+-} tree that comprises all direct and indirect instances of the indexed type. This is basically what was adhered to in the ASR definitions; however Kim, Kim, and Dale 1989 developed a special structure of the leaf nodes, which is sketched as follows:

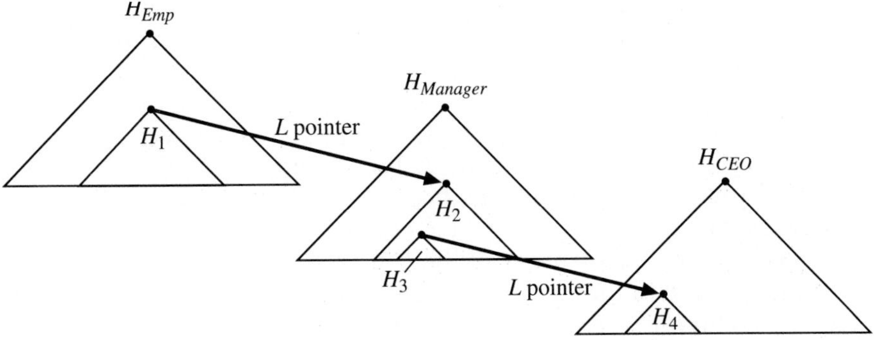

FIGURE 9–4
Three Nested H-Trees

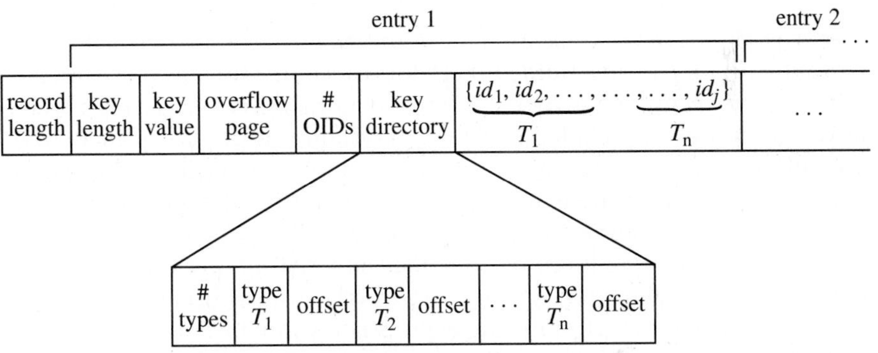

This layout of the leaf nodes provides support for extracting the (OIDs of) objects of a particular type by jumping to the corresponding offset, which is maintained in the key directory.

Low, Ooi, and Lu 1992 developed a sophisticated indexing scheme, called *H*-trees, for combining type hierarchy indexing with single type indexing. The basic idea consists of nesting B^+-trees—that is, nesting the index tree of a subtype within the tree of the supertype. For our example, this is graphically shown in Fig. 9–4, where the three *H*-trees, H_{Emp} for direct `Emp` instances, $H_{Manager}$ for direct `Manager` instances, and H_{CEO} for `CEO` instances, are sketched

The nesting is achieved by incorporating so-called *L* pointers, which refer from the supertype index to the subtype index tree. There are two essential conditions for a valid *H*-tree nesting:

1. The range of the subtree referenced by an *L*-pointer must be contained in the range of the referencing node of the supertype tree. In terms of our example, the range of the subtree H_2 must be contained in the range of H_1, and the range of H_4 must be contained in the range of H_3.

2. All leaf nodes of a subtype tree have to be covered by the supertype tree. This means that all leaf nodes have to be reachable by following L-pointers emanating from the supertype tree.

A single type lookup on H-trees is carried out by searching in the corresponding H-tree and simply ignoring the L-pointers. A type hierarchy lookup is carried out by searching in the H-tree of the root type (over which the query is stated) and traversing the L-pointers to subtype trees.

Of course, the maintenance of the H-trees imposes a severe overhead on update operations, the exact penalty of which still has to be investigated more thoroughly.

9.4 Function Materialization

Let us now discuss an optimization technique that is devised to expedite the evaluation of queries containing function invocations, such as our example query Q_3. The technique is rooted in view materialization, which is a well-known technique in relational database systems. Here, we present the basics of *function materialization*, a similar, yet more powerful, optimization concept for object-oriented data models. Exploiting the object-oriented paradigm—namely, *classification*, *object identity*, and *encapsulation*—facilitates a rather easy incorporation of function materialization into (existing) object-oriented systems. Only those types (classes) whose instances are involved in some materialization are appropriately modified and recompiled —thus leaving the remainder of the object system invariant. Furthermore, the exploitation of encapsulation (information hiding) and object identity provides for additional performance tuning measures that drastically decrease the invalidation and rematerialization overhead incurred by updates in the object base.

9.4.1 Storing Materialized Results

If several functions that share all argument types are materialized, the results of these functions may be stored within the same data structure. This provides more efficiency when evaluating queries that access results of several of these functions and, further, avoids the need to store the arguments redundantly. These thoughts lead to the following definition:

DEFINITION 2.6 (Generalized Materialization Relation, GMR) Let $t_1, \ldots t_n, t_{n+1}, \ldots, t_{n+m}$ be types and let $f_1, \ldots f_m$ be side-effect-free functions with $f_j : t_1, \ldots t_n \rightarrow t_{n+j}$, for $1 \leq j \leq m$. Then the generalized materialization relation $<f_1, \ldots f_m>$ for the functions $f_1, \ldots f_m$ is of arity $n + 2 * \text{m}$ and has the following form:

$<f_1, \ldots, f_m> : [O_1 : t_1, \ldots, O_n : t_n, f_1 : t_{n+1} V_1 : bool, \ldots, f_m : t_{n+m}, V_m : bool]$

Intuitively, the attributes $O_1, \ldots, O_n$ store the arguments (i.e., values if the argument type is atomic or references to objects if the argument type is complex); the attributes $f_1, \ldots f_m$ store the results or—if the result is of complex type—references to the result objects of the invocations of the functions $f_1, \ldots f_m$; and the attributes $V_1, \ldots, V_m$ (standing for *validity*) indicate whether the stored results are currently valid.

An extension of the GMR $<f_1, \ldots f_m>$ is consistent if a *true* validity indicator implies that the associated materialized result is currently valid—that is,

$$\forall \tau \in \langle f_1, \ldots, f_m \rangle : \tau.V_j = true \Rightarrow \tau.f_j = f_j(\tau.O_1, \ldots, \tau.O_n)$$

In the remainder of this chapter we consider only consistent GMR extensions.

The above definition of consistency provides some tuning measure with respect to the invalidation and rematerialization of results. Upon an update to a database object that invalidates a materialized function result, we have two choices:

1. *Immediate rematerialization.* The invalidated function result is immediately recomputed as soon as invalidation occurs.
2. *Lazy rematerialization.* The invalidated function result is only marked as being invalid by setting the corresponding V_i attribute to *false*. The rematerialization of invalidated results is carried out as soon as the load of the object base management system falls below a predetermined threshold or at the next time the function result is needed.

In this presentation we will discuss only the materialization of functions with complex argument types. As can easily be seen, it is not practical to materialize a function for all values of an atomic argument type (e.g., *float*). Therefore, Kemper, Kilger, and Moerkotte 1994 proposed *restricted GMRs* for materializing functions for selected arguments only.

An example of a GMR comprising only a single materialized function (`Emp.skill`) is shown below:

⟨Emp.skill⟩		
$O_1 : OID_{Emp}$	$skill : int$	$V_{skill} : bool$
id_4	9	*true*
id_5	8	*true*
id_6	3	*true*
...	...	...
id_{12}	3	*true*
id_{13}	10	*true*

It should now be obvious that the example query Q_3 can be evaluated as

$$\pi_{O_1} (\sigma_{skill=10} \langle Emp.skill \rangle)$$

as long as the GMR `<Emp.skill>` contains the valid `skill` result for *all* `Emp` instances.

9.4.2 Storage Representation of GMRs

The flexible retrieval operations on the GMRs require appropriate index structures to avoid exhaustive search of GMR extensions. For that, well-known indexing techniques from relational database technology can be utilized. The easiest way to support flexible and efficient access to any combination of GMR fields would be a single multidimensional index structure, denoted *MDS*, over the fields $O_1, \ldots, O_n, f_1, \ldots f_m$:

MDS	O_1	...	O_n	f_1	...	f_m	V_1	...	V_m

Here, the first $n + m$ columns constitute the $(n + m)$-dimensional keys of the multidimensional storage structure. The m validity bits $V_1, \ldots, V_m$ are additional attributes of the records being stored in the MDS.

Unfortunately, the currently existing multidimensional storage structures, such as the Grid-File of Nievergelt, Hinterberger, and Sevcik 1984, are not well suited to support more than three or four dimensions. Therefore, more conventional indexing schemes have to be utilized to expedite access on GMRs of higher arity. The index structures are chosen according to the expected query mix, the number of argument fields in the GMR, and the number of functions in the GMR. A good proposal for multidimensional indexing relying on conventional B-trees is described by Lum 1970.

9.4.3 Invalidation and Rematerialization of Function Results

When the modification of an object o is reported, the GMR manager must find all materialized results that become invalid. This task is equivalent to determining all materialized functions f and all argument combinations $o_1, \ldots o_n$ such that the modified object o has been accessed during the materialization of $f(o_1, \ldots o_n)$. Note that in GOM—as in most other object models—references are unidirectional; there is no efficient way to determine from an object o the set of objects that reference o via a particular path. Therefore, the GMR manager maintains reverse references from all objects that have been used in some materialization to the appropriate argument objects in a relation called *Reverse Reference Relation* (RRR). The RRR contains tuples of the following form:

RRR		
O	*F*	*A*
id_0	Emp.skill	(id_4)
id_1	Emp.skill	(id_4)
id_4	Emp.skill	(id_4)
id_2	Emp.skill	(id_5)
id_3	Emp.skill	(id_6)
...	...	...

⟨Emp.skill⟩		
$O_1 : OID_{Emp}$	*skill* : *int*	V_{skill} : *bool*
id_4	9	*true*
id_5	8	*true*
id_6	3	*true*
...	...	...
id_{12}	3	*true*
id_{13}	10	*true*

FIGURE 9–5
The Data Structures of the GMR Manager

$$[id(o), f, (id(o_1), \ldots, id(o_n))]$$

Herein, *id(o)* is the identifier of an object *o* utilized during the materialization of the result $f(o_1, \ldots\ o_n)$. Note that *o* needs not be one of the arguments $o_1, \ldots\ o_n$; it could be some object related (via attributes) to one of the arguments. Thus, each tuple of the RRR constitutes a reference from an object *o* influencing a materialized result to the tuple of the appropriate GMR in which the result is stored. We call this a *reverse reference,* as there exists a reference chain in the opposite direction in the object base.

DEFINITION 2.7 (Reverse Reference Relation) The reverse reference relation RRR is a set of tuples of the form

$$[O : OID, F : FunctionId, A : \textbf{List}(OID)]$$

For each tuple r ∈ RRR the following condition holds: The object (with the identifier) *r.O* has been accessed during the materialization of the function *r.F* with the argument list *r.A*. (The angle brackets < ... > denote the list constructor in GOM syntax.)

The reverse references are inserted into the RRR during the materialization process. Therefore, each materialized function *f* and all functions invoked by *f* are modified—the modified versions are extended by statements that inform the GMR manager about the set of accessed objects. During a (re)materialization of some result, the modified versions of these functions are invoked.

For our example object base `Company`, a part of the RRR that controls the invalidation of precomputed results in the GMR <`Emp.skill`> is shown in Fig. 9–5. Each time an object is updated in the object base, the RRR is inspected to determine which materialized results have to be invalidated (lazy rematerialization) or recomputed (immediate rematerialization). Kemper, Kilger, and Moerkotte 1994 describe ways to detect object updates by schema modification and efficient algorithms for maintaining the RRR—which, of course, changes as a result of object base updates.

9.4.4 Strategies to Reduce the Invalidation Overhead

The invalidation mechanism outlined so far is (still) rather unsophisticated and, therefore, induces unnecessarily high update penalties upon object modifications. Four dual techniques to reduce the update penalty—consisting of invalidation and rematerialization—by better exploiting the potential of the object-oriented paradigm are developed by Kemper, Kilger, and Moerkotte 1994. The techniques described there are based on the following ideas:

1. *Isolation of relevant object properties.* Materialized results typically depend on only a small fraction of the state of the objects visited in the course of materialization. For example, the materialized `skill` certainly does not depend on the `sex` and `name` attributes of an `Emp`.
2. *Reduction of RRR lookups.* The unsophisticated version of the invalidation process has to check the RRR each time any object *o* is updated. This leads to many unnecessary table lookups that can be avoided by maintaining more information within the objects being involved in some materialization—and thus restricting the lookup penalty to only these objects.
3. *Exploitation of strict encapsulation.* By strictly encapsulating the representation of objects used by a materialized function, the number of update operations that need be modified can be reduced significantly. Since internal subobjects of a strictly encapsulated object cannot be updated separately—without invoking an outer-level operation of the strictly encapsulated object—we can drastically reduce the number of invalidations by triggering the invalidation only by the outer-level operation.
4. *Compensating updates.* Instead of invoking the materialized function to recompute an invalidated result, specialized compensating actions can be invoked that use the old result and the parameters of the update operation to recompute the new result in a more efficient way.

9.4.5 Related Work

The details of function materialization, including a quantitative assessment, were described by Kemper, Kilger, and Moerkotte 1994. Function materialization is similar to materialization of views in the relational context. The most important work is reported by Blakeley, Coburn, and Larson 1989. Further work in precomputing queries and database procedures was done in Postgres. Here, the "QUEL as a Datatype" attributes are precomputed and cached in separate data structures. The control concepts are discussed by Stonebraker, Anton, and Hanson 1987; Jhingran 1988; and Sellis 1988.

9.5 Object Placement

The idea of *clustering* is to place objects that are logically related (i.e., frequently used together) physically close to each other. The effectiveness of clustering is measured in terms of the number of page faults occurring during an application. The lower the number of page faults the better. The interconnectivity of objects in object bases demands new clustering techniques.

There are two different approaches to clustering: *sequence-based clustering* and *partition-based clustering*. The former relies on algorithms producing an object sequence. The latter relies on partitioning algorithms that partition the object net into partitions such that each one fits into a single page. We discuss each of these approaches. Then we provide a discussion.

9.5.1 Sequence-Based Clustering

The sequence-based approach to clustering stores objects in a specific sequence onto disk. All known sequence-based clustering strategies can be seen as instances of a generic sequence-based clustering strategy consisting of two phases: (1) the *presort* stage, which is followed by (2) the *traversal* phase. During the first stage, all objects to be clustered are sorted. In the second stage, the sorted objects serve as roots for the traversal algorithm. All objects reachable from the root object are appended to the clustering sequence—mostly directly on disk—according to their visiting order. Traversals may end for two reasons: No more objects can be reached from the current root object, and no more objects fit into the current page. In both cases, a new traversal starts with the next (not yet placed) object in the presorted object sequence as the root. Of course, special care has to be taken in order to prevent objects from being stored twice.

Obviously, the presort order must depend on some information associated with each object. This information has to be taken from an ordered domain. A first source of information is the object's time of creation (*toc*). Depending on whether we sort by increasing or decreasing time of creation, the two presort orders *toc* and toc^{-1} are derived. Another common set of presort orders is derived from—often user-specified—type orders. This results in a partial order only, since objects that are instances of the same type remain unordered. The user should be allowed to specify the presort order. The most common example is presort orders that are based on attribute values and that typically sort objects within type extents.

The most popular traversal algorithms are *depth first, breadth first,* and *best first* traversals. The *best first* traversal is successively applied to (not already stored) objects of the presort sequence until all objects are placed. The traversal depends on the information about which links to follow and, if there exist several possible links, which one to choose. Link weights

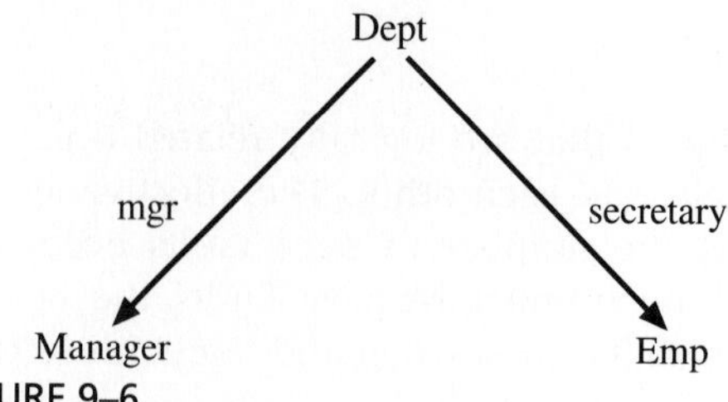

FIGURE 9–6
Sample Placement Tree

between 0 and 1 for each link provide sufficient information (the *best first* algorithm follows the one with the highest weight).

If we require that the weights take the values 0 and 1 only and all objects visited during one traversal fit into a single page, the traversal algorithm can be specified by a *placement tree*. A *placement tree* is a tree with nodes labeled by types and edges labeled by attribute names. For the *Company* extension shown in Fig. 9–2, the example placement tree storing departments together with their managers and secretaries (see Fig. 9–6) results in the following object placement (we assume that three objects fit into a single page):

$$[\ id_8, id_{11}, id_4], [id_9, id_{12}, id_6], [id_{10}, id_{13}, —]$$

9.5.2 Partition-Based Clustering

The clustering problem is closely related to the partitioning problem in which a graph is to be partitioned into several disjunct subgraphs (partitions). The optimization problem consists of finding partitions such that the sum of the weights of all outgoing references (i.e., references to vertices contained in other partitions) is minimal. In partition-based clustering, the weights for the references can be determined in the same way as for sequence-based clustering. Given the weights, partitioning algorithms are applied to determine a partitioning under the constraint that the objects contained in each partition fit into a single page.

The first partitioning algorithm applied to clustering was Kernighan and Lin 1970's graph partitioning heuristic. It starts with an arbitrary partitioning and then iterates over each pair of partitions. During each iteration, objects are swapped between the partitions, if this results in a decrease in the total weight of all outgoing references. Problems occur if the objects cannot be swapped due to their sizes and the space left in the pages of the partitions. Another disadvantage of this algorithm is its high asymptotic complexity of $O(n^{2.4})$.

These disadvantages led to the development of fast greedy graph partitioning algorithms based on Kruskal's algorithm for computing minimum-weight spanning trees. The basic version of such a greedy graph partitioning algorithm—called *ggp*—is outlined as follows:

```
define ggp(objectNet) is
    partitions := <>;
    place each object in objectNet into a different page;
    insert these pages into partitions;
    Let edgeList be a list of tuples of the form (o1, o2,
        wo1,o2)
          where wo1,o2 is the total weight of all edges
              between o1 and o2;
    Sort edgeList by descending weights;
    foreach ((o1, o2, wo1,o2) in edgeList) do
    begin
      Let P1, P2 be the partitions containing objects o1, o2;
      if (P1 ≠ P2 and the total size of all objects of P1 and
          P2 is less than the page size)
      begin
        Move all objects from P2 to P1;
        Remove P2 from partitions;
      end if;
    end foreach;
    return partitions;
end ggp;
```

The first step of this algorithm consists of assigning each object to a new (separate) partition. All these partitions are maintained in the variable *partitions*. Then, for all pairs of objects (o_1, o_2) in the object net with at least one reference between them, a tuple (o_1, o_2, $w_{o1,o2}$) is inserted into the list *edgeList* where $w_{o1,o2}$ is the accumulated weight of all references between o_1 and o_2. All tuples of *edgeList* are visited in the order of descending weights. Let (o_1, o_2, $w_{o1,o2}$) be the current tuple. Let P_1, P_2 be the partitions to which the objects o_1 and o_2 are assigned. If $P_1 \neq P_2$ and the total size of all objects assigned to P_1 and P_2 is less than the page size, the two partitions are joined.[4] Otherwise, the edge is merely discarded—and the partitions remain invariant. For e being the number of edges in the clustering graph, the complexity of the greedy graph partitioning algorithm is $O(e \log e)$. For further improvements of this heuristic see Gerlhof et al. 1993.

9.5.3 Discussion

There exist a few possibilities for the time of object placement:

- objects are stored at their creation time
- objects are stored at the end of the creating transaction
- reclustering occurs at an arbitrary point in time

4. Partitions are represented as binary trees to accelerate the join operation.

If an object is stored immediately at its creation time, it can only be stored (clustered) with objects that have been created prior to it. Further, there exist no references from other objects to it. Hence, the clustering strategies described in this section do not apply. In order to have some control over object placement, user hints are implemented—that is, the user may specify an (existing) object close to which the newly created object is to be placed. Closeness is measured as being in the same page or not. Of course, this approach puts the burden of good object placement on the shoulders of the programmer. It has been implemented in, for example, Exodus [Carey et al. 1986], ObjectStore [Lamb et al. 1991], and ORION [Kim 1990].

If objects are placed at the end of a creating transaction, they can be stored not only together with objects created before them but also with objects created later within the same transaction. Hence, possibly a whole set of objects, most likely referencing each other, is to be placed at the end of a transaction. Further, it is also likely that the creating transaction will not only create new objects but also assign values to their attributes and establish references between the newly created and existing objects and vice versa. In this case, any of the clustering strategies can either be restricted to the newly created objects or involve already created objects also. The former case is easier to handle. As soon as already created objects come into play, decisions have to be made about which of these objects are taken into consideration for (re)clustering. Thus, the problems of reclustering (see below) have to be faced at each commit time. This might impose an unacceptable run-time penalty. The only practical choice is to apply a clustering strategy of low run-time complexity to only the newly created objects. One choice is to apply *placement trees* as implemented in O_2 by Benzaken and Delobel 1990.

Reclustering is mainly a question of cost. Since reclustering should take place only if all the objects to be considered for the new object placement exist, any clustering strategy can be applied. It could be up to the database administrator (DBA) to select the best time for reclustering and the best strategy for the given application. The DBA should consider the clustering performance and the run-time overhead of the different clustering strategies. But there is another crucial point: If the system relies on logical object identifiers (i.e., object identifiers that are independent of the actual physical location of the objects), there is no need to adjust the references to objects moved during reclustering. This is not true for physical object identifiers, where the actual address of the object is encoded in the identifier. Here, all references to the objects that are re-placed must be adjusted. This can be prohibitively expensive. In the worst case, the whole object base has to be searched for references to be updated. In case backward references exist, this might be affordable.

Sequence-based clustering strategies are used in several object base systems, such as Cactis [Hudson and King 1989], Encore [Hornick and

Zdonik 1987], and ORION [Banerjee et al. 1988]. To our knowledge, partition-based clustering strategies have not (yet) been incorporated into any system. Partition-based clustering was first introduced by Tsangaris and Naughton 1991, 1992. There the Kernighan and Lin 1970 graph partitioning algorithm is applied. Several greedy graph partitioning algorithms were introduced by Gerlhof et al. 1993 and compared with other variants of graph partitioning algorithms.

9.6 Object Storage Models: Decomposition and Replication

In this section we will sketch different storage models for object bases. The goal, of course, is to expedite access to the relevant parts of an object base while at the same time keeping the overhead for updates tolerable. The subsequent discussion of three alternative storage representations is largely based on a proposal by Valduriez, Khoshafian, and Copeland 1986. A quantitative evaluation of some of the proposed storage schemes for one benchmark application is reported by Teeuw et al. 1993.

9.6.1 NSM: N-ary Storage Model

This storage model was assumed in the graphical representation of our example object base `Company` in Fig. 9–2. In this storage model, objects are considered as N-ary tuples where the tuples comprise *all* the attributes constituting the structural representation of the object. Note that this includes the structural representation of inheritance—as illustrated for objects of type `Manager` in Fig. 9–2.

It may be tempting to map complete type extensions into a single dedicated file. However, this may violate the clustering objective.

9.6.2 DSM: Decomposition Storage Model

While the NSM scheme bundles entire objects, the DSM model of Copeland and Khoshafian 1985 decomposes an object such that each attribute value is stored separately. Thus, the storage model consists of triples

(*OID, attribute, value*)

where the value is either an atomic value or the OID of the referenced object. In terms of our example object base extension, (part of) the storage representation looks as follows:

(id_0, *duration*, 12)
(id_0, *competence*, 10)
...

$(id_4$, *name*, "*Sander*")
$(id_4$, *worksIn*, $id_8)$
$(id_4$, *salary*, 90000)
$(id_4$, *sex*, '*F*')
$(id_4$, *jobHistory*, $id_0)$
$(id_4$, *jobHistory*, $id_0)$
...

In this normalized representation, even the set-valued attribute `jobHistory` is flattened by unnesting the set containing references to *Task* objects.

Except for distributed database applications, this representation scheme appears to be impractical. Therefore, a hybrid of the two aforementioned representations is described in the following section.

9.6.3 Fragmentation and Replication

Valduriez, Khoshafian, and Copeland 1986 proposed the P-DSM (partial DSM) storage scheme as a hybrid between the decomposition (DSM) and the N-ary (NSM) storage schemes. Under P-DSM, objects are vertically fragmented based on attribute affinities such that attributes that are frequently used together are stored in the same fragment. In the relational context, there exists a large body of work on deriving these affinities from the work load (e.g., Hoffer and Severance 1975 and Navathe et al. 1984).

The P-DSM model naturally leads to replication when attributes are incorporated in more than one fragment of an object. Of course, replication incurs an additional update penalty.

A sample fragmentation with selective replication for some objects of our `Company` object base is shown below:

$(id_4$, *name*, "*Sander*") $(id_4$, *worksIn*, $id_8)$ $(id_4$, *salary*, 90000) $(id_4$, *jobHistory*, $\{id_0, id_1\})$	$(id_4$, *name*, "*Sander*") $(id_4$, *salary*, 90000) $(id_4$, *sex*, '*F*')	
$(id_{11}$, *name*, "*Boss*") $(id_{11}$, *worksIn*, $id_8)$ $(id_{11}$, *salary*, 150000) $(id_{11}$, *jobHistory*, {...})	$(id_{11}$, *name*, "*Boss*") $(id_{11}$, *salary*, 150000) $(id_{11}$, *sex*, '*F*')	$(id_{11}$, *name*, "*Boss*") $(id_{11}$, *backUp*, $id_5)$

Here, the `Emp` object id_4 is fragmented into two partially overlapping fragments while the `Manager` object id_{11} is split into three overlapping fragments. The fragments are presumably derived according to some attribute affinities obtained from the object base usage profile.

A natural fragmentation boundary is given by the subtype/supertype hierarchy. One could bundle all attributes defined in one type of the inheritance hierarchy within a separate fragment. Then a CEO instance would be modeled by four fragments: one comprising the attributes defined in `Person`, one for `Emp`, one for `Manager`, and one for attributes specific to a `CEO` object.

9.7 Future Research

In this chapter we described several physical object management techniques that have been proposed to optimize object base applications. While each one of these techniques is fairly well understood, their interaction in one system still requires research. For example, indexes and clustering are affected by updates. Either they are totally invalidated (i.e., indexes and materialized functions) or they exhibit a lower effectiveness (i.e., clustering). Nevertheless, up to now each technique has its own dedicated way to detect and handle updates. A better way would be to factor out the detection/invalidation mechanism and develop a general mechanism that can then be directly supported by lower levels of the object base system—resulting, one hopes, in better performance.

From the discussion in this chapter, it should be clear that each of the techniques requires tuning; the task of tuning a physical object base when these techniques are combined is much more difficult. Therefore, tools need to be developed for aiding the database administrator in the task of deriving an effective physical object base design for a given usage profile. One of the prerequisites for such a tool is the ability to characterize the application behavior by monitoring, sampling, or (static) application analysis. Another requirement is a comprehensive cost model that takes the interdependencies of the various physical object management techniques into account.

Given the fact that many advanced applications do not rely on ad hoc usage but, instead, access and manipulate the database by predefined programs, one might infer that the profile of these applications can be very specific. As an example, consider production in manufacturing where the production process is well organized and deterministic and imposes real-time requirements. Given its deterministic nature, the profile is very specific. Given the real-time requirements, the database system must be very efficient for the given profile. Since performance is highly influenced by the physical organization of the data, the physical organization should be very specifically tailored to the profile. Hence, for a given logical schema and profile, it should be possible to explicitly define a fine-grained physical schema. This has several implications: First, the physical data structures must be much more specifically tailored to specific application profiles than in traditional applications. Being provocative, one could state that today's storage structures and indexes are broad-band techniques applicable to a broad range of applications. Developing finer-grained techniques implies the necessity of refining benchmarking techniques. Second, languages are needed that allow one to specify the physical schema at a grain required by the application and supported by the storage structures. Third, if for example the production phase is reorganized, the physical database design must be reorganized as well. Hence, reorganization issues must be investigated more thoroughly. The requirements induced by reorganization needs become much harder. Considering manufacturing, the production phase runs 24 hours a day, 7 days a week. For these nonstop applications with real-time constraints, incremental reorganization becomes a hard issue.

ACKNOWLEDGMENTS

This work was supported in part by the German Research Council (DFG) under contracts Ke 401/6-1 and SFB 346.

REFERENCES

Banerjee, J., Kim, W., Kim, S.J., and Garza, J.F. 1988. Clustering a DAG for CAD Databases. *IEEE Trans. Software Eng.*, Vol. 14, No. 11, 1684–1699.

Benzaken, V., and Delobel, C. 1990. Enhancing Performance in a Persistent Object Store: Clustering Strategies in O_2. In *Implementing Persistent Object Bases.* A. Dearle, G. Shaw, and S. Zdonik, eds. 403–412. Morgan Kaufmann, San Mateo, Cal.

Bertino, E., and Kim, W. 1989. Indexing Techniques for Queries on Nested Objects. *IEEE Trans. Knowledge and Data Engineering,* Vol. 1, No. 2, 196–214.

Blakeley, J.A., Coburn, N., and Larson, P.A. 1989. Updating Derived Relations: Detecting Irrelevant and Autonomously Computable Updates. *ACM Trans. on Database Systems,* Vol. 14, No. 3, 369–400.

Carey, M., DeWitt, D., Richardson, J., and Shekita, E. 1986. Object and File Management in the EXODUS Extensible Database System. *Proceedings of the International Conference on Very Large Data Bases (VLDB),* Kyoto, Japan, 91–100.

Copeland, G., and Khoshafian, S. 1985. A Decomposition Storage Model. *Proceedings of the ACM-SIGMOD International Conference on Management of Data,* Austin, Tex., 268–279.

Gerlhof, C., Kemper, A., Kilger, C., and Moerkotte, G. 1993. Partition-Based Clustering in Object Bases: From Theory to Practice. *Proceedings of the International Conference on Foundations of Data Organization and Algorithms (FODO),* Chicago, Ill.

Härder, T. 1978. Implementing a Generalized Access Path Structure for a Relational Database System. *ACM Trans. on Database Systems (TODS),* Vol. 3, No. 3, 285–298.

Hoffer, J.A., and Severance, D.G. 1975. The Use of Cluster Analysis in Physical Database Design. *Proceedings of the International Conference on Very Large Data Bases (VLDB).*

Hornick, M., and Zdonik, S. 1987. A Shared, Segmented Memory System for an Object-Oriented Database. *ACM Trans. Office Inf. Syst.*, Vol. 5, No. 1, 70–95.

Hudson, S.E., and King, R. 1989. Cactis: A Self-Adaptive, Concurrent Implementation of an Object-Oriented Database Management System. *ACM Trans. on Database Systems (TODS)*, Vol. 14, No. 3, 291–321.

Jhingran, A. 1988. A Performance Study of Query Optimization Algorithms on a Database System Supporting Procedures. *Proceedings of the International Conference on Very Large Data Bases (VLDB)*, Los Angeles, 88–99.

Kemper, A., Kilger, C., and Moerkotte, G. 1994. Materialization of Functions in Object Bases: Design, Implementation and Assessment. *IEEE Trans. Knowledge and Data Engineering* (in print; an excerpt appeared in *Proceedings of the ACM-SIGMOD International Conference on Management of Data*, May 1991, 258–268).

Kemper, A., and Moerkotte, G. 1990. Access Support in Object Bases. *Proceedings of the ACM-SIGMOD International Conference on Management of Data*, Atlantic City, N.J., 364–374

Kemper, A., and Moerkotte, G. 1992. Access Support Relations: An Indexing Method for Object Bases. *Information Systems*, Vol. 17, No. 2, 117–146.

Kemper, A. and Moerkotte, G. 1994. *Object-Oriented Database Management: Applications in Engineering and Computer Science*. Prentice Hall, Englewood Cliffs, N.J.

Kemper, A., Moerkotte, G., and Peithner, K. 1993. A Blackboard Architecture for Query Optimization in Object Bases. *Proceedings of the International Conference on Very Large Data Bases (VLDB)*, Dublin, Ireland.

Kernighan, B., and Lin, S. 1970. An Efficient Heuristic Procedure for Partitioning Graphs. *Bell System Technical Journal*, Vol. 49, No. 2, 291–307.

Kifer, M., Kim, W., and Sagiv, Y. 1992. Querying Object-Oriented Databases. *Proceedings of the ACM-SIGMOD International Conference on Management of Data*, 393–402.

Kim, W. 1990. *Introduction to Object-Oriented Databases*. MIT Press, Cambridge, Mass.

Kim, W., Kim, K.C., and Dale, A. 1989. Indexing Techniques for Object-Oriented Databases. In *Object-Oriented Concepts, Databases, and Applications*. W. Kim and F. H. Lochovsky, eds. 371–394, Addison-Wesley, Reading, Mass.

Lamb, C., Landis, G., Orenstein, J., and Weinreb, D. 1991. The ObjectStore Database System. *Communications of the ACM*, Vol. 34, No. 10, 50–63.

Low, C.C., Ooi, B.C., and Lu, H. 1992. H-Trees: A Dynamic Associative Search Index for OODB. *Proceedings of the ACM-SIGMOD International Conference on Management of Data*, 134–143.

Lum, V.Y. 1970. Multi-Attribute Retrieval with Combined Indexes. *Communications of the ACM*, Vol. 13, 660–665.

Maier, D., and Stein, J. 1986. Indexing in an Object-Oriented DBMS. *Proceedings IEEE International Workshop on Object-Oriented Database Systems*, K.R. Dittrich and U. Dayal, eds., Asilomar, Pacific Grove, Cal.

Navathe, S., Ceri, S., Wiederhold, G., and Jinglie, D. 1984. Vertical Partitioning Algorithms for Database Design. *ACM Trans. on Database Systems*, Vol. 9, No. 4, 680–710.

Nievergelt, J., Hinterberger, H., and Sevcik, K.C. 1984. The Grid File: An Adaptable, Symmetric Multikey File Structure. *ACM Trans. on Database Systems (TODS)*, Vol. 9, No. 1, 38–71.

Sellis, T.K. 1988. Intelligent Caching and Indexing Techniques for Relational Database Systems. *Information Systems,* Vol. 13, No. 2, 175–186.

Shekita, E.J. and Carey, M.J. 1989. Performance Enhancement Through Replication in an Object-Oriented DBMS. *Proceedings of the ACM-SIGMOD International Conference on Management of Data,* Portland, 325–336.

Stonebraker, M., Anton, J., and Hanson, E. 1987. Extending a Database System with Procedures. *ACM Trans. on Database Systems (TODS),* Vol. 12, No. 3, 350–376.

Teeuw, W.B., Rich, C., Scholl, M.H., and Blanken, H.M. 1993. An Evaluation of Physical Disk I/Os for Complex Object Processing. *Proceedings IEEE Conference on Data Engineering,* Vienna, Austria, 363–372.

Tsangaris, M.M., and Naughton, J.F. 1991. A Stochastic Approach for Clustering in Object Bases. *Proceedings of the ACM-SIGMOD International Conference on Management of Data,* Denver, 12–21.

Tsangaris, M.M., and Naughton, J.F. 1992. On the Performance of Object Clustering Techniques. *Proceedings of the ACM-SIGMOD International Conference on Management of Data,* San Diego, 144–153.

Valduriez, P. 1987. Join Indices. *ACM Trans. on Database Systems (TODS),* Vol. 12, No. 2, 218–246.

Valduriez, P., Khoshafian, S., and Copeland, G. 1986. Implementation Techniques of Complex Objects. *Proceedings of the International Conference on Very Large Data Bases (VLDB),* Kyoto, Japan, 101–110.

Zdonik, S., and Maier, D. 1989. Fundamentals of Object-Oriented Databases. In *Readings in Object-Oriented Databases,* S. Zdonik and D. Maier, eds. 1–32. Morgan Kaufmann, San Mateo, Cal.

10

Requirements for a Performance Benchmark for Object-Oriented Database Systems

WON KIM
JORGE F. GARZA

There are widely used benchmarks for relational database systems and online transaction processing systems. There are also a few proposed benchmarks for object-oriented database systems. The current proposals for object-oriented database systems have two problems. First, they focus excessively on the pointer traversal type of operation that is supported in first-generation object-oriented database systems (i.e., persistent storage systems for object-oriented programming languages). Second, they do not provide a basis for a performance comparison between object-oriented database systems and relational database systems. In this chapter, we summarize requirements for a benchmark for full-blown object-oriented database systems that removes these serious shortcomings. A benchmark designed to meet these requirements can even serve as a guide for the design and development of second-generation object-oriented database systems.

10.1 Introduction

The University of Wisconsin benchmark [Bitton, DeWitt, and Turbyfill 1983] is a fairly well-adopted basis for establishing performance characteristics of relational database systems. The TP-1 benchmark [A Measure of Transaction Processing Power 1985] is widely accepted for measuring the raw performance of online transaction processing systems. There are a few proposed benchmarks [Carey, DeWitt, and Naughton 1993; Cattell and Skeen 1992] for object-oriented database systems [Kim 1990, Kim and Lochovsky 1989]. They have been useful as starting points for a more comprehensive and meaningful benchmark for object-oriented database systems. However, the current proposals are deficient in two important respects.

First, there is an excessive emphasis on the pointer traversal type of operations that first-generation object-oriented database systems support but an inadequate coverage of operations that full-fledged database systems should (and do) provide but that first-generation object-oriented database systems happen not to provide.

Second, the current proposals provide no basis for a meaningful comparison of performance between an object-oriented database system and a relational database system. In other words, they can be used only to compare the performance of persistent storage systems (also known as first-generation object-oriented database systems); however, they are not designed to establish a performance comparison between object-oriented database systems and relational database systems. An object-oriented data model is a superset of the relational data model. Therefore, a full-fledged object-oriented database system should provide all the features of a relational database system (such as a join query, a nested subquery, a query with a group-by clause and aggregation functions, an update or delete based on a query, etc.). Further, some of the operations that are the staple of object-oriented database systems (such as fetching a single object using an object identifier, traversing related objects using object pointers embedded in objects, loading a method) can actually be simulated (albeit inefficiently) using the facilities provided in relational database systems (such as a single table query, join queries, and a stored procedure). As such, benchmarks designed for full-blown object-oriented database systems should make it possible to compare the performance of the relational subset of an object-oriented database system against that of a relational database system. It should also make it possible to compare the performance of a relational database system against an object-oriented database system for those object-oriented operations that can be simulated using the facilities of relational database systems.

The objective of this chapter is to offer a summary of requirements for a comprehensive benchmark for second-generation object-oriented database systems that removes these two major shortcomings in the current benchmark proposals. The remainder of this chapter is organized as follows. In section 10.2, we summarize all fundamental operations that a benchmark for second-generation object-oriented database systems should include. In section 10.3, we discuss how some of the operations that are the staple of object-oriented database systems can be simulated using the facilities of relational database systems. Section 10.4 provides some observations for further consideration in the actual implementation of a benchmark incorporating the requirements summarized in this chapter.

10.2 Essential Operations for Object-Oriented Database Systems

In this section, we will identify and briefly describe all essential operations in object-oriented database systems that merit inclusion in a performance benchmark. Some of these are difficult to perform efficiently using relational database systems.

10.2.1 Fetching a Single Object (from the Database) Using Its OID

In object-oriented systems, every object has a unique object identifier (OID), and an object, object-1, is linked to another object, object-2, by storing the OID of object-2 within object-1. Once an application retrieves an object from the database, it can retrieve other objects that are linked to it by submitting their OIDs to the database.

To quickly fetch a single object from the database given its OID, systems maintain a hash table (usually an extendible hash table) that maps each OID to its physical address on disk.

10.2.2 Traversing a Nested Object (in the Database) Using Embedded OIDs

It is often necessary to retrieve many (or all) of the reachable objects from a given object—that is, to retrieve a nested object. Conceptually, this can be done by a depth-first or breadth-first traversal of a single nested object—that is, a sequence of single-object fetches by successively submitting OIDs of objects to be fetched. To properly support the retrieval of nested objects, the system needs to physically cluster components of a nested object. Further, it is useful to allow a partial retrieval of a nested object as well as a full retrieval. A partial retrieval of a nested object means the retrieval of some of the components of a nested object up to a certain nesting depth.

The ability to traverse a nested object is different from fetching successive tuples through a cursor in relational database systems. The cursor mechanism allows a sequence of records to be retrieved that satisfy a query. It is not a means of fetching tuples in different tables that are linked together. Since a tuple in a relational database does not ordinarily contain identifiers of other tuples, it is difficult in any event to efficiently fetch tuples linked to a given tuple.

10.2.3 Navigation of Memory-Resident Objects

First-generation object-oriented database systems automatically convert OIDs stored in objects to memory pointers to other objects when they load objects from the database to application workspace in memory. This conversion of an OID to a memory pointer is commonly known as *pointer swizzling* [Kim et al. 1988; White and DeWitt 1992]. Pointer swizzling makes possible efficient navigation of linked objects residing in memory.

Relational database systems do not do pointer swizzling, largely because tuples in a table in a relational database do not contain OIDs (or tuple identifiers) to refer to logically related tuples in other tables.

10.2.4 Traversing an Inheritance Hierarchy

The schema of an object-oriented database is a directed acyclic graph of classes (often called a class hierarchy). Given a class, it is often important to quickly traverse the class hierarchy to determine all its immediate superclasses, all its ancestor classes, all immediate subclasses, or all subclasses.

For example, when an object-oriented database system receives a method invocation on an object, it must first determine the class to which the object belongs and then determine if the method being invoked was defined on the class. If the method is found not to have been defined for the class, a superclass in which the method was defined must be identified.

Further, an object-oriented database system needs to determine all subclasses of a class when, for example, it needs to set locks on them when the definition of the class is to be updated (e.g., an attribute of the class is dropped, a new method is added) or when a query is issued against the class and all its subclasses [Kim and Garza 1988].

10.2.5 Reverse Navigation of Objects (in the Database and in Memory)

Since it is possible to fetch an object, say object-2, through its OID stored in an object, say object-1, it is sometimes useful to be able to perform the reverse operation—that is, to find object-1 given object-2.

This can be easily done if objects contain reverse OIDs or if a data structure is separately maintained to map each pair of objects in each direction—for example, object-1 to object-2 and object-2 to object-1. Due to the update overhead, some systems do not directly support the reverse navigation of objects.

10.2.6 Dynamic Loading of Methods

Object-oriented database systems allow user-written programs to be attached to classes. The inheritance mechanism allows applications to reuse the programs when defining subclasses of the classes. The systems typically store the programs as object files in the host file system and automatically load and execute them.

Relational database systems have recently added a facility called *stored procedures*. A stored procedure is much like a method. However, a stored procedure is not associated with any table, and it obviously cannot be inherited.

10.2.7 Retrieval and Update of Large Objects (BLOBs)

Although the retrieval and update of a BLOB (binary large object) is not a requirement due to object-oriented data modeling, a modern database system, whether it is relational or object oriented, must provide facilities for storing, retrieving, and updating multimedia data. A BLOB is a special data type that represents any large datum (typically a multimedia datum such as a bit-mapped image, an audio passage, or a textual document). Relational database systems all support BLOBs, and object-oriented database systems must support them, too.

Applications should be able to retrieve an entire BLOB or a part of a BLOB and be able to update a BLOB by appending data to a BLOB, inserting data into a BLOB, replacing a part of a BLOB with a given data, and deleting an entire BLOB. Further, database systems should support automatic concurrency control and recovery of transactions involving updates to a BLOB.

10.2.8 Queries and Updates

Besides the types of queries and updates that are supported in relational database systems, object-oriented database systems must support four additional types of queries and updates that arise as consequences of object-oriented data modeling [Kim 1989]. These include path queries, class-hierarchy queries, queries involving set-valued attributes, and queries containing methods. Further, database systems, object-oriented or not, should support queries involving regular expressions against textual data.

Path Queries

A path query is a query that includes a path expression in a search predicate. A path expression [Kifer, Kim, and Sagiv 1992] is a concatenation of attribute names along a composition hierarchy. For example, Manufacturer.President.Name is a path expression, where President is an attribute of a class, say Company, which is the data type of the Manufacturer attribute, while Name is an attribute of a class, say Employee, which is the data type of the President attribute.

A path expression is essentially an abbreviated form of a join of classes. In object-oriented database systems, the fact that objects store OIDs of other objects as values of attributes makes it potentially efficient to process a path query.

Class-Hierarchy Queries

A class-hierarchy query is a query that retrieves objects not only from a specified class but also all or some of its subclasses in a class hierarchy rooted at the class. For example, suppose that the class Person is the superclass of the classes Student and Faculty, and the classes Student and Faculty are superclasses of the class GraduateStudent. Then a class-hierarchy query issued against the class Person will retrieve qualified objects from the all of these classes, rather than just the class Person.

Queries Involving Set-Valued Attributes

Like retrieval and update of BLOBs, support of queries involving set-valued attributes is not a requirement due to any object-oriented concept. However, the first normal form restriction in relational database systems has proven to be a major impediment to applications that need to model columns that contain more than one value (such as the Children column in an Employee table, the Manager column in a Company table).

Object-oriented database systems allow set-valued attributes. A set-valued attribute may store more than one value. A set-valued attribute comes in at least three flavors: a standard set (which does not allow duplicate data), a multiset (also called a bag, which allows duplicate data), and a sequence (also called a list, which allows duplicate data and maintains ordering of data). Further, a set-valued attribute may be homogeneous or heterogeneous. A homogeneous set allows data of only one data type, whereas a heterogeneous set allows data of more than one data type.

Operations on a set-valued attribute include retrieval and update of the entire set or any subset of the set (e.g., first element, last element, any element) and retrieval and update of objects using search predicates that include set-valued attributes (e.g., Employee.Children contains {Tom, Mary}). The search predicates may also involve the existential and universal quantifiers. The existential quantifier refers to some of the elements in a set (e.g., Employee.Children contains some_of {Tom, Mary}); while the universal quantifier refers to all of the elements in a set (e.g., Employee.Children contains all_of {Tom, Mary}).

Queries Involving Methods

A method that returns a boolean value (true, false) may be used as a search predicate in a query. A method may also take the place of an attribute name in a predicate. Further, a method may even take the place of the comparison operator in a predicate.

Queries Involving Regular Expressions

Applications that deal with textual documents often need to issue queries involving regular expressions in search predicates. For example, an application may wish to determine if a given document contains the words *data base* or *database* or find all documents that contain any word that starts with the characters *comput.*

We note that the requirement for supporting queries involving regular expressions is a special case of a more general requirement for queries with search predicates that involve multimedia data. Since today's hardware and software technologies do not allow pattern-match search predicates involving general multimedia data (e.g., Person.Picture is_like <image of a passport size photo of a person>), only queries against textual data are included as a requirement here.

10.2.9 Dynamic Schema Changes

Relational database systems allow a few simple types of dynamic schema change, changes to the schema without a system shutdown. These include adding or dropping a table and adding or dropping a column in a table. Although those object-oriented database systems that are persistent storage systems for the C++ programming language do not support dynamic schema changes, full-blown object-oriented database systems really should support a reasonable set of dynamic schema changes. The set of dynamic schema changes includes adding or dropping a class, adding or dropping an attribute, adding or dropping a method, and adding or deleting a superclass to an existing class [Banerjee et al. 1987].

Since object-oriented database systems that support pointer swizzling manage memory-resident objects, a dynamic schema change will require the flushing of memory-resident objects to the database if they belong to the class whose definition has been changed.

10.2.10 Transaction Commit and Abort

Since object-oriented database systems that support pointer swizzling manage memory-resident objects, a transaction commit requires updated memory-resident objects to be flushed to the database. This overhead may cause commits to be slower in object-oriented database systems than in relational database systems.

Transaction commits and aborts should be measured for transactions involving updates to BLOBs, nested objects, and schema changes, as well as to the standard numeric and short string data that relational database systems deal with.

10.3 A Unified Benchmark for Relational and Object-Oriented Database Systems

A benchmark for relational databases, such as the University of Wisconsin benchmark, may be used straightforwardly to test the data definition facilities, transactions (commit, abort), and queries and updates involving only relationlike classes for object-oriented databases (i.e., classes that do not include any set-valued attributes and that include only those attributes with primitive numeric or short string data types). However, object-oriented database systems include additional operations that result from object-oriented data modeling (singe object fetch using an OID, traversal of a nested object, traversal of a class hierarchy, etc.) and advanced data management facilities (such as BLOBs, regular expression matching, dynamic schema changes, set-valued attributes) that relational database benchmarks typically do not include.

The remainder of this section will discuss how those operations that belong to object-oriented database systems as a result of object-oriented modeling can be simulated in relational databases for performance comparison between a relational database system and an object-oriented database system.

10.3.1 Single-Object Fetch

For a relational database, this can be easily simulated by a query that is guaranteed to return one, and only one, entire tuple from a table. Since a relational query will return an entire tuple, for a fair comparison, a request to fetch the contents of an object rather than just its OID should be issued against an object-oriented database.

10.3.2 Reverse Navigation of Objects

For a relational database, this can be approximated by a query that, given the value *V* of a particular attribute in a tuple of table, will return tuples of other tables that contain *V* as the value in one designated attribute.

10.3.3 Composition-Hierarchy Retrieval

A composition hierarchy of classes can be fairly easily simulated by a set of tables related through the foreign-key constraint. Whereas the traversal of a composition hierarchy can be done through a path query or a sequence of single-object fetches in object-oriented database systems, in relational databases a comparable operation can only be done through explicit joins of the tables that correspond to the classes in the composition hierarchy.

10.3.4 Navigation of Memory-Resident Objects

Relational database systems do not support pointer-based navigation of memory-resident objects. All that can be done to simulate this using a relational database system is the explicit joins of tables that are necessary to simulate the traversal of a composition hierarchy (as described above), with the retrieved tuples pinned in page buffers.

10.3.5 Class-Hierarchy Traversal

Relational database systems do not directly support the IS-A relationship and inheritance of attributes among tables. All classes in a class hierarchy can of course be simulated as a set of tables in a relational database. Since relational database systems do not understand inheritance, however, all inherited attributes in a class must be defined explicitly in a table to which the class is mapped. Note that this is not an entirely fair simulation either, since a class in an object-oriented database consists of not only attributes but also of methods and inheritance—that is, the system overhead in maintaining the schema information in object-oriented database systems is inherently higher than that for relational database systems.

Since relational database systems do not understand the superclass/subclass relationship, it is not meaningful to simulate the traversal of a class hierarchy to determine supertables or subtables of a given table. But the need to traverse a class hierarchy still exists to support class-hierarchy queries.

10.3.6 Queries and Updates

Path Queries

A path query can of course be simulated straightforwardly by explicit joins involving the classes on the path expression in the query.

Class-Hierarchy Queries

A class-hierarchy query may be easily (but tediously) simulated by a set of queries, each involving only one class in the class hierarchy of concern to the query.

A join of two class hierarchies must be simulated by M × N separate joins, where M is the number of classes on one class hierarchy and N is the number of classes on the other class hierarchy.

Queries Involving Set-Valued Attributes

A set-valued attribute is not allowed in a relational database. One way to represent a set is to duplicate tuples. A query involving a set-valued attribute in an object-oriented database can therefore be formulated as a query that searches or retrieves these duplicate tuples in a relational database.

Queries Involving Methods

Relational database systems do not directly support queries involving methods. Using those relational database systems that support stored procedures, however, a combination of queries that do not involve stored procedures and some computations using stored procedures on the results of the queries, it may be possible to simulate queries that directly include methods in search predicates. Note, however, that the optimization of a query that involves a method in an object-oriented database system is to be performed automatically by the system. The hand-coding of the computations involving stored procedures on query results in the relational simulation may destroy fairness in the comparison.

10.4 Guidelines for Designing a Benchmark Database

We offer the following general guidelines for the design of a benchmark database for object-oriented database systems.

1. It should be designed to allow the testing of all of the operations that object-oriented database systems should support (rather than only the common set of operations supported by all commercial object-oriented database systems).
2. It should also be designed to allow the testing of all major operations supported in today's relational database systems (since object-oriented database systems should support all major operations found in relational database systems).
3. It should be designed to establish the performance characteristics of a large database in a multiuser environment; the smallest tolerable database should be one gigabyte, and the number of concurrent users should be 20. We offer the following set of parameters as a guideline for creating a benchmark database:

- number of classes: 100–200
- levels of the class hierarchy: 20
- number of immediate subclasses of a class: 1–10
  — this defines the fan-out of a class hierarchy
- number of immediate superclasses of a class: 1–3
- levels of a composition hierarchy: 1–10
- number of methods in a class: 0–5

- number of elements (values) in a set-valued attribute: 1–200
- number of set-valued attributes in a class: 0–5
  — one should be a standard set, one a multiset, and one a sequence
  — some should be a set of primitive data and others should be a set of OIDs
  — further, one should be a heterogeneous set
- number of attributes in a class whose data types are arbitrary classes: 0–5
  — this defines the fan-out of a composition hierarchy
- number of attributes in a class whose data types are a BLOB: 0–1
- size of a BLOB: 10–100 megabytes
- number of attributes in a class: same as in relational database benchmarks
- number of objects in a class: same as in relational database benchmarks
- sizes of attributes: same as in relational database benchmarks
- distribution of data types of the attributes in a class: same as in relational database benchmarks
- distribution of attributes on which indexes are maintained: same as in relational database benchmarks
- data page size: same as in relational database benchmarks

10.5 Observations About Meaningful Benchmarking

Vendors of database systems often use the results of a benchmark measurement against competing database systems to establish the relative performance superiority of their systems. A performance benchmark has a great potential for misleading prospective customers of database systems if it is not properly designed and run or if the results of measurements are open to misinterpretation. As a way of closing this chapter, we offer a few observations about meaningful benchmarking.

It is obviously important to design a benchmark database properly and to include a comprehensive set of operations against the benchmark database. If the benchmark database is small or the set of operations measured against the database is only a small fraction of a comprehensive set of operations that should be measured, then the benchmark is meaningless.

Further, benchmarks are often designed for and run in a single-user environment and therefore do not yield any result regarding the performance characteristics of database systems in a multiuser environment. A multiuser environment with a large database is the production environment for which a database benchmark should be designed and run. Clearly, a database system that does not support a multiuser environment (e.g., automatic concurrency control, authorization) is not very useful.

There is one important problem with existing benchmarks for both relational and object-oriented database systems besides the two major deficiencies in the current benchmark proposals for object-oriented database systems. It is that they do not provide any means of differentiating feature-rich systems from feature-poor systems. For example, a relational database system that supports joins is relatively feature rich compared to a system that does not. First-generation object-oriented database systems typically do not support queries, views, authorization, triggers, dynamic schema changes, the Unique and Null integrity constraints, and so on. A benchmark should not be designed (or at least the results of running a benchmark should not be reported) such that a database system that does not support, for example, authorization or Unique constraint, to be a better system than a system that may be somewhat slower because of the need to check authorization or uniqueness of values being inserted, respectively. To counterbalance a possible performance degradation in feature-rich systems due to additional database services they provide over relatively feature-poor systems, the set of operations to run against a benchmark database should perhaps include operations that can affect the performance of other operations that more clearly merit inclusion in the benchmark. Such auxiliary operations that are typically missing in performance benchmarks include those for exposing the availability of dynamic schema changes, authorization, semantic integrity (referential integrity, Unique, Null, and triggers), database replication, dual logging for higher availability, and the like. When a particular database system does not support a particular feature (e.g., a join query), the system should simply receive either "feature not supported" or "infinity" for the time taken to run the operation, rather than forcing a hand-coded simulation of the missing feature.

REFERENCES

A Measure of Transaction Processing Power, *Datamation*, 1985.

Banerjee, J., Kim, W., Kim, H., and Korth, H. 1987. Semantics and Implementation of Schema Evolution in Object-Oriented Databases. *Proceedings of ACM-SIGMOD International Conference on Management of Data* 1987, San Francisco.

Bitton, D., DeWitt, D., and Turbyfill, C. 1983. Benchmarking Database Systems, a Systematic Approach. *Proceedings of the International Conference on Very Large Data Bases*, November 1983.

Carey, M., DeWitt, D., and Naughton, J. 1993. The OO7 Benchmark. *Proceedings of ACM-SIGMOD International Conference on Management of Data* 1993, Washington, D.C.

Cattell, R., and Skeen., D. 1992. Object Operations Benchmark. *ACM Trans. on Database Systems,* Vol. 17, No. 1.

Kifer, M., Kim, W., and Sagiv, Y. 1992. Querying Object-Oriented Databases. *Proceedings of ACM-SIGMOD International Conference on Management of Data* 1992, San Diego.

Kim, W. 1989. A Model of Queries for Object-Oriented Databases. *Proceedings of the International Conference on Very Large Data Bases,* Amsterdam.

Kim, W. 1990. *Introduction to Object-Oriented Databases.* MIT Press, Cambridge, Mass.

Kim, W., and Garza, J. F. 1987. Transaction Management in an Object-Oriented Database System. *Proceedings of ACM-SIGMOD International Conference on Management of Data* 1987, Chicago.

Kim, W., and Lochovsky, F. 1989. *Object-Oriented Concepts, Applications, and Databases.* Addison-Wesley, Reading, Mass.

Kim, W., et al. 1988. Integrating an Object-Oriented Programming System with a Database System. *Proceedings of International Conference on Object-Oriented Programming Systems, Languages, and Applications,* San Diego.

White, S., and DeWitt, D. 1992. A Performance Study of Alternative Object Faulting and Pointer Swizzling Strategies. *Proceedings of International Conference on Very Large Data Bases,* Vancouver.

11

An Object-Oriented DBMS War Story: Developing a Genome Mapping Database in C++

NATHAN GOODMAN

The Computing Group of the Whitehead Institute/MIT Center for Genome Research has developed an object-oriented database that supports several large genome mapping projects. The database is implemented in C++ on top of a C++-based DBMS product. The database supports applications written in multiple languages—Perl, C++, C, and Smalltalk—running on several kinds of Unix workstations, Apple Macintosh computers, and IBM PC-compatible computers. Contrary to conventional wisdom, our experience suggests that it is a mistake to make the database too smart by implementing complex programs as methods inside database objects. Our experience also indicates that C++ is a poor language for implementing databases, with problems related to the mechanics of defining attributes, the mechanics of referring to objects in a systematic way, the lack of a garbage collector, and subtle traps in the inheritance model. We also found that current C++-based DBMSs lack important database functions, and to compensate for this, we were forced to provide our own simple implementations of standard DBMS functions: transaction logging for roll-forward recovery, a multithread transaction monitor, a query language and query processor, and storage structures. In effect, we used the C++-based DBMS as an object-oriented storage manager and built a data management system specialized for large-scale genome mapping on top of it. Despite these difficulties, we were able to develop a successful object-oriented system.

11.1 Introduction

The Center for Genome Research at the Whitehead Institute for Biomedical Research, affiliated with MIT, is engaged in large-scale biological research projects as part of the Human Genome Project [Frenkel 1991; Lander, Langridge, et al. 1991; Office of Technology Assessment 1988]. To support these projects, the Computing Group of the Genome Center has developed an object-oriented database called MapBase [Goodman, Reeve, et al. 1992;

Goodman, Rozen, et al. 1993]. MapBase is implemented in C++ [Ellis and Stroustrup 1990; Stroustrup 1986] on top of a commercially available C++-based DBMS product (ObjectStore [Lamb, Landis, et al. 1991] from Object Design, Inc.). This chapter describes our experience in developing MapBase and in integrating it with other software elements of the Genome Center information system. This experience has convinced us that object-oriented techniques are effective in principle but cumbersome in practice.

One very fundamental problem that we encountered concerns the overall architecture of the information system. With classical database techniques, the boundary between database and application is perfectly clear: The database stores data as passive elements, and the application contains all program logic. With object-oriented techniques, this distinction evaporates because an object-oriented database stores objects that may contain data and programs [Cattell 1991; Kim 1990].

A related problem concerns the semantic richness of an object-oriented database. Object-oriented techniques make it possible to represent a wealth of real world detail in a natural way [Goodman 1991; Rumbaugh, Blaha, et al. 1991]. The database designer can create customized data types and data structures that are ideally suited for a given application domain. The danger is that such richness will lead to database designs that are too complex—too expensive to develop and too hard to maintain.

The key unanswered questions are: Which programs should be implemented inside the database, and which should remain in the application? How smart should the database be?

A more pragmatic problem concerns the specific technology that is commercially available today. C++ has emerged as the *de facto* standard object-oriented data model. There are four or five C++-based DBMS products, and almost every non-C++-based product provides a C++ coupling. Smalltalk is running a distant second: There is one native Smalltalk-based DBMS product and two other products that provide a Smalltalk coupling. All other object models are one of a kind. The dominance of C++ concerns us because—despite its growing popularity as a general-purpose programming language—we have found it to be a bad language for creating database schemas. It is relatively straightforward to create a rough draft database in C++, but it takes enormous expertise and energy to convert this into a robust production system.

In the same vein, we encountered serious problems due to the lack of important DBMS functions in current C++-based DBMS products. We were forced to implement our own functions for certain aspects of transaction management, query processing, and storage structures. We found performance to be enigmatic as well. It is easy to get superb performance on a small, single-user database, but it is hard to retain this performance as the database grows and concurrent use expands. All told, about 40 percent of our database code is devoted to working around problems in the DBMS.

We begin with a brief description of our application and the architecture of our information system. The next section discusses the pragmatic problems we encountered with the DBMS and C++. Section 11.4 explores more fundamental problems caused by the fuzzy boundary between the database and the application.

11.2 Background

11.2.1 The Application

The Whitehead Institute/MIT Center for Genome Research is constructing maps of the human and mouse genomes [Copeland, Gilbert, et al. 1993]. A *genome map* is essentially a road map of the chromosomes of a genome. A genome map contains some number of mapped features and indicates spatial relationships over those features. Some mapped features are pointlike, analogous to small towns on a road map. Others are linelike, analogous to roads.

Figure 11–1 illustrates one kind of genome map, called a *genetic map*. The vertical line represents a single mouse chromosome. The labels to the right of the vertical line are arbitrary names of the features that have been mapped on this chromosome, and the numbers to the left of the line indicate the distances between the features. All the features in this map are very short DNA segments that can be uniquely identified. The segments are short enough that we may treat them as points with no loss of usability. Figure 11–2 illustrates another kind of map, called a *physical map*. In this map, there are two kinds of mapped features. The dotted vertical lines represent very short DNA segments just like those in Fig. 11–1. The horizontal lines represent DNA segments that are 1000 times larger than the short segments. The intersection of a dotted vertical line with a horizontal line indicates that the short DNA segment represented by the vertical line is contained in the large segment represented by the horizontal line. The different shadings of the horizontal lines indicate levels of confidence for the various containment relationships. The maps shown in these figures were constructed by our Genome Center and were current as of late 1993.

These projects will require the completion of more than 5 million experiments, each of which requires the completion of several steps. As experiments are completed, the results must be analyzed and combined to produce the requisite maps.

The Computing Group of the Genome Center develops a variety of software to support these projects. The software has four major tasks. One is to automate the collection of data from each experimental step and the flow of information from step to step. The second task is to analyze the results and produce the desired maps. Third, we must provide information to per-

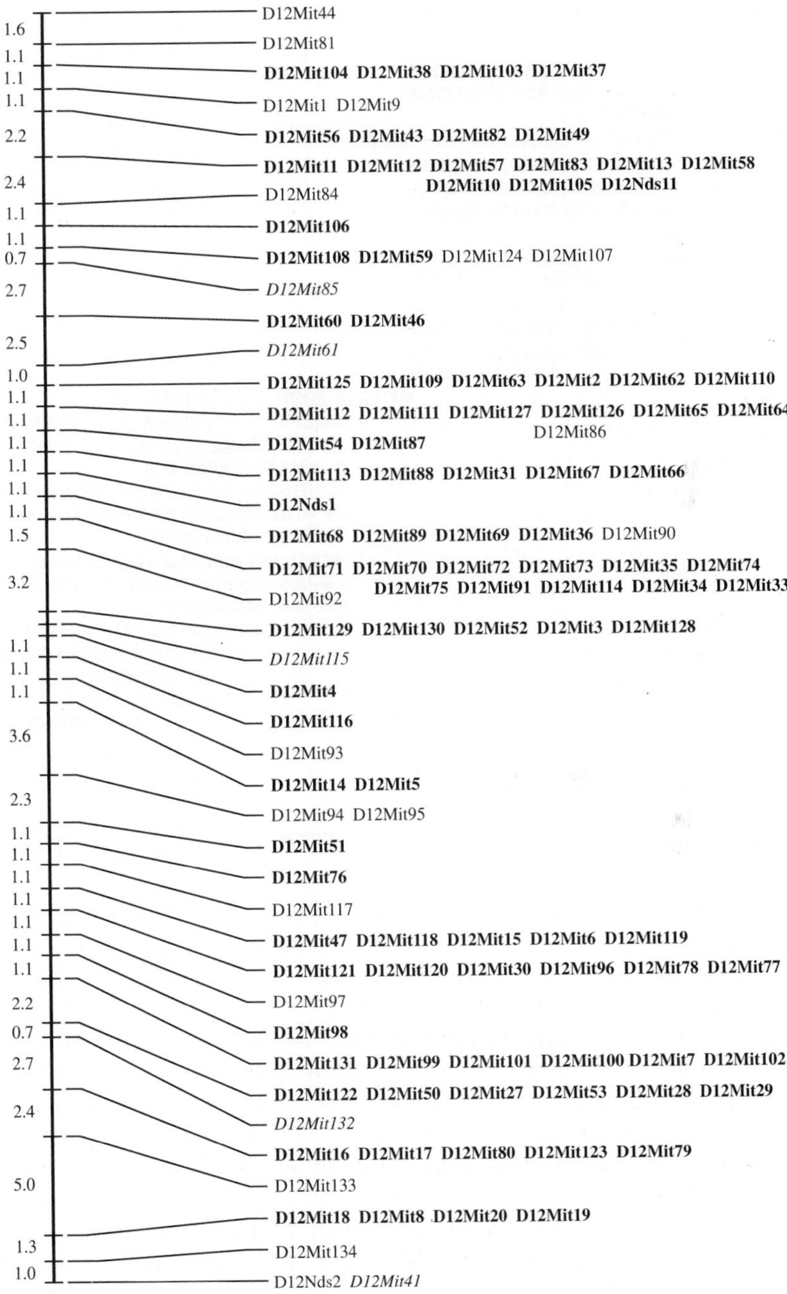

FIGURE 11–1
Genetic Map

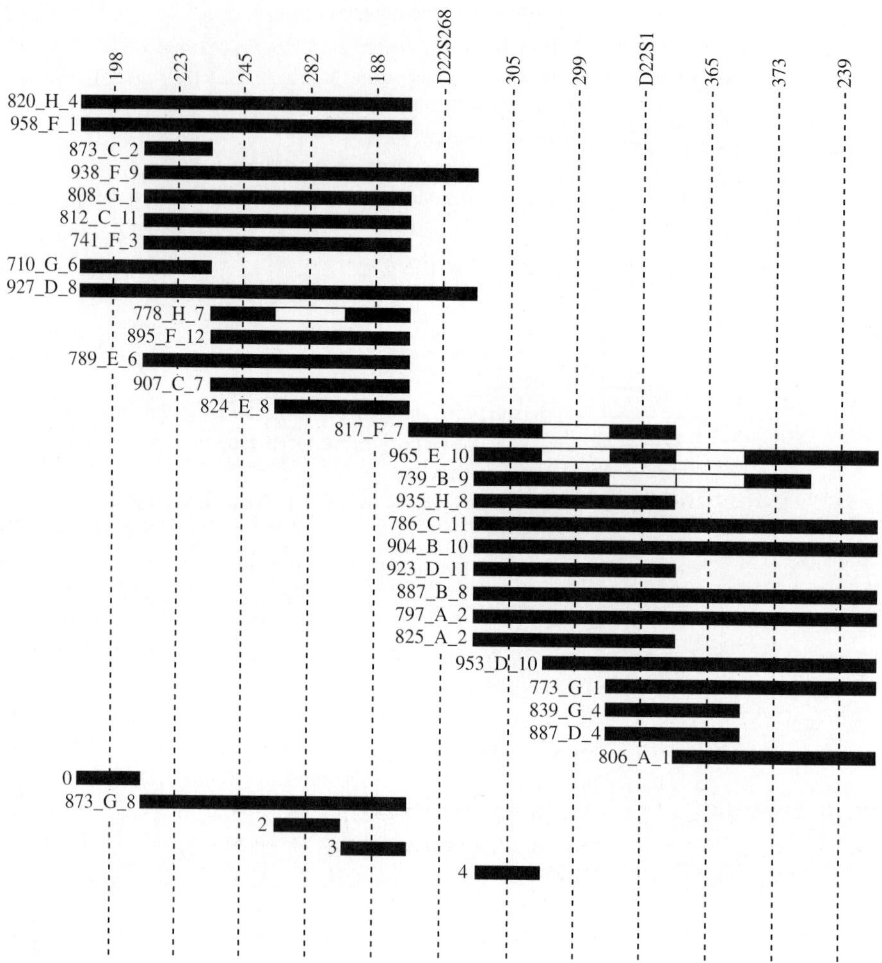

FIGURE 11–2
Physical Map

sonnel within the Center regarding the progress of each experiment. Finally, we must disseminate the results of the project to the biological community at large.

Our software also supports several smaller projects: (1) genetic mapping of the rat genome, (2) genetic mapping of the zebrafish genome, (3) construction of a high-resolution physical map of the human Y chromosome, and (4) a number of focused projects to map specific genes.

The system is inherently multiplatform and multilingual. In addition to the MapBase database, the system includes a map construction program called MAPMAKER [Lander, Green, et al. 1987] for genetic maps, another program for constructing physical maps [Reeve, Kaufman, et al. 1993], a program called PRIMER [Lincoln, Daly, et al. 1991] for analyzing the short DNA segments on our maps, numerous small application programs, user interface programs, and programs to control laboratory machines. For pragmatic and historical reasons, these programs are written in a variety of programming languages. MapBase and some application programs are written in C++. Our map construction programs, PRIMER, and some application programs are written in C. Many small application programs are written in Perl. The database runs on a Sun Unix workstation. Most other programs are able to run on Sun, DEC Ultrix, and DEC Alpha workstations, although a few programs run only on Macintoshes or PCs. MAPMAKER is a large, compute-intensive program; we prefer to run it on an Alpha workstation, which is the most powerful machine we presently have; when making large maps, we often run MAPMAKER on multiple workstations simultaneously. The Macintosh is the desktop platform of choice among our users, and we have designed our user interface software to run on these machines.

The database size is modest. At present, the database occupies about 50 megabytes. The database is naturally divided into partitions for each project. The largest of these partitions is 25 megabytes. We expect the database to grow 10 times larger over the life of the project.

The performance load is modest, too. There are rarely more than five concurrent users per partition. The peak update load is currently fewer than 1000 transactions per day per partition; this translates into fewer than 50 bytes per second per partition. The peak retrieval load occurs during map construction. At present, the construction of our largest map requires that 500 kilobytes be transferred from the database to the map construction program; the system accomplishes this in less than a minute. We expect the peak update and retrieval rates to grow by a factor of 10 over the life of the project.

Ad hoc queries fall into a few categories. *Name queries* retrieve information about a single mapped feature identified by a unique name. *Status queries* retrieve information about features based on which experimental steps have been completed for the feature. *Positional queries* retrieve information about features that lie in a given region of a map. Name and status queries are very fast because the database maintains suitable indexes for these. Positional queries are also fast, because the database maintains a map data structure that can be searched by position. Queries that do not fall into these categories require a sequential scan of the database.

Performance expectations are high. Our users have grown up with computers on their desks and expect our information system to be as responsive as a typical desktop application. They expect to be able to access our shared database as efficiently as they can access local data on their desktop Macintoshes.

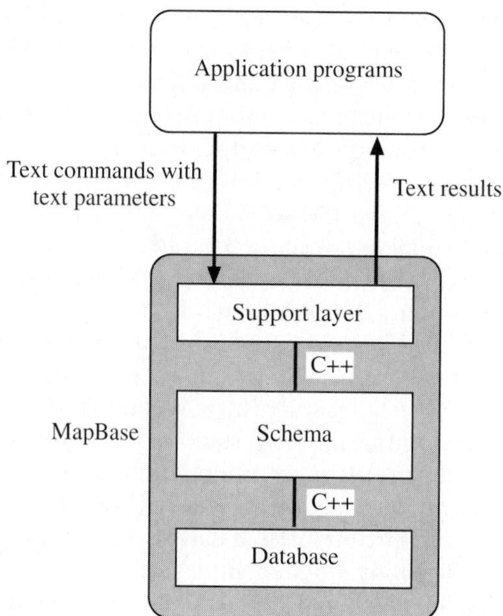

FIGURE 11–3
System Architecture

11.2.2 System Architecture

Because we are using a C++-based DBMS, the database schema is a library of C++ classes. These classes together with a suite of support functions are packaged into a program we call MapBase. See Fig. 11–3.

The MapBase program operates as a network-accessible database server. To use the database, an application program connects to MapBase (by connecting to a designated socket). Once connected, the application program accesses the database by issuing commands to the MapBase server. This command interface is the only way into the database; there are no back doors. We run a separate MapBase server process for each database partition.

The interface between application programs and MapBase is entirely text based; all commands and data are expressed in standard ASCII text[1]. Commands may be updates, retrievals, or control messages (such as "set date" or "commit transaction") and usually take parameters. To put data into the database, an application program converts the data to text and

1. We have not dealt with the problems of images and other nontextual data types.

sends it as parameters to appropriate MapBase update commands. To get data from the database, the program executes a retrieval command; MapBase responds with a stream of textual results that the program converts to the desired internal representation. An alternate approach would be to use a remote procedure call mechanism (RPC) for this interface [Bloomer 1991].

In effect, MapBase functions as a multiconnection database server. Applications are clients and communicate with MapBase using a text-based command language. This is virtually identical to the way applications access a SQL-based relational database. Instead of SQL, the application uses the command language we have developed. We have left unsolved the many hard problems of distributed object management. When a program retrieves data, any connection to the underlying objects in the database is lost. If the program changes the data, it is responsible for translating the change into a series of MapBase commands to update the underlying objects.

This structure directly solves our need for distributed, multiplatform, multilingual access. Programs written in any language and running on any machine can access MapBase by connecting to the appropriate socket and emitting text commands. The performance penalty imposed by this architecture is in the range of 30–50 percent—that is, MapBase spends that much time managing its communication with clients and converting parameters and results to and from text.

The program consists of about 40,000 lines of code divided into six major modules, as shown in the table below. The *collections* module implements several setlike classes. *Values* implements user-defined data types, such as strings and DNA sequences. *Taxonomy* defines a simple taxonometric classification of the organisms we are mapping. *Map strategy, map,* and *workflow* define different aspects of the various mapping procedures used in the center: workflow models the specific experimental steps used by each mapping procedure; map strategy defines the central concepts of each procedure independent of the detailed steps; the map module represents maps themselves. *Support* implements the command language, communications manager, and other system-support functions, some of which are described later.

Module	Percent of Total
Collections	2%
Values	13%
Taxonomy	3%
Map strategy	12%
Map	4%
Workflow	26%
Support	40%

11.3 Pragmatic Considerations

11.3.1 Challenges Imposed by the DBMS

The DBMS we are using provides no way to *roll forward* from a backup copy of the database[2]. A disk crash or serious DBMS crash can destroy all updates since the last database backup. To work around this problem, we implemented a simple logging scheme. MapBase captures each command as it comes in and copies the command to a sequential log file. To recover a database partition, we create a new empty partition and replay the log file in its entirety. This currently takes about 30 minutes. This logging scheme ignores the race conditions that arise when there is an operating system or hardware crash while MapBase is executing a command [Bernstein, Hadzollacos, et al. 1987]. Despite this simplification, the scheme works well enough for our purposes.

Second, there is no support for *schema evolution*. A schema change can invalidate the database, making it inaccessible. The DBMS provides no way to reload the database when this happens[3]. In other words, a schema change can have the same effect as a disk crash! The logging scheme described above solves this problem, too. When a new schema is released, we rebuild the database from scratch just as if the database had been lost. An advantage of this solution is that the database recovery code is exercised on a regular basis. Having lived through 10 or 20 schema migrations, we are confident that the logging scheme works! A major disadvantage is that a schema change may also affect the format of previously logged commands. When this happens, we write ad hoc programs that massage the logs into the new format. This is probably just as hard as writing ad hoc programs to dump, reformat, and reload the database directly.

Third, the *query language*, though elegant in design, suffers a serious practical limitation: Queries must refer directly to data members of objects; queries may not invoke methods or overloaded functions. This violates a key precept of object-oriented design—the encapsulation principle [Atkinson, Bancilhon, et al. 1989]—by exposing an object's internal structure to the outside world and renders the query language unusable for our purposes. This led us to develop our own simple query language. The query language is designed to retrieve information about mapped features and, in particular, to retrieve all laboratory results that pertain to a given mapped feature. The query language is vaguely SQL-like. A query has a *condition list* that filters the data being retrieved and a *target list* that specifies the information to be retrieved for each mapped feature. Alternatively, it is possible

---

2. The vendor claims this problem is fixed in the latest release of the product.
3. The vendor claims this problem is fixed in the latest release of the product.

to count the number of mapped features that satisfy a condition list or to store the selected elements in a named set for further processing. It is also possible to sort the results. The condition list is a conjunction of *selection clauses*, each of which compares a data element to a constant (or a pair of constants). The comparison operators are the usual <, ≤, and the like, plus regular expression matching on strings, positional comparisons for maps, and other operators customized for our application. We also provide canned queries and reports for retrievals that are not handled by the query language. For example, there are canned queries to dump the data needed to construct a map and to retrieve whole maps in various formats.

Fourth, the *collection library* was apparently designed to sit under the query language; it lacks low-level structures and control mechanisms that are needed when used outside the query language. The query optimizer decides when to use indexes, but there is no way for a programmer to use an index explicitly. The DBMS performs automatic index maintenance, but there is no way for a programmer to step in and do this directly. There are B-tree secondary indexes but no B-tree primary structures. There is no sorted list data structure. There are hashed secondary and primary structures, but the programmer cannot directly control hash table parameters. Having built our own query language, we found the DBMS-supplied collection library to be unsuitable as well. This led us to implement our own simple storage structures for setlike objects and indexes. Sets are implemented as expandable arrays of pointers. Duplicate detection is optional and, if performed, requires a sequential scan of the set. In most cases, duplicates are prevented as a natural consequence of the program logic. In some cases, the program using the set does duplicate detection by consulting a suitable index. The only index structure we support is static hashing.

Single-user performance is excellent provided the database fits in a main memory cache but degrades rapidly when the database exceeds the cache. To its credit, the DBMS is designed to exploit very large caches and allows the system administrator to easily control the cache size. As the database grows, we deal with the performance impact by simply increasing the cache size as follows: When a MapBase server process begins execution, it sets its cache size to be 1 megabyte more than the current size of its database partition. The largest database partition is presently 25 megabytes and is expected to exceed 100 megabytes by the end of the project. It is cheaper for us to buy more memory than to devise a cleverer solution to the problem.

Multiuser performance is troublesome because of lock contention. The DBMS employs page-level two-phase locking. We have found it difficult to avoid hot spots in storage allocation and other low-level areas. To work around the contention problem, we implemented a multiconnection transaction monitor that allows multiple concurrent users to share a single MapBase process. The unit of atomicity is a single MapBase command—there are no multicommand transactions. This greatly simplifies the transaction management problem but has obvious limitations.

Transaction commits are another performance problem. We have found that commits incur two main costs: (1) the commit itself takes time, presumably as updates are written to disk; (2) the *next* transaction runs slowly for a period of time, which is caused, we believe, by the fact that the DBMS unlocks all cached data upon commit and must reacquire those locks as the new transaction runs. We have run tests in which we vary the commit interval, committing after every *n* updates, for *n* ranging from 1 to 10,000 or more. The details depend on the precise nature of the test, but the basic conclusion is that for low values of *n*, the cost of committing a transaction is 10–20 times greater than the cost of executing the transaction. To work around this cost, we do not commit after every transaction but rather issue commits periodically—normally, every 10 minutes. Naturally, uncommitted updates are at risk during this interval and will be lost if there is a crash. In most cases, updates can be recovered from the log file.

The sum total of these decisions is that we are using the DBMS as an object-oriented, transaction-protected storage manager. The DBMS provides persistent storage of C++ objects, page-level two-phase locking, and page-level transaction logging. We have implemented our own very specialized data management system on top of these capabilities. Most of our algorithms are simplistic but work well enough for our purposes.

11.3.2 Challenges Imposed by C++

C++ was never meant to be used as a database language. The language was designed for general-purpose programming. It lacks elementary database capabilities, and its object model poses difficulties for typical database classes.

C++ does not directly support the notion of an attribute of an object. Suppose we wish to code a Person class with two attributes, `name` and `address`. In SQL, this takes three lines of code:

```
CREATE TABLE Person (
  name varchar (100),
  address varchar (200))
```

A minimal C++ version is almost as short:

```
class Person {
  public:
    String name;
    String address;
    Person (String n, String a) : name (n), address (a) {} };
```

In this example, we assume that `String` is a variable-length string class. The lines

```
String name;
String address;
```

define data elements for the Person's name and address, both of type String. The line

```
Person (String n, String a) : name (n), address (a) {}
```

defines a *constructor* function that is used to create new Person objects; this function is analogous to the SQL INSERT verb but must be supplied by the programmer. The keyword public: indicates that the data elements and constructor are visible to programs outside the class. In most cases, a class also needs a *destructor* function, analogous to SQL's DELETE, to destroy objects.

Unfortunately, this minimal design violates a basic object-oriented design principle by allowing data elements to be visible outside the object. Instead, we are well advised to bury the data elements inside the protected part of the object and provide *accessor* and *mutator* functions to operate on these elements. The resulting class is much larger than the SQL design. Each attribute must be mentioned 8 to 10 times in the class[4]: once to define the data element that stores the attribute, twice in the constructor, once in the destructor, twice in the accessor function, and 2–4 times in the mutator function. This problem, though conceptually trivial, leads to an enormous explosion in the size of the schema. It also makes schema maintenance more arduous: To change the name of an attribute, you have to edit 8 or 10 occurrences of the name! What is conceptually a one-line change turns into an 8–10 line change.

A second problem is that C++ provides three ways to refer to an object—by value, by reference, and by pointer—and important language features work differently for different subsets of these modes. The details are too technical for this presentation, but the conclusion is that no mode of referral is uniformly best. There is a temptation to mix and match these modes, using each where it works best. We have found this too error prone and have opted to use pointers throughout. This means that we give up important language features such as general operator overloading and automatic initialization and deinitialization of local variables.

A third problem is that C++ does not have an automatic garbage collector. A program that uses an object must know whether it was dynamically allocated—and so must be deleted—or whether it is part of the permanent database—and so must not be deleted. This makes it difficult to change the way objects are implemented as the database evolves.

4. That is, either the name of the attribute or the name of a surrogate, such as a formal parameter, must appear this many times in the class definition.

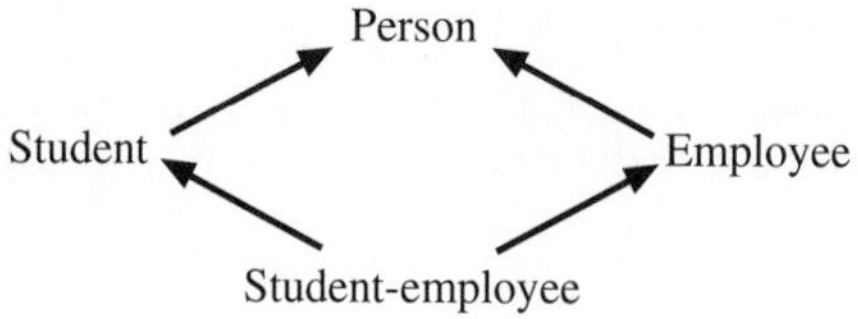

FIGURE 11–4
Class Hierarchy with Multiple Inheritance

Multiple inheritance is another problem area. Consider the well-worn university personnel example illustrated in Fig. 11–4. The `Person` class has subclasses `Student` and `Employee`, which have a common subclass `Student-Employee`. To make this work as expected, the `Student` and `Employee` classes must declare `Person` to be a *virtual base class*. This declaration introduces some hidden storage overhead, it causes constructor functions to work differently, and it disallows certain data type conversions that would otherwise be legal. These effects make it difficult to introduce this kind of inheritance into an extant schema.

Late binding of functions can also lead to surprises. C++ allows the programmer to specify whether a function is to be bound late or early. When a subclass inherits a late bound function, it is allowed to change the implementation of the function but not the types of parameters or the result. If the subclass does change parameter or result types, late binding is turned off. This makes it difficult to create functions or to define attributes that become more specialized as we work down an inheritance hierarchy.

11.4 How Much Semantics?

Object-oriented techniques allow programs to be implemented as part of the database schema—that is, as functions inside classes that are part of the schema—or outside of it. In our system architecture, programs inside the schema are below the command interface and can directly access the database using C++. Programs outside the schema are above the command interface and may only access the database through our limited, text-based command language. Is there a rational basis for deciding which programs go where? We have struggled with this question and have no solid answer. We offer some examples.

11.4.1 DNA Sequence Analysis

Recall from section 11.2 that many of the features we map are short DNA segments. These DNA segments are produced in the laboratory by cutting the genome into millions of random small segments and randomly selecting

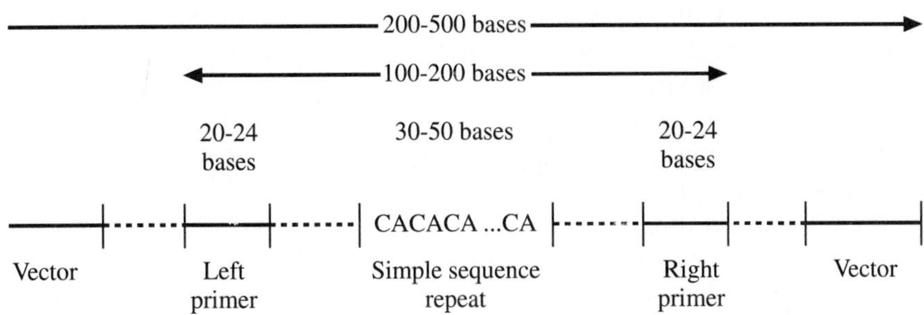

FIGURE 11–5
Anatomy of a Sequence Tagged Site (STS)

a few tens of thousands of these to use in the project. Each selected segment is sequenced, and the sequence is put into the database. Each sequence is analyzed by software to ensure that the segment is suitable for the experiment. Unsuitable sequences remain in the database but are flagged appropriately. Figure 11–5 illustrates the structure of these short segments, which are technically called *sequence tagged sites* (STS) [Olson, Hood, et al. 1989]. The figure is discussed further in the text below.

The central step in our mapping experiments is a chemical reaction called the *polymerase chain reaction* (PCR). This reaction can be used, for example, to determine whether a given short DNA segment is contained in a large segment. The physical map shown earlier in Fig. 11–2 was constructed by exactly this procedure. To perform this reaction, the short segment must contain even shorter stretches near its left- and right-hand ends that can be used as so-called *primers* for the reaction. The suitability of a short stretch for this purpose depends on properties such as the temperature at which the short stretch melts and freezes. We have written a program, called PRIMER [Lincoln, Daly, et al. 1991], that predicts these properties and determines whether suitable primers exist. Having identified the primer sequences, it is possible to purchase synthetic DNA with that sequence from a chemical supply company. This synthetic DNA is a key ingredient in the PCR procedure.

To be usable as a mapped feature, a DNA segment must be unique—that is, it must appear exactly once in the genome. The human genome contains a number of segments that are repeated thousands or even hundreds of thousands of times[5]. Sometimes the repeated sequences are exactly the same, but usually they are only approximately equal. The biological purpose of these repeats is unknown, but many have been identified by researchers in the field. We have compiled a list of about 100 known repeated sequences. When we insert a new sequence into the database, we

5. The genomes of most higher organisms contain such repeats.

compare it against the list of known repeats using a well-known approximate search algorithm, FASTA [Pearson and Lipman 1988]. If the new sequence matches a known repeat, it is likely to be nonunique, and we flag it as such.

Repeated segments are not always bad. For one of our mapping projects—genetic mapping—we require that segments contain a simple repetitive stretch in the middle. Refer to Fig. 11–5. In our work, the repeating sequence is typically of the form CACA...CA[6]. These so-called *simple sequence repeats* (SSRs) have no known biological function but are quite useful for mapping [Weber and May 1989]. These sequences are scattered throughout the human and mouse genomes. The length of such repetitive sequences tends to vary between individuals. Using the polymerase chain reaction, it is possible to measure the distance between the primers and hence the length of the repeated region. This makes it possible to track how the segments are inherited from generation to generation, which is the essential step in genetic mapping. Note that although the CA part of the segment is repetitive, the rest of the segment must be unique. The two arms of the sequence are run through the repeat checker described above to ensure this.

The beginning and ending parts of the sequence are artifacts of the laboratory procedure and are completely irrelevant to the problem at hand. These artifacts arise as follows. After the DNA of the genome is cut into small segments of the desired size, each segment is infused into a microorganism that has been genetically engineered to store and replicate the segment as needed; when the segment is sequenced, one inevitably ends up with a small amount of sequence that derives from the microorganism. The sequence of the microorganism is completely known. We use software to search for the known microorganism sequence at the beginning and end of the segment—called *vector*—and conceptually remove it before any other analysis is done. Refer again to Fig. 11–5. For technical reasons, different microorganisms with different vector sequences are used for different groups of DNA segments. The software consults the database to determine which microorganism and vector were used for the present segment.

Occasionally, the same DNA segment is selected twice. Sometimes this happens because the segment is part of a repeated segment. It also happens as a result of bias in the process used to select segments[7]. Because we need to detect when this happens to avoid wasting time and money processing

---

6. C and A are two of the four possible DNA bases.

7. If the selection process were truly random, the chances of picking a duplicate segment would be vanishingly small. In reality, there are severe selection biases, and the rate of duplicate sequences is high enough to warrant attention. During normal operation, we see 1–10 percent duplicates; there are occasional bad periods when the duplicate rate may reach 40 percent or more. When the duplicate rate gets too high, the genome is resampled, which resets the selection bias.

the same piece of DNA twice, we developed a program to check for duplicate sequences. The program examines each new sequence that is put into the database and conceptually compares it to each existing sequence in the database. To improve the efficiency of this process, the program maintains an indexed filter that identifies potential duplicates. For each potential duplicate, the program retrieves the old sequence and compares it to the new one, using a well-known dynamic programming algorithm for approximate sequence matching [Needleman and Wunsch 1970; Waterman 1984].

The various programs we have described could, in principle, be implemented as part of the schema or as application programs outside the database. For historical reasons, most were implemented outside the database. One exception is the duplicate checking program. We originally implemented this program inside the schema as a function inside the DNA segment class. It seemed a natural place to put it for two reasons. First, it seemed natural for the DNA segment class to be responsible for knowing what constitutes a duplicate sequence and how to identify it. Second, the program accesses a lot of persistent data—namely, the indexed filter and the sequences of potential duplicate segments. This decision turned out to be a mistake. There were several problems. First, the indexed filter was larger than the rest of the database! This destroyed locality of reference for the entire database and led to severe thrashing. Second, the program takes about 2 minutes to check a new sequence against a database of 1000 existing sequences. When inside the schema, the program was below the command interface, and the cost was paid every time the recovery logs were replayed. This caused database reloads to consume almost 20 hours, as opposed to about 30 minutes when the program is removed. Third, the program uses a fussy algorithm that needs occasional fiddling. When we changed the algorithm, the program would sometimes find previously unknown duplicates in the existing database and would occasionally miss ones that were previously known. Both occurrences are significant and need human attention. When the program is inside the schema, it makes these new discoveries during database reloads, which is not a good time to carefully examine new findings. We have since moved the program out of the schema.

A basic premise of the object data model is that objects should contain data and programs that operate on that data [Atkinson, Bancilhon, et al. 1989]. During the early days of the project, we took this premise seriously and sought to implement inside the schema all programs that naturally seemed to belong. Naïvely, all the programs described in this section seem to fit this bill. Our experience suggests otherwise. The one program that was originally implemented inside the schema has been removed, and the reasons why it was removed would apply to the other programs, too.

We have since adopted a firm rule that most programs are implemented outside the database. Programs are implemented inside the data-

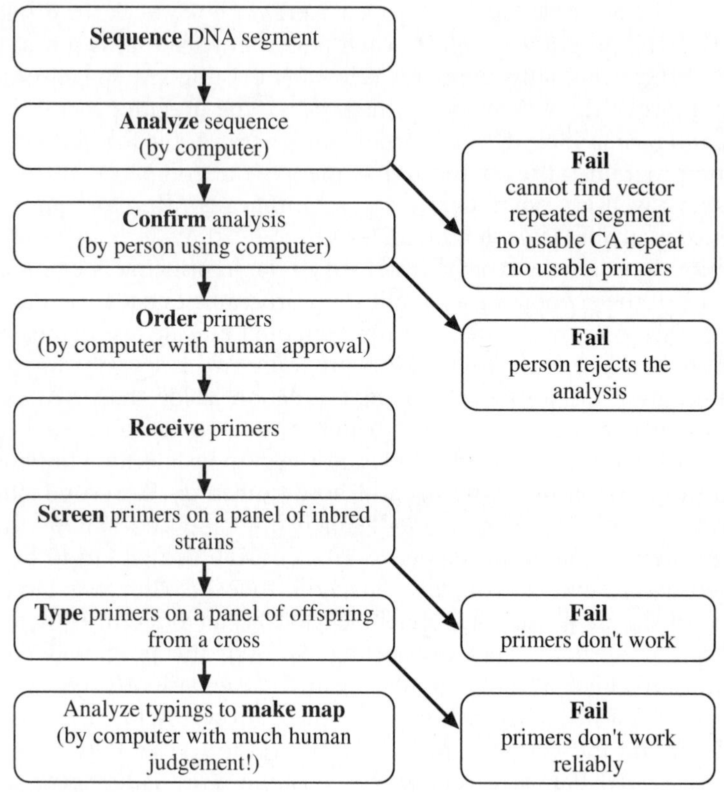

FIGURE 11–6
Idealized Workflow Model

base only if there is a compelling efficiency reason. Though this violates a basic premise of the object model, it is a more modular way to develop the complete system. As new needs arise, it is easier to modify an application program than to modify the schema. It is also easier to reuse programs in other contexts. For example, we can use the programs to analyze sequences obtained from outside sources without first storing the sequences in the database.

11.4.2 Workflow Model

As mentioned in section 11.2, there is a part of the schema, called the workflow module, that models the experimental steps involved in our mapping procedures. Figure 11–6 illustrates an early version of the model for the genetic mapping procedure. We originally modeled the genetic mapping process for a given DNA segment as a simple finite state machine. There is a

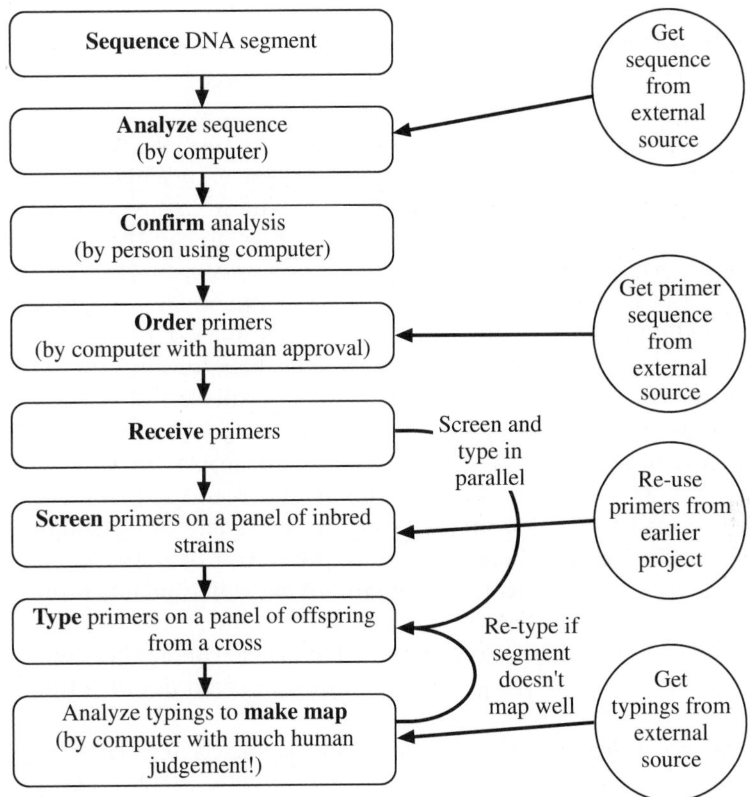

FIGURE 11–7
More Realistic Workflow Model

main line sequence of states that represents the normal experimental flow from one step to the next. States branching off the main line represent steps that failed in the laboratory. The database enforced the order dependencies implicit in the finite state machine diagram by rejecting updates for a later step until all earlier steps had been completed.

This model was implemented in an early release of the system and was a complete disaster. We came to realize that the workflow model in Fig. 11–6 was an idealized textbook version of the laboratory procedure. What really went on in the laboratory was quite different. People did not always do steps in the prescribed order and sometimes skipped steps entirely. Sometimes they would do the work but not enter the data for several days. People could discover a problem at almost any step and terminate the process or back up to an earlier step. Fig. 11–7 shows a more complex workflow model, including the most common alternate paths through the process.

At this point we were faced with two choices: Either make the model more complex by capturing all legal alternate paths or make it simpler by allowing all paths to be legal. The pressure of time forced us to choose the latter.

The simpler model contains two main classes: ProcessStep represents the completion of a basic laboratory step, and Process represents the execution of a sequence of steps for a given DNA segment; a Process object contains a list of ProcessStep objects. The model enforces no constraints on the order or multiplicity of steps—a Process object allows steps to be executed in any order and to be repeated any number of times. Each ProcessStep object is signed and dated—that is, the object records who performed the step and when it was completed. The Process object uses this information to reconstruct the history of the experiment. There is a subclass of ProcessStep for each kind of basic laboratory step. Each ProcessStep subclass stores data elements that chronicle the results of the step. For example, the subclass for "sequence DNA segment" has a data element that is the sequence of the segment. For each ProcessStep subclass, there is an update command in the MapBase textual interface language. To store the results of an experimental step in the database, an application program invokes the update command for its ProcessStep subclass. The update command creates the corresponding ProcessStep object and adds it to the correct Process. The application program is responsible for enforcing any constraints on the order or multiplicity of steps.

Process and ProcessStep are semantically weak classes. They record experimental results in an essentially flat structure with little knowledge of how results are linked together. The effect is to move the semantics of the workflow model from the database out to the applications. The resulting simpler model has been quite successful and is still in use.

In the early days of the project, we tried to create a semantically rich schema. We separated map strategy from map workflow, expecting the former to embody general concepts of our mapping scheme independent of the experimental protocol and the latter to define the details of specific protocols. It did not work out that way. Over time, the map strategy module has atrophied while the workflow module has ballooned. When we need to store a new kind of data in the database, it is a simple matter to add a new ProcessStep subclass or to add new data elements to an existing subclass. There are now about 35 ProcessStep subclasses. This semantically weak class hierarchy stores almost the entire database.

11.5 Conclusion

An object-oriented database schema is more than an object-oriented program coupled to a database. We have found that guidelines and design rules recommended for object-oriented programs do not always work for schemas. Our experience suggests that it is a bad idea to make the database too smart by implementing too many programs as part of the schema. Programs that are inside the schema are harder to modify because schema modifications often force a database reload. Such programs also tend to be less portable and less reusable because they are generally coded with DBMS requirements in mind. A typical database class is much simpler than a typical class in a general program; it is important to be able to define simple classes in a straightforward, uniform way. A schema and its database are a shared resource that must be accessible to many different programs written in different languages and running on different computers; it is not practical to insist that all database programs be written in a single language, no matter how good the language may be. It is important to have a mechanism for application programs to invoke database programs; we implemented a text-based command language for this purpose; remote procedure call (RPC) would be another good choice. It is also important to have a query language or something similar for ad hoc queries.

Current tools for building object-oriented databases are barely adequate. Until recently, the DBMS we are using lacked roll-forward recovery and tools for schema evolution. It provides an elegant query language and collection class library that proved unusable for our purposes. Performance is excellent if the database fits in a main memory cache and if care is taken to avoid concurrency control hot spots. We regularly evaluate other DBMS products and generally find that each product comes with its own multitude of serious ills. C++ has emerged as the de facto standard object data model, which is unfortunate because C++ is a poor database language. Some of the problems with C++ are conceptually trivial but pragmatically important; for example, it takes several lines of code to define a simple attribute of an object. Other problems, such as the lack of a garbage collector and limitations in the inheritance model, are more profound.

Despite these problems, we were able to use current techniques and tools to develop a successful object-oriented database and information system. The system is used routinely and plays an essential role in several large genome mapping projects at the Whitehead Institute/MIT Center for Genome Research. We remain convinced that object-oriented techniques are a good idea. We anxiously await the next generation of object-oriented database tools and techniques.

REFERENCES

Atkinson, M. P., et al. 1989. The Object Oriented Database System Manifesto. *First Deductive and Object Oriented Database Conference*, Kyoto, Japan.

Bernstein, P. A., Hadzollacos, V., et al. 1987. *Concurrency Control and Recovery in Database Systems*. Addison-Wesley, Reading, Mass.

Bloomer, J. 1991. *Power Programming with RPC*. O'Reilly & Associates, Sebastol, CA.

Cattell, R. G. G. 1991. *Object Data Management: Object-Oriented and Extended Relational Database Systems*. Addison-Wesley, Reading, Mass.

Copeland, N. G., Gilbert, D. J., et al. 1993. Genome Maps IV. *Science*, No. 262, 67–82.

Ellis, M. A., and Stroustrup, B. 1990. *The Annotated C++ Reference Manual*. Addison-Wesley, Reading, Mass.

Frenkel, K. A. 1991. The Human Genome Project and Informatics. *Communications of the ACM*, Vol. 34, No. 11, 40–51.

Goodman, N. 1991. The Object Database Debate. *InfoDB*, Vol. 5, 13–18.

Goodman, N., Reeve, M. P., et al. 1992. *The Design of MapBase: An Object Oriented Database for Genome Mapping*. Whitehead Institute for Biomedical Research, Cambridge, Mass.

Goodman, N., Rozen, S., et al. 1993. *Requirements for a Deductive Query Language in the MapBase Genome-Mapping Database*. Workshop on Programming with Logic Databases, Vancouver, B.C.; Computer Sciences Department, University of Wisconsin.

Kim, W. 1990. *Introduction to Object-Oriented Databases*. Massachusetts Institute of Technology, Cambridge, Mass.

Lamb, C., Landis, G., et al. 1991. The ObjectStore Database System. *Communications of the ACM*, Vol. 34, No. 10, 50–63.

Lander, E. S., Green, P., et al. 1987. MAPMAKER: An Interactive Computer Package for Constructing Genetic Linkage Maps of Experimental and Natural Populations. *Genomics*, Vol. 1, No. 2, 174–181.

Lander, E. S., Langridge, R., et al. 1991. Mapping and Interpreting Biological Information. *Communications of the ACM*, Vol. 34, No. 11, 32–39.

Lincoln, S. E., Daly, M. J., et al. 1991. *PRIMER: A Computer Program for Automatically Selecting PCR Primers*. Whitehead Institute for Biomedical Research, Cambridge, Mass.

Needleman, S. B., and Wunsch, C. 1970. A General Method Applicable to the Search for Similarities in the Amino Acid Sequences of Two Proteins. *Proceedings of the National Academy of Science*, Vol. 48, 444–453.

Office of Technology Assessment. 1988. Mapping Our Genes, The Genome Projects: How Big, How Fast. Office of Technology Assessment, Congress of the United States.

Olson, M. V., Hood, L., et al. 1989. A Common Language for Physical Mapping of the Human Genome. *Science*, Vol. 245, No. 4925, 1434–1445.

Pearson, W. R. and Lipman, D. J. 1988. Improved Tools for Biological Sequence Comparison. *Proceedings of the National Academy of Science*, Vol. 85, No. 8, 2444–2448.

Reeve, M. P., Kaufman, A., et al. 1993. A Contig Assembly Algorithm for Mapping the Human Genome. *Proceedings of the 1993 Conference on MacroMolecules, Genes, and Computers*, Waterville Valley, N.H.

Rumbaugh, J., Blaha, M., et al. 1991. *Object-Oriented Modeling and Design*. Prentice-Hall, Englewood Cliffs, N.J.

Stroustrup, B. 1986. *The C++ Programming Language*. Addison-Wesley, Reading, Mass.

Waterman, M. S. 1984. Efficient Sequence Alignment Algorithms. *Journal of Theoretical Biology*, Vol. 108, No. 3, 333–337.

Weber, J., and May, P. E. 1989. Abundant Class of Human DNA Polymorphisms Which Can Be Typed Using the Polymerase Chain Reaction. *American Journal of Human Genetics*, Vol. 44, No. 3, 388–396.

12

Where Object-Oriented DBMSs Should Do Better: A Critique Based on Early Experiences

ANGELIKA KOTZ-DITTRICH
KLAUS R. DITTRICH

Though still young on the market, object-oriented DBMSs have already attracted a lot of interest and raised many expectations on the customer side. In this chapter, we try to point out, based on early experiences, to what extent these expectations have been met so far. We focus on the major conceptual shortcomings that are still inherent in today's OODBMSs and suggest directions for improvement that should be followed in order to completely fulfill the promises of this technology.

12.1 Introduction

After several years of research and prototype development, object-oriented DBMS products have now been offered in the marketplace for some time. There are several approaches (and companies) that compete, standardization efforts have not led to tangible results yet, and of course—consider the short period of time since their emergence—available products are less mature today than their relational counterparts, which have had some 10 years more to reach their present state. Nevertheless, OODBMS vendors report success, the number of installed copies increases remarkably, and market prognoses look rather bright.

It is thus interesting to have a look at how OODBMSs have been doing in applications that used the new technology in a rather early stage. Unfortunately, users developing and running real applications in practice typically do not have the time or interest to prepare detailed written accounts of why and where their solutions failed or succeeded and to publish those in the open literature. Furthermore, most applications of OODBMSs are still in a rather experimental phase. The material we present here is therefore mainly based on personal observations (though not from large-scale real-life applications) and on input received from several professional applications; while most of it should extend to other applications as well, we do not claim that it is representative of all OODBMSs in use today.

We are less interested in enumerating in detail advantages of OODBMSs that have been sufficiently reiterated in vendor advertisements and the relevant literature [Bancilhon, Delobel, and Kanellakis 1992; Cattell 1991; Kim 1990] or shortcomings typically encountered due to the relative immaturity of systems (like suboptimal performance or functional restrictions due to implementation weaknesses or missing tools). Instead, we will point out some issues where (most of) today's OODBMSs fall short conceptually and where future systems or releases should improve in order to fulfill the promises of the technology and serve targeted applications better.

12.2 Framework of Discussion

OODBMS technology is still in a state of flux, and so it is difficult to pinpoint pros and cons of specific properties (as they may have changed in the next release of an existing system or in a new one), and it is likely that one would find counterexamples and diverging positions for each of the aspects we are going to treat. It is thus appropriate to clearly specify the framework of the subsequent discussion.

- It is difficult to make general statements. Systems are rather heterogeneous, and most experiences pertain to special features of one product or a class of products (that may be completely different in others). For example, statements made about a Smalltalk-based product may differ fundamentally from those about a product based on C++.
- The assessment of OODBMS features depends very much on the group of people one talks to. Programming language users would expect different features from DBMS users. Programming language users may consider features as useful or sufficient that are considered useless or insufficient by DBMS users and vice versa. Along the same line, some vendors consider OODBMSs with a rather narrow focus, assuming that their data model should have exactly the features that are known from object-oriented programming languages (though there are differences among them). Others take a broader view and include additional features or relax others [Atkinson et al. 1989].
- Our discussion relates largely to the so-called pure object-oriented DBMSs (i.e., C++-based OODBMSs) and not to systems that combine relational and object-oriented DBMSs.
- Many results of an OODBMS evaluation will depend on what the system is supposed to be used for: as a mere storage manager for objects produced by means of an object-oriented programming language, as a repository for various kinds of objects (from various sources), or as a full-fledged database manager with a powerful data model, providing all popular DBMS features [Bancilhon 1992]. Requirements and their fulfillment by a given product will be quite different for various cases.

- Likewise, requirements and thus product satisfaction will be different depending on the application area considered. Currently, OODBMSs are mainly used or experimented with in technical areas like CAD/CAM, CASE, network management, decision support, geographic information systems, and the like, but to a much lesser extent in more traditional business-oriented areas. We will thus primarily have requirements of the former in mind when looking at shortcomings of current systems.
- It shows that current OODBMSs already offer a number of advantages in that they allow representation of complex worlds of interest in a more straightforward way than relational systems. This includes the representation of additional semantics by means of object structures (based on object identity), inheritance structures, and user-defined classes including application-oriented operations (methods) which are often superior to generic data-structure-oriented operations.

  Further advantages that are generally claimed for object-oriented systems and should thus apply to OODBMSs as well, like the reuse of designs, will need more experience to be judged because a reasonable supply of classes has to be realized before anything can be reused. However, this is not a system issue (the needed concepts do exist) but an issue for making appropriate use of what is here.

  In this chapter, we will not further address those advantages (which is typically done in vendor presentations and publications) but highlight some of the weaker points instead. Note that this is not meant to indicate that OODBMSs show more negative than positive aspects.
- For some current shortcomings like meta data access, query languages, and the like, improvements can be foreseen with new product versions in the near future.

12.3 Areas for Future Improvement

In this section, we discuss several areas that should—according to our own and collected experience—be subject to further improvements as current solutions do not fulfill all application requirements. The syntax used in the examples is supposed to be self-explanatory for readers familiar with object-oriented programming languages and database systems; it is not taken from any system.

12.3.1 Query Language and Query Optimization

From the very beginning, OODBMSs were mainly targeted at technical applications for which navigational access is a central requirement. For example, it is typical for a VLSI designer to select a chip layout identified by

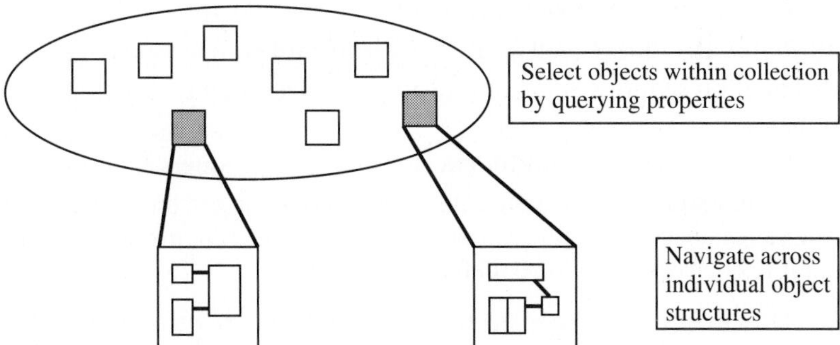

FIGURE 12–1
Set-Oriented and Navigational Access to Objects

some name or number and work on it for a long period of time, traversing and modifying the structures within this plan, and adding to them. The same is true for mechanical CAD, CASE, and the like. It is the strength of OODBMSs and one of their main goals to support this navigational access within large coherent data structures.

Because of these typical access features, the use of set-oriented queries on object databases has been neglected for a long time. Only slowly, the idea came up that a query language might be beneficial and even necessary for an OODBMS, especially—but not only—when used in nontechnical fields. The combination of associative access (find objects with certain properties in the database) and navigational access (to further investigate the objects found) is indispensable for future applications. Figure 12–1 illustrates both kinds of access. (Note that the set of objects symbolized by the oval may itself be part of an even more complex structure.)

The needs of early applications, however, have not been the only limiting factor for the development of a query language. The formalization and algebraic description of the object model (or of some object model) is far more difficult than, say, the relational algebra and has not yet been achieved in a commonly accepted form. Especially when it comes to the use of method calls in queries, the formalization is all but clear. As a consequence, the optimization of object-oriented queries is extremely hard to solve and is still in a research stage. There are, however, promising research results that may lead to a practically applicable methodology [Cluet and Delobel 1992; Graefe et al. 1992; Mitchell, Zdonik, and Dayal 1993; Pirahesh, Hellerstein, and Hasan 1992].

Today's OODBMSs offer restricted query facilities on object collections with rather simple optimization strategies (some products being more advanced than others). We still do not have an object query standard, though there are efforts to come up with an object SQL. Features offered by the majority of products today are:

- path expressions on object attributes
- attribute/attribute as well as attribute/constant comparisons
- exploitation of indexes for simple attribute access and path expressions
- arbitrary queries (without indexes) executed by sequential scan
- no optimization of joins (the interobject access via attributes that are not materialized by explicit object references can be considered equivalent to the relational join operation)

It is rather convenient to execute queries that suit the object structure — that is, exploit the reference paths between objects. However, queries that are formulated on object relationships not directly modeled by references are executed inefficiently. As an example, think of a document database with three classes `document`, `author` and `city`; and two sets collecting all the documents and all the cities.

```
class document (
      string name;
      person author;
      int no_of_lines, no_of_pages;
)

class person (
      string name;
      city home;
)

class city (
      string name;
)
set <document> all_documents;
set <city> all_cities;
```

It is common for today's OODBMSs to support and optimize simple queries like:

Select all documents with more than 1000 lines or more than 15 pages

```
set <document> long_documents =
       all_documents [no_of_lines > 1000 or no_of_pages > 15]
```

Select all documents with authors living in NY

```
set <document> NY_documents =
       all_documents [ author.home.name == "New York"]
```

However, when queries are formulated in the direction not supported by references (as from `city` via `author` to `document`), the system will do no special query optimization. The query will be processed by a sequential scan.

Select all cities with at least one document produced there

```
set <city> author_cities =
        all_cities [ all_documents [ author.home.name == name]
                != 0]
```

Select all cities where more documents are produced than in NY

```
set <city> more_than_NY_cities =
        all_cities [(all_documents [ author.home.name ==
                name]).size >
                (all_documents [ author.home.name ==
                        "New York"]).size]
```

12.3.2 Complex Objects

One of the central ideas in the early research on OODBMSs was to support *complex* objects (or *composite, structured, molecular* objects)—that is, potentially complex hierarchies or networks of objects related by "part_of" or similar relationships [Dittrich 1990; Kim, Bertino, and Garza 1989]. It was considered useful to differentiate between the cases where a subobject is an integral part of the containing object and when it is not. In the first case, operations like copy or delete would work on the whole complex object, including the subobjects; in the second case, this would not work. For many applications it is useful if the DBMS can handle truly complex objects like whole machine parts, program modules, chip layouts, and the like.

However, most existing OODBMS products do not support the full functionality of complex objects. As in programming languages, the relationship between objects is often supported by reference only. One can navigate across the reference and code one's own operations using it, but there are no predefined generic operations exploiting different reference semantics. Basically, all references are to independent objects, and the semantics of special relationships within complex objects are hidden within the user-supplied operations.

In the simple example of the document database above, this might be just the desired behavior. When deleting or copying a `document`, one will usually not want to delete the corresponding `author` and his or her home `city`. However, there are many cases where the objects referenced by an object should be treated as true subparts. Imagine an extension of the document database in which each `document` references its `chapters` and each `chapter` its `paragraphs`.

```
class document (
        ...
        set <chapter> chapters;
)
```

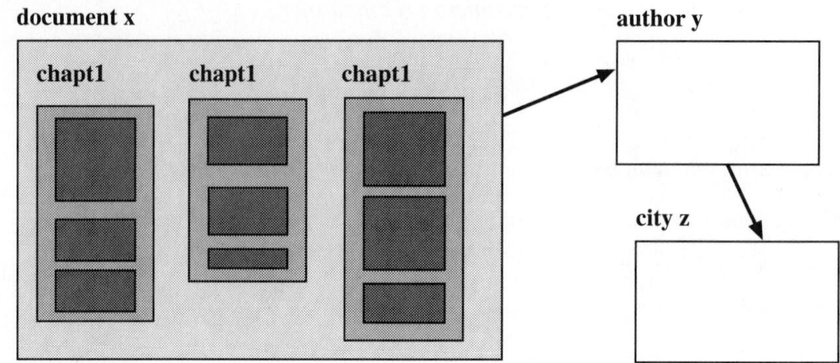

FIGURE 12–2
Example of a Complex Object

```
class chapter (
      set <paragraph> paragraphs;
)
class paragraph (
      ...
)
```

A document together with its hierarchy of chapters and paragraphs forms a typical complex object, while the author and his or her home city do not form part of it but are just referenced (see Fig. 12–2). It is not desirable that a chapter or paragraph object should exist in the database without a corresponding document—that is, when object of class document is deleted, all its parts have to be deleted, too. The semantics of copying a document is a deep copy, including all subparts. Also, application-specific operators like format or print should be applied recursively to all subparts. This is not supported by common OODBMS products, nor can users add this functionality in regularly defined classes later on (at least not in its entirety). The least that is needed are two or more different kinds of references (with and without operation propagation along them).

Some OODBMSs offer the feature of inverse relationships to express the fact that there exists a mutual reference between two objects (i.e., a binary relationship). The system will automatically ensure referential integrity by, for example, establishing the corresponding reference as soon as a reference is created. It is even possible to automatically propagate deletion via these references. However, other operations cannot exploit the difference between normal and inverse relationships.

Figure 12–3 shows a possible scenario where the attributes used_by and uses of a part object are modeled by an inverse relationship. We suppose that the uses reference is handled manually, while the system manages the inverse reference used_by automatically. The opposite or a mixed way to proceed would also be possible. As an option, the deletion of part1 may

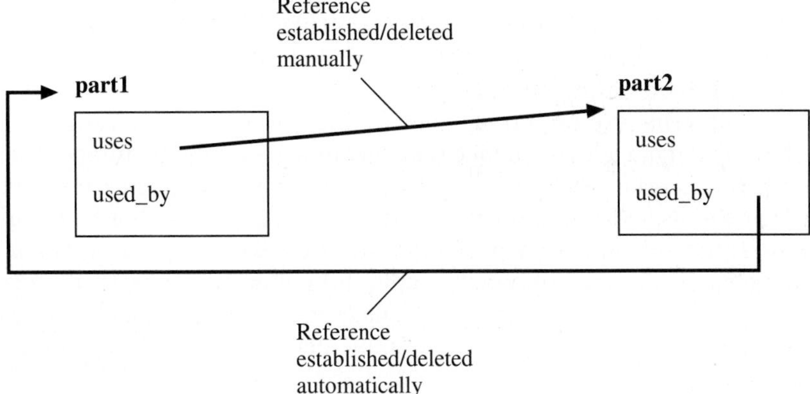

FIGURE 12–3
Example of an Inverse Relationship

induce the deletion of part2. However, a copy operation on part1 will not copy part2 but only the reference to this object (unless the user explicitly programs a deep copy operation).

```
class part (
      set <part> uses inverse used_by;
      set <part> used_by inverse uses;
)
```

Some systems make a distinction between values and objects. A value can be used as part of a complex object, but it lacks the properties of an object in its own right (it has no identity, it cannot be shared, etc.). Therefore, values are not suited to achieve the same functionality as with complex objects built from other real objects.

12.3.3 Openness of Language

Most existing OODBMS products are closely tied to a specific programming language, in particular, C++, Smalltalk, and Lisp. The programming language is either used directly at the DBMS interface, or it has been modified and/or extended to yield a specialized DBMS language.

This is convenient for programmers of the corresponding language who are just interested in a persistent store for their program objects. However, when several application languages are to be used with the same DBMS, the closed nature of the language is clearly a drawback. This means that when changing one's programming language, one has also to change the OODBMS. If one is not prepared to do this, one will have to put up with awkward interfaces (it is usually possible to interface, but typically many nice features are lost). As a consequence, the choice of a programming language may depend not on the application needs but on the OODBMS already installed. The DBMS no longer acts as an independent data repository (which is the successful philosophy of RDBMS and will most likely be crucial for any subsequent technology, too) but very much as part of the application programming system.

There seems to be no agreement among OODBMS vendors on whether the language dependency is an advantage or a disadvantage. There is certainly a market for products that are specialized and therefore optimized for the use with one specific programming language. For some programmers, this may be just what they want. However, when true database functionality is needed for which application independence is a central requirement, systems with formal, language-independent models are necessary. These should allow for method implementation in various programming languages.

12.3.4 Methods Stored in Database

Most OODBMSs (mainly those based on C++) only store the structure of objects—that is, the attributes or data members—in the database. The corresponding methods are not treated by the DBMSs and are stored in regular files (i.e., source files created by the user, object and executable files created by compiler and linker, respectively) outside the database. Methods have to be linked conventionally to the application program. Again, for a number of applications this may be sufficient, but it requires additional organizational mechanisms. The user has to ensure that all programs link in the correct methods corresponding to the current schema. Consistency and security issues arise that might otherwise have been handled by the DBMS. Data management facilities like recovery, versioning, and querying are not applicable for methods. The original idea of the OODBMS as a central repository of abstract data types has not been fulfilled.

In a system that allows the storage of methods, it is sufficient for a user to just open a database. No additional linking of the application programs is necessary. This also has an advantage related to the openness of the language. It is irrelevant for the application program in which language the stored methods are written because only a formalized method call is passed to the DBMS. The different principles of the two approaches are contrasted in Fig. 12–4.

12.3.5 Meta Data Access

A number of current OODBMSs (again, mainly those based on C++) do not treat meta data as full-fledged objects. By meta data, we mean the definition of classes, attributes, and methods (as we just saw, the methods may not even be part of the database). As a consequence, the user cannot query the properties of classes as he or she can query normal objects or apply other DBMS functions to them.

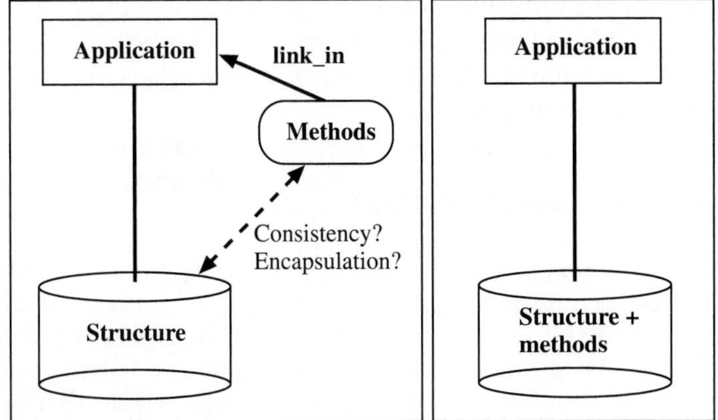

FIGURE 12–4
Methods Outside Versus Methods Inside the Database

To extend our former example to meta data access, we assume that the DBMS automatically maintains the meta classes class and attribute.

```
class class (
      string name;
      int no_of_attributes;
      set <attribute> attributes;
)
class attribute (
      string name;
      bool set_valued;
      class attr_type;
)
set <class> all_classes;
```

If this kind of meta data was made available for querying, the user could retrieve information like:
Select all classes with more than 10 attributes

```
set <class> big_classes =
        all_classes [no_of_attributes > 10]
```

Select all classes where at least one attribute type is a set of objects of class "person"

```
set <class> person_ref_classes =
        all_classes [ attributes [set_valued == TRUE and
             attr_type.name == "person"] != 0]
```

Meta data management is a feature OODBMS vendors are striving to improve. New product versions will provide better support for meta data access, which is useful for end users as well as for third-party vendors who need this feature to provide tools on top of the DBMS. The problem of meta data management is most difficult to solve in OODBMSs based on C++, as this programming language does not treat classes as regular objects. Therefore, vendors have to provide workarounds for meta data access that do not fit neatly into the programming interface.

12.3.6 Dynamic Class Definition

Closely related to the problem of meta data access is the issue of dynamic class definition and modification. OODBMSs in the C++ context usually require that all classes be known at compile time. If the user wants to add, modify, or delete any classes, he or she has to recompile the schema statically (as far as schema modification is supported at all). While dynamic class definition is a feature of low necessity for many applications, there are others for which this additional flexibility would be helpful, especially to build higher-level interfaces on top of OODBMSs. In the example from section 12.2.5, this would require operations like

- create new objects of class class and attribute
- modify attributes like no_of_attribute, attr_type, or name
- delete objects of class class and attribute

12.3.7 Consistency Constraints

The idea of doing all consistency checking within the methods has been rather popular in the field of OODBMSs. It is true that the possibility of defining methods offers computational completeness for user-defined consistency checks. However, this has led to the fact that OODBMSs do not offer additional declarative mechanisms for consistency rules. In most systems, only implicit constraints specific to the data model are supported (like type constraints on attributes). There are no mechanisms to declare

- key properties of attributes or uniqueness constraints
- explicit consistency constraints (invariants)
- pre- and postconditions of methods
- triggers or similar active elements

As pointed out above, this could all be expressed in methods. However, as is always the case with declarative versus procedural features, explicit consistency constraints would be more user friendly, less error prone, more easily accessible for inspection and modification, and so on. For example, it is rather inconvenient that an attribute of a class cannot be declared the primary key of the class (this also has to do with the fact that many OODBMSs do not manage class extensions; see below). In some systems, uniqueness constraints may be expressed when creating indexes—that is, on the physical instead of the logical schema level.

In our document database, a simple example of what might be expressed by consistency constraints but cannot be done in today's OODBMSs is:

```
class document (
      string name;
      person author;
      int no_of_lines, no_of_pages;
      set <chapter> chapters;

      key name;
      author not null;
      no_of_lines >= no_of_pages;
)
```

Furthermore, consistency constraints may exist that extend beyond just one object or class; they are again only inconveniently dealt with in the absence of facilities for explicit declarative constraint handling.

12.3.8 Management of Class Extensions

In an RDBMS, it is rather straightforward to keep all data in the form of extensions of the defined relations. It is far less straightforward how to manage extensional data in OODBMSs. The extension of each class consists of all its instances. While there are applications—for example, in the technical field—where the user is not interested in this complete set of instances, other applications require frequent access to class extensions.

Many existing OODBMSs do not offer automatic management of class extensions. The user may define arbitrary object collections that can be queried, iterated upon, and so on. If a class extension is needed, the user has to define a collection for it and keep it up to date on insertion and deletion.

When class extensions are of frequent interest (e.g., the extension of all accounts, all cities, all customers, etc.), this is rather awkward. It would therefore be desirable for OODBMSs to offer at least the option of automatic extension management. According to the application needs, the user should be able to decide for each class whether to store the extension or not. Few products offer this feature so far.

12.3.9 View Mechanism

Existing OODBMSs do not provide view mechanisms like those found in relational DBMS. There are several reasons behind this:

- There has been the opinion that data encapsulation and inheritance make explicit view definitions unnecessary.
- Views in relational DBMSs are treated like predefined queries. As OODBMSs do not provide elaborate query languages, there is no powerful declarative language to define views.
- Views in relational DBMSs can be considered as a means of access control. For a long time, access control has been of low interest to the OODBMS vendors, due to the typical CA* applications where rather coarse security mechanisms were considered sufficient.
- The treatment of views is a problem of considerable complexity in the context of method invocation and inheritance.

However, at least to use OODBMSs in nontechnical areas, a view mechanism would be helpful if not an important requirement. In connection with a more comprehensive access control mechanism (see below), it could help to make OODBMSs more popular in security-critical areas (in our document class, it might for example be desirable to create a view on class document leaving out the author attribute, in case some users are not allowed to access or not interested in seeing this information). In the research area, the problem of views in OODBMSs has already been studied; see, for example, [Scholl, Schek, and Tresch 1992 and Bertino 1992].

12.3.10 Integration with Existing OO Programming Systems

Some vendors claim that it is easy to rewrite object-oriented programs to make use of their OODBMS for persistent data management. This is usually true only for simple applications. When porting larger systems, many problems may arise, such as

- naming conflicts
- rewriting of class hierarchies (especially in OODBMSs with persistence by inheritance[1])
- references between persistent and temporary objects
- overwriting of system operations (OODBMSs tend to overwrite system operations and rely on the applications never to do the same—which is certainly not realistic. For example, both the application system and the OODBMS may redefine the basic operators `new` and `delete` to

1. Persistence by inheritance requires each class with persistent objects to be derived from a special superclass. Therefore, persistence by inheritance requires restructuring of the class hierarchy. In contrast, persistence by allocation (by storage class) allows one to create persistent objects of arbitrary classes.

introduce their own special form of memory management. Conflicts like that are rather hard to eliminate.)

Hence, it is nontrivial to rewrite large application systems to work with present OODBMSs. Primarily, OODBMS vendors should give more support for the smooth integration of name spaces and should not rely on applications restraining from the modification of system operations. The relationship of temporary and persistent object space is also an area for improvement.

12.3.11 Interoperability with Non-OODBMSs

Future industrial scenarios will certainly see a variety of heterogeneous DBMSs. Relational DBMSs and even CODASYL DBMSs will stay with us for a long time, with OODBMSs coming into play for appropriate new applications. The success of OODBMSs will depend—among others—on the ability to interact with the other DBMSs. In current OODBMS products, we do not see much support for cooperation in heterogeneous environments. Interoperability with relational systems is of especially great importance and might be supported in various forms:

- Provide an SQL interface by means of methods of the OODBMS to directly access relational data (either these data may be materialized and encapsulated in objects or the access may be passed through to a relational DBMS).
- Load objects from relations via some sort of gateway.
- Execute distributed transactions on OODBSs and RDBSs.
- Develop a federated database system that may adopt a data model that is a superset of the relational and object-oriented models.

It is up to both relational and object-oriented vendors to develop suitable mechanisms for interoperability.

12.3.12 Access Control

In technical applications OODBMSs have mainly targeted, authorization and access control were considered to be rather minor issues. This is why corresponding mechanisms in OODBMSs are not adequate today. Most of them are based on file or segment level, and the user cannot grant rights on individual objects or classes. If OODBMSs are going to expand into more business-oriented fields (banks, insurance applications, etc.), this is a feature to be improved. Objects lend themselves easily as units of access control, and there exist a number of research results on this issue [Brueggemann 1991; Rabitti, et al. 1991]. Therefore, it may be possible for OODBMS vendors to provide system solutions.

12.4 Other Arguments That are Decisive for OODBMS Use in Industry

The list of issues discussed in the previous section has comprised technical features of OODBMSs. Not surprisingly, to users concerned with professional applications, a number of rather different aspects matter as well and are often even more important than the technical excellence of a system:

- reliability of vendors (which of the current products will still be supported five years from now?)
- existence of reference installations
- (non)existence of standards (users are reluctant to tie themselves to a special model)
- interoperability with relational (and CODASYL) DBMSs
- success of object-oriented technology in other fields (programming, design, etc.)
- support for designing object-oriented databases (rather little work has been done in this area so far)
- availability on various platforms
- after-sales customer support

Good solutions to these problems seem to be as (or even more!) important for the success of systems (and of OODBMS technology as a whole) than improvements in most technical questions. However, this should not be taken as an excuse for not doing better with respect to the issues discussed in this chapter.

12.5 Summary

Though OODBMSs meet a number of special requirements and are thus already well received in niche markets, they do not provide all the important features their targeted application areas would like to use or that are even commonly expected of this class of systems. Interestingly, most concepts and fundamental implementation techniques needed for further improvements have been extensively researched and tested in (partly even early) academic and industrial prototypes [Cardenas and McLeod 1990; Dittrich 1988; Dittrich, Dayal, and Buchmann 1991; Zdonik and Maier 1990].

It is thus up to the next wave of systems to make OODBMS technology more appealing, and current work on standardization should also reflect the issues discussed in this chapter.

ACKNOWLEDGMENTS

We would like to thank the users of OODBMS technology who shared their insights with us, especially the contributors to the workshop "Object-Oriented Database Systems at Work" held in Zurich in October 1992, and A. Duppenthaler and his team at Byron Informatik, Basel.

REFERENCES

Atkinson, M., et al. 1989. The Object-Oriented Database System Manifesto. *Proceedings of the International Symposium on Deductive and Object-Oriented Databases '89*, Elsevier (reprinted in Bancilhon, Delobel, and Kanellakis, 1992).

Bancilhon, F. 1992. Object-Oriented Database Systems: The Market and the Applications. Presentation at the SI-DBTA Workshop "Object-Oriented Database Systems at Work," Zurich, October 1992.

Bancilhon, F., Delobel, C., and Kanellakis, P., eds. 1992. *Building an Object-Oriented Database System—The Story of O_2*. Morgan Kaufmann, Los Altos, Calif.

Bertino, E. 1992. A View Mechanism for Object-Oriented Databases. *Proceedings of the International Conference on Extending Data Base Technology '92*, Springer.

Brueggemann, H. H. 1991. Rights in an Object-Oriented Environment. *Proceedings of the IFIP WG 11.3 Conference on Database Security*, Shepherdstown.

Cardenas, A. F., and McLeod, D. 1990. *Research Foundations in Object-Oriented and Semantic Database Systems*. Prentice Hall, Englewood Cliffs, N.J.

Cattell, R. G. G. 1991. *Object Data Management—Object-Oriented and Extended Relational Database Systems*. Addison-Wesley, Reading, Mass.

Cluet, S., and Delobel, C. 1992. A General Framework for the Optimization of Object-Oriented Queries. *Proceedings of the ACM-SIGMOD International Conference*.

Dittrich, K. R., Dayal, U., and Buchmann, A.P., eds. 1991. *On Object-Oriented Database Systems*. Springer-Verlag, Berlin.

Dittrich, K. R., ed. 1988. Advances in Object-Oriented Database Systems. *Lecture Notes in Computer Science* 334, Springer-Verlag, Berlin.

Dittrich, K. R. 1990. Object-Oriented Database Systems: The Next Miles of the Marathon. *Information Sytems*, Vol. 15, No. 1, 161–167.

Graefe, G., et al. 1992. Extensible Query Optimization and Parallel Execution in Volcano. In: *Query Processing for Advanced Database Applications*. J. C. Freytag, G. Vossen, D. Maier, eds. Morgan-Kaufmann, Los Altos, Calif.

Kim, W., Bertino, E., and Garza, J. 1989. Composite Object Revisited. *Proceedings of the ACM-SIGMOD International Conference*.

Kim, W. 1990. *Introduction to Object-Oriented Databases*. MIT Press, Cambridge, Mass.

Mitchell, G., Zdonik, S.B., and Dayal, U. 1993. An Architecture for Query Processing in Persistent Object Stores. *Proceedings of the Hawaii Conference on Systems Sciences*.

Pirahesh, H., Hellerstein, J. M., and Hasan, W. 1992. Extensible Rule-Based Query Rewrite Optimization in Starburst. *Proceedings of the ACM-SIGMOD International Conference.*

Rabitti, F., Bertino, E., Kim, W., and Woelk, D. 1991. A Model of Authorization for Next-Generation Database Systems. *ACM Trans. on Database Systems,* Vol. 16, No. 1, 88-131.

Scholl, M. H., Schek, H.-J., and Tresch, M. 1992. Object Algebra and Views for Multi-Objectbases. *Proceedings of the International Workshop on Distributed Object Management.* Morgan Kaufmann, Edmonton, Alberta.

Zdonik, S. B., and Maier, D., eds. 1990. *Readings in Object-Oriented Database Systems.* Morgan Kaufmann, Los Altos, Calif.

13

Object-Oriented Database Systems: Promises, Reality, and Future

WON KIM

During the past decade, object-oriented technology has found its way into programming languages, user interfaces, databases, operating systems, expert systems, and the like. Products labeled as object-oriented database systems have been in the market for several years, and vendors of relational database systems are now declaring that they will extend their products with object-oriented capabilities. A few vendors are now offering database systems that combine relational and object-oriented capabilities in one database system. Despite these activities, there are still many myths and much confusion about object-oriented database systems, relational systems extended with object-oriented capabilities, and even the necessities of such systems among users, trade journals, and even vendors. The objective of this chapter is to review the promises of object-oriented database systems and examine the reality and how their promises may be fulfilled through unification with the relational technology.

13.1 Definitions

Object-oriented technologies in use today include object-oriented programming languages (e.g., C++ and Smalltalk), object-oriented database systems, object-oriented user interfaces (e.g., Macintosh and Microsoft Windows systems, Frame and Interleaf desktop publishing systems), and so on. An object-oriented technology is a technology that makes available to the users facilities that are based on object-oriented concepts. To define *object-oriented concepts,* we must first understand what an *object* is.

The term *object* means a combination of *data* and *program* that represents some real-world entity. For example, consider an employee named Tom; Tom is 25 years old, and his salary is $25,000. Then Tom may be represented in a computer program as an object. The data part of this object would be (`name: Tom, age: 25, salary: $25,000`). The program part

Reprinted with permission from Proc. of the International Conference on Very Large Databases, August 1993, Dublin, Ireland.

of the object may be a collection of programs (hire, retrieve the data, change age, change salary, fire). The data part consists of data of any type. For the "Tom" object, string is used for the name, integer for age, and monetary for salary; but in general, even any user-defined type, such as Employee, may be used. In the "Tom" object, the name, age, and salary are called *attributes* of the object.

Often, an object is said to *encapsulate* data and program. This means that the users cannot see the inside of the object capsule but can use the object by calling the program part of the object. This is not much different from procedure calls in conventional programming; the users call a procedure by supplying values for input parameters and receive results in output parameters.

The term *object-oriented* roughly means a combination of object encapsulation and inheritance. The term *inheritance* is sometimes called *reuse.* Inheritance means roughly that a new object may be created by extending an existing object. Now let us understand the term *inheritance* more precisely. An object has a data part and a program part. All objects that have the same attributes for the data part and same program part are collectively called a *class* (or *type*). The classes are arranged such that some class may inherit the attributes and program part from some other classes.

Tom, Dick, and Harry are each an Employee object. The data part of each of these objects consists of the attributes Name, Age, and Salary. Each of these Employee objects has the same program part (hire, retrieve the data, change age, change salary, fire). Each program in the program part is called a *method.* The term *class* refers to the collection of all objects that have the same attributes and methods. In our example, the Tom, Dick, and Harry objects belong to the class Employee since they all have the same attributes and methods. This class may be used as the type of an attribute of any object. At this time, there is only one class in the system —namely, the class Employee; and three objects that belong to the class— namely, Tom, Dick, and Harry objects.

Now suppose that a user wishes to create two sales employees, John and Paul. But sales employees have an additional attribute—namely, Commission. The sales employees cannot belong to the class Employee. However, the user can create a new class, Sales_Employee, such that all attributes and methods associated with the class Employee may be reused and the attribute Commission may be added to Sales_Employee. The user does this by declaring the class Sales_Employee to be a subclass of the class Employee. The user can now proceed to create the two sales employees as objects belonging to the class SalesEmployee. The users can create new classes as subclasses of existing classes. In general, a class may inherit from one or more existing classes, and the inheritance structure of classes becomes a directed acyclic graph (DAG); but for simplicity, the inheritance structure is called an *inheritance hierarchy* or *class hierarchy.*

The power of object-oriented concepts is delivered when encapsulation and inheritance work together.

- Since inheritance makes it possible for different classes to share the same set of attributes and methods, the same program can be run against objects that belong to different classes. This is the basis of the object-oriented user interface that desktop publishing systems and windows management systems provide today. The same set of programs (e.g., `open`, `close`, `drop`, `create`, `move`, etc.) apply to different types of data (image, text file, audio, directory, etc.).
- If the users define many classes, and each class has many attributes and methods, the benefit of sharing not only the attributes but also the programs can be dramatic. The attributes and programs need not be defined and written from scratch. New classes can be created by adding attributes and methods to existing classes, rather than by modifying the attributes and methods of existing classes, thereby reducing the opportunity to introduce new errors to existing classes.

13.2 Promises of OODBs

An object-oriented programming language (OOPL) provides facilities to create classes for organizing objects, to create objects, to structure an inheritance hierarchy to organize classes so that subclasses may inherit attributes and methods from superclasses, and to call methods to access specific objects. Similarly, an object-oriented database system (OODB) should provide facilities to create classes for organizing objects, to create objects, to structure an inheritance hierarchy to organize classes so that subclasses may inherit attributes and methods from superclasses, and to call methods to access specific objects. Beyond these, an OODB, because it is a database system, must provide standard database facilities found in today's relational database systems (RDBs), including nonprocedural query facility for retrieving objects, automatic query optimization and processing, dynamic schema changes (changing the class definitions and inheritance structure), automatic management of access methods (e.g., B+-tree index, extensible hashing, sorting, etc.) to improve query processing performance, automatic transaction management, concurrency control, recovery from system crashes, and security and authorization. Programming languages, including OOPLs, are designed with one user and a relatively small database in mind. Database systems are designed with many users and very large databases in mind; hence performance, security and authorization, concurrency control, and dynamic schema changes become important issues. Further, database systems are used to maintain critical data accurately; hence, transaction management, concurrency control, and recovery are important facilities.

Insofar as a database system is a system software whose functions are called from application programs written in some host programming languages, we may distinguish two different approaches to designing an OODB. One is to store and manage objects created by programs written in an OOPL. Some of the current OODBs are designed to store and manage objects generated in C++ or Smalltalk programs. Of course, an RDB can be used to store and manage such objects. However, RDBs do not understand objects—in particular, methods and inheritance. Therefore, what may be called an *object manager* or an *object-oriented layer* software needs to be written to manage methods and inheritance and to translate objects to tuples (rows) of a relation (table). But the object manager and RDB combined are in effect an OODB (with poor performance, of course)!

Another approach is to make object-oriented facilities available to users of non-OOPLs. The users may create classes, objects, inheritance hierarchy, and so on, and the database system will store and manage those objects and classes. This approach in effect turns non-OOPLs (e.g., C, FORTRAN, COBOL, etc.) into object-oriented languages. In fact, C++ has turned C into an OOPL, and CLOS has added object-oriented programming facilities to CommonLISP. An OODB designed using this approach can of course be used to store and manage objects created by programs written in an OOPL. Although a translation layer would need to be written to map the OOPL objects to objects of the database system, the layer should be much less complicated than the object manager layer that an RDB would require.

In view of the fact that C++, despite its growing popularity, is not the only programming language that database application programmers are using or will ever use, and there is a significant gulf between a programming language and a database system, the second approach is a more practical basis of a database system that will deliver the power of object-oriented concepts to database application programmers. Regardless of the approach, OODBs, if done right, can bring about a quantum jump in the productivity of database application programmers and even in the performance of the application programs.

One source of the technological quantum jump is the reuse of a database design and program that object-oriented concepts make possible for the first time in the evolving history of database technologies. Object-oriented concepts are fundamentally designed to reduce the difficulty of developing and evolving complex software systems or designs. Encapsulation and inheritance allow attributes (i.e., database design) and programs to be reused as the basis for building complex databases and programs. This is precisely the goal that has driven the data management technology from file systems to relational database systems during the past three decades. An OODB has the potential to satisfy the objective of reducing the difficulty of designing and evolving very large and complex databases.

Another source of the technological jump is the powerful data type facilities implicit in the object-oriented concepts of encapsulation and inheritance. The data type facilities in fact are the keys to eliminating three of the important deficiencies of RDBs. These are summarized below. I will discuss these points in greater detail later.

- RDBs force the users to represent hierarchical data (or complex nested data or compound data) such as bill of materials in terms of tuples in multiple relations. This is awkward to start with. Further, to retrieve data thus spread out in multiple relations, RDBs must resort to joins, a generally expensive operation. The data type of an attribute of an object in OOPLs may be a primitive type or an arbitrary user-defined type (class). The fact that an object may have an attribute whose value may be another object naturally leads to nested object representation, which in turn allows hierarchical data to be naturally (i.e., hierarchically) represented.
- RDBs offer a set of primitive built-in data types for use as domains of columns of relations, but they do not offer any means of adding user-defined data types. The built-in data types are basically all numbers and short symbols. RDBs are not designed to allow new data types to be added and therefore often require major surgery to the system architecture and code to add any new data type. Adding a new data type to a database system means allowing its use as the data type of an attribute—that is, storage of data of that type, querying, and updating of such data. Object encapsulation in OOPLs does not impose any restriction on the types of data that the data part of an object may hold—that is, the types of data may be primitive types or user-defined types. Further, new data types may be created as new classes, possibly even as subclasses of existing classes, inheriting their attributes and methods.
- Object encapsulation is the basis for the storage and management of programs as well as data in the database. RDBs now support *stored procedures*—that is, they allow programs to be written in some procedural language and stored in the database for later loading and execution. However, the stored procedures in RDBs are not encapsulated with data—that is, they are not associated with any relation or any tuple of a relation. Further, since RDBs do not have the inheritance mechanism, the stored procedures cannot automatically be reused.

13.3 Reality of OODBs

There is a number of commercial OODBs. These include GemStone from Servio Corporation; ONTOS from ONTOS; ObjectStore from Object Design, Inc.; Objectivity/DB from Objectivity, Inc.; Versant from Versant Object Technology, Inc.; Matisse from Intellitic International (France); Itasca (commercial version of MCC's ORION prototype) from Itasca Systems, Inc.; O_2 from O_2 Technology (France). These products all support an object-oriented data model. Specifically, they allow the user to create a new class with attributes and methods, have the class inherit attributes and methods from superclasses, create instances of the class each with a unique object identifier, retrieve the instances either individually or collectively, and load and run methods.

These products have been in the market since as early as 1987. However, most of them have been in evaluation and preliminary prototype application development—that is, they have not been seriously used for many mission-critical applications. Further, a fairly large number of copies of the products have been given away for free trial, artificially boosting the total count of product installations. The worldwide market size for all the current OODBs combined is estimated to be $20–30 million—a tiny fraction of the $3 billion worldwide market size for all database products. To be sure, the past several years have been a gestation period for object-oriented technology in general and object-oriented database technology in particular. Further, the technical market and OOPL market the current OODBs have targeted are new markets that have not been previously relied on database systems. However, the lack of maturity of the initial (and to a good extent, the current) OODB offerings has also contributed significantly to their slow acceptance in mission-critical applications.

13.3.1 Limitations

Limitations as Persistent Storage Systems

One key objective and, therefore, selling point of most of the current OODBs is the support of a unified programming and database language—that is, one language (e.g., C++ or Smalltalk) in which to do both general-purpose programming and database management. This objective was the result of the current situation in which application programs are written in a combination of a general-purpose programming language (mostly, COBOL, FORTRAN, PL/I, or C), and database management functions are embedded within the application programs in a database language (e.g., the SQL relational database language). A general-purpose programming language and a database language are very different in syntax and data model (data structures and data types), and the necessity of having to learn and use two very different languages to write database application programs has been frequently regarded as a major nuisance. Since C++ and Smalltalk already include facilities for defining classes and a class hierarchy (i.e., for data definition), in effect these languages are a good basis for a unified programming and database language. The first step that most of the vendors of the early OODBs took was to make the classes and instances of the classes persistent—that is, to store them on secondary storage and make them accessible even after the programs that defined and created them were terminated.

Current OODBs that are designed to support OOPLs place various restrictions on the definition and use of objects. In particular, most systems treat persistent data differently from nonpersistent data (e.g., they make it illegal for a persistent object to contain the OID of a nonpersistent object) and therefore require the users to explicitly declare whether an object is persistent or not. Further, they cannot make certain types of data persistent and therefore prohibit their use.

Limitations as Database Systems

The second, much more severe, source of immaturity of most of the current OODBs products is the lack of basic features that users of database systems have become accustomed to and therefore expect. The features include a full nonprocedural query language (along with automatic query optimization and processing), views, authorization, dynamic schema changes, and parameterized performance tuning. Besides these basic features, RDBs offer support for triggers, meta data management, and constraints such as UNIQUE and NULL—features that most OODBs do not support.

- Most of the OODBs suffer from the lack of query facilities; in those few systems that do provide significant query facilities, the query language is not ANSI SQL-compatible. Typically, the query facilities do not include nested subqueries, set queries (union, intersection, difference), aggregation functions and group by, and even joins of multiple classes, and so on—facilities fully supported in RDBs. In other words, these products allow the users to create a flexible database schema and populate the database with many instances, but they do not provide a powerful enough means of retrieving objects from the database.
- RDBs support views as dynamic windows into the stored database. The view definition includes a query statement to specify the data that will be fetched to constitute the view. A view is used as a unit of authorization. No OODB today supports views.
- RDBs support authorization—that is, they allow the users to grant and revoke privileges to read or change the tuples in the tables or views they created to other users, or to change the definition of the relations they created to other users. Most OODBs do not support authorization.
- RDBs allow the users to dynamically change the database schema using the ALTER command; a new column may be added to a relation, a relation may be dropped, and a column can sometimes be dropped from a relation. However, most of the current OODBs do not allow dynamic changes to the database schema, such as adding a new attribute or method to a class, adding a new superclass to a class, dropping a superclass from a class, adding a new class, and dropping a class.

- RDBs automatically set and release locks in processing query and update statements the users issue. However, some of the current OODBs require the users to explicitly set and release locks.
- RDBs allow the installation to tune system performance by providing a large number of parameters that can be set by the system administrator. The parameters include the number of memory buffers, the amount of free space reserved per data page for future insertions of data, and so forth. Most of the OODBs offer a limited capability for parameterized performance tuning.

Because of the deficiencies outlined above, most of these products will require major enhancements. It is safe to assume that the vendors of these products will make the required changes to their current software rather than rewriting the products from scratch. The extent of the changes that will be required to bring these products to full-fledged database systems that can at least match the level of database functionality expected of today's database systems is so great that it is not expected that the enhanced products will attain the robustness and performance required for mission-critical applications within the next three or four years.

Upgrading most of the current OODBs to true database systems poses not only major technical difficulties as outlined above but also a serious philosophical difficulty. As we have seen already, most of the current OODBs are closer to being merely persistent storage systems for some OOPL than database systems. The term OODB was not deliberately designed to be misleading and confusing since the OODBs were designed to manage a database of objects generated by programs written in OOPLs. However, the database users have been trained during the past two decades to think of a database system as software that allows a large database to be queried to retrieve a small portion of it, that does not require any hint from the user about how to process any given query, that allows a large number of users to simultaneously read and update the same database, that automatically enforces database integrity in the presence of multiple concurrent users and system failures, that allows the creator of a portion of a database to grant and revoke access privileges to his or her data to other users, that allows the installation to tune the performance of a database system by adjusting various system parameters, and so forth. For this reason, the term *OODB* has become a misnomer for most of the current OODBs.

Most of the current OODBs have essentially extended the OOPLs with a run-time library of database functions. These functions must be called from the application programs, with appropriate specifications of the input and output parameters. The syntax of the calling functions is made consistent with the application programming language. As the current OODBs are upgraded to true database systems, a major extension to the current library of database functions will be necessitated to support query facilities. Today's programming languages, including object-oriented languages, simply are not designed with database queries in mind. A database query may return an indeterminate number of records or objects that satisfy user-specified search conditions. Therefore, the application program must be designed to step through the entire set of records or objects that are turned until there is no more left. This is what led to the introduction of the cursor mechanism in database systems. The result of a database query must therefore be assigned to some data structure and accompanying algorithm that can store and step through an indefinite number of objects. Further, there will arise the need to provide facilities to specify nested subqueries, postprocessing on the result of a query (corresponding to GROUP BY, aggregation functions, correlation queries, etc.), and set queries (union, intersection, difference). In the name of a unified programming and database language, presumably, all these facilities will be made available to the programmers in a syntax that is consistent with the programming languages. In other words, the unified language approach does not eliminate the need for any of the database facilities; rather, it merely makes the facilities available to the users in a different syntax. Further, the syntax, to be consistent with the host programming languages, is at a low, procedural level. A procedural syntax is always more difficult for non-technical users to learn and use. Therefore, it is not clear if ultimately the unified language approach offers any advantages over that of embedding a database language in host programming languages.

13.3.2 Myths

There are many myths about OODBs. Many of these myths are totally without merit and are the result of the unfortunate label *database system* that has been attached to most of the current OODBs that are not full-fledged database systems comparable to the current RDBs. Some of the myths are the result of the evolving nature of the technology. Yet others represent concerns from purists that in my view are not practically useful.

OODBs Are 10 to 100 Times Faster than RDBs

Vendors of OODBs often make the claim that OODBs are between 10 and 100 times faster than RDBs, and they back up the claim with performance numbers. This claim can be misleading unless it is carefully qualified. OODBs have two sources of performance gain over RDBs. In an OODB, the value of an attribute of an object X whose domain is another object Y is the object identifier (OID) of the object Y. Therefore, if an application has already retrieved object X and now would like to retrieve object Y, the database system may retrieve object Y by looking up its OID. Figure 13–1a illustrates two instances of the class Person, and two instances of the class Company, such that the class Company is the domain of the attribute

Person

oid	name	age	salary	worksfor
115	John	25	25000	002
267	Chen	30	25000	001

Company

oid	name	age	president	location
001	Acme	15	Cohen	NY
002	UniSQL	3	Kim	Austin

(a) Object representation in an OODB

Person

name	age	salary	worksfor
John	25	25000	UniSQL
Chen	30	25000	Acme

Company

name	age	president	location
Acme	15	Cohen	NY
UniSQL	3	Kim	Austin

(b) Tuple representation in an RDB

FIGURE 13–1
Object Versus Tuple Representation

Worksfor in the class Person. The value stored in the Worksfor attribute is the OID of an object of the class Company. If the OID is a physical address of an object, the object may be directly fetched from the database; if the OID is a logical address, the object may be fetched by looking up a hash table entry (assuming that the system maintains a hash table that maps an OID to its physical address).

The current RDBs allow only a primitive data type as the domain of an attribute of a relation. As such, the value of an attribute of a tuple can only be primitive data (such as a number or string) and can never be another tuple. If a tuple Y of a relation R2 is logically the value of an attribute A of a tuple X of a relation R1, the actual value stored in attribute A of tuple X is a value of attribute B of tuple Y of relation R2. If an application has retrieved tuple X and would now like to retrieve tuple Y, the system must in effect execute a query that scans the relation R2 using the value of attribute A of tuple X. Figure 13–1b is an equivalent representation in an RDB of the object-oriented database in Figure 13–1a. The domain of the attribute Worksfor in the relation Person is the primitive data type String. If an application has retrieved the Person tuple for "John" and would like to retrieve the Company tuple for "UniSQL," it needs to issue a query that will scan the Company relation. Imagine that the Company relation has thousands or tens of thousands of tuples. If no index is maintained on attribute B (Name) of relation R2 (Company), the entire relation R2 must be sequentially searched to find tuple Y (for "UniSQL"). If an index is maintained on attribute B, tuple Y may be retrieved about as fast as in OODBs that resort to a hash table lookup but less efficiently than in OODBs that implement OIDs as physical addresses (and therefore do not require any hash table lookup).

A second source of performance gain in OODBs over RDBs is that most OODBs convert the OIDs stored in an object to memory pointers

Person					Company				
oid	**name**	**age**	**salary**	**worksfor**	**oid**	**name**	**age**	**president**	**location**
115	John	25	25000	002	001	Acme	15	Cohen	NY
267	Chen	30	25000	001	002	UniSQL	3	Kim	Austin

(a) Object representation in database

Person					Company				
addr	**name**	**age**	**salary**	**worksfor**	**addr**	**name**	**age**	**president**	**location**
040	John	25	25000	020	004	Acme	15	Cohen	NY
080	Chen	30	25000	004	020	UniSQL	3	Kim	Austin

(b) Object representation in memory

FIGURE 13–2
Object Representation in Databases and in Memory

when the object is loaded into memory. Suppose that both objects X and Y have been loaded into memory, and the OID stored as the value of attribute A of object X is converted to a virtual memory pointer that points to object Y in memory. Then navigating from object X to object Y—that is, accessing object Y as the value of attribute A of object X—becomes essentially a memory pointer lookup. Figure 13–2a illustrates the database representation of the objects of the classes Person and Company. Figure 13–2b illustrates the memory representation of the same objects. The OIDs stored in the Worksfor attribute of the Person objects have been converted to memory addresses. Imagine that hundreds or thousands of objects have been loaded into memory and that each object contains memory pointers to one or more other objects in memory. Further, imagine that navigation from one object to other objects is to be performed repeatedly. Since RDBs do not store OIDs, they cannot store in one tuple memory pointers to other tuples. The facility to navigate through memory-resident objects is a fundamentally absent feature in RDBs, and the performance drawback that results from it cannot be neutralized by simply having a large buffer space in memory. Therefore, for applications that require repeated navigation through linked objects loaded in memory, OODBs can dramatically outperform RDBs.

If all database applications require only OID lookups with database objects or memory-pointer chasing among objects in memory, the two to three orders of magnitude performance advantage for OODBs over RDBs is very valid. However, most applications that require OID lookups also have database access and update requirements that RDBs have been designed to meet. These requirements include bulk database loading; creation, update, and delete of individual objects (one at a time); retrieval from a class of one or more objects that satisfy certain search conditions; joins of more than one class (as we will see shortly); transaction commit; and so forth. For such applications, OODBs do not have any performance advantage to offer. In fact, even for the example database of Fig. 13–1, if the objective of the application is to fetch Person objects, along with the related Company objects, that satisfy certain conditions (e.g., all Persons whose Age is greater than 25 and whose Salary is less than 40000—i.e., a general query) rather than fetching a specific Company object for a given Person object (i.e., a simple navigation), OODBs may not enjoy any performance advantage at all, depending on how the OIDs are implemented and whether the query optimizer is designed to exploit the OIDs in processing queries.

OODBs Eliminate the Need for Joins

OODBs significantly reduce the need for joins of classes (comparable to joins of relations in RDBs); however, they do not eliminate the need altogether. In OODBs the domain of an attribute of a class C may be another class D. However, in RDBs the domain of an attribute of a relation R1 cannot be another relation R2. Therefore, to correlate a tuple of one relation with a tuple of some other relation, RDBs always require the users to explicitly join the two relations. OODBs replace this explicit join with an implicit join—namely the fetching of the OIDs of objects in a class that are stored as the values of an attribute in another class. The examples in Fig. 13–1 illustrated this point. The specification of a class D as the domain of an attribute of another class C in an OODB is in essence a static specification of a join between the classes C and D.

The relational join is a general mechanism that correlates two relations on the basis of the values of a corresponding pair of attributes in the relations. Since two classes in an OODB may in general have corresponding pairs of attributes, the relational join is still useful and, therefore, necessary in OODBs. For example, in Fig. 13–1, the classes Person and Company both have attributes Name and Age. Although the Name and Age attributes of the class Company are not the domains of the Name and Age attributes of the class Person and vice versa, the user may wish to correlate the two classes on the basis of the values of these attributes (e.g., find all Person objects whose Age is less than the Age of the Company the Person Worksfor).

Object Identity Eliminates the Need for Keys

Object identity has received more attention that it merits. Object identity is merely a means of representing an object and also guaranteeing uniqueness of each individual object. An OID does not carry any additional semantics. Even if the OID lends uniqueness to each object, the OID is generated automatically by the system and usually is not even made visible to the users. Therefore, it does not offer a convenient means of fetching specific desired objects from a large database (i.e., when the user does not know the OIDs of the objects). It is more convenient for the user to be able to fetch one or more objects using user-defined keys. For example, in the database of

Fig. 13–1, if the Name attribute is a primary key, the user may fetch one Person object by issuing a query that searches for a specific Name.

OODBs Eliminate the Need for a (Nonprocedural) Database Language

This myth came about because most of the current OODBs offer only limited query capabilities. Vendors of the OODBs elected to focus their development efforts on the performance of database navigation and on making objects persistent. The commands necessary to invoke the limited database facilities have been presented to the users as calls to a library of database functions—that is, a procedural language. Upgrading most of the current OODBs to true database systems, in particular adding full query facilities comparable to those supported in RDBs, will necessitate a nonprocedural query language, which will be very difficult to hide. OODB vendors are now attempting to provide nonprocedural query languages, generally labeled as *Object SQL*.

Query Processing Will Violate Encapsulation

One objective of encapsulating data and program into an object in OOPLs is to force the programmers to access objects only by invoking the program part of the objects and to keep the programmers from making use of knowledge of the data structures used to store the objects or the implementation of the program part. In the course of processing a query, the database system must read the contents of objects, extract OIDs that may be stored in some attributes of the objects, and retrieve objects that correspond to those OIDs. Object purists regard this as violating object encapsulation since the database system examines the contents of objects. This view is not practical or useful. First, it is the database system that examines the contents of objects, not any ordinary user. Second, the act of examining the values stored in attributes of objects may be regarded as invoking the "get (or read)" method implicitly associated with every attribute of every class. If purity of objects must be preserved at all cost, then every single numeric and string constant used must be explicitly assigned an OID! But no known OOPL or OO application system does that.

OODBs Can Support Versioning and Long-Duration Transactions

There is a general misunderstanding that somehow OODBs can support versioning and long-duration transactions, and, by implication, versioning and long-duration transactions cannot be supported in RDBs. Although the paradigm shift from relations to objects does eliminate key deficiencies in RDBs, it does not address the issues of versioning and long-duration transactions. The object-oriented paradigm does not include versioning and long-duration transactions, just as the relational model of data does not include them. Simply put, C++ and Smalltalk do not include any versioning facilities or long-duration transaction facilities.

The reason versioning and long-duration transactions have become associated with OODBs is simply that they are database facilities that have been missing in RDBs and that have been identified as requirements for those applications that OODBs, with their more powerful data modeling facilities and object navigation facilities, can satisfy much better than RDBs (e.g., computer-aided engineering system, computer-aided authoring system, etc.). In fact, most OODBs do not even support versioning and long-duration transactions. The few OODBs that do offer what are labeled as versioning and long-duration transactions provide only primitive facilities.

Versioning and long-duration transactions can be supported in both OODBs and RDBs with equal ease or difficulty. Let us consider a few aspects of versioning. If an object is to be versioned, often a timestamp and/or version identity needs to be maintained. This can be implemented by creating system-defined attributes for the timestamp and/or version identity. Clearly, this can be done both for each versioned object in a class in OODBs and each versioned tuple in a relation in RDBs. Similarly, version-derivation history may be maintained in the database. Further, such versioning facilities as version derivation, version deletion, version retrieval, and so on may be expressed by extending the database language of OODBs and RDBs.

Next, let us consider long-duration transactions. A transaction is simply a collection of database reads and updates that are treated as a single unit. RDBs have implemented transactions with the assumption that they will interact with the database only for a few seconds or less. This assumption becomes invalid and long-duration transactions become necessary in environments where human users interactively access the database over much longer durations (hours or days). Regardless of the duration of a transaction, a transaction is merely a mechanism for ensuring database consistency in the presence of simultaneous accesses to the database by multiple users and in the presence of system crashes. What differentiates an OODB from an RDB is the data model—that is, how data are represented (i.e., attributes and methods and classes and class hierarchy in an OODB versus attributes and relations in an RDB). It should be clear that the paradigm difference between RDBs and OODBs does not solve the problems that transactions are designed to solve.

OODBs Support Multimedia Data

OODBs are a much more natural basis than RDBs for implementing functions necessary for managing multimedia data. *Multimedia data* is broadly defined as data of arbitrary type (number, short string, Employee, Company, image, audio, text, graphics, movie, a document that contains images and text, etc.) and arbitrary size (1 byte, 10K bytes, 1 gigabyte, etc.). The reason that OODBs handle multimedia data more naturally than RDBs do is that OODBs allow arbitrary data types to be created and used—the first requirements for managing multimedia data.

However, the object-oriented paradigm (i.e., encapsulation, inheritance, methods, arbitrary data types—collectively or individually) does not solve the problems of storing, retrieving, and updating very large multimedia objects (e.g., an image, an audio passage, a textual document, a movie, etc.). OODBs must solve exactly the same engineering problems that RDBs have had to solve to allow the BLOB (binary large object) as the domain of a column in a relation, including incremental retrieval of a very large object from the database (the page buffer in general cannot hold the entire object), incremental update (a small change in an object should not result in copying the entire object), concurrency control (more than one user should be able to access the same large object simultaneously), and recovery (logging should not lead to copying an entire object).

13.4 Fulfilling the Promises of OODBs

Today, both the deficiencies of RDBs and the promises of OODBs are fairly well understood. However, OODBs have not had significant impact in the database market. Two of the reasons are that most of the current OODBs lack maturity as database systems (i.e., they lack many of the key database facilities found in RDBs) and that they are not sufficiently compatible with RDBs (i.e., they do not support a superset of ANSI SQL).

The emerging industry and market consensus is that object-oriented technology can indeed bring about a quantum jump in database technology, but there are at least three major conditions that must be met before it can deliver on its promises.

First, new database systems that incorporate an object-oriented data model must be full-fledged database systems that are compatible with RDBs (i.e., whose database language must be a superset of SQL).

Second, application development tools and database access tools must be provided for such database systems, just as they are critical for the use of RDBs. The tools include graphical application (form) generator, graphical browser/editor/designer of the database, graphical report generator, database administration tool, and possibly others.

Third, a migration path (a bridge) is needed to allow coexistence of such systems with currently installed RDBs, so that the installations may use RDBs and new systems for different purposes and also to gradually migrate from their current products to the new products.

In this section, I will provide an outline of how an object-oriented database system may be built that is fully compatible with RDBs and how a migration path may be provided from RDBs to such a new database system.

UniSQL, Inc. has a commercial database system, UniSQL/X, that supports a superset of ANSI SQL with full object-oriented extensions. UniSQL, Inc. also offers graphical database access tools and an application generation tool for use with UniSQL/X. Further, UniSQL, Inc. offers a commercial federated (multi) database system, UniSQL/M, that allows coexistence of UniSQL/X with RDBs, while giving the users a single-database illusion. I will use UniSQL/X and UniSQL/M to illustrate key concepts in this section.

Unification of the relational and object-oriented technologies is most definitely the underpinning for postrelational database technology. ORACLE Corporation recently announced plans to develop an object-oriented extension to SQL. The ANSI SQL3 standards committee is currently designing object-oriented extensions to SQL2. The objective of SQL3 is exactly the same as the one that guided the development of the UniSQL/X database language. SQL3 is about three to four years away. Further, HP's OpenODB supports a database programming language called OSQL that is based on a combination of SQL and a functional data model (rather than a relational data model). There is also a proposal and initial implementation from Texas Instruments for a database programming language called ZQL[C++] that extends C++ with SQL-like query facility. The vendors of some OODBs are also preparing to develop "SQL-like" languages, generally labeled as *Object SQL*, that include facilities for defining and querying object-oriented databases, as an add-on to their existing OODBs. This represents a major direction change in their product strategy. Just a few years ago, these vendors merely attempted to provide gateways between their OODBs and some RDBs.

13.4.1 Unifying RDBs and OODBs

Unification Architectures

Broadly, there are three possible approaches to bringing together OODBs and RDBs: gateway, OO-layer on RDB engine, and single engine. In the gateway approach, an OODB request is simply translated and routed to a single RDB for processing, and the result returned from the RDB is sent to the user issuing the original request. The gateway appears to the RDB as an ordinary user of the RDB. The current implementations of gateways impose various restrictions on the OODB requests; they accept only read requests, or only one request (rather than a sequence of requests as a single transaction), or only simple requests (i.e., not all types of queries comparable to those RDBs are capable of processing). Although the gateway approach makes it possible for an application program to use data retrieved from both an OODB and an RDB, it is not a serious alternative for unifying relational and object-oriented technologies. Its performance is unacceptable because of the cost of translating requests and returned data and the communication overhead with the RDB. Further, its usability is unacceptable because the application programmers or users have to be aware of the existence of two different databases.

In the OO-layer approach (exemplified by HP's OpenODB), the user interacts with the system using an OODB database language (in the case of OpenODB, an ObjectSQL), and the OO layer performs all translations of the object-oriented aspects of the database language to their relational equivalents for interaction with the underlying RDB. The translation overhead can be significant, and this architecture inherently compromises performance. For example, the OO layer would map objects to tuples of relations and generate the OIDs of objects and pass them to the RDB as an attribute of the tuple, using the interface the RDB makes available; it would also map an OID found in an object to its corresponding object stored in the RDB, again using the RDB interface; and so forth. An RDB consists of two layers: data manager layer and storage manager layer. The data manager layer processes the SQL statements, and the storage manager layer maps the data to the database. The OO layer may be interfaced with either the data manager layer (i.e., talk to the RDB via SQL statements) or the storage manager layer (i.e., talk to the RDB via low-level procedure calls). The data manager interface is much slower than the storage level interface. (OpenODB uses the data manager interface between its OO layer and the underlying RDB.) Since this approach assumes that the underlying RDB will not be modified to better accommodate the needs of the OO layer, it can incur serious performance and operational problems when sophisticated database facilities need to be supported. For example, if a large number of classes in a class hierarchy must be locked (e.g., to support dynamic schema changes), the OO layer must either acquire locks one at a time (incurring a performance penalty and risking deadlocks) since an RDB has no provision for locking a class hierarchy atomically (roughly, in one command), or lock the entire database with one call to the underlying RDB (potentially preventing any other user from accessing any part of the database). Neither option is desirable. Further, if the OO layer is to support updates to objects in memory and automatically flush updated objects to the database when the application's transaction commits (finishes), the individual objects must be inserted back into the database one at a time, using the RDB interface.

The rationale for the OO-layer approach is to be able to port the OO layer on top of a variety of existing RDBs; this flexibility is obtained at the expense of performance. The OO-layer approach is the basis of a database system that makes a variety of databases appear to be a single database to application programs. Such a database system is known as a *multidatabase system*. The OO-layer approach can be used as a basis of a multidatabase system that makes it possible for application programs to work with data retrieved from OODBs and RDBs. I note that OpenODB currently is not a multidatabase system. Its OO layer can connect to only one RDB.

The unified approach melds the OO layer and the RDB into a single layer, while making all necessary changes in both the storage manager layer and the data manager layer of the RDB. The database system must fully support all the facilities the database language allows, including dynamic schema changes, automatic query optimization, automatic query processing, access methods (including B+-tree index, extensible hashing, external sorting), concurrency control, recovery from both soft and hard crashes, transaction management, and granting and revoking of authorizations. The richness of the unified data model added to implementation difficulties.

Unifying the Data Models

A relational database consists of a set of relations (tables), and a relation in turn consists of rows (tuples) and columns. A row/column entry in a relation may have a single value, and the value may belong to a set of system-defined data types (e.g., integer, string, float, date, time, money). The user may impose further restrictions, called integrity constraints, on these values (e.g., the integer value of an employee age may be restricted to between 18 and 65). The user may then issue a nonprocedural query against a relation to retrieve only those tuples of the relation the values of whose columns satisfy user-specified conditions. Further, the user may correlate two or more relations by issuing a query that joins the relations on the basis of a comparison of the values in user-specified columns of the relations.

UniSQL/X generalizes and extends this simple data model in three ways, each reflecting a key object-oriented concept. A basic tenet of an object-oriented system or programming language is that the value of an object is also an object. The first UniSQL/X extension reflects this by allowing the value of a column of a relation to be a tuple of any arbitrary user-defined relation, rather than just an element of a system-defined data type (number, string, etc.). This means that the user may specify an arbitrary user-defined relation as the domain of a column of a relation. The first CREATE TABLE statement in Fig. 13–3 shows the specification of an `Employee` relation under the relational model. The values of the `Hobby` and `Manager` columns are restricted to character strings. The second CREATE TABLE in Fig. 13–3 reflects data-type extension for the columns of a relation. The value for the `Hobby` column no longer needs to be restricted to a character string; it may now be a tuple of a user-defined relation `Activity`. Similarly, the data type for the `Manager` attribute of the relation `Employee` can even be the `Employee` relation itself.

Allowing a column of a relation to hold a tuple of another relation (i.e., data of arbitrary type) directly leads to nested relations; that is, the value of a row/column entry of a relation can now be a tuple of another relation, and the value can in turn be a tuple of another relation, and so forth, recursively. In Fig. 13–1 we saw how this conceptually simple extension may result in significant performance gain when retrieving data. This

```
1. CREATE TABLE Employee
    (Name CHAR(20), Job CHAR(20), Salary FLOAT,
         Hobby CHAR(20), Manager CHAR(20));

2. CREATE TABLE Employee
    (Name CHAR(20), Job CHAR(20), Salary FLOAT,
         Hobby Activity, Manager Employee);

          CREATE TABLE Activity
             (Name CHAR(20), NumPlayers INTEGER,
                  Origin CHAR(20));

3. CREATE TABLE Employee
    (Name CHAR(20), Job CHAR(20), Salary FLOAT,
         Hobby Activity, Manager Employee)
    PROCEDURE RetirementBenefits FLOAT;

4. CREATE TABLE Employee
    (Job CHAR(20), Salary FLOAT, Hobby Activity,
         Manager Employee)
    PROCEDURE RetirementBenefits FLOAT
    AS CHILD OF Person;

          CREATE TABLE Person
             (Name CHAR(20),SSN CHAR(9),Age INTEGER);
```

FIGURE 13–3
Successive Extensions to the Relation Model

also gives a database system the potential to support such applications as multimedia systems (which manage image, audio, graphic, text data, and compound documents that comprise of such data), scientific data processing systems (which manipulate vectors, matrices, etc.), engineering and design systems (which deal with complex nested objects), and so forth. This is the basis for bridging the large gulf in data types supported in today's programming languages and database systems.

The second UniSQL/X extension is the object-oriented concept of encapsulation—that is, combining data and program (procedure) to operate on the data. This is incorporated by allowing the users to attach procedures to a relation and have the procedures operate on the column values in each tuple. The third CREATE TABLE statement in Fig. 13–3 shows the PROCEDURE clause for specifying a procedure, `RetirementBenefits`, which computes the retirement benefit for any given employee and returns a floating-point numeric value. Procedures for reading and updating the value of each column are implicitly available in each relation.

A relation now encapsulates the state and behavior of its tuples; the state is the set of column values, and the behavior is the set of procedures that operate on the column values. The user may write any procedure and attach it to a relation to operate on the values of any tuple or tuples of the relation. There is virtually unlimited application of procedures.

The third UniSQL/X extension is the object-oriented concept of inheritance hierarchy. UniSQL/X allows the users to organize all relations in the database into a hierarchy such that between a pair of relations `P` and `C`, `P` is made the parent of `C`, if `C` is to take (*inherit*) all columns and procedures defined in `P`, besides those defined in `C`. Further, it allows a table to have more than one parent relation from which it may take columns and procedures. The child relation is said to inherit columns and procedures from the parent relations (this is called *multiple inheritance*). The hierarchy of relations is a directed acyclic graph (rather than a tree) with a single system-defined root. Further, an IS-A (generalization and specialization) relationship holds between a child relation and its parent relation. In the fourth CREATE TABLE in Fig. 13–3, the `Employee` relation is defined as a CHILD OF another user-defined relation `Person`. The `Employee` relation automatically inherits the three columns of the `Person` relation; that is, the `Employee` relation will have the `Name`, `SSN`, and `Age` columns, even if they are not specified in its definition.

The relation hierarchy offers two advantages over the conventional relational model of a simple collection of largely independent (unrelated) relations. First, it makes it possible for a user to create a new relation as a child relation of one or more existing relations; the new relation inherits (reuses) all columns and procedures specified in the existing relations and their ancestor relations. Further, it makes it possible for the system to enforce the IS-A relationship between a pair of relations. RDBs require the users to manage and enforce this relationship.

Now, let us change the relational terms as follows. Change "relation" to "class," "tuple of a relation" to "instance of a class," "column" to "attribute," "procedure" to "method," "relation hierarchy" to "class hierarchy," "child relation" to "subclass," and "parent class" to "superclass." The UniSQL/X data model described above is an object-oriented data model! An object-oriented data model can be obtained by extending the relational model. The terms "object-oriented data model," "extended relational data model," and "unified relational and object-oriented data model" ("unified," for brevity) become synonymous if the data model is obtained by augmenting the conventional relational data model with the first three extensions described above. However, an extended relational model (system) is not an object-oriented model (system) if it does not include all three extensions. Further, it is important to note that a database system based on such a model, because of its relational foundation, may be built by adapting all the theoretical underpinnings of the relational database technology that have been developed during the past two decades.

Although each of the three extensions individually may appear to be minor, the consequences of the extensions, individually and collectively, with respect to ease of application data modeling and/or subsequent increase in query performance can be significant. The nested relation extension eliminates the need for cumbersome workarounds that users of RDBs have had to resort to. The procedure and relation hierarchy extensions open up significant new possibilities in application data modeling and application programming. Further, the nested relation and relation hierarchy extensions reflect the powerful data type facilities of OOPLs.

Query and Data Manipulation

Of course, it is not enough just to define a data model that allows the users to represent complex data requirements. Once the database schema has been defined using the data definition facilities, the database may be populated with a large number of user-defined objects. The power of a database system comes into play when the users can retrieve and update tiny fractions of the database efficiently. To allow this, a database system provides query and data manipulation (insert, update, delete) facilities.

The UniSQL/X query language, unlike mere SQL-like object query languages, is a superset of ANSI SQL, and as such, if the extensions are removed from the syntax, it degenerates to ANSI SQL. By a "SQL-like" language I mean a database language that is either a subset of SQL or that does not support the semantics of SQL. A SQL-like language that is a subset of SQL is one, for example, that does not support nested subqueries in the WHERE clause or aggregation functions in the SELECT clause, and so on. It is also one that does not include facilities for defining and using views, or facilities for dynamically making changes to the database schema, or facilities for specifying the UNIQUE and NULL constraints on attributes of a class, or facilities for granting and revoking authorizations, and so forth. A SQL-like database language that does not support the semantics of SQL is one, for example, that treats NULL values differently from SQL, or that refuses to commit a transaction after accepting all read and update requests from the user without any complaints, or that introduces a restriction that does not exist in SQL (e.g., the DROP CLASS command does not allow a class to be dropped if any objects still belong to a class, while the DROP TABLE command in SQL results in dropping a table and all its tuples, whether or not there are tuples), and so forth.

If a set of classes are defined just as relations in conventional relational databases, the users of the UniSQL/X query language may issue all queries in ANSI SQL syntax, including joins and nested subqueries, queries that group and order the results, and queries against views. Let us consider two simple examples using Fig. 13–4. In the figure, the class `Employee` is defined as a subclass of the class `Person`, and the class `Activity` is the domain of the attribute `Hobby` of the class `Employee`. The first query finds all employees who earn more than 50000 and are over 30 years of age and

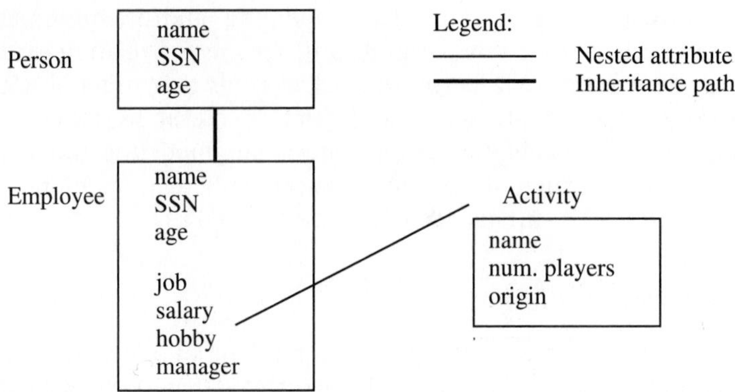

FIGURE 13–4
An Example Database Schema

outputs the average salary of all such employees by job category. The second query is a join query, which finds the names of all employees who earn more than their managers.

```
SELECT    Job, Avg (Salary)
FROM      Employee
WHERE     Salary < 50000 AND Age > 30
GROUP BY       Job;
```

```
SELECT    Employee.Name
FROM      Employee
WHERE     Employee.Salary > Employee.Manager.Salary;
```

The UniSQL/X query language also allows the formulation of a number of additional types of queries that become necessary under the unified data model (i.e., queries that are not applicable under the relational model). The unified data model is richer, and thus it gives rise to query expressions that do not arise in RDBs. In particular, it allows *path queries*—that is, queries against nested classes; queries that include methods as part of search conditions; queries that return nested objects; and queries against a set of classes in the class hierarchy.

An example of a query on a class hierarchy is retrieving instances from a class and all its subclasses. In the following query, the keyword *ALL* causes the query to be evaluated against the class `Person` and its subclass `Employee`.

```
SELECT    Name, SSN
FROM      ALL Person
WHERE     age > 50;
```

An example of a path query that retrieves nested objects, using Fig. 13–4, is "Find the names of all employees and their employers for those employees who earn more than $50,000 and whose hobby is tennis."

This query is evaluated against the nested objects defined by the classes `Employee` and `Activity`. The query is formulated by associating the predicate (Name = 'tennis') with the class `Activity`, and the predicate `'Salary > 50000'` with the class `Employee`. The query returns all attributes of `Employee` from the nested `Employee` objects that satisfy the query conditions.

```
SELECT    *
FROM      Employee
WHERE     Salary > 50000 AND Hobby.Name = "Tennis";
```

The dot notation in the predicate (`Hobby.Name = "Tennis"`) extends the standard predicate expression to account for the nesting of attributes through the use of arbitrary data types.

Support for Object Navigation

Like some OODBs that are designed to make OOPL objects persistent, UniSQL/X provides workspace management facilities to automatically manage a large number of objects in memory (called a workspace or an object buffer pool). In particular, UniSQL/X automatically converts the storage format of objects between the database format and the memory format, automatically converts the OIDs stored in objects to memory pointers when objects are loaded from the database into memory, and automatically flushes (writes) objects updated in memory to the database when the transaction that updated them finishes.

These workspace management facilities in UniSQL/X make it possible for database application programs to navigate memory-resident objects via memory-pointer chasing and to propagate changes to individual objects collectively to the database. RDB applications must resort to explicit queries that either join two relations or at least search a single relation to emulate the simple navigation from one object to another related object. Further, RDB applications must also propagate updated tuples one at a time to the database via the RDB interface (either the data manager level or the storage manager level). When a transaction finishes, UniSQL/X automatically sends all objects created or updated by the transaction to the database to make them persistent. UniSQL/X application programs do not need to do anything to propagate the changes to the database.

I note that, unlike most OODBs that also provide workspace management facilities, UniSQL/X supports full query facilities and full dynamic schema evolution. Since at any point in time an object may exist both in the database and in the workspace, and the "copy" in the workspace may have been updated, a query must be evaluated against the "copies" in the workspace for those objects that have been loaded into the workspace and against the database objects for those objects that have not been loaded into the workspace. Further, if the user makes a schema change (e.g., drop an attribute of a class, or add an attribute to a class), the "copies" of objects in the workspace become invalid. UniSQL/X takes full account of these considerations in its support of automatic query processing and dynamic schema evolution.

Further, workspace management facilities are essential for making objects persistent and for supporting the performance requirements in object navigation for application programs written in OOPLs. Although UniSQL/X is not wedded to any particular OOPL, the sophisticated workspace management facilities provided in UniSQL/X mean that a rather simple translation layer may be implemented on top of UniSQL/X to support any particular OOPL (e.g., C++ or Smalltalk).

13.5 Interoperating with RDBs

The gateway approach that I discussed as an (unsatisfactory) alternative for unifying an OODB with RDBs serves one useful purpose. It allows an OODB and RDBs to coexist, and it can potentially make it possible for one application program to work with data retrieved from both an OODB and one or more RDBs. As I remarked already, however, the current OODB-RDB gateways typically pass requests to only one RDB (e.g., to Sybase or to ORACLE) and do not treat the separate requests to an OODB and to RDB as a single transaction (i.e., collection of requests that is treated as a single unit).

A multidatabase system (MDBS) is logically a full generalization of a gateway. An MDBS is actually a database system that controls multiple gateways. It does not have its own database; it merely manages remote databases through the gateways, one gateway for each remote database. An MDBS presents the multiple remote databases as a single virtual database to its users. Since an MDBS does not have its own real database, certain database facilities, such as those for managing access methods (creating and dropping B+-tree index, extendible hash table, etc.) and parameterized performance tuning, become meaningless.

However, an MDBS is a nearly full-fledged database system. An MDBS must provide data definition facilities so that the virtual database may be defined on the basis of the remote databases. The data definition facilities need to include means to harmonize (homogenize) the different representations of the semantically equivalent data in different remote databases. An MDBS user may query the definition of the virtual database and query and update the virtual database (requiring query optimization and query processing mechanisms). Multiple MDBS users may simultaneously query, update, and even populate the virtual database (requiring concurrency control mechanisms); the users may submit a collection of queries and updates as a single transaction against the virtual database (requiring transaction management mechanisms); the users would grant and revoke authorizations on parts of the database to other users (requiring authorization mechanisms).

To translate MDBS queries and updates to equivalent queries and updates that can be processed by remote database systems, an MDBS requires gateways for remote database systems. The gateways in an MDBS are often called *drivers* and remote database systems are called *local* database systems, and the single virtual database that an MDBS presents to its users is called a *global* database. Further, an MDBS is said to *integrate* multiple local databases into a single global database.

UniSQL/M is a multidatabase system from UniSQL, Inc. that integrates multiple UniSQL/X databases and multiple relational databases. UniSQL/M is UniSQL/X augmented to access external relational databases and UniSQL/X databases; as such, it is a full-fledged database system, and UniSQL/M users can query and update the global database in the SQL/X database language. UniSQL/M maintains the global database as a collection of views defined over relations in local RDBs and classes in local UniSQL/X databases. UniSQL/M also maintains a directory of the local database relations and classes, their attributes and data types, and methods that have been integrated into the global database. Using the information in the directory, UniSQL/M translates the queries and updates to equivalent queries and updates for processing by local database systems that manage the data that the queries and updates need to access. The local database drivers pass the translated queries and updates to local database systems and pass the results to UniSQL/M for format translation, merging, and any necessary postprocessing (e.g., sorting, grouping, and joining). Further, UniSQL/M supports distributed transaction management over local databases, which means that all updates issued within one UniSQL/M transaction, even when they result in updates to multiple local databases, are simultaneously committed or aborted.

RDB vendors today offer gateways of different levels of sophistication. Some gateways allow SQL queries to be passed to a hierarchical database system (namely, IMS) or to file systems such as DEC's RMS. Some gateway is currently being upgraded to accept both queries and updates and even to support distributed transaction management over local databases. However, none of these gateways are designed to pass SQL queries to OODBs; there has been little need to develop such gateways.

UniSQL/M differs from the gateways currently offered by RDB vendors and OODB vendors in three major ways.

- UniSQL/M is a full-fledged database system rather than a mere gateway, supporting queries, updates, authorization, and transaction management over the global database (the specifications of views defined over local database tables and classes and directory of information about local database tables and classes). Most current gateways do not accept updates.

- UniSQL/M connects to and coordinates queries and updates to multiple local databases for a single UniSQL/M transaction; in particular, it supports distributed transaction management over local databases. Most current gateways pass requests to only one local database or do not allow simultaneous updates to multiple local databases within a single transaction when they do support multiple local databases.

There is one more powerful advantage that UniSQL/M offers over any of the current gateways. UniSQL/M extends, although not fully (due to theoretical limitations), local RDBs to UniSQL/X—that is, UniSQL/M converts the tuples retrieved from relational local databases into objects by augmenting them with object identifiers and allowing the users to attach methods to them. In this way, UniSQL/M makes key object-oriented facilities provided in UniSQL/X indirectly available to local RDBs—in particular, SQL/X path queries, methods, and workspace management for objects in UniSQL/M memory.

UniSQL/M may be used in at least three different contexts. First, it may be used to allow coexistence of UniSQL/X with RDBs. Second, it may be used to turn a collection of RDBs (or a collection of UniSQL/Xs) into a distributed database system. Third, when interfaced to a single RDB, it acts as the object management layer for the RDB engine, turning the RDB into UniSQL/X.

14

The POSC Solution to Managing E&P Data

VINCENT J. KOWALSKI

The requirements of managing and accessing Exploration & Production (E&P) data in the petroleum industry exceed the scope and capabilities of most current database technologies and standards. This chapter presents what these special requirements are and then discusses how the POSC Epicentre Data Model in conjunction with POSC's Data Access and Exchange API address these requirements.The POSC solution is put in the context of current DBMS standards and technologies.

14.1 Introduction

The Petrotechnical Open Software Corporation (POSC) is a not-for-profit membership company dedicated to the provision of a software integration platform (SIP) for the upstream Exploration and Production (E&P) industry. The scope of POSC offerings includes:

- definition of the computing environment for E&P technical applications
- an integrated, industry-wide, multidiscipline E&P data model (Epicentre)
- data access interface specifications for accessing the POSC Epicentre Data Model
- specification and endorsement of E&P data exchange formats
- E&P specific common user interface components
- a software development environment specification for E&P developers

These offerings form the Petrotechnical Software Integration Platform Specifications [POSC 1991a; POSC 1992c].

Currently, POSC has published the following specifications to support the above:

- POSC Software Integration Platform Specification, Base Computer Standards—Version 1.0 [POSC 1991a]

- POSC Software Integration Platform Specification, Epicentre Data Model, Version 1.0 [POSC 1994a]
- POSC Software Integration Platform Specification, Data Access and Exchange, Version 1.0 [POSC 1994b]
- POSC Software Integration Platform Specification, Exchange Format, Version 1.0 [POSC 1994c]
- POSC Software Integration Platform Specification, E&P User Interface Style Guide, Version 1.0 [POSC 1994d]

The purpose of this chapter is to describe E&P data and show how the access requirements for this data are addressed by the POSC Epicentre Data Model and Data Access and Exchange API. The Data Access and Exchange Application Programming Interface (API) provides a standard means of accessing data defined by the POSC Epicentre Data Model [POSC 1992b] and managed within a POSC Data Store or POSC Exchange Format (PEF) file [POSC 1992e]. In turn, the data model is represented in the EXPRESS information modeling language [ISO 1992a]. However, support of extra constructs that are defined in the Epicentre Data Model is included, while some EXPRESS constructs that Epicentre does not require may not be supported.

14.2 The Size, Shape, and Composition of E&P Data

The character and related requirements of E&P data are described in this section. The business of E&P is very broad, and therefore several kinds of data must be supported in an E&P data model. In addition to the straightforward tabular (i.e., relational) entities, an E&P data model must be able to support:

- large aggregates (arrays, sets, etc.) of scientific measurements
- complex data types
- context
- units, representations, and coordinate systems
- spatial data types

In addition, merely modeling each entity with the correct structure is not adequate. The full suite of entities defined in the data model must interrelate in meaningful and useful ways as well. Each of the above topics is covered individually in the sections that follow.

14.2.1 Large Aggregations of Scientific Measurements

Approximately 70–80 percent of the volume of E&P data may be categorized as identifiable aggregations of scientific values. Such aggregations of scientific values are often measurements of a property or set of properties taken over some given index (e.g., time, space, etc.).

Because of the sheer size of E&P data aggregates, the ability of a computing system to store, load, and perform operations on such objects efficiently and quickly is an important requirement.

The large size of E&P aggregates often imposes the requirement for subset operations. This requirement has been more a constraint of applications and the systems they run on than on the conceptual nature of the data. Nevertheless, subsetting of large aggregates has been and continues to be an important requirement.

14.2.2 Complex Data Types

E&P data at the attribute level do not tend to always be flat. In other words, given an attribute of some E&P entity, it is possible that the attribute has substructure. The components that make up this substructure may themselves appear as entities or attributes do at the respective higher levels. The ability to manipulate such complex data types as singular values as well as the ability to investigate the substructure and its values are both requirements imposed by this kind of E&P data.

14.2.3 Context

E&P data are generally accessed in terms of one or more contexts. These contexts are very often motivated by business needs (e.g., who works with whom on this data, how much of this data store is of interest to my project, what transforms have been applied to these data since they were acquired from the field, etc.). The most important of these contexts are data collections, versions, process history, and preferences.

Data Collections

E&P data are commonly organized into scopes termed *projects*. Project data may be defined to be all data within a given geographic area, work process, organizational responsibility, or almost any constraint determined by some business requirement. Such collections may be managed for data administration functions such as archives and restoration. In addition, data collections may be convenient for creating a focus of attention for data processing tasks that manipulate E&P data.

Versions

E&P data have a life cycle in which, like all other data, they are created, queried, updated, and destroyed. E&P data have the additional requirement that their creations and updates are very often related to both the ancestor data and the processes that are involved. For example, given an array of seismic data, it is not usually enough to know which ordinal version it is, but which processes (i.e., algorithms) transformed which predecessor seismic data to arrive at the given array.

Process History

Given the above discussion of versions, it is clear that processes, their associated algorithms, and the data they transform must be managed in a coordinated fashion. There is a need to know what the status of given data is and a requirement to reproduce and adjust results. Such requirements arise from the kind of if . . . then analysis that is often performed in E&P.

Preferences

Sometimes referred to as *profiling*, the ability to store preferences is necessary by E&P data consuming and producing software processes. The quantity of parametric information that goes into the processing of E&P data is often quite large. In addition, many processes, once defined and refined, are run repetitively for similar sets of data. As a result, mechanisms for storing and accessing E&P data processing preferences, not unlike those for storing and accessing user preferences in modern graphical user interfaces, are required.

14.2.4 Units, Representations, and Coordinate Systems

Some of the most important characteristics that distinguish scientific measurements from purely mathematical or other measurement quantities are units of measure, representations, and coordinate systems.

Units of Measure

Scientific measurements are given meaning by the units in which they are recorded. Although linear transformations exist for most conceivable unit conversions, it is usually desirable to access related data in the same unit system (e.g., SI). Both the assertion of the units associated with given data types and the conversion to other units of measure are required operations.

Representations

Representations are the various ways of expressing the same entity. This goes beyond mere changes in units, however. For example, a geometric surface may be expressed as grid, mesh, or set of isovalues. Representations are not always convertible in straightforward, linear ways, as are units. At the same time, however, there is a requirement to perform such conversions.

Coordinate Systems

As most scientific data values are ultimately expressed graphically, it is difficult to conceive of such data exclusive of some set of coordinates. E&P data often are used in the context of simple coordinates such as rectilinear or spherical systems. But significantly, E&P data are also very often accessed in the context of geographic coordinates. Geographic coordinates have the inherent complexity that the earth is not a simple geometric shape. Earth coordinates are based on, in addition to other quantities, an approximation of the earth's surface to a simpler geometric shape and an estimate of actual earth dimensions. As such, transformations between geographic coordinates often have the difficulties that they may be nonreversible, nonlinear, heuristic, and may have a large family of possible solutions.

14.2.5 Spatial Data Types

Much E&P data must be described and interrelated spatially. The two fundamental views of spatial data are geometric and topological.

Geometric

Fundamentally, the geometry of a spatial object is the mathematical description of the location of the object. The description of the location of such an object is expressed as a collection of points or functions that generate points within a specified coordinate system.

Topological

The topology of a spatial object has two important facets: classification and association.

The classification of the topology of an object encompasses such characteristics as the openness or closedness of an object. These classifications determine the types of relationships that are possible with other spatial objects.

Topological associations define how two spatial objects are related. Examples of such associations are overlap, contain, and meet.

It is often the case that topological relationships are derived from the relative geometries of two or more objects. However, this is not mandatory (e.g., it may be known that Houston is contained in Texas even though the coordinates of Houston and Texas are unknown).

14.2.6 Integration: How It All Fits Together

There is an ever-increasing need for data to be shared among the various component disciplines of E&P. Therefore, an E&P data model must have the means to interrelate entity definitions as well as accommodate different views of the same entity. These requirements have led to the need for a highly integrated E&P data model.

14.2.7 Relationships

The semantics that bind one entity to another comprise an important form of data model integration. Relationships may be either explicit or implicit, and an E&P data model needs to support both. Explicit relationships are needed for well-known, definable paths between entities. Relationships that are not known a priori but may be useful to specific applications should not have explicit paths defined, but need the capability of being constructed for the purpose at hand.

14.2.8 Reuse of Entity Definitions

Certain E&P entity definitions may be useful in a number of more specialized entity definitions. It is clear that there is a need for both consistency of the higher-level entity definitions and a means for easily adding entities that are specializations of the existing entity definitions. Reuse of entity definitions also has the benefits of producing a more coherent, compact, and verifiable data model.

14.3 How E&P Data Are Used

In addition to the special data access and exchange requirements imposed by the nature of E&P data themselves, the way in which those data are used imposes further requirements. The following present broad classes of E&P applications software and what requirements they bring with them, the requirements of integrating E&P applications.

14.3.1 Acquisition of E&P Data

Data acquisition is the original recording of E&P data. This often takes the form of recording measurements made in the field or laboratory. For Data Access and Exchange, there is a requirement to trace E&P data back to this acquisition origin.

14.3.2 Loosely Coupled Sharing of Data

Producers and consumers of E&P data are often disjoint in terms of time, space, or computing environment. Nevertheless, data very often must be shared between such disconnected partners. Such sharing generally takes the form of writing to and reading from a transportable storage medium such as tape or floppy disk. Loose interchange of data requires both the producer and the consumer either to know the format of the exchanged data or to have software that can access the exchanged data in a way that encapsulates the underlying data format. For an exchange format to have widest applicability, it must be highly self-describing and, at the same time, extensible.

All systems that manage data must have some mechanism for identifying instances of those data. In an environment where data is exchanged in a loosely coupled manner, the requirement for data identification persists, but the additional problem exists that there can be no dependence on some central, automatic means for assigning or managing such identification.

14.3.3 Tightly Coupled Sharing of Data

When a given set of applications access the same data store concurrently, they are said to share that data in a tightly coupled manner. Analogous to the loosely coupled interchange described above, applications that tightly share data must have knowledge of the structural and semantic contents of the data store or have data access software that encapsulates the details of the underlying data.

Increasingly in E&P, tightly coupled data sharing means that data may be transferred from application to application in a high-speed, asynchronous manner. Such interapplication communication presents yet another set of requirements for data format definition (i.e., the messaging protocols) and data access functionality.

14.3.4 Finding Data Relevant to a Given Project

Given the notion of context described in the previous section, the definition of a project generally involves the assertion of some combination of such contexts. In an integrated data store that has all the data required by a project plus the mechanisms for performing operations that are closed for the set of data defined by the project, finding relevant data is done, by definition, automatically. However, if the data required by a project are distributed across multiple data stores or, worse, multiple disjoint computing environments, the search for project data may be nontrivial. Once located, standard exchange formats and data model definition and the related access software are needed for consolidating such data into a single project data store.

14.3.5 Data Preparation: Edit, Filter, Merge, Transform

E&P data that are recorded in the field are generally not usable in their raw form for analysis or interpretation. For a given type of E&P data there may be several steps in which data are altered to become more suitable for analytical or interpretive work. Some of these steps may be algorithmic, as in the application of certain mathematical filters, while some such changes can only be determined by an earth scientist with knowledge of the data.

In order for data to be edited, they must be located in the data store, presumably according to some search criteria, and retrieved. Once the data are transformed, they must then be stored back into the data store. These are the main requirements of Data Access and Exchange.

Various approaches to managing the steps taken to arrive at corrected data exist within different E&P application systems. The main requirement, however, is that for a given E&P object there must be a means for determining what has taken place (i.e, the processes, ancestor data, parameters, etc.) to arrive at the current state of the object.

14.3.6 Graphical Display of Data

As most E&P data consist of scientific measurements, the graphical display of such data is essential in any set of E&P applications software. To display data, they must be located, typically according to some search criteria, and retrieved. In addition, graphical display of E&P data is often done in a geographic context. This requires the ability to query and retrieve data based on such a context (e.g., find and display all wells in the state of Texas).

14.3.7 Quality Control of Data

Quality control can be applied either internally or externally relative to a data consumer. Internally, the processes that have edited, filtered, or otherwise transformed a given set of data can be monitored for accuracy and corrected if necessary. Externally, the data acquired from a producer are checked against control data, sanity checks, and knowledge of related data. Both types of quality control require a means for recording and traversing the life cycle or history of a set of data.

14.3.8 Calculating Results

Calculating results is the producing of new data from some given set of inputs. It is different from data preparation in that data preparation is a fix-up of given data, while calculating results creates new objects. However, the data access requirements for calculating results are exactly the same as those for data preparation.

14.3.9 Analysis and Interpretation of Data

Analysis and interpretation of E&P data are generally dependent on other processes, such as data preparation, graphical display of data, and calculations. As such, the Data Access and Exchange requirements of analysis and interpretation of data are determined by those other processes.

14.3.10 Saving or Discarding Results

The saving or discarding of E&P data has generally two main criteria: whether the data are globally interesting (i.e., will they be of interest outside the project they are currently defined to be part of) and whether the data need to be revisited. If the data will have global interest or will be revisited, they most likely will be saved. Otherwise, they can be discarded. These requirements imply the need for data creation and update operations. In addition, E&P data make this problem of saving data more interesting in that data are often required to be saved according to some context (i.e., version, project, etc.).

14.3.11 Application Integration

Increasingly, there is a requirement to have all the above functionality accessible from the same computing platform. This implies that applications must interoperate on several important dimensions. The ability of applications to access data that are guaranteed to be in a standard format in a consistent way is an important one of these interoperability dimensions.

14.4 Epicentre Meta Model Concepts

To address the structural requirements of E&P data, POSC has defined a meta model for the Epicentre Data Model. The meta model provides all the basic constructs for defining the specific content of Epicentre [POSC 1992b]. The meta model consists of two essential parts: EXPRESS-based concepts and addition meta data (i.e., concepts in addition to EXPRESS).

14.4.1 EXPRESS-Based Concepts

Much of the Epicentre Meta Model is based on EXPRESS. EXPRESS is an information modeling language that consists of elements that allow an unambiguous object definition and specification of constraints on the objects defined [International Organization for Standardization 1991a]. The concepts in Epicentre that are drawn from EXPRESS are:

- entity
- supertype and subtype
- attribute, explicit, and inverse
- defined data type
- simple type
- aggregate type
- where rule
- uniqueness rule
- global rule
- schema
- algorithm

These concepts are used in Epicentre as they are defined in EXPRESS. The EXPRESS concepts of select types and derived attributes have been deliberately excluded to provide a better match to available technology.

In addition, it should be noted that in EXPRESS the concept of relationship between entities is represented using attributes. EXPRESS also assigns importance to the direction of a relationship in that such relationship attributes may be either explicit or inverse. This distinction means that an inverse attribute can be created only as a consequence of creating its corresponding explicit attribute.

14.4.2 Additional Meta Data

The Epicentre Meta Model adds to the concepts that are provided in EXPRESS by providing epicentre data types, natural identifiers, reference entities, and number ranges.

Epicentre Data Types

Epicentre data types have been defined to allow data behavior common in E&P activities to be specified by referring to the appropriate data type. The concept is to define such types so that they may be treated as simple types that are in EXPRESS (e.g., STRING). The following are the Epicentre data types:

- date
- time
- yearmonthinterval

- daytimeinterval
- complex
- rational
- ratio
- quantity
- anyquantity
- angle
- money
- location
- point
- line
- surface, which includes
  - — triangulated MESH
  - — grid
  - — contour
- volume
- element
- sparse
- sample

For the most part, these data types provide the basis for the spatio-temporal data that may be stored in Epicentre.

Natural Identifiers

A natural identifier consists of one or more attributes such that the combination of attribute values of an instance is unique within the instance base. Since this concept is not directly supported by EXPRESS, a convention has been adopted in Epicentre for naming natural identifiers.

Reference Entities

Reference entities enable information such as enumerated code lists to be specified and described once in a standard way and be common to all applications without duplication.

There are three types of reference:

- POSC Fixed—a fixed number of POSC defined instances. All and only the standard instances will be present.
- POSC Open—same as POSC Fixed, except unspecified additions are allowed.
- Local—no POSC-specified instances, and unspecified additions are allowed.

Number Ranges

To facilitate implementation on available technology, number ranges have been defined in Epicentre that are more restrictive than those allowed in EXPRESS.

14.5 Epicentre High Level Model Concepts

The concepts represented in the high level model, though not strictly structural as are the meta-model concepts, pervade the Epicentre Data Model. From another perspective, the high level model entities are at or near the top of the inheritance hierarchy in Epicentre.

The following subsections present brief descriptions of the high level model entities that are particularly applicable to the requirements set out in section 14.2.

14.5.1 E_and_P_data

E_and_P_data is the superclass of all entities in Epicentre except for reference information and environmental entities that have less to do with the E&P business and more to do with the computing environment within which a given data store is located.

14.5.2 Object_of_interest

Object_of_interest is an entity that is used to define all things used within an E&P business. As it is an entity, Object_of_interest has attributes and relationships. Other data that may describe an Object_of_interest that could be changed without giving rise to a new Object_of_interest instance are specified as relationships to instances of Property.

14.5.3 Property

A Property describes the nonidentifying characteristics of an Object_of_interest. As Property is defined as an entity, a given Property (e.g., temperature) may have one or more specializations (e.g., average temperature, maximum temperature, etc.).

An instance of a Property may have several representations. The different Properties range from, for example, describing the same length in feet or meters to describing a three-dimensional surface as a triangulated mesh or as a mathematical function.

14.5.4 Data_collection

The Data_collection entity allows a group of E_and_P_data instances to be identified. Instances of data may belong to zero, one, or more Data_collections. An instance of a Data_collection may not be a member of its own collection, but Data_collections may contain other Data_collections.

14.5.5 Activity

Activity is defined as a continuous action or a process. An Event_activity is an instantaneous change of a perceived state. Changes resulting from Activities are specified by Event_activities.

Activities can be aggregates of other Activities, meaning that the aggregate parts are carried out between the start and end of the parent Activity. This provides a means of addressing the process history requirement stated in section 14.2.

Activities use and create Data_collections, Objects_of_interest, and Properties.

14.5.6 Association

Association is the supertype of entities expressing relationships among E_and_P_data entities.

14.5.7 Spatial_object

Spatial_objects (a specialization of Object_of_interest) enable Business_objects (another specialization of Object_of_interest) to be described in terms of topological entities such as Face, Ring, Region, Shell, Edge, and Vertex. Spatial_object classes are included primarily to support the description of pieces of the earth.

Geometric representations of Spatial_objects, together with any property characteristics, are intended to be handled as subclasses of Property.

14.6 POSC Data Access and Exchange API

The Data Access and Exchange API [POSC 1992d] provides the basic data-related services required by the types of applications described in section 14.3.

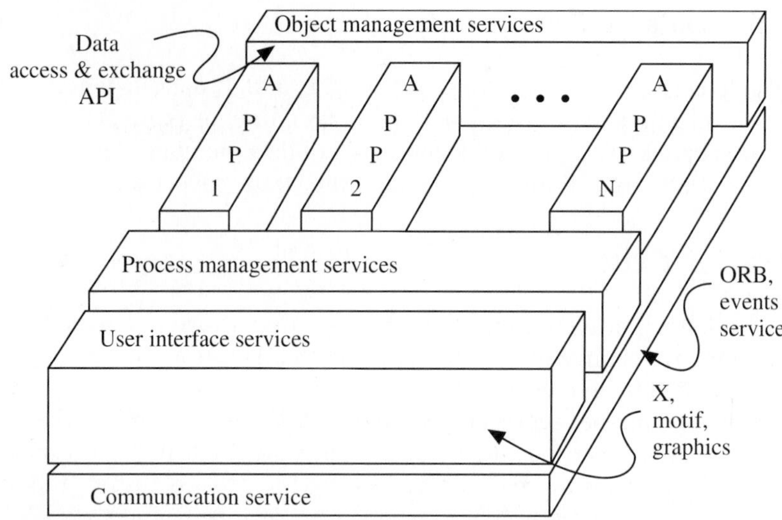

FIGURE 14–1
ECMA/NIST SEE Framework Applied to POSC SIP

14.6.1 Data Access and Exchange API Architecture

There are two important architectural aspects of the Data Access and Exchange API. First, the API fits into a larger set of services that forms the platform in which E&P applications are developed and interoperate. Second, the API itself has substructure where layers representing different levels of abstraction have been defined. Each of these architectural perspectives is presented, in order, below.

Architectures on which standards are being based are the NIST/ECMA SEE reference model [ECMA 1991] and OMG's Object Services Architecture [OMG 1992]. These architectures provide a broad perspective of the standards necessary to support application interoperability. They provide a coherent model for communication between applications and between an application and services. The API addresses some of the Object Management Services as described in the SEE reference model (Fig. 14–1).

Standards related to the SEE reference model, PCTE [ECMA 1990], and ATIS [ANSI 1991] are monolithic and currently have few implementations. OMG is starting a phased approach to standardize particular object services that would seem easier for suppliers and users to implement. The Object Events Service may provide a base for many of the Inter-Application Communication requirements.

Other standards for implementation are defined in the POSC Base Standards Document [POSC 1991a]. In addition, POSC is tracking OMG's Common Object Request Broker Architecture [OMG 1991] as a means of

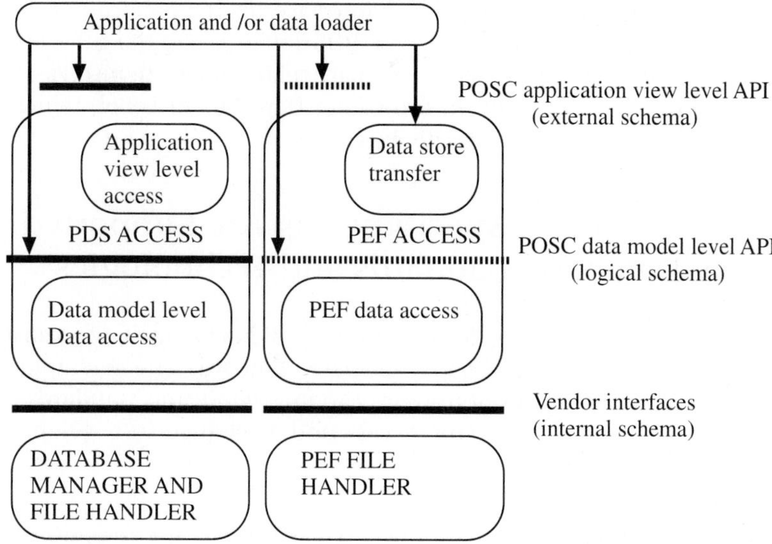

FIGURE 14–2
POSC Data Access and Exchange API Components

implementing services in a heterogeneous network within the communications services layer of the SEE reference model (Fig. 14–1).

The API has substructure where layers representing different levels of abstraction have been defined. Each of these architectural perspectives is presented, in order, below.

Two different levels, as depicted in Fig. 14–2, are defined within the Data Access and Exchange API: Data Model Level and Application View Level.

A request to the Data Model Level API specifies a mapping from the data constructs on which the Data Model is built to the data structures that are used by an application. All the constructs used in building the Data Model need to be available with an adequate set of operations to define the mappings.

At this level, the mappings are often defined using a data manipulation language. However, with relationships explicit in the model, an interface that can directly manipulate individual instances and navigate across relationships between instances is also appropriate.

The Application View Level API has semantics meaningful to E&P applications. A request to this API will operate on all the data in some view —a subset and/or specialization of the Data Model for a particular business function. The view, then, includes the semantics of the Data Model rather than just dealing with the underlying constructs. This interface hides the mappings necessary to transform from the data model to the view from the application and thus provides a simpler interface for the application developer. For the Application View Level API, POSC will specify the rules for the creation of views but not specify any particular views themselves. The Application View Level is built on top of the Data Model Level, which, in turn encapsulates any vendor-specific interface.

14.7 How POSC's Specifications Are Supported by Database Standards and Technologies

The POSC Specifications are derived from and have much in common with several existing and emerging database standards and technologies. The overlap of the features found in certain significant standards and technologies with the POSC Data Access and Exchange is developed in this section.

14.7.1 Standards

EXPRESS

The EXPRESS information modeling language [ISO 1991a] maps rather well to the Epicentre meta-model. The concepts of aggregate and complex data types, inheritance, and rules are all supported in EXPRESS. EXPRESS does not support, however, the following concepts that are used in Epicentre: multidimensional arrays, methods, and natural identifiers.

Version 2 of EXPRESS is expected to have methods defined as part of the language. Nevertheless, as a standard means of delivering Epicentre, EXPRESS has been found to be quite suitable.

STEP Data Access Interface (SDAI)

The STEP standardization effort has produced an API specification not unlike the POSC Data Access and Exchange API direct manipulation interface. The most conspicuous difference between SDAI and the POSC API is that SDAI does not have functions that execute query language statement strings (similar to POSC's language execution calls). This is a serious deficiency as the SAG CLI and APIs based on it are becoming more widely accepted. In addition, SDAI does not provide relational operations such as those in the data access language of the POSC API.

SQL-89 (SQL1 or SQL-92 Entry Level)

As most DBMSs do not yet conform to the full language defined in SQL-92, SQL-89 [ISO 1989] (or the Entry Level defined in SQL-92 [ANSI 1992]) is the most widespread standard on which database products are based. Much of the entity-attribute-relationship conceptual content of the Epicentre meta-model is well supported by SQL-89.

SQL-92 (or SQL2)

Although SQL-92 (or SQL2) [ANSI 1992] has many powerful new features beyond those of SQL-89, it does not have the object-oriented concepts required by the Epicentre meta-model or the aggregates provided by EXPRESS. One important development in the evolution of SQL-92 has been the adoption of the SQL Access Group's Call Level Interface as an addendum to the language. This means that a call interface similar to the language execution calls defined in the POSC Data Access and Exchange API has been adopted as part of an ANSI standard.

SQL3

SQL3 [ISO 1992a] is the logical extension of SQL-92. It is currently being defined by the ANSI X3H2 Technical Committee. POSC has representation in ANSI X3H2. SQL3 will have several object-oriented features, including inheritance, complex data types, and aggregates. It therefore will have a good mapping to the Epicentre meta-model.

SQL Access Group Call Level Interface (SAG CLI)

The language execution calls in the POSC API are based on the SQL Access Group Call Level Interface [SAG 1992]. In addition, the SAG CLI has been adopted by X/Open as a standard and by ANSI X3H2 as an addendum to the SQL language definition. An increasing number of vendors is developing APIs based on the SAG CLI.

As a means for binding attributes of simple data types and executing the relational subset of the data access language, the SQL Access Group's Call Level Interface is adequate. To better integrate with other POSC specifications, it was necessary to alter and extend the SAG CLI to include binding to aggregates as well as the execution of POSC's own data access language.

American Petroleum Institute RP66

The American Petroleum Institute RP66 [Wilhelmsen 1992] is a standard for the exchange of E&P data. Though the standard was originally designed for the exchange of well log data, it has been extended and generalized to a point where it may be applied to a wide range of E&P data. POSC has derived its own POSC Exchange Format (PEF) from the API RP66 standard. The POSC PEF goes beyond RP66 in that the PEF defines mappings from the Epicentre Data Model to structures defined in RP66 (termed Logical

Records). In a general sense, the PEF allows the schema that defines the exchanged data to be carried along with the exchanged data.

Object Management Group (OMG) Common Object Request Broker Architecture (CORBA)

The Common Object Request Broker Architecture (CORBA) of the Object Management Group (OMG) specifies an Interface Definition Language (IDL) for distributed access to objects. The Object Request Broker provides mechanisms by which objects make requests and receive responses. This mechanism is provided in a heterogeneous distributed environment and provides interoperability among the applications running in such an environment [OMG 1991; OMG 1992].

POSC acknowledges the importance of CORBA to distributed computing environments of the future and has attempted to specify nothing that will preclude the use of ORBs by POSC-compliant applications.

POSC maintains membership in OMG.

CAD Framework Initiative (CFI), Error Handling Programming Interface, and Inter-Tool Communication Programming Interface

The CAD Framework Initiative has specified two programming interfaces that have been used as a basis for the POSC Data Access and Exchange API: CFI Error Handling Programming Interface and CFI Inter-Tool Communication Programming Interface.

POSC monitors specifications under development at CFI and is a member of CFI.

14.7.2 Technologies

Relational Database Management Systems

Relational database management systems (RDBMSs) are commercially available data management systems that are usually based on SQL or a derivation thereof. Such systems are fairly well suited to the entity-attribute-relationship aspects of the Epicentre meta-model but fall far short of its object-oriented requirements.

Aggregated data values are often stored in RDBMSs through the use of some form of a Binary Large Object or BLOB. Utilization of a BLOB, however, imposes the additional requirement of implementing (often) complex logic to transform the BLOB to and from values that are semantically meaningful to applications. In this regard, SQL-92 has done some standardization and has defined the BIT STRING construct. Unfortunately, much of the definition of BIT STRINGs (e.g., the length) is left to the discretion of the implementor.

Object-Oriented Database Management Systems

Object-oriented database management systems (OODBMSs) exist primarily as a means for making objects, instantiated on the basis of C++ classes, persist beyond the bounds of the execution of the application that created them.

Such systems have a low impedance mismatch between the application code and the data access code; they are expressed in the same language. In addition, since C++ defines multidimensional arrays, OODBMSs generally address the requirement for large aggregates rather well.

Unfortunately, aside from the standardization of the C++ language itself, there is little standardization of such technologies and very poor portability from one such OODBMS to another.

Unified Relational and Object-Oriented Database Management Systems

Hybrid database technology adds object-oriented concepts to SQL-based query language. Since this is similar to the approach taken by the ANSI X3H2 committee in defining SQL3, these technologies are well positioned to converge with SQL3 when it is actually standardized. One important advantage of this unification is that such systems will support older relational data store definitions and applications while allowing newer data models and applications to be defined using object-oriented methodology. In addition, these technologies include aggregates, which most RDBMSs do not.

In evaluating technologies submitted to POSC in response to a Data Access and Exchange Request for Technology (RFT) [POSC 1991b, 1992a], unified relational and object-oriented database management systems were found to map most closely to both the Epicentre meta-model and the requirements put forth in the RFT. For these reasons, POSC selected Hewlett-Packard's OpenODB [Hewlett-Packard 1991] and UniSQL's UniSQL/X [UNISQL 1991a, 1991b] products as the bases for the Data Access and Exchange API.

14.8 Conclusion

Though the requirements of E&P data modeling and access stretch and often transcend most existing database technologies and standards, there exists much that can be applied meaningfully to address such requirements. In places where standards or technologies do not provide a direction, a pro-active approach to influencing those technologies and standards is called for. This two-pronged approach of adopting where possible and influencing where appropriate has placed POSC in a position to voice the needs of its members who have previously had few opportunities to have direct impact on advances in data management technologies and standards.

REFERENCES

American National Standards Institute. 1991. Working Draft Information Resource Dictionary System—ATIS, ANSI X3H4.

American National Standards Institute. 1992. Database Language SQL X3.135-1992, ANSI X3H2.

CAD Framework Initiative. 1992a. CFI Error Handling Programming Interface, Version 0.9.

CAD Framework Initiative. 1992b. CFI Candidate Standard Inter-Tool Communication Programming Interface, Version 0.9.3-102892.

European Computer Manufacturers Association. 1990. Portable Common Tool Environment (PCTE), Standard ECMA-149.

European Computer Manufacturers Association and National Institute of Standards and Technology, United States Department of Commerce. 1991. *Reference Model for Frameworks of Software Engineering Environments.* NIST Special Publication 500-201—Technical Report ECMA TR/55, 2nd edition.

Hewlett-Packard Company. 1991. OpenODB Preliminary Developer Release Reference Document.

International Organization for Standardization. 1989. ISO9075:1989, Database Language SQL.

International Organization for Standardization. 1990. ISO/IEC 9899:1990 C Language Standard.

International Organization for Standardization. 1991a. EXPRESS Language Reference Manual, ISO TC84/SC4/WG5 Document 14.

International Organization for Standardization and American National Standards Institute. 1992. (ISO/ANSI) Working Draft Database Language SQL (SQL3), DRAFT—ANSI X2H2, ISO/IEC JTC1/SC21/WG3.

Object Management Group and X/Open. 1991. The Common Object Request Broker: Architecture and Specification, OMG Document Number 91.12.1—Revision 1.1.

Object Management Group and X/Open. 1992. Object Services Architecture, OMG Document Number 92.8.1—Draft Revision 5.0.

Petrotechnical Open Software Corporation. 1991a. Software Integration Platform Specification—Base Computer Standards, Version 1.0.

Petrotechnical Open Software Corporation. 1991b. Software Integration Platform—Data Access Request for Comments, POSC EPDA-3.

Petrotechnical Open Software Corporation. 1992a. Software Integration Platform—Request for Technology, POSC EPDA-4.

Petrotechnical Open Software Corporation. 1992b. POSC E&P Data Model Methodology.

Petrotechnical Open Software Corporation. 1992c. Technical Program Overview, POSC Document TR-1.

Petrotechnical Open Software Corporation. 1992d. Software Integration Platform Specification, Volume 3 (API), Version 1.0 Snapshot.

Petrotechnical Open Software Corporation. 1992e. Software Integration Platform Specification, Volume 4 (PEF), Version 1.0 Snapshot.

Petrochemical Open Software Corporation. 1994a. POSC Software Integration Platform Specification, Epicentre Data Model, Version 1.0. PTR Prentice Hall, Englewood Cliffs, N.J.

Petrochemical Open Software Corporation. 1994b. POSC Software Integration Platform Specification, Data Access and Exchange, Version 1.0. PTR Prentice Hall, Englewood Cliffs, N.J.

Petrochemical Open Software Corporation. 1994c. POSC Software Integration Platform Specification, Exchange Format, Version 1.0. PTR Prentice Hall, Englewood Cliffs, N.J.

Petrochemical Open Software Corporation. 1994d. POSC Software Integration Platform Specification, E&P User Interface Style Guide, Version 1.0. PTR Prentice Hall, Englewood Cliffs, N.J.

SQL Access Group. 1992. Call Level Interface, Base Document Version 2.1.2, CLI-92-014.

UniSQL, Inc. 1991a. UniSQL/X Users Manual Release 1.0 1991.

UniSQL, Inc. 1991b. UniSQL/X Application Programmers Interface Manual Release 1.0.

Wilhelmsen, D. 1992. An Introduction to American Petroleum Institute Recommended Practice 66. In press.

15

The Changing Database Standards Landscape

CRAIG THOMPSON

As database technology scales to meet enterprise needs, standards are becoming increasingly important in the database marketplace. Two trends are changing the current picture. Both the relational database community and the object database community are responding to the need for object database standards. At the same time, the frameworks and enterprise integration communities are segmenting database systems into collections of object services. Both trends are affecting the boundaries of the field. This chapter describes these trends, circa mid-1993.

15.1 Introduction

As our computing world becomes more complex and we understand more about it, there is a continuing need to consolidate what we know in a form that will allow next-generation computing systems to build on what we have learned. This chapter addresses the standardization process as a way to capture this knowledge and make it useful to wide communities for reasonable cost. In particular, it focuses on two trends that are having major impact on database standardization: the trend toward extending DBMSs to support object technology and the trend toward segmenting monolithic standards to simpler component standards that can be composed.

Section 15.2 broadly describes the need for and economics of standards and the standardization process. Section 15.3 describes the trend toward adding objects to DBMSs, focusing on the effort to extend SQL to SQL3 and the parallel effort to standardize OODBs by the Object Data Management Group. Section 15.4 describes the trend toward decomposing monolithic database standards and systems into simpler, interoperable parts. Section 15.5 predicts future trends.

15.2 Background on Standards

A *standard* is a quantifiable interface, model, rule, or representation established by authority, custom, or general consent to permit common interchange. In information technology, common standards are intended to precisely define the syntax and semantics of a programming or database language, a representation, an instruction set, or even a software architecture.

Economic forces are the driver for standards development. In the last several years, to stay competitive, governments and corporations increasingly buy COTS (commercial off the shelf) software rather than build custom software. There is a parallel trend to require standards wherever possible since they preserve investment (longer shelf life, lower cost, less risk with second sourcing, lower training costs). Without standards of some kind, there is chaos: Groups cannot share information or insulate applications from each other to port them to later generations. Interfaces provide insulating boundaries; standard interfaces allow wider communities to take advantage of these boundaries.

There are several kinds of standards. *Base,* or *component,* standards have limited scope and are developed by committees of experts. *Profiles* are suites of referenced base standards that accomplish some larger function in an integrated, interoperable way.

Proprietary standards are closely held by one or a few organizations and may be protected by intellectual property laws; documentation is restricted but may be available by commercial license. In the open marketplace, dominant vendors' products may become *de facto,* or *market,* standards. Documentation may exist, but there may be no exact definition of the standard. The need to grow or open a closed market may drive organizations to cooperate as *consortia* to register, develop, and sometimes implement potential standards. *Formal (voluntary) standards* are developed by an accredited national or international standards organization through a public process. Due process and consensus criteria required can slow the process. Documentation is publicly available. The aim is a well-defined definition. *Regulatory standards* are developed by some organization, often the government, to manage some kinds of competition or meet internal needs.

Reactionary standards lag the marketplace. They react to de facto marketplace practices and seek to consolidate proprietary or de facto standards into a voluntary standard. Participants have experience. One approach is a least-common denominator approach in which the common features of relevant systems are codified. *Anticipatory standards* lead the marketplace and create or expand markets. Technical sufficiency may be unknown until implemented. Timing is tricky and there is an art in reaching consensus before marketplace trends are evident. There is always some danger in premature standards—they may be ignored or may impede progress. One approach is to create a layered migration path in which defined levels of capability are specified.

The International Standards Organization (ISO) coordinates many international computer standards. Voting is by country. In the United

States, the American National Standards Institute (ANSI) accredits standards-producing organizations. IEEE and X3 are key standards-development organizations (SDOs) and both produce a variety of computer software standards, including standards for C++, Smalltalk, Lisp, Cobol, SQL, repositories, distributed systems, and object models. Several other SDOs exist. National and international SDOs usually attempt to maintain coordination so that their standards do not deviate.

Participants in voluntary standards are often organizations. Truly unaffiliated individuals are rare. Many organizations participate as standards producers; they view the standards process as a means to attract customers who will invest in their complying products. Other organizations participate as standards consumers; they may be concerned with profiles of standards that will interoperate—that is, work together—and they often participate in component standards definition in order to make their requirements known and to influence standards directions. Many industrial organizations now have Standards Councils that actively seek to profile standards that meet an organization's needs and that set strategies for developing standards for competitive advantage.

Ultimately, standards may be successful in allowing industries to mature and grow, or they may fail to make an impact if never accepted by industry. Organizations need to continually evaluate how to get the most value from the standardization process: when to lead, when to follow, and when to choose to deviate. Advantages to participation are positioning and meeting the competition on neutral ground; there is no advantage to being ignorant of standards.

15.3 The Trend Toward Combining DBMS Standards and Object Technology

This section focuses on the trend toward adding objects to database standards.

15.3.1 The SQL Family of Standards

ISO JTC1/SC21/WG3 (Information Processing/Open Systems Interconnection/Database Working Group) and X3H2 (ANSI Accredited Standards Committee X3/Database) are the two parallel committees that coordinate to provide standards for SQL.

Before 1986–1987, there were *no* database standards, international or domestic. SQL 86 provided a reactionary baseline, least-common denominator standard. It provided a programming language-independent tabular data model, schema definition, views, and cursors for a row-at-a-time programming language interface.

SQL 89 is currently the standard commercial relational database language that has wide market acceptance. It is more complete functionally than SQL 86 in that it provides referential integrity (to insure foreign keys match corresponding primary keys). It also provides SQL embeddings for Ada, C, COBOL, FORTRAN, Pascal, and PL/1.

SQL2, completed in 1992, is anticipatory in that it goes beyond today's commercial offerings [Date and Darwen 1993; Melton 1993a]. It adds an executable DDL, dynamic SQL via PREPARE and EXECUTE statements, outer join, cascaded update and delete, temporary tables, set operations union, intersection and difference, domain definitions in schemas, new built-in data types (including Datetime, National, and Varchar), transaction consistency levels, deferred constraint checking, scrolled cursors, and SQL diagnostics.

SQL3, targeted for completion in 1995 or beyond, is upwards compatible to SQL2 and at the same time adds support for objects [Melton 1993b]. SQL3 is computationally complete (unlike OMG IDL and its derivatives — see sections 15.3.2 and 15.4.2). The SQL3 specification is actively undergoing revision. It is very likely changes will be made that make even the brief description in this chapter incorrect.

SQL3 objects are instances of Abstract Data Types (ADTs), which are patterned semantically after C++ class definitions. SQL3 ADTs support multiple inheritance; public, private, and protected members; and operations. Parameterized ADTs are supported. In SQL3, ADTs themselves are not objects. Some schema evolution operations are provided to add, alter, or drop members or add or drop superclasses.

SQL3 is a hybrid language similar to other hybrids like C++, which extends C, and Common Lisp Object System, which extends Common Lisp. Procedures are supported for compatibility with SQL2. The very notion of object is influenced by SQL2. SQL3 supports three sorts of objects. For compatibility with SQL2, objects include rows in tables where there is no OID and objects are accessible by primary key. Alternatively, objects (rows) can have unique, immutable system-generated OIDs visible as the first column in tables. Finally, vendors can support hidden OIDs not visible to the user that are not unique or immutable.

Tables are *Multisets* of rows—that is, an unordered collection that allows duplicates. All rows are of the same type. *Sets* (with no duplicates) and *Lists* (with order) are treated as special cases of tables.

Relationships are provided by REF types of members, which are OID-valued instead of key values. References can be to Multisets, Sets, Lists, or objects. Literals do not have OIDs.

SQL3 operators are divided into mutator operations, which can change state; observer operations, which cannot change state; and actor operations, which may be either observer or mutator operations.

The SQL3 ADT scheme is extensible. A new project has been proposed to define a collection of standard ADT packages (class library) including

```
interface Course: Atomic_Object       //e.g., Course inherits from Atomic_Object
  {extent courses;                    //named set of all instances,optional
   attribute string[32] name;         //generates get and set methods
   relationship set<section> sections//a one-many relationship
                inverse section_of;   //and its inverse
   total_enrollment()}                //operation to sum enrollment across
                                          sections
```

FIGURE 15–1
Example ODMG ODL Interface Definition

Vectors, Matrices, Geographic and Spatial, Text and Document, Graphics, Pictures, Audio, Video, Hypermedia, and ASN.1 data types.

Issues for SQL3 include: Is it necessary to invent a new object model, a new syntax, and a new computationally complete language, all modeled on C++ but not the same as or extensions to C++ (or OMG IDL)? Would it be possible instead to reuse C++/IDL more directly for this purpose? What will language bindings look like for C++ and for other languages with somewhat different object models? Will there be a market in developing reusable ADT libraries that is distinct from the similar markets for libraries in C++ or PDES/STEP Express (see section 15.4.4)?

15.3.2 ODMG-93

Object Database Management Group is a consortium of five OODB vendors and a number of reviewers, formed in the fall of 1991, with the objective of putting in place a *de facto* OODB interface standard by late 1993 [Cattell 1993]. The absence of an OODB standard is viewed by the group as a road-block to widespread adoption of OODB technology. The collaboration on a joint ODMG-93 specification is aimed at jump-starting a more formal standards process. The five OODB vendors involved in development of the specification include Object Design, Objectivity, Ontos, 0_2, and Versant; no implementation of ODMG-93 currently exists, but all five vendors have claimed that they would implement the specification by mid-1994.

The premise of OODBMSs differs from the premise of extended relational database systems (and from SQL3) in that OODBMSs are closely integrated with programming language syntax, semantics, and compilers for existing programming languages, including C++, C, Smalltalk, Common Lisp, and Ada.

Like the SQL3 specification, the ODMG-93 specification is undergoing revision. As a consequence, the following description is expected to change before the specification is stabilized.

ODMG begins by defining a programming language independent Object Definition Language (ODL) that is similar to C++ class definitions and is an extension of OMG IDL (see section 15.4.4). Figure 15–1 is an example ODMG ODL interface definition.

A built-in type hierarchy consists of *Denotable_Object* and *Characteristics*. *Denotable_Objects* are either *Objects* or *Literals*. *Objects* are either atomic or structured. *Structured_Objects* include either *Structures* or parameterized *Collections[T]*, like *Set, Bag, List, MultiList,* and *Array*. *Literals* may be atomic, including *Integer, Float, Character,* and *Boolean,* or they may be immutable structures or collections. Immutable structures include *Date* and *Time*. *Characteristics* include *Properties*, which may be *Attributes* or *Relationships*, and *Operations*.

The ODMG Object Manipulation Language (OML) supports operations on OML types. OML types are by default declared to be persistent, meaning instances may be either transient or persistent. If declared transient, all instances of an OML type must be transient.

The type *Database* supports operations *open()* and *close()*, which connect repositories of objects to the program run-time. Associated with a database are three sorts of entry points into the database: the *schema* of types of objects stored in the database, *extents* associated with types, and a *namespace* that associates user-specified names with persistent objects. Associated with the *type* object are operations for accessing meta data (e.g., name, has_supertypes, has_properties, has_operations).

OML supports a pessimistic, lock-based concurrency control model in which nested transactions control access to persistent data. In addition to *commit* and *abort* operations, a checkpoint operation can be used to commit all modified objects to the database while retaining all locks held by the transaction instance.

An Object Query Language (OQL) supports the ODMG data model. ODMG's OQL is declarative and has a concrete syntax that is SQL-like. It permits operations on collections other than just sets. OQL only covers queries; operations to create collections or insert or remove elements are treated normally as operations on types.

The ODMG specification provides two initial programming language bindings, the C++ Binding and the Smalltalk Binding. The overriding ODMG design principle for language bindings is that the programmer should feel that he or she is using one language and not two separate languages with bindings between them. That is, there should be a unified type system between the programming language and the database. Individual objects of common types can be persistent or transient. The binding respects the language, naturally extends it, and does not duplicate functionality already in the base language; expressions in the OML binding freely compose with expressions in the base language.

The ODMG specification is actively undergoing revision. At present, there are two candidate C++ bindings. One involves using handles, called *refs*, to manipulate OML objects. The other is more seamless; objects are made persistent at allocation time, but references to OML and C++ persistent or transient objects are the same. In the C++ binding, pointers from persistent to transient objects are set to NULL at commit. In the Smalltalk binding, objects can be made persistent at any time at or after object creation. Any objects referenced from a persistent object become persistent.

The ODMG specification is a good first step in building consensus for an OODB standard. More work is needed to distinguish how the OMG ODL and the native object models in C++ and Smalltalk relate to each other to simultaneously provide seamlessness (where the database and programming language use the same data models) and interlanguage sharing (since ODL, C++, and Smalltalk are not one-to-one data models). More work is also needed to determine whether and how the ODMG object model and object query language and SQL3 can be aligned since they are similar in coverage. Finally, more work will be needed to determine how OMG's object services architecture relates to ODMG's specification (see section 15.4.2).

15.4 The Trend Toward Segmentation of Database Standards

This section describes the second main trend, the trend towards decomposing monolithic standards (like those described in section 15.3) into simpler component standards that can interoperate. This trend is similar to that in stereos or the automobile industry, in which best-of-class suppliers supply key components to system integrators who assemble products from them. The thesis of this trend is that database standards are becoming more open, providing an opportunity for groups other than just major vendors to assemble database products from parts supplied by best-of-service providers.

15.4.1 X3/SPARC/DBSSG/OODB Task Group

OODBTG was a study group, formed in January 1989 with a charter to characterize OODBs and recommend to X3 whether and what standards activities to initiate in the OODB area. Individuals from about 40 organizations, including several OODB vendors, met quarterly to complete a final report, which was published by National Institute for Standards and Technology (NIST) in September 1991 [Fong et al. 1991]. Around 800 copies were distributed.

The group organized two public workshops on OODB standardization to gather consensus, sponsored a survey of OODB systems, and completed several reports. The OODB Task Group Final Report contains a glossary of OODB terms, a reference model characterizing OODBs, and a set of recommendations for standardization.

```
Object Data Management
 General Characteristics of Object Models
 |---Objects: Operations, Requests, Messages,
 |   Methods, and State
 |---Binding and Polymorphism
 |---Encapsulation
 |---Identity
 |---Types and Classes
 |---Inheritance and Delegation
 |---Noteworthy Objects: Relationships, Attributes,
 |   Literals, Containment, and Aggregates
 |---Extensibility
 |---Integrity Constraints
 |---Object Language

 Data Management Characteristics
 |---Persistence
 |---Concurrency and Transactions
 |---Distribution
 |---ODM Object Languages and Queries
 |---Data Dictionary and Namespace
 |---Change Management: Versions, Configurations,
 |   Dependencies, Schema Evolution
 |---Reliability and Recovery
 |---Security

 ODM System Characteristics
 |---Class Libraries
 |---Program and User Interfaces
 |---User Roles
```

FIGURE 15–2
ODM Design Space

In the standardization process, reference models play an intermediate role. They serve to delimit the shape and scope of a potential standard and provide an abstract semantics and description that allows people to understand and compare systems. It differs from a standard in that specific interfaces that allow machines to communicate still need to be specified. The OODBTG Object Data Management Reference Model played a role similar to the more familiar earlier OODB Manifesto [Atkinson et al. 1989] but was more comprehensive. The document describes an OODB as a collection of characteristics (see Fig. 15–2).

OODBTG came to two main conclusions about future standardization of OODBs. First, they recognized that several fields are simultaneously extending their standards by adding object technology. These include programming languages, network management, operating systems, design methodologies, user interfaces, and others. Most characteristics of OODB object models are shared with object models developed for other purposes and are not special to OODBs. This is not unexpected when one considers the goal of OODBs to provide seamlessness (in which the database and programming language use the same data models). Nevertheless, database and other groups are proposing new and different object models that may not provide interoperability guarantees. OODBTG proposed that X3 initiate an effort to guide ongoing and future object model standardization efforts toward convergence where possible (see section 15.4.4).

Second, they recognized that, while OODBs may depend on several data management characteristics (e.g., persistence, transactions, distribution, meta data, change management, security), several of these characteristics are orthogonal to each other, may or may not be present in a given OODB, are not special to OODBs, and may be needed by systems other than those that persistently store large volumes of small objects. The group's conclusion was that, rather than develop a monolithic OODB standard, simpler reusable component standards should be developed that could be composed to become an OODB or could be reused by other communities.

15.4.2 Object Management Group

The Object Management Group (OMG) is a nonprofit consortium of over 300 companies formed in 1989 with the objective of developing an industrywide architectural framework populated with supporting detailed interface specifications. The specifications are based on an object management paradigm and are intended to drive industry toward an interoperable, reusable, and portable software base that will reduce complexity, lower costs, and speed the introduction to new distributed, enterprise-level software applications. In 1990, OMG completed its Object Management Architecture (OMA) Reference Model [Soley 1993]. Figure 15–3 shows the Object Request Broker (ORB), a software backplane that provides message dispatch and hides distribution. Applications can be composed from application-specific software and collections of reusable Object Services accessible via the ORB.

In 1991, a detailed interface specification for the ORB, called CORBA, was completed. Part of the CORBA specification included the definition of an object definition language called Interface Description Language (IDL), similar to C++ class definitions.

In 1992, an abstract object model was defined that is characterized by a core object model and a collection of component extensions. The core has been specified, but the components have not yet been agreed upon, though groups like ODMG are identifying extensions to IDL that are candidate components (e.g., extents, relationships).

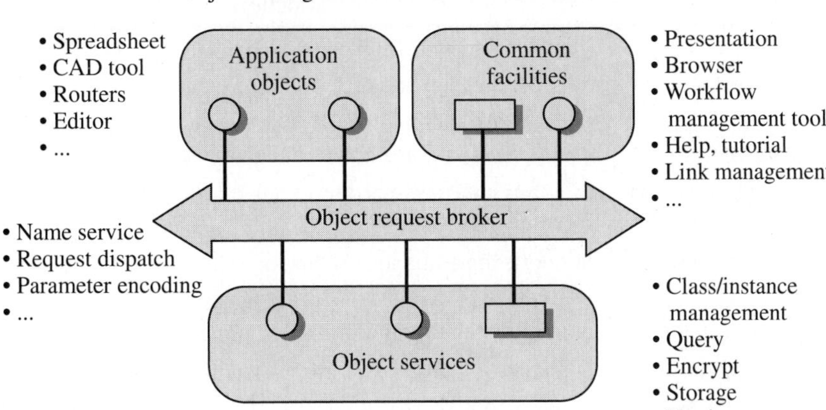

FIGURE 15–3
OMG Object Model Architecture (from OMA Guide)

Also in 1992, OMG completed a detailed description of a collection of object services that will initially populate the OMA architecture (see Table 15–1) [OMG 1992]. Interestingly, many of the object services identified by OMG are one to one with the services or characteristics identified by OODB Task Group (see Fig. 15–2) and the functional capabilities identified by ODMG.

Like OODBTG, OMG recognizes that it can populate the specifications in stages and that groups other than database systems need distribution, name services, replication, relationships, and other services that overlap. A series of OMG Requests for Proposals is in progress to populate OMG's object services architecture (OSA). The first covers the lifecycle, event, name, and persistence services; the second covers transactions, concurrency, relationships, and externalization.

The advantage of an OSA to the end user is that it extends the advantages of common look-and-feel of some graphical user interfaces to provide a common, familiar semantics for many applications. They can learn how to do queries, use help, and so on, just once, and those capabilities extend across many applications. The advantage to the application developer is the ability to reuse common services and protocols to more quickly build applications that are more robust. An advantage to enterprises is that OSAs are scalable and can accommodate heterogeneity, legacy applications, and services and can provide migration paths. An advantage to research groups is that they can focus on improving individual elements of a services architecture without rearchitecting a monolithic system. An advantage for standards is that OSAs can be standardized modularly and do not lead to

Table 15–1: Categories of Object Services

Service	Function
Archive	Supports mapping between active and backup object stores
Backup/restore	Supports backup and recovery of objects
Change management	Supports identification and consistent evolution of objects, including version and configuration management
Concurrency control	Supports concurrent access to one or more objects by one or more objects
Data interchange	Supports the exchange of some or all of an object's visible state between two objects
Event notification	Supports notification of events to interested objects
Externalization	Supports object externalization and internalization
Implementation repository	Supports the management of object implementations
Installation and activation	Provides mechanisms for distributing, activating, deactivating, and relocating managed objects
Interface repository	Supports the management of object interface definitions
Licensing	Supports license management
Lifecycle	Supports object create, delete, copy, and equivalence
Naming	Supports mapping between names and objects
Operational control	Supports controlling the dynamic behavior of managed objects

monolithic standards. A disadvantage of OSAs is that industry still lacks experience since OSAs are relatively new and we do not yet know definitively whether best-of-class OODBs, RDBs, repositories, CASE tools, and related information management systems can be composed from standard OSA toolkits.

15.4.3 Other Evidence for the Trend Toward Database Standards Segmentation

While OODBTG recommended modular component standards and OMG is developing them, these are not the only groups working toward more open database technology standards.

X/Open XA

X/Open is an industry consortium that profiles collections of standards that will interoperate. X/Open *brands* compliant systems. The X/Open XA standard is motivated by the need for transactions that span DBMS and transac-

Table 15–1: Categories of Object Services (con.)

Service	Function
Persistence	Supports persistence of an object independent of both the lifetime of the client applications that access the object and the implementation that realizes the object's methods
Properties	Provides dynamic named attributes associated with an object
Query	Supports operations on sets and collections that return sets and collections. Supports indexing
Relationships	Supports associations between two or more objects
Replication	Supports explicit replication of objects in a distributed environment and the management of consistency of the copies
Sagas	Supports long-running transactions with possible intermediate checkpoints
Security	Supports access control on objects
Startup services	Supports bootstrapping and termination of object services
Threads	Supports multiple threads of execution control
Time	Supports synchronization of clocks in a distributed system
Trading	Supports matching of provided services to the service needs of a client object
Transactions	Supports atomic execution of one or more operations

tion processing systems. The objective is to develop a protocol that allows an external transaction controller to poll systems that have their own transaction support to insure that when they all are ready to commit, they do so atomically. This requires that all such component systems support messages like *prepare-to-commit*. The XA protocol is data-model independent in that relational, object, and other forms of database system can be engineered to follow this protocol. Formerly closed systems are now becoming more open to support this form of cooperation. This trend toward openness is driven by the economic need to scale transaction processing so that transactions provide normal ACID properties but span data repositories within and between organizations.

X3H2.1 Remote Data Access

A work item related to X3H2 involves providing mechanisms for one relational system to communicate with another. This involves standardizing on system catalogs and on issuing embedded queries. As with X/Open XA, RDA has the effect of separating a database capability from its DBMS implementation. In this case, a gateway is created that allows applications to talk to a single SQL application program interface (API), which then connects to different target relational DBMS systems, thus insulating applications from DBMS implementations. An industrial consortium, SQL Access Group, was instrumental in accelerating agreement on this standard. Two specifications based on RDA are competing in the marketplace, Microsoft's ODBC and Borland's IDAPI. Both provide gateways to multiple backend relational DBMS systems.

X3H4 Information Resource Dictionary Systems (IRDS)

IRDS is a standard for meta data models. The standard is evolving from being SQL-based to adopting an architecture that views an IRDS as dependent on a collection of object services, similar to a subset of OMG services.

15.4.4 The Broader Standards Landscape

Workshop on Application Integration Architectures (AIA):

The AIA Workshop was held in February 1993 to assess whether enterprise integration standards, including database standards, will converge to allow interoperation of standards-based products [Thompson and Hodges 1993]. There are no global mechanisms (other than the marketplace) that insure this outcome. Many standards development organizations and consortia have local perspectives, and there is some overlap between groups. Different groups operate in different time frames with different objectives. One important conclusion of the workshop was that many groups can cast their work as part of an object services architecture. A few of the standards groups and consortia developing standards that relate to object database technology are briefly described in this section.

Change Management

Change management is the ability to efficiently manage historical versions, configurations and compositions, and derivation dependencies. Some view change management as part of an object model; others view it as an object service. Change management is an example of overlap where several groups have focused on providing some level of support. These groups include X3H4 (IRDS), X3H6 (CASE Integration Services), PDES/STEP, PCTE, CAD Framework Initiative, OMG, and X3J13 (Common Lisp).

PDES/STEP and CASE Data Interchange Format (CDIF)

Common databases are only part of the problem in sharing information within and between organizations. Several applications areas (including product data, electrical engineering, manufacturing, petrochemical, and computer-aided software engineering) are defining common schemas (like class libraries) for sharing common object types across applications on a vertical industrywide basis. PDES/STEP, CDIF, and some similar communities define an E-R or OO data model for defining schemas, generic interchange formats for bulk transfer of the data, and mappings to programming languages and database systems.

Portable Common Tools Environment (PCTE)

PCTE is a European Computer Manufacturers Association (ECMA) standard. In several ways similar to OMG, PCTE provides an entity-relationship interface to file systems (large-grain objects) and is moving toward supporting fine-grain objects with an object model.

X3H7 Object Information Management

One of the important conclusions of the AIA Workshop was that there are many standards development organizations and consortia that are developing their own object models. This was also a conclusion of OODB Task Group. As a result of their recommendation to X3, a new technical committee, X3H7 Object Information Management was formed in January 1993. The group meets quarterly, usually in conjunction with other standards groups working on object model standards. Two efforts are under-way. One involves a careful comparison of existing object models via a feature comparison matrix. Object models vary semantically in dozens of ways (e.g., rules of inheritance, rules for encapsulation, support for relation-ships, binding-time issues, flexibility in meta models). Some differences between object models are accidental; some are requirements of an application area. Examples of the latter are support in object models for dynamic and/or asynchronous dispatch of methods. X3H7 is also considering how to accommodate heterogeneous object models since they are a fact of life in programming-in-the-large. They have identified several situations in which applications written in object models in different programming languages need to interact (e.g., when a Lisp application wants to use a user-interface management system written in C++) and are working to develop approaches to handle these situations. Developing a new object model (which OMG, ODMG, and SQL3 are all doing) is one approach.

15.5 Conclusions

The economic impact of standards is their reason for existence. Standards are necessary for scaling information systems to provide enterprise integration. Formal standards groups and industry consortia are sometimes criticized as uncreative, tedious and glacially slow, expensive in time and travel, vehicles for dominant vendors, and irrelevant. To be sure, these criticisms are sometimes valid. But standardization can also be a force for the good, can provide a forum where good ideas are reviewed to become better, can be steered by those with an industrywide vision, and can produce large shifts in industry directions.

The jury is still out deciding exactly what will happen next in the OODB standardization area. It appears safe to conclude that some form of hybrid OODB-RDB will eventually result. The established relational community is adding objects in SQL3, building on past database standards. The newcomer ODMG consortium and the OODB vendors are building more directly on programming language standards, proposing to extend them with database services including queries based on SQL. The groups are not miles apart conceptually. ODMG has introduced a programming-language-neutral object model that is an extended OMG IDL, which is itself a relative of C++, and SQL3 is moving to a programming-language-neutral object model that is also related to C++.[1] Both specifications make objects persistent without requiring them to be parts of collections. ODMG provides much more seamless interfaces to programming languages, and their standard is more closely based on experience. SQL3, while anticipatory in the area of objects, builds from a much larger installed base. Neither group has yet demonstrated how to simultaneously preserve seamlessness and support interoperation across different object models. No implementations of either standard yet exist, though ODMG implementations are expected by mid-1994. There is a real opportunity for convergence of these efforts.

The trend towards segmentation may result in a much more radical change in how we view database technology. The OODB trend towards merging the boundaries between databases and programming languages is one instance. In general, extending the database to capture more meaning can be viewed as database-centric when other groups are extending programming languages or operating systems or distributed systems to capture similar meaning. By viewing a database as a composition of object services that are also useful for other purposes, database systems may be rebuilt via more general and more powerful object services architectures. Instead of monolithic standards, we expect compositional standards that reflect the increased openness of the architecture. The openness can result in acceleration of improvement to the parts. Experimental reference implementations of object services architectures that can be composed to form OODBs add

---

1. The term *programming-language-neutral object model* is actually a misnomer, though it is widely used. It is intended to indicate an object model that is neutral with respect to existing object-oriented programming languages. There is an assumption that sharing information among existing programming languages will be accomplished using the neutral object model. This is analogous to the use of the relational model in RDBMSs, where it provides a neutral representation with respect to host programming languages. Actually, the newly invented *neutral* object model becomes yet-another-object-model (YAOM), to which database programming languages are fitted, as is the direction for SQL3. This considerably weakens the argument for inventing a new "neutral" model.

credibility to this trend [Wells et al. 1992]. This trend may well affect and may even force convergence of SQL3 and ODMG as OMG adopts separate but composable specifications for persistence, transactions, relationships, queries, and other object services in 1994.

Standing back still further, we can identify another major consequence of these two trends. At present, a tiny fraction of data is stored in object databases, a larger fraction in relational databases, but most data is still stored in file systems, and this is increasing with the trend towards downsizing to decentralize corporate networks. File system technology has undergone only modest change over the last 25 years. Yet it is possible to view a file system as a degenerate lightweight OODB with name space, weak typing, support mainly for large objects, and no support for inheritance or behavior. Several groups are beginning to work on next generation object-file systems that add object services and models on top of and under file systems. The twin trends identified in this chapter may well be just an intermediate step on the road toward an information system that unifies file systems with relational and object databases.

REFERENCES

Atkinson, M., Bancilhon, F., DeWitt, D., Dittrich, K., Maier, D., and Zdonik, S. 1989. The Object-Oriented Database System Manifesto. *Proceedings of DOOD'89*, Kyoto, Japan.

Cattell, R., ed. 1993. The Object Database Standard: ODMG-93. Morgan Kaufmann.

Date, C., and Darwen, H. 1993. *A Guide to the SQL Standard*, 3rd edition. Addison-Wesley, Reading, Mass.

Fong, E., Kent, W., Moore, K., and Thompson, C., eds. 1991. X3/SPARC/DBSSG OODB Task Group Final Report. *NIST Technical Report*, National Institute of Standards and Technology. (Hardcopy available from Elizabeth Fong at fong@ecf.ncsl.nist.gov).

Melton, J., ed. 1993a. *American National Standard Database Language SQL (SQL2)*. X3.135-1992.

Melton, J., ed. 1993b. *ISO/ANSI Working Draft Database SQL (SQL3)*, X3H2-93-091/ ISO DBL YOK-003.

Object Management Group. 1992. OMG Object Services Architecture, Revision 6.0. OMG Document 92.8.4.

Soley, R., ed. 1993. Object Management Architecture Guide, Revision 2.0, 2nd edition. OMG TC Document 92.11.1.

Thompson, C., and Hodges, B., eds. 1993. Report on the Workshop on Application Integration Architectures. *NIST Technical Report*, National Institute of Standards and Technology.

Wells, D., Blakeley, J., and Thompson, C. 1992. Architecture of an Object-Oriented Database Management System. *IEEE Computer*, Vol. 25, No. 10.

16

Multimedia Information Systems: Issues and Approaches

STAVROS CHRISTODOULAKIS
LEONIDAS KOVEOS

We present an overview of issues that are important for the design and implementation of multimedia information systems. We outline current approaches and longer-term research issues. Finally, we present an ongoing project, KYDONIA, for the design and implementation of all the layers of an object-oriented multimedia information system.

16.1 Introduction

The methods that have been employed in order to improve communication and information exchange between people were limited in capabilities due to the limitations of the media used. Before the wide use of computers, information was formed in static structures (books, papers, etc.) that are difficult to modify or update. The computer ability to manage information and data and present them in a variety of structures has broken the static structures' monopoly.

The first computing systems dealt only with information that was represented in alphanumeric forms. PCs added the ability to work in graphics mode at a low-resolution analysis that was incapable of displaying text. With the technological advance in storage devices, graphics and video adapters, the size of main memory, and processing power, it was possible to manage and display text and high-quality graphics, allowing the production of user-friendly interfaces. In addition, new peripherals such as mice, scanners, and laser printers began making an impact in the computer industry. The last decade introduced the concepts of advanced graphics interfaces, hyperlinking, and object orientation. Effective nonlinear representation of and navigation through complex multimedia information became possible.

It is very difficult to define the term *multimedia*. We can define it very loosely as any system that we can use to present information in more than one form: text, graphics, still image, animation, sound, video, special computer-generated effects. The system has user-friendly interactive interfaces that help the communication of complex ideas and complex knowledge structures. *Multimedia* are extensively used, nowadays, for entertainment, public information, advertising, and education. In the future, integrated electronic systems, composed of computers, digital TVs, optical disks, electronic detectors, and other electronic units will be used for presentation and interaction with the user via multimedia.

Multimedia information systems are the information systems that manage multimedia information, facilitate multimedia for presentations, and use specific tools for the storage, management, and retrieval of multimedia information. Systems for storing and retrieving *multimedia information* have been designed and developed for different application areas in the last decade. Several different approaches for the management and presentation of multimedia information have been adopted and utilized in the context of these systems.

16.2 Requirements for Multimedia Information Management Systems

In this section, we present several requirements on multimedia information management, such as storage and retrieval of multimedia data, synchronization issues, query specification, modeling, structuring, content addressability, and others.

16.2.1 Multimedia Data Storage and Retrieval

There is a number of problems associated with the design of the storage manager of an efficient multimedia object server:

- There are several kinds of magnetic and optical storage devices that are appropriate for different kinds of multimedia applications. These types of storage devices, which may have diverse properties, should be uniformly modeled and integrated into a single multimedia storage manager.
- Multimedia data typically require very large storage. In some application environments, they force the use of tertiary storage and multilevel storage hierarchies. Uniform and effective integration of multilevel storage with respect to the requirements of multimedia applications is of considerable importance.
- Some of the performance characteristics of real-time retrieval of multimedia objects demand substantial run-time support. Appropriate scheduling and resource allocation algorithms should be developed that allow good performance for environments with a mixture of delay-sensitive and non-delay-sensitive data.

- The multimedia data (large volumes and real-time retrieval characteristics) impose very demanding requirements in the system. Effective use of storage and processing parallelism is essential for good performance of such systems.
- Many important multimedia information systems applications are distributed in nature. To guarantee good performance for multimedia data retrieval, distributed system support is required.

These features are not supported well by existing systems. In this subsection, we discuss requirements of multimedia information systems.

Management of Multimedia Data in Large-Capacity Devices

Multimedia data require very large storage capacities. Optical disks of various kinds are used in the archiving of multimedia data. They provide inexpensive storage, large storage capacities, and reasonably fast random access. There are currently analog and digital optical disk storage devices in the market. Digital optical storage of multimedia data has major advantages in the long run. Within the category of digital optical storage devices, one can find devices better suited to publishing (CD-ROMs), to archiving information (WORMs), or to changing information (rewritables), as well as variations in between. With present technology, it is often not possible for any single device to store the large volume of multimedia data produced and processed daily by organizations. For this reason, optical disks are organized in larger arrangements (jukeboxes) from which disks are fetched on demand via a (slow) control mechanism [Byte 1990].

Optical disks have performance characteristics different from those of magnetic disks. Therefore, their retrieval performance must be understood clearly and modeled to allow maximum utilization of their capabilities [Christodoulakis 1987]. Based on the performance models developed, better solutions to database performance problems may be found. One such problem is that of optimal data placement, for which it was shown that the solution for the CLV-type disks (constant linear velocity disks) is very different from the solution for the CAV-type disks (constant angular velocity disks) [Ford and Christodoulakis 1990].

Several other performance optimizations have to be done in order to achieve the performance level required by very large multimedia databases in the future. Such optimizations involve good usage of tertiary storage, exploitation of parallelism (in both main memory and secondary storage), usage of cache memory, migration algorithms, scheduling, and query optimization [Christodoulakis et al. 1991].

A multimedia storage manager should support *expandability* and *storage transparency*. It should operate in environments of rewritable magnetic disks, rewritable optical disks, write-once optical disks, read-only optical disks, CD-WOs, and CD-rewritable disks (defined by the new international standards from Philips and Sony). It should be able to easily accommodate storage devices with new characteristics. The storage manager should be able to manage (i.e., insert, delete, update, etc.) information on top of these devices, provided that these devices obey the international device interconnection standards, as well as the standards describing the information allocation on top of such devices. The basic operations of the storage manager should be translated *transparently* into appropriate operations for each different kind of device. Thus, a formal generalized model of storage is required that is able to capture the characteristics of the different device types and map a generalized set of operations into the corresponding set of operations for the particular device type.

Long Data Management

Multimedia data can be very large. The system should provide efficient manipulation for multimedia data [Lehman and Linsday 1989].

To optimize retrieval performance, the system should make an effort to store the parts of a *long multimedia object* (such as image, video, etc.). However, it may be difficult and slow for the system to find contiguous space on secondary storage to store these objects at insertion time. Thus, in order to have a good response time for writes, the system should try to write the parts of the long object as inexpensively as possible. It should then try to optimize the reads in the background by clustering together (as well as near other related objects) the long object. Such a design, which involves both read and write optimization, has several variations depending on the importance of the two types of optimization.

Different types of long multimedia objects are usually used differently as well. For example, images are usually shown to the user as a whole; for example, the user interface usually does not project parts of an image while waiting for the other parts to be retrieved (the exception is progressive retrieval interfaces). This implies that it is not efficient to fetch parts of images, then serve another request, then fetch the remaining parts of the images [Gemmell and Christodoulakis 1992]. Images will often have to be fetched as a whole. This is not the case with audio and video objects, where large blocks containing parts of the objects may be prefetched waiting for their use after the previous parts of the objects have been played.

In multimedia information retrieval environments, it is also often the case that a large portion of objects satisfying a query will not be used by the user who finds what he or she wants in a subset of the data and then interrupts the search.[1] In this case, a retrieval strategy in which long objects are not transferred to main memory except if explicitly requested seems more

1. This is typical in information retrieval environments.

profitable. For images, this implies retrieval on demand after a request, while for other data types, such as video, it implies starting the retrieval on demand. In addition, due to their large main-memory requirements and their small probability of reuse, the long data items should free the main-memory space soon after their use.[2]

For very long objects, retrieval of parts may be necessary. This is often the case with long pieces of audio, video, and the like, but it may be the case for very long images or graphics, where only a windowful of an image is shown. For example, in a large cartographic map, a miniature can show the whole map, while positioning a small window on the miniature will allow the user to identify an area that he or she wants to see in detail. The system should support efficient retrieval of parts of larger objects. In turn, this implies appropriate data clustering and indexing within a large multimedia object.

Large multimedia objects are frequently compressed to reduce storage requirements and disk and bus bandwidth requirements. Different compression algorithms and standards (like JPEG, MPEG, px64) for compression exist [Fox 1992]. Retrieval of parts of compressed images is harder. Playback or playing from an arbitrary point is more difficult in compressed video or audio when interframe compression methods are used. System support is needed for good performance.

In some environments, long multimedia objects may have multiple representations to satisfy various user needs or device presentation characteristics. For example, the existence of high-resolution screens and low-resolution screens in client workstations may imply that a different quality image has to be sent to the users. When and how different representations should be kept is a system optimization feature.

It is clear that the retrieval of long objects may result in retrieval delays due to the data-transfer time involved. The system should try to reduce delays by exploiting secondary storage parallelism. The diverse nature of the different multimedia data types implies that different data placement algorithms could be more profitable for different data types. For example, while stripping seems appropriate for images, it does not seem appropriate for video. In addition, data compression, varying data representations, and progressive retrieval may have different effects on the parallel data placement and retrieval.

Multilevel Storage Hierarchies

The storage manager should be able to handle *multilevel storage hierarchies* efficiently and transparently. Main memories are fast and are becoming

---

2. There are some exceptions, however, where an object is played cyclically (e.g., music repetition), and they should be recognized by the storage manager.

larger. They will be used to store some active portions of the database on a long-term basis. The second level of the storage hierarchy will typically be composed of optical and magnetic disks, which will store multimedia data that have relatively high probability of access. The third level (i.e., jukeboxes) will hold data that are less frequently accessed. Each jukebox has a number of read and write drives associated with it. There may be more than one jukebox in larger configurations.

The third level of storage hierarchy (jukeboxes) has much higher storage capacities, and it is able to accommodate the requirements of space-demanding multimedia database applications, but it is also much slower (e.g., 5 to 10 seconds for a disk exchange). It should also be clear that there is a significant retrieval performance difference between the first and the second levels of the storage hierarchy.

It is therefore important to design and implement tools that manage the data in a multilevel storage hierarchy to guarantee fast response times. This implies movement of data across storage hierarchy levels according to the frequency of access. *Migration* from one level of the storage hierarchy to another may have to take place because of space limitations, changing access patterns, prescheduled organizational procedures, and so on. It may also require data conversions (e.g., pointer swizzling, different data compression, different indexing, different clustering, etc.). Thus, tools for access monitoring, data migration, and data conversion across the levels of a multilevel storage hierarchy are required. In addition, efficient scheduling algorithms for concurrent access of data from tertiary storage should be employed.

Real-Time Multimedia Data Transfer and Synchronization Issues

Multimedia data often pose real-time transfer and synchronization requirements. The real-time transfer requirements are soft. It is desirable for data always to reach the receiver end (within the workstation itself or across the network) in time so that there are no interruptions in the presentation [Anderson and Homsy 1991; Gemmell and Christodoulakis 1992; Little and Ghafoor 1991]. For example, if voice or video is retrieved from a secondary storage device, the next chunk to be presented should reach the receiver end before the currently played chunk finishes; otherwise, interruptions in the presentation will be heard or seen. In the case where two or more different multimedia data types are retrieved for presentation, there may be a synchronization problem at the receiver end. In the case of video with associated voice and text captions, all three data types must be synchronized. The video chunk should reach the receiver's end together with its associated audio chunk and its associated text caption.

The real-time transfer and synchronization issues will depend on the distribution of compression rates of the various data types, the buffer space allocated, the scheduling algorithms used, the data placement on secondary storage devices, the distribution of data on devices across the network, and the bandwidth allocated in the communication channel.

Some researchers adopt the approach of finding conditions that guarantee real-time transfer and synchronization of information at the receiver's end. This is easier to achieve when the receiver is on the same workstation (although it is still a hard problem in its generality [Gemmell and Christodoulakis 1992]). It is more difficult to achieve when the receiver is across a network because of the unpredictability of the network load. In this case, one may be forced to sacrifice some quality of the information in order to guarantee real-time delivery and synchronization.

There are several factors affecting the performance of real-time data transfer and synchronization. In order to pursue comprehensive studies in this area, performance-oriented models of multimedia data as well as models describing the multimedia data absorption from users have to be developed, in addition to data placement, retrieval models, and so on.

With the evolution of technology, the speed of secondary storage devices as well as that of the communication channels increases. Fiber optics technology promises to deliver hundreds of megabits per second. However, it has been proved in the past that users quickly consume any extra resources they are given. It is thus important to develop and study algorithms guaranteeing good real-time delivery and synchronization of multimedia information. The algorithms could exploit reduced quality as well as usage of cache memory across the network and should use performance-oriented models of multimedia information (or synthetic workloads) as well as user absorption models.

16.2.2 Modeling, Structuring, Content Addressability, and Browsing

An important problem in future large multimedia data bases will be to provide mechanisms that will allow the user to locate efficiently the information he or she wants. With trillions of bytes stored on very large optical archives, it becomes clear that the user needs good tools to help find and retrieve relevant information. A large amount of information must be captured at the time of data insertion (or soon after) in order to achieve effective and efficient information retrieval later. Typical methods of information capturing include recognition, typing, clustering, and establishing explicit relationships.

Database systems allow users to find information using types, attributes, and relationships of their elements. On the other hand, information-retrieval techniques rely mainly on text content. In addition to traditional text pattern-matching techniques, a variety of similarity-based techniques have been developed. Loosely speaking, similarity-retrieval techniques allow one to retrieve a document if the document's keywords are close to the ones specified in the user's query. The important difference is that database retrieval is based on facts; for example, for an entity to be retrieved, it has to have a value or an explicit relationship specified in a user query. The information-retrieval approach suggests that an entity may be retrieved because it is relevant, although it may not have a value or a relationship that appears explicitly in the user query [Salton 1989].

Recently, emphasis has been given to hypertext or hypermedia-based approaches. Hypertext or hypermedia approaches are ways of structuring the contents of the information base. Information is retrieved traversing links of a particular type in forward or backward directions [Caudillo and Mainguenaud 1991]. The hypertext/hypermedia data model is close to the object-oriented database models. Hypertext/hypermedia-oriented models often suggest a method of navigation for retrieving the information from the information base.

Furthermore, efforts were made to provide content addressability in more complex data types such as images [Narasimhalu and Christodoulakis 1991]. Since it is difficult to access information in real time using pattern-recognition techniques, most methods provide a content descriptor for the image, which is examined against a user request. The content descriptor can be a simple text descriptor, or it can contain some more structured information describing the contents of the image. In some cases, similarity-retrieval techniques can be employed to match the database contents with a graphics filter that the user provides.

Currently, content-based retrieval for voice and scanned documents is limited by the capabilities of current speech and document recognition technology.

The area of content addressability of multimedia objects is profound. It encompasses difficult problems in computer science and engineering, like natural language understanding, speech processing, vision, and user modeling. It is, however, crucial to extend the known techniques or heuristics developed in different application areas (e.g., databases, information retrieval, natural language understanding, and psychology) to achieve a better and uniform way of effectively locating multimedia information in the large information repositories of the future.

Finally, content addressability has to be supplemented with good browsing techniques (e.g., miniatures), since it is unlikely in many environments that the user will be able to specify precisely what he or she wants. The means of information browsing and its granularity are important system design aspects for effective information finding.

16.2.3 Query Specification and Refinement and Human-Computer Interaction (HCI)

Effective query specification for various classes of users ranging from naïve to expert is important in information systems. Query refinement plays an important role in HCI. In information-retrieval environments, query refinement is used

- to better focus the query (if too many documents are retrieved using the original filter)
- to expand the original filter if too few documents qualify
- to redirect the search if the original filter is inappropriate

In modern database environments, a combination of set-oriented searching and navigation-oriented browsing techniques is usually employed. Finally, hypertext/hypermedia-oriented systems use links to navigate through the database in order to find relevant concepts. Thesaurus and relevance feedback are techniques that have been explored in the information-retrieval environments to build a user profile that is used for more effective query specification and refinement [Salton 1989]. In multimedia information systems, query specification is not restricted to specifying attribute values in terms of ASCII character strings.

The HCI techniques that have been explored in traditional database and information retrieval environments will evolve into multimedia HCI techniques. There are already many different kinds of input devices and sensors that can be used for effective man-machine interaction, and more will be developed in the future (e.g., eye tracking). Advances in speech processing, natural language understanding, recognition of handwritten input, and the like will open new possibilities for multimedia query specification and refinement. More traditional techniques for thesaurus construction, relevance feedback, and hypertext will be expanded to utilize multimedia and will be used as components of uniformly integrated multimedia information systems.

16.2.4 Information Presentation and Artificial Reality

Information may be captured by various sources and stored in an internal representation form that facilitates content addressability, effective presentation, and information extraction. The objective of information extraction and presentation is to extract the relevant information from the contents of the information base and to present it to the user in its most appropriate form. Often this process involves transformation of information. For example, alphanumeric data of experiments may have to be extracted, converted, and presented on a graphics screen in the form of graphs or pie charts. The objective of this presentation is to allow users a fast understanding of a large quantity of data by means of a diagram. If the user is not satisfied with the presentation form that was automatically chosen by the system, he or she may be allowed to choose an alternative representation (say a pie chart instead of a graph), which will result in the system making the conversion from its internal representation (numbers) to the new presentation form (pie chart) [Christodoulakis et al. 1986].

The principle of alternative presentations of the internal information has many applications in different areas. For example, in a teaching system for physics, the internal representation may be in the form of rules describing principles of physics. The external presentation may allow students to see the results of their actions in terms of diagrams or animations presented on the screen. The system may allow them to choose parameters of the experiment and observed variables.

In the future, information extraction and presentation will utilize diverse and interrelated multimedia information. Extraction may generally involve several different parts of the database. The extracted information may be used to synthesize, according to certain rules, a complex multimedia information base and the navigation and interaction rules in it. Information may be converted automatically from one representation to another in order to adapt to user profiles, existence of the required presentation devices at the destination site, uniformity of presentation, and so on.

Complex, time-dependent, natural phenomena will be described using an internal information representation method and will be presented to users in a multimedia fashion. Although they require tremendous computing power, simulations of this kind find significant applications in teaching, training, and entertainment. In addition to modeling natural phenomena, the behavior of living objects may be captured (possibly semiautomatically) and represented internally in the computer. The internal representation of the behavior may be accompanied by pictures, video, sound, and 3-D graphics that can be used according to rules to effectively present simulations of living objects or societies in an interactive environment, where the user and the objects interact with each other. The design and implementation of such systems require input from several fields of science and engineering as well as advanced software engineering techniques.

16.3 Development Approaches

Systems for storing and retrieving multimedia information have been designed and developed for different application areas in the last decade, and different approaches have also been followed for this purpose. In terms of the development approach and application areas, we can classify multimedia information systems into two general categories:

1. Those that extend existing information systems:
   - extensions of relational database management systems
   - extensions of object-oriented database management systems
   - extensions of information retrieval systems
2. Those that are developed from scratch:
   - new multimedia document systems
   - hypermedia systems with significant multimedia support

We combine these classifications and describe several systems that provide diverse functionalities and features. In each category, we briefly explain how multimedia information systems' requirements are fulfilled by following diverse development approaches. The systems described, though not unique, are representative of the category in which they are classified despite the fact that there is no clear distinction among those categories in every single case. We start with multimedia document systems that have been initiated in order to provide pure multimedia functionality.

16.3.1 Multimedia Document Management Systems

One of the earliest approaches to multimedia information systems comes from office automation. The objective of these systems is to provide flexible retrieval from large repositories of *multimedia documents,* which are text documents enhanced with raster images, graphics, and audio annotations. Two examples are MINOS [Christodoulakis et al. 1986] and MULTOS [Thanos 1990]. Both systems offer the following features: modeling of complex object structure, content-based retrieval, and differentiation of internal (logical) and external (layout/presentation) representations.

MINOS: MINOS (**M**ultimedia **IN**formation **O**ffice **S**ystem) was one of the first integrated document management systems developed in the early 1980s [Christodoulakis et al. 1986a; Christodoulakis et al. 1986b; Tsichritzis et al. 1983]. It introduced an object-oriented approach to model the content and presentation aspects of multimedia documents that were composed of short attributes, text, graphics, bitmaps, and sound. The system allowed creation, filing, and extraction of components of complex documents. The filing system (ODAS—**O**ptical **D**isk **A**rchival **S**ystem) supported WORM optical disk file management [Christodoulakis et al. 1987]. Access methods for text and attributes appropriate for an archival office environment were developed [Christodoulakis 1984; Faloutsos and Christodoulakis 1987]. Later versions of the system supported a client/server architecture, caching, and scheduling [Bradshaw 1989; Mok 1991].

MULTOS: MULTOS (**MULT**imedia **O**ffice **S**erver) [Thanos 1990] was an experimental system (developed in the late 1980s) that was designed to enhance multimedia document retrieval. It was based on multilevel conceptual modeling principles for semantic structuring. It incorporated principles of the Office Document Architecture (ODA) model specifying the logical and layout levels of document modeling. MULTOS supported dynamic and archive filing (integrating WORM optical disks) for documents containing text components only. The final prototype provided extensive system functionality: Multimedia documents could be created in the client subsystem, classified automatically, and stored in the server subsystem. The same documents could be retrieved using text, image, and document attributes.

16.3.2 Multimedia Database Systems

The previous systems developed multimedia document management systems from scratch. A different approach is to develop multimedia document management applications on top of existing database management systems. This approach makes available all the functionality already provided by a DBMS, and the same DBMS can be used for other applications as well.

Conventional relational databases can be very inefficient at retrieving documents. They are designed to support the retrieval of information that has simple, repetitive structures. Documents have more complex structures than conventional data, and they are usually large. In addition, the types of queries supported by document databases are different from those supported by conventional databases. Most documents contain several sections, each of which may contain several subsections or other logical units such as paragraphs or tables. Such structures are difficult to store and retrieve efficiently in conventional database systems. This is why many existing systems that support text retrieval are not based on the relational model.

Object-Oriented Approaches

There are two types of requirements that multimedia applications impose on a database system [Woelk et al. 1986]. One is the requirement for a data model that allows a natural and flexible definition and evolution of the schema that can represent the composition of the complex relationships among parts of a multimedia document. Another is the requirement for the sharing and manipulation (storage, retrieval, and transmission) of multimedia information. An object-oriented approach is an elegant basis for addressing all data modeling requirements of the multimedia applications [Christodoulakis et al. 1991; Klas et al. 1990; Woelk et al. 1986]. Here we briefly describe Woelk and Kim 1987, which first presented and implemented the idea.

ORION Multimedia Information Manager: ORION [Kim et al. 1990] is a series of database systems that have been prototyped at MCC as vehicles for research into the next-generation database architecture and the integration of programming languages and databases. The ORION systems support a rich set of database features for the next-generation data-intensive application environments. These include an object-oriented data model, transaction management, queries and automatic query optimization, version control, change notification, composite objects, and multimedia data management. The latest version of ORION is a distributed object-management system in which all computers in the network participate in the management of a shared persistent database.

ORION supports multimedia objects [Woelk and Kim 1987; Woelk et al. 1986]. Multimedia information is captured, stored, and presented in ORION using lattices of classes that represent capture devices, storage devices, captured objects, and presentation devices. A message protocol for the representation and capture of multimedia information using ORION classes is defined.

A descriptor object is used in ORION to describe the disk location of the associated long data stored on disk pages. The long data are usually too large to place in their entirety in the object buffer pool. Instead, only pieces (i.e., pages) of long data are cached in the page buffer pool. For this reason, a page buffer pool is also defined in each client for exclusive use by the long data manager part of the object subsystem. Concurrency, transaction, and validation mechanisms have been developed for long data as well [Woelk and Kim 1987].

Nested Relational Approaches

Another effective approach to managing documents is nested (non-first normal form) relational database systems. Nested relational systems permit hierarchically structured objects such as documents to be represented in a natural way. We can identify three possible schemas for representing a document database using a nested relational database system [Zobel et al. 1991]:

- *Monolithic schema*—each document is represented by a single tuple with a nested table of sections, and each section has a nested table of subsections. The text in each section and subsection is stored in a nested table of fragments.
- *Segmented schema*—each document is represented by a number of tuples, each containing title information, the current section and subsection name, and a single fragment.
- *Duplex schema*—each document is represented by a *title* tuple containing title information and a nested table of sections and subsections. Each subsection includes a nested table of foreign keys of fragments containing the text of that subsection.

The schemas described above assume that each document will have a certain structure. More flexible nested relational schemas can also be designed, permitting storage of document collections containing documents of arbitrary structure.

TITAN+: TITAN+ is a nested relational database system prototyped at the Key Centre for Knowledge Based Systems [Zobel et al. 1991]. TITAN+ uses multiorganizational bit-sliced signature file indexing to provide access by content. The approach taken by the TITAN+ system is to break documents into fragments, which are blocks of text holding logical units such as paragraphs. The main reason to follow this approach is that the size of fragments is small, and they are inexpensive to retrieve from disk. However, the use of fragments increases database size, and some types of queries become more expensive to evaluate. A fragment consists of a logical unit of text such as a sentence, a paragraph, or a table.

DASDBS: DASDBS (**DA**rma**S**tadt **D**ata **B**ase **S**ystem) [Paul et al. 1987] is conceived as a family of application-specific database systems on top of a common database kernel. The kernel provides mechanisms to efficiently store hierarchically structured complex objects and offers operations that are set oriented and can be processed in a single scan through the objects. In order to achieve high concurrency in a layered system, a multilevel transaction methodology is applied.

Other Approaches

Durr and Lang [1991] presented a *Data Schema Approach to Multimedia Database System Architecture*, which is derived from the structure of the data to be stored. They distinguish objects of different abstraction layers, represent them in appropriate data schemas, and map these schemas to corresponding architecture layers.

They identify three types of multimedia objects, thus emphasizing the features of single media objects, structurally oriented multimedia objects, and multimedia objects with behavioral relationships. Every single media object belongs to one medium (i.e., an abstract data type). Multimedia objects are composed of single media objects or already existing multimedia objects, and they have distinguishable structurally oriented and behaviorally oriented relationships. For each of the three types, they present appropriate data schemas that express important characteristics. The architecture of the MDBMS is then derived by a straightforward mapping of data schemas to architectural layer.

A prototype integration component has been implemented on top of the relational database system RDB/VMS. Data schemas are specified as ER diagrams and then simply mapped to relations of the database system.

16.3.3 Multimedia Information Retrieval Systems

In addition to the database approach for storage and retrieval of multimedia information (which has already been presented), one can use information-retrieval techniques for the same purpose. As Rabitti and Savino 1992 explain, retrieval in database management systems is based on the exact evaluation of a boolean combination of predicates on attributes. Each attribute has a well-defined domain and predicates that can be applied on it. The answer to a query is the set of database records for which the query conditions evaluate to true.

The information-retrieval approach to document retrieval consists of retrieving all documents whose properties are similar to those present on the query. These documents are delivered to the users in decreasing order of their similarity to the query. Historically, information-retrieval research has focused on the problem of retrieving unstructured text documents from large and static document archives [Salton 1989].

There exist several systems that use information-retrieval techniques, such as the Manchester Multimedia Information System [Goble et al. 1992], the I^3R system [Croft and Thompson 1987], and also the prototype system presented in Rabitti and Savino 1992. The approach followed by this last prototype is an extension of the approach used in the implementation of the MULTOS prototype.

Most of the systems that use information-retrieval techniques concentrate on image and text retrieval and content addressability. In general, the performance and user satisfaction they achieve for these types of requests is remarkable.

16.3.4 Authoring and Hypermedia Systems

Some recent approaches from hypertext/media systems propose to relax the strong typing and structuring modalities for documents as a way to allow reading and writing documents on line. Hypermedia links with system-defined semantics are considered as a way to represent both the organization of the documents and structured database coupling. These systems focus on tools for *authoring* (creation of multimedia documents) and tools for *interlinking* media components (hypermedia). Existing hypermedia capabilities facilitate better visualization of information on the screen, and the functionality available to the user for handling the system includes many possibilities to integrate different metaphors. There are several systems following similar approaches under the same idea—for example, Intermedia [Yankelovich et al. 1988], SEPIA [Streitz et al. 1992], and Harmony [Shimojo et al. 1991]. Furthermore, significant efforts have been made toward presenting unified models for hypermedia/multimedia systems [Caudillo and Mainguenaud 1991]. Below, we briefly describe the is-News Multimedia Information System, which follows the aforementioned approach.

The is-News Multimedia Information System [Putz and Neuhold 1991] is an experimental system that has been developed by the Integrated Publication and Information Systems Institute (IPSI) of the GMD, the German Research Centre of Computer Science. The system focuses on electronic publishing, integrating multimedia aspects, access to heterogeneous multimedia databases and remote online databases, as well as a hypertext writing environment.

In the is-News system, two different aspects of multimedia systems are considered. The first refers to different information types. Specifically, is-News supports time-independent information (text, images) and time-dependent information (video). The second aspect refers to multimedia support for user interface. In this case, the visualization of the information on the screen and the user's functionality for handling the system include many possibilities to integrate hypermedia structures. The document model that has been used is based in the standard SGML. This model is mapped to an object-oriented database.

16.4 The KYDONIA Project

The aim of the KYDONIA project is to develop the technology for the next generation of multimedia information systems. In this effort, which started in 1991 in MUSIC, the requirements described in the previous sections of this chapter are taken into account. The methodology followed is to develop in parallel several multimedia information-system applications (several local and international multimedia application projects are currently run by MUSIC) in order to generate more detailed requirements and tests for the system. These requirements are passed through the layers of the architecture and result in specific implementation options. Since we have developed all the layers of the architecture within MUSIC, we are in a good position to modify and extend them when the need arises.

The system[3] is currently operational on a single-site basis, but a client-server architecture will be operational soon. It is implemented in C++ and currently runs on SUN workstations (SunOS 4.0 and 4.1), HP workstations (HP-UX 8.05), Silicon Graphics Indigo (Irix), and also PCs (Windows) [Christodoulakis et al. 1992a]. It will soon be ported to on a parallel machine (Parcytec). The overall architecture follows an object-oriented philosophy with extensions and optimizations appropriate for multimedia. All

---

3. This system has been developed in the context of the ESPRIT II (P2424)—KIWIs project and the AIM (A2024)—MILORD project.

well-known features of object-oriented architectures are supported (complex objects, object identification, encapsulation, multiple inheritance, methods, overriding, and extensibility).

The current system consists of three separable basic modules: the *Object Manager (OM)*, the *Storage Manager (SM)*, and the *Interface Module (IM)*.

The OVM Language (LOVM): The interface module of the OVM kernel is a fully object-oriented database programming language *(LOVM)*. It supports the most important features of the known object-oriented programming languages as well as extensions for supporting database capabilities (e.g., querying, rule creation and manipulation, etc.). Using this language, one is able to interact with the kernel by sending (precompiled) messages to objects and obtaining the results. Via LOVM, the OVM kernel ensures a uniform access to all system objects and functions as well as for regular data objects.

The Object Manager (OM): The Object Manager (OM) is the module of the system that handles persistent and temporary complex objects with identity. This module includes several submodules that implement the presentation manager that ensures compatibility with the data model, queries, version control, imperative rule management (i.e., triggers, constraints), multimedia object management, index management, and the message-passing manager.

The Storage Manager (SM): The Storage Manager module is a file management system developed for use by object-oriented multimedia applications [Christodoulakis et al. 1993]. SM is divided into three layers: logical file layer, physical file layer, and device layer. Logical files group together related data. The physical file layer allows different ordering and placement of the data of a logical file, and the device layer allows efficient device management for small and large data types.

To provide an interface between the object manager and SM, a dual-buffering scheme is implemented. A cluster is the basic data unit of the buffer pool (controlled by SM), and object is the basic data unit of the object pool, controlled by the object manager. For performance reasons, retrieval of an object from secondary storage is not performed independently of the other objects of the same cluster. A physical file may be placed on one or more (possibly removable) devices. This mapping operates on a three-level store: main memory, magnetic disks, and tertiary storage (i.e., optical disks). Additionally, the ability to place physical units on different devices allows for supporting device parallelism.

In the device layer [Christodoulakis et al. 1992b], SM provides storage-device transparency, so that it can operate in environments with different types of disks (magnetic, optical, etc.). For this reason, the Disk Drive Manager (DDM) is implemented. DDM provides a formal model that captures the characteristics of the different device types and maps a generalized set of operations to the corresponding set of operations for the particular device type. Furthermore, SM provides disk cartridge self-containment so that cartridges can be completely removed from a running file system and stored or transported to another installation.

REFERENCES

Anderson, D., and Homsy, G. 1991. A Continuous Media I/O Server and Its Synchronization Mechanism. *IEEE Computer* (special issue on multimedia information systems).

Bradshaw, D. P. 1989. *Retrieval Optimization in the MINOS Distributed Testbed.* Master's thesis, Department of Computer Science, University of Waterloo.

Byte. 1990. State of the Art Report on Magnetic Versus Optical Disk Technologies. *BYTE*.

Caudillo, R., and Mainguenaud, M. 1991. An Hypertex-Like Multimedia Document Data Model. *Proceedings of the ACM International Conference on Multimedia Information Systems 1991*, McGraw-Hill.

Christodoulakis, S. 1984. An Experimental Multimedia Information System for an Office Environment. *IEEE Database Engineering*, Vol. 7, No. 3.

Christodoulakis, S. 1987. Analysis of Retrieval Performance for Records and Objects Using Optical Disk Technology. *ACM Transactions on Database Systems*, 137–169.

Christodoulakis, S., et al. 1992a. *The OVM System: Design Documentation and User Manual.* Deliverable for the Project KIWIs, Tech. Report, Technical University of Crete.

Christodoulakis, S., Ailamaki, A., Anestopoulos, D., and Argyropoulos, S. 1992b. *The Device Layer of MILORD.* Report on the activity D2 of the MILORD project.

Christodoulakis, S., Anestopoulos, D., and Argyropoulos S. 1993. Data Organization and Storage Hierarchies in a Multimedia Server. *IEEE COMPCON*, Spring.

Christodoulakis, S., Ho, F., Theodoridou, M., Papa, M., and Pathria, A. 1986a. Multimedia Document Presentation, Information Extraction and Document Formation in MINOS: A Model and a System. *ACM Transactions on Office Information Systems (TOOIS)*, Oct., 345–383.

Christodoulakis, S., Ho, F., and Theodoridou, M. 1986b. The Multimedia Object Presentation Manager of MINOS: A Symmetric Approach. *Proceedings of the ACM-SIGMOD Conference 1986.*

Christodoulakis, S., Koveos, L., Fragonikolakis, M., Ailamaki, N., and Kapetanakis, G. 1991. The Design and Performance Studies for a Multimedia Information Server. *IEEE Data Engineering Bulletin*, Sept.

Christodoulakis, S., Ledoux, E., and Ng, R. 1987. *A WORM Optical Disk Based Document Filing System*. Tech. Report, Multimedia Lab, University of Waterloo.

Croft, W., and Thompson, R. 1987. I^3R: A New Approach to the Design of Document Retrieval Systems. *Journal of the American Society for Information Science*.

Durr, M., and Lang, S. M. 1991. A Data Schema Approach to Multimedia Database System Architecture. *International Conference on Multimedia Information Systems*, Singapore.

Faloutsos, C., and Christodoulakis, S. 1987. Description and Performance Analysis of Signature File Methods. *ACM Transactions on Office Information Systems (TOOIS)*, Aug.

Ford, D., and Christodoulakis, S. 1990. Optimal Data Placement on CLV Optical Disks. *ACM Transactions on Office Information Systems (TOOIS)*, Sept.

Fox, E. A. 1992. Advances in Interactive Digital Multimedia Systems. *IEEE Computer* (special issue on multimedia information systems).

Gemmell, J., and Christodoulakis, S. 1992. Principles of Storage and Retrieval for Delay Sensitive Data. *ACM Transactions on Office Information Systems (TOOIS)*, Jan.

Goble, C., O'Docherty, M., Crowther, P., Ireton, M., Oakley, J., and Xydeas, C. 1992. The Manchester Multimedia Information System. *Proceedings of 3rd International Conference on Extending Database Technology*, Vienna.

Kim, W., Garza, F., Ballou, N., and Woelk, D. 1990. Architecture of the ORION Next-Generation Database System. *IEEE Transactions on Knowledge and Data Engineering*, Apr.

Klas, W., Neuhold, E. J., and Schrefl, M. 1990. Using an Object-Oriented Approach to Model Multimedia Data. *Computer Communications*, Vol. 13, No. 4.

Lehman, T., and Linsday, B. 1989. The Starburst Long Field Manager. *Proceedings of the 15th International Conference on Very Large Data Bases*, Amsterdam.

Little, T. D. C., and Ghafoor, A. 1991. Spatio-Temporal Composition of Distributed Multimedia Objects for Value-Added Networks. *IEEE Computer* (special issue on multimedia information systems).

Mok, S. C. W. 1991. *Protocols for Data Archival and Retrieval in the MINOS Distributed Testbed*. Master's Thesis, Department of Computer Science, University of Waterloo.

Narasimhalu, A. D., and Christodoulakis, S., eds. 1991. *Proceedings of the ACM International Conference on Multimedia Information Systems 1991*, McGraw-Hill.

Paul, H. B., Schek, H. J., Scholl, M. H., Weikum, G., and Deppisch, U. 1987. Architecture and Implementation of the Darmstadt Kernel System. *Proceedings of the International Conference ACM-SIGMOD*, San Franscisco.

Putz, W., and Neuhold, E. 1991. is-News: a Multimedia Information System. *IEEE Data Engineering Bulletin*, Sept.

Rabitti, F., and Savino, P. 1992. An Information Retrieval Approach for Image Databases. *Proceedings of the International Conference on Very Large Databases*, Vancouver, B.C.

Salton, G. 1989. *Automatic Text Processing: The Transformation, Analysis and Retrieval of Information by Computer*. Addison-Wesley, Reading, Mass.

Shimojo, S., et al 1991. A New Hyperobject System Harmony: Its Design and Implementation. *ACM International Conference on Multimedia Information Systems*, Singapore.

Streitz, N., Haake, J., Hannemann, J., Lemeke, A., Schuler, W., Schutt, H., and Thuring, M. 1992. SEPIA: A Cooperative Hypermedia Authoring Environment. *Proceedings of the 4th ACM European Conference on Hypertext (ECHT)*, Dec.

Thanos, C., ed. 1990. *Multimedia Office Filing: The Multos Approach*. Nort-Holland, Amsterdam.

Tsichritzis, D., Christodoulakis, S., Economopoulos, P., Faloutsos, C., Lee, A., Lee, D., Vandenbroek, J., and Woo, C. 1983. A Multimedia Office Filing System. *Proceedings of the 9th International Conference on Very Large Data Bases,* Florence.

Woelk, D., and Kim, W. 1987. Multimedia Information Management in an Object-Oriented Database System. *Proceedings of the 13th International Conference on Very Large Data Bases,* Brighton.

Woelk, D., Kim, W., and Luther, W. 1986. An Object-Oriented Approach to Multimedia Information Databases, *Proceedings of the ACM-SIGMOD Conference,* (May).

Yankelovich, N., et al. 1988. Intermedia: The Concept and the Construction of a Seamless Information Environment. *IEEE Computer,* Jan.

Zobel, J., Thom, J., and Sacks-Davis, R. 1991. Efficiency of Nested Relational Document Database Systems. *Proceedings of the 17th International Conference on Very Large Databases,* Barcelona.

17

Spatial Data Models and Query Processing

HANAN SAMET
WALID G. AREF

An overview is presented of the issues in building spatial databases. The focus is on data models and query processing. Query optimization in a spatial environment is also briefly discussed.

17.1 Introduction

Not so long ago the term *database management system (DBMS)* was a euphemism for distinguishing commercial applications (e.g., banking, insurance, etc.) from scientific applications (e.g., number crunching). Today the distinction is rapidly disappearing as users try to come to grips with an information explosion that increasingly involves the world around them. Some new application areas include geographic information systems (GIS), engineering information systems, CAD/CAM, remote sensing, environmental modeling, and image databases. The common thread behind all of these applications is that they make use of spatial data.

Spatial data is a term used to describe data that pertain to the space occupied by objects in a database. These data are geometric and varied. They consist of points, lines, rectangles, polygons, surfaces, volumes, time, and data of even higher dimension. Spatial data are usually found in conjunction with what is known as *attribute* or *nonspatial* data (e.g., the name of a river, the type of soil found in a region, the current speed during a time interval, etc.).

Spatial data can be discrete or continuous. When they are discrete (e.g., points in a multidimensional space or specific instances of time), then they can be modeled using traditional techniques from relational DBMSs. In particular, the coordinate values of the point or the time instant can be treated as additional attributes in a tuple. In contrast, such data as lines, regions, time intervals, and the like are continuous. By *continuous* we mean that the data span a region in space or time. In other words, the attribute value holds at more than just one point or instance of time.

In this chapter, we focus on the modeling of spatial data and their integration into a DBMS. The result is termed a *spatial database*. Since the application domain is so wide, we restrict ourselves to the requirements and examples for a geographic information system. This chapter is organized as follows. Section 17.2 gives a brief overview of the type of queries that a spatial database must be able to handle. Section 17.3 presents a number of different methods of interacting with a spatial database, although the emphasis is on SQL, as it is the most commonly used method. Section 17.4 discusses the integration of spatial and nonspatial data to build a spatial database system. The examples are primarily in the context of relational databases, as this is where most of the work has been done. Section 17.5 describes some of the issues that must be addressed when building a query optimizer for an environment that contains spatial and nonspatial data. Note that we do not elaborate on temporal data, although we do briefly mention the close relationship between temporal and spatial data, especially when they are both present (known as a *spatiotemporal database* [Al-Taha et al. 1993]). We also do not dwell on the representation of spatial data. This is the subject of Chapter 18, on spatial data structures.

17.2 Typical Queries

There are several levels at which queries to a spatial database such as a geographic information system (GIS) can be described. At the highest level, the most common queries are to display the data, to find a pattern in the data, and to predict the behavior of the data at another location or instance of time. These queries are so general that often their execution does not require interacting with a spatial database. Frequently, they can be answered directly. On the other hand, other queries are at such a low level that they do not require use of a DBMS, either (e.g., digitization, conversion between different data formats, map projections, enhancement, etc.).

The remainder of the queries fall in an area where a DBMS is useful. These queries can be viewed as dealing with a hierarchy of data [Tomlin 1990]. At the highest level, we have a library of maps (more commonly referred to as *layers*), all of which are in registration (i.e., they have a common origin), and the goal is to perform a sequence of operations on them. Each layer is partitioned into zones (regions) where the zones are sets of locations with a common attribute value. For example, for a given map, we can have a land-use layer, a road network layer, and a pollution layer. In the land-use layer, land is divided into land-use zones (e.g., wetland, river, desert, city, park, and agricultural zones). The road network layer contains the roads that pass through the portion of space that is covered by the map. The pollution layer contains regions with different degrees of pollution. Other possible map layers correspond to vegetation, fire stations, roads, rivers, elevations, and the like. Each layer can be viewed as a relation in a relational DBMS (or a class of objects in an object-oriented DBMS). The attributes in the different layers reflect some property of the map. For example, the land-use layer can have the attributes zip code, soil type, and land usage and a spatial attribute of some geometric data type that represents the shape or boundary of each land-use region.

The different queries can be classified in terms of this hierarchy [Tomlin 1990]. Local queries involve locations that are coincident on various layers (e.g., what combination of features is found at location *x*?). Zonal queries are in terms of groups of locations that have the same attribute value on the same layer (e.g., where does wheat grow?). Focal queries deal with neighborhoods of locations on the same layer. The extent of the neighborhood is usually limited by distance, direction, or possibly time (e.g., find all wheat growing regions within 10 miles of the boundaries of rice-growing regions). These queries are analogs of range queries in a conventional database management system. The difference is that the shape of the range depends on the extent of a spatial feature (i.e., the area spanned by it) rather than being a hyper-rectangle as in a conventional DBMS (e.g., find all people between the ages of 30 and 35 and who weigh between 150 and 180 pounds).

Using these classifications, we can describe in greater depth some of the analytic capabilities that a spatial database must have in order to be able to respond to the queries that are expected to be posed[1]. Local queries consist of retrieval, classification and possibly recoding, generalization (i.e., reducing detail), and measurement (e.g., area, perimeter).

Another important query is known as *polygon overlay* or simply *overlay*. In this case, two layers involving different nonspatial attributes are overlaid and a function is applied to the corresponding attribute values at each location. For example, we can overlay the land-use and pollution layers in order to generate a new layer of land-use/pollution regions. In this case, a wetland region can be decomposed into several regions, each with a different degree of pollution. Recalling our analogy between layers and relations (or objects), the effect is much like a join operation where the common spatial attribute is the space spanned by the two layers. Thus the result is like a cartesian product of the two layers. This operation is a special case of what we term a *spatial join*, although the spatial join is far more general since it can involve relations more general than layers as long as the operand relations have spatial attributes that span the same underlying space.

Zonal queries are often used to implement a special case of polygon overlay. A typical zonal query involves three layers. The first two layers are the operands to the query, while the third layer contains the result. The first

---

1. These queries are typical of a GIS environment and where necessary we give a brief definition in parentheses.

layer serves as a mask that partitions the second layer into zones where the value of each location in the third layer is the result of the application of the designated zonal query to all locations in the second layer that coincide with each zone. An example of a zonal query is to find the average rainfall for each region where a particular crop or crops are grown. Notice the distinction from the polygon overlay in that a zonal operation does not create new zones, whereas a polygon overlay does since its result is the cartesian product of the two operand layers. Thus the result of a zonal operation is more like a spatial selection.

Focal queries include search, proximity determination (e.g., Voronoi diagrams that, given a set of points termed *sites*, partition the plane into regions such that each point in a given region is closer to a particular site than to any other site), spatial region queries (also known as *buffers* or *corridors*), interpolation, generation of triangulated irregular networks (*TINs*) for dealing with surface data, and so on. Connectivity queries are also closely related to focal queries. They involve factors such as flow and visibility.

An alternative, and even simpler, way to classify queries is on the basis of whether they are location based (e.g., what grows at location *x*?) or attribute based (e.g., where does wheat grow?). This classification has a direct bearing on the way the spatial data are organized and is discussed in greater detail in the chapter on spatial data structures.

17.3 Spatial Query Languages

The design of a proper query language (termed *interaction method* here) for a spatial database is a nontrivial task. For the sake of this discussion, we say that the interaction takes the form of a *command* or a *probe*. We use the identity and sophistication of the user to distinguish between these two rather similar concepts. In the case of a command, the user generally knows exactly what he or she wants to do, and there is a premium on the avoidance of ambiguity. Thus the command can be given using a predefined syntax that simplifies its processing. The objective is to be concise and exact. On the other hand, in the case of a probe, the user does not know exactly what he or she wants. He or she is performing data exploration. Frequently, he or she has little or no knowledge of the nature of the data that is stored in the database and even less about how it is represented. However, he or she may have a visual concept of what he or she is trying to achieve. Thus the querying may use the display of previous results by means such as pointing.

Attention must also be paid to the actual interaction with the spatial database. Surprisingly, in most systems this is usually an afterthought. Natural language is one approach. However, its drawback is its inherent ambiguity. This can be overcome by using a graphical user interface (e.g., Scholl and Voisard 1992; Vijlbrief and van Oosterom 1992). Unfortunately, designing a graphical user interface to a GIS involves more than just replacing typed commands by menus. It is important to realize that spatial data are characterized by geometry and map display. Tabular concepts and representations, as are common in some SQL-based approaches, do not play as prominent a role. Instead, we may need to develop some uniformly accepted iconic representations for spatial concepts.

Several interaction methods are possible. They range from SQL to queries by example. In most cases, the emphasis is on retrieving data using a standardized language. This is coupled with a desire to provide sophisticated methods to formulate more complex commands and logical combinations thereof. Some of the issues that arise are a result of the presence of abstractions of spatial data that are more complex than relations. Also, there is a need to support the graphical display of the results of queries. For example, in the case of points, it is preferable to display them rather than to list the values of their coordinates. Further utility is provided by also displaying some context with the points or even highlighting them by use of techniques such as reverse video, blinking, or simple circling or boxing.

Interaction with spatial data should be graphical. This means that both the input and the output should be graphical. One interaction technique is for the user to draw the shape of the desired output. Selection can be achieved by pointing; however, this is ambiguous if several objects are associated with the same region. Selection can also be accomplished by wandering around an area (e.g, a pan operation) or by zooming. The use of graphical renderings is also important. For example, using the same rendering for different objects at different locations conveys a notion of similarity, while the dissimilarity of renderings emphasizes differences between the objects. Of course, a legend is also needed to convey the semantics of the different renderings.

A good inspiration for the design of the interface is to make use of classical cartographic concepts [Tufte 1983, 1990]. For example, color is often used to indicate depth and height. A legend is useful to convey information about a map. Operations between maps are usually performed by overlaying them. This means that the individual map layers should be iconized and a hierarchical mechanism developed to facilitate the expression of their interrelationship. The key is to study the daily workings of a cartographer.

Here we focus on the use of SQL, as it is the most commonly used method of interacting with a relational database. In fact, at times, it is also used to interact with an object-oriented database (e.g., Deux et al. 1990). Thus it is often proposed to use it with a spatial database as well (e.g., Aref and Samet 1991a; Gadia 1993; Roussopoulos et al. 1988; Scholl and Voisard 1992). Note that it has been argued (e.g., Egenhofer 1992) that SQL is the wrong approach. These arguments are based on the inability to refer to the results of previous operations or on how the output is to be displayed. Similarly, selection by pointing is difficult to achieve. The problem is that SQL is primarily a means to retrieve from a tabular representation, while spatial applications often require retrieval from a graphical representation. This is a reformulation of our earlier criticism that spatial data cannot always be represented as points in a higher dimensional space (which is what a tuple really is—for more details on these issues, see the section on spatial indexing in Chapter 18, on spatial data structures).

Of course, in order to use SQL with spatial data, we need to extend it. There is a number of choices. Some systems extend the SQL grammar by adding a set of spatial operators (e.g., PSQL [Roussopoulos et al. 1988]). In essence, the idea is to extend the standard `select` ... `from` ... `where` ... syntax to also include spatial operators and relations involving spatial data. Its drawback is that operators cannot be added at run-time, which limits its extensibility. An alternative approach is for the query language to permit user-defined functions and operators that are made known to the DBMS at run-time (termed *registering* [Haas et al. 1990; Stonebraker and Rowe 1986]). They can be scalar (e.g., area) or multivalued, in which case the result can be a relation (termed a *table function* [Haas et al. 1990]).

In the rest of this section we discuss how to incorporate the spatial attributes into the relation. For the present, let us associate the spatial attributes with the tuple [Aref and Samet 1991a; Roussopoulos et al. 1988]. In this case, the spatial attributes appear at the same conceptual level as the nonspatial attributes. Thus the value of a particular spatial attribute is common to all the nonspatial attributes in the tuple.

17.3.1 One Spatial Extension to SQL

Spatial Data Definition

Using the above method of incorporating spatial attributes, we now show how SQL would be used in a spatial database by examining a typical situation. Consider a set of objects (e.g., points and lines) in two-dimensional space and a set of features that partition the space into nonoverlapping or overlapping regions. We use the following two schemas. The first schema is for a relation containing line segments called `roads` and the second is for a relation containing areas called `regions`. The `roads` relation has one spatial attribute, `road_coords` of type `LINE_SEGMENT`. The `regions` relation has one spatial attribute, `region_location` of type `REGION`. Of course, other spatial data types are available, such as `POINT`, `POLYGON`, `BOX`, and the like.

```
create table roads
      (road_id NUMBER,
       road_name CHAR(30),
```

```
        road_type CHAR(30),
        road_coords LINE_SEGMENT);/* spatial attribute */

create table regions
       (region_id NUMBER,
        region_name CHAR(30),
        region_zip_code NUMBER,
        region_utilization CHAR(30),
        region_importance NUMBER,
        region_location REGION); /* spatial attribute */
```

Spatial Data Manipulation

The standard relational operations such as projection, selection, and join are available in the nonspatial domain and are also adapted to the spatial domain. There are many ways of characterizing an SQL predicate as being spatial or relational (equivalent to nonspatial). Here we characterize a predicate as spatial if the condition (i.e., in the `where` clause) involves at least one of the spatial attributes or a spatial operation (e.g., intersection); otherwise, the predicate is characterized as relational. This is the case even if the predicate results in a map, as is the case whenever all the attributes are selected and at least one of the attributes is spatial. This can be seen by the following example, which selects all regions whose importance is greater than 5. In particular, the result is a new relation, which means a new region map as well. This new relation and map contain all the tuples selected in the operation (i.e., they will contain the regions with importance values > 5).

```
select all
       from regions
       where region_importance>5;
```

Spatial and relational projections are distinguished in the same way as spatial and relational selections. The difference is that in the case of projection, only a subset of the attributes is selected. In fact, if none of the selected attributes is spatial, then only a relation results (and not a map).

Spatial conditions typically consist of comparisons involving the result of the application of functions of spatial attributes. Some examples are given below:

```
area(region_attr)>val
perimeter(spatial_attr)
centroid(region_attr)
object_at(spatial_attr,location)
in_circle(spatial_attr,location,radius)
nearest_to(spatial_attr)=a
length(line_attr)>val
in_window(spatial_attr,x1,y1,x2,y2
```

The Window Operation

As an example of the use of a spatial condition, consider the following command, which combines a spatial selection (i.e., a window operation, which is the same as a rectangular range query) with a nonspatial selection. The result is a map containing just the part of the freeways contained in the space spanned by the window. In addition, we have a new relation whose tuples correspond to the freeways that lie in the window.

```
select all
      from roads
      where in_window(road_coords,w) and
            road_type=freeway;
```

The window operation is a special case of a set-theoretic operation in that we are taking the intersection of the space spanned by a regular map and an otherwise empty map containing the space spanned by the window. The attribute values of the regular map in the selected area are retained as a result of this operation. Using our classification of operations, it is a local operation as it involves corresponding locations in two layers. Given one or more spatial attributes, set-theoretic operations can be applied to them as well. For example, suppose we wish to find the names of all the roads that pass through College Park. It is executed by intersecting the `region_location(s)` of the tuple(s) whose `region_name` is `College Park` with the `road_coords` attribute of the road map.

```
select road_name
      from roads regions
      where region_name=College Park
            and intersect(region_location,road_coords);
```

Spatial Join

When the intersection involves more than one spatial attribute, the operation is a spatial join rather than a spatial selection. The reason is that we are now combining two relations. In particular, we know that a θ-join is a join that involves comparisons between attributes that are θ-comparable, where θ is a comparator. If the comparator is based on spatial attributes, then the command is said to be a *spatial join*, while if the comparator is based on a nonspatial attribute, then the operation is called a *nonspatial* or *relational join*.

To understand the meaning of the spatial join better, suppose that in our example we selected all the attributes instead of just the road names (i.e., we ignore the projection implied by the fact that we only selected the nonspatial attribute corresponding to the names of the roads). The result of the join is a new relation consisting of a merge of all tuples whose corresponding spatial attributes are in College Park. This new relation contains all the attributes of the two participating relations including the two spatial attributes (i.e., `region_location` and `road_coords`) and their corresponding maps. Some other examples of spatial join operations include determining all spatial features that are adjacent to other spatial features, within a certain distance of other spatial features, contained in other spatial features, and so on. Interestingly, the spatial join may involve the same relations. For example, to find all regions adjacent to universities we would use the following command.

```
select all
       from l regions, k regions
       where adjacent_to(l.region_location,k.region_location)
            and l.region_utilization=university;
```

In this case, the resulting relation will have two spatial attributes corresponding to `region_location` and two maps—that is, one map for the university regions and one map for the neighboring regions.

It is interesting to note that in the literature, the term *spatial join* has a number of meanings. For example, in Orenstein and Manola 1988, the term *spatial join* is used to mean, in the context of this chapter, the spatial join intersection operation. Ooi 1988 does not distinguish between spatial join and spatial selection. They use the term *spatial join* to mean both *join* and *selection*. They perform selections by fixing one of the arguments of the spatial join. However, no join action, in the conventional database sense, takes place in this case. In fact, a window operation can be viewed as a selection operation rather than a spatial join with a constant object (the window) that has no further nonspatial attributes. Güting 1989 defines spatial joins and spatial selections in essentially the same way as done here.

17.3.2 An Alternative Spatial Extension

The approach we have described above associates the spatial attributes with the tuple. In particular, the spatial attributes appear at the same conceptual level as the nonspatial attributes—that is, the value of a particular spatial attribute is common to all of the nonspatial attributes in the tuple. An alternative approach associates the spatial attributes as a subhierarchy of the nonspatial attributes [Gadia 1993]. This is equivalent to distributing the spatial attribute across all of the nonspatial attributes. The drawback is that we have now established a hierarchy where the spatial attributes are subservient to the nonspatial attributes.

As an example of this alternative, consider the `regions` relation. Let us add the attribute `region_soil`. In this case, the spatial attribute `region_location` no longer appears with the nonspatial attributes in the schema. Instead, `region_location` is declared at the top level with the name of the relation. Let the new relation be called `new_regions`. This

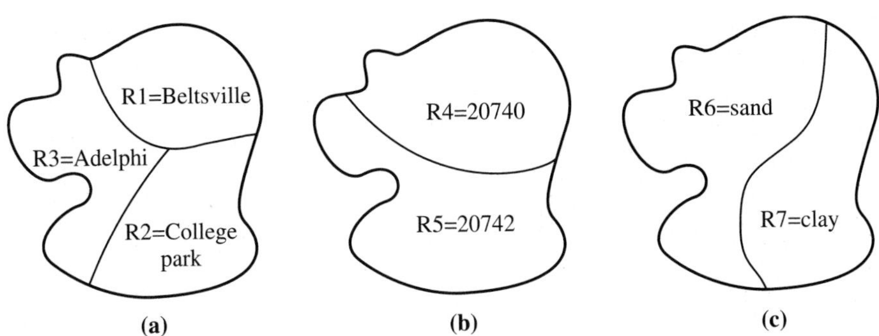

FIGURE 17–1
Three Partitions of the Same Region: (a) By Region Name; (b) By Zip Code; and (c) By Soil Type

means that `region_location` is to be distributed across the nonspatial attributes, and `region_location` has a value for every nonspatial attribute in each tuple. In fact, the nonspatial attributes in each tuple may now have several values if the corresponding spatial attribute requires decomposition. This is the case when the `region_name`, `region_zip_code`, and `region_soil` values are not the same for the entire region represented by the tuple.

```
create table new_regions
      (spatial_attribute: region_location REGION)
      (region_id NUMBER,
       region_name CHAR(30),
       region_zip_code NUMBER,
       region_utilization CHAR(30),
       region_importance NUMBER,
       region_soil CHAR(30));
```

For example, suppose that we have a tuple *t* with `region_utilization = university`, `region_id = 55`, and `region_importance = 5`. This area has more than one name (e.g. `R1` is `Beltsville`, `R2` is `College Park`, and `R3` is `Adelphi`), more than one zip code (e.g., `R4` is `20740` and `R5` is `20742`), and more than one soil type (e.g., `R6` is `sand` and `R7` is `clay`). Figure 17–1 shows the resulting decompositions of the region. Tuple *t* now has multiple-valued attributes. This must be expressed in the tuple. One way to incorporate this approach in an instance (i.e., tuple) of the `new_regions` schema is given below.

```
tuple in table new_regions
     (region_id: 55,
      region_name:
        {R1: Beltsville,
         R2: College Park,
         R3: Adelphi},
```

```
region_zip_code:
  {R4: 20740,
   R5: 20742},
region_utilization: university,
region_importance: 5,
region_soil:
  {R6: sand,
   R7: clay});
```

Using this approach, we can also separate the spatial conditions from the nonspatial conditions. This is the approach taken by Gadia 1993, who adds a `restricted to` clause to the standard SQL command. In this case, the command takes the form `select` ... `restricted to` ... `from` ... `where` .... The condition in the `where` clause only includes the nonspatial attributes, while the condition in the `restricted to` clause deals with the spatial data.

For example, suppose that we wish to find the name of the regions covering a university whose soil type is `sand` and are in the `20742` zip code. The query is formulated as follows:

```
select region_name from new_regions
       restricted to region_soil=sand ∩ region_zip_code=20742
       where region_utilization=university;
```

This query is executed by first selecting all the tuples whose `region_utilization` value is `university` and then examining their corresponding spatial attributes. In particular, we restrict our view to the locations that are of soil type `sand` and in zip code `20742`. Now we return the names of the regions that overlap these locations. This can be achieved by intersecting the result of the `restricted` clause with the corresponding spatial attribute value of `region_name`. Notice that what we have done is define the semantics of a projection operation in such an environment.

Gadia 1993 proposes to use this approach to deal with spatiotemporal data. The temporal attribute is treated in the same way as the spatial attribute. The difference is that the temporal attribute is restricted to points or intervals by the very nature of the time dimension. In contrast, there is no such restriction on the spatial dimension. It is also interesting to note that SQL commands can be nested within the `restricted` clause.

17.4 Integration of Spatial and Nonspatial Data

The key issue in building a spatial DBMS is deciding how to integrate the representation of spatial and nonspatial data. In section 17.3, a number of methods for interacting with such a database were proposed. This was done in a manner that was largely independent of the underlying architecture of the system. In this section we discuss a number of spatial DBMS architectures. Since the field is still developing, most of these architectures are research prototypes rather than commercial systems.

Some researchers use the classifications *dedicated, dual, layered,* and *integrated* to distinguish among the different architectures [Vijlbrief and van Oosterom 1992]. In the following, we first give an overview of the issues that arise when using these architectures. This is followed by a more detailed comparative discussion of features of some research prototypes.

17.4.1 Dedicated Systems

Many prototype systems are suggested that support spatial objects. The principal shortcoming of these systems is their development path. One common path is as a dedicated system with the purpose of supporting applications in a specific domain (e.g., CAD databases) without a full understanding of database issues such as the absence of high-level data definition facilities (e.g., Shaffer et al. 1990; Tomlin 1990). Also, these systems are not easily extendible in the sense that it is difficult to modify them to perform actions not previously envisioned by the system's designers. An alternative path is a general database tool that supports a wide variety of applications often without a complete understanding of the requirements of such applications. In both cases, the mentioned shortcomings lead to a reduction in the efficiency of the data processing capabilities of the system.

17.4.2 Dual Architectures

Dual architectures are based on distinguishing between the spatial and nonspatial data by using different data models for them. Examples are ARC/INFO [Peuquet and Marble 1990] and SICAD [Schilcher 1985]. Communication between the systems is via common identifiers. The shortcomings are traditional database issues such as synchronization, locking, integrity (e.g., the results of actions in the spatial data model might not be reflected in the nonspatial data model, etc.).

A dual architecture implies the existence of two storage managers. This can be avoided by storing spatial data in a purely relational data model. This means that spatial data must be transformed (e.g., by use of methods such as representative points) or decomposed into constituent pieces (e.g., a region boundary into a sequence of line segments or a region interior into a set of blocks or pixels). This approach implies a hierarchy and in fact is the basis of the layered architecture. In this case, we have a GIS at the top layer, followed by a spatial support layer, followed by a relational DBMS at the bottom layer. Examples of this approach include SIRO-DBMS [Abel 1989] and GEOVIEW [Waugh and Healey 1987]. Of course, the relative order of some of the elements in the hierarchy can be changed. For example, in Gadia 1993, spatial and temporal data are placed below the relational layer (see the discussion at the end of section 17.3).

17.4.3 Integrated Architectures

An integrated architecture is the most general. It involves users extending the DBMS with their own abstract data types so as to provide better support for spatial applications. This extension frequently involves making use of an extensible database management system (e.g., Carey et al. 1988; Güting 1989; Haas et al. 1990; Schek and Waterfeld 1986; Stonebraker and Rowe 1986) as well as object-oriented DBMSs (e.g., Deux et al. 1990). Such systems attempt to provide a generalized DBMS that facilitates the support of unconventional applications such as spatial databases. These systems add some new constructs to offer additional modeling power. Included among the new constructs is support for abstract data types (e.g., Carey et al. 1988), procedural fields (e.g., Stonebraker and Rowe 1986), complex objects (e.g., Carey et al. 1988; Kim et al. 1987), set-valued attributes (e.g., Zaniolo 1983), and so on.

Users of integrated architectures are motivated in part by a belief that each of the data types (i.e., spatial and nonspatial) should be represented by an appropriate data structure that suits its operational needs. This has been done primarily by extending the relational model (e.g., see Stonebraker 1986). At times, the extensions are such that the result is a layered architecture. In such cases, the system can be described as belonging to both architectures. Nevertheless, we describe it in conjunction with integrated systems, as we feel that being an extension of the relational model is the systems' most important characteristic.

17.4.4 Prototype Systems

SIRO-DBMS [Abel 1989], GEOVIEW [Waugh and Healey 1987], SAND [Aref and Samet 1991a], Gral [Güting 1989], Probe [Orenstein and Manola 1988], GEOQL [Ooi 1988], Geo-Kernel [Schek and Waterfeld 1986], and GEO++ [Vijlbrief and van Oosterom 1992] are examples of systems based on extending the relational model. Some systems (e.g., Abel 1989; Orenstein and Manola 1988; Waugh and Healey 1987) implement a spatial database on top of a relational DBMS with minor changes to the relational system. Changes are in the form of shells outside the DBMS (as in Abel 1989). In most of these systems, spatial data are flattened into the relational format, which means that spatial data are treated as if they are regular attribute data.

GEO++ [Vijlbrief and van Oosterom 1992] is built on top of the Postgres [Stonebraker and Rowe 1986] extensible DBMS. It makes use of the primitive data types point, line segment, path, and box provided by Postgres to define other data types as well as operators.

Probe [Dayal and Smith 1986; Orenstein and Manola 1986, 1988] contains a general geometric object class: a point set but no specific types (e.g., point, line, etc.). It treats space and time as generic types with the same status as integers, floating point numbers, strings, and the like. Probe does not have a spatial query language. However, Probe does provide a general method for indexing the space by linearizing the spatial index to one dimension through the use of bit-interleaving techniques and storing the resulting values into an attribute that is indexed by a B-tree. The user can add spatial data types based on application needs as a specialization of the point set type and index the underlying space using this general spatial attribute. One disadvantage is that Probe limits itself to space-filling curve representations of spatial data when there are other interesting spatial data structures that could be used.

Geo-Kernel [Schek and Waterfeld 1986; Wolf 1989] implements a geometric data model on top of the DASDBS kernel system [Schek and Waterfeld 1986; Wolf 1989] that supports Non-First-Normal-Form (NF^2) relations [Schek and Scholl 1989]. The implementation focuses on efficient processing of window queries with possible feature selection from the window. Also, in contrast to the assumptions made in other systems (e.g., SAND [Aref and Samet 1991a]), Geo-Kernel models sets of objects (e.g., a set of points, a set of lines, or a set of regions) as atomic objects. A set of objects is the atomic unit of processing for each geometric operator.

Other systems (e.g., Gral [Güting 1989] and GEOQL [Ooi 1988]) extend the relational model a step further to achieve efficient spatial data processing. Spatial data is stored in separate spatial data structures. Spatial operations are executed on top of these structures. They build on the early work and ideas in Stonebraker 1986.

Gral [Güting 1989] permits user-defined data types and operations. It provides an integrated data model and query language for geometric applications. The user interface is algebraic and procedural. It uses a many-sorted algebra both as an algebraic query language and as an executable language to describe query plans (although with lower-level primitives and operators).

17.4.5 Linking Spatial and Nonspatial Data

One important issue that arises in the design of systems based on an integrated architecture is how to link the spatial data description (stored in some data structure) of an object with the rest of the object's nonspatial description. Many systems are biased toward either the spatial or the nonspatial aspect of the system (e.g., GEOQL [Ooi 1988]). GEOQL extends SQL to support spatial applications. The underlying architecture is composed of

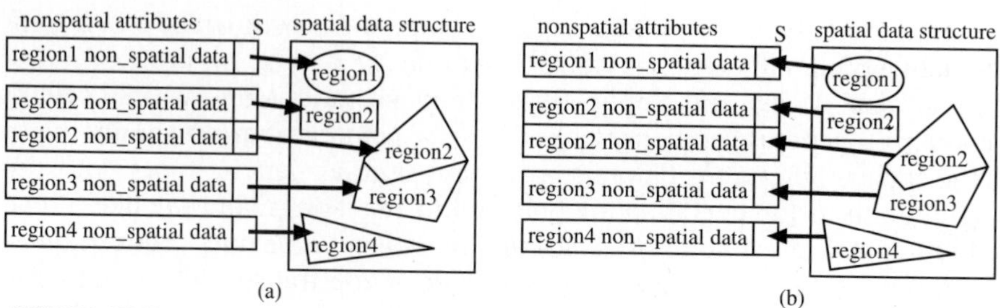

FIGURE 17–2
(a) Forward Links and (b) Backward Links for the Region's Relation

an SQL backend, a spatial processor, and an extended optimizer. In GEOQL, each relation is assumed to have only one spatial attribute. Multiple spatial representation of an object is difficult under this model (e.g., modeling a city once as a point in a point map and once as a region by defining its bounding perimeter). GEOQL is biased toward the relational component in several aspects. In particular, even though spatial data structures are maintained, spatial operations cannot be composed directly without building intermediate database relations. This limits the efficiency of spatial query processing.

In SAND [Aref and Samet 1991a], spatial and nonspatial data are linked bidirectionally. A spatial data structure is associated with each spatial attribute in the schema and is used to store all data instances of that spatial attribute over the set of homogeneous objects (e.g., line data in a road network). The spatial data structure that is chosen depends on the attribute's spatial data type (e.g., point, line, region, etc.). The spatial data structure serves as an index for spatial objects and an environment for the execution of spatially related operations (e.g., image rotation and scaling, polygon intersection, area computation, proximity queries).

The data instances of the set of nonspatial attributes are stored in database relations. Each tuple in the relation corresponds to one object. Two logical links are maintained between the spatial and nonspatial data instances of an object: *forward* and *backward* links (see Fig. 17–2). The linked instances and the links form what is termed a *spatial relation*. Forward links are used to retrieve the spatial information of an object given the object's nonspatial information. Backward links are used to retrieve the nonspatial information of an object given the object's spatial information. Since the nonspatial information of an object is stored in a tuple, the backward link can be the tuple-id. On the other hand, since spatial data structures contain all the spatial information necessary to identify an object, the forward link can be a representative value of one part of the object that uniquely selects the object. For example, in the case of nonoverlapping region data, an example of a forward link is a candidate point inside the region.

Maintaining forward and backward links between the spatial and nonspatial parts of a set of objects facilitates browsing in the two parts and permits efficient query processing. Flexibility in the interaction between spatial and nonspatial attributes enables operations (whether spatial or nonspatial) to be performed in their most natural environment.

The need to support bidirectional links between database objects was realized as early as hierarchical and network database management systems (e.g., IMS [McGee 1977] and CODASYL DBTG [CODASYL 1971]). They are also proposed in Lorie and Meier 1984. In Lorie and Meier 1984, arbitrary links (via references and identifiers that could be used to implement bidirectional links) are adapted to geographical databases where a geographical object is represented by a tuple having some unique identifier and a long field to store the geographic representation of the object in addition to other nonspatial attributes. Links are used to express explicit relationships between geographical objects (e.g., parent-child or reference relationships).

Bidirectional links are also used in Geo-Kernel [Schek and Waterfeld 1986; Wolf 1989] in order to allow each of the spatial and nonspatial parts of an object to access the other part. Spatial objects are partitioned into cells. Cells are clustered according to their two-dimensional neighborhood. The address of the nonspatial description of an object is stored with each cell of this object. Since Geo-Kernel uses nested relations [Schek and Scholl 1989], an attribute of type relation (i.e., a subrelation) is used in order to store all the addresses of the cells comprising a spatial object. This resembles a forward link in a spatial relation in SAND [Aref and Samet 1991a]. However, in contrast to subrelations, in a spatial relation only one spatial identifier is stored as a forward link, and it is the responsibility of the spatial data structure (or its encapsulating spatial process or ADT) to extract the rest of the spatial description of an object. This greatly reduces the storage overhead from the relational side as well as reduces the cost that must be borne in systems such as Geo-Kernel to maintain the set of addresses stored in a subrelation that refer to different cells of the same object.

The idea of introducing abstract data types (ADTs) as new attribute domains into a relational database system and supporting user-defined index structures appears in Stonebraker 1986. Following this approach, spatial data structures are viewed in many extensible database systems (e.g., Güting 1989; Roussopoulos et al. 1988; Stonebraker and Rowe 1986) as indexing structures. As a result, only backward links (i.e., from the index structure to the actual tuple) are needed in these architectures. In contrast, it is important to note that in SAND's spatial relations [Aref and Samet 1991a], user-defined data structures serve not only as spatial indexes for speeding up operations but also as containers for the full description of spatial data. In the latter, the bidirectional links between corresponding components of the ADT can be used for efficient access. Spatial relations can be viewed as a merge of the ADT work in Stonebraker 1986 and the complex object support in Lorie and Meier 1984. In a spatial relation, a spatial attribute is an ADT that is implemented by user-defined data structures. Functions may be applied to an instance of one spatial attribute in a given tuple (e.g., computing the area or perimeter of a region where a particular crop is grown) or to the whole relation (e.g., find all the crops that are grown in a particular query).

Gral [Güting 1989] avoids forward links (and hence does not use containers) by employing spatial data structures as indexes that approximate spatial objects (e.g., by using bounding boxes). In addition, the full description of the spatial object (e.g., the coordinate values of the vertices of a polygon) is stored with the object's corresponding tuple in an on-line format (i.e., formatted in a memory-mapped image such that when the tuple is loaded into main memory, the spatial description of the object is ready for use without any additional format conversions). In this case, when a query is posed, the spatial data structure is used as a filtering step that produces a set of candidate objects; then the full description of these objects is used as a refinement step to produce the final answer to the query. The performance of these alternative data architectures with respect to spatial query processing and optimization is an interesting research problem. One drawback of this approach, though, is that every time a tuple participates in a join, the full description of the spatial object needs to be duplicated as well (in many cases, the size of this spatial description of an object is large; for example, this is the case with polygon objects).

17.4.6 Prototypes Based on Object-Oriented Systems

The object-oriented model can also be used as a basis of a spatial database. In the object-oriented approach, information is highly structured by the introduction of classes and inheritance concepts. Data encapsulation and overloading facilitate data manipulation and make the physical and logical representations of the data independent of each other. In the case of a spatial database, concepts such as classes, inheritance, encapsulation, type, and method extensions are handy. The different spatial data types can be implemented as classes with inheritance used to define subclasses (e.g., the class for a polygon with holes inherits from the more general polygon class). Complex objects can be defined from simpler ones (e.g., a road is composed of several line segments).

Scholl and Voisard 1992 describe a GIS built on top of the O_2 object-oriented DBMS [Deux et al. 1990]. However, their implementation makes little use of object-oriented techniques. Instead, they implement an extended relational system on top of O_2 where by *extended* we mean supporting relations with abstract data types to encapsulate geometric data types. Spatial data are modeled at two levels: map and geometric. A spatial database consists of a set of maps, where a map is a relation that has at least one spatial attribute. Map operations are implemented as methods on map objects. The geometric level corresponds to the spatial attributes that are represented by geometric abstract data types (e.g., points, lines, regions, etc.).

17.5 Query Processing and Optimization

Query optimization for spatial databases is a relatively undeveloped field. It is heavily dependent on the application. Frequently, there is no special treatment for spatial data, in the sense that the optimization strategies for the underlying DBMS are used with few special provisions being made for the difference in the data. A cost model and framework for comparing different optimization strategies is needed.

One issue is how to take into account the effect of the different representations and spatial access methods. For example, for a given set of spatial queries, representations based on computing a minimum bounding rectangle can be compared with representations based on storing an exact description, on storing increasing levels of details, and transformations into points in a higher-dimensional space.

Another equally important issue is the nature of the datasets. For example, clustering of the data may alter the selectivity of a window operation (i.e., what is the expected percentage of the tuples that will be selected for output). Such clustering can be detected by distinguishing between a rural and an urban area. For point and line data, data density is important. For region data, skewness, roundness, connectedness, and topology (e.g., number of holes) come into play. As an example of the importance of skewness, it is useful to distinguish between querying a map of rivers and a map of lakes.

Of course, a tighter grip on the issue of estimating the cost of spatial operations is also needed. This depends on two factors. The first consists of the execution time of the underlying algorithm and I/O. The second is the time needed to produce the output. The latter is facilitated by a knowledge of selectivity factors. For example, consider the following two different spatial selection operations:

1. `nearest_to`(p), which finds the nearest object to point p.
2. `object_at`(p), which finds the object stored at point p.

Assume that spatial indexes exist for each operation. In this case, the selectivities are the same for both operations—that is, each returns just one object and thus takes $O(1)$ time to produce the output. However, the execution times of the algorithms can be quite different. In particular, depending on the underlying representation of the spatial data, `nearest_to` may require $O(n)$ I/O operations, while `object_at` may require just $O(\log n)$ I/O operations.

A number of recently suggested spatial database architectures address the issue of spatial query optimization (e.g., SAND [Aref and Samet 1991b], Gral [Güting 1989], GEOQL [Ooi 1988], and Geo-Kernel [Wolf 1989]). However, they differ in the capabilities and degrees of freedom they provide to the spatial query optimizer as a result of the manner in which they integrate spatial data with nonspatial data. In particular, the underlying architecture may limit some feasible strategies for spatial query processing.

GEOQL's spatial query optimizer [Ooi 1988] extends the well-known query decomposition technique [Wong and Youssefi 1976] to handle spatial queries as well. However, GEOQL is biased towards the relational side. In particular, every relation is supported by at most one spatial attribute that is implicit and is always associated with the relation. Each query is decomposed into disjoint subqueries that consist entirely of either spatial or nonspatial conditions. The nonspatial subqueries are executed by an SQL backend, while spatial queries are executed by a spatial processor. Additional SQL subqueries are introduced to merge multiple partial results (i.e., temporary relations). Spatial operations cannot be composed directly—that is, each operation returns a relation, and no further optimization is possible. GEOQL's optimizer only estimates the cost of nonspatial operations and does not take the I/O cost of spatial operations into account (i.e., only their selectivities). Different query execution plans are attempted. Heuristics are used to prune the number of plans whose costs are to be estimated (e.g., the cost of subqueries in an AND-clause that have no overlap is not affected by their order of execution).

In Geo-Kernel [Wolf 1989], spatial information is stored in textual form as an attribute value in a relation. For example, a polygon relation can be expressed as an attribute. This is potentially quite costly from a storage point of view (i.e., spatial data is usually voluminous) as a join may cause the same spatial data to be stored with different records. Nevertheless, during query evaluation, appropriate spatial data structures are used to operate on spatial data. Thus in Geo-Kernel there is a need for conversion procedures to toggle between these data structures and the textual or byte-string form for each spatial data type. Notice that in order to perform the operation *intersects* or *closest*, for example, the entire set of spatial objects in the relevant relations must be downloaded into the spatial data structures. This is an expensive task, and its cost has to be included when considering different query evaluation plans. As a result, the query optimizer prefers to perform relational selections before spatial selections in order to lower the cost of spatial data conversion (i.e., downloading) by reducing the number of qualifying tuples.

Gral [Becker and Güting 1989; Güting 1989] uses an algebraic query language at both the query description and execution levels. It uses a rule-based optimizer to normalize and optimize at the descriptive algebra level. Some examples include exchanging the order of operations using a predefined partial order of operations (e.g., selects before joins) and finding a good order for performing joins using selectivity estimates. The optimizer also translates the query to an executable algebraic form and optimizes at that level (e.g., by combining selection operations). It only takes the selectivity of the operation into account and thus ignores the actual cost of performing the operation. For example, it prefers performing a closest operation to a select operation since closest reduces the number of tuples, although its I/O execution cost may be considerably higher.

Systems such as GEO++ [Vijlbrief and van Oosterom 1992] are implemented on top of Postgres [Stonebraker and Rowe 1986]. Postgres allows users to add application-dependent operators. The operators are characterized so that the query optimizer can decide which optimization techniques should be applied. This is done by using cost estimates. Some of the characterizations include precedence, associativity, whether or not the operator is hash joinable, commutator and negator operators, and select and join selectivities. The operator and index characteristics are stored in tables. Based on these characteristics, the optimizer maps the operators (if possible) into existing database methods (e.g., hardwired join algorithms).

SAND's query processing and optimization strategies [Aref and Samet 1991b] include the ability to reorder operations as well as merging. Merging is useful when a query contains two conditions (can be spatial or nonspatial) and the user wants to perform them independently and merge the results. Merging can be either homogeneous (i.e., the conditions are both spatial or both nonspatial) or nonhomogeneous (i.e., one condition is spatial while the other is nonspatial). The former is implemented by intersecting the sets resulting from the operations. For the latter, the execution can be either spatial driven or relational driven. The one that is chosen depends, in part, on selectivity factors. For example, in the case of a spatial-driven merge, the spatial data structure is traversed and only the spatial objects (and their tuples) that satisfy the spatial condition and whose tuples satisfy the relational condition are retained.

Other optimizations that SAND is capable of performing include combining successive spatial operations or successive relational operations as well as making use of pipelining and composition. At times, an operation may not be very selective, in which case it is preferable to delete the unselected items from the map rather than create a new map containing the multitude of selected items. Early projection is also useful when it is known that some of the attributes are no longer needed. Frequently, the optimization is application dependent. For example, when part of the condition involves the computation of the nearest object, it may be preferable to rank order all the objects at once rather than compute the nearest object anew each time.

17.6 Concluding Remarks

An overview has been presented of some of the issues that arise in building spatial databases. As we saw, they consist, in part, of finding better ways to interact with the database, integrating the spatial and nonspatial data, and optimizing the processing of the queries. It should be clear that such databases are still in their infancy in the sense that much remains to be done before the ideas explored in research prototypes will find their way into commercial systems.

ACKNOWLEDGMENT

This work was supported in part by the National Science Foundation under Grant IRI-9017393

REFERENCES

Abel, D.J. 1989. SIRO-DBMS: A Database Tool-Kit For Geographical Information Systems. *International Journal of Geographical Information Systems,* Vol. 3, No. 2, 103–116.

Al-Taha, K. K., Snodgrass, R. T., and Soo., M. D. 1993. Bibliography on Spatiotemporal Databases. *SIGMOD Record,* Vol. 22, No. 1, 59–67.

Aref, W. G., and Samet, H. 1991a. Extending a DBMS with Spatial Operations. In: *Advances in Spatial Databases,* 299–318. O. Günther and H. J. Sheck, eds. Lecture Notes in Computer Science 525. Springer-Verlag, Berlin.

Aref, W. G., and Samet, H. 1991b. Optimization Strategies for Spatial Query Processing. *Proceedings of the 17th International Conference on Very Large Databases,* Barcelona, 81–90.

Becker, L., and Güting, R. H. 1989. Rule-Based Optimization and Query Processing in an Extensible Geometric Database System. Technical Report 312, Dortmund University, Dortmund, Germany.

Carey, M., DeWeitt, D., and Vandenberg, S. 1988. A Data Model and Query Language for EXODUS. *Proceedings of the 1988 ACM-SIGMOD International Conference on Management of Data,* Chicago, Vol. 17, 413–423.

CODASYL. 1971. CODASYL Data Base Task Group. *ACM.*

Dayal, U., and Smith, J. J. 1986. A Knowledge-Oriented Database Management System. In: *On Knowledge Base Management Systems: Integrating Artificial Intelligence and Database Technologies,* 227–257. M. L. Brodie and J. Mylopoulos, eds. Springer-Verlag, New York.

Deux, O. et al. 1990. The Story of O_2. *IEEE Transactions on Knowledge and Data Engineering,* Vol. 2, No. 1, 91–108.

Egenhofer, J. J. 1992. Why Not SQL! *International Journal of Geographical Information Systems,* Vol. 6, No. 2, 71–85.

Gadia, S. K. 1993. Parametric Databases: Seamless Integration Oof Spatial, Temporal, Belief, and Ordinary Data. *SIGMOD Record,* Vol. 22, No. 1, 15–20.

Güting, R. H. 1989. Gral: An Extensible Relational System for Geometric Applications. *Proceedings of the 15th International Conference on Very Large Databases (VLDB),* Amsterdam, 33–44.

Haas, L. J., Chang, W., Lohman, G. M., McPherson, J., Wilms, P. F., Lapis, G., Lindsay, B., Pirahesh, H., Carey, M. J., and Shekita, E. 1990. Starburst Mid Flight: As The Dust Clears. *IEEE Transactions on Knowledge and Data Engineering,* Vol. 2, No. 1, 143–160.

Kim, W., Banerjee, J., Chou, H., Garza, J., and Woelk, D. 1987. Composite Object Support in an Object-Oriented Database System. *Proceedings of the 2nd ACM OOPSLA Conference,* Orlando, 118–125.

Lorie, R., and Meier, A. 1984. Using a Relational DBMS for Geographical Databases. *GeoProcessing,* Vol. 2, 243–257.

McGee, W. C. 1977. The IMS/VS System. *IBM Systems Journal,* Vol. 16, No. 2, 84–168.

Ooi, B. C. 1988. *Efficient Query Processing for Geographic Information Systems.* Ph.D. thesis, Monash University, Victoria, Australia. (Also *Lecture Notes in Computer Science* 471, Springer-Verlag, Berlin, 1990.)

Orenstein, J. A., and Manola, F. A. 1986. Spatial Data Modeling and Query Processing in PROBE. Technical Report CCA-86-05, Computer Corporation of America, Cambridge, Mass.

Orenstein, J. A., and Manola, F. A. 1988. PROBE Spatial Data Modeling and Query Processing in an Image Database Application. *IEEE Transactions on Software Engineering,* Vol, 14, No. 5, 611–629.

Peuquet, D. J. and Marble, D. F. 1990. ARC/INFO: An Example of a Contemporary Geographic Information System. In: *Introduction Readings In Geographic Information Systems,* 90–99. D. J. Peuquet and D. F. Marble, eds. Taylor and Francis, London.

Roussopoulos, N., Faloutsos, C., and Sellis, T. 1988. An Efficient Pictorial Database System for PSQL. *IEEE Transactions on Software Engineering,* Vol. 14, No. 5, 639–650.

Schek, H., and Scholl, M. 1989. The Two Roles of Nested Relations in the DASDBS Project. In: *Nested Relations and Complex Objects in Databases,* 50–68. S. Abiteboul, P. C. Fischer, and H. J. Schek, eds. Springer-Verlag, Berlin. (Also in *Lecture Notes in Computer Science* 361.)

Schek, H., and Waterfeld, W. 1986. A Database Kernel System for Geoscientific Applications. *Proceedings of the 2nd International Symposium on Spatial Data Handling,* Seattle, 273–288.

Schilcher, M. 1985. Interactive Computer Graphic Data Processing in Cartography. *Computers & Graphics,* Vol. 9, No. 1, 57–66.

Scholl, M., and Voisard, A. 1992. Object-Oriented Database Systems for Geographic Applications: An Example with O_2. In: *Geographic Database Management Systems,* 103–137. G. Gambosi, M. Scholl, and H. W. Six, eds., Springer-Verlag, Berlin.

Shaffer, C. A., Samet, H., and Nelson, R. C. 1990. QUILT: A Geographic Information System Based on Quadtrees. *International Journal of Geographical Information Systems,* Vol. 4, No. 2, 103–131.

Stonebraker, M. 1986. Inclusion of New Types in Relational Database Systems. *Proceedings of the 2nd International Conference on Data Engineering,* Los Angeles, 262–269.

Stonebraker, M., and Rowe, L. 1986. The Design of Postgres. *Proceedings of the 1986 ACM-SIGMOD International Conference on Management of Data,* Washington, D.C., Vol. 15, 340–355.

Tomlin, C. D. 1990. *Geographic Information Systems and Cartographic Modeling.* Prentice Hall, Englewood Cliffs, N.J.

Tufte, E. R. 1983. *The Visual Display of Quantitative Information.* Graphics Press, Cheshire, Conn.

Tufte, E. R. 1990. *Envisioning Information.* Graphics Press, Cheshire, Conn.

Vijlbrief, T., and van Oosterom, P. 1992. The GEO++ System: An Extensible GIS. *Proceedings of the 4th International Symposium on Spatial Data Handling,* Charleston, Vol. 1, 40–50.

Waugh, T. C., and Healey, R. G. 1987. The GEOVIEW Design: A Relational Data Base Approach to Geographical Data Handling. *International Journal of Geographical Information Systems,* Vol. 1, No. 2, 101–118.

Wolf, A. 1989. The DASDBS GEO-Kernel: Concepts, Experiences, and the Second Step. *Design and Implementation of Large Spatial Databases, Proceedings of the First Symposium SSD '89,* Santa Barbara, 67–88. (Also *Lecture Notes in Computer Science* 409, Springer-Verlag, Berlin, 1990.)

Wong, E., and Youssefi, K. 1976. Decomposition—A Strategy for Query Processing. *ACM Transactions on Database Systems,* Vol. 1, No. 3, 223–241.

Zaniolo, C. 1983. The Database Language GEM. *Proceedings of the 1983 ACM-SIGMOD International Conference on Management of Data,* San Jose, Vol. 12, 207–218.

18

Spatial Data Structures

HANAN SAMET

An overview is presented of the use of spatial data structures in spatial databases. The focus is on hierarchical data structures, including a number of variants of quadtrees, which sort the data with respect to the space occupied by it. Such techniques are known as *spatial indexing methods*. Hierarchical data structures are based on the principle of recursive decomposition. They are attractive because they are compact and, depending on the nature of the data, they save space as well as time and also facilitate operations such as search. Examples are given of the use of these data structures in the representation of different data types such as regions, points, rectangles, lines, and volumes.

18.1 Introduction

Spatial data consist of spatial objects made up of points, lines, regions, rectangles, surfaces, volumes, and even data of higher dimension, which includes time. Examples of spatial data include cities, rivers, roads, counties, states, crop coverages, mountain ranges, and parts in a CAD system. Examples of spatial properties include the extent of a given river or the boundary of a given county. Often it is also desirable to attach nonspatial attribute information such as elevation heights or city names to the spatial data. Spatial databases facilitate the storage and efficient processing of spatial and nonspatial information ideally without favoring one over the other. Such databases are finding increasing use in applications in environmental monitoring, space, urban planning, resource management, and geographic information systems (GIS) [Buchmann et al. 1990; Günther and Schek 1991].

A common way to deal with spatial data is to store them explicitly by parametrizing them and thereby obtaining a reduction to a point in a possibly higher dimensional space. This is usually quite easy to do in a conventional database management system since the system is just a collection of records, where each record has many fields. In particular, we simply add a field (or several fields) to the record that deals with the desired item of spatial information. This approach is fine if we just want to perform a simple retrieval of the data.

However, if our query involves the space occupied by the data (and hence other records by virtue of their proximity), then the situation is not so straightforward. In such a case we need to be able to retrieve records based on some spatial properties that are not stored explicitly in the database. For example, in a roads database, we may not wish to force the user to specify explicitly which roads intersect which other roads or regions. The problem is that the potential volume of such information may be very large and the cost of preprocessing it high, while the cost of computing it on the fly may be quite reasonable, especially if the spatial data is stored in an appropriate manner. Thus we prefer to store the data implicitly so that a wide class of spatial queries can be handled. In particular, we need not know the types of queries a priori.

Being able to respond to spatial queries in a flexible manner places a premium on the appropriate representation of the spatial data. In order to be able to deal with proximity queries, the data must be sorted. Of course, all database management systems sort the data. The issue is which keys they sort on. In the case of spatial data, the sort should be based on all the spatial keys, which means that, unlike conventional database management systems, the sort is based on the space occupied by the data. Such techniques are known as *spatial indexing* methods.

One approach to the representation of spatial data is to separate it structurally from the nonspatial data while maintaining appropriate links between the two [Aref and Samet 1991a]. This leads to a much higher bandwidth for the retrieval of the spatial data. In such a case, the spatial operations are performed directly on the spatial data structures. This provides the freedom to choose a more appropriate spatial structure than the imposed nonspatial structure (e.g., a relational database). In such a case, a spatial processor can be used that is specifically designed for efficiently dealing with the parts of the queries that involve proximity relations and search, and a relational database management system can be used for the parts of the queries that involve nonspatial data. Its proper functioning depends on the existence of a query optimizer to determine the appropriate processor for each part of the query [Aref and Samet 1991b].

As an example of the type of query to be posed to a spatial database system, consider a request to "find the names of the roads that pass through the University of Maryland region." This requires the extraction of the region locations of all the database records whose "region name" field has the value "University of Maryland" and build a map *A*. Next, map *A* is intersected with the road map *B* to yield a new map *C* with the selected roads. Now create a new relation with just one attribute, which is the relevant road names of the roads in map *C*. Of course, there are other approaches to answering the above query. Their efficiency depends on the nature of the data and their volume.

In the rest of this review we concentrate on the data structures used by the spatial processor. In particular, we focus on hierarchical data structures. They are based on the principle of recursive decomposition (similar to *divide-and-conquer* methods). The term *quadtree* is often used to describe many elements of this class of data structures. We concentrate primarily on region, point, rectangle, and line data. For a more extensive treatment of this subject, see Samet 1990a and 1990b.

Our presentation is organized as follows. Section 18.2 describes a number of different methods of indexing spatial data. Section 18.3 focuses on region data and also briefly reviews the historical background of the origins of hierarchical spatial data structures such as the quadtree. Sections 18.4, 18.5, and 18.6 describe hierarchical representations for point, rectangle, and line data, respectively, and give examples of their utility. Section 18.7 contains concluding remarks in the context of a geographic information system that makes use of these concepts.

18.2 Spatial Indexing

Each record in a database management system can be conceptualized as a point in a multidimensional space. This analogy is used by many researchers (e.g., Hinrichs and Nievergelt 1983; Jagadish 1990) to deal with spatial data by mapping the spatial object (henceforth we just use the term *object*) into a point (termed a *representative point*) in either the same (e.g., Jagadish 1990), lower (e.g., Orenstein and Merrett 1984), or higher (e.g., Hinrichs and Nievergelt 1983) dimensional spaces. This analogy is not always appropriate for spatial data. One problem is that the dimensionality of the representative point may be too high [Orenstein 1989]. One solution is to approximate the spatial object by reducing the dimensionality of the representative point. Another more serious problem is that use of these transformations does not preserve proximity.

To see the drawback of just mapping spatial data into points in another space, consider the representation of a database of line segments. We use the term *polygonal map* to refer to such a line segment database, consisting of vertices and edges, regardless of whether or not the line segments are connected to each other. Such a database can arise in a network of roads, power lines, rail lines, and the like. Using a representative point (e.g., Jagadish 1990), each line segment can be represented by its endpoints[1]. This means that each line segment is represented by a tuple of four items (i.e., a pair of x coordinate values and a pair of y coordinate values). Thus, in effect, we have constructed a mapping from a two-dimensional space (i.e., the space from which the lines are drawn) to a four-dimensional space (i.e., the space containing the representative point corresponding to the line).

1. Of course, there are other mappings, but they have similar drawbacks. We shall use this example in the rest of this section.

This mapping is fine for storage purposes and for queries that only involve the points that comprise the line segments (including their endpoints)—for example, finding all the line segments that intersect a given point or set of points or a given line segment. However, it is not good for queries that involve points or sets of points that are not part of the line segments, as they are not transformed to the higher dimensional space by the mapping. Answering such a query involves performing a search in the space from which the lines are drawn rather than in the space into which they are mapped.

As a more concrete example of the shortcoming of the mapping approach, suppose that we want to detect if two lines are near each other or, alternatively, to find the nearest line to a given point or line. This is difficult to do in the four-dimensional space since proximity in the two-dimensional space from which the lines are drawn is not necessarily preserved in the four-dimensional space into which the lines are mapped. In other words, although the two lines may be very close to each other, the Euclidean distance between their representative points may be quite large.

Thus we need different representations for spatial data. One way to overcome these problems is to use data structures that are based on spatial occupancy. Spatial occupancy methods decompose the space from which the data is drawn (e.g., the two-dimensional space containing the lines) into regions called *buckets*. They are also commonly known as *bucketing methods*. Traditionally, bucketing methods such as the grid file [Nievergelt et al. 1984], BANG file [Freeston 1987], LSD trees [Henrich et al. 1989], buddy trees [Seeger and Kriegel 1990], and the like have always been applied to the transformed data (i.e., the representative points). In contrast, we are applying the bucketing methods to the space from which the data is drawn (i.e., two dimensions in the case of a collection of line segments).

There are four principal approaches to decomposing the space from which the data is drawn. One approach buckets the data based on the concept of a minimum bounding (or enclosing) rectangle. In this case, objects are grouped (hopefully by proximity) into hierarchies and then stored in another structure such as a B-tree [Comer 1979]. The R-tree (e.g., Beckmann et al. 1990; Guttman 1984) is an example of this approach.

The R-tree and its variants are designed to organize a collection of arbitrary spatial objects (most notably two-dimensional rectangles) by representing them as d-dimensional rectangles. Each node in the tree corresponds to the smallest d-dimensional rectangle that encloses its son nodes. Leaf nodes contain pointers to the actual objects in the database instead of sons. The objects are represented by the smallest aligned rectangle containing them.

Often the nodes correspond to disk pages and, thus, the parameters defining the tree are chosen so that a small number of nodes is visited during a spatial query. Note that the bounding rectangles corresponding to different nodes may overlap. Also, an object may be spatially contained in

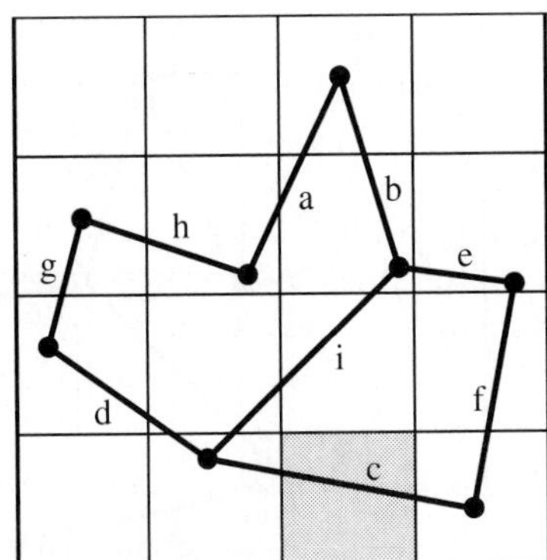

FIGURE 18–1
Example Collection of Line Segments Embedded in a 4 × 4 Grid

several nodes, yet it is only associated with one node. This means that a spatial query may often require several nodes to be visited before ascertaining the presence or absence of a particular object.

The basic rules for the formation of an R-tree are very similar to those for a B-tree. All leaf nodes appear at the same level. Each entry in a leaf node is a 2-tuple of the form (R,O) such that R is the smallest rectangle that spatially contains object O. Each entry in a non-leaf node is a 2-tuple of the form (R,P) such that R is the smallest rectangle that spatially contains the rectangles in the child node pointed at by P. An R-tree of order (m,M) means that each node in the tree, with the exception of the root, contains between $m \leq \lceil M/2 \rceil$ and M entries. The root node has at least two entries unless it is a leaf node

For example, consider the collection of line segments given in Fig. 18–1 shown embedded in a 4×4 grid. Let $M = 3$ and $m = 2$. One possible R-tree for this collection is given in Fig. 18–2a. Figure 18–2b shows the spatial extent of the bounding rectangles of the nodes in Fig. 18–2a, with broken lines denoting the rectangles corresponding to the subtrees rooted at the non-leaf nodes. Note that the R-tree is not unique. Its structure depends heavily on the order in which the individual line segments were inserted into (and possibly deleted from) the tree.

The drawback of these methods is that they do not result in a disjoint decomposition of space. The problem is that an object is only associated with one bounding rectangle (e.g., line segment `i` in Fig. 18–2 is associated with rectangle `R5`, yet it passes through `R1`, `R2`, `R4`, and `R5`). In the worst case, this means that when we wish to determine which object is associated with a particular point (e.g., the containing rectangle in a rectangle database or an intersecting line in a line segment database) in the two-dimensional space from which the objects are drawn, we may have to search the entire database.

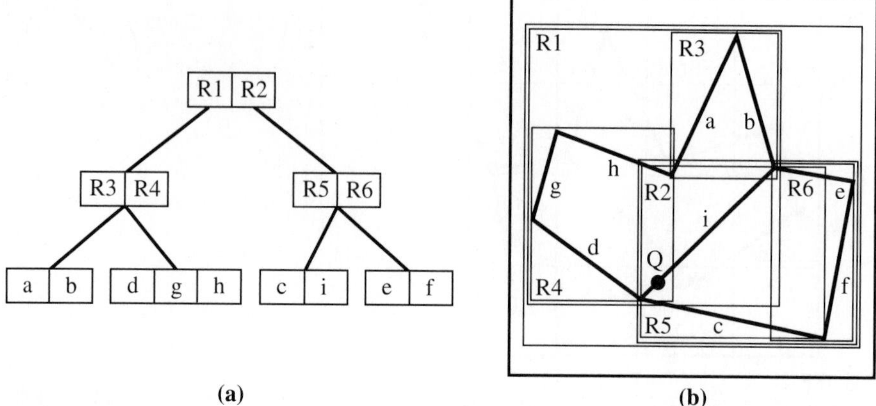

FIGURE 18–2
(a) R-Tree for the Collection of Line Segments in Fig. 18–1, and (b) The Spatial Extents of the Bounding Rectangles

For example, suppose we wish to determine the identity of the line segment in the collection of line segments given in Fig. 18–2 that passes through point `Q`. Since `Q` can be in either `R1` or `R2`, we must search both of their subtrees. Searching `R1` first, we find that `Q` could only be contained in `R4`. Searching `R4` does not lead to the line segment that contains `Q` even though `Q` is in a portion of bounding rectangle `R4` that is in `R1`. Thus, we must search `R2`, and we find that `Q` can only be contained in `R5`. Searching `R5` results in locating `i`, the desired line segment.

The other approaches are based on a decomposition of space into disjoint cells, which are mapped into buckets. Their common property is that the objects are decomposed into disjoint subobjects such that each of the subobjects is associated with a different cell. They differ in the degree of regularity imposed by their underlying decomposition rules and by the way in which the cells are aggregated. The price paid for the disjointness is that in order to determine the area covered by a particular object, we have to retrieve all the cells it occupies. This price is also paid when we want to delete an object. Fortunately, deletion is not so common in these databases. A related drawback is that when we wish to determine all the objects that occur in a particular region, we often retrieve many of the objects more than once. This is particularly problematic when the result of the operation serves as input to another operation via composition of functions. For example, suppose we wish to compute the perimeter of all the objects in a given region. Clearly, each object's perimeter should only be computed once. Eliminating the duplicates is a serious issue (see Aref and Samet 1992 for a discussion of how to deal with this problem in a database of line segments).

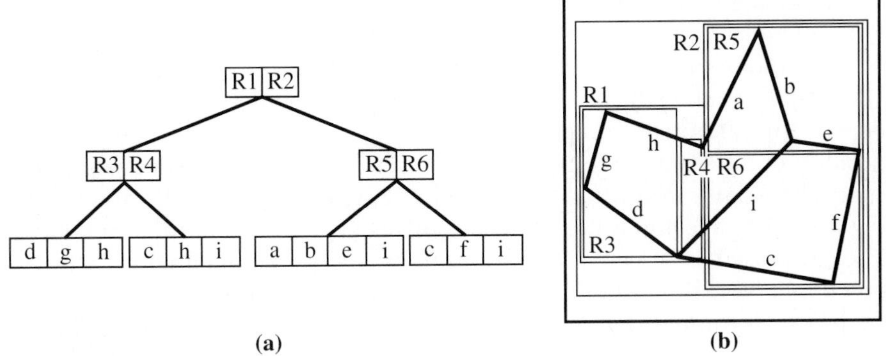

(a) (b)

FIGURE 18–3
(a) R⁺-Tree for the Collection of Line Segments in Fig. 18–1 and (b) The Spatial Extents of the Bounding Rectangles

The first method based on disjointness partitions the objects into arbitrary disjoint subobjects and then groups the subobjects in another structure such as a B-tree. The partition and the subsequent groupings are such that the bounding rectangles are disjoint at each level of the structure. The R^+-tree [Sellis et al. 1987] and the cell tree [Günther 1988] are examples of this approach. They differ in the data they deal with. The R^+-tree deals with collections of objects that are bounded by rectangles, while the cell tree deals with convex polyhedra.

The R^+-tree is an extension of the k-d-B-tree [Robinson 1981]. The R^+-tree is motivated by a desire to avoid overlap among the bounding rectangles. Each object is associated with all the bounding rectangles that it intersects. All bounding rectangles in the tree (with the exception of the bounding rectangles for the objects at the leaf nodes) are nonoverlapping[2]. The result is that there may be several paths starting at the root to the same object. This may lead to an increase in the height of the tree. However, retrieval time is sped up.

Figure 18–3 is an example of one possible R^+-tree for the collection of line segments in Fig. 18–1. This particular tree is of order (2,3), although in general it is not possible to guarantee that all nodes will always have a minimum of 2 entries. In particular, the expected B-tree performance guarantees are not valid (i.e., pages are not guaranteed to be *m/M* full) unless we are willing to perform very complicated record insertion and deletion procedures. Notice that line segments `c` and `h` appear in two different nodes,

2. From a theoretical viewpoint, the bounding rectangles for the objects at the leaf nodes should also be disjoint. However, this may be impossible (e.g., when the objects are line segments where many line segments intersect at a point).

while line segment `i` appears in three different nodes. Of course, other variants are possible since the R^+-tree is not unique.

Methods such as the R^+-tree and the cell tree (as well as the R^*-tree [Beckmann et al. 1990]) have the drawback that the decomposition is data dependent. This means that it is difficult to perform tasks that require composition of different operations and data sets (e.g., set-theoretic operations such as overlay). In contrast, the remaining two methods, while also yielding a disjoint decomposition, have a greater degree of data independence. They are based on a regular decomposition. The space can either be decomposed into blocks of uniform size (e.g., the uniform grid [Franklin 1984]) or adapt the decomposition to the distribution of the data (e.g., a quadtree-based approach such as Samet and Webber 1985). In the former case, all the blocks are of the same size (e.g., the 4×4 grid in Fig. 18–1). In the latter case, the widths of the blocks are restricted to be powers of 2, and their positions are also restricted.

The uniform grid is ideal for uniformly distributed data, while quadtree-based approaches are suited for arbitrarily distributed data. In the case of uniformly distributed data, quadtree-based approaches degenerate to a uniform grid, albeit with a higher overhead. Both the uniform grid and the quadtree-based approaches lend themselves to set-theoretic operations, and thus they are ideal for tasks that require the composition of different operations and data sets. In general, since spatial data is not usually uniformly distributed, the quadtree-based regular decomposition approach is more flexible. The drawback of quadtreelike methods is their sensitivity to positioning in the sense that the placement of the objects relative to the decomposition lines of the space in which they are embedded affects their storage costs and the amount of decomposition that takes place. This is overcome to a large extent by using a bucketing adaptation that decomposes a block only if it contains more than n objects.

All the spatial occupancy methods discussed above are characterized as employing spatial indexing because with each block the only information that is stored is whether or not the block is occupied by the object or part of the object. This information is usually in the form of a pointer to a descriptor of the object. For example, in the case of a collection of line segments in the uniform grid of Fig. 18–1, the shaded block only records the fact that a line segment crosses it or passes through it. The part of the line segment that passes through the block (or terminates within it) is termed a *q-edge*. Each q-edge in the block is represented by a pointer to a record containing the endpoints of the line segment of which the q-edge is a part [Nelson and Samet 1986]. This pointer is really nothing more than a spatial index—hence the use of this term to characterize this approach. Thus no information is associated with the shaded block as to what part of the line (i.e., q-edge) crosses it. This information can be obtained by clipping [Foley et al. 1990] the original line segment to the block. This is important, for often the precision necessary to compute these intersection points is not available.

18.3 Region Data

A region can be represented either by its interior or by its boundary. In this section we focus on the representations of regions by their interior, while the use of a boundary is discussed in section 18.6 in the context of collections of line segments as found, for example, in polygonal maps. The most common region representation is the image array. In this case, we have a collection of picture elements (termed *pixels*). Since the number of elements in the array can be quite large, there is interest in reducing its size by aggregating similar (i.e., homogeneous or equal-valued) pixels. There are two basic approaches. The first approach breaks up the array into $1 \times m$ blocks [Rutovitz 1968]. This is a row representation and is known as a *runlength code*. A more general approach treats the region as a union of maximal square blocks (or blocks of any other desired shape) that may possibly overlap. Usually the blocks are specified by their centers and radii. This representation is called the *medial axis transformation* (*MAT*) [Blum 1967].

When the maximal blocks are required to be disjoint, to have standard sizes (squares whose sides are powers of two), and to be at standard locations (as a result of a halving process in both the x and y directions), the result is known as a *region quadtree* [Klinger 1971]. It is based on the successive subdivision of the image array into four equal-size quadrants. If the array does not consist entirely of 1s or entirely of 0s (i.e., the region does not cover the entire array), it is then subdivided into quadrants, subquadrants, and so on, until blocks are obtained (possibly 1×1 blocks) that consist entirely of 1s or entirely of 0s. Thus, the region quadtree can be characterized as a variable resolution data structure.

As an example of the region quadtree, consider the region shown in Fig. 18–4a, which is represented by the $2^3 \times 2^3$ binary array in Fig. 18–4b. Observe that the 1s correspond to pixels that are in the region and the 0s correspond to pixels that are outside the region. The resulting blocks for the array of Fig. 18–4b are shown in Fig. 18–4c. This process is represented by a tree of degree 4.

In the tree representation, the root node corresponds to the entire array. Each son of a node represents a quadrant (labeled in order NW, NE, SW, SE) of the region represented by that node. The leaf nodes of the tree correspond to those blocks for which no further subdivision is necessary. A leaf node is said to be BLACK or WHITE, depending on whether its corresponding block is entirely inside or entirely outside of the represented region. All non-leaf nodes are said to be GRAY. The quadtree representation for Fig. 18–4c is shown in Fig. 18–4d. Of course, quadtrees can also be used

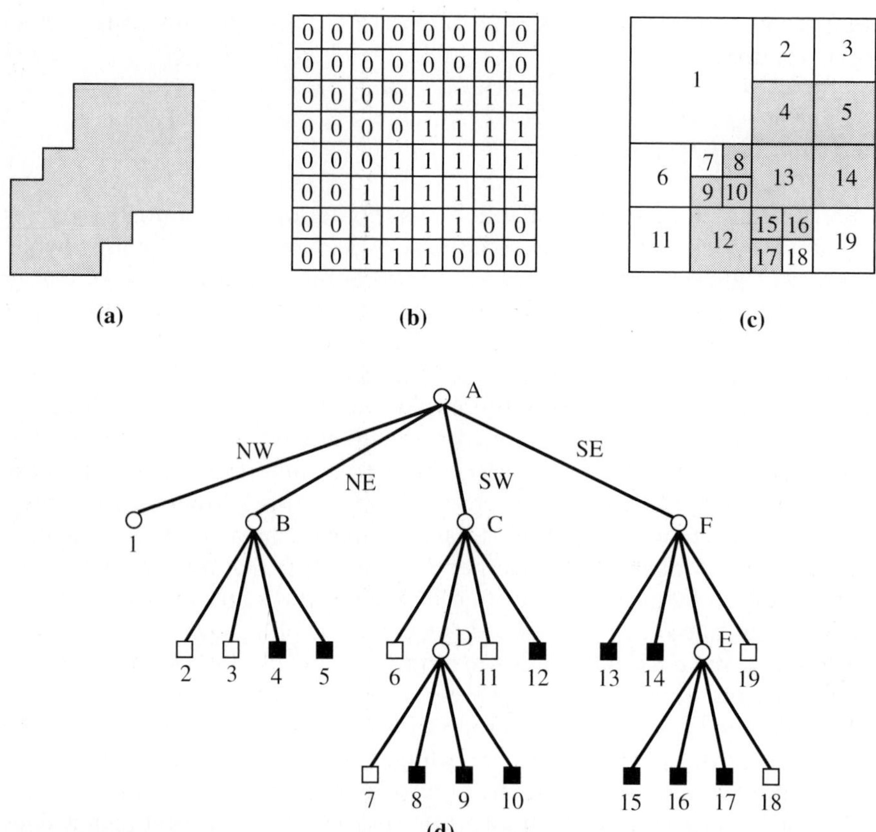

FIGURE 18–4
(a) Sample Region, (b) Its Binary Array Representation, (c) Its Maximal Blocks with the Blocks in the Region Being Shaded, and (d) The Corresponding Quadtree

to represent nonbinary images. In this case, the same merging criteria are applied to each color. For example, in the case of a land-use map, simply merge all wheat-growing regions, and likewise for corn, rice, and the like [Samet et al. 1984].

The term *quadtree* is often used in a more general sense to describe a class of hierarchical data structures whose common property is that they are based on the principle of recursive decomposition of space. They can be differentiated on the following bases:

1. The type of data they are used to represent.
2. The principle guiding the decomposition process.
3. The resolution (variable or not).

Currently, they are used for points, rectangles, regions, curves, surfaces, and volumes (see the remaining sections for further details on the adaptation of the quadtree to them). The decomposition may be into equal parts on each level (termed a *regular decomposition*), or it may be governed by the input. The resolution of the decomposition (i.e., the number of times that the decomposition process is applied) may be fixed beforehand, or it may be governed by properties of the input data.

Unfortunately, the term *quadtree* has taken on more than one meaning. The region quadtree, as shown above, is a partition of space into a set of squares whose sides are all a power of 2 long. A similar partition of space into rectangular quadrants is termed a *point quadtree* [Finkel and Bentley 1974]. It is an adaptation of the binary search tree to two dimensions (which can be easily extended to an arbitrary number of dimensions). It is primarily used to represent multidimensional point data where the rectangular regions need not be square. The quadtree is also often confused with the pyramid [Tanimoto and Pavlidis 1975]. The pyramid is a multiresolution representation that is an exponentially tapering stack of arrays, each one quarter the size of the previous array. In contrast, the region quadtree is a variable resolution data structure.

The distinction between a quadtree and a pyramid is important in the domain of spatial databases and can be easily seen by considering the types of spatial queries. There are two principal types [Aref and Samet 1990]. The first is location based. In this case, we are searching for the nature of the feature associated with a particular location or in its proximity. For example, "What is the feature at location X?" or "What is the nearest city to location X?" or "What is the nearest road to location X?" The second is feature based. In this case, we are probing for the presence or absence of a feature, as well as seeking its actual location. For example, "Does wheat grow anywhere in California?" or "What crops grow in California?" or "Where is wheat grown in California?"

Location-based queries are easy to answer with a quadtree representation as they involve descending the tree until the object is found. If a nearest neighbor is desired, then the search is continued in the neighborhood of the node containing the object. This search can also be achieved by unwinding the process used to access the node containing the object. On the other hand, feature-based queries are more difficult. The problem is that there is no indexing by features. The indexing is only based on spatial occupancy. The goal is to process the query without examining every location in space. The pyramid is useful for such queries since the nodes that are not at the maximum level of resolution (i.e., at the bottom level) contain summary information. Thus we could view these nodes as feature vectors that indicate whether or not a feature is present at a higher level of resolution. Therefore, by examining the root of the pyramid (i.e., the node that represents the entire image), we can quickly tell if a feature is present without having to examine every location.

For example, consider the block decomposition of the nonbinary image in Fig. 18–5a. Its truncated pyramid is given in Fig. 18–5b. The values

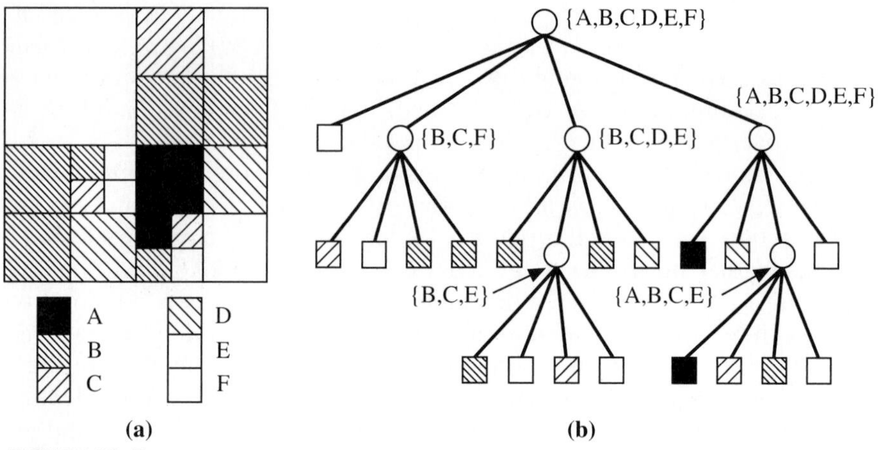

FIGURE 18–5
(a) Sample Nonbinary Image, and (b) Its Corresponding Truncated Pyramid

of a non-leaf node *p* in the truncated pyramid indicate if the feature is present in the subtrees of *p*. In the interest of saving space, the pyramid is not shown in its entirety here.

Quadtreelike data structures can also be used to represent images in three dimensions and higher. The octree [Hunter 1978; Meagher 1982] data structure is the three-dimensional analog of the quadtree. It is constructed in the following manner. We start with an image in the form of a cubical volume and recursively subdivide it into eight congruent disjoint cubes (called *octants*) until blocks are obtained of a uniform color or a predetermined level of decomposition is reached. Figure 18–6a is an example of a simple three-dimensional object whose raster octree block decomposition is given in Fig. 18–6b and whose tree representation is given in Fig. 18–6c.

The quadtree is particularly useful for performing set operations as they form the basis of most complicated queries. For example, to find the names of the roads that pass through the University of Maryland region, we will need to intersect a region map with a line map. For a binary image, set-theoretic operations such as union and intersection are quite simple to implement [Hunter and Steiglitz 1979].

In particular, the intersection of two quadtrees yields a BLACK node only when the corresponding regions in both quadtrees are BLACK. This operation is performed by simultaneously traversing three quadtrees. The first two trees correspond to the trees being intersected, and the third tree represents the result of the operation. If any of the input nodes are WHITE, then the result is WHITE. When corresponding nodes in the input trees are GRAY, then their sons are recursively processed and a check is made for the mergibility of WHITE leaf nodes. The worst-case execution time of this algorithm is proportional to the sum of the number of nodes in the two input

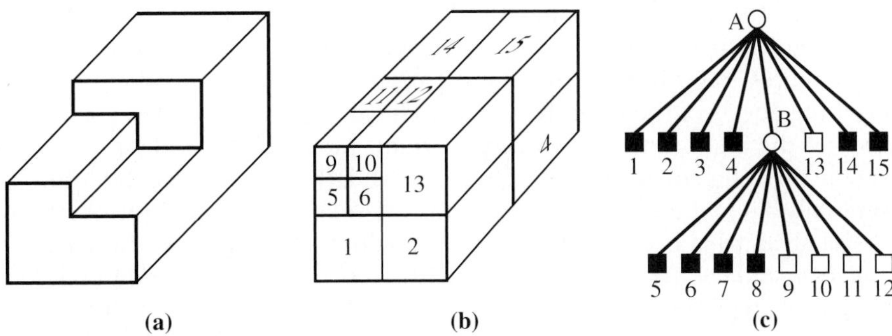

FIGURE 18–6
(a) Example Three-Dimensional Object; (b) Its Octree Block Decomposition; and (c) Its Tree Representation

quadtrees, although it is possible for the intersection algorithm to visit fewer nodes than the sum of the nodes in the two input quadtrees.

Performing the set operations on an image represented by a region quadtree is much more efficient than when the image is represented by a boundary representation (e.g., vectors) as it makes use of global data. In particular, to be efficient, a vector-based solution must sort the boundaries of the region with respect to the space they occupy, while in the case of a region quadtree, the regions are already sorted.

One of the motivations for the development of hierarchical data structures such as the quadtree is a desire to save space. The original formulation of the quadtree encodes it as a tree structure that uses pointers. This requires additional overhead to encode the internal nodes of the tree. In order to further reduce the space requirements, two other approaches have been proposed. The first treats the image as a collection of leaf nodes where each leaf is encoded by a pair of numbers. The first is a base 4 number termed a *locational code*, corresponding to a sequence of directional codes that locate the leaf along a path from the root of the quadtree (e.g., Gargantini 1982). It is analogous to taking the binary representation of the x and y coordinates of a designated pixel in the block (e.g., the one at the lower left corner) and interleaving them (i.e., alternating the bits for each coordinate). The second number indicates the depth at which the leaf node is found (or alternatively its size).

The second, termed a *DF-expression*, represents the image in the form of a traversal of the nodes of its quadtree [Kawaguchi and Endo 1980]. It is very compact as each node type can be encoded with two bits. However, it is not easy to use when random access to nodes is desired. For a static collection of nodes, an efficient implementation of the pointer-based representation is often more economical spacewise than a locational code representation [Samet and Webber 1989]. This is especially true for images of higher dimension.

Nevertheless, depending on the particular implementation of the quadtree, we may not necessarily save space (e.g., in many cases a binary array representation may still be more economical than a quadtree). However, the effects of the underlying hierarchical aggregation on the execution time of the algorithms are more important. Most quadtree algorithms are simply preorder traversals of the quadtree and, thus, their execution time is generally a linear function of the number of nodes in the quadtree. A key to the analysis of the execution time of quadtree algorithms is the *quadtree complexity theorem* [Hunter 1978], which states that the number of nodes in a quadtree region representation is $O(p+q)$ for a $2^q \times 2^q$ image with perimeter p measured in pixel widths. In all but the most pathological cases (e.g., a small square of unit width centered in a large image), the q factor is negligible and, thus, the number of nodes is $O(p)$.

The quadtree complexity theorem holds for three-dimensional data [Meagher 1980] where perimeter is replaced by surface area, as well as for objects of higher dimensions d for which it is proportional to the size of the $(d-1)$-dimensional interfaces between these objects.

The quadtree complexity theorem also directly impacts the analysis of the execution time of algorithms. In particular, most algorithms that execute on a quadtree representation of an image instead of an array representation have an execution time that is proportional to the number of blocks in the image rather than the number of pixels. In its most general case, this means that the application of a quadtree algorithm to a problem in d-dimensional space executes in time proportional to the analogous array-based algorithm in the $(d-1)$-dimensional space of the surface of the original d-dimensional image. Therefore, quadtrees act like dimension-reducing devices.

18.4 Point Data

Multidimensional point data can be represented in a variety of ways. The representation ultimately chosen for a specific task is influenced by the types of operations to be performed on the data. Our focus is on dynamic files (i.e., the amount of data can grow and shrink at will) and on applications involving search. In section 18.3 we briefly mentioned the point quadtree. In higher dimensions (i.e., greater than 3) it is preferable to use the k-d tree [Bentley 1975] as every node has degree 2 since the partitions cycle through the different attributes.

There are many different representations for point data. Most of them are some variants of the bucket methods discussed in section 18.2. These include the grid file and EXCELL, which are described in section 18.6. For more details, see Samet 1990b. In this section we present the PR quadtree (P for point and R for region) [Orenstein 1982; Samet 1990b] as it is based on

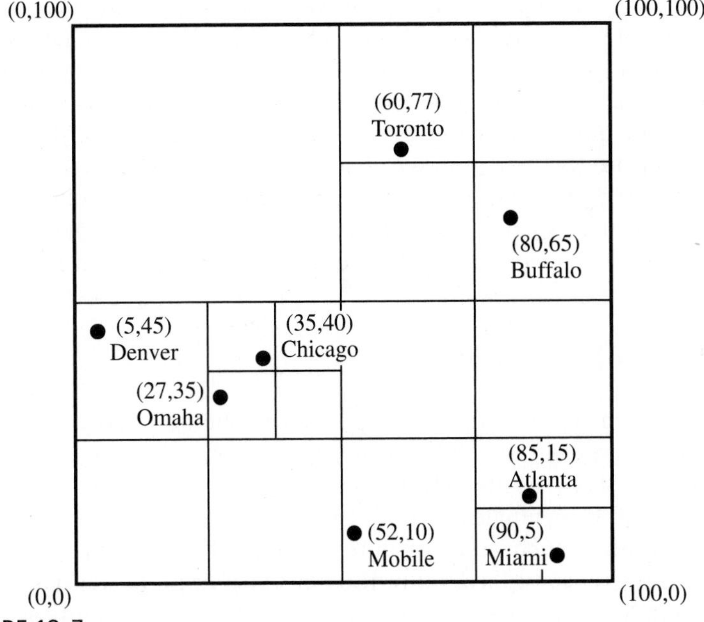

FIGURE 18–7
A PR Quadtree

a regular decomposition. It is an adaptation of the region quadtree to point data that associates data points (that need not be discrete) with quadrants. The PR quadtree is organized in the same way as the region quadtree. The difference is that leaf nodes are either empty (i.e., WHITE) or contain a data point (i.e., BLACK) and its coordinate values. A quadrant contains at most one data point. For example, Fig. 18–7 is a PR quadtree corresponding to some point data.

The shape of the PR quadtree is independent of the order in which data points are inserted into it. The disadvantage of the PR quadtree is that the maximum level of decomposition depends on the minimum separation between two points. In particular, if two points are very close, then the decomposition can be very deep. This can be overcome by viewing the blocks or nodes as buckets with capacity *c* and only decomposing a block when it contains more than *c* points. Of course, bucketing methods such as the R-tree and the R^+-tree can also be used.

PR quadtrees, as well as other quadtreelike representations for point data, are especially attractive in applications that involve search. A typical query is one that requests the determination of all records within a specified distance of a given record—for example, all cities within 100 miles of Washington, D.C. The efficiency of the PR quadtree lies in its role as a pruning device on the amount of search that is required. Thus, many records will not need to be examined. For example, suppose that in the hypothetical database of Fig. 18–7 we wish to find all cities within 8 units of a data point with coordinates (84,10). In such a case, there is no need to search the NW, NE, and SW quadrants of the root [i.e., (50,50)]. Thus, we can restrict our search to the SE quadrant of the tree rooted at root. Similarly, there is no need to search the NW, NE, and SW quadrants of the tree rooted at the SE quadrant [i.e., (75,25)]. Note that the search ranges are usually orthogonally defined regions such as rectangles, boxes, and the like. Other shapes are also feasible, as the above example demonstrated (i.e., a circle).

18.5 Rectangle Data

The rectangle data type lies somewhere between the point and region data types. Rectangles are often used to approximate other objects in an image for which they serve as the minimum rectilinear enclosing object. For example, bounding rectangles can be used in cartographic applications to approximate objects such as lakes, forests, and hills. In such a case, the approximation gives an indication of the existence of an object. Of course, the exact boundaries of the object are also stored, but they are only accessed if greater precision is needed. For such applications, the number of elements in the collection is usually small, and most often the sizes of the rectangles are of the same order of magnitude as the space from which they are drawn.

Rectangles are also used in VLSI design rule checking as a model of chip components for the analysis of their proper placement. Again, the rectangles serve as minimum enclosing objects. In this application, the size of the collection is quite large (e.g., millions of components) and the sizes of the rectangles are several orders of magnitude smaller than the space from which they are drawn.

The representation that is used depends heavily on the problem environment. If the environment is static, then frequently the solutions are based on the use of the plane-sweep paradigm [Preparata and Shamos 1985], which usually yields optimal solutions in time and space. However, the addition of a single object to the database forces the reexecution of the algorithm on the entire database. We are primarily interested in dynamic problem environments. The data structures that are chosen for the collection of the rectangles are differentiated by the way in which each rectangle is represented.

One representation discussed in section 18.2 reduces each rectangle to a point in a higher dimensional space and then treats the problem as if we have a collection of points [Hinrichs and Nievergelt 1983]. Each rectangle is a cartesian product of two one-dimensional intervals where each interval is represented by its centroid and extent. Each set of intervals in a particular dimension is, in turn, represented by a grid file [Nievergelt et al. 1984].

The grid file is a two-level grid for storing multidimensional points. It uses a grid directory (a two-dimensional array of grid blocks for two-dimensional point data) on disk indicating the address of the bucket (i.e., page) that contains the data associated with the grid block. A set of linear scales (actually a pair of one-dimensional arrays in the case of two-dimensional data) is kept in core. The linear scales access the grid block in the grid directory (on disk) that is associated with a particular point. The grid file guarantees access to any record with two disk operations — that is, one for each level of the grid. The first access is to the grid block, while the second access is to the grid bucket. The linear scales are necessary because the grid lines in the grid directory can be in arbitrary positions.

In contrast, EXCELL [Tamminen 1981] also guarantees access to any record with two disk operations but makes use of regular decomposition. This means that the linear scales are not necessary. However, a grid partition results in doubling the size of the grid directory.

The second representation is region based in the sense that the subdivision of the space from which the rectangles are drawn depends on the physical extent of the rectangle—not just one point. Representing the collection of rectangles, in turn, with a treelike data structure has the advantage that there is a relation between the depth of node in the tree and the size of the rectangle(s) that are associated with it. Interestingly, some of the region-based solutions make use of the same data structures that are used in the solutions based on the plane-sweep paradigm.

There are three types of region-based solutions currently in use. The first two solutions adapt the R-tree and the R^{+}-tree (discussed in section 18.2) to store rectangle data (i.e., in this case, the objects are rectangles instead of line segments as in Figs. 18–2 and 18–3). The third is a quadtree-based approach and uses the MX-CIF quadtree [Kedem 1982].

In the MX-CIF quadtree, each rectangle is associated with the quadtree node corresponding to the smallest block that contains it in its entirety. Subdivision ceases whenever a node's block contains no rectangles. Alternatively, subdivision can also cease once a quadtree block is smaller than a predetermined threshold size. This threshold is often chosen to be equal to the expected size of the rectangle [Kedem 1982]. For example, Fig. 18–8 is the MX-CIF quadtree for a collection of rectangles. Note that rectangle F occupies an entire block and, hence, it is associated with the block's father. Also, rectangles can be associated with both terminal and nonterminal nodes.

It should be clear that more than one rectangle can be associated with a given enclosing block and, thus, often we find it useful to be able to differentiate between them. This is done in the following manner [Kedem 1982]. Let *P* be a quadtree node with centroid (*CX*,*CY*), and let *S* be the set of rectangles associated with *P*. Members of *S* are organized into two sets according to their intersection (or collinearity of their sides) with the lines passing through the centroid of *P*'s block — that is, all members of *S* that intersect

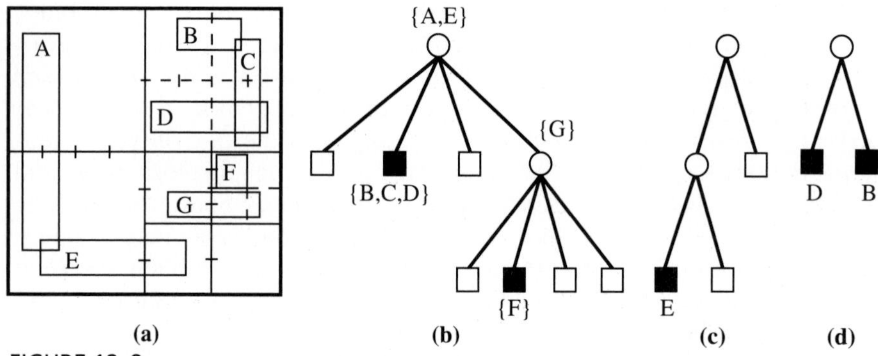

FIGURE 18–8
(a) Collection of Rectangles and the Block Decomposition Induced by the MX-CIF Quadtree; (b) The Tree Representation of (a); The Binary Trees for the *y* Axes Passing Through the Root of the Tree in (b), and (d) The NE Son of the Root of the Tree in (b)

the line $x = CX$ form one set and all members of S that intersect the line $y = CY$ form the other set.

If a rectangle intersects both lines (i.e., it contains the centroid of P's block), then we adopt the convention that it is stored with the set associated with the line through $x = CX$. These subsets are implemented as binary trees (really tries), which in actuality are one-dimensional analogs of the MX-CIF quadtree. For example, Fig. 18–8c and Fig. 18–8d illustrate the binary trees associated with the *y* axes passing through the root and the NE son of the root of the MX-CIF quadtree of Fig. 18–8c, respectively. Interestingly, the MX-CIF quadtree is a two-dimensional analog of the interval tree [Edelsbrunner 1980], which is a data structure that is used to support optimal solutions based on the plane-sweep paradigm to some rectangle problems.

18.6 Line Data

Section 18.3 was devoted to the region quadtree, an approach to region representation that is based on a description of the region's interior. In this section, we focus on a representation that specifies the boundaries of regions. The simplest representation is the polygon consisting of vectors that are usually specified in the form of lists of pairs of *x* and *y* coordinate values corresponding to their start and end points. The vectors are usually ordered according to their connectivity. One of the most common representations is the chain code [Freeman 1974], which is an approximation of a polygon's boundary by use of a sequence of unit vectors in the four principal directions. Using such representations, given a random point in space, it is very difficult to find the nearest line to it as the lines are not sorted. Nevertheless, the vector representation is used in many

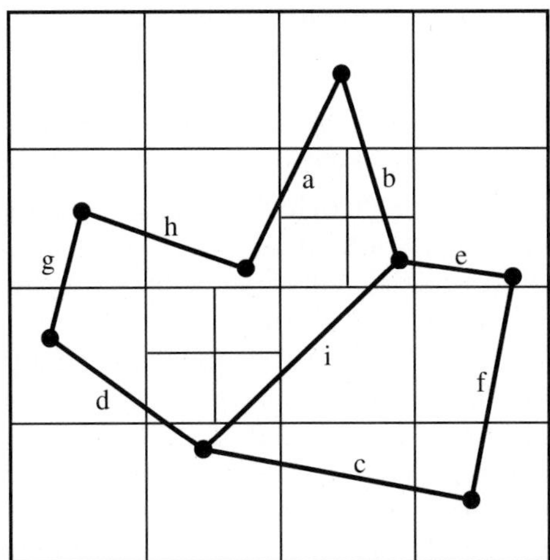

FIGURE 18–9
PM_1 Quadtree for the Collection of Line Segments of Fig. 18–1

commercial systems (e.g., ARC/INFO [Peuquet and Marble 1990]) because of its compactness.

In this section we concentrate on the use of bucketing methods. There is a number of choices (see Hoel and Samet 1992 for an empirical comparison). The first two are the R-tree and the R^+-tree, which have already been explained in section 18.2. The third uses regular decomposition to adaptively sort the line segments into buckets of varying size. There is a one-to-one correspondence between buckets and blocks in the two-dimensional space from which the line segments are drawn. There is a number of approaches to this problem [Samet 1990b]. They differ by being either vertex based or edge based. Their implementations make use of the same basic data structure. All are built by applying the same principle of repeatedly breaking up the collection of vertices and edges (making up the polygonal map) into groups of four blocks of equal size (termed *brothers*) until a subset is obtained that is sufficiently simple that it can be organized by some other data structure. This is achieved by successively weakening the definition of what constitutes a legal block, thereby enabling more information to be stored in each bucket.

The PM quadtree family [Samet and Webber 1885] is vertex based. We illustrate the PM_1 quadtree. It is based on a decomposition rule stipulating that partitioning occurs as long as a block contains more than one line segment, unless the line segments are all incident at the same vertex that is also in the same block (e.g., Fig. 18–9). A similar representation has been devised for three-dimensional images (e.g., Ayala et al. 1985). The decomposition criteria are such that no node contains more than one face, edge, or vertex unless the faces all meet at the same vertex or are adjacent to the same edge. This representation is quite useful since its space requirements for polyhedral objects are significantly smaller than those of a conventional octree.

The PMR quadtree [Nelson and Samet 1986, 1987] is an edge-based variant of the PM quadtree (see also edge-EXCELL [Tamminen 1981]). It makes use of a probabilistic splitting rule. A block is permitted to contain a variable number of line segments. The PMR quadtree is constructed by inserting them one by one into an initially empty structure consisting of one block. Each line segment is inserted into all the blocks it intersects or occupies in its entirety. During this process, the occupancy of each affected block is checked to see if the insertion causes it to exceed a predetermined *splitting threshold*. If the splitting threshold is exceeded, then the block is split *once*, and only once, into four blocks of equal size. The rationale is to avoid splitting a node many times when there are a few very close lines in a block. In this manner, we avoid pathologically bad cases. For more details, see Nelson and Samet 1986.

A line segment is deleted from a PMR quadtree by removing it from all the blocks it intersects or occupies in its entirety. During this process, the occupancy of the block and its siblings (the ones that were created when its predecessor was split) is checked to see if the deletion causes the total number of line segments in them to be less than the splitting threshold. If the splitting threshold exceeds the occupancy of the block and its siblings, then they are merged and the merging process is recursively reapplied to the resulting block and its siblings. Notice the asymmetry between splitting and merging rules.

Figure 18–10e is an example of a PMR quadtree corresponding to a set of nine edges labeled *a–i* inserted in increasing order. Observe that the shape of the PMR quadtree for a given polygonal map is not unique; instead, it depends on the order in which the lines are inserted into it. In contrast, the shape of the PM_1 quadtree is unique. Figure 18–10a–e shows some of the steps in the process of building the PMR quadtree of Fig. 18–10e. This structure assumes that the splitting threshold value is 2. In each part of Fig. 18–10a–e, the line segment that caused the subdivision is denoted by a thick line, while the gray regions indicate the blocks where a subdivision has taken place. The insertion of line segments *c, e, g, h,* and *i* cause the subdivisions in parts a, b, c, d, and e, respectively, of Fig. 18–10. The insertion of line segment *i* causes three blocks to be subdivided (i.e., the SE block in the SW quadrant, the SE quadrant, and the SW block in the NE quadrant). The final result is shown in Fig. 18–10e. Note the difference from the PM_1 quadtree in Fig. 18–9—that is, the NE block of the SW quadrant is decomposed in the PM_1 quadtree while the SE block of the SW quadrant is not decomposed in the PM_1 quadtree.

The PMR quadtree is very good for answering queries such as finding the nearest line to a given point [Hoel and Samet 1991]. It is preferred over

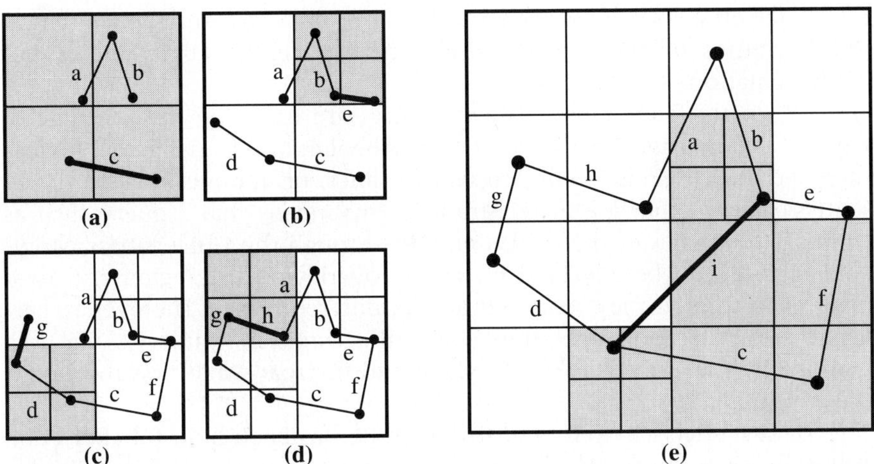

FIGURE 18–10
PMR Quadtree for the Collection of Line Segments of Fig. 18–1 (a)–(e) Illustrate Snapshots of the Construction Process, with the Final PMR Quadtree Given in (e)

the PM_1 quadtree as it results in far fewer subdivisions. In particular, in the PMR quadtree there is no need to subdivide in order to separate line segments that are very close or whose vertices are very close, which is the case for the PM_1 quadtree. This is important since four blocks are created at each subdivision step. Thus, when many subdivision steps occur, many empty blocks are created and, thus, the storage requirements of the PMR quadtree are considerably lower than those of the PM_1 quadtree. Generally, as the splitting threshold is increased, the storage requirements of the PMR quadtree decrease while the time necessary to perform operations on it will increase. Another advantage of the PMR quadtree over the PM_1 quadtree is that by virtue of being edge based, it can easily deal with nonplanar graphs.

Observe that although a bucket in the PMR quadtree can contain more line segments than the splitting threshold, this is not a problem. In fact, it can be shown [Samet 1990b] that the maximum number of line segments in a bucket is bounded by the sum of the splitting threshold and the depth of the block (i.e., the number of times the original space has been decomposed to yield this block).

18.7 Concluding Remarks

The use of hierarchical data structures in spatial databases enables the focussing of computational resources on the interesting subsets of data. Thus, there is no need to expend work where the payoff is small. Although many of the operations for which they are used can often be performed equally as efficiently, or more so, with other data structures, hierarchical data structures are attractive because of their conceptual clarity and ease of implementation.

When the hierarchical data structures are based on the principle of regular decomposition, we have the added benefit of a spatial index. All features, be they regions, points, rectangles, lines, or volumes, can be represented by maps that are in registration. This means that a query such as "finding the names of the roads that pass through the University of Maryland region" can be executed by simply overlaying the region and road maps even though they represent data of different types. The overlay performs an intersection operation where the common feature is the area spanned by the University of Maryland and the roads that pass through it (i.e., a spatial join).

In fact, such a system, known as QUILT, has been built [Shaffer et al. 1990] for representing geographic information using the quadtree variants described here. In this case, the quadtree is implemented as a collection of leaf nodes where each leaf node is represented by its locational code, which is a spatial index. The collection is in turn represented as a B-tree. There are leaf nodes corresponding to region, point, and line data.

The disadvantage of quadtree methods is that they are shift sensitive in the sense that their space requirements are dependent on the position of the origin. However, for complicated images, the optimal positioning of the origin will usually lead to little improvement in the space requirements. The process of obtaining this optimal positioning is computationally expensive and is usually not worth the effort [Li et al. 1982].

The fact that we are working in a digitized space may also lead to problems. For example, the rotation operation is not generally invertible. In particular, a rotated square usually cannot be represented accurately by a collection of rectilinear squares. However, when we rotate by 90°, then the rotation is invertible. This problem arises whenever one uses a digitized representation. Thus, it is also common to the array representation.

ACKNOWLEDGMENT

The assistance of Erik G. Hoel in the preparation of the figures is greatly appreciated.

REFERENCES

Aref, W. G., and Samet, H. 1990. Efficient Processing of Window Queries in the Pyramid Data Structure. *Proceedings of the Ninth ACM SIGACT-SIGMOD-SIGART Symposium on Principles of Database Systems (PODS)*, Nashville, 265–272.

Aref, W. G., and Samet, H. 1991a. Extending a DBMS with Spatial Operations. In: *Advances in Spatial Databases*, 299–318. O. Günther and H. J. Schek, eds., *Lecture Notes in Computer Science* 525. Springer-Verlag, Berlin.

Aref, W. G., and Samet, H. 1991b. Optimization Strategies for Spatial Query Processing. *Proceedings of the Seventeenth International Conference on Very Large Databases (VLDB)*, Barcelona, 81–90.

Aref, W. G., and Samet, H. 1992. Uniquely Reporting Spatial Objects: Yet Another Operation for Comparing Spatial Data Structures. *Proceedings of the Fifth International Symposium on Spatial Data Handling*, Charleston, Vol. 1, 178–189.

Ayala, D., Brunet, P., Juan, R., and Navazo, I. 1985. Object Representation by Means of Nonminimal Division Quadtrees and Octrees. *ACM Transactions on Graphics*, Vol. 4, No. 1, 41–59.

Beckmann, N., Kriegel, H. P., Schneider, R., and Seeger, B. 1990. The R*-Tree: An Efficient and Robust Access Method for Points and Rectangles. *Proceedings of the ACM-SIGMOD Conference*, Atlantic City, 322–331.

Bentley, J. L. 1975. Multidimensional Binary Search Trees Used for Associative Searching. *Communications of the ACM*, Vol. 18, No. 9, 509–517.

Blum, H. 1967. A Transformation for Extracting New Descriptors of Shape. In: *Models for the Perception of Speech and Visual Form*, 362–380. W. Wathen-Dunn, ed. MIT Press, Cambridge, Mass.

Buchmann, A., Günther, O., Smith, T. R., and Wang, Y.-F., eds. 1990. *Design and Implementation of Large Spatial Databases. Lecture Notes in Computer Science* 409. Springer-Verlag, Berlin.

Comer, D. 1979. The Ubiquitous B-tree. *ACM Computing Surveys*, Vol. 11, No. 2, 121–137.

Edelsbrunner, H. 1980. Dynamic Rectangle Intersection Searching. Institute for Information Processing Report 47, Technical University of Graz, Graz, Austria.

Finkel, R., and Bentley, J. 1974. Quad Trees: A Data Structure for Retrieval on Composite Keys. *Acta Informatica*, Vol. 4, No. 1, 1–9.

Foley, J. D., van Dam, A., Feiner, S. K., and Hughes, J. F. 1990. *Computer Graphics: Principles and Practice*, 2nd ed. Addison-Wesley, Reading, Mass.

Franklin, W. R. 1984. Adaptive Grids for Geometric Operations. *Cartographica*, Vol. 21, Nos. 2 and 3, 160–167.

Freeman, H. 1974. Computer Processing of Line-Drawing Images. *ACM Computing Surveys*, Vol. 6, No. 1, 57–97.

Freeston, M. 1987. The BANG File: A New Kind of Grid File. *Proceedings of the ACM-SIGMOD Conference*, San Francisco, 260–269.

Gargantini, I. 1982. An Effective Way to Represent Quadtrees. *Communications of the ACM*, Vol. 25, No. 12, 905–910.

Günther, O. 1988. Efficient Structures for Geometric Data Management. Ph.D. thesis, Electronics Research Laboratory, College of Engineering, University of California at Berkeley. (*Lecture Notes in Computer Science* 337, Springer-Verlag, Berlin, 1988.)

Günther, O., and Schek, H. J., eds. 1991. *Advances in Spatial Databases. Lecture Notes in Computer Science* 525. Springer-Verlag, Berlin.

Guttman, A. 1984. R-Trees: A Dynamic Index Structure for Spatial Searching. *Proceedings of the ACM-SIGMOD Conference*, Boston, 47–57.

Henrich, A., Six, H. W., and Widmayer, P. 1989. The LSD Tree: Spatial Access to Multidimensional Point and Non-Point Data. *Proceedings of the Fifteenth International Conference on Very Large Databases (VLDB)*, Amsterdam, 45–53.

Hinrichs, K., and Nievergelt, J. 1983. The Grid File: A Data Structure Designed to Support Proximity Queries on Spatial Objects. *Proceedings of the WG'83 International Workshop on Graphtheoretic Concepts in Computer Science*, Truner Verlag, Linz, Austria, 100–113.

Hoel, E. G., and Samet, H. 1991. Efficient Processing of Spatial Queries in Line Segment Databases. In: *Advances in Spatial Databases*, 237–256. O. Günther and H. J. Schek, eds. *Lecture Notes in Computer Science* 525. Springer-Verlag, Berlin.

Hoel, E. G., and Samet, H. 1992. A Qualitative Comparison Study of Data Structures for Large Line Segment Databases. *Proceedings of the ACM-SIGMOD Conference*, San Diego, 205–214.

Hunter, G. M. 1978. Efficient Computation and Data Structures for Graphics. Ph.D. thesis, Department of Electrical Engineering and Computer Science, Princeton University, Princeton, N.J.

Hunter, G. M., and Steiglitz, K. 1979. Operations on Images Using Quad Trees. *IEEE Transactions on Pattern Analysis and Machine Intelligence*, Vol. 1, No. 2, 145–153.

Jagadish, H. V. 1990. On Indexing Line Segments. *Proceedings of the Sixteenth International Conference on Very Large Databases (VLDB)*, Brisbane, 614–625.

Kawaguchi, E., and Endo, T. 1980. On a Method of Binary Picture Representation and Its Application to Data Compression. *IEEE Transactions on Pattern Analysis and Machine Intelligence*, Vol. 2, No. 1, 27–35.

Kedem, G. 1982. The Quad-CIF Tree: A Data Structure for Hierarchical On-Line Algorithms. *Proceedings of the Nineteenth Design Automation Conference*, Las Vegas, 352–357.

Klinger, A. 1971. Patterns and Search Statistics. In: *Optimizing Methods in Statistics*, 303–337. J. S. Rustagi, ed. Academic Press, New York.

Li, M., Grosky, W. I., and Jain, R. 1982. Normalized Quadtrees with Respect to Translations. *Computer Graphics and Image Processing*, Vol. 20, No. 1, 72–81.

Meagher, D. 1980. Octree Encoding: A New Technique for the Representation, the Manipulation, and Display of Arbitrary 3-D Objects by Computer. Technical Report IPL-TR-80-111, Electrical and Systems Engineering Technical Report, Rensselaer Polytechnic Institute, Troy, N.Y.

Meagher, D. 1982. Geometric Modeling Using Octree Encoding. *Computer Graphics and Image Processing*, Vol. 19, No. 2, 129–147.

Nelson, R. C., and Samet, H. 1986. A Consistent Hierarchical Representation for Vector Data. *Computer Graphics*, Vol. 20, No. 4, 197–206.

Nelson, R. C., and Samet, H. 1987. A Population Analysis for Hierarchical Data Structures. *Proceedings of the ACM-SIGMOD Conference*, 270–277.

Nievergelt, J., Hinterberger, H., and Sevcik, K. C. 1984. The Grid File: An Adaptable, Symmetric Multikey File Structure. *ACM Transactions on Database Systems*, Vol. 9, No. 1, 38–71.

Orenstein, J. A. 1982. Multidimensional Tries Used for Associative Searching. *Information Processing Letters,* Vol. 14, No. 4, 150–157.

Orenstein, J. A. 1989. Redundancy in Spatial Databases. *Proceedings of the ACM-SIGMOD Conference,* Portland, 294–305.

Orenstein, J. A., and Merrett, T. H. 1984. A Class of Data Structures for Associative Searching. *Proceedings of the Third ACM SIGACT-SIGMOD Symposium on Principles of Database Systems,* Waterloo, Ontario, 181–190.

Peuquet, D. J., and Marble, D. F. 1990. ARC/INFO: An Example of a Contemporary Geographic Information System. In: *Introductory Readings in Geographic Information Systems,* 90–99. D. J. Peuquet and D. F. Marble, eds., Taylor & Francis, London.

Preparata, F. P., and Shamos, M. I. 1985. *Computational Geometry: An Introduction.* Springer-Verlag, New York.

Robinson, J. T. 1981. The k-d-B-Tree: A Search Structure for Large Multidimensional Dynamic Indexes. *Proceedings of the ACM-SIGMOD Conference,* Ann Arbor, 10–18.

Rutovitz, D. 1968. Data Structures for Operations On Digital Images. In: *Pictorial Pattern Recognition,* 105–133. G. C. Cheng, et. al., ed. Thompson Book Co., Washington, D.C.

Samet, H. 1990a. *Applications of Spatial Data Structures: Computer Graphics, Image Processing, and GIS.* Addison-Wesley, Reading. Mass.

Samet, H. 1990b. *The Design and Analysis of Spatial Data Structures.* Addison-Wesley, Reading, Mass.

Samet, H., Rosenfeld, A., Shafer, C. A., and Webber, R. E. 1984. A Geographic Information System Using Quadtrees. *Pattern Recognition,* Vol. 17, No. 6, 647–656.

Samet, H., and Webber, R. E. 1985. Storing a Collection of Polygons Using Quadtrees. *ACM Transactions on Graphics,* Vol. 4, No. 3, 182–222.

Samet, H., and Webber, R. E. 1989. A Comparison of the Space Requirements of Multi-Dimensional Quadtree-Based File Structures. *Visual Computer,* Vol. 5, No. 6, 349–359.

Seeger, B., and Kriegel, H. P. 1990. The Buddy-Tree: An Efficient and Robust Access Method for Spatial Data Base Systems. *Proceedings of the Sixteenth International Conference on Very Large Databases (VLDB),* Brisbane, 590–601.

Sellis, T., Roussopoulos, N., and Faloutsos, C. 1987. The R^+-Tree: A Dynamic Index for Multi-Dimensional Objects. *Proceedings of the Thirteenth International Conference on Very Large Databases (VLDB),* Brighton, England, 507–518.

Shaffer, C. A., Samet, H., and Nelson, R. C. 1990. QUILT: A Geographic Information System Based on Quadtrees. *International Journal of Geographical Information Systems,* Vol. 4, No. 2, 103–131.

Tamminen, M. 1981. The EXCELL Method for Efficient Geometric Access to Data. *Acta Polytechnica Scandinavica,* Mathematics and Computer Science Series, No. 34, Helsinki.

Tanimoto, S., and Pavlidis, T. 1975. A Hierarchical Data Structure for Picture Processing. *Computer Graphics and Image Processing,* Vol. 4, No. 2, 104–119.

19

Temporal Object-Oriented Databases: A Critical Comparison

RICHARD SNODGRASS

Adding time support to object-oriented databases has been an active area of research for the past decade. This chapter surveys the 16 temporal object-oriented query languages that have been proposed. Support for the three kinds of time—user-defined time, valid time, and transaction time—is examined; schema versioning is also considered. The central conundrum remains unresolved: Do the increased efficiency and ease of use justify the added complexity of explicit temporal constructs in the data model and query language?

19.1 Introduction

Time is an important aspect of all real-world phenomena. Events occur at specific points in time; objects and the relationships among objects exist over time. The ability to model this temporal dimension of the real world is essential to many computer applications, such as econometrics, banking, inventory control, accounting, law, medical records, land and geographical information systems, and airline reservations.

Conventional databases represent the state of an enterprise at a single moment of time. Although the contents of a database continue to change as new information is added, these changes are viewed as modifications to the state, with the old, out-of-date data being deleted from the database. The current contents of the database may be viewed as a snapshot of the enterprise. In such systems, the attributes involving time are manipulated solely by the application programs; the database management system (DBMS) interprets dates as values in the base data types. No conventional system interprets temporal domains when deriving new relations.

Application-independent DBMS support for time-varying information has been an active area of research for about 15 years, with approximately 650 papers generated thus far [Bolour et al. 1982; Kline 1993; McKenzie 1986; Soo 1991; Stam and Snodgrass 1988; Tansel et al. 1993]. This chapter examines proposals for adding time to object-oriented (OO) databases.

We first examine the time domain: its structure and dimensionality (interestingly, there are three time dimensions), followed by issues of supporting each dimension. We briefly discuss and compare the 16 extant proposals of temporal object-oriented query languages. We adopt a broad definition of *object oriented* and include entity-relationship and complex object query languages. We conclude with a summary of the major accomplishments and unmet challenges of research into temporal OO databases.

In this chapter we focus on OO data models and query languages; most query languages are defined over their own data models. Within these two topics we discuss only those aspects related to temporal support. We discuss temporal OO query processing only briefly and storage structures not at all, as those topics have scarcely been mentioned in the literature.

19.2 The Time Domain

In this section we focus on time itself: how it is modeled and how it is represented. The next section will combine time with facts, to model time-varying information.

19.2.1 Structure

We initially assume that there is one dimension of time. The distinctions we address here will apply to each of the several dimensions we consider in the next section.

Early work on *temporal logic* centered around two structural models of time, *linear* and *branching* [Van Benthem 1982]. In the linear model, time advances from the past to the future in a totally ordered fashion. In the branching model, also termed the *possible futures* model, time is linear from the past to now, where it then divides into several time lines, each representing a potential sequence of events [Worboys 1990]. Along any future path, additional branches may exist. The structure of branching time is a tree rooted at now. The most general model of time in a temporal logic represents time as a partially ordered set. Additional axioms can be introduced to specify other, more refined models of time. For example, linear time can be specified by adding an axiom imposing a total order on this set. Recurrent processes may be associated with a *cyclic* model of time [Chomicki and Imelinski 1989; Lorentzos 1988; Lorentzos and Johnson 1988].

Axioms may also be added to temporal logics to characterize the *density* of the time line [Van Benthem 1982]. Combined with the linear model, *discrete* models of time are isomorphic to the natural numbers, implying that each point in time has a single successor [Clifford and Tansel 1985]. *Dense* models of time are isomorphic to the rationals or the reals: Between any two moments of time another moment exists. *Continuous* models of time are isomorphic to the reals—that is, they are both dense and, unlike the rationals, contain no gaps. In the continuous model, each real number corresponds to a point in time; in the discrete model, each natural number corresponds to a nondecomposable unit of time with an arbitrary duration. Such a nondecomposable unit of time is referred to as a *chronon* [Jensen et al. 1993]. A chronon is the smallest duration of time that can be represented in this model. It is not a point but a line segment on the time line. Although time itself is generally perceived to be continuous, most proposals for adding a temporal dimension to object-oriented data models are based on the discrete time model.

Axioms can also describe the *boundedness* of time. Time can be bounded orthogonally in the past and in the future.

Models of time may include the concept of *distance* (most temporal logics do not do so, however). Both time and space are *metrics* in that they have a distance function satisfying four properties: (1) the distance between any two points is nonnegative; (2) the distance between any two nonidentical points is nonzero; (3) the distance from time point α to time point β is identical to the distance from β to α; (4) the distance from α to γ is less than or equal to the distance from α to β plus the distance from β to γ (the triangle inequality).

With distance and boundedness, restrictions on range can be applied. The scientific cosmology of the Big Bang posits that time began with the Big Bang, 14 ± 4 billion years ago. There is much debate on when it will end, depending on whether the universe is *open* or *closed* (Hawking provides a readable introduction to this controversy [Hawking 1988]). If the universe is closed, then time will have an end when the universe collapses back onto itself in what is called the *Big Crunch*. If it is open, then time will go on forever.

Finally, one can differentiate *relative* time from *absolute* time (more precise terms are *unanchored* and *anchored*). For example, "9am, January 1, 1992" is an absolute time, whereas "9 hours" is a relative time, also termed a *span*. This distinction, though, is not as crisp as one would hope, because absolute time is absolute only with respect to another time (in this example, midnight, January 1, A.D. 1). Relative time differs from distance in that the former has a direction (e.g., one could envision a relative time of –9 hours) whereas a distance is unsigned.

19.2.2 Dimensionality

In the context of databases, two time dimensions are of general interest [Snodgrass and Ahn 1986]. *Valid time* concerns the time a fact was true in reality. The valid time of an event is the time at which the event occurred in the real world, independent of the recording of that event in some database. Valid times can also be in the future, if it is expected that some fact will be true at a specified time in the future. *Transaction time* concerns the time the fact was stored in the database. The transaction time (an interval) of a fact begins with the transaction that inserted the fact into the database and ends with the transaction that removed this fact from the database.

These two dimensions are orthogonal. A data model supporting neither dimension is termed *snapshot,* as it captures only a single snapshot in time of both the database and the enterprise that the database models [Jensen et al. 1993]. A data model supporting only valid time is termed, logically, a *valid-time* model; one that supports only transaction time is termed a *transaction-time* model; and one that supports both valid and transaction time is termed a *bitemporal* model (*temporal* is a generic term implying some kind of time support). As an example, a bitemporal database could store the information that Melanie was employed in the OODBMS project from June through September and that this information was entered into the database in July.

While valid time may be bounded or unbounded (as we saw, cosmologists feel that it is at least bounded in the past), transaction time is bounded on both ends. Specifically, transaction time starts when the database is created (before the creation time, nothing was stored) and doesn't extend past the present (no facts are known to have been stored in the future). Changes to the database state are required to be stamped with the current transaction time. Hence, transaction time and bitemporal relations are *append only,* since no information is ever overwritten, making them prime candidates for storage on write-once optical disks. As the database state evolves, transaction times grow monotonically. In contrast, successive transactions may mention widely varying valid times in the past, present, and future.

The two time dimensions are not homogeneous; transaction time has a different semantics from valid time. Valid and transaction time *are* orthogonal, though there are generally some application-dependent correlations between the two times. As a simple example, consider the situation where a fact is recorded as soon as it becomes valid in reality. In such a *specialized* bitemporal database, termed *degenerate* [Jensen and Snodgrass 1994], valid and transaction time are identical. As another example, if a measurement is recorded at most two days after it was valid in reality, and if it takes at least six hours from the measurement time to record the measurement, then such a relation is termed *delayed strongly retroactively bounded with bounds six hours and two days.*

There is a third kind of time that may be included: *user-defined time.* This term refers to the fact that the semantics of these values are known only to the user and are not interpreted by the DBMS, as differentiated from valid and transaction time, whose semantics are supported by the DBMS.

19.3 Temporal Object-Oriented Query Languages

Table 19–1 lists the OO query languages that support time. Not included are knowledge representation languages, such as Telos [Mylopoulos et al. 1990] or TSOS [Barbic and Pernici 1985], which, while supporting either valid or transaction time or both, are not strictly OO query languages. Also not included, for the same reason, are nested relational query languages and data models, such as HQuel [Tansel 1991], HRDM [Clifford and Croker 1987], HTQuel [Gadia 1988], TempSQL [Gadia and Nair 1993] and TBE [Tansel et al. 1989].

While many of the languages listed in the table each have several associated papers, we have indicated the most comprehensive or most readily available reference. The third column identifies the underlying data model; for some of the query languages, this model is not named. The conventional query language or data model on which the temporal query language/data model is based is named in the next column. Interestingly, about half of the query languages are based on the *relational* query languages DAPLEX [Shipman 1981], Quel [Held et al. 1975] and SQL [Date 1989], rather than on existing non-temporal OO query languages. The fifth column indicates whether the language has been implemented. The final column ascribes a name to each query language for later reference.

In the remainder of this chapter, we use a simple example. There are three object types: `employee`, `department`, and `project`. Here, instances of `employee` are associated with a single instance of `department` at a time; they can be associated with several `project` instances at any time. In a DBMS supporting valid time, we record the employee history: the departments and projects they are currently associated with, as well as the projects and departments they were associated with in the past. All information in the database is up to date. If we find that an employee has been associated with, say, an incorrect department in the past, we update the database to fix that error. The challenge is to augment an OO data model to capture the history of objects and their attributes and to augment an OO query language to permit queries over this history.

We first examine user-defined time, as it is the most straightforward aspect of time to support, in both the data model and the query language. Subsequent sections consider valid and transaction time.

19.4 User-Defined Time

User-defined time is supported by most of the commercial relational DBMSs as another domain that can be associated with attributes [Oracle 1987; Tandem 1983]. Date and time support in the SQL-92 standard [Melton and Simon 1993] is very similar to that in DB2 [Date 1988]. A `Date` has a granularity of a day; a `Time` has a granularity of a second but a range of only

Table 19–1: Temporal Query Languages

Query Language	Citation	Underlying Data Model	Based On	Impl.	Identifier
OSQL	[Beech & Mahbod 1988]		SQL	X	IRIS
MATISSE	[ADB 1992]		SQL	X	MATISSE
OODAPLEX	[Wuu & Dayal 1992]	OODAPLEX	DAPLEX		OODAPLEX
OOSTSQL	[Cheng & Gadia 1992]	OOSTM	DAPLEX/SQL		OOSTSQL
OQL	[Käfer & Schöning 1992a]	OVM	SQL	X	OQL
OQL/T	[Su & Chen 1991]	OSAM*/T	OSAM*/OQL		OQL/T
Orion	[Kim et al. 1990]		SQL	X	Orion
Postquel	[Stonebraker et al. 1990]		Quel	X	Postquel
SERQL	[Wuu 1991]		ER	X	SERQL
—	[Elmasri & Wuu 1990]	TEER	EER/GORDAS		TEER
TMQL	[Käfer & Schöning 1992b]	TMAD	SQL		TMQL
TOSQL	[Rose & Segev 1991]	TOODM	SQL		TOSQL
TOOSQL	[Rose & Segev 1993a]	TOODM	SQL	X	TOOSQL
—	[Sciore 1991]		annotations		Sciore1
—	[Sciore 1994]		EXTRA/EXCESS		Sciore2
VISION	[Caruso & Sciore 1988]	VISION	meta-functions	X	VISION

100 hours; a `DateTime` combines the range of a `Date` with the granularity of a second (there is also a fractional `DateTime` with a granularity of a microsecond). Hewlett-Packard's object-oriented query language OSQL [Lyngbaek 1991] and UniSQL [Kim 1993] continue in the SQL tradition by including `Date`, `Time`, and `DateTime` as literals.

Overmyer proposed making time an abstract data type (ADT), with its own set of operations [Overmyer and Stonebraker 1982]. Many of the object-oriented query languages (e.g., Postgres [Stonebraker et al. 1990] and ZQL[C++] [Blakeley 1991]) can support user-defined time in just this fashion. One can also realize most of the benefits of time as an ADT without requiring an extensible DBMS [Soo and Snodgrass 1992].

Others have advocated that various notions of time (see section 19.2) should be supported more directly, as either a regular or a primitive class (i.e., a class with no attributes). The primary benefit is that the power of the object-oriented data model (with subtyping, inheritance, and polymorphic functions with late binding) can be used to express the semantics of time appropriate to the application.

OODAPLEX [Dayal 1989] is an object-oriented data model and query language based on the DAPLEX functional data model [Shipman 1981], in which time types can be defined as subtypes of `point`. The two operations defined for `point`, a comparison operator (=) and an ordering relationship (<), can be inherited and may also be overridden by the subtypes. The specific ordering relationship chosen determines the different time structures (e.g., linear versus branching, dense versus discrete). In this approach, time is not accorded special status within the model; it is simply another type, which can be supported in code by either the system or the application.

In the Temporal Object-Oriented Data Model (TOODM), `Time` is a primitive system-defined class, with subclasses `Absolute` and `Relative` [Rose and Segev 1991]. User-defined subtypes (e.g., `Date`, a subtype of `Absolute`) can be added, with relevant associated methods.

19.5 Valid Time

Valid time has been added to many data models. By far the majority of work in temporal databases is based on the relational model. We first briefly review work with this model, then turn our focus to the entity-relationship and object-oriented data models.

19.5.1 Relational Extensions

Over two dozen extensions to the relational model to incorporate time have been proposed over the last 15 years. Most support only valid time; a few only support transaction time or support both kinds of time.

These models may be compared along the valid-time dimension by asking three basic questions: How is valid time represented, how are facts associated with valid time, and how are attribute values represented? Here we list some of the many answers to these questions. More details on extensions to the relational data model, including a comprehensive comparison, may be found elsewhere [McKenzie and Snodgrass 1991; Snodgrass 1987, 1992].

Valid times can be represented with single chronon identifiers (i.e., event timestamps), with intervals (i.e., as interval timestamps), or as valid-time elements, which are finite sets of intervals. Valid time can be associated with entire tuples or with individual attribute values. A third alternative, associating valid time with sets of tuples (i.e., relations) has not been incorporated into any of the proposed data models, primarily because it lends itself to high data redundancy.

There are six basic alternatives to representing attribute values.

- *Atomic valued*—values do not have any internal structure—for example, `'Melanie'`
- *Set valued*—values are sets of atomic values—for example, `{'Melanie','Eric'}`

- *Functional, atomic valued*—values are functions from the valid-time domain to the attribute domain—for example, 1993 → `'Melanie'`, 1994 → `'Eric'`
- *Ordered pairs*—values are an ordered pair of a value and a timestamp—for example, (`'Melanie'`, 1993)
- *Triplet valued*—values are a triple of attribute value, valid-from time, and valid-to time—for example, (`'Melanie'`, January 1993, March 1994). This is similar to the ordered pairs representation, except that only one interval may be represented.
- *Set-triplet value*—values are a set of triplets—for example, {(`'Melanie'`, January 1993, March 1994), (`'Eric'`, February 1992, December 1993) }. This is more general than ordered pairs, in that more than one value can be represented, and more general than functional valued, since more than one attribute value can exist at a single valid time.

In the conventional relational model, if attributes are atomic valued, they are considered to be in *first normal form* [Codd 1972]. Hence, only the data models placed in the first category may be considered to be strictly in first normal form. However, in most of the other models, the non-atomicity of attribute values comes about solely because time is added. We will see aspects of these approaches when considering how time has been supported in object-oriented data models.

There have been three general approaches to adding valid-time support to an OO data model and query language. We discuss each in turn.

19.5.2 Using the Object Model Directly

The first approach utilizes the substantial expressive power of the OO data model directly and thus requires no changes either to the model or to the query language to support time-varying information. The OODAPLEX type system, supporting parameterized types like set, multiset, tuple, and function, is sufficient for modeling temporal information. For example, attribute-value timestamping could be used to specify that `dept` and `projects` are time varying.

```
type employee is object
    function name(e:employee→n:string)
    function dept  (e:employee→f:(t:time→d:department))
    function projects  (e:employee→f:(t:time→d:{project}))
```

The `name` attribute is a function that maps a particular `employee` instance to a particular `string`. The `dept` function, when applied to a particular `employee`, returns a function that, when provided a `time`, returns a `department`. The range of `projects` is a function that returns a set of `projects` (hence the "{}" syntax). These functions can be invoked in the query language. Other functions are provided by the system. The extent function returns the instances of a specified type. The following query lists the department(s) that Melanie worked in when she was on the OODBMS project (syntactic sugar can make this query somewhat shorter).

```
for the e in extent(employee) where name(e) = 'Melanie'
    for the p in extent(project) where name(p) = 'OODBMS'
        for each t where p in projects(e)(t)
            dept(e)(t)
        end
    end
end
```

As an alternative, object timestamping [Clifford and Croker 1988] could have been employed, by using a state function in the employee object that takes a time and evaluates to a snapshot_employee object, containing nontemporal dept and projects functions.

```
type employee is object
    function name(e:employee→n:string)
    function state(e:employee→f:(t:time→d:snapshot_employee))
type snapshot_employee is object
    function dept(e:employee→department))
    function projects (e:employee→{project}))
```

The advantages of either approach are that various semantics of valid time can be specified by the user (as also holds for user-defined time), and the schema specification and query languages remain uncluttered with additional time-specific clauses, assuming, of course, that the necessary features, including functions and sets as first-class citizens, are available. The downside is that users have to roll their own support for time when specifying the schema, and also when specifying queries, and the query optimizer has to work much harder since there are no hints provided in the language that access methods or storage structures oriented towards time-varying values should be employed.

19.5.3 Using Other Extensions to Support Time

A second approach is to include general extensions to the data model and query language for other reasons, and then show how these extensions may be used to support time-varying information.

Sciore has advocated the use of *annotations* (introduced several years earlier [Stefik et al. 1986]) to support the various kinds of versioning, including histories, revisions, and alternatives [Sciore 1991]. Here we are concerned only with histories, which are defined over valid time; the other two aspects are defined over transaction time. Sciore has also extended the EXTRA data model [Carey et al. 1988] with the keyword versioned, to partition the attributes between those that have exactly one value and those for which all previous values should be retained [Sciore 1994]. Generic and specific references are supported. Sciore extended the EXCESS query language (itself an extension of Quel [Held et al. 1975]) to include an iterator (`inall`) over all versions; queries expressed in the original EXCESS operate on the default version of the object. Then predicates in the `where` clause can be used to select the desired version(s). We focus here on annotations; generic references will be discussed in the context of the Chou-Kim versioning model in section 19.6.1.

Sciore's proposal supports annotations by associating a *hidden variable* with each conventional variable. Each hidden variable is bound to an object from an *annotation class*, which is a conventional class. The `employee` object type can be represented as follows.

```
class employee inherits object =
 variables
   name:string;
   dept:HistoryFn, department;
   projects:HistoryFn, {project};
end employee;
```

Here, the `name` variable is unannotated; the `dept` and `projects` variables are annotated with the `HistoryFn` annotation class, which supports versioning.

Normally, annotations are invisible to the user. If the `dept` variable is accessed, a method of the `HistoryFn` is invoked behind the scenes on the hidden variable associated with `dept`, evaluating to a particular `department`. In this case, the user is unaware of the presence of the hidden variable. On the other hand, when querying over the history of an attribute's value, various methods of the annotation class must be used explicitly. The example query given previously in OODAPLEX could be expressed using annotations as follows.

```
((employee select:[:e|e.name = 'Melanie']).↑dept choose:
    (project.↑name timeWhen:[:n|n = 'OODBMS'])
).value
```

The symbol '.↑' selects the history variable, which has associated with it the `choose:` and `timeWhen:` methods, used to select values at specified times and to extract the times when certain values were valid, respectively. Here the name of the class is used to denote all the instances of the class.

Annotations, as well as the `HistoryFn` class, make support of valid time easier to implement. Query optimization is still difficult, as all manipulation of time is done by user-defined functions (which themselves could perhaps be individually optimized).

The VISION system adopted a similar approach [Caruso and Sciore 1988, 1990]. As with OODAPLEX, attributes are functions in the VISION data model. But the data model takes the additional step of treating functions as objects. Functions can then have functions associated with them; these latter functions are called *meta-functions*, which are very similar to the methods associated with the annotation classes just discussed.

19.5.4 Direct Incorporation of Time into the Data Model

In contrast to the previous approaches, most researchers have proposed specific data modeling and query language constructs to support information varying over valid time. Seven such proposals have been identified in the literature, all since 1990. In this section we review each very briefly, and then compare them.

Two proposals extend query languages for the Entity-Relationship model [Chen 1976]. Elmasri's Temporal Extended Entity-Relationship (TEER) model incorporates an extension to GORDAS [Elmasri and Wiederhold 1983] to support valid time. TEER timestamps both entities and relationships with temporal elements [Elmasri and Wuu 1990; Elmasri et al. 1990]. The target list and the where clause are augmented with additional constructs to manipulate temporal elements. In addition, Wuu has defined a separate query language based on the basic E-R model and on SQL, termed Structured Entity-Relationship Query Language, or SERQL [Wuu 1991].

Käfer proposed a complex-object data model and query language with temporal constructs, to be implemented on top of a non-temporal complex object data model termed MAD [Käfer and Schöning 1992b].

The remaining query languages are defined over OO data models. TOODM, the data model behind TOSQL and TOOSQL, encodes attribute values as `time sequences`, which are sequences of (value, temporal element) pairs [Rose and Segev 1991, 1993b]. The OQL/T query language for the temporal object-oriented knowledge representation model OSAM*/T incorporates an optional WHEN clause as well as a set of temporal functions and operators [Su and Chen 1991]. Sciore has extended the EXTRA data model [Carey et al. 1988] to differentiate between versioned and unversioned attributes and has made several changes to the EXCESS query language to support selection of times and default times, termed *contexts* [Sciore 1994]. Finally, Gadia et al. have proposed an object-oriented spatiotemporal structured query language (OOSTSQL), an extension of SQL, which supports both spatial and temporal data [Cheng and Gadia 1992; Cheng et al. 1992].

To provide a feel for these languages, we express the previously discussed query in three languages. The following TOOSQL query lists the department(s) that Melanie worked in when she was on the OODBMS project.

```
SELECT e.dept, e.dept.vt
FROM e:employee, p:projects
```

```
WHERE e.name = 'Melanie' WHEN e.dept.vt.DURING(e.projects.vt)
  AND p.name = 'OODBMS' IN e.project
```

The same query in TMQL is as follows.

```
SELECT d WHILE(p.name = 'OODBMS')
FROM e(employee) - (d(department), p(project))
WHERE e.name = 'Melanie' AND p.name = 'OODBMS'
```

Finally, here is what the query looks like in OOSTSQL.

```
SELECT dept(e)
RESTRICTED TO [['OODBMS' IN project-name(projects(e))]]
FROM employee e
WHERE name(e) = 'Melanie'
```

19.6 Transaction Time

Transaction time concerns when facts were logically present in the database, as opposed to when the facts were true in reality. Supporting transaction time is necessary when one would like to *roll back* the state of the database to a previous point in time. Transaction time is also useful when storing versions, say, of an engineering design. In such situations, transaction time is often branching, versus the linear time model underlying valid time.

Transaction time has a quite different semantics from valid time. When utilizing valid time, we store the history of employees in the database. We could then query the database to determine what departments and projects an employee was associated with now, or in the past. Errors would be corrected by modifying the database. If, instead, transaction time were supported, *versions* would be stored, rather than *histories*. The current department for each employee would be stored. As that department changed, new information would be written to the database, indicating that the old information was no longer correct. In such a database, we could still ask what department an employee is currently in. We could not ask what department an employee was in in the past. Instead, the question would have to be of the form, what department did we *think* (i.e., was stored in the database) the employee was in as of some date in the past. Effectively, the database is rolled back to that date, and the question "What is the current department?" is asked. Errors in the past cannot be corrected since they were not known to be errors in the past. Transaction and valid time are orthogonal, and support for both provides the greatest modeling and querying power.

In considering support for transaction time, an important distinction must be made: Are the object instances or their attributes, versioned (termed *extension versioning*) or are the *definitions* of those objects versioned (termed *schema versioning*)? If extension versioning is adopted, then schema versioning may or may not be supported. If extension versioning is not supported, then schema versioning is not relevant, as only the most recent version of the schema need be retained.

19.6.1 Extension Versioning

As with support for valid time, there are three general approaches to support extension versioning. The first is to use the model directly, making no changes to the data model or query language. OODAPLEX follows this approach. Since the semantics of time is arbitrary (the user can implement whatever is desired), transaction time can be accommodated by always appending a new value to the f function when an attribute's value changes.

In the second approach, general extensions to the data model and query language are exploited to support time-varying information. Sciore's annotations, discussed earlier, can be used to support revisions and alternatives (i.e., branching transaction time). He proposes the annotation class `RevisionFn`, methods such as `asOf:`, `checkin:`, and `checkout:`, and the annotation class `AlternativeFn`, for branching transaction time. Generic references are also capable of supporting transaction time [Sciore 1994], as are also the meta-functions in VISION [Caruso and Sciore 1988].

In the third approach, the data model and language are modified to explicitly support transaction time. As with valid time, the majority of proposals are in this camp. The MATISSE OODBMS timestamps the entire object graph [ADB 1993]. Conceptually, the object graph is copied on each transaction; versions are shared in the physical implementation. Käfer differentiates *object attributes* from *version attributes*, the latter's values varying among the versions of the object [Käfer and Schöning 1992a]. In the TOODM, an attribute type of `TS[]` is a set of 3-tuples, of the object ID, history, and corrections [Rose and Segev 1991]. Both the history and the corrections are sets of 3-tuples, containing the object ID of the history value, the attribute value, and a temporal element timestamp. The information in the history and correction sets enables the history at any prior point in transaction time to be reconstructed. In Postgres, the DBMS supporting the Postquel query language, tuples are associated with two transaction timestamps, specifying the interval in which they were logically present in the database [Stonebraker et al. 1990]. Ong and Goh have shown that a DBMS that has support for linear transaction time, rules, procedures, and union queries can support the major version concepts, including simulating branching transaction time [Ong and Goh 1990].

The Chou-Kim versioning model [Chou and Kim 1986; Kim 1990] has garnered the widest acceptance; it has been implemented in ORION [Kim et al. 1990], in the IRIS object-oriented DBMS [Beech and Mahbod 1988; Wilkinson et al. 1990] (though this support has not yet been incorporated into the commercial version and its query language OSQL), and in OQL [Käfer 1992].

The Chou-Kim model adopts object versioning. A keyword is used to indicate that a class is versionable. Both conventional and composite objects (the latter, a heterogeneous collection of objects related via the part-of relationship [Kim et al. 1987; Kim 1989]) may be versioned, though implementations don't generally support versioning of composite objects. Versions are numbered automatically by the system, starting at 1. Versions are associated with names, timestamps, and a status. Versions may be distinguished into a *transient* version, which can be updated at any time; a *working* version, which can be shared but not updated; and a *released* version, which cannot be updated or deleted. Versions can be *promoted* or *demoted* among these classifications.

The model differentiates between generic and specific references. A *generic reference* points to an object and all its versions and can be used to delay the binding of the attribute to a specific version. A *specific reference* points to a fixed version of the object.

Versions can be related to each other, generating an acyclic graph of versions associated with each generic object. The data model automatically maintains two relationships, a *version-of* relationship between a versionable object and all its versions, and a *derived-from* relationship between a version and the versions directly derived from it. In the stored data, the system maintains a *generic* object, which contains (among other information) the version-derivation hierarchy, which is a tree of *version descriptors*, each of which contains the version number of the version and the object identifier of the version. In the terminology of section 19.2.1, objects are versioned with branching transaction time, with the added feature of two versions being merged to create a new version (hence transaction time is truly a graph rather than a tree).

19.6.2 Schema Versioning

In schema *evolution*, the schema can change in response to the varying needs of the application. In schema *versioning*, several schemas are present at different transaction times. As an example, suppose that on May 1 we decide to add a `NumChildren` attribute to the `employee` class. If only schema evolution were supported, a value for this attribute would be added to all instances of that class and, perhaps, a default value for this attribute.

There are two ways to implement schema evolution. In MATISSE, the conversion is *eager*, in that all instances are immediately changed to include the new attribute [ADB 1993]. In Orion, the conversion is *lazy* [Banerjee et al. 1987]. When the schema in ORION is modified, no disk-resident data instances need be updated. Instead, when an instance is referenced by an application program and fetched into memory, it is transformed into an instance conforming to the scheme currently in effect. In both cases, only one schema is logically in effect; Orion's implementation simply spreads the burden of updating the data in a scheme change across subsequent retrievals.

In schema versioning, there are multiple schemas logically in effect. In the example, data stored before May 1 would not need to have a `NumChildren` attribute. Rolling back the database to April 1 also rolls back the schema. This behavior is consistent with the semantics of transaction time, which concerns the state of the database. Schema versioning has been examined both in the context of relational databases [Ben-Zvi 1982; McKenzie and Snodgrass 1990; Roddick 1992] and in the context of OO databases. Multiple schemas may also be defined via *object-oriented views* [Bertino 1992] or *semantic contexts* [Andany et al. 1991] (which should be differentiated from Sciore's contexts [Sciore 1994]). An essential difference between these approaches and schema versioning is that in the latter, an object created in a specific schema version is only visible in that schema version rather than in all views or contexts [Bertino and Martino 1993].

Three OO data models support schema versioning. In MATISSE, the entire schema is timestamped with a transaction time [ADB 1993]. Postgres implements schema versioning by specifying that the system catalog consists of transaction-time relations [Stonebraker et al. 1990]. Both view transaction time as linear.

The Chou-Kim versioning model accommodates a more extensive form of schema versioning [Kim and Chou 1988]. This model is similar to MATISSE and Postgres in that it views the entire schema (the class lattice) as a versioned object; it differs in that it associates a status (transient or working) to each schema and it maintains a version-derivation hierarchy (hence, transaction time is branching). The model includes rules specifying which schema version owns each object created under it, as well as through which schema(s) each object may be accessed. Schema versioning under the Chou-Kim model has not yet been implemented, though detailed data structures, storage representations, and object accessing algorithms have been presented [Kim and Chou 1988].

19.7 Comparison

Table 19–2 provides more detail on each language. The second and fourth columns indicate what is timestamped ("N/A" denotes no support for the indicated kind of time). Those with "arbitrary" indicated require the user to decide what granularity of data should be timestamped. Timestamps are associated with attributes, with groups of attributes, with entire objects, with the entire object graph, and with the schema. The third and fifth columns indicate how timestamps are represented. Those with "arbitrary" indicated support time with user- or system-provided classes; hence, anything is possible. Only a few explicitly support user-defined time, though as was mentioned in section 19.4, such support is not difficult to provide. Time-stamps can be version identifiers, events, intervals, temporal elements

Table 19–2: Temporal Query Languages

Identifier	What Is Valid-Time Timestamped	Valid Timestamp Representation	What Is Transaction-Time Timestamped	Transaction Timestamp Representation	Underlying Algebra
IRIS	N/A	N/A	objects	event, identifier	
MATISSE	N/A	N/A	object graph + schema	event, identifier	
OODAPLEX	arbitrary	arbitrary	arbitrary	arbitrary	[Dayal & Wuu 1992]
OOSTSQL	attributes	spatiotemporal element	N/A	N/A	
OQL	N/A	N/A	groups of attributes	version identifier	
OQL/T	objects	interval	N/A	N/A	TA-algebra
Orion	N/A	N/A	objects	version hierarchy	
Postquel	N/A	N/A	tuples, schema	interval	
SERQL	objects	interval	N/A	N/A	
TEER	objects	valid-time element	N/A	N/A	
TMQL	elementary objects	interval	N/A	N/A	
TOSQL	attributes	temporal element	attributes	temporal element	[Rose & Segev 1993b]
TOOSQL	attributes	temporal element	attributes	temporal element	[Rose & Segev 1993b]
Sciore1	attributes	arbitrary	attributes	arbitrary	
Sciore2	groups of attributes	event	groups of attributes	event	[Carey et al. 1988]
VISION	attributes	event	attributes	event	

(sets of intervals), or a position in branching transaction time. A few proposals provide an algebra for their query language.

Returning to the alternatives listed in section 19.5.1 for representing attribute values, we find the alternatives are more limited in the OO data models than in the relational models.

- *Atomic valued*—with time associated with entire objects or sets of attributes, instead of individual attributes: IRIS, Orion, OQL/T, OQL, Postquel, Sciore2, SERQL, TEER, and TMQL. MATISSE timestamps the entire object graph
- *Sets of ordered pairs*—of values and timestamps: TOSQL and TOOSQL

- *Functions from a timestamp domain*—OODAPLEX and OOSTSQL
- *Functions represented by class instances*—Sciore1 and VISION

Five of the sixteen query languages support only valid time, five support only transaction time, and a (slight) plurality of six languages supports both valid and transaction time. Of the seven that have been implemented, four query languages support only transaction time, reflecting an emphasis on supporting versioning for engineering applications.

19.8 Standards

Support for time in conventional relational database systems (e.g., Oracle 1987; Tandem 1983) is entirely at the level of user-defined time (i.e., attribute values drawn from a temporal domain). These implementations are limited in scope and are, in general, unsystematic in their design [Date and White 1990; Date 1988]. Date and time support in SQL-92 [Melton and Simon 1993] is very similar to that in DB2. SQL-92 corrects some of the inconsistencies in the time support provided by DB2 but inherits its basic design limitations [Soo and Snodgrass 1992]. The SQL3 standard, currently in flux, is expected to incorporate object-oriented aspects. It, however, remains conservative with respect to temporal support, addressing only user-defined time.

None of the other object-oriented database standards, including OMG's IDL data model supporting CORBA [OMG and Xopen 1992], support valid or transaction time. In fact, this data model doesn't even support user-defined time.

19.9 Conclusion

A decade ago, research on temporal object-oriented data models was launched under the guise of versions in an engineering database [Plouffe et al. 1983]. Five years later, the first paper on valid-time support appeared [Caruso and Sciore 1988]; this system is still one of only two implemented languages that support both valid and transaction time. The past half decade of research, with almost 20 temporal OO query languages proposed, can be visualized as three branches off this initial trunk. The first branch, containing OODAPLEX, attempted to and succeeded in obtaining full temporal support by paring down the model still further. Functions, less general than VISION's meta-functions, were shown to be sufficient to support all three kinds of time: user-defined, valid, and transaction time (both linear and branching).

The second branch concerns Sciore's subsequent work with generic references and with annotations, subtly molding the data model and query language while retaining the ability to support valid and transaction time.

The bulk of the work, the third branch, advocates the addition of specific time-oriented constructs in the data model and query language. Two implicit factors argue that such constructs are required. First, the OODBMS should help the user by providing a means to express important features of the application, its time-varying nature being one. Second, execution and storage efficiency are important. The DBMS may require indications in the schema and in the queries that time is present. The query languages in this group are much easier to optimize and to support with efficient data structures because more information is specified and is thus available to the DBMS optimizer.

So the central, and as yet unresolved, conundrum facing the temporal OODBMS community is this: Do the increased efficiency and ease of use justify the added complexity of explicit temporal constructs in the data model and query language? If not, then the solutions in the left and middle branches should be merged into a clear, sparse approach in which the temporal semantics is left pretty much to the user. On the other hand, if the added complexity is justified, then the difficult task of merging the many disparate approaches present in the right branch should be undertaken.

We conclude with a list of accomplishments and a list of challenges, which lead to future work. There have been many significant accomplishments over the past five years of temporal OO database research.

- The semantics of the time domain, including its structure and dimensionality, is well understood.
- A significant amount of research has been expended on temporal OO data models, addressing complex and subtle design problems.
- Over a dozen temporal OO query languages have been proposed.
- Several commercial temporal OODBMSs are now on the market.

There have also been some unmet challenges.

- The user-defined time support in the SQL2 standard is poorly designed. The emerging SQL3 standard does not appear to be addressing the central issues of temporal support.
- In contrast to temporal relational query languages, the specification of temporal OO query languages is quite informal. No temporal OO data model or query language has a formal semantics.
- Empirical studies are needed to compare storage and query evaluation strategies that support time-varying data.

Obviously, these issues should be addressed. The place to start is the fundamental question of whether explicit temporal constructs in the data model and query language are required to achieve high usability and efficiency.

ACKNOWLEDGMENTS

This work was supported in part by NSF grants ISI-8902707 and ISI-9302244. Comments on a previous draft from José Blakeley, Curtis Dyreson, Christian S. Jensen, Wolfgang Käfer, Won Kim, Ellen Rose, Arie Segev, Michael Soo, and Stanley Su, as well as comments from Dan Fishman, Shashi Gadia, Edward Sciore, and Michael Stonebraker helped improve the presentation and identify inaccuracies.

REFERENCES

ADB *MATISSE Versioning*. 1993. Technical Report, ADB/Intellitic.

Andany, J., Leonard, M., and Palisser, C. 1991. Management of Schema Evolution in Databases. *Proceedings of the Conference on Very Large Databases,* Barcelona, 161–170.

Banerjee, J., Kim, W., Kim, H. K., and Korth, H. F. 1987. Semantics and Implementation of Schema Evolution in Object-Oriented Databases. *Proceedings of the ACM-SIGMOD International Conference on Management of Data,* San Francisco, 311–322.

Barbic, F., and Pernici, B. 1985. Time Modeling in Office Information Systems. *Proceedings of the ACM-SIGMOD International Conference on Management of Data,* 51–62.

Beech, D., and Mahbod, B. 1988. Generalized Version Control in an Object-Oriented Database. *Proceedings of the International Conference on Data Engineering,* IEEE, 14–22.

Ben-Zvi, J. 1982. *The Time Relational Model.* Ph.D. dissertation. Computer Science Department, UCLA.

Bertino, E. 1992. A View Mechanism for Object-Oriented Databases. *Proceeedings of the International Conference on Extending Database Technology,* Vienna.

Bertino, E., and Martino, L. 1993. *Object-Oriented Database Systems.* International Computer Science Series. Addison-Wesley, Reading, Mass.

Blakeley, J. A. 1991. *ZQL[C++]: Extending a Persistent C++ Language with a Query Capability.* Technical Report ITB-91-10-01. Computer Science Laboratory, Texas Instruments Inc.

Bolour, A., Anderson, T. L. , Dekeyser, L. J., and Wong, H. K. T. 1992. The Role of Time in Information Processing: A Survey. *SigArt Newsletter,* Vol. 80, 28–48.

Carey, M. J., DeWitt, D. J., and Vandenburg, S. L. 1988. A Data Model and Query Language for EXODUS. *Proceedings of the ACM-SIGMOD International Conference on Management of Data,* Chicago, 413–423.

Caruso, M., and Sciore, E. 1988. Meta-Functions and Contexts in an Object-Oriented Database Language. *Proceedings of the ACM-SIGMOD International Conference on Management of Data,* Chicago, 56–65.

Caruso, M., and Sciore, E. 1990. The Vision Object-Oriented Database Management System. *Advances in Database Programming Languages*. ACM Press, New York.

Chen, P. P-S. 1976. The Entity-Relationship Model—Toward a Unified View of Data. *ACM Transactions on Database Systems*, Vol. 1, No. 1, 9–36.

Cheng, T. S., and Gadia, S. K. 1992. *A Seamless Object-Oriented Model for Spatio-Temporal Databases*. Technical Report TR-92-41, Computer Science Department, Iowa State University.

Cheng, T. S., Gadia, S. K., and Nair, S. 1992. *Relational and Object-Oriented Parametric Databases*. Technical Report TR-92-42, Computer Science Department, Iowa State University.

Chomicki, J., and Imelinski, T. 1989. Relational Specifications of Infinite Query Answers. *Proceedings of the ACM-SIGMOD International Conference on Management of Data*, 174–183.

Chou, H.-T., and Kim, W. 1986. A Unifying Framework for Version Control in a CAD Environment. *Proceedings of the Twelfth International Conference on VLDB*, 336–344.

Clifford, J., and Croker, A. 1987. The Historical Relational Data Model (HRDM) and Algebra Based on Lifespans. *Proceedings of the International Conference on Data Engineering*, 528–537. IEEE Computer Society Press, Los Angeles.

Clifford, J., and Croker, A. 1988. Objects in Time. *IEEE Data Engineering*, Vol. 7, No. 4, 189–196.

Clifford, J., and Tansel, A. U. 1985. On an Algebra for Historical Relational Databases: Two Views. *Proceedings of the ACM-SIGMOD International Conference on Management of Data*, 247–265.

Codd, E. F. 1972. Further Normalization of the Data Base Relational Model. In: *Data Base Systems. Vol. 6 of Courant Computer Symposia Series*. Prentice Hall, Englewood Cliffs, N.J.

Date, C. J. 1988. A Proposal for Adding Date and Time Support to SQL. *SIGMOD Record*, Vol. 17, No. 2, 53–76.

Date, C. J. 1989. *A Guide to the SQL Standard*, 2nd Edition. Addison-Wesley, Reading, Mass.

Date, C. J., and White, C. J. 1990. *A Guide to DB2*, Vol. 1, 3rd Edition. Addison-Wesley, Reading, Mass.

Dayal, U. 1989. Queries and Views in an Object-Oriented Data Model. *Proceedings of the Second Workshop on Database Programming Languages*.

Dayal, U., and Wuu, G. T. J. 1992. A Uniform Approach to Processing Temporal Queries. *Proceedings of the Conference on Very Large Databases*, Vancouver.

Elmasri, R., El-Assal, I., and Kouramajian, V. 1990. Semantics of Temporal Data in an Extended ER Model. *Ninth International Conference on Entity-Relationship Approach*, Lausanne, Switzerland.

Elmasri, R., and Wiederhold, G. 1983. GORDAS: A Formal High-Level Query Language for the Entity-Relationship Model. *Proceedings of the Conference on Entity-Relationship Approach to Software Engineering*.

Elmasri, R., and Wuu, G. 1990. A Temporal Model and Query Language for ER Databases. *Proceedings of the Sixth International Conference on Data Engineering*, 76–83.

Gadia, S. K., 1988. A Homogeneous Relational Model and Query Languages for Temporal Databases. *ACM Transactions on Database Systems,* Vol. 13, No. 4, 418–448.

Gadia, S., and Nair, S. 1993. Temporal Databases: A Prelude to Parametric Data. In: *Temporal Databases: Theory, Design, and Implementation.* Benjamin/Cummings, A. Tansel, et al. eds., Redwood City, Cal.

Hawking, S. 1988. *A Brief History of Time.* Bantam Books, New York.

Held, G. D., Stonebraker, M., and Wong, E. 1975. INGRES—A Relational Data Base Management System. *Proceedings of the AFIPS National Computer Conference,* 409–416. AFIPS Press, Anaheim, Cal.

Jensen, C. S., Clifford, J., Elmasri, R., Gadia, S. K., Hayes, P., and Jajodia, S., eds. 1993. *A Consensus Glossary of Temporal Database Concepts.* Technical Report R 93-2035, Department of Mathematics and Computer, Institute for Electronic Systems.

Jensen, C. S., and Snodgrass, R. 1994. Temporal Specialization and Generalization. *IEEE Transactions on Knowledge and Data Engineering* (in press).

Käfer, W. 1992. *History and Version Management of Complex Objects* (in German). Ph.D. dissertation. Fachbereich Informatik, University Kaiserslautern.

Käfer, W., and Schöning, H. 1992a. Mapping a Version Model to a Complex-Object Data Model. *Proceedings of the International Conference on Data Engineering,* Tempe, Arizona, 348–357.

Käfer, W., and Schöning, H. 1992b. Realizing a Temporal Complex-Object Data Model. *Proceedings of the ACM-SIGMOD International Conference on Management of Data,* San Diego, 266–275.

Kim, W. 1989. Composite Objects Revisited. *Proceedings of the ACM-SIGMOD International Conference on Management of Data,* 337–347.

Kim, W. 1990. *Introduction to Object-Oriented Databases,* MIT Press, Cambridge, Mass.

Kim, W. 1993. *On Object-Oriented Database Technology.* Technical Report. UniSQL, Inc.

Kim, W., Banerjee, J., Chou, H.-T., Garza, J. F., and Woelk, D. 1987. Composite Object Support in an Object-Oriented Database System. *OOPSLA '87 Proceedings,* 118–125.

Kim, W., and Chou, H.-T. 1988. Versions of Schema in OODB. *Proceedings of the Conference on Very Large Databases,* Long Beach, 148–159.

Kim, W., Garza, J. F., Ballou, N., and Woelk, D. 1990. Architecture of the ORION Next-Generation Database System. *IEEE Transactions on Knowledge and Data Engineering,* Vol. 2, No. 1, 109–124.

Kline, N. 1993. An Update of the Temporal Database Bibliography. *ACM-SIGMOD Record,* Vol. 22, No. 4, 66–80.

Lorentzos, N. A. 1988. *A Formal Extension of the Relational Model for the Representation of Generic Intervals.* Ph.D. dissertation, Birkbeck College.

Lorentzos, N. A., and Johnson, R. G. 1988. Requirements Specification for a Temporal Extension to the Relational Model. *Data Engineering,* Vol. 11, No. 4, 26–33.

Lyngbaek, P. 1991. *OSQL: A Language for Object Databases.* Technical Report HPL-DTD-91-4. Hewlett-Packard Laboratories.

McKenzie, E. 1986. Bibliography: Temporal Databases. *ACM-SIGMOD Record,* Vol. 15, No. 4, 40–52.

McKenzie, E., and Snodgrass, R. 1990. Schema Evolution and the Relational Algebra. *Information Systems,* Vol. 15, No. 2, 207–232.

McKenzie, E., and Snodgrass, R. 1991. An Evaluation of Relational Algebras Incorporating the Time Dimension in Databases. *ACM Computing Surveys,* Vol. 23, No. 4, 501–543.

Melton, J., and Simon, A. R. 1993. *Understanding the New SQL: A Complete Guide.* Morgan Kaufmann Publishers, San Mateo, Cal.

Mylopoulos, J., Borgida, A., Jarke, M., and Koubarakis, M. 1990. Telos: Representing Knowledge About Information Systems. *ACM Trans. on Office Information Systems,* Vol. 8, No. 4, 325–362.

OMG and Xopen. 1992. *The Common Object Request Broker: Architecture and Specification.* Object Management Group and X/Open, Framingham, Mass. and Reading Berkshire, UK.

Ong, L.-P., and Goh, Jeffrey K. S. 1990. *A Unified Framework for Version Modeling Using Production Rules in a Database System.* Memorandum, UCB/ERL M90/33. Electronics Research Laboratory, College of Engineering, University of California.

Oracle Computer, Inc. 1987. *ORACLE Terminal User's Guide.*

Overmyer, R., and Stonebraker, M. 1982. Implementation of a Time Expert in a Database System. *ACM-SIGMOD Record,* Vol. 12, No. 3, 51–59.

Plouffe, W., Kim, W., Lorie, R., and McNabb, D. 1983. *Versions in an Engineering Database System.* IBM Research Report RJ4085, IBM Research.

Roddick, J. F. 1992. Schema Evolution in Database Systems—An Annotated Bibliography. *ACM-SIGMOD Record,* Vol. 21, No. 4, 35–40.

Rose, E., and Segev, A. 1991. TOODM—A Temporal Object-Oriented Data Model with Temporal Constraints. *Proceedings of the Tenth International Conference on the Entity Relationship Approach.*

Rose, E., and Segev, A. 1993a. TOOSQL—A Temporal Object-Oriented Query Language. *Proceedings of the Tenth International Conference on the Entity-Relationship Approach,* Dallas.

Rose, E., and Segev, A. 1993b. TOOA—A Temporal Object-Oriented Algebra. *Proceedings of the European Conference on Object-Oriented Programming.*

Sciore, E. 1991. Using Annotations to Support Multiple Kinds of Versioning in an Object-Oriented Database System. *ACM Transactions on Database Systems,* Vol. 16, No. 3, 417–438.

Sciore, E. 1994. Versioning and Configuration Management in an Object-Oriented Data Model. *VLDB Journal,* Vol. 3, No. 1, 77–106.

Shipman, D. W. 1981. The Functional Data Model and the Data Language DAPLEX. *ACM Transactions on Database Systems,* Vol. 6, No. 1, 140–173.

Snodgrass, R. T. 1987. The Temporal Query Language TQuel. *ACM Transactions on Database Systems,* Vol. 12, No. 2, 247–298.

Snodgrass, R. T. 1992. Temporal Databases. In: *Theories and Methods of Spatio-Temporal Reasoning in Geographic Space.* A. U. Frank, I. Campari, and U. Formentini, eds. *Lecture Notes in Computer Science,* 639. Springer-Verlag.

Snodgrass, R. T., and Ahn, I. 1986. Temporal Databases. *IEEE Computer,* Vol. 19, No. 9, 35–42.

Soo, M. D. 1991. Bibliography on Temporal Databases. *ACM-SIGMOD Record,* Vol. 20, No. 1, 14–23.

Soo, M. D., and Snodgrass, R. 1992. *Mixed Calendar Query Language Support for Temporal Constants.* TempIS Technical Report 29. Computer Science Department, University of Arizona.

Stam, R., and Snodgrass, R. 1988. A Bibliography on Temporal Databases. *Database Engineering,* Vol. 7, No. 4, 231–239.

Stefik, M., Bobrow, D., and Kahn, K. 1986. Integrating Access-Oriented Programming into a Multiparadigm Environment. *IEEE Software,* Vol. 3, No. 1, 10–18.

Stonebraker, M., Rowe, L., and Hirohama, M. 1990. The Implementation of POSTGRES. *IEEE Transactions on Knowledge and Data Engineering,* Vol. 2, No. 1, 125–142.

Su, S. Y. W., and Chen, H. M. 1991. A Temporal Knowledge Representation Model OSAM*T and Its Query Language OQL/T. *Proceedings of the Conference on Very Large Databases.*

Tandem Computers, Inc. 1983. *ENFORM Reference Manual.* Cupertino, Cal.

Tansel, A. U. 1991. A Historical Query Language. *Information Sciences,* No. 53, 101–133.

Tansel, A. U., Arkun, M. E., and Özsoyovglu, G. 1989. Time-By-Example Query Language for Historical Databases. *IEEE Transactions on Software Engineering,* Vol. 15, No. 4, 464–478.

Tansel, A. U., Clifford, J., Gadia, S., Jajodia, S., Segev, A., and Snodgrass, R., eds. 1993. *Temporal Databases: Theory, Design, and Implementation.* Database Systems and Applications Series. Benjamin/Cummings, Redwood City, Cal.

Van Benthem, J. F. K. 1982. A. *The Logic of Time.* D. Reidel Publishing Co., Hingham, Mass.

Wilkinson, K., Lyngbaek, P., and Hasan, W. 1990. The Iris Architecture and Implementation. *IEEE Transactions on Knowledge and Data Engineering,* Vol. 2, No. 1, 63–75.

Worboys, M. F. 1990. Reasoning About GIS Using Temporal and Dynamic Logics. *Temporal GIS Workshop.* University of Maine, Orono, Me.

Wuu, G. 1991. SERQL: An ER Query Language Supporting Temporal Data Retrieval. *Proceedings of the Tenth International Phoenix Conference on Computers and Communications,* 272–279.

Wuu, G., and Dayal, U. 1992. A Uniform Model for Temporal Object-Oriented Databases. *Proceedings of the International Conference on Data Engineering,* Tempe, Arizona, 584–593.

20

Cooperative Transactions for Multiuser Environments

GAIL E. KAISER

This chapter surveys extended transaction models proposed to support long duration, interactive, and/or cooperative activities in the context of multiuser software development and CAD/CAM environments. Many of these are variants of the checkout model, which addresses the long duration and interactive nature of the activities supported by environments but still isolates environment users, making it difficult for them to collaborate while their activities are in progress. However, a few cooperative transaction models have been proposed to facilitate collaboration, usually while maintaining some guarantees of consistency.

20.1 Introduction

Conventional database transactions guarantee atomicity in two senses: concurrency atomicity, for consistent concurrent access, and failure atomicity, for consistent persistence. Unfortunately, these atomicity properties severely limit the applicability of the transaction concept with respect to modern database applications such as software development and CAD/CAM environments, even though these applications still need consistent concurrent access and persistence.

From a transactional perspective, multiuser environments are characterized by:

- *Long duration*—activities consisting of sequences of database accesses may last from minutes to months. Rollback of long transactions, either for concurrency control or failure recovery, is generally unacceptable due to the economic and morale costs of lost work.
- *Interactive control*—users choose the actions within their activities as they go along. It is usually inconvenient to plan transaction schedules a priori, and automatic redo of activities is often infeasible.
- *Cooperation among users*—users share partial results of their activities while still in progress. Serializability is sometimes incompatible with consistency, when concerted effort is necessary to take the database from one semantically consistent state to another.

One widely accepted approach to long and interactive activities is the checkout model, in which users copy objects from the shared repository to private work areas for manipulation. A user might reserve these objects exclusively until a later checkin, or multiple users might later merge their updates to the same (or semantically related) objects. Neither mechanism, however, directly addresses cooperative activities—so users are tempted to communicate outside system control. This chapter surveys proposed approaches to all three problems, with particular emphasis on supporting cooperation. We are primarily concerned with concurrency control and do not explicitly address failure recovery, although recovery of some sort is usually required. Most of the papers mentioned are relatively recent, but note that many of their ideas were foreshadowed in the 1970s [Davies 1973, 1978].

The reader is assumed to be familiar with the conventional atomic transaction model [Bernstein et al. 1987] and its main implementation mechanisms, such as two-phase locking [Eswaran et al. 1976], multiversion timestamp ordering [Reed 1978], optimistic validation [Kung and Robinson 1981], multigranularity locking [Gray et al. 1975], and nested transactions [Moss 1982]. We start with a small motivating example, which will be referred to throughout the chapter. Next, we explain the checkout model in more detail and consider some extensions, which provide a range of functionality for coordinating the long duration, interactive activities of multiple environment users (i.e., only the first two requirements above). This is followed by a brief synopsis of a generic model that supplies primitives for constructing a range of checkoutlike nested transaction models. We then describe some proposals that address synergistic cooperation among the users while their work is in progress (thus addressing all three of the requirements). A table summarizes all the models surveyed, and then the chapter ends with a brief discussion of research directions.

20.2 Motivating Example

Two programmers, Alice and Bob, are developing the same program consisting of three modules: X, Y, and Z. Modules X and Y consist of procedures and declarations that comprise the main code of the program; module Z is a library of procedures called in modules X and Y. When the program is tested, two bugs are discovered. Bob is assigned the task of fixing one bug that is suspected to be in module X. He starts working on X. Alice's task is to explore a possible bug in the code of module Y, so she starts browsing Y. After a while, Bob finds that the bug in X is caused by bugs in some of the procedures in the library module. After editing Z, Bob proceeds to compile and test the modified code.

Alice finds a bug in module Y and modifies various parts of the module's code to fix it. Alice now wants to test the new Y. She is not concerned with the modifications that Bob made in X because she believes they are unrelated to her problem. However, she wants to access Bob's changes to module Z because some procedures in Z are called from Y: Bob's edits might have introduced semantic inconsistencies with Y's code. But since Bob is still working on modules X and Z, Alice will either have to access module Z at the same time that Bob is working on it or wait until he is done. Let's assume waiting is unacceptable because then Alice would be idle until Bob finishes his task.

If traditional concurrency control based on two-phase locking were used, Bob and Alice would not be able to access module Z at the same time. They could concurrently lock modules Y and X, respectively, since they work in isolation on these modules. But these users need to work *cooperatively* on module Z, and thus neither of them can lock it for the duration of his or her task. Recall that Bob writes Z and Alice reads it, and write and read locks are normally considered incompatible. Even if the locks were at the finer granularity of individual procedures, they would still have a problem because Bob and Alice need to access the same procedures (e.g., to recompile the module).

A variant of multiversion timestamp ordering might seem to solve the problem by supporting parallel versions of module Z. Alice would access the previously compiled version while Bob works on a new version. But this would require Alice to later retest her code after the new version of Z is released, resulting in unnecessary work, at least as undesirable as the waiting suggested above. Or optimistic validation could be employed, implicitly introducing parallel versions accessed by Bob and Alice. Here the read/write conflict would be detected only after Bob's work was completed, rolling back (throwing away) his changes! Any other mechanism for implementing conventional transactions would also run into difficulties because it would necessarily enforce serializability of Alice's and Bob's tasks.

Since this example is trivial, there are many obvious workarounds. But few scale up to even medium scale systems with perhaps hundreds of modules and tens of programmers. The next section discusses the checkout model and several extensions, variants of which are typically used in practice—even though they have serious limitations with respect to cooperation while work is in progress.

20.3 Coordination

When a small team of environment users works together on a project, the members of the team work autonomously, for the most part, but trust the others to act in a reasonable way. There are only a few rules that need to be enforced to maintain smooth interactions among the members of a small team. The environment should provide a means of orchestrating the interactions of the users, with the goal that information and effort are neither lost nor duplicated as a result of their simultaneous activities. In particular, it is necessary to *coordinate* the concurrent access to the shared repository in which the project components are stored [Perry and Kaiser 1991].

20.3.1 Basic Checkout Model

The basic checkout model, in tandem with versions and configurations, is supported by numerous commercially marketed tools for software development (e.g., Adele [Estublier et al. 1984], DSEE [Leblang and Chase 1987], SMS [Schwanke et al. 1989]). Katz 1990 gives a comprehensive overview of version and configuration systems oriented towards CAD/CAM environments. Most of these provide some of the capabilities outlined here, but in the text we cite only representative (and often early) examples.

Versions

The simplest form of coordination among members of a design or development team is to control the access to shared objects so that only one user can modify any particular object at a time. The *checkout/checkin* approach has been implemented by widely used version control tools like SCCS [Rochkind 1975] and RCS [Tichy 1985]. Each object is considered to be a collection of multiple *versions*. A version represents the state of the object at some time in the history of its development. The versions of an object are usually stored together in a compact representation that allows the reconstruction of any specific version when it is needed.

A version may become *immutable*, which means that it can no longer be modified. Instead, a new successor version can be created after checking out (reserving) the object. The initial reservation makes a copy of the indicated version and gives the owner of the reservation exclusive access to the copy so that he or she can modify it and check it in (deposit it) as a new version. Other users who need to access the same object must wait until the new version has been deposited (and the reservation released) or reserve another version. Two or more users can modify the same object only by working on parallel versions, creating *branches* in the version history. Branching ensures write-serializability among the versions of an object. The result of consecutive reserves, deposits, and branches is a version tree that records the full history of development of the single conceptual object. Branches of the version tree can be merged to combine the changes with respect to the least common ancestor along two or more paths.

This scheme is pessimistic since it does not allow access conflicts to occur on what is intended to be the same version (rather than allowing them to occur and then correcting them as in optimistic schemes; see section 20.3.3). It is conceptually optimistic, on the other hand, in the sense that it allows multiple parallel versions of the same object to be created even though it is known that these versions will have to be merged later. That is, it assumes any semantic conflicts between version branches can be adequately resolved (usually by one user manually constructing a new version to reflect the changes introduced in several versions, although some progress has been made in automatic merging [Horwitz et al. 1989]).

Considering our example, Bob and Alice would checkout modules X and Y, respectively; Bob would later checkout module Z when he discovered it was also needed for his task. Since Alice does not need to modify Z, she could use whatever commands are provided by the version management tool to access the most recently checked in version of Z in read-only mode and simply release her reservation when done, so a new version branch would not be created. As in the multiversion timestamp ordering approach mentioned in section 20.2, Alice would initially test with the old code for Z and then repeat her tests after Bob checked in his new version of Z. The unnecessary work might go even further, though, since Alice could find errors in Z during her testing and repair them herself in a parallel version (in which case she does create a new branch)—even though Bob may already be fixing the same problems! Alternatively, Alice could negotiate with Bob (outside control of the tool), asking him to checkin his changes to Z while maintaining his reservation of X. Then Alice could use the new version of Z for her testing. But this may result in incompatible versions of X and Z since there is nothing forcing Bob to eventually checkin a consistent version of X, or even checkin X at all as opposed to releasing his reservation.

The basic checkout model provides minimal coordination between multiple users. Like the classical transaction model, it does not rely on semantic information about the objects or the computations performed on these objects. The model suffers from two main problems as far as concurrency control is concerned. First, it does not support any notion of aggregate or composite objects, forcing the user to reserve and deposit each subobject individually. This can lead to problems if a user reserves several objects, all of which belong conceptually to one aggregate object; creates new versions of each of them; makes sure that they are consistent as a set; and then neglects to deposit some of the objects. Second, the reserve/deposit mechanism often does not provide any control over reserved objects beyond locking them in the public database. Thus, once an object has been reserved by a user, it may become available outside the concurrency control mechanism. The owner of the reservation can decide to let other users access and even modify that object (e.g., through permissions granted on the private work area via the file system).

Itasca (previously ORION-2 [Kim et al. 1991]) solves the second problem through a distributed database incorporating *private databases* into which objects are checked out from the shared database, as well as a query facility that distinguishes between private and shared databases. There is no

```
          TAlice      TBob
   |
   |                  read(X)
   |      read(Y)     read(Z)
   |      write(Y)    write(Z)
   |                  write(X)
   |      read(Z)     write(X)
   |      write(Y)
   v
 Time
```

FIGURE 20–1
Domain Relative Addressing Schedule

access to objects outside of system control. However, Itasca's support for composite objects, in the sense of maintaining references between objects, does not attach any semantics to the references. In particular, it allows subobjects of a composite object to be reserved and deposited independently by the same or different users, so the first problem remains.

Configurations

The key omission is not keeping track of which versions of objects are consistent with each other. For example, if each component (object) of a program has multiple versions, it would be impossible to find out which versions of the components actually contributed to producing a particular executable that is being tested. It is necessary to group sets of versions that are consistent with each other or otherwise used together into *configurations*.

Walpole et al. 1988a introduced *domain relative addressing*, which supports versions of configurations by extending Reed 1978's notion of time-relative addressing (multiversion concurrency control). Whereas Reed's algorithm synchronizes accesses to objects with respect to their timestamp, domain relative addressing does so with respect to their domain. A *domain* is essentially a configuration, consisting of one selected version for each of a related set of objects. Domains are consistent, by definition, since a (long) transaction reads only those versions in its input domain and writes new versions generating an output domain [Walpole et al. 1988b]. Even when multiple transactions employ the same input domains concurrently, they produce distinct output domains.

To illustrate this approach, consider the two long transactions T_{Alice} and T_{Bob} of Fig. 20–1. The schedule shown is serializable, with T_{Alice} either before T_{Bob} or vice versa. Applying domain relative addressing, however, the checkout operation is implicitly invoked by the first read of an object, but checkin is triggered only on explicit commit and has thus not occurred yet (it is not automatically invoked by a write). So T_{Alice} is necessarily serialized before T_{Bob}, meaning she reads the old version of Z before Bob's changes. Although we still have the retesting issue, it is not possible for Bob to introduce a semantic inconsistency by checking in only his changes to Z (or X) and aborting his changes to X (or Z). Instead, an entire configuration representing all checked out versions must be deposited atomically as a new version of the configuration.

20.3.2 Semantic Coordination

Configuration management assumes that the versions of objects contained in the same configuration are semantically consistent, just as the classical transaction model assumes that a transaction's actions take the database objects it accesses from one semantically consistent state to another. But neither enforces any particular integrity constraints because those are necessarily specific to the application.

Enforcing Consistency

Smile [Kaiser and Feiler 1987] is a multiuser software development environment for C programming. As in Itasca, Smile maintains private work areas for individual users as well as a shared repository, and supports global queries encompassing both the user's private database and the shared database. As in domain relative addressing, Smile requires the entire contents of a private work area (called an *experimental database*) to be checked in atomically. Unlike domain relative addressing, however, it does not support versions of either objects or configurations. Instead, there is always one public configuration in the *main database*, consisting of the only public version of each object, and any number of private configurations containing private versions that have not yet been deposited.

Smile's novel aspect is that it adds semantics-based consistency enforcement to the checkout model. The database contains C program components—for example, functions, type definitions, and variable declarations—collected into modules corresponding roughly to a C source file plus a C header file. The module is the unit of checkout/checkin, and additional modules can be added to the user's experimental database at any time. When the user requests checkin of his or her experimental database, Smile analyzes all its modules using the Lint tool [Johnson 1978], recompiles them, and links them together with the unmodified modules in the main database. If any errors are detected during this process, the checkin operation is automatically aborted; the user is expected to repair the problems and try again.

Considering our example, Bob starts a long transaction T_{Bob}, which creates a new experimental database EDB_{Bob}, and copies module X into this database. He later requests to add module Z to his experimental database. Now X and Z are exclusively reserved to T_{Bob}, and no other transaction can also reserve them. Other long transactions, however, can continue to read the baseline versions of these modules from the main database. For example, Alice can connect directly to the main database to perform read-only queries, or she can start her own update transaction on Y in EDB_{Bob}. Bob then proceeds to edit the bodies of X and Z. When the modification process is complete, he requests a deposit operation to copy the updated X and Z to the main database and thus make his changes available to other users.

Smile analyzes and compiles the new X and Z together with Y in the main database (i.e., a module in an experimental database might import from a module in the main database). The baseline might have changed while T_{Bob} was in operation, if Alice checked in an experimental database in the meantime, overwriting the previous baseline. If the analysis and compilation both succeed, the modules are deposited and T_{Bob} commits. Otherwise, Bob is informed of the errors and the deposit is aborted; Bob has to fix the errors in his modules and repeat the deposit operation when he is ready. The commit of T_{Bob} does not automatically delete EDB_{Bob}, so the user can continue to manipulate its copies of the modules, if desired, but it is not possible to checkin anything further from EDB_{Bob} into the main database or checkout any other modules from the main database into EDB_{Bob}.

Smile not only enforces consistency among the objects accessed within the same long transaction, but it also enforces global consistency with respect to all other objects. The description above considers only a posteori consistency checking, at the time of (intended) deposit, after the changes have already been made. To minimize unsuccessful deposits, with their recompilation overhead, Smile also enforces consistency in an a priori manner: A user is not permitted to change the *interface* of a module unless he or she has reserved all other modules that depend on that interface—or, actually, on the portion of the interface intended to be changed (in the sense of smart recompilation [Tichy 1986]). For example, say function f of module Z is called by function g of module Y. The internal code of f can be changed once Z has been reserved, but Bob also has to reserve module Y before he can modify f's external signature (parameter and return types). If another long transaction T_{Alice} has already reserved module Y in another experimental database EDB_{Alice}, the operation to edit f's signature is aborted. T_{Bob} is forced to either wait until T_{Alice} deposits Y, at which point T_{Bob} can reserve it as an addition to EDB_{Bob}, or to work on another task that does not affect Z. From this example, it should be clear that enforcing semantics-based consistency leads Smile to restrict concurrency possibly even more than the previously discussed variants of the checkout model.

Multi-Level Consistency

Infuse [Kaiser et al. 1989] is another multiuser environment for C programming. As in Smile, copies of modules are checked out into experimental databases representing work areas; unlike Smile's, Infuse's experimental databases are not necessarily private to a single user. Instead, Infuse supports a *multilevel hierarchy*: All modules are reserved from the main database into the same top-level experimental database shared among all users, from which modules may be reserved into child experimental databases representing groups of users, which may in turn have their own child experimental databases for subgroups, until eventually reaching leaf experimental databases where actual changes are normally made by individuals. The top-level experimental database corresponds roughly to a top-level nested transaction.

Infuse further extends Smile from static (compilation-time) to dynamic (execution-time) consistency checking. Within a given experimental database, no checking is initiated until all its child experimental databases have been successfully deposited. Then the locally reserved modules are compiled and linked against *stub* modules. The interfaces of stub modules represent the corresponding modules from the baseline (or reserved elsewhere in the hierarchy), but their functionality is sufficient only for testing of the locally reserved modules—for example, a function defined by a stub module might perform no computation but only prompt the user for its return value. The modules reserved in an experimental database cannot be deposited into the parent experimental database until they have passed an appropriate test suite. The entire system is compiled and tested in the top-level experimental database, before deposit of the changed modules into the main database to replace the baseline.

Let's reconsider our example, where Bob is assigned module X and Alice module Y. Either user creates a top-level experimental database $EDB_{X,Y}$, into which X and Y are reserved. Bob creates a child experimental database EDB_X in which he reserves X, and Alice creates EDB_Y in which she reserves Y. Again, Bob later adds Z, this time to both the top-level experimental database, now $EDB_{X,Y,Z}$ and his private area $EDB_{X,Z}$. Bob again changes the interface of function f—for example, by adding a new parameter. Unlike Smile, Infuse permits Bob to make this change even while Alice is simultaneously modifying module Y (recall that function g of module Y calls f in module Z). After Bob completes his changes, he deposits the contents (X and Z) of $EDB_{X,Z}$ into $EDB_{X,Y,Z}$. This operation automatically initiates recompilation and testing using local stub modules, if that had not been performed previously.

Alice separately finishes her changes and deposits Y (EDB_Y) into $EDB_{X,Y,Z}$. Semantic checking is performed only with respect to Y in isolation, so no errors are found at this point. However, when either Bob or Alice attempts to deposit the modules in $EDB_{X,Y,Z}$ to the main database, the compiler reports that modules Y and Z are not consistent with each other because of function f's new parameter. At that point, either Bob or Alice must create a child experimental database EDB_Y' (the previous EDB_Y has been discarded) in which he or she can fix the problem, by modifying the call to f in function g. Infuse thus allows greater concurrency than Smile at the cost of potentially greater inconsistency—and the need for a later round of changes to reestablish consistency.

Infuse provides additional features useful for large-scale projects. For example, authorized users can issue read-only queries, called *transcendent transactions* [Kaiser and Perry 1991], against any subset of the experimental databases in the hierarchy. This permits a manager to keep tabs on the progress of the work. Infuse also provides a facility whereby users can define *workspaces* [Kaiser and Perry 1987] that temporarily group together any two or more experimental databases *anywhere* in the hierarchy for the purpose of early consistency checking among the modules represented by those databases. This is akin to the various group models explained in section 20.5.2, in the sense that the normal isolation among long transactions is relaxed among members of a group, but Infuse workspaces permit the groupings to be formed and destroyed on the fly as needed.

20.3.3 Optimistic Coordination

The extended transaction models presented so far severely restrict concurrent access to the same object. There is usually read-only access to previously checked in versions, but no more than one transaction can modify the same version at the same time. Although a sequence of parent transactions reserves a module in Infuse, the module can be edited only in a leaf transaction (i.e., one with no children of its own). It is often the case in software development efforts, however, that two or more users in the same group need to change the same object concurrently. Since these users are typically familiar with each other's plans, they are assumed to be able to resolve any conflicts they introduce during their concurrent accesses by *merging* their changes into a single consistent version. Note that this is different from domain relative addressing, where transactions may read the same version but always write distinct versions.

Like Infuse, the Network Software Environment (NSE) [Honda 1988] operates on a hierarchical database structure. Each node of this structure is called an *environment* (not to be confused with a software development or CAD/CAM environment). An environment presents a read-only view of (potentially) the entire file system but requires updates to be made on private copies of files. Rather than generating permanent configurations as in domain relative addressing, NSE's concurrency control policy permits multiple sibling environments to checkout simultaneously what is conceptually the *same* version of an object and, when conflicts are discovered at checkin, merge their updates back into the shared file system.

The first environment to finish its work on a particular file deposits its copy as the new version of the file in its parent environment; the second child environment to finish has to merge its copy with the first environment's version, creating a newer version. The third environment to commit

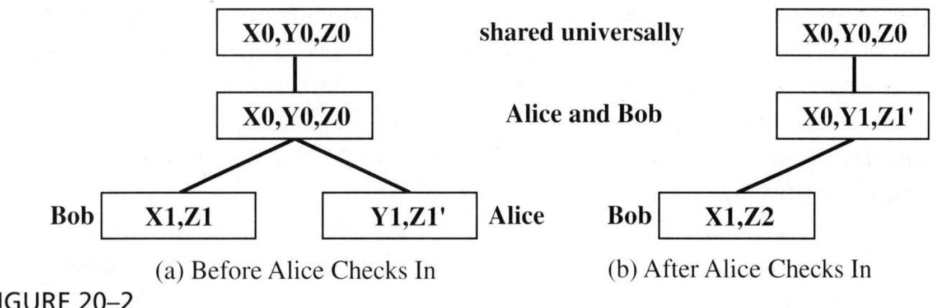

FIGURE 20–2
NSE Environments

will merge its copy with this newer version, and so on. This is distinct from creating branching versions, since all the checked in copies add versions to the original branch. (NSE uses the SCCS tool internally to manage these versions.) In effect, the validation phase of the conventional optimistic concurrency control scheme is modified to replace rollback of conflicting transactions with merging of updates. Adams et al. 1989 refer to this approach as *copy/modify/merge.*

Illustrating this approach, either Bob or Alice creates a top-level environment $ENV_{X,Y}$ to fix X and Y. Bob then creates his own child environment ENV_X to edit X. Z is added later, resulting in $ENV_{X,Y,Z}$ and $ENV_{X,Z}$. Alice controls her own child environment, ENV_Y. (Note that there is nothing preventing Z from being checked out at the same time as X, but here we follow the scenario of section 20.2.)

When Alice needs to compile and link the program for testing, she normally accesses the old version of Z in $ENV_{X,Y,Z}$. However, as in the basic checkout model, she can negotiate directly with Bob to retrieve his in-progress copy of Z or to ask him to deposit it early. Say she uses the old version, finds some bugs tickled by her own changes to Y, and decides to fix them herself. In NSE, she can checkout Z for updates even though Bob already has it checked out, generating $ENV_{Y,Z}$. But this introduces a race to determine which of Alice and Bob checks in Z first. The loser becomes responsible for correctly merging the changes, and it is still necessary for Alice to retest Y using the resulting version of Z. An instance where Alice wins the race and Bob merges the two variants is illustrated in Fig. 20–2.

20.4 Modeling Coordination

Domain relative addressing, Smile, and Infuse all support an explicit atomic transaction model in the sense that a (long) transaction begins, work proceeds within that transaction, and eventually the transaction either commits or aborts. Either all the changes made during the transaction are retained or none of them are. In contrast, the basic checkout model, Itasca, and NSE all allow individual objects to be reserved and deposited independently, with no formal notion of maintaining consistency among multiple objects. Walter 1984 proposes a middle ground, with the basic structure of nested transactions but a more flexible relationship between parent and child transactions.

In his model, the interface between a parent transaction and a child transaction can be either *single request,* where the parent in effect issues a query or update to the child and waits until the child returns the full result atomically, or *conversational,* meaning the control alternates between the parent that generates a series of requests and the child that answers these requests individually. The conversational interface necessitates grouping the parent and child transactions in the same *backout sphere* because if the child transaction is aborted (for any reason) in the middle of a conversation, not only does the system have to rollback the changes of the child transaction, but the parent transaction has to be rolled back (or backed out) to the point before the entire conversation began (not just the current request). In general, a backout sphere includes all transactions that are involved in a chain of conversations, where all of them must be backed out if any one of them is.

In contrast, the single-request interface supported by the traditional nested transaction model does not require rolling back the parent because the child transaction's computation does not affect the computation in progress in the parent transaction. In this framework, the basic checkout model can be viewed as supporting a multiple-request interface where there can be multiple outstanding requests at the same time, each of the requests concerns only a single object, and a child transaction multitasks among computations towards answering the pending requests. A child transaction might never abort in toto but can rollback its changes to an individual object since its last deposit of that object.

In addition to backout spheres, Walter also proposed the idea of *commit spheres*. Any transaction within a commit sphere can commit only if all other transactions in its sphere also commit. One can imagine extended transaction models where child transactions are not necessarily in the same commit sphere as their parents (e.g., the transactions resulting from the split operation are not in the same commit sphere), so a child could commit persistently even though its parent aborts.

Finally, Walter investigated the *synchronization* between parent and child transactions. His single-request and conversational interfaces as described above assume synchronous interaction, as does our suggested multiple-request extension, but asynchronous communication between the parent and child is also plausible. Here computation continues in the parent transaction while the child transaction is also active. Thus there arises the need for controlling concurrent access to objects shared between the parent and child, via locking or some other scheme.

Given these three aspects—interface, dependency, and synchronization—Walter presented a nested transaction model in which each subtransaction has three attributes defined when it is created. The first attribute, reflecting the interface criterion, can be set to either `BACKOUT` or `NOBACKOUT`, with `BACKOUT` indicating that the child transaction is associated with its own backout sphere and `NOBACKOUT` meaning that it shares a backout sphere with its parent transaction. The dependency attribute is set to either `COMMIT` or `NOCOMMIT`, and the third attribute, reflecting the synchronization mode, is set to either `SYNC` or `NOSYNC`. The eight combinations of these attributes define levels of coordination between a transaction and its subtransactions. For example, a subtransaction created with the attributes `BACKOUT`, `COMMIT`, and `SYNC` is independent of its parent since it possesses its own backout sphere and its own commit sphere, and locking is needed to synchronize access to objects shared with its parent.

Walter claims that it is possible to define all other nested transaction models within his model. The classical nested transaction model, for example, is defined as creating subtransactions with attributes set to `BACKOUT`, `NOCOMMIT`, and `SYNC`. Infuse and NSE arguably could both be defined using `BACKOUT`, `NOCOMMIT`, and `NOSYNC`, even though their behavior is substantially different—Walter's model is apparently insufficient for distinguishing between them. In particular, Infuse's interface attribute is `BACKOUT` because the single-request interface inherently places the parent and child in different backout spheres. NSE's interface attribute is also `BACKOUT` because the multiple-request interface places the parent and child in different backout spheres with respect to each distinct request—that is, releasing a reservation without checkin has no effect on previous checkins of the same file by either the same or different child environments. Neither Infuse nor NSE allows a subtransaction to commit its changes to the shared repository without depositing through the multiple levels of ancestors—thus `NOCOMMIT`. Finally, there is no synchronization `NOSYNC` between a parent and child transaction, in Infuse because there cannot be any work done in a parent experimental database until all the children have committed and thus the synchronization issue does not arise, and in NSE because concurrent updates to the same file are permitted (and merged later).

20.5 Cooperation

As the size of a project grows, the interactions among the team members increase both in number and in complexity. Although small teams can allow a great deal of freedom, assuming cooperation is effected by frequent direct communications outside system control, larger populations require complicated rules and regulations with their attendant restrictions on individual freedom. Large teams are typically subdivided into several groups, each responsible for a part of the design or development task. Members of a group then cooperate with each other to complete their parts, so it is necessary for the environment to support cooperation among members of the same group as well as coordination of multiple groups [Perry and Kaiser 1991]. The mechanisms described in section 20.4 generally handle the former well but are relatively weak regarding the latter. (Although Infuse was intended for large teams divided into smaller groups, it focuses on the coordination among groups without much concern for the cooperation within groups, so is described in section 20.3 with the other approaches concentrating on coordination.)

20.5.1 Cooperation Primitives

Walter's primitives described in section 20.4 form a framework for *reasoning about* different transaction models, but the imprecision in distinguishing Infuse from NSE points to some difficulty regarding how they might be used to *implement* such models. However, others have proposed primitives that are, at least in principle, intended to be employed directly in implementing new transactional systems.

Notification

One approach to maintaining consistency, while still allowing some cooperation, is to support notification and interactive conflict resolution rather than enforcing serializability. The Gordion database system [Ege and Ellis 1987] provides a notification primitive that can be used in conjunction with other primitives to implement cooperative concurrency control policies. Notifications alert users about interesting events such as an attempt to lock an object that has already been locked in an exclusive mode or to create a new version of an object that is already checked out.

Two policies that use notification in conjunction with nonexclusive locks and versions were implemented in the Gordion system: *immediate notification* and *delayed notification* [Yeh et al. 1987]. Immediate notification alerts the affected users of any attempt at conflicting access as soon as the conflict occurs. Delayed notification alerts the users of all the conflicts that have occurred only when one of the conflicting (long) transactions attempts to commit. (NSE supports an intermediate point, through its `resync` command, to request any pending notifications on demand.) Gordion resolves conflicts by instigating a "phone call" between the two parties with the assumption that they can interact directly to resolve the conflict (it might be more practical to send electronic mail, or allow the user to have specified an appropriate action for each class of notification in advance [Leblang and Chase 1984]).

These policies incorporate humans as part of the conflict resolution algorithm. On the one hand, this enhances concurrency when many of the tasks are interactive. On the other hand, it can degrade consistency because humans cannot always be relied on to correctly resolve conflicts. It might be preferable for the environment to support some form of automatic consistency checking, as in Smile and Infuse, or intelligent tools, such as NSE's merge utility (see section 20.3).

Dynamic Restructuring

Two new operations, `split-transaction` and `join-transaction`, have been proposed for restructuring long, interactive transactions while they are in progress [Kaiser and Pu 1992]. The basic idea is that all sequences of database accesses that are included in a set of concurrent transactions are performed in a schedule that is serializable at the point when the transactions are committed. The schedule, however, may include new transactions that result from splitting and joining the original transactions. Thus, the committed set of transactions may not correspond in a simple way to the originally initiated set.

A `split-transaction` operation divides an ongoing transaction into two or more serializable transactions by dividing the actions and the resources (e.g., locked objects) between the new transactions. The resulting transactions can proceed independently from that point on, perhaps controlled by different users, and behave as if they had been independent all along. The original transaction disappears entirely, as if it had never existed. The `split-transaction` operation can be applied only when it is possible to generate two transactions that are serializable with each other as well as all other transactions.

One application of `split-transaction` is to commit one of the new transactions in order to release all its resources so that they can be acquired by other transactions [Pu et al. 1988]. In this case, the splitting of a transaction reflects the fact that the user who controlled the original transaction has decided that he or she is done with some of the resources reserved by the transaction—so these resources can be treated as held by a separate transaction that now commits. The splitting of a transaction generally results from new information determined while the transaction is in progress—in this case, the dynamic access pattern of the transaction (the fact that it no longer needs some resources). Thus it would not have been possible to initiate the eventually split transactions as independent top-level transactions a priori (as in Garcia-Molina and Salem 1987, where a *saga* consists of a sequence of conventional transactions, and interleaving among sagas is permitted at transaction boundaries).

To clarify this technique, suppose that Alice and Bob start long transactions T_{Bob} and T_{Alice} to modify the modules X and Y, respectively. Again, T_{Bob} later decides to also edit module Z, and, after a while, Alice discovers that she too needs to access Z. We assume environmental support for notifi-

```
        T_Alice              T_Bob                        T_BobA
 |
 |                           begin
 |      begin                read(X)
 |      read(Y)              read(Z)
 |      write(Y)             write(Z)
 |                           write(X)
 |      request read(Z)      corresponding notify(Z)
 |                           split((Z),(X))
 |                           commit(Z)
 |      actual read(Z)                                    write(X)
 |      write(Y)
 |
 |                                                        commit(X)
 |      commit(Y,Z)
 v
Time
```

FIGURE 20–3
Split-Transaction Schedule

cation similar to that described above. On being notified that T_{Alice} would like to see the new code of module Z, Bob decides that he can give up that module since he has finished his changes to it. So he splits T_{Bob} into T_{Bob} and T_{BobA}, and then commits T_{BobA}, thus committing his changes to Z while retaining X. Bob should do this only if the changes to Z do not depend in any way on the previous or planned changes to X, which might later be aborted. Alice can now read Z and use it for testing her code, and she eventually commits T_{Alice}, releasing Z as well as Y. This schedule is shown in Fig. 20–3.

`Join-transaction` performs the reverse operation of `split-transaction`, merging the ongoing work of two or more independent transactions as if these transactions had always been a single transaction. A `split-transaction` followed by a `join-transaction` in one of the newly separated transactions can be used to transfer resources among particular in-progress transactions without even temporarily making the resources available to other transactions. The above example could therefore be modified to transfer Z from Bob to Alice without committing it—for example, if it is not in a final (i.e., self-consistent) state but instead Alice intends to take over the work of editing it.

20.5.2 Group Transactions

Most extended transaction models intended to encompass synergistic cooperation—that is, concerted effort among multiple concurrent transactions toward a common goal, are based on some notion of a *group*. Transactions within a group can cooperate in ways not permitted for transactions outside the group or among groups. Perhaps it is not coincidence that most group-based approaches also extend the lock modes available far beyond the conventional read and write.

Group-Oriented Model

The *group-oriented model* [Klahold et al. 1985] categorizes long transactions into *group transactions* (GTs) and *user transactions* (UTs). Every UT is a subtransaction of some GT. The model provides primitives to define groups of users, with the intention of associating each GT with a user group. A GT reserves objects from the public database into the corresponding group database, within which individual users create their own user databases and invoke UTs to reserve objects from the group database into their user database. The structure is similar to Smile, but there are two levels of experimental databases rather than just one; note that exactly two levels are permitted, not the arbitrary hierarchies of Infuse and NSE (see section 20.3).

Groups are isolated from each other—that is, one user group cannot see the work of another user group until the relevant group database has been deposited into the public repository. GTs are thus serializable with respect to each other. Within a group transaction, multiple UTs can run concurrently and are serializable unless users intervene to cooperate in a nonserializable schedule. The basic mechanism provided for relaxing serializability is a version facility that supports parallel development (branching) and notification. Versions can be derived, deleted, and modified by a user only after being locked in any one of a range of lock modes.

The model supports five lock modes on a version of an object: (1) read-only, which makes a version available only for reading; (2) read/derive, which allows multiple users to either read the same version or derive a new (modifiable) version from it; (3) shared derivation, which allows the owner of the lock to both read the version and derive a new version, while allowing parallel reads of the same version and derivation of different new versions by other users; (4) exclusive derivation, which allows the owner to read a version of an object and derive a new version, and allows only parallel reads of the original version; and (5) exclusive lock, which allows the owner to read, modify, and derive a version and allows no operations by other users on that version.

Users can access objects only as part of a (long) transaction. Each transaction is two phase, consisting of an acquire phase and a release phase, as in the conventional transaction model. Locks can be strengthened (i.e., converted into a more exclusive mode) only during the acquire phase and weakened (converted into a more flexible lock) only during the release phase. If a transaction requests a lock on a particular object and the object is already locked with an incompatible lock by another transaction, the request is rejected and the initiator of the requesting transaction is informed of the rejection. This avoids the problem of deadlock, which would be caused by blocking transactions that request unavailable resources. Instead, the user is notified later when the object becomes available.

The group-oriented transaction model also provides a special read operation that breaks any lock by allowing a user to read a version, knowing that it might soon be changed. This gives the user the ability to observe the progress of a task without impinging on the task's progress. In the scenario of our motivating example, Alice might take advantage of this facility to read Bob's (changing) version of the library module Z as needed for her compilation and testing of Y. She would realize that Z will continue to change and may not even be internally consistent (e.g., it might not compile successfully) but perhaps would prefer the recent snapshot of Z to the old version as it was before Bob began his task.

Transaction Groups

The ObServer database system [Hornick and Zdonik 1987] replaces classical locks with a rich set of lock modes and communication modes that can be paired, in principle, to support an implementation framework for cooperative transactions. The lock modes indicate whether the transaction intends to read or write the object and whether it is willing to read while another transaction writes, write while other transactions read, or accept multiple writers of the same object. The communication modes specify whether the transaction wants to be notified if another transaction requests a specific lock on the object or if another transaction has updated the object.

A *transaction group* [Fernandez and Zdonik 1989] is a process that controls database access by a set of cooperating transactions and transaction (sub)groups (collectively members of the transaction group). Within each transaction group, member transactions and subgroups are synchronized according to an *input protocol* that defines some semantic correctness criteria appropriate for the application. The criteria are specified by semantic patterns and enforced by a recognizer and a conflict detector. The recognizer ensures that a lock request from a member transaction matches an element in the set of locks that the group may grant to its members. The conflict detector ensures that a request to lock an object in a certain mode does not conflict with the locks already held on the object.

If a transaction group member requests an object that is not currently locked by its group, the group must request a lock on the object from its parent (if any, otherwise the database itself). The input protocol of the parent group might be different from that of the child group, as in the constraints of the cooperating CAD transactions model. In that case, the child group must transform its requested lock mode into a different mode accepted by the parent's input protocol. The transformation is carried out by an *output protocol,* which consults a lock translation table to determine how to transform a lock request into one that is acceptable to the parent group.

To illustrate, consider the example depicted in Fig. 20–4. Bob and Alice are together assigned the task of updating modules X, Y, and Z, while Charlie is responsible for updating the documentation of the project. Alice and Bob need to cooperate while working on their modules (recall the shar-

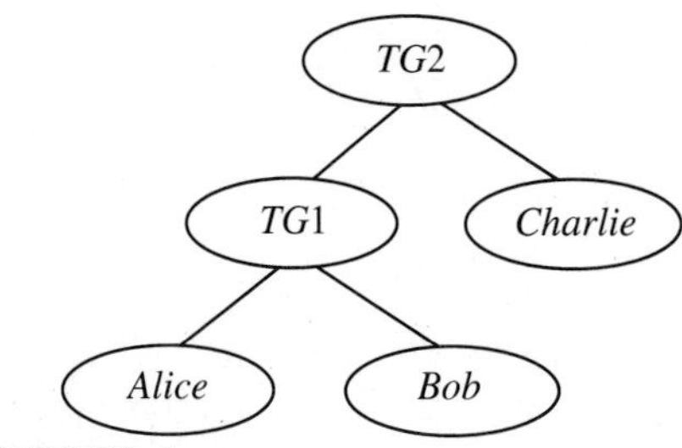

FIGURE 20–4
Transaction Groups

ing of Z from previous sections), whereas Charlie only needs to access the final result of the modifications in order to verify that the modules match the documentation. Two transaction groups are defined, TG1 and TG2. TG2 has $T_{Charlie}$ and TG1 as its members, and TG1 includes T_{Bob} and T_{Alice}. The output protocol of TG1 states that changes made by the transactions within TG1 are committed with respect to TG2 only when all the transactions of TG1 have either committed or aborted. The input protocol of TG1 accepts lock modes that allow T_{Alice} and T_{Bob} to cooperate (e.g., see each other's partial results) while isolation is maintained within TG2 (to prevent $T_{Charlie}$ from accessing the partial results of the transactions in TG1).

Participant Transactions

The transaction groups model determines cooperation opportunities in terms of nonstandard lock modes and how the remaining lock conflicts are handled. A related approach is to define each (long) transaction as a *participant* in a specified *domain*, where participant transactions in the same domain need not appear to have been performed in some serial order with respect to each other [Kaiser 1990]. (Participation domains should not be confused with the domains of domain relative addressing.) A domain would typically represent the set of transactions controlled by the users collaborating on a common task. However, unlike transaction groups, there is no implication that all the transactions in a domain commit together or even that all of them commit (some may abort) [Kaiser 1991]. Those transactions that are not participants in a particular domain are considered *observers* with respect to that domain. Observer transactions must be serialized with respect to the transactions in the domain and, furthermore, should not view any anomalous behavior due to the interactions among participants.

Say a domain D is defined to respond to the modification request of section 20.2, and Alice and Bob start long transactions T_{Alice} and T_{Bob} that participate in D. The schedule shown in Fig. 20–5 is not serializable according to any of the conventional concurrency control mechanisms. T_{Alice} reads the updates T_{Bob} made to module Z, which are written but are not yet

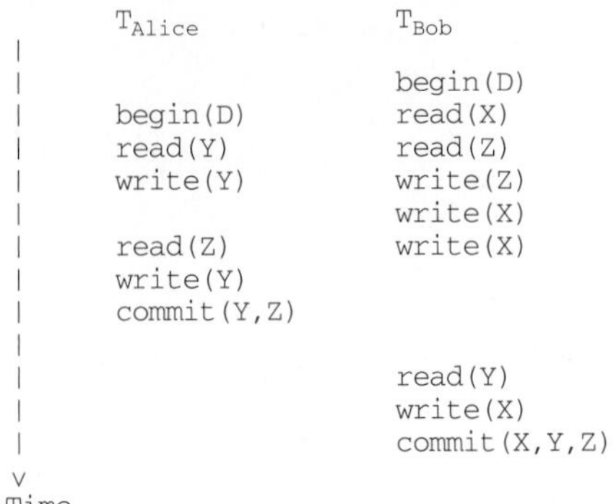

T_Alice
T_Bob
begin(D)
begin(D)
read(X)
read(Y)
read(Z)
write(Y)
write(Z)
write(X)
read(Z)
write(X)
write(Y)
commit(Y,Z)
read(Y)
write(X)
commit(X,Y,Z)
Time

FIGURE 20–5
Participant Transaction Schedule

committed by T_{Bob}, modifies parts of module Y, and then commits. T_{Bob} reads the changed Y (e.g., to test his own code in the context of the entire program) and continues to modify X after T_{Alice} has committed. Since T_{Alice} and T_{Bob} participate in the same domain D, the schedule is legal according to the participant transactions model.

Now say that our third user, Charlie, starts a long transaction $T_{Charlie}$ in domain E, so it is an observer for domain D. Assume the sequence of events shown in Fig. 20–6, where Charlie does not work on documentation but instead modifies library module Z. The transaction schedule is legal to this point, since $T_{Charlie}$ thus far could be serialized before T_{Bob} (but not after, since Bob reads Charlie's updates to Z). But then $T_{Charlie}$ attempts to read module Y, which has been modified and committed by T_{Alice}. This would be illegal even though T_{Alice} has already committed! The reason is that T_{Alice} cannot be serialized before $T_{Charlie}$, and thus before T_{Bob}, because T_{Alice} reads the uncommitted changes to module Z written by T_{Bob}. In fact, T_{Alice} cannot be serialized either before or after T_{Bob}. This would not be a problem if it was unnecessary to serialize T_{Alice} with any transactions outside the shared domain D; the serializability of transactions within a participation domain need be enforced only with respect to what can actually be observed by transactions that are not participants in the domain.

20.6 Research Directions

We saw in section 20.4 a formalism that intends to model the class of nested transaction models. Since there are several cooperative transaction models but no consensus on which one is best, or even that there *is* one approach that is universally superior for all environment applications, it would be desirable to develop an analogous formalism for cooperation. Such a for-

```
|       T_Alice        T_Bob         Charlie
|
|                                    begin(E)
|                      begin(D)      read(Z)
|       begin(D)       read(X)       write(Z)
|       read(Y)        read(Z)
|       write(Y)       write(Z)
|                      write(X)
|       read(Z)        write(X)
|       write(Y)
|       commit(Y,Z)
|
|                                    read(Y)
|
v
Time
```

FIGURE 20–6
Participant Transaction Schedule

malism should provide a relatively small number of primitives that could be combined in different ways to specify the characteristics of a wide range of extended transaction models. Further, the formalism should be *executable* in the sense that it would be possible to prototype constructed models, albeit not necessarily in the most efficient manner. For example, Salem 1993 proposed a toolkit that seems feasible for implementing a range of extended transaction models but concerned only with long duration and to some extent interactive control, without the possibility of cooperation.

The ACTA framework [Chrysanthis and Ramamritham 1990] meets the first criterion, but was never intended to be executable. Skarra 1991 proposed a formalism, as a sample input/output protocol for transaction groups, for recognizing required and prohibited patterns of transaction interactions using finite state automata. She concedes, though, that the implementation is unwieldy and unlikely to scale up. Barghouti 1992 suggested condition/action rules for recognizing and resolving transaction conflicts. A proof-of-concept implementation was included in the Marvel 3.1 software development environment, which also supports user-defined lock modes [Ben-Shaul et al. 1993]. Heineman 1993 is currently developing a formalism that provides a superset of the repair primitives used in the actions to support (at least) dynamic restructuring and participant transactions; it remains to be seen whether this approach will be practical. Thus, cooperation modeling remains an important open problem for future research.

ACKNOWLEDGMENTS

The author is supported by grants from the National Science Foundation, Andersen Consulting, AT&T Foundation, Bull HN Information Systems and IBM Canada Ltd., and by the New York State Center for Advanced Technol-

Mechanism	System	Consistency	Long	Interactive	Cooperative
Classical Transactions	numerous	Yes	No	No	No
Checkout	RCS	No	Yes	Yes	No
Distributed Checkout	Itasca	Possible	Yes	Yes	No
Domain Relative Addressing	Cosmos	Minimal	Yes	Limited	No
Single-level Consistency	Smile	Yes	Yes	Yes	No
Multi-level Consistency	Infuse	Yes	Yes	Yes	Limited
Copy/Modify/ Merge	NSE	No	Yes	Yes	No
Backout and Commit Spheres	N/A	Possible	Yes	Yes	Unclear
Notification	Gordion	No	Yes	Yes	Limited
Dynamic Restructuring	in progress	Yes	Yes	Yes	Limited
Group-Oriented Trans.	unknown	Minimal	Yes	Yes	Limited
Transaction Groups	ObServer	Possible	Yes	Limited	Yes
Participant Trans.	in progress	Minimal	Yes	Yes	Yes

FIGURE 20–7
Proposed Concurrency Control Approaches

ogy in Computers and Information Systems. This chapter is based in part on material gathered by Naser Barghouti for Barghouti and Kaiser 1991.

REFERENCES

Adams, E. W., Honda, M., and Miller, T. C. 1989. Object Management in a CASE Environment. *Eleventh International Conference on Software Engineering,* 154–163. IEEE Computer Society Press, Pittsburgh.

Barghouti, N. S. 1992. *Concurrency Control in Rule-Based Software Development Environments.* Ph.D. thesis, Columbia University.

Barghouti, N. S., and Kaiser, G. E. 1991. Concurrency Control in Advanced Database Applications. *ACM Computing Surveys,* Vol. 23, No. 3, 269–317.

Ben-Shaul, I. Z., Kaiser, G. E., and Heineman, G. T. 1993. An Architecture for Multi-User Software Development Environments. *Computing Systems, The Journal of the USENIX Association,* Vol. 6, No. 2, 65–103.

Bernstein, P. A., Hadzilacos, V., and Goodman, N. 1987. *Concurrency Control and Recovery in Database Systems*. Addison-Wesley, Reading Mass.

Chrysanthis, P. K., and Ramamritham, K. 1990. ACTA: A Framework for Specifying and Reasoning about Transaction Structure and Behavior. *1990 ACM-SIGMOD International Conference on Management of Data,* 194–203. Atlantic City.

Davies, C. T., Jr. 1973. Recovery Semantics for A DB/DC System. *Twenty-eighth ACM National Conference,* 136–141. Atlanta.

Davies, C. T., Jr. 1978, Data Processing Spheres of Control. *IBM Systems Journal,* Vol. 17, No. 2, 179–198.

Ege, A., and Ellis, C. A. 1987. Design and Implementation of Gordion, an Object Base Management System. *Third International Conference on Data Engineering,* 226–234. Los Angeles.

Estublier, J., Ghoul, S., and Krakowiak, S. 1984. Preliminary Experience with a Configuration Control System for Modular Programs. In: *ACM SIGSOFT/SIGPLAN Software Engineering Symposium on Practical Software Development Environments,* 149–156. P. Henderson, ed.

Eswaran, K. P., Gray, J. N., Lorie, R. A., and Traiger, I. L. 1976. The Notions of Consistency and Predicate Locks in a Database System. *Communications of the ACM,* Vol. 19, No. 11, 624–632.

Fernandez, M. F., and Zdonik, S. B. 1989. Transaction Groups: A Model for Controlling Cooperative Work. *Third International Workshop on Persistent Object Systems: Their Design, Implementation and Use,* 128–138. Queensland, Australia.

Garcia-Molina, H., and Salem, K. 1978. SAGAS. *ACM-SIGMOD 1987 Annual Conference,* 249–259, San Francisco.

Gray, J., Lorie, R., and Putzolu, G. 1975. Granularity of Locks and Degrees of Consistency in a Shared Database. *International Conference on Very Large Data Bases,* 428–451. Morgan Kaufmann.

Heineman, G. T. 1993. *A Transaction Manager Component for Cooperative Transaction Models.* Technical Report CUCS-017-93, Columbia University Department of Computer Science.

Honda, M. 1988. Support for Parallel Development in the Sun Network Software Environment. *Second International Workshop on Computer-Aided Software Engineering,* 5-5–5-7.

Hornick, M. F., and Zdonik, S. B. 1987. A Shared, Segmented Memory System for an Object-Oriented Database. *ACM Transactions on Office Automation Systems,* Vol. 5, No. 1, 70–95.

Horwitz, S., Prins, J., and Reps, T. 1989. Integrating Noninterfering Versions of Programs. *ACM Transactions on Programming Languages and Systems,* Vol. 11, No. 3, 345–387.

Johnson, S. C. 1978. Lint, a C Program Checker. *Unix Programmer's Manual.* AT&T Bell Laboratories.

Kaiser, G. E. 1990. A Flexible Transaction Model for Software Engineering. *Sixth International Conference on Data Engineering,* 560–567. IEEE Computer Society Press, Los Angeles.

Kaiser, G. E. 1991. Interfacing Cooperative Transactions to Software Development Environments. *Office Knowledge Engineering,* Vol. 4, No. 1, 56–78.

Kaiser, G. E., and Feiler, P. H. 1987. Intelligent Assistance Without Artificial Intelligence. *Thirty-second IEEE Computer Society International Conference*, 236–241. IEEE Computer Society Press, San Francisco.

Kaiser, G. E., and Perry, D. E. 1987. Workspaces and Experimental Databases: Automated Support for Software Maintenance and Evolution. *Conference on Software Maintenance*, 108–114. IEEE Computer Society Press, Austin.

Kaiser, G. E., and Perry, D. E. 1991. Making Progress in Cooperative Transaction Models. *Data Engineering*, Vol. 14, No. 1, 19–23.

Kaiser, G. E., Perry, D. E., and Schell, W. M. 1989. Infuse: Fusing Integration Test Management with Change Management. *COMPSAC 89: The Thirteenth Annual International Computer Software and Applications Conference*, 552–558. IEEE Computer Society Press, Orlando.

Kaiser, G. E., and Pu, C. 1992. Dynamic Restructuring of Transactions. In: *Database Transaction Models for Advanced Applications*, 265–295. A. K. Elmagarmid, ed. Morgan Kaufmann, San Mateo, Cal.

Katz, R. H. 1990. Toward a Unified Framework for Version Modeling in Engineering Databases. *ACM Computing Surveys*, Vol. 22, No. 4, 375–408.

Kim, W., Ballou, N., Garza, J. F., and Woelk, D. 1991. A Distributed Object-Oriented Database System Supporting Shared and Private Databases. *ACM Transactions on Information Systems*, Vol. 9, No. 1, 31–51.

Klahold, P., Schlageter, G., Unland, R., and Wilkes, W. 1985. A Transaction Model Supporting Complex Applications in Integrated Information Systems. *ACM-SIGMOD 1985 International Conference on Management of Data*, 388–401, Austin.

Kung, H. T., and Robinson, J. 1981. On Optimistic Methods for Concurrency Control. *ACM Transactions on Database Systems*, Vol. 6, No. 2, 213–226.

Leblang, D. B., and Chase, R. P., Jr. 1984. Computer-Aided Software Engineering in a Distributed Workstation Environment. In: *ACM SIGSOFT/SIGPLAN Software Engineering Symposium on Practical Software Development Environments*, 104–112. P. Henderson, ed. ACM Press.

Leblang, D. B., and Chase, R. P., Jr. 1987. Parallel Software Configuration Management in a Network Environment. *IEEE Software*, Vol. 4, No. 6, 28–35.

Moss, J. E. B. 1982. Nested Transactions and Reliable Distributed Computing. *Second Symposium on Reliability in Distributed Software and Database Systems*, 33–39. IEEE Computer Society Press, Pittsburgh.

Perry, D. E., and Kaiser, G. E. 1991. Models of Software Development Environments. *IEEE Transactions on Software Engineering*, Vol. 17, No. 3, 283–295.

Pu, C., Kaiser, G. E., and Hutchinson, N. 1988. Split-Transactions for Open-Ended Activities. *Fourteenth International Conference on Very Large Data Bases*, 26–37. Morgan Kaufman, Los Angeles.

Reed, D. P. 1978. Naming and Synchronization in a Decentralized Computer System. Ph.D. dissertation, Massachusetts Institute of Technology.

Rochkind, M. J. 1975. The Source Code Control System. *IEEE Transactions on Software Engineering* SE-1, 364–370.

Salem, K. 1993. *Implementing Extended Transaction Models Using Transaction Groups*. Technical Report CS-TR-3051, University of Maryland Department of Computer Science.

Schwanke, R. W., Cohen, E. S., Gluecker, R., Hasling, W. M., Soni, D. A., and Wagner, M. E. 1989. Configuration Management in BiiN SMS. *Eleventh International Conference on Software Engineering,* 383–393. IEEE Computer Society Press, Pittsburgh.

Skarra, A. H. 1991. Localized Correctness Specifications for Cooperating Transactions in an Object-Oriented Database. *Office Knowledge Engineering,* Vol. 4, No. 1, 79–106.

Tichy, W. F. 1985. RCS M: A System for Version Control. *Software M Practice & Experience,* Vol. 15, No. 7, 637–654.

Tichy, W. F. 1986. Smart Recompilation. *ACM Transactions on Programming Languages and Systems,* Vol. 8, No. 3, 273–291.

Walpole, J., Blair, G. S., Malik, J., and Nicol, J. R. 1988a. A Unifying Model for Consistent Distributed Software Development Environments. In: *ACM SIGSOFT/SIGPLAN Software Engineering Symposium on Practical Software Development Environments,* 183–190. P. Henderson, ed.

Walpole, J., Blair, G. S., Malik, J., and Nicol, J. R. 1988b. Maintaining Consistency in Distributed Software Engineering Environments. *Eighth International Conference on Distributed Computing Systems,* 418–425. IEEE Computer Society Press, San Jose.

Walter, B. 1984. Nested Transactions with Multiple Commit Points: An Approach to the Structuring of Advanced Database Applications. *Tenth International Conference on Very Large Data Bases,* 161–171. Morgan Kaufmann, Singapore.

Yeh, S., Ellis, C., Ege, A., and Korth, H. 1987. *Performance Analysis of Two Concurrency Control Schemas for Design Environments.* Technical Report STP-036-87, MCC.

21

Active Database Systems

UMESHWAR DAYAL
ERIC HANSON
JENNIFER WIDOM

Integrating a production rules facility into a database system provides a uniform mechanism for a number of advanced database features, including integrity constraint enforcement, derived data maintenance, triggers, alerters, protection, version control, and others. In addition, a database system with rule-processing capabilities provides a useful platform for large and efficient knowledge-base and expert systems. Database systems with production rules are referred to as *active database systems*, and the field of active database systems has indeed been active. This chapter summarizes current work in active database systems; topics covered include active database rule models and languages, rule execution semantics, and implementation issues.

21.1 Introduction

Conventional database systems are *passive*: They only execute queries or transactions explicitly submitted by a user or an application program. For many applications, however, it is important to monitor situations of interest and to trigger a timely response when the situations occur. For example, an inventory control system needs to monitor the quantity in stock of items in the inventory database, so that when the quantity in stock of some item falls below a threshold, a reordering activity may be initiated. This behavior could be implemented over a passive database system in one of two ways, neither of which is satisfactory. First, the semantics of condition checking could be embedded in every program that updates the inventory database, but this is a poor approach from the software engineering perspective. Alternatively, an application program can be written to poll the database periodically to check for relevant conditions. However, if the polling frequency is too high, this can be inefficient, and if the polling frequency is too low, conditions may not be detected in a timely manner.

An *active database system*, in contrast, is a database system that monitors situations of interest and, when they occur, triggers an appropriate response in a timely manner. The desired behavior is expressed in *production rules* (also called *event-condition-action rules*), which are defined and stored in the database. This has the benefits that the rules can be shared by many application programs, and the database system can optimize their implementation.

The production rule paradigm originated in the field of artificial intelligence (AI) with expert systems rule languages such as OPS5 [Brownston et al. 1985]. Typically, in AI systems, a production rule is of the form:

condition → *action*

An inference engine cycles through all the rules in the system, *matching* the condition parts of the rules with data in working memory. Of all the rules that match (the *candidate set*), one is selected using some *conflict resolution policy,* and this selected rule is *fired*—that is, its action part is executed. The action part may modify the working memory, possibly according to the matched data, and the cycle continues until no more rules match.

This paradigm has been generalized to event-condition-action rules for active database systems. These are of the form

```
on event
if condition
then action
```

This allows rules to be triggered by events such as database operations, by occurrences of database states, and by transitions between states (among other things), instead of being evaluated by an inference engine that cycles periodically through the rules. When the triggering event occurs, the condition is evaluated against the database; if the condition is satisfied, the action is executed. Rules are defined and stored in the database and evaluated by the database system, subject to authorization, concurrency control, and recovery.

Such event-condition-action rules are powerful and uniform mechanisms for a number of useful database tasks: They can enforce integrity constraints, implement triggers and alerters, maintain derived data, enforce access constraints, implement version control policies, gather statistics for query optimization or database reorganization, and more [Eswaran 1976; Morgenstern 1983; Stonebraker et al. 1982]. Previous support for these features, when present, provided little generality and used special-purpose mechanisms for each. In addition, the inference power of production rules makes active database systems a suitable platform for building large and efficient knowledge-base and expert systems.

While the power of active database systems was recognized some time ago, a true research field did not emerge until relatively recently [Dayal 1988]. However, the field has quickly blossomed, and it currently enjoys considerable activity and recognition. A number of powerful research prototypes have been built [Anwar and Mangis 1993; Beeri and Milo 1991; Chakravarthy et al. 1989; Dayal et al. 1988; Delcambre and Etheredge 1988; Gatziu and Geppert 1991; Gehani and Jagadish 1991; Hanson 1992; McCarthy and Dayal 1989; Stonebraker et al. 1990; Stonebraker and Kemnitz 1991; Widom et al. 1991; Widom and Finkelstein 1990]. In this chapter, we will illustrate the features of active database systems using *Ariel* [Hanson 1992], *HiPAC* [Chakravarthy et al. 1989; Dayal et al. 1988; McCarthy and Dayal 1989], *Postgres* [Stonebraker et al. 1990; Stonebraker and Kemnitz 1991], and *Starburst* [Widom et al. 1991; Widom and Finkelstein 1990] as representative of the field. Limited production rule capabilities are now appearing in commercial database products such as *Ingres* [INGRES 1992], *InterBase*, *Oracle* [ORACLE 1992], *Rdb* [Rdb 1991], and *Sybase* [Howe 1986], and in the SQL2 and emerging SQL3 standards.

This chapter provides a broad survey of current work in active database systems. The discussion is divided into three technical areas. Rule models and language design are discussed in section 21.2, rule execution semantics in section 21.3, and implementation issues in section 21.4. section 21.5 concludes and discusses areas for future research.

21.2 Rule Models and Languages

This section describes the issues involved in designing a database production rule language and explains how those issues have been addressed in various active database systems. We also describe the rule language features proposed for SQL2 and SQL3, which are indicative of the state of commercial practice.

Some of the differences among rule languages stem from differences in the underlying data models supported by the different systems. In relational systems such as Ariel, Postgres, Starburst, and the commercial products, rules are defined (and named) as metadata in the schema, together with tables, views, integrity constraints, and the like. As with other metadata, operations are provided to add, drop, or modify rules. In object-oriented systems such as HiPAC, rules are treated as first-class objects that are instances of rule types defined in the schema. These rule types are subtypes of a generic type **rule**. Rules are structured objects with events, conditions, and actions as their components. Like any object, rules can be created, deleted, or modified. In addition, rule objects have some special operations, including **fire**, which causes a rule to be triggered; **enable**, which causes a rule to be activated; and **disable**, which causes a rule to be deactivated (so that it won't be triggered even if its triggering event occurs).

Database rule languages vary considerably in the complexity of specifiable events, conditions, and actions. In some languages, the triggering event may be implicit—any relevant change to the database that can cause the condition to become true is treated as a triggering event. However, a key advantage of making events explicit is the flexibility gained in expressing transitions. For example, suppose it is desired to keep the salaries of two employees, Alice and Bob, the same. Suppose further that the following semantics are desired: If the constraint is violated because Alice's salary is changed by a user transaction, then change Bob's as well; however, if the constraint is violated because Bob's salary is changed by a user transaction, then abort the transaction. With explicit events, it becomes possible to specify these separate transitions.

In addition, some languages provide mechanisms whereby data (parameters) can be *bound* in the event and/or condition part of a rule and then passed to the condition and/or action. Some languages provide *rule ordering* as a conflict resolution mechanism. Finally, some languages provide mechanisms for organizing a large rule base. In the remainder of this section, we address each of these issues in further detail.

21.2.1 Event Specification

The most common triggering events in active database rule languages are modifications to the data in the database. In relational database systems, these modifications take place through **insert**, **delete**, and **update** commands; in object-oriented database systems, these modifications may also take place through method invocations. All active database systems support rules that are explicitly or implicitly triggered by database modifications. In a relational database system, a rule explicitly triggered by database modifications might look like:

```
define rule MonitorNewEmps
on insert to employee
if ...
then ...
```

where `employee` is a table of employee information. In an object-oriented database system, a rule explicitly triggered by database modifications might look like:

```
define rule CheckRaises
on employee.salary-raise()
if ...
then ...
```

where `salary-raise` is a method defined over objects in an `employee` class.

Some rule languages also allow rules to be triggered by data retrieval:

```
define rule MonitorSalAccess
on retrieve salary
from employee
if ...
then ...
```

Other database operations, such as transaction **commit**, **abort**, or **prepare-to-commit**, are allowed by some languages.

Some languages support rules triggered by *temporal events*. These might be absolute (e.g., `08:00:00 hours on 1 January 1994`), relative (e.g., `5 secs. after takeoff`), or periodic (e.g., `17:00:00 hours every Friday`).

Finally, a number of languages allow *composite events*, ranging from simple disjunctions of modification events to arbitrary combinations of events specified by powerful event composition operators.

The SQL2 standard allows *assertions* to be defined on tables. Each assertion is a simple rule that is triggered by one of the following events: **before commit**, **after insert**, **after delete**, or **after update** of a table. In the case of updates, a subset of the table's columns may be specified, so that the rule is triggered only when those columns are updated. The proposed SQL3 standard introduces **triggers** in addition to assertions (the difference will become clear when we discuss the action parts of these rules). The allowed triggering events are **before** or **after** an insertion, deletion, or update of a table.

The triggering events allowed in most relational research prototypes are similar to those for SQL2 assertions (although commit events typically are not allowed). Additionally, in Starburst, a rule may specify more than one modification operation on the same table; the rule is triggered when any of the operations occur (i.e., the event is a disjunction). In Ariel, the event may be omitted from a rule, in which case triggering is defined implicitly by the rule's condition. (Any event that causes the condition to be satisfied triggers the rule.) Postgres allows single explicit triggering events, which may be updates, some disjunctions of updates, or retrieval operations.

The object-oriented active database systems typically support a richer event specification language. In HiPAC, events can be generic database operations (**retrieve**, **insert**, **delete**, **update**), type-specific operations (method invocations) including operations on rule objects, transaction operations, temporal events, external events such as messages or signals from devices, and various compositions of these events, including disjunction, sequence, and repetition. Also, in HiPAC, events are defined to have formal parameters [e.g., `salary-raise(e:employee, oldsal:`

integer, newsal:integer)] has three parameters, e of type employee, and oldsal and newsal of type integer). When an instance of this event type occurs, the formal parameters are bound to a specific employee (the one whose salary is being updated) and two specific integers (this employee's old salary and new salary). Other object-oriented systems (e.g., DOM, Ode, Adam, Samos, and Sentinel) have proposed similar capabilities.

21.2.2 Condition Specification

In all database production rule languages, the condition part of a rule specifies a predicate or query over the data in the database. The condition is satisfied if the predicate is true or if the query returns a nonempty answer. When the event is explicit, the condition may often be omitted, in which case it is always satisfied. Many database rule languages allow conditions in rules triggered by database modifications to refer both to the modified data and to the database state preceding the triggering event. These mechanisms are described in section 21.2.4. With such mechanisms, *transition conditions*, which are conditions over changes in the database state, may be expressed.

In the commercial systems and in Ariel, Postgres, and Starburst, rule conditions are arbitrary predicates over the database state; modified data also can be referenced, so transition conditions can be specified. An example of such a rule is the following:

```
define rule MonitorRaise
on update to employee.salary
if employee.salary > 1.1 * old employee.salary
then ...
```

In SQL2 assertions, the condition also is a predicate, but the condition is satisfied if the predicate is false. In HiPAC, rule conditions are sets of predicates or queries on the database; if all the predicates are satisfied and all the queries' results are nonempty, then the condition is satisfied. Transition conditions may be expressed in HiPAC using the event parameter mechanism described in section 21.2.1.

21.2.3 Action Specification

The action part of a database production rule specifies the operations to be performed when the rule is triggered and its condition is satisfied. In AI rule languages, the action part of a rule usually inserts, deletes, or updates data in the working memory based on data matching the rule's condition. However, most database production rule languages allow more general rule actions.

In SQL2 assertions, the action part is implicit. When the condition is satisfied (i.e., when the predicate is false), the implicit action is to abort the current transaction.

In SQL3 triggers, Ariel, Postgres, and Starburst, rule actions can be arbitrary sequences of retrieval and modification commands over any data in the database. Rule actions also may specify **rollback** to abort the current transaction. All of these languages have a mechanism whereby rule actions can refer to the data whose modification caused the rule to be triggered (see section 21.2.4). Hence, if desired, rule actions can be based on triggering data as in AI rule languages. An example of this is the following:

```
define rule FavorNewEmps
on insert to employee
then delete employee e where e.name = employee.name
```

This rule is triggered whenever a new employee is inserted; its action deletes any existing employees with the same name. In Postgres, a rule's action may be tagged with the keyword **instead**, indicating that the action is to be executed instead of the triggering operation.

Rule actions in HiPAC can contain arbitrary database operations, transaction operations, rule operations, signals that user-defined events have occurred, or calls to application procedures.

21.2.4 Event-Condition-Action Binding

In AI rule languages such as OPS5, there is a link between the data that match a rule's condition and the behavior of the rule's action. Each time an OPS5 rule is executed, the variables in the condition are bound to data items in working memory that satisfy the condition, and these are then passed to the action.

Since database production rule languages may have explicitly specified events, and since they have different and more varied conditions and actions than OPS5 rules, the notion of binding also is different and more varied. In HiPAC, the triggering event of a rule may be parameterized, and these parameters may be referenced in the rule's condition and action. For example, if a rule is triggered by `salary-raise(e:employee, oldsal: integer, newsal:integer)`, then `e` in the condition or action refers to the employee object on which the method was invoked, and `oldsal` and `newsal` refer to the integers bound when the event occurred. For composite events, the parameters have to be accumulated before being passed to the condition and action. For example, for the repetition event `salary-raise*(e:employee, oldsal:integer, newsal:integer)`, which allows the `salary-raise` event to occur one or more times, the data passed to the condition is a multiset of 3-tuples of (`e`, `oldsal`, `newsal`) values, one for each occurrence of the `salary-raise` event. Recall that rule conditions in HiPAC can be sets of queries. The results of these queries can also be referenced (along with the event parameters) in rule actions.

In SQL2/SQL3, Ariel, Postgres, and Starburst, rules are (explicitly or implicitly) triggered by insertions, deletions, and/or updates on a particular table. Hence, each rule language has a mechanism whereby the inserted, deleted, or updated tuples can be referenced in rule conditions and actions.

In SQL2/SQL3 and Ariel, when a rule is triggered by a change to a table *T*, then any reference to *T* in the rule condition or action implicitly references the changed tuple. This is illustrated by the following SQL3 trigger:

```
create trigger DeptDel
before delete on department
when department.budget < 100,000
delete employee where employee.dno = department.dno
```

This rule is triggered before the deletion of a department; the condition (**when clause**) and action refer to the department being deleted.

Old and new values of updated tuples can also be referenced in the condition and action parts, as illustrated by rule MonitorRaise in section 21.2.2. SQL2 assertions use the keywords **old** and **new**. SQL3 triggers allow the trigger definition statement to give specific correlation names to the old and new values; these names are then used in the condition and action. In Ariel, the old value is referenced using the keyword **previous**. The entire table on which the change occurs, rather than just the changed tuples, can also be referenced in the condition and action parts. This is achieved through the use of *tuple variables* or *synonyms* as illustrated by the rule FavorNewEmps in section 21.2.3.

In Postgres, the event-condition binding is similar: A reference to the table whose change triggered the rule implicitly references the changed tuple. However, in the action part, a reference to the table whose change triggered the rule produces the entire table. To reference the modified tuple before and after the triggering event, Postgres uses the special tuple variables **new** and **old**. For example, the FavorNewEmps rule in section 21.2.3 would be written in Postgres as follows:

```
define rule FavorNewEmps
on append to employee
then delete employee where employee.name = new.name
```

In Starburst, a single rule triggering may involve arbitrary combinations of inserted, deleted, and updated tuples (as will be described in section 21.3). These changes may be referenced in the condition and action part of a Starburst rule using *transition tables*. Transition tables are logical tables that are referenced just like database tables. At rule execution time, transition table **inserted** contains the tuples that were inserted to trigger the rule, transition table **deleted** contains the tuples that were deleted to trigger the rule, and transition tables **new-updated** and **old-updated** contain the new and old values, respectively, of the tuples that were updated to trigger the rule. As an example, the following Starburst rule aborts the transaction whenever the average of updated employee salaries exceeds 100:

```
define rule AvgTooBig
on update to employee.salary
if (select avg(salary) from new-updated) > 100
then rollback
```

21.2.5 Rule Ordering

SQL2 and SQL3 do not allow more than one rule to be defined with the same triggering event, hence conflict resolution is never needed. However, most other rule languages do not impose such a severe syntactic restriction. In many active database systems, the choice of which rule to execute when more than one is triggered is made more or less arbitrarily, although some languages do provide features whereby the rule definer can influence conflict resolution.

Various features have been considered for Postgres, including *numeric priorities* and *exception hierarchies*, but none have been incorporated to date. In Starburst, rules are *partially ordered*. That is, for any two rules, one rule can be specified as having higher priority than the other rule, but an ordering is not required. In Ariel, rules have numeric priorities. Each rule is assigned a floating point number between -1000 and 1000; if no number is specified explicitly then a default of 0 is assigned. HiPAC departs from other active database systems in that multiple triggered rules are executed concurrently (see section 21.3.5). Even so, HiPAC includes a mechanism whereby rules can be relatively ordered to influence the serialization order of concurrent execution.

21.2.6 Rule Organization

Since the number of rules defined in an active database system may be very large, some languages include mechanisms for organizing the collection of rules. Also, some include mechanisms for selectively activating and deactivating rules as a way of controlling the number of rules that must be monitored by the system at any given time.

In relational systems, rules are defined in the schema. Rules refer to particular tables, and so are subject to the same controls as other metadata objects (e.g., views, constraints); thus, if a table is dropped, all rules defined for it are no longer operative. No special mechanisms are provided for organizing the rules in a schema.

In HiPAC, rules are first-class objects. Hence, they can be organized in types like any other objects. Rule types can participate in subtype hierarchies, they can have attributes, and they can be related to other objects. Like other objects, rules can be included in collections, which may be explicitly named or defined by queries. For example, one can define the collection

```
{r in Flight-rule where Effective-date(r) after 1/1/90}
```

where `Flight-rule` is a rule type and `Effective-date` is an attribute defined for this type. Collections of rules can be selectively activated and deactivated using the **enable** and **disable** operations. These can be invoked from within a user transaction or in the actions of other rules.

21.3 Rule Execution Semantics

The semantics of a database production rule language determines how rule processing will take place at run-time once a set of rules has been defined, including how rules will interact with the arbitrary database operations and transactions that are submitted by users and application programs. Even for relatively small rule sets, rule behavior can be complex and unpredictable, so a precise execution semantics is very important.

As explained in section 21.1, in AI rule languages, rules are processed by an inference engine that cycles through all rules in the system, in each cycle finding those rules whose conditions are true and choosing one such rule whose action is then executed. In active database systems, this approach is not always appropriate or adequate. Most importantly, unlike in AI systems, in active database systems rule processing is integrated with conventional database activity—queries, modifications, and transactions—and it is this activity that causes rules to become triggered and initiates rule processing. Furthermore, during rule processing in an active database system, it may be too inefficient to determine, in each cycle, the entire set of rules whose conditions are true.

As with the rule language itself, there are a number of alternatives for rule execution, and there is considerable variance in the semantics taken by existing active database systems. One issue considered by active database system designers is the *granularity* of rule processing, especially for rules that are triggered by modification events. Since in most database system languages, operations work on sets of tuples (or sets of objects), there is a choice of firing the rule after each tuple (or object) is modified or once for the entire set of modifications specified by the operation. Other choices are possible; for instance, rules may be fired at the end of an entire transaction.

Another issue is whether more than one rule can be triggered by the same event; some languages preclude this, and others allow it. If it is allowed, then is the execution sequential, using some form of conflict resolution to select one rule at a time, or can rules execute concurrently? Some languages have sequential execution semantics, while others allow concurrent execution. With either sequential or concurrent execution semantics, there is also the issue of whether one rule can trigger the execution of another rule or of (another instance of) the same rule. Clearly, if such nested triggering is allowed, termination is a concern.

Finally, the interplay between rule execution and the execution of user-initiated transactions is also an issue. Some systems execute rules within the scope of the triggering transaction—that is, the transaction in which the triggering event occurred. Others allow more flexible scoping of rules and transactions.

In this section, we separately consider the four example active database systems we have been discussing—Ariel, Postgres, Starburst, and HiPAC—and describe each system's approach to run-time rule execution. We also describe the semantics of rule execution in SQL2 and SQL3 and briefly consider the issue of error recovery during rule processing. For convenience, in the remainder of this section we use the term database *user* to mean user or application program.

21.3.1 Ariel

In Ariel, rules are triggered by *transitions*, which are database modifications induced either by a single database command or by a sequence of commands grouped together by the user to delineate rule processing. Since a single data modification command in relational systems such as Ariel is a set-oriented **insert**, **delete**, or **update** operation, the minimum granularity of rule processing in Ariel is a set of tuple-level operations. Commands grouped together may constitute an entire transaction, but they may not span transactions, so the maximum rule-processing granularity is an entire transaction. Rule processing is invoked automatically at the end of each transition and takes place as part of the transaction containing the transition. Once rule processing begins, Ariel uses a cycling inference engine similar to that used by AI rule languages.

Recall from section 21.2.4 that Ariel rule actions can reference the data whose modification triggered the rule. Since Ariel rules may be triggered by sets of changes, these references may correspond to sets of tuples rather than single tuples. As an example, consider the following rule:

```
define rule MonitorNewBobs
on insert to employee
if employee.name = "Bob"
then retrieve employee
```

If multiple tuples are inserted into the employee table before this rule is executed, then the rule's action will retrieve all of the inserted tuples whose value in column `name` is `Bob`. In general, when a triggered rule is executed in Ariel, the rule processes the entire set of triggering changes, including both the user-generated changes that initiated rule processing and any subsequent changes made by rule actions. If a rule is executed multiple times during rule processing (e.g., because it is retriggered by another rule's changes or because it triggers itself), then each time it executes, it processes all matching changes since the last time it executed. If **rollback** is executed in a rule action, then rule processing terminates and the transaction is aborted.

Recall from section 21.2.5 that each Ariel rule is assigned a numeric priority but that the assignments need not be unique. Hence, when multiple rules are triggered, conflict resolution in Ariel proceeds as follows:

1. Pick the rule(s) with highest numeric priority.
2. If there's a tie, pick the rule(s) most recently matched by changes.
3. If there's still a tie, pick the rule(s) whose condition is the most selective.
4. If there's still a tie, pick a rule arbitrarily.

Finally, note that when Ariel rules are processed after a transition, the rules actually consider the *net effect* of the modifications in the transition, rather than the individual modifications. In most cases the net effect is the same as the individual modifications. However, in some cases there is a difference: If a tuple is updated several times in a transition, the net effect is a single update; if a tuple is updated and then deleted, the net effect is deletion of the original tuple; if a tuple is inserted and then updated, the net effect is insertion of the updated tuple; and if a tuple is inserted and then deleted, the net effect is no modification at all.

21.3.2 Postgres

In Postgres, rule processing is invoked immediately after any modification to any tuple that triggers and satisfies the condition of one or more rules. This sometimes is referred to as *tuple-oriented* rule processing, as opposed to Ariel's *set-oriented* rule processing. Recall that rule actions in Postgres are arbitrary database operations. Hence, when a rule's action is executed, it may modify multiple additional tuples, each of which may (immediately) trigger additional rules. Consequently, rule processing in Postgres is inherently recursive and synchronous (similar to a procedure call mechanism), rather than sequential as in Ariel. The basic rule-processing algorithm in Postgres is described as follows:

1. Some (user- or rule-generated) tuple modification occurs.
2. The modification triggers and satisfies the conditions of rules R_1, R_2, ..., R_n.
3. For each rule R_i execute R_i's action.

As mentioned above, action execution (step 3) can perform tuple modifications that recursively invoke this rule processing algorithm. There is no conflict resolution mechanism in Postgres—triggered rules are executed in arbitrary order. If **rollback** is executed in a rule action, then rule processing terminates and the transaction is aborted.

As a simple example of the difference between tuple-oriented and set-oriented rule processing in relational systems, consider the following rule:

```
define rule SetSalary
on insert to employee
then begin
      starting-salary := select avg(salary)
           from employee) - 10 ;
      update employee (salary = starting-salary)
           where employee.id = new.id
     end
```

This rule is triggered by insertions into the employee table; its action sets the starting salary for inserted employees to 10 less than the average employee salary. Suppose a set of new employees is inserted. In a tuple-oriented rule system such as Postgres, this rule is triggered once for each inserted employee, so the salaries of the new employees differ. In a set-oriented rule system such as Ariel, this rule is triggered only once, so the salaries of the new employees are the same.

21.3.3 Starburst

In Starburst, rule processing is invoked automatically at the end of each user transaction that triggers one or more rules. In addition, users can invoke rule processing within transactions by issuing special commands. Hence, as in Ariel, the minimum rule-processing granularity is a single relational database command (i.e., a set of tuple-level operations) and the maximum granularity is an entire transaction.

We first explain end-of-transaction rule processing in Starburst and then describe rule processing within transactions in response to user commands. Recall that Starburst rules may be triggered by inserts, deletes, and/or updates; a rule is triggered whenever one or more of its triggering operations occurs. During Starburst rule processing, the first time a triggered rule is executed it considers all modifications since the start of the transaction, including the user modifications and any subsequent modifications made by rules. If the rule is triggered additional times, it considers all modifications since the last time it was triggered. Like Ariel's, Starburst's rules consider the net effect of sets of modifications, rather than the individual modifications (recall section 21.3.1).

Starburst rule processing uses an inference engine similar to AI rule languages and to Ariel. However, in each cycle Starburst determines the rules that are triggered but does not eliminate those whose condition is false—a triggered rule's condition is not evaluated until the rule is selected for consideration. For conflict resolution, recall that Starburst rules may be assigned relative priorities. Hence, when a triggered rule is selected for condition evaluation and possible execution, it is selected such that no other triggered rule has higher priority.

In addition to automatic rule processing at the end of each transaction, rule processing in Starburst is invoked within transactions when the user issues one of three commands: **process rules**, **process ruleset** *S*, or **process rule** *R*. Command **process rules** invokes the same rule-processing algorithm that is invoked at transaction end. Command **process ruleset** S also invokes rule processing but only for those rules in the user-defined rule set *S*. Command **process rule** *R* is similar, except that only rule *R* can be triggered or executed. Regardless of whether a rule is executed in response to one of these commands or in response to end-of-transaction rule processing, the semantics is the same: The rule considers the entire set of modifications since it was last considered within the transaction or since the start of the transaction if it has not yet been considered. As in the other systems, if **rollback** is executed in a rule action, then rule processing terminates and the transaction is aborted.

21.3.4 SQL2 and SQL3

SQL2 and SQ3 permit both tuple-level and set-level processing of assertions and triggers. The choice is made at rule definition time by specifying a **for each row** option (which induces tuple-level processing) or omitting it. Recall that assertions can be defined with a database modification command as the triggering event or with the special event **before commit**. In either case, the condition is evaluated over the current state of the database, including all modifications made since the start of the transaction. Triggers are triggered by database modifications; they can refer to the states of the modified table prior to (**old**) or immediately following (**new**) the modification.

Rule processing is strictly sequential. No conflict resolution is necessary since no two rules can be defined to have the same triggering event. Further, additional syntactic restrictions on rule definitions ensure that the same table cannot be modified multiple times in a sequence of rule firings, thereby ensuring termination. Note that none of the other systems guarantees termination.

	C-A Mode		
E-C Mode	immediate	deferred	decoupled
immediate	condition checked and action executed after event	condition checked after event, action executed at end of transaction	condition checked after event, action executed in separate transaction
deferred	not allowed	condition checked and action executed at end of transaction	condition checked at end of transaction, action executed in separate transaction
decoupled	condition checked and action executed in separate transaction	not allowed	condition checked in one separate transaction, action executed in a different separate transaction

FIGURE 21–1
Coupling Modes in HiPAC

21.3.5 HiPAC

Before describing run-time rule processing in HiPAC, it is necessary to introduce the concept of *coupling modes.* Coupling modes originated in the HiPAC project but subsequently have been discussed in the context of other active database systems, (e.g., Anwar and Mangis 1993; Buchmann 1990; Gatziu and Geppert 1991; Gehani and Jagadish 1991; Schreier et al. 1991). Coupling modes determine how rule events, conditions, and actions relate to database transactions. Whereas in Ariel, Postgres, Starburst, and many other active database systems, rule conditions are evaluated and actions are executed in the same transaction as the triggering event, in HiPAC this is not always the case. The rule definer has the flexibility of deciding whether or not the conditions and actions should execute in the triggering transaction.

Let *E, C,* and *A* denote the event, condition, and action, respectively, of a rule. Associated with each HiPAC rule is an *E-C coupling mode* and a *C-A coupling mode*. The E-C coupling mode determines when the rule's condition is executed with respect to the triggering event, and the C-A coupling mode determines when the rule's action is executed with respect to the condition. Each coupling mode is *immediate,* indicating immediate execution; *deferred,* indicating execution at the end of the current transaction; or *decoupled,* indicating execution in a separate transaction. Not all combinations of coupling modes make sense; Fig. 21–1 shows the seven combinations that are allowed and the two that are not. For each of these combinations, it is relatively easy to construct an active database application for which that behavior seems most appropriate. In addition, for the decoupled mode, a *causality* constraint can optionally be specified; if specified, this constraint means that the triggered transaction can commit only if the triggering transaction commits, and the triggered transaction must follow the triggering transaction in the serialization ordering.

Rule processing in HiPAC is invoked whenever any event occurs that triggers one or more rules. As mentioned in section 21.2.5, HiPAC differs considerably from most other active database systems in its handling of multiple triggered rules. Rather than selecting one triggered rule to execute using some form of conflict resolution, HiPAC executes all triggered rules concurrently. If, during rule execution, additional rules are triggered, they also are executed concurrently. To do this, HiPAC uses an extension of the *nested transaction* model of execution [Moss 1985], which lends itself well to this rule-processing semantics and to the realization of coupling modes.

The basic rule-processing algorithm in HiPAC is described as follows:

1. Some (user- or rule-generated) event triggers rules R_1, R_2,..., *Rn*.
2. For each rule R_i schedule a transaction to
   a. evaluate R_i's condition
   b. if the condition is true, schedule a transaction to execute R_i's action

Transaction scheduling in step 2 is based on R_i's E-C coupling mode, while transaction scheduling in step 2b is based on R_i's C-A coupling mode: Immediate mode causes a nested subtransaction to be spawned immediately, deferred mode causes a nested subtransaction to be spawned at the commit point of the current transaction, and decoupled mode causes a separate (top-level) transaction to be spawned. Note that both condition evaluation and action execution (steps 2a and 2b) can generate events that recursively invoke this rule-processing algorithm. Finally, as mentioned in section 21.2.5, HiPAC rules may have relative ordering, and this ordering is used to influence the serialization order of concurrently executing nested subtransactions.

21.3.6 Error Recovery

One issue not yet fully addressed in many active database systems is the semantics of error recovery during rule processing. A database rule may generate an error during its execution for a number of reasons—for example, because data it read has been deleted, because data access privileges have been revoked, because concurrently executing transactions have created a deadlock, because of a system-generated error, or because the rule action itself has uncovered an error condition.

Errors such as missing data or revoked privileges can usually be avoided in any database system with a sophisticated enough dependency-tracking facility. In such systems, when a data item is deleted or privileges ɔked, rules that depend on their existence are invalidated. Most ꞓ rule systems handle errors during rule processing by aborting the current transaction, since this is how conventional database systems typically handle errors during transaction processing. However, in the case of error conditions produced by rule actions, this is not the only possible reasonable behavior. Other alternatives are to terminate execution of that rule and continue rule processing, to return to the state preceding rule processing and resume database processing, or to restart rule processing.

The nested transaction model used in HiPAC allows some of these possibilities. When a rule execution subtransaction fails, the failure event is returned to its parent, which has the option of spawning a sibling subtransaction to repair the error (this may be accomplished through the firing of another rule that is triggered by the failure event). Alternatively, failure can be propagated up the transaction tree all the way to the root (top) transaction.

Another issue is how to recover events after system crashes. For events that are database operations, there is no problem: These are recovered as part of normal transaction recovery. For temporal or external events (such as those supported by HiPAC), events have to be declared to be recoverable or not; for recoverable events, their occurrences and parameter bindings have to be reliably logged. As part of recovery, uncommitted transactions (for the decoupled conditions and actions) triggered by the recovered event signals have to be restarted.

21.4 Implementation Issues

Active database systems must support all the features provided by conventional database systems, including data definition, data manipulation, storage management, transaction management, concurrency control, and crash recovery. In addition, active database systems must provide mechanisms for event detection and rule triggering, for condition testing, for rule action execution, and for user development of rule applications.

21.4.1 Characteristics of Representative Systems

The Ariel active database system is built using the *Exodus* database toolkit [Carey et al. 1991]. The focus of Ariel's implementation is on efficient condition testing, which is achieved by incorporating a highly tuned *discrimination network* that extends the *Rete* and *TREAT* networks used by AI rule languages [Wang and Hanson 1992]. When data modification commands are executed in Ariel, the modified tuples are packaged as *tokens* and passed to the discrimination network, where rule conditions are tested. In addition, the Ariel architecture includes the following components:

- A *rule manager/rule catalog* for handling rule definition and manipulation tasks.
- A *rule execution monitor* for maintaining the set of triggered rules and scheduling their execution.
- A *rule action planner*, which is invoked by the rule execution monitor to produce optimized execution strategies for database commands occurring in rule actions; these commands are executed by the same query processor that executes user commands.

In Postgres, two different mechanisms are implemented for rules: *tuple-level* processing and *query rewrite*. When a rule is created, the user selects which mechanism is to be used for that rule. Tuple-level processing places a *marker* on each tuple for each rule that has a condition matching that tuple. When a tuple is modified or retrieved, if the tuple has one or more markers on it, then the rule or rules associated with the marker(s) are located and their actions are executed. Markers must be installed and removed when rules and data are created, deleted, and modified. In contrast, the query rewrite implementation consists of a module between the command parser and the query processor. This module intercepts each user command and augments it with additional commands reflecting the effects of rules triggered by the original command. Since the additional commands also may trigger rules, query rewrite must be applied recursively; in some cases, it may not terminate. However, when applicable, the compile-time approach of query rewrite can be considerably more efficient than the run-time approach of tuple-level processing. Unfortunately, the semantics can differ between the two approaches, as explained in Stonebraker and Kemnitz 1991.

The Starburst database system has as one of its primary goals *extensibility* [Haas et al. 1990], and the rule system implementation relies on Starburst's extensibility features. The *attachment* feature is used to monitor data modifications that are of interest to rules. These modifications are stored in a main-memory data structure called a *transition log*. When rules are processed at the end of a transaction or in response to a user command, the transition log is consulted to determine which rules are triggered. Triggered rules are indexed in a sort structure reflecting rule priorities; rule conditions are evaluated and actions are executed through Starburst's normal query processor. References to transition tables (recall section 21.2.4) are implemented using Starburst's *table function* feature: Table functions for each of the four transition tables use the transition log to produce appropriate tuples at run time. The Starburst rule system also includes components for concurrency control, authorization, and crash recovery.

The HiPAC architecture extends an object-oriented database system with a *rule manager*, which coordinates rule processing, and *event detectors* for the different types of events. It also extends the functions of the *object manager* to store rule objects and implement operations on them and the functions of the transaction manager to implement the coupling modes of the execution model and to provide concurrency control and recovery for rule objects in addition to data objects. Algorithms for incremental evaluation of rule conditions after database modifications were also developed. There are three different main-memory prototype implementations of HiPAC. The most substantial of these is a Smalltalk-80 implementation, which includes both a rule manager and a transaction manager. Concurrent transactions are implemented as Smalltalk *threads* (i.e., lightweight processes). A unique feature of this implementation is its support for bidirectional interaction between application programs and the database rule system: Applications can invoke database operations, and rules running inside the database can invoke application operations.

21.4.2 Rule Programming Support

The implementation of an active database system can include many useful features that support the rule programmer. Features for analyzing rule processing include the abilities to trace rule execution, to display the current set of triggered rules, to query and browse the set of rules, and to cross-reference rules and data. Other useful features include the abilities to control errors in rule programs, to activate and deactivate selected rules or groups of rules while the database system is processing transactions, and to experiment with rules on an off-line subset of a working database. Simple versions of some of these features exist in some active database systems, while more sophisticated and complete versions will certainly emerge over time.

21.4.3 Rule Termination

Rule processing is subject to infinite loops—that is, rules may trigger one another indefinitely. In a database system, this behavior can be catastrophic; for example, rules could erroneously fill the disk with data by repeatedly performing inserts on a table, eventually crashing the system. At the very least, a transaction in which rules are looping would surely inhibit concurrency (by holding locks on data) and saturate memory buffers, slowing system throughput. Recall that SQL2 and SQL3 avoid this problem by imposing sufficient syntactic restrictions on rule definitions; however, these restrictions are very strong and limit the expressiveness of the rule language. In general, given the power of the other rule languages discussed in this survey, it is an undecidable problem to determine in advance whether rules are guaranteed to terminate, although conservative algorithms have been proposed that warn the rule programmer when looping is possible [Aiken et al. 1992]. A run-time solution to detecting and preventing infinite loops is to provide a rule triggering limit. In this case, the number of rules executed during rule processing is monitored; if the limit is reached, rule processing is terminated. Most active database systems provide such a limit, specified by the user and/or by a system default. Another mechanism is to detect if the same rule is triggered a second time with the same set of parameters.

21.5 Conclusions and Future Directions

This chapter has provided an overview of active database systems, including database production rule models and languages, rule execution semantics, and implementation issues. The rules provided by active database systems can be used for integrity constraint enforcement, derived data maintenance, authorization checking, versioning, and many other database system applications; they also enable more advanced and powerful applications, and they provide a platform for large and efficient knowledge-base and expert systems.

The theory and technology of active database systems is still maturing. There are several areas that researchers and practitioners will likely address in the future, particularly as active databases emerge in the commercial arena. These include the following:

Support for application development: In section 21.4.2, we described a number of features, not present in many active database system prototypes, that are vital for the development of database rule applications. One suggested approach to application development treats database rules as assembly language, automatically generating rules from higher-level specifications [Ceri 1992; Ceri and Widom 1990, 1991]. While this approach works well for a number of standard applications, there will always be a need to develop applications using rules directly. In addition, considerable work is needed on increasing the communication capability between database rules and applications.

Increasing the expressive power of rules: Some applications may need the ability to define rules with more complex triggering events, conditions, or actions than currently can be expressed in database rule languages. Methods for increasing the expressiveness of database rule language while maintaining an efficient implementation deserve further study.

Improved algorithms: Efficient algorithms for processing rules are crucial for delivering the functionality of active databases without excessively degrading the performance of conventional database processing. While some work has been done in this area, continued improvements are needed.

Distribution and parallelism: So far, active databases have been considered primarily in centralized database environments. An initial consideration of the problem of rule processing in distributed and parallel environments appears in Ceri and Widom 1992, but this is only a theoretical study relating to a particular rule language. Many issues arise when considering a distributed or parallel active database system, including the distribution and fragmentation of rules and algorithms that guarantee equivalence with centralized rule processing. Note that, even in centralized database systems, parallelism might be exploited to improve the performance of rule processing.

REFERENCES

Aiken, A., Widom, J., and Hellerstein, J. M. 1992. Behavior of Database Production Rules: Termination, Confluence, and Observable Determinism. *Proceedings of the ACM-SIGMOD International Conference on Management of Data.*

Anwar, E., and Maugis, S. C. 1993. A New Perspective on Rule Support for Object-Oriented Databases. *Proceedings of the ACM-SIGMOD International Conference on Mangement of Data.*

Beeri, C., and Milo, T. 1991. A Model for Active Object Oriented Database. *Proceedings of the Seventeenth International Conference on Very Large Data Bases.*

Brownston, L., Farrell, R., Kant, E., and Martin, N. 1985. *Programming Expert Systems in OPS5: An Introduction to Rule-Based Programming.* Addison-Wesley, Reading, Mass.

Buchmann, A. 1990. Modelling Heterogeneous Systems as a Space of Active Objects. *Proceedings of the Fourth International Workshop on Persistent Object Bases.*

Carey, M., et al. 1991. The Architecture of the Exodus Extensible DBMS. In: *Object-Oriented Database Systems.* K. Dittrich, U. Dayal, and A. Buchmann, eds. Springer-Verlag, Berlin.

Ceri, S. 1992. A Declarative Approach to Active Databases. *Proceedings of the Eighth International Conference on Data Engineering.*

Ceri, S., and Widom, J. 1990. Deriving Production Rules for Constraint Maintenance. *Proceedings of the Sixteenth International Conference on Very Large Data Bases.*

Ceri, S., and Widom, J. 1991. Deriving Production Rules for Incremental View Maintenance. *Proceedings of the Seventeenth International Conference on Very Large Data Bases.*

Ceri, S., and Widom, J. 1992. Production Rules in Parallel and Distributed Database Environments. *Proceedings of the Eighteenth International Conference on Very Large Data Bases.*

Chakravarthy, S., et al. 1989. *HiPAC: A Research Project in Active, Time-Constrained Database Management (Final Report).* Technical Report XAIT-89-02, Xerox Advanced Information Technology, Cambridge, Mass.

Cohen, D. 1989. Compiling Complex Database Transition Triggers. *Proceedings of the ACM-SIGMOD International Conference on Management of Data.*

Dayal, U. 1988. Active Database Management Systems. *Proceedings of the Third International Conference on Data and Knowledge Bases.*

Dayal, U., et al. 1988. The HiPAC Project: Combining Active Databases and Timing Constraints. *SIGMOD Record*, Vol. 17, No. 1, 51–70.

Delcambre, L. M. L., and Etheredge, J. N. 1988. The Relational Production Language: A Production Language for Relational Databases. *Proceedings of the Second International Conference on Expert Database Systems.*

Diaz, O., Patom, N., and Gray, P. 1991. Rule Management in Object-Oriented Databases: A Uniform Approach. *Proceedings of the Seventeenth International Conference on Very Large Data Bases.*

Eswaran, K. P. 1976. *Specifications, Implementations and Interactions of a Trigger Subsystem in an Integrated Database System.* Technical Report RJ 1820, IBM Research Laboratory, San Jose, Cal.

Gatziu, A. S., and Geppert, K. D. 1991. Integrating Active Concepts into an Object-Oriented Database System. *Proceedings of the Third International Workshop on Database Programming Languages.*

Gehani, N., and Jagadish, H. V. 1991. Ode as an Active Database: Constraints and Triggers. *Proceedings of the Seventeenth International Conference on Very Large Data Bases.*

Haas, L., et al. 1990. Starburst Mid-Flight: As the Dust Clears. *IEEE Transactions on Knowledge and Data Engineering*, Vol. 2, No. 1, 143–160.

Hanson, E. N. 1992. Rule Condition Testing and Action Execution in Ariel. *Proceedings of the ACM-SIGMOD International Conference on Management of Data.*

Howe, L. 1986. *Sybase Data Integrity for On-Line Applications.* Technical report, Sybase Inc.

INGRES. 1992. *INGRES/SQL Reference Manual*, Version 6.4. ASK Computer Co.

Kotz, A. M., Dittrich, K. R., and Mulle, J.A. 1988. Supporting Semantic Rules by a Generalized Event/Trigger Mechanism. *Proceedings of the International Conference on Extending Data Base Technology.*

McCarthy, D. R., and Dayal, U. 1989. The Architecture of an Active Database Management System. *Proceedings of the ACM-SIGMOD International Conference on Management of Data.*

Morgenstern, M. 1983. Active Databases as a Paradigm for Enhanced Computing Environments. *Proceedings of the Ninth International Conference on Very Large Data Bases.*

Moss, E. 1985. *Nested Transactions: An Approach to Reliable Distributed Computing.* MIT Press, Cambridge, Mass.

ORACLE. 1992. *ORACLE7 Reference Manual.* ORACLE Corporaton.

Rdb. 1991. *Rdb/VMS—SQL Reference Manual.* Digital Equipment Corporation.

Schreier, U., Pirahesh, H., Agrawal, R., and Mohan, C. 1991. Alert: An Architecture for Transforming a Passive DBMS into an Active DBMS. *Proceedings of the Seventeenth International Conference on Very Large Data Bases.*

Simon, E., Kiernan, J., and de Maindreville, C. 1992. Implementing High-Level Active Rules on Top of Relational Databases. *Proceedings of the Eighteenth International Conference on Very Large Data Bases.*

Stonebraker, M., et al. 1982. A Rules System for a Relational Database Management System. *Proceedings of the Second International Conference on Databases.*

Stonebraker, M., Jhingran, A., Goh, J., and Potamianos, S. 1990. On Rules, Procedures, Caching and Views in Data Base Systems. *Proceedings of the ACM-SIGMOD International Conference on Management of Data.*

Stonebraker, M. and Kemnitz, G. 1991. The Postgres Next-Generation Database Management System. *Communications of the ACM,* Vol. 34, No. 10, 78–92.

Wang, Y.-W., and Hanson, E. N. 1992. A Performance Comparison of the Rete and TREAT Algorithms for Testing Database Rule Conditions. *Proceedings of the Eighth International Conference on Data Engineering.*

Widom, J., Cochrane, R. J., and Lindsay, B. G. 1991. Implementing Set-Oriented Production Rules as an Extension to Starburst. *Proceedings of the Seventeenth International Conference on Very Large Data Bases.*

Widom, J., and Finkelstein, S. J. 1990. Set-Oriented Production Rules in Relational Database Systems. *Proceedings of the ACM-SIGMOD International Conference on Management of Data.*

22

Management of Uncertainty in Database Systems

AMIHAI MOTRO

As models of the real world, databases are often permeated with forms of uncertainty, including imprecision, incompleteness, vagueness, inconsistency, and ambiguity. This chapter addresses issues of database uncertainty. It defines basic terminology, and it classifies the various kinds of uncertainty. It then surveys solutions that have been attempted, and it speculates on the reasons that have hindered the development of general-purpose database systems with powerful uncertainty capabilities. Finally, it describes challenging new applications that will require such capabilities, and it points to promising directions for research.

22.1 Introduction

Database systems model our knowledge of the real world.[1] This knowledge is often permeated with uncertainty. Hence, database systems must be able to deal with uncertainty. And, indeed, most database systems include capabilities for dealing with some kinds of uncertainty—for example, many systems are able to represent missing values with nulls, and most query languages admit some form of uncertain queries by allowing users to substitute patterns for constants.

Yet these capabilities are weak in comparison with the variety and degree of uncertainty that are encountered in practice. While the research community has shown persistent interest in this subject, most of these efforts have yet to transcend experimental prototypes. By and large, commercial database systems have been slow to incorporate capabilities for dealing with uncertainty.

Nevertheless, many new applications require uncertainty capabilities (see section 22.5), and without general systems that possess these capabilities, these applications are usually handled in an ad hoc manner. Undoubtedly, the development of a suitable database theory to deal with uncertain

1. We use the term *database system* in a broad sense, to include related types of information systems such as *information retrieval systems* and *expert systems*.

database information and uncertain database transactions, and the successful deployment of this theory in an actual database system, remain challenges that have yet to be met.

This chapter addresses issues of database uncertainty. It defines basic terminology and classifies the various kinds of uncertainty. It then surveys solutions that have been attempted, and it speculates on the reasons that have hindered the development of general-purpose database systems with powerful uncertainty capabilities. Finally, it describes new challenging applications that will require such capabilities, and it points to promising directions for research.

Undoubtedly, the best known issue of uncertainty is the representation of unknown values with nulls and the evaluation of queries in the presence of such nulls. Yet uncertainty permeates many additional aspects of databases, including the definitions of database transactions and even the processing of transactions.

We therefore devote a substantial part of this chapter (sections 22.2, 22.3, and 22.4) to study the different forms of uncertainty and to evaluate the work that has already been done in this area. Section 22.2 provides basic definitions, including a simple and general model of database systems. This model allows us to classify uncertainty into three main categories: *Description uncertainty* refers to uncertainty in the information stored in databases (e.g., data, constraints, or rules), *transaction uncertainty* refers to uncertainty in the operations that manipulate this information (e.g., queries, updates, and re-structuring operations), and *processing uncertainty* refers to uncertainty arising in the application of transactions to descriptions. The main approaches are then studied in sections 22.3 and 22.4. In sections 22.5 and 22.6, we speculate on the reasons commercial database systems have been slow to incorporate capabilities for dealing with uncertainty. We then describe several applications that challenge present database systems by requiring more powerful methods for dealing with uncertainty, and we point to some promising areas of research; in particular, we postulate that suitable solutions could come from fusing database technology with various theories of artificial intelligence.

22.2 Terminology

Our discussion of uncertainty in database systems begins with definitions of database systems and uncertainty.

22.2.1 Database System

A database system is a computer model of some portion of the real world. Like any other model, it abstracts reality to a level warranted by the expected applications. Usually, such models include a declarative component for *describing* the real world and an operational component for *manipulating* this description. Typical manipulations are (1) *modifications* of the description, either to refine the model or to track any changes that may have occurred in the real world; and (2) *transformations* of the description, to derive implied descriptions.

Thus, a database system can be abstracted as a description D of the real world, a stream of modifications, and a stream of transformations. Each modification m replaces the present description with a new description; each transformation t computes a new description from the present description (without changing the present description). A computer system S is responsible for maintaining the description reliably and for processing the modifications and transformations correctly and efficiently.

As an example, in a relational database system a description is a set of tables (i.e., a database); a modification can affect either the definition or the contents of tables (i.e., restructuring or update); and a transformation reduces the set of tables into a single table (i.e., query evaluation).

22.2.2 Uncertainty

We assume that uncertainty permeates our *models* of the real world, not the real world itself. In other words, the real world is always certain; it is our knowledge of it that is sometimes uncertain. We use the term *uncertainty* to refer to any element of the model that cannot be asserted with complete confidence. In particular, uncertainty can be expected (1) in the descriptions of the real world, (2) in the modifications and transformations of these descriptions, and (3) in the execution of these operations. Referring again to the example of relational database systems, these correspond to the data, the definitions of restructuring, update and query transactions, and the processing of transactions.

We have offered the general term *uncertainty* to describe any element of the model that cannot be asserted with complete confidence. Within this general condition, we observe several distinct types of uncertainty:[2]

- *Uncertainty*—it is not possible to determine whether an assertion in the model is *true* or *false*. For example, there might be uncertainty about the database fact "the age of John is 38."
- *Imprecision*—the information available in the model is not as specific as it should be. For example, when a distinct value is required, the information available might be a *range* (e.g., "the age of John is between 37 and 43"), *disjunctive* (e.g., "the age of John is either 37 or 43"), *negative*

2. One of these specific types will also be termed *uncertainty*; thus, depending on the context, this term will be used both generically and specifically.

(e.g., "the age of John is not 37"), or even *unknown* (often referred to as *incompleteness*).

- *Vagueness*—the model includes elements (e.g., predicates or quantifiers) that are inherently vague; for example, "John is in early middle age." A particular formalization of vagueness is based on the concept of *fuzziness*.
- *Inconsistency*—the model contains two or more assertions that cannot be true at the same time; for example, "the age of John is between 37 and 43" and "the age of John is 35."
- *Ambiguity*—some elements of the model lack complete semantics, leading to several possible interpretations. For example, it may not be clear whether stated salaries are per year or per month.

The objective of a database system is to provide its users with the information they need. In our terminology, such information is always the result *t(D)* of transforming a description *D* with a transformation *t*. Thus, it is the quality of *t(D)*, rather than the quality of *D*, that should concern the designers and users of database systems. A result *t(D)* may be uncertain because *D* is uncertain, or because *t* is uncertain, or because the application of *t* to *D* involves uncertainty.[3]

We name these categories of uncertainty, respectively, *description uncertainty, transaction uncertainty,* and *processing uncertainty.* These categories serve as a framework for classifying the work that has been done in the area of uncertainty in database systems. This work is discussed in the next two sections.

22.3 Description Uncertainty

Undoubtedly, uncertainty that permeates the information stored in databases has received the most attention. In this section we consider some basic aspects of description uncertainty, and we review some of the more important solutions that have been suggested.

22.3.1 Introduction

Our discussion of description uncertainty begins by considering three issues: the different *elements* of descriptions that might be affected by uncertainty, the different *sources* for uncertainty, and the different *degrees* of uncertainty.

3. In turn, the uncertainty of *D* may owe to uncertainty either in the initial description or in some later modification *m*.

Roughly, we ask *what* is uncertain, *why* is it uncertain, and *how* uncertain is it?

Elements Affected by Uncertainty

Depending on the model used, descriptions may take different forms, and uncertainty could affect each of them.

Consider, for example, relational databases. The structures of the relational model admit different kinds of uncertainty. The first kind involves uncertainty at the level of data values; for example, some values of `DEPARTURE_TIME` in the relation `FLIGHT (FLIGHT_NUMBER, DEPARTURE_TIME)` might be uncertain. The second kind involves uncertainty at the level of the tuple; for example, there might be uncertainty regarding the membership of some tuples in the relation `DIRECT_CONNECTION (ORIGIN, DESTINATION)`. A third kind involves uncertainty at the level of the relation (the structure); for example, there might be uncertainty whether a flight may have more than one destination, and hence what should be the proper description of this relationship [Borgida 1985].

As another example, consider an information retrieval system that models each document with an identifier and a vector of keywords. There might be uncertainty at the level of a keyword (i.e., the appropriateness of a specific keyword to a given document might be questionable). In addition, there might be uncertainty at the level of an entire document (i.e., the existence of a document might be in doubt).

As a third example, consider an expert system that models real-world knowledge with facts and rules expressed in logic. There might be uncertainty about specific facts (similar to the tuple uncertainty in relational databases) and about specific rules (i.e., a rule might be only an approximation of the behavior of the real world).

Sources of Uncertainty

Having excluded the possibility that reality itself is subject to uncertainty, we can assume that a perfect description of any real-world object always exists. Thus, uncertain descriptions are solely due to the *unavailability* of these perfect descriptions. For example, the precise salary of Tom might be unknown, or the true relationship between Bordeaux wine and good health might be unclear. Yet within this generic unavailability we observe several specific sources of uncertainty [Kwan et al. 1992].

Uncertainty might result from using *unreliable information sources*, such as faulty reading instruments, or input forms that have been filled out incorrectly (intentionally or inadvertently). In other cases, uncertainty is a result of *system errors*, including transmission noise, delays in processing update transactions, imperfections of the system software, and corrupted data owing to failure or sabotage.

At times, uncertainty is the unavoidable result of information-gathering methods that require *estimation* or *judgment*. Examples include the determination of the subject of a document, the digital representation of a continuous phenomenon, and the representation of a phenomenon that is constantly varying.

In other cases, uncertainty is the result of restrictions imposed by the *model*. For example, if the database schema permits storing at most two occupations per employee, descriptions of occupation might exhibit uncertainty. Similarly, the sheer *volume* of the information that is necessary to describe a real-world object might force the modeler to turn to approximation and sampling techniques.

Degrees of Uncertainty

The relevant information that is available in the absence of certain information may take different forms, each exhibiting a different level of uncertainty. The following discussion is independent of the particular structure affected by uncertainty. It assumes that an element *e* of the description models an object *o* of the real world. The element *e* might be a value, a fact, a tuple, a rule, and so on.

Uncertainty is highest when the mere *existence* of some real-world object is in doubt. The simplest solution is to ignore such objects altogether. This solution, however, is unacceptable if the model claims to be *closed world* (i.e., objects not modeled do not exist).

Uncertainty is reduced somewhat when elements of the model may be assigned values in a prescribed range, to indicate the certainty that the objects they model exist. When the element is a fact, this value can be interpreted as the *confidence* that the fact holds; when it is a rule, this value can be interpreted as the *strength* of the rule (percent of cases where the rule applies).

Assume now that existence is assured, but some or all of the information with which the model describes an object is *unknown*. Such information has also been referred to as *incomplete, missing,* or *unavailable.*

Uncertainty is reduced when the information that describes an object is known to come from a limited set of alternatives (possibly a range of values). This uncertainty is referred to as *disjunctive* information. Note that when the set of alternatives is simply the entire domain of admissible values, disjunctive information reverts to unknown information.

Uncertainty is reduced even further when each alternative is accompanied by a number describing the probability that it is indeed the true description (and the sum of these numbers for the entire set is 1). In this case, the uncertain information is *probabilistic*. Again, when the probabilities are unavailable, probabilistic information reverts to disjunctive information.

22.3.2 Solutions

Space considerations forbid discussion of all the different solutions that have been attempted for accommodating uncertainty in descriptions. We sketch here five approaches that are different from each other; they also exhibit sufficient generality to be applicable in different kinds of information systems.

Null Values

Most data models insist that similar real-world objects be modeled with similar descriptions. The simplest example of this approach are models that use tabular descriptions. Each such table models a set of similar real-world objects: Each row describes a different object, and the columns provide the different components of the description. Often, some elements of a particular description cannot be stated with certainty. Occasionally, this problem may be evaded simply by not modeling any object whose description is incomplete. Often, however, the consequences of this approach are unacceptable, and incomplete descriptions must be admitted. Not surprisingly, incompleteness is a lesser issue in models that do not rely on mandatory information.

The least ambitious approach to admitting incomplete descriptions is to ignore all partial information about the uncertain parts of a description that may be available and to model them with a pseudo-description, called *null*, that denotes uncertainty [Date 1986; Imielinski 1989; Maier 1983; Zicari 1992].

Once null values are admitted into descriptions, the model must define the behavior of transformations and modifications in the presence of nulls. This is not always a simple task. For example, an extension to the relational calculus that is founded on a three-valued logic [Codd1979] has been the subject of criticism [Date 1990]. Inference in incomplete databases is discussed in Demolombe and Farinas del Cerro 1988. Updates of incomplete databases are discussed in Abiteboul and Grahne 1985.

Various refinements to this approach have been suggested. For example, a distinction has been made between incompleteness due to *unavailability* and incompleteness due to *inapplicability*.[4] Similarly, it has been suggested to use *distinct* nulls for unavailable descriptions that are known to be identical. These and other refinements constitute attempts to apply whatever partial information is available.

4. Strictly speaking, however, inapplicability is not a case of uncertainty. Inapplicability indicates that specific objects cannot be accommodated in the general description schemes used in the model.

Certainty Factors

Certainty factors denote confidence in various elements of the description. They offer a simple tool for representing uncertainty and have thus been applied in both information retrieval systems and expert systems.

In information retrieval systems, certainty factors (often called *weights*) have been used to denote confidence that a specific keyword describes a given document (or alternatively, to denote the strength with which this keyword applies to the document) [van Rijsbergen 1979; Salton and McGill 1983; Turtle and Croft 1992]. Methods have even been developed for computing certainty factors automatically, by scanning documents and applying keyword counting techniques. The manipulation of these certainty factors is relatively simple, as they are easily accommodated in the vector space models that are often used in information retrieval.

In expert systems, certainty factors have been used to denote confidence that stated facts and rules indeed describe real-world objects [Harmon and King 1985]. Such factors are usually declared by the knowledge engineers as part of the knowledge acquisition process, but they can also be derived automatically as part of a knowledge discovery process [Piatetsky-Shapiro 1991]. The manipulation of certainty factors in expert systems is often straightforward; for example, assuming certainty factors in the range [0,1], when a rule with certainty p is applied to a fact with certainty q, the generated fact is assigned a certainty factor $p \cdot q$. Pragmatic considerations may have been the reason that commercial expert systems often prefer this mostly informal representation of uncertainty over more formal approaches that are based on probability theory. However, many objections have been raised against certainty factors, showing that the lack of firm semantics may lead to unintuitive results [Pearl 1988].

Possibility and Probability

Fuzzy set theory offers a comprehensive approach to modeling uncertainty in information systems. The approach described here is derived from Prade and Testemale 1984; Raju and Majumdar 1988; and Zemankova and Kandel 1985.

The basic concept of fuzzy set theory is the *fuzzy set*. A fuzzy set F is a set of elements where each element has an associated value in the interval [0,1] that denotes the *grade* of its membership in the set. For example, a fuzzy set may include the elements 20, 30, 40, and 50, with grades of membership 1.0, 0.7, 0.5, and 0.2, respectively.

As a relation is a subset of the product of several domains, one approach is to define relations that are fuzzy subsets of the product of several domains. Since each such relation is a fuzzy set, each of its tuples is associated with a membership grade. This definition admits uncertainty at the tuple level. For example, the tuple **(Dick, Pascal)** could belong to the relation `PROFICIENCY(PROGRAMMER, LANGUAGE)` with membership grade

0.9 (alternatively, this tuple may be interpreted as stating that Dick's proficiency in Pascal is 0.9).

Consider the fuzzy set defined earlier, and assume it is named YOUNG. It is also possible to interpret this set as the definition of the term *young*: It is a term that refers to 20-year-olds with possibility 1.0, to 30-year-olds with possibility 0.7, and so on. Thus, fuzzy sets may be applied to describe vague terms.

Consider now standard (nonfuzzy) relations, but assume that the elements of the domains are not values but fuzzy sets of values. This definition admits uncertainty at the data-value level. Having fuzzy sets for values permits specific cases where a value is one of four kinds:

1. A set or a range—for example, the value of DEPARTMENT can be **{shipping, receiving}**, or the value of SALARY can be **40,000-50,000**. Note that the interpretation of such sets and ranges is purely *disjunctive*: Exactly one element of the set or range is the correct value.
2. A fuzzy value—for example, the value of AGE can be **young**.
3. A null value.
4. A simple value (no uncertainty).

Finally, by defining a fuzzy relation as a fuzzy subset of the product of domains of fuzzy sets, both kinds of uncertainty can be accommodated.

To manipulate fuzzy databases, the standard relational algebra operators must be extended to fuzzy relations. The first approach, in which relations are fuzzy sets but elements of domains are crisp, requires simple extensions to these operators. The second approach, in which relations are crisp but elements of domains are fuzzy, introduces more complexity because the softness of the values in the tuples creates problems of value identification (e.g., in the join or in the removal of replications after projections). Also, in analogy with standard mathematical comparators such as = or <, which are defined via sets of pairs, the second approach introduces fuzzy comparators such as *similar-to* or *much-greater-than*, which are defined via fuzzy sets of pairs. These fuzzy operators offer the capability of expressing fuzzy (uncertain) retrieval requests.

In Barbara et al. 1992, a model is described that handles uncertainty with traditional probability distributions (rather than the possibility distributions of the fuzzy models). A *probability distribution function* of a variable X over a domain D assigns each value $d \in D$ a value between 0 and 1, as the probability that $X = d$. One important difference between probability and possibility distribution functions is that the sum of the probabilities assigned to the elements of X must be exactly 1. The definition of a probabilistic database is similar to the second definition of fuzzy databases: standard relations but with domain values that are, in general, probability distribution functions. A feature of this model is that it allows probability distributions that are incompletely specified: Each such distribution is complemented with a *missing value* that is assigned the balance of the probability.

Distances

An approach to uncertainty that has been applied successfully to both databases systems and information retrieval systems handles uncertainty with *distance*. The basic idea is to model the real world with apparently certain descriptions and to rely on definitions of distances among descriptions to create *neighborhoods* of descriptions.

Thus, any uncertainty about a real-world object *o* is ignored, and an apparently certain description of it *e* is stored. It is then hoped that this negligence would be compensated by having *e* somewhere in the neighborhood of the true description. When a request for information specifies this true description, *e* would be retrieved along with the other neighbors of the true description.

As an example, consider an information retrieval system that describes documents with sets of keywords [Salton and McGill 1983; Turtle and Croft 1992; van Rijsbergen 1979]. Such systems often represent keyword sets with vectors: The dimension of each vector is the number of possible keywords, and a specific vector position is 1 if a particular keyword is in the set and 0 otherwise. Often, there is uncertainty whether a specific vector is the true description of a given document. By establishing a distance among document descriptions, usually with some vector metric, and retrieving all the information in the neighborhood of a request-vector, the negative effects of inaccuracies in the description are diminished.

As another example, consider relational database systems. Such systems describe objects with tuples, and often there is uncertainty regarding the value of some attribute in a given tuple. It is possible to establish a distance among the elements of the domain of this attribute. Then, when a query specifies a value of this attribute, all the tuples would be retrieved whose value for that attribute is in the neighborhood of the specified value [Motro 1988].

We assumed here that descriptions are subject to uncertainty (which is ignored) and requests are certain. The same solution applies when descriptions are certain and requests are subject to uncertainty. Such requests would be specified with apparent certainty and would be answered with the neighborhood of the request. Again, the negative effects of inaccuracies in the request would be moderated. Uncertainty in requests is discussed in more detail in section 22.4.1.

A refinement of this general method is to admit certainty factors (section 22.3.2) in the descriptions and in the requests. For example, vectors describing keyword sets use values in the range [0,1] to denote the certainty that a specific keyword applies to the given document (or, alternatively, to denote the strength with which this keyword applies). Similarly, request-vectors use such values to denote the weights of various keywords in the overall request.

Soundness and Completeness

The final approach we discuss has been developed in the context of relational databases [Motro 1989]. Instead of modeling imperfections in the information (i.e., uncertainty), it suggests declaring the portions of the database that are prefect models of the real world (and thereby the portions that are possibly imperfect).

Thus, like distances and unlike incompleteness, certainty factors, or fuzziness, the descriptions themselves have no special features for uncertainty (i.e., they appear certain). However, meta-information provides the distinction between certain and uncertain information. (Recall that fuzziness and distances also require meta-information: the definitions of fuzzy terms or the measures of proximity.)

With this information included in the database, the database system can *qualify* the accuracy of the answers it issues in response to queries: Each answer is accompanied by statements that define the portions that are guaranteed to be perfect.

This approach interprets certainty, which it terms *integrity*, as a combination of *soundness* and *completeness*. A description is sound if it includes *only* information that occurs in the real world; a description is complete if it includes *all* the information that occurs in the real world. Hence, a description has integrity if it includes the whole truth (completeness) and nothing but the truth (soundness).

The approach uses the mechanism of *views* to declare the portions of the database or the portions of an answer that have integrity. It describes a technique for inferring the views of individual answers that are guaranteed to have integrity from the views of the entire database that are known to have integrity.

The concept of view completeness is similar to an assumption that a certain view of the database is *closed world* [Reiter 1978]; the notion of view soundness is shown to be a generalization of standard database integrity constraints.

22.4 Transaction Uncertainty and Processing Uncertainty

While most of the work in uncertainty has focused on description uncertainty, transaction and processing uncertainty have just as important impact on the quality of the information delivered to users. In this section we discuss briefly issues and solutions that concern uncertainty in the definition of transformations (e.g., queries), in the definition of modifications (e.g., updates or restructuring operations), and in the processing of such transactions.

22.4.1 Transformations

Transformations are operations that derive new descriptions from stored descriptions. The most frequent type of transformation is requests from users for information (queries). Uncertain requests may occur for different reasons.

At times, users of database systems have insufficient knowledge of the database and database system they are using: They might not have a clear idea of the information available in the database (or how it is organized), or they might not know how to formulate their requests with the tools provided by the system.

Requests for information formulated by such *naïve* users exhibit a high level of uncertainty. They range from requests that cannot be interpreted by the system (for reasons that are either syntactic or semantic) to requests that do not achieve correctly the intentions of the users (or achieve them only in part).

Regardless of their level of expertise, occasionally users may try to access a database system with only a *vague* idea of the information they seek. For example, a user may be accessing an electronic catalogue for a product that would be interesting or exceptional. Alternatively, users could have a clear idea of the information they want but might lack the information necessary to specify it to the system. An example is a user who wishes to look up the meaning of a word in a dictionary but cannot provide its correct spelling.

To summarize, we distinguish among (1) uncertainty about the *information available* (or how it is organized), (2) uncertainty about the *information needed* (or how to denote it in terms acceptable to the system), and (3) uncertainty about the *system languages and tools* that are used to formulate requests.

To address all these, the approach has been to develop alternative access tools. Browsers allow users to access information in either situation discussed above [D'Atri et al. 1992; Motro 1986; Rogers and Cattell 1987]. Interactive query constructors conduct user-system dialogues to arrive at satisfactory formulations of user requests [Williams 1984]. Vague query processors allow users to embed uncertain specifications in their requests (e.g., neighborhood queries) [Ichikawa and Hirakawa 1986; Motro 1988]. Error-tolerant interfaces use relaxed formalisms in their interpretation of requests [Motro 1990].

As mentioned above, even after a request for information has been accepted by the system and its answer delivered to the user, uncertainty might still persist because it is not always possible to verify that the request has indeed achieved correctly the intention of the user. Often, the only assurance that the information delivered is the information needed is that the user is somewhat familiar with it. In the absence of such familiarity, uncertainty will persist.

Hence, one must accept that there would be frequent instances where the answer that is delivered is inaccurate, yet both the system and the user are unaware of this inaccuracy. Often, the uncertainty of apparently certain answers is revealed only when a conflicting answer to the same request is received from another information system.

22.4.2 Modifications

Modifications (update and restructuring) are operations that affect the descriptions stored in information systems. Like transformations (queries), modifications are defined by users, and here also we distinguish among three main sources of uncertainty: (1) insufficient knowledge of the system, (2) insufficient knowledge of the specific database that is being modified, and (3) uncertainty about the information embedded in a modification.

Many of the approaches aimed at alleviating the problems of transformation uncertainties (section 22.4.1 above) are also applicable to modification uncertainties. However, fewer tools have been developed to address modification uncertainties. A possible explanation is that, while modifications may be attempted by users at all levels of expertise, it is often assumed that users who modify databases should have good familiarity with the database and database system.

The third source of uncertainty, vague or imprecise modifications, is unrelated to expertise. One example is a request to add information that is uncertain—for example, "the new manager is either Paul or John." Another example is a request to delete information, with uncertainty about what exactly should be deleted—for example, "some of the telephone numbers are no longer valid."

However, this kind of uncertainty is not any different from the description uncertainty that was the subject of section 22.3. Thus, the first request would be accommodated as any information of the kind "exactly one of the following values holds," and the second request would be accommodated as any information of the kind "some of the following values hold." (Of course, if the system cannot model these kinds of uncertainty, then it would not be able to handle these modifications.)

22.4.3 Processing

Even when a description D and a transformation t are free of uncertainty, the result $t(D)$ may be uncertain because of the methods used by the system to process requests. In certain applications, an information system might allocate only limited computational resources to process a request [Imielinski 1987]. For example, a recursive query to a genealogical database to list all the ancestors of a specific individual might be terminated after a predetermined period of time (presumably the number of ancestors retrieved by then would be sufficient). In other applications, query processing might involve randomizations, sampling, or other estimation techniques [Kwan et al. 1992]. For example, a statistical database system might introduce perturbations into its answers deliberately, for reasons of security. In each case, the answers would exhibit uncertainty.

Finally, it is sometime considered advantageous to sacrifice accuracy for the sake of *simplicity*. Recent research on *intensional answers* [Cholvy and Demolombe 1986; Shum and Muntz 1988; Pirotte et al. 1991; Motro 1994] has focused on the generation of abstract answers that describe the exhaustive answers compactly albeit imperfectly. For example, a query to list the employees who earn over $50,000 might be answered simply and compactly "engineers," even when the set of engineers and the set of employees who earn over $50,000 are not exactly the same (e.g., when the two sets overlap substantially or when one set contains the other).

22.5 Hindrances and Challenges

Commercial database systems have been slow to incorporate uncertainty capabilities. While solutions based on fuzzy set theory are gaining acceptance in several technologies, commercial database systems have not embraced this solution yet. Often, the only capabilities widely available are for handling null values and for specifying specifying uncertain queries by allowing the substitution of patterns for constants.

Examining the possible reasons for this slow acceptance may suggest directions for further research. First, database systems practitioners are concerned primarily with the *performance* of their systems. Here, many of the algorithms for matching uncertain data or for processing uncertain requests are highly complex and inefficient.

Practitioners are also concerned with *compatibility*. This dictates that capabilities for accommodating uncertainty should be offered as strict extensions of existing standards. Additionally, database practitioners have often been dissatisfied with various *idiosyncratic implementations* of uncertainty capabilities. This may have had a chilling effect on further implementations.

Another hindrance for database systems with uncertainty capabilities may lie in the *expectations of users*. A fundamental principle of database systems has been that queries and answers are never open to subjective interpretations, and users of database systems have come to expect their queries to be interpreted unambiguously and answered with complete accuracy. In contrast, users of information retrieval systems would be pleased with a system that delivers a high rate of recall (proportion of relevant material retrieved) and precision (proportion of retrieved material that is relevant). Similarly, users of expert systems are aware that conclusions offered by automated experts are often questionable, and they would be satisfied with systems that have shown to have a high rate of success. A database system that must adhere to the principles of unambiguity and complete accuracy cannot accommodate the full range of uncertain information; for example, it can accommodate null values or disjunctive data but not (because of its more subjective nature) probabilistic or possibilistic data.

Recently, new applications have emerged that require database systems with uncertainty capabilities. Several of these challenging applications are described below. Their description is followed by a discussion of a possible source of uncertainty technology and the challenges involved in adapting it for database systems.

22.5.1 Heterogeneous Database Environments

In recent years, the integration and interchange of information among heterogeneous database systems has been recognized as an important area of database system research and development. Multidatabase environments present a strong case for having uncertainty management capabilities. While individual database systems are usually careful to avoid internal inconsistencies (mostly with methodical design that avoids repeating the same information at multiple locations in the system), when information from independent systems with overlapping information is integrated, inconsistencies will often surface. Thus, even when individual answers are free from any uncertainty, their integration in a global answer would introduce uncertainty. Therefore, database systems in a multidatabase environment should be capable of combining conflicting answers into a single (uncertain) answer and then storing and manipulating such information [Motro 1993].

In a heterogeneous multidatabase environment, the integration and interchange of information requires protocols for translating information among the different models. The possibility of having database systems that are based on different uncertainty formalisms presents an additional challenge: to develop protocols for finding *common* uncertainty formalisms so that uncertain information can be integrated with minimal loss of information.

22.5.2 Multimedia Databases

As discussed in section 22.3, retrieval from traditional databases is usually based on *exact matching,* where a request for data establishes a specific retrieval goal, and the database system retrieves the data that match it exactly. Presently, the management of image databases largely follows the same paradigm: While images are stored (in digitized form) in large databases, retrieval is performed on *textual descriptions* of these images that are stored along with the images themselves.

A more ambitious approach, such as IBM's Query By Image Content (QBIC) [Faloutsos et al. 1994], is to retrieve images that match a given *image*. Image-matching techniques are usually based on algorithms of *best matching*. As with the information retrieval systems discussed earlier, the use of uncertainty formalisms is essential. A similar problem is to match handwritten addresses against a database of addresses.

22.5.3 Imputation and Knowledge Discovery

In various applications, notably in scientific and statistical projects, it is necessary to estimate missing data (nulls) from other data that are available. For example, a missing measurement is estimated by other measurements made by the same instrument at other times, as well as by measurements made by other instruments at the same time. This process, usually referred to as *imputation*, yields information of varying degrees of uncertainty. The management of this information cannot be done by traditional database techniques and requires the use of uncertainty techniques.

The inference of missing values from their contexts is related to the more general issue of discovering new knowledge in large databases. Database knowledge is usually *declared*: Rules and constraints are assumed to be definite and accurate and to hold in any database instance (exceptions, if any, must be stated). In contrast, *discovered* knowledge is always subject to uncertainty: The patterns and rules are often tenuous and could be refuted by future data. Again, the management of such information requires uncertainty techniques.

22.5.4 Adapting Artificial Intelligence for Databases

Modeling uncertainty in database systems involves a classical dilemma. On one hand, we want a model as rich and powerful as possible—for example, a single concept of information that is capable of representing elegantly all known kinds of uncertain information, as well as certain information. On the other hand, database systems must abide by crucial constraints of simplicity and efficiency, of both their descriptions and the manipulations of their descriptions.

Like database systems, the field of artificial intelligence has been concerned with modeling accurately our knowledge of the real world. Numerous uncertainty theories have been developed; mostly they are founded on nonclassical logics, on probability theory, on belief functions, or on possibility theory [Lea Sombe 1991; Motro and Smets 1992; Smets and Clarke 1991; Smets and Motro 1993].

It might be said that, traditionally, research in artificial intelligence has been emphasizing rich and powerful models, striving to model accurately all the minute nuances of reality. On the other hand, research in database systems has been emphasizing economical representations with lower expressivity but with small representational overhead and high processing efficiency.

A notable case in point is the so-called *semantic data models* that were defined in the late 1970s to enhance the modeling capabilities of early database systems [Hammer and McLeod 1981; Hull and King 1987]. These models incorporated modeling features, such as generalization and aggregation hierarchies, that had been adapted from research in artificial intelligence. An even earlier example is the adaptation of *semantic networks* for databases [Roussopoulos and Mylopoulos 1975]. A third and more recent example is *knowledge-rich database systems* that incorporate inference rules expressed in mathematical logic [Ullman 1988; Ullman 1989; Ceri et al. 1990]. Not surprisingly, a major research thrust among database researchers who have been working in this area has been the development of *highly efficient* inference techniques for a *limited* class of rules.

Thus, database systems may be said to have embraced poor-person's AI or, more graciously, to have adapted AI concepts to work under the strict constraints of database systems. The adaptation of uncertainty theories that have been developed for artificial intelligence to working database techniques is an important challenge for database researchers. The recent success of several information-extensive diagnostic and decision-support systems, such as QMR-BN [Henrion and Suermondt 1993], hints at the possible rewards that research in this direction may provide.

22.6 Conclusion

Database systems of the current generation are not designed to manage information that is permeated with uncertainty. Uncertain data is stored as null values or it must be excluded from the database, and users with uncertain requests can use queries with simple patterns or they must browse the database to find their answers.

To provide satisfactory solutions to new applications, such as information integration in multidatabase environments, retrieval of images by content, and inference of missing values or new knowledge, future database systems would have to include stronger capabilities for dealing with uncertainty.

To assure the success of any future endeavors in this area, various hindrances must be overcome; in particular, issues of performance and compatibility must be addressed. Research into uncertainty in the field of artificial intelligence may provide a suitable source of technology for database systems.

ACKNOWLEDGMENTS

This work was supported in part by NSF Grant No. IRI-9007106 and by a ARPA grant, administered by the Office of Naval Research under Grant No. N0014-92-J-4038.

REFERENCES

Abiteboul, S., and Grahne, G. 1985. Update Semantics for Incomplete Databases. *Proceedings of the Eleventh International Conference on Very Large Data Bases,* Stockholm, 1–12.

Barbara, D., Garcia-Molina, H., and Porter, D. 1992. The Management of Probabilistic Data. *IEEE Transactions on Knowledge and Data Engineering,* Vol. 4, No. 5, 487–502.

Borgida, A. 1985. Language Features for Flexible Handling of Exceptions in Information Systems. *ACM Transactions on Database Systems,* Vol. 10, No. 4, 565–603.

Ceri, S., Gottlob, G., and Tanka, L. 1990. *Logic Programming and Databases.* Springer-Verlag, Berlin.

Cholvy, L., and Demolombe, R. 1986. Querying a Rule Base. *Proceedings of the First International Conference on Expert Database Systems,* Charleston, South Carolina, 365–371.

Codd, E. F. 1979. Extending the Database Relational Model to Capture More Meaning. *ACM Transactions on Database Systems,* Vol. 4, No. 4, 397–434.

Date, C. J. 1986. *Relational Database: Selected Writings.* Addison-Wesley, Reading, Mass.

Date, C. J. 1990. NOT is Not "Not"! In: *Relational Database Writings 1985-1989.* Addison-Wesley, Reading, Mass.

D'Atri, A., Motro, A., and Tarantino, L. 1992. ViewFinder: An Object Browser. Technical report, Department of Information and Software Systems Engineering, George Mason University.

Demolombe, R., and Farinas del Cerro, L. 1988. An Algebraic Evaluation Method for Deduction in Incomplete Data Bases. *Journal of Logic Programming,* Vol. 5, 183–205.

Faloutsos, C., Equitz, W., Flickner, M., Niblack, W., Petkovic, D., and Barber, R. 1994. Efficient and Effective Querying by Image Content. *Journal of Intelligent Information Systems* (in press).

Hammer, M., and McLeod, D. 1981. Database Description with SDM: A Semantic Database Model. *ACM Transactions on Database Systems,* Vol. 6, No. 3, 351–386.

Harmon, P., and King, D. 1985. *Expert Systems—Artificial Intelligence in Business.* John Wiley & Sons, New York.

Henrion, M., and Suermondt, J. 1993 Probabilistic and Bayesian Representations of Uncertainty in Information Systems: A Pragmatic Introduction. *Proceedings of the Workshop on Uncertainty Management in Information Systems: From Needs to Solutions,* Avalon, Cal., 71–90.

Hull, R., and King, R. 1987. Semantic Database Modeling: Survey, Applications and Research Issues. *Computing Surveys,* Vol. 19, No. 3, 201–260.

Ichikawa, T., and Hirakawa, M. 1986. ARES: A Relational Database with the Capability of Performing Flexible Interpretation of Queries. *IEEE Transactions on Software Engineering,* SE-12(5), 624–634.

Imielinski, T. 1987. Intelligent Query Answering in Rule Based Systems. *Journal of Logic Programming,* Vol. 4, No. 3, 229–257.

Imielinski, T. 1989. Incomplete Information in Logical Databases. *Data Engineering,* Vol. 12, No. 2, 29–40.

Kwan, S., Olken, F., and Rotem, D. 1992. Uncertain, Incomplete, and Inconsistent Data in Scientific and Statistical Databases. *Proceedings of the Workshop on Uncertainty Management in Information Systems: From Needs to Solutions,* Mallorca, Spain, 64–91.

Lea Sombe, et al. 1991. Special issue on reasoning under incomplete information in artificial intelligence. *International Journal of Intelligent Systems,* Vol. 5, No. 4.

Maier, D. 1983. *The Theory of Relational Databases.* Computer Science Press, Rockville, Md.

Motro, A. 1986. BAROQUE: A Browser for Relational Databases. *ACM Transactions on Office Information Systems,* Vol. 4, No. 2, 164–181.

Motro, A. 1988. VAGUE: A User Interface to Relational Databases That Permits Vague Queries. *ACM Transactions on Office Information Systems,* Vol. 6, No. 3, 187–214.

Motro, A. 1989. Integrity = Validity + Completeness. *ACM Transactions on Database Systems,* Vol. 14, No. 4, 480–502.

Motro, A. 1990. FLEX: A Tolerant and Cooperative User Interface to Databases. *IEEE Transactions on Knowledge and Data Engineering,* Vol. 2, No. 2, 231–246.

Motro, A. 1993. A Formal Framework for Integrating Inconsistent Answers from Multiple Information Sources. Technical Report ISSE-TR-93-106, Department of Information and Software Systems Engineering, George Mason University.

Motro, A. 1994. Intensional answers to database queries. *IEEE Transactions on Knowledge and Data Engineering* (in press).

Motro, A., and Smets, P., eds. 1992. *Proceedings of the Workshop on Uncertainty Management in Information Systems: From Needs to Solutions,* Mallorca, Spain.

Pearl, J. 1988. *Probabilistic Reasoning in Intelligent Systems: Networks of Plausible Inference.* Morgan Kaufmann, San Mateo, Cal.

Piatetsky-Shapiro, G. 1991. Discovery, Analysis and Presentation of Strong Rules. In: *Knowledge Discovery in Databases,* 227–248. G. Piatetsky-Shapiro and W. Frawley, eds. AAAI Press/MIT Press, Menlo Park, Cal.

Pirotte, A., Roelants, D., and Zimanyi, E. 1991. Controlled Generation of Intensional Answers. *IEEE Transactions on Knowledge and Data Engineering,* Vol. 3, No. 2, 221–236.

Prade, H., and Testemale, C. 1984. Generalizing Database Relational Algebra for the Treatment of Incomplete or Uncertain Information and Vague Queries. *Information Sciences,* Vol. 34, No. 2, 115–143.

Raju, K. V. S. V. N., and Majumdar, A. 1988. Fuzzy Functional Dependencies and Lossless Join Decomposition of Fuzzy Relational Database Systems. *ACM Transactions on Database Systems,* Vol. 13, No. 2, 129–166.

Reiter, R. 1978. On Closed World Data Bases. In: *Logic and Databases,* 55–76. Plenum Press, New York.

Rogers, T. R., and Cattell, R. G. G. 1987. Object-Oriented Database User Interfaces. Technical report, Information Management Group, Sun Microsystems.

Roussopoulos, N., and Mylopoulos, J. 1975. Using Semantic Networks for Data Base Management. *Proceedings of the First International Conference on Very Large Data Bases,* 144–172.

Salton, G., and McGill, M. J. 1983. *Introduction to Modern Information Retrieval.* McGraw-Hill, New York.

Shum, C. D., and Muntz, R. 1988. An Information-Theoretic Study on Aggregate Responses. *Proceedings of the Fourteenth International Conference on Very Large Data Bases,* Los Angeles, 479–490.

Smets, P., and Clarke, M. R. B. 1991. Special issue on uncertainty, conditionals, and non-monotonicity. *Journal of Applied Non-Classical Logics,* Vol. 1, No. 2.

Smets, P., and Motro, A., eds. 1993. *Proceedings of the Workshop on Uncertainty Management in Information Systems: From Needs to Solutions,* Avalon, Cal.

Turtle, H. R., and Croft, W. B. 1992. Uncertainty in Information Retrieval Systems. *Proceedings of the Workshop on Uncertainty Management in Information Systems: From Needs to Solutions,* Mallorca, Spain, 111–137.

Ullman, J. D. 1988. *Database and Knowledge-Base Systems, Volume I.* Computer Science Press, Rockville, Md.

Ullman, J. D. 1989. *Database and Knowledge-Base Systems, Volume II.* Computer Science Press, Rockville, Md.

van Rijsbergen, C. J. 1979. *Information Retrieval,* 2nd Edition. Butterworths, London.

Williams, M. D. 1984. What Makes RABBIT Run? *International Journal of Man-Machine Studies,* Vol. 21, No. 4, 333–352.

Zemankova, M., and Kandel, A. 1985. Implementing Imprecision in Information Systems. *Information Sciences,* Vol. 37, Nos. 1–3, 107–141.

Zicari, R. 1992. Databases and Incomplete Information. *Proceedings of the Workshop on Uncertainty Management in Information Systems: From Needs to Solutions,* Mallorca, Spain, 52–63.

23

Distributed Databases

HECTOR GARCIA-MOLINA
MEI HSU

In this chapter we briefly survey current distributed database systems, their key components as well as the state of the art in commercial systems, and explore some of the remaining open problems.The problem areas considered include new transaction models, very large systems, mobile systems, and the use of text and other unstructured data.

23.1 Introduction

Communication networks make it feasible to access remote data or databases, allowing the sharing of data among a potentially large community of users. There is also a potential for increased reliability: When one computer fails, data at other sites are still accessible. Critical data may be replicated at different sites, making it available with higher probability. Multiple processors also open the door to improved performance. For instance, a query can be executed in parallel at several sites.

We have so far avoided the term *distributed database*. For some people, this term implies a particular type of distributed data management system in which users are given transparent, integrated access to a collection of databases. In other words, a user is given the illusion of a single database with one global schema. Queries on this database are automatically translated into queries on the underlying databases. In the early days (before 1980), this was thought to be the ultimate goal for all distributed data management systems, and hence the term *distributed database* became associated with transparency and integration. Nowadays most researchers agree that transparency and integration may be incompatible with requirements for autonomy and diversity of implementations. They are using the term *distributed database* in a more general sense to mean a collection of possibly independent or federated database systems. Each system has some set of facilities for exchanging data and services with other members. In this chap-

An earlier and shorter version of this chapter appeared in *ACM-SIGMOD Record,* Vol. 19, No. 4, December 1990, pp. 98–103.

ter we take the broader meaning of distributed databases in order to cover a wider spectrum of the challenging problems facing researchers.

We start by giving in section 23.2 a brief summary of the key problems that arise in distributed databases. In section 23.3 we then review the current state of the art in commercial distributed databases systems. Finally, in section 23.4 we discuss the future directions for development and research.

Before starting we would also like to clarify that due to space limitations this will not be a survey of relevant papers and work. In the references section we have included a few good sources of information on distributed database systems. These include references to most of the current work in the area.

23.2 Key Problems

Distributed database systems come in a great variety of forms and shapes. As discussed in the introduction, systems may provide differing levels of transparency. Distributed database systems may run on different hardware architectures, from a collection of tightly coupled computers connected over a high-speed network to a set of geographically distributed machines connected by low bandwidth lines. The data themselves may be represented in a variety of models. In spite of all this variety, there is a fundamental feature that makes a distributed database different from a conventional database: The data are partitioned and stored at separate computers. This introduces two key problems:

1. To answer a query, data residing at separate computers may have to be combined and moved.
2. Since the data are under the control of separate computing elements, it may be necessary to coordinate transactions to preserve data consistency.

In the next two subsections we review these two problems and the possible solutions.

23.2.1 Parallel and Distributed Query Processing

When a database system receives a query, it constructs a query-processing plan and executes the plan to produce the answer to the query. The plan dictates the sequencing of the operations as well as the choice of access paths to be used in accessing the physical data records. The query optimizer generates potential plans, estimates their costs, and chooses one that minimizes the estimated costs.

Distributed database systems add two more considerations to the problem of constructing a query plan: maximize parallelism and minimize network data transfer. We illustrate some of the issues in distributed query processing through an example. Consider the following query:

Select * from *A*, *B* where *A.u* > 100 and *A.x* = *B.x*

Suppose relations *A* and *B* are on two different nodes N_1 and N_2. This query involves a select operation on relation *A* and a join operation on *A* and *B*. One strategy is to employ a pipelining mechanism:

Node N_1: Select * from *A* where *A.u* > 100;
    pipe above tuples to N_2;
Node N_2: receive piped tuples from N_1;
    join received tuples with *B* tuples on *x*;

With the above strategy, node N_1 is dedicated to the select operation, and when a tuple in *A* is found to satisfy the condition, it is sent over to node N_2. Node N_2 is dedicated to the join operation, receiving tuples from N_1 and joining them with tuples in *B* to produce the result. In the pipelining mechanism, nodes are connected via pipelines of tuples, and all nodes are utilized concurrently for processing the query.

Suppose both relations *A* and *B* above are large, but the result of their join based on *A.x* = *B.x* is relatively small. In this situation, there may be many tuples in *A* that are transferred to *B* but do not participate in the result relation (i.e., cannot find tuples in *B* that have a matching value on *x*). In such a situation, consider the following alternative query plan:

(step 1) On Node N_2:
    Send (Select *B.x* from *B*) to N_1 as *TEMP*;
(step 2) On Node N_1:
    Select *A*.* from *A*, *TEMP*
    where *A.x* = *TEMP.x* and *A.u* > 100;
    pipe above tuples to N_2;

  On Node N_2:
    receive pipelined tuples from N_1;
    join received tuples with *B* tuples on *x*;

The above plan first transfers a (hopefully small) *TEMP* relation from N_2 to N_1. The *TEMP* relation is used on N_1 to cut down the number of tuples in *A* that are sent over to N_2 since any tuple in *A* that does not have an *x* attribute value matching a value in *TEMP* will be discarded. This two-step multisite join mechanism is called the semijoin mechanism. In the above example, the semijoin method is effective in reducing the network transfer cost because the size of *TEMP* is much smaller than the size of the subrelation A satisfying $A.u > 100$. In general, the distributed query optimizer must have knowledge of the sizes of the relations, the image sizes of the attributes, and the transfer costs to be able to intelligently take advantage of such more sophisticated methods.

Consider the same query but a finer-grained distribution configuration, where relation A is partitioned horizontally, based on some criterion of the value of x, into m segments that are stored on nodes NA_1 to NA_m, and relation B is similarly partitioned and stored on nodes NB_1 to NB_m. To join A and B, a tuple with a given x value at NA_1 only needs to be matched with NB_1 tuples, since only B tuples with the same x value would have to be stored there. The same holds true for the other segments. Thus, a smart query plan will direct node NA_1 to pipe the tuples to NB_1, NA_2 to NB_2, and so on, and have each NB node send the joined tuples to the query site. The plan exploits the knowledge of the distribution schema to maximize concurrency and minimize data movement.

Many other factors can be taken into account for distributed query optimization. They include, for example, work load among nodes, physical data layout and access paths (e.g., how data is clustered on the disk and whether data is indexed), and properties of the desired result relations (e.g., whether the result should be sorted by certain attribute).

23.2.2 Distributed Transactions

In a centralized database system, the transaction manager ensures that user programs or transactions are executed with ACID properties (atomicity, consistency, isolation, durability). This is typically achieved by using (1) a concurrency control mechanism such as two-phase locking to ensure that concurrent transactions do not interfere with each other, and (2) a logging mechanism to ensure that a transaction can be either completed or fully aborted after a failure (hardware, software, or transaction).

With a distributed database, we may have transactions operating on data residing at different computers. The portion of a transaction done at one computer or site is called a *subtransaction*. Each site can ensure, using conventional logging, that its subtransactions are executed atomically. However, it is now necessary to coordinate the decisions made at each site, so that they all decide to commit (complete) all the subtransactions of a transaction, or they all decide to abort (undo) all the subtransactions.

This agreement is typically reached via a two-phase commit protocol (2PC). Here is one way it could work: A coordinator site asks all participants to execute their corresponding subtransactions. When each participant finishes, it enters a prepared-to-commit state where it has enough logged information to either undo or to successfully complete its subtransaction.

Once it is prepared, a site sends a prepared-to-commit message to the coordinator. When the coordinator has received prepared-to-commit messages from all participants, it makes a commit entry in its log and sends commit messages to all sites. When a participant receives a commit message, it completes its subtransaction. If any of the participants cannot or do not want to complete their subtransactions, the coordinator writes an abort record and sends abort messages to all sites.

In terms of concurrency control, many conventional strategies work in a distributed environment. In particular, two-phase locking transactions need to request locks (shared or exclusive) for all the objects they access. The lock for object X is managed by the site where X is stored. Thus, the lock for X can be requested when X is accessed, just as in a centralized system. The transaction can release its locks as part of the final phase of the two-phase commit protocol.

Replicated data represents one key complication to the strategy described in the previous paragraph. Specifically, consider an object X that has three copies, X_1, X_2, and X_3, each at a different site. If a transaction wishes to update X, the standard protocol requires that exclusive locks be acquired at all three sites. There are two disadvantages: (1) three locks have to be acquired for a single object, and (2) if copy X_i is not available, then the transaction cannot proceed.

To reduce the redundant locking and data availability problems, a number of replicated data management algorithms have been suggested. They vary in the way they perform concurrency control and how they commit transactions. For example, in some cases, locking is only performed at a primary copy; in others, locking is done at all available sites (i.e., to update object X, one requests locks at all sites that hold a copy of X and that are operational). For commitment, instead of requiring participation by all sites with a copy of X, only a fixed subset may be necessary, only the available sites may be necessary, or a subset determined by voting may be required (e.g., if there are five copies, any three may be sufficient to commit a transaction). The goal of all these protocols is to guarantee *one-copy* semantics; that is, the execution of transactions should be as if there were a single copy of each object and all read and writes were directed to that copy.

To conclude this section, we note that actual distributed database systems may or may not have the facilities we have described here. (This will become apparent in the next section, where we describe commercial systems.) For instance, a system may not have a query optimizer or a mechanism for managing replicated data. This means users must cope with the problems on their own, for example, by either doing their own query optimization or managing copies on their own, or with poor performance or inconsistent data.

23.3 Capabilities of Commercial DDBMS Systems

In this section we review historical and current trends in commercial development of distributed databases.

23.3.1 Client-Server Architecture for Distributed Processing

Many commercial DBMSs today offer a distributed client-server architecture in which multiple client applications in client nodes are connected to a database server on a server node. The client applications issue SQL queries, which are executed on the server node. An example of a client-server relational database product is Ingres/Net, introduced in 1983.

In addition to accessing database servers using SQL, some commercial relational DBMSs (e.g., Sybase, Informix, Oracle) also offer built-in support for stored procedures. Stored procedures are database application routines that reside and execute on the DB server node. A client application sends a remote procedure invocation request to the DB server node, and the DB server node invokes the appropriate application routine. The routine typically executes a sequence of database queries on the DB server and returns an answer to the client via a remote procedure return message.

Invoking stored procedures on the DB servers insulates the DB clients from the specific database structures and languages supported on the DB servers. This improves node autonomy and can be used as the basis for integration of heterogeneous DB servers.

Most existing client-server database access protocols are vendor proprietary. The advantage of vendor-proprietary protocols is that each vendor is able to tune the protocol to maximize performance. However, this makes it difficult for database client applications to migrate from one database server to another. Standard database server access protocols are emerging. One popular example is the SQL Access Group's SQL Access API and Message Format. Commercial support for such standards in database servers is expected in the near future.

In a client-server architecture, a client may be connected to multiple database servers simultaneously and thus be able to access and correlate information from distributed sources. This paradigm effects a form of distributed processing and supports a certain degree of integration of distributed data. However, when a client is connected to multiple database servers, properly correlating the data from various sources is the client's responsibility. Furthermore, it is difficult for the client to achieve atomicity of a transaction that spans multiple database servers. A distributed DBMS overcomes these difficulties by providing data location transparency and distributed transaction management.

23.3.2 Distributed Transaction Management

Distributed transaction management has been present in transaction processing monitors (TPM, e.g., IBM's CICS and IMS/DC, Tandem's Guardian, and DEC's ACMS) [Bernstein 1990] since the late 1970s. The early TPMs integrate homogeneous databases on proprietary platforms and provide functions for logging, commit, and recovery. Clients send requests to a TPM, which processes the request by internally coordinating local and remote applications that access multiple databases. Two-phase commit (2PC) is supported by the proprietary DBMSs accessed in a TPM, allowing the TPM to coordinate the commit processing of a multisite request.

Commercial relational DBMSs have only recently begun to offer the 2PC functionality for their own DBMSs residing on distributed sites. Ingres was the first such vendor to support automatic 2PC for distributed Ingres database sites (in 1990). Informix Version 5.0 and Oracle Release 7 have also added automatic 2PC support. Sybase, on the other hand, has offered a server library that allows user-developed server-based application procedures, including those that operate on the Sybase engine or those that operate on foreign DBMSs to be networked together. While one may argue that Sybase's server library mimics a TP monitor, it does not yet offer automatic 2PC capability.

Existing commercial 2PC support is mostly for coordinating commit of transactions that span homogeneous (in particular, single-vendor) DBMSs. Transaction management on distributed heterogeneous databases can be facilitated by having DBMSs support standard distributed transaction processing protocols. The XA protocol in the X/Open protocol suite [XOpen 1991] allows a DBMS to communicate with a standard transaction manager, which coordinates transaction commit for multiple DBMSs. The ISO/TP protocol [ISOTP 1991] allows multiple transaction managers to commit a transaction together.

DBMSs that comply with transaction management standards are only beginning to emerge. However, this represents a critical trend in commercial development. Informix has been compliant with the evolving XA standard since 1991, while Oracle Release 7, introduced recently, is also claimed to be XA compliant. Other major vendors have indicated intention to follow suit.

23.3.3 Data Location Transparency

In contrast to the top-down assumptions used in early distributed database research, where a single global database schema is decomposed into multiple physical fragments to be distributed to multiple sites, commercial DBMSs have approached distributed data management in a bottom-up fashion. After multiple databases residing on distributed sites have been deployed as independent database systems, an *integration server* may be installed that offers a global schema on top of multiple existing local database schemata.

Location transparency is offered by the integration server. Ingres/Star is an example of an integration server product. The client of an integration server can issue SQL queries based on the global schema without regard to where the data referenced in the global schema actually resides. The integration server then maps and decomposes the query on the global schema into subqueries on local schemata supported by underlying database servers. The integration server acts as a client to the underlying database servers in requesting the execution of subqueries. The local databases remain unaware of the existence of other local databases, and they communicate only with the integration server. A local database may be registered at multiple integration servers, thus participating in multiple global schemata.

23.3.4 Distributed Query Processing

The local databases combined with an integration server appear as a distributed database system to a client of the integration server. Distributed query optimization has been utilized in some of the commercial integration servers. For example, in Ingres/Star, the parameters that are taken into account in decomposing the global query include statistical distribution of data, amount of data being transported, speed of the communication links, existence of primary and secondary indexes, and some storage structure parameters. Some of these parameters are obtained from the local databases when the latter are registered with the integration server. These parameters guide the integration server in constructing a distributed query execution plan.

The integration server approach focuses primarily on data retrieval. Support for database update via a global schema is not emphasized.

23.3.5 Distributed Data Replication

Commercial support for data replication is still primitive. Most of such support is in the form of a database snapshot feature that generates and refreshes read-only copies of a data set at specified time intervals. A database snapshot is a materialized view. For example, snapshots may be created with the following commands (exact syntax may vary):

Create materialized_view *v1* as
select * from *work* where *assigned_to* = ME
refresh *incremental* cycle *1 hour*;

```
Create materialized_view v2 as
select work.* from work, work_data where
work.id = work_data.id and work_data.amount > 500
refresh complete cycle 1 day;
```

In the above example, *v1* is a snapshot that involves only one relation. This snapshot is refreshed every hour with *incremental* updates (specified with the "refresh incremental cycle 1 hour" clause); that is, at the refresh time, only the incremental updates to the relation *work* since the last refresh are sent to the replication site. Snapshot *v2* involves two relations. The specification "refresh complete" means that at the refresh time, a new copy of *v2* is sent to the replication site.

The Oracle's snapshot facility and the VMS Data Distributor, a DEC product for Rdb, are two examples of commercial products offering snapshot-based replication. More sophisticated data replication support such as transactional updates across multiple copy sites (section 23.2.2) is presently being evaluated by vendors.

23.3.6 Site Autonomy Revisited

While standard transaction management protocols hold promise for achieving atomic commit of a transaction that spans multiple heterogeneous DBMSs, they may not be universally practical. Not only will their commercial deployment take time, but there is also the argument that 2PC violates site autonomy. Similar arguments can be extended to the universal practicality of standard access protocols such as SQL Access.

As the scale of distributed DBMSs grows, it will become increasingly important to explore other dimensions of distributed data integration services. They include, for example, data and behavior encapsulation, alternative transaction models, and active event notification. These ideas are discussed in the following section.

23.4 Future Directions

23.4.1 Distributed Data Architecture

Consider a user local to a database management system. Consider also a second remote database that the user wishes to access. How should the local system present the remote data? As discussed in the introduction, under a transparent, fully integrated architecture, the remote database is made to appear as part of the local one. Operations on the remote data, for example, joining a remote table with a local one, can be done (at least from the point of view of the user) as easily as fully local operations. At the other end of the spectrum, the remote site may simply offer a set of services that may be invoked by explicit calls. For example, if the remote computer handles an airline database, it may let a user request the schedule for a given flight or reserve a seat on a flight.

Transparency is not an all or nothing issue. It can be provided at various levels, and each level requires a particular type of agreement among all the participants. In the fully transparent case, the sites must agree on the data model, the schema interpretation, the data representation, the available functionality, and where the data are located. In the nontransparent service model, there is only agreement on the data exchange format and on the functions that are provided by each site.

The tradeoffs involved in providing transparency revolve around simplicity of access and ability to integrate data from diverse sources versus issues of site autonomy and specialized functions. Clearly, from the point of view of a user who wants remote access, a transparent architecture is desirable. All the data at the remote site are accessible, just as if they were local. However, from the point of view of the administrator of the remote site, transparency provides access that is difficult to control. The remote site could only make visible certain views on its data, but view mechanisms in many systems are not powerful enough to provide the desired protection. For instance, at a bank site, funds transfer may only be allowed if the account balance is positive and the customer has a good credit rating. A simple view mechanism cannot express this.

It is much easier to provide these checks within a procedure that is called remotely. Although the data may be freely accessible to local users, remote users see the data encapsulated by a set of procedures, much as in an object-oriented programming environment. This type of remote service or federated architecture is simpler to implement than full transparency. Less agreement is needed among the participants, and complex algorithms such as a multisite join need not be implemented. Sites have greater autonomy to change the services they provide or how they provide them.

The research challenge in this area is to fully understand the spectrum of alternatives. While we have sketched the two extreme solutions (full transparency and a service model), the intermediate models are not well defined. The fundamental issue is the *level* at which remote requests and responses are exchanged. Great care is needed to avoid weakening remote access functionality to the lowest common denominator while, at the same time, avoiding a proliferation of service and implementation-specific protocols. Fruitful research directions include extending data access and manipulation protocols to support database procedures (to encapsulate services and policies), authentication standards, and relaxed serializability levels (with special authorization required for full serializability). In addition, further research is needed on technologies for exporting type definitions and *behav-*

ior to allow remote users to exploit the semantic content of retrieved information (i.e., object distribution).

23.4.2 New Transaction Models

In a federated database architecture, computers provide services to other sites. The glue that ties together the system is the transaction management system. It coordinates a sequence of interactions with different nodes, providing data consistency and atomicity.

Conventional transaction models based on locking and two-phase commit (section 23.2.2) may be inadequate. One reason is that they force participants to use the same model and to possibly give up their autonomy. For instance, a participant in a two-phase commit must become a subordinate of the coordinator(s), not releasing resources held by a transaction (locks) until instructed to do so. Another problem is that a large transaction may last for a long time, holding up critical resources. In a sense, this is a problem of scale: As the number of participants in the protocol grows or the amount of work each participant must do grows, the time resources are tied up also grows. This is unacceptable if these are critical, often-accessed resources.

The need for relaxed concurrency control protocols in the local case has been recognized in some products and standards proposals. For distributed systems, there have already been numerous proposals [Elmagarmid 1992; IEEE 1993] for weaker transaction models that give participants more autonomy and improve performance, while still guaranteeing some basic correctness properties. For example, a sequence of steps at various sites can be considered a saga and not a full-fledged transaction. After each step completes, a local transaction commits. If the saga needs to be aborted later on, a compensating step is run at nodes where transactions committed. This eliminates the need for two-phase commit. However, sagas can now see intermediate results of other sagas, so programming such applications may be trickier. Also, the need for compensating steps creates more work for the application programmers. Tools for developing applications in a saga environment would be a very valuable contribution.

Without global transactions (as is the case with sagas and similar approaches), only consistency constraints local to a single site are maintained. Global constraints, for example, object *X* at site *A* must be a copy of object *Y* at site *B*, are not necessarily guaranteed. If the intersite constraints are known, it is possible to maintain them in an approximate way—for example, making *X* approximately equal to *Y* or *X* equal to a relatively recent value of *Y*. Such approximate constraints may be adequate for some applications—for example, an automated teller machine may not need to know precisely how much money a customer has in his or her account; a rough estimate may be enough to make the decision whether funds can be withdrawn. Approximate constraints may make it possible to operate without two-phase commit for many steps or subtransactions, improving autonomy and performance.

In general terms, there is a need for more options for transaction management in a distributed database. For each option, it is necessary to precisely define the type of correctness it provides and to evaluate the performance and autonomy it yields.

23.4.3 Very Large Systems

Current trends indicate that the number of databases is rapidly growing, while at the same time their size is also increasing. Some database and distributed data algorithms do not scale up nicely as the number of components in the system grows. In a conventional database, for example, one may need to place data off line to make a backup or for reorganization. Typically, this is done during the night. As the database grows in size, the backup or reorganization time grows, and a night is no longer long enough.

In a distributed database, one is faced with such problems of scale as individual databases grow and also as the number of databases and the scope of the system grows. For instance, in a worldwide distributed system, there is no nighttime to do reorganizations or backups. Key system algorithms may break down in larger systems. For example, in a small system, it may be feasible to search for a particular file of interest by broadcasting a request to all nodes. In a very large system, this becomes impractical. Having a central directory of all resources is also a bad idea, not just because of its large size, but because it is prone to failures and because not all sites may want to advertise their resources to everyone. Thus, the problem of resource finding in a very large distributed data system is quite challenging. When one starts a search, one not only does not know where the resource is, but one does not know what directories are available for this type of resource.

As an illustrative example, consider a scientist searching for a database of ozone readings over Antarctica for the year 1980. (For one thing, *Antarctica* and *ozone* are denoted differently in Russian databases.) Different organizations have directories of their own databases, but there is no reliable directory of organizations. Heterogeneity is an added complication here: It is not clear how to make our query understandable to different organizations and, if a relevant database is found, how to know what it really contains, expressed in our terms. While some progress has been made with yellow and white pages servers, the mechanisms for describing data resources in human- or machine-readable form are quite crude. One only needs to try to use today's bibliographic search systems to realize that capturing and encoding the semantic or technical essence of data collections is not well advanced.

In addition to the resource finding protocols, there are other algorithms that may not scale up. The challenge is to identify them and to find alternatives. For instance, what deadlock detection, query processing, or transaction processing algorithm will work best in a very large system or in a system with very complex queries or with many participants in a transaction?

Administration of large distributed databases is another problematic area. As the number of components, users, and transactions rapidly grows, it becomes harder and harder to manage the system effectively. The volume of accounting, billing, and user authentication information grows. The number of choices for improving or speeding up a system grows. The size and number of database schemas grows. It becomes harder to evaluate the performance of the system and to predict its behavior under changes. Upgrading or installing new software also is harder, as there are more sites that are affected and it is impractical to halt the entire system to do an operating or database system upgrade. A related problem is the management of the underlying computer communication network. The problems are analogous: handling growing information on links, protocols, and performance. Also, key network algorithms do not scale up—for example, those for initializing a network after its failure.

23.4.4 Mobile Systems and Disconnected Operations

The advent of powerful laptop computers and cellular communications has introduced many challenging distributed database problems. Here we discuss three possible scenarios.

Mobile Computing

We have a collection of mobile computers that are linked by low-bandwidth radio links. In this scenario, we assume that computers can always communicate. For example, we may have a fleet of taxis, each with a small computer and cellular radio link. We can view the data at each site (e.g., the position of the taxi, the destination, fuel left) as part of a large and rapidly changing distributed database. The challenge here is to efficiently perform queries on this changing data (e.g., find the closest taxi to this street corner). The fact that communication bandwidth is low complicates things; for instance, it may not be feasible to have each site constantly report its location and data changes to all sites that may have queries. Two additional complications may arise in this scenario: (1) the available electric power may be limited; in this case, one must minimize not only the number of bytes transmitted but also the power consumed in answering queries and propagating updates; and (2) the sites may be frequently turned off to save power (or for other reasons, e.g., security); this is equivalent to having sites fail, but since these "failures" are more frequent, mechanisms have to be devised for rapidly and efficiently bringing each site up to date when it resumes processing.

Disconnected Operation

In this scenario, sites may become disconnected. For example, a user may unplug his or her computer from the network, take it home and work there (with no network connection), and then later reconnect to the network. The complication here is that a disconnected site may contain a part of the distributed database, and that part may be updated during the disconnected period. For example, a user may have a copy of some files on his or her laptop computer and modify the files at home. Traditional concurrency control and recovery algorithms (section 23.2.2) may be too restrictive or simply inappropriate. For instance, while a user has checked out a file for laptop use, no one else may be able to read the file. It may be more desirable to allow other readers to see an older version of the file or even to have multiple sites update objects concurrently (violating one-copy semantics). The challenge here is to devise appropriate algorithms and notions of correctness.

Combined Scenarios

One can also consider scenarios with features from the above two. For example, one could have disconnected operation and low-bandwidth communications during connections (e.g., when a user connects his or her laptop, he or she uses a 1200-baud telephone modem).

23.4.5 Nontraditional Applications

Distributed systems are increasingly used for retrieving information on a wide variety of topics ranging from stock prices to cars for sale, from news items to jokes. In some cases, the information is stored in commercial database services and a fee is paid. In other cases, computers are interconnected in ad hoc networks and information exchanged between end users, as in "net-news" or in bulletin boards. In still other cases, the communications companies themselves are providing information services. This is the case of MiniTel in France. Traditionally, these information networks have not been considered a distributed database. However, there is no reason why the mechanisms developed for formal distributed databases could not be extended to informal and/or loosely coupled information repositories.

In simple terms, the problem of information management is one of matchmaking. On one hand, we have a user who wants some type of information (e.g., who has found this bug in this program?). On the other hand, we have suppliers of information that may fully or partially match those needs. The goal is to make a connection between the supplier and the consumer. The problem is related to that of resource finding described in section 23.3, but there are added complications.

Sometimes information requests are not for a single item but are standing orders—for example, send me all future news items on this topic. This means the system must not only find the appropriate sources, but it must also set up the data paths for ongoing communication. Batching data transmissions is also important. For example, if two users at neighboring computers request the same information, it may be more effective to route the information to one computer and to then forward it to the other. Existing systems such as net-news provide batching, but they make many restrictions as to what users may read and when they can read.

A provider of information often wishes not only to track who has received it but also may need to be able to control how it is to be used. This will require facilities for access tracking and for contracting with the recipient. Important social, legal, political, and scientific issues must be addressed before open information distribution systems can be used for anything other than the exchange of trivial information.

Existing information systems usually do not provide reliability. In particular, a user may miss information if his or her machine is down. Thus, one challenge is to incorporate exiting distributed database crash recovery technology into information networks.

Distributed data and information can also be used in nontraditional ways—that is, more than simply submitting queries and getting replies. For instance, electronic newsletters with user contributions are one such interaction. Users submit articles or news items to an editor or a group of editors. The editors check the articles, trimming them or eliminating uninteresting ones. The accepted articles are then distributed on the network to subscribers or are made available for queries. There has also been interest in systems to support distributed collaboration—for example, to help a collection of researchers share information and conduct their research. Clearly, shared, distributed data must play a critical role here. The challenge is to expand the models and mechanisms of distributed database to encompass these new applications.

23.5 Conclusions

In order to extend data distribution to large-scale environments, the requirements and characteristics of different DBMS implementations and information-collecting organizations must be addressed. The challenge is to support integration of information from diverse sources without retreating to a low-function common protocol (e.g., NFS) while, at the same time, avoiding a proliferation of high-level, service-specific interfaces. Future research should consider carefully the role of remotely invoked procedures (which might have interfaces similar to other, general data accessing interfaces) as a mechanism to respond to organizational autonomy and control issues. Such interfaces could encapsulate local control procedures but execute in the context of a larger information interchange environment (e.g., authenticated user, transactions, accounting, data exchange formats, etc.).

We also believe that any success in providing distributed information-processing facilities in a heterogeneous environment will probably rely, ultimately, on standard protocols for authentication, accounting/billing/contracting, data access specifications, schema exchange, typed object transport, and information resource characterizations. Accommodating multiple data models will increase the difficulty of developing mechanisms for information exchange and integration. The alternative is to provide the user with an array of information accessing tools, each of which can extract or manipulate data in a single type of DBMS using a unique user interface and communication protocol. Information integration from different sources in such an environment would be the user's problem.

Finally, we believe that one fruitful direction for data distribution technology is the extension of data semantics. This means that mechanisms for defining type-specific behavior (procedures, functions, or methods) should, somehow, be extended to allow data objects to retain their semantic qualities as they are transported from one location to another. In some sense, this challenge echoes the earlier efforts to develop seamless functional distribution for the data model and its operations. Without techniques for transmitting objects without loss of their semantic qualities, information is pinned to the environment in which it is created and cannot interact (be integrated) with information (objects) from other cultures (environments).

ACKNOWLEDGMENTS

Bruce Lindsay contributed to an earlier version of this chapter. Also, Va-On Tam provided many valuable suggestions. This research was partially supported by the Defense Advanced Research Projects Agency of the Department of Defense under Contract No. DABT63-91-C-0025 and by the Center for Integrated Systems at Stanford University.

REFERENCES

Bell, D., and Grimson, J. 1992. *Distributed Database Systems*. Addison-Wesley, Reading Mass.

Bernstein, P. A. 1990. Transaction Processing Monitors. *CACM*, Vol. 33, No. 11, 75–86.

Breitbart, Y., Garcia-Molina, H., and Silberschatz, A. 1992. Overview of Multidatabase Transaction Management. *VLDB Journal*, Vol. 1, No. 2, 181–240.

Ceri, S., and Pelagatti, G. 1989. *Distributed Databases: Principles and Systems.* McGraw-Hill, New York.

Elmagarmid, A. K., ed. 1992. *Database Transaction Models for Advanced Applications.* Morgan Kaufmann, Los Altos, Cal.

Gray, J., and Reuter, A. 1993. *Transaction Processing: Concepts and Techniques.* Morgan Kaufmann Publishers, Los Altos, Cal.

IEE. 1987. Special issue on distributed databases. *IEEE Proceedings.*

IEE. 1993. Special issue on workflow and extended transaction systems. *IEEE Data Engineering*, Vol. 16, No. 2.

ISOTP. 1991. *ISO/IEC 10026, Information Technology—Open Systems Interconnection—Distributed Transaction Processing.*

Özsu, M.T., and Valduriez, P. 1991. *Principles of Distributed Database Systems.* Prentice Hall, Englewood Cliffs, N.J.

X/Open Company, Ltd. 1991. *X/Open Snapshot: X/Open DTP: XA Interface.*

24

Parallel Relational Database Systems

EDWARD OMIECINSKI

The motivation behind the development of parallel database systems is to provide increased performance of database system software by using high-performance parallel computers. The use of parallelism will be fundamental to achieving good performance for users accessing very large (e.g., terabyte size) databases. In this chapter, we examine some of the important contributions made in the parallel database area within the context of system design and query processing. We also discuss some of the issues that need to be addressed in future work in parallel database systems.

24.1 Introduction

There has been a dramatic increase in the use of relational database systems over the past 10 years and, with that, an increase in the amount of data stored, retrieved, and processed. A single relation size of a few gigabytes as well as a relational database size of several terabytes will not be uncommon in the near future. To maintain a suitable level of performance with such large databases, high performance parallel computers will have to be used. Relational database systems have been designed and implemented not only for general purpose multiprocessor computers in a university/research setting (e.g., Gamma, Bubba, Grace) but also in industry, where commercial products have already appeared on the market (e.g., by Teradata and Tandem).

General purpose high-performance multiprocessor systems provide a large number of fast processors, which a database system can take advantage of, but of more importance for database processing is the need for the multiprocessor system to provide some sort of parallel I/O capability. With database systems, in the past as well as in the future, it has been and will be important to minimize I/O. This need to minimize the I/O overhead has led various commercial multiprocessor systems to provide such a capability (e.g, with variations of disk arrays).

In this chapter we will examine some of the important contributions to the parallel database area. The chapter is divided into two major topics: system architecture and query processing. We start with system architecture in section 24.2, where we discuss general models (e.g., shared nothing and shared everything) as well as specific implementations (e.g., Gamma, Bubba, and SDC). We present the topic of parallel relational query processing in section 24.3. Some of the issues we discuss are inter and intra query parallelism, join processing and data placement. We discuss future work regarding parallel relational database systems in section 24.4 and present conclusions in section 24.5.

24.2 System Architecture

Three major architectures have been proposed for parallel database systems [Stonebraker 1986]. These include shared-everything, shared-disks, and shared-nothing system designs. The three different models are depicted in Fig. 24–1.

24.2.1 Models

At one end of the spectrum, there is the shared-everything model, where all the processors have direct access to a common memory and direct access to all the secondary storage devices, which we refer to as *disks*. At the other end of the spectrum, there is the shared-nothing model. With the shared-nothing model, each processor has its own directly accessible memory as well as its own directly accessible disk(s). Processors communicate with each other by way of message passing. As an alternative to these two models, the shared-disks model allows direct access to all the disks by any of the processors but associates a private memory with each processor. So a processor can directly access only its own memory.

The shared-nothing model appears to be the most dominant of the three. Its main advantage is that of scalability—that is, hundreds and even thousands of processors might be interconnected in such a system. On the other hand, scalability appears to be a problem with shared-everything and shared-disks models. Latency and network traffic also become potential problems with those two models.

24.2.2 Implementations

In this section, we present six prominent parallel database system projects based on two of the models presented in the preceding section. Although there has been work on systems based on the shared-disks model, it has not been of primary interest to database researchers. The same can be said of system development based on the shared-everything model. As we will see, five of the parallel database systems we consider are based on the shared-

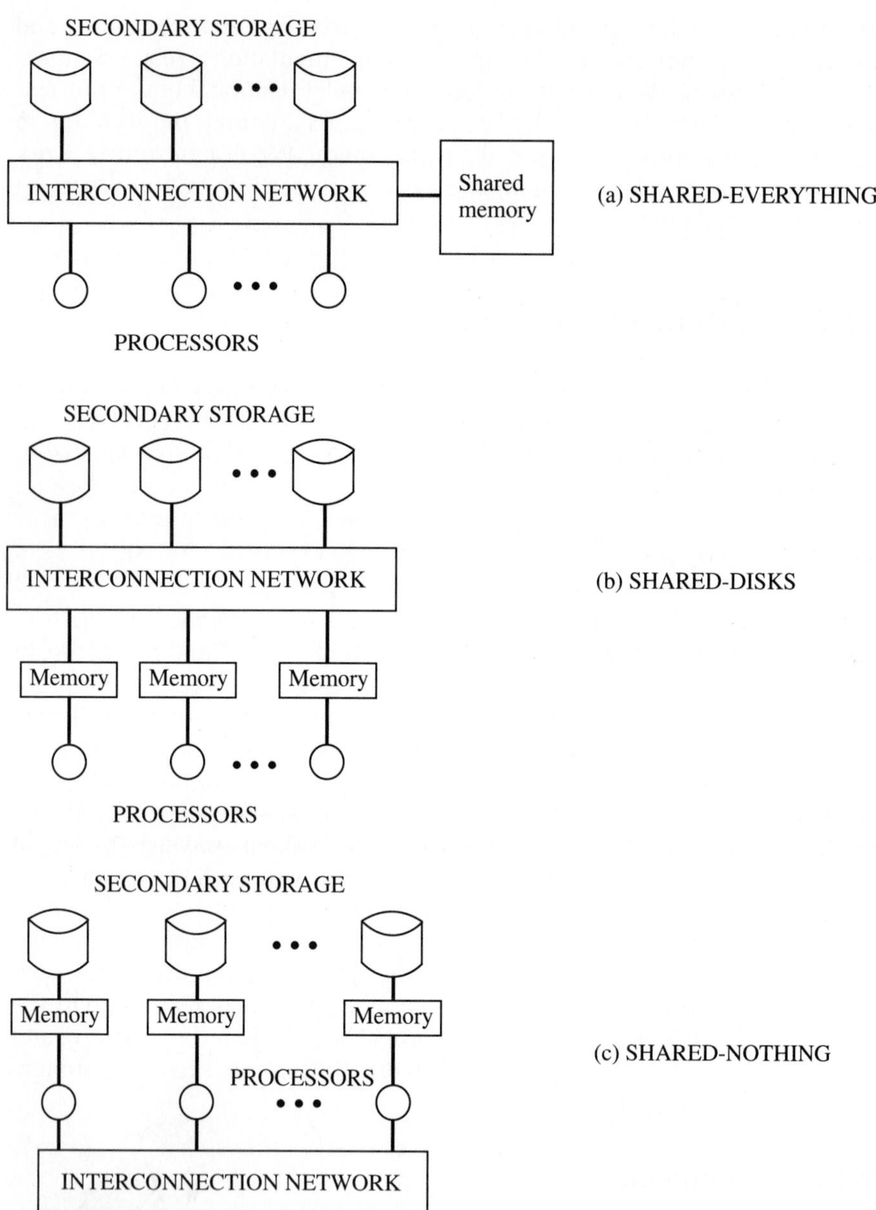

FIGURE 24–1
Shared-Everything, Shared-Disks, and Shared-Nothing Architectures

nothing model and only one is based on the shared-everything model. As a point of interest, a parallel database system differs from a distributed database system running on a local area network in a number of ways. Typically, parallel database systems have no notion of site autonomy, have a centralized schema, and have a single point for initiating the execution of all queries.

DBC/1012

The DBC/1012 [Neches 1984; Teradata 1985] from Teradata Corporation is a commercially available parallel database system. The DBC/1012 consists of a set of interface processors (IFPs), access module processors (AMPs), and disk storage units (DSUs). The IFPs communicate with the host, parse, optimize, and direct the execution of user requests. They also broadcast data to and accumulate results from the AMPs. The AMPs perform the actual storage and retrieval of data on the DSUs. All relations on the Teradata machine are horizontally partitioned across multiple AMPs, although it is possible to limit the number of AMPs over which relations are partitioned. IFPs and AMPs are interconnected by a dual redundant, tree-structured interconnection called the *Ynet*. The Ynet is an active bus whose bus modules contain logic able to perform selection and sorting operations. Using the Ynet, operation requests are broadcast to the appropriate access modules. Results from the access modules are sorted when they return up the Ynet and then broadcast back to the requesting interface module. The Teradata machine uses four alternative join algorithms [Teradata 1985]. One computes an outer-join, while the other two are used only in special cases (for example, when the inner relation contains a single tuple). The fourth and most common way in which the join is executed involves redistributing the two source relations by hashing on the joining attributes. The tuples are stored in a temporary file sorted in hash key order on each AMP. After the redistribution step, each AMP uses a sort-merge join algorithm to complete the join.

Gamma

Gamma [DeWitt et al. 1990] is a fully operational prototype designed at the University of Wisconsin. It is based on the experience from the earlier multiprocessor database machine prototype, Direct. The original version of Gamma consisted of 17 VAX 11/750 processors, each with two megabytes of memory, along with another VAX serving as a host machine, all connected by a token ring. A disk drive is attached to every eight processors. Recently, Gamma [DeWitt et al. 1990] has been ported to a 32-processor iPSC/2 Intel hypercube with a disk attached to each node.

Relations in Gamma are horizontally partitioned across all disks in the system—referred to as *declustering*. Four methods [Ghandeharizadeh and DeWitt 1990a] for declustering are used in Gamma and will be discussed in detail in section 24.3.2. Once a relation has been partitioned, Gamma provides the normal mechanism for creating primary and secondary indexes on each fragment of the relation. A special multiprocessor index is also constructed if the relation is range partitioned. When an operator process begins execution, it continuously reads tuples from its input stream, operates on each tuple, and uses a split table to route the resulting tuples to the process indicated in the split table. Consider the case of a join operation utilizing the results from a selection operation. If the join is to be executed by *N* processes, the split table will contain *N* entries. The selection process applies a hash function to the joining attribute of the tuples that survive the selection to produce a value between 1 and *N*. This value is used as an index into the split table to obtain the address of the process that expects the tuple and to execute the join.

Bubba

The Bubba project [Boral et al. 1990] at MCC (which ended in 1989) had as its goal the development of a scalable, high-performance, and highly available database system. The Bubba parallel database system is based on the shared-nothing model and is implemented on a 40-node Flex/32 multiprocessor where each node has its own disk. Bubba utilizes three types of nodes: interface processors, intelligent repositories, and checkpoint-and-log intelligent repositories. The interface processors communicate with external host machines and coordinate the execution of user requests. The intelligent repositories store the database and perform most of the work in transaction execution. The checkpoint-and-log intelligent repositories maintain database checkpoints and update for database recovery logs that are used if an intelligent repository experiences a failure.

The Bubba design effort emphasizes four major areas: data placement, automatic parallelization, dataflow control, and data recovery. Similar to other shared-nothing systems, data placement is an important component of Bubba [Copeland et al. 1988]. Since the data is declustered across the disks to allow for parallelism, the data operations are executed where the data reside. This directly affects the load across the nodes and hence Bubba's performance. So, data placement in Bubba is determined by workload patterns.

Since Bubba depends on a general database programming language, FAD [Boral et al. 1990], it is important that the transaction programs rely on automatic parallelization. The FAD compiler accomplishes this by decomposing FAD programs into multithreaded parallel programs. The idea of having a general purpose database programming language is to allow the execution of more of the application transaction directly in Bubba without excessive data movement, as might occur in the traditional host language-embedded query language approach.

In Bubba, a dataflow operation may execute in parallel on many nodes. So, when one operation is done, dataflow control is needed to coordinate the sending and receiving of data produced by that operation to a subsequent operation that uses the data.

To provide for high availability, data recovery techniques become a central issue in the Bubba design. Techniques are developed to allow for continued system processing in the face of node failures and the restoration of nodes after a failure.

Grace/SDC

Grace [Kitsuregawa et al. 1984], developed at the University of Tokyo, was one of the first database machines implemented. Its goal was to achieve high performance through data stream oriented processing. It is also one of the first multiprocessor database machines to apply hashing as a way to execute a join.

The Grace machine consists of four types of fundamental modules: processing modules, memory modules, disk modules, and control modules. The processing modules are responsible for executing the relational operators. The memory modules provide storage for the data streams during processing while the disk modules provide persistent storage for the database. The control modules, as their name indicates, control the machine.

The various modules are connected by two loops (buses): the staging ring and the processing ring. For example, consider the processing of a join operator. As previously mentioned, the join is executed by way of hashing. First, the disk modules filter and hash the relevant data, through the staging ring, into the appropriate memory modules. Next, dynamic hash clustering is used to partition tuples into buckets, which are distributed to memory modules. Each processor is assigned a bucket to process. Once the bucket distribution is complete, the tuples of a bucket are gathered by processing modules in a pipelining fashion. Once tuples are received in a processing module, they are sorted by a pipeline merge sort unit and are output when the processing of a bucket is completed.

In the recent work [Kitsuregawa and Ogawa 1990] on the Super Database Computer, the researchers at the University of Tokyo again take a combined hardware and software approach to the performance problem. They capitalize on their previous work [Kitsuregawa et al. 1989] to design a parallel database machine with an improved performance. SDC is a shared-nothing system, consisting of several processing modules. Although each processing module looks like a shared-everything system—that is, multiple CPUs, a specialized hardware sorter, shared memory, and a disk subsystem. The various processing modules are interconnected by a specialized communication network, the omega network. As with Grace, hashing is of prime importance with SDC. Data skew is a problem for Grace, so to handle this problem in SDC they develop a strategy called *bucket spreading*. Instead of using a static allocation of buckets to processing modules, they employ a dynamic allocation based on the size of the buckets so as to balance the load between different processing modules.

Volcano

The Volcano system [Graefe 1990] is from the University of Colorado. It is a dataflow query processing system that is extensible and incorporates parallelism. It employs an operator model of parallelism, specifically it has an exchange operator that parallelizes all other operators. The encapsulation of parallelism in Volcano allows for new query-processing algorithms to be coded for single-process execution but run in a highly parallel environment without modifications. Volcano allows intraoperator parallelism on partitioned datasets and both vertical and horizontal interoperator parallelism. With intraoperator parallelism, several processors perform the same operation on different subsets of a stored dataset. Vertical parallelism allows the pipelining of data between processes. Horizontal parallelism is achieved by having different processors execute different subtrees of a complex query tree. Volcano does not currently support interquery parallelism.

Volcano consists of modules for a file system, buffer management, sorting, B+ trees, and two algorithms each for various relational algebra operators such as natural join, outer join, division, union, and so on. The algebra operators are implemented as iterators—that is, they support a simple open-next-close protocol. Operators do not need to know what kind of operator produces its input or whether its input comes from an intermediate result or a file. This concept is referred to as *streams* and allows any number of operators to be combined to evaluate a complex query.

Some experimental results are reported in Graefe 1990 concerning the overhead of the Volcano exchange operator when executed on a shared memory multiprocessor. The results indicate that the exchange operator is very fast. The granularity of data exchange between processors is also examined. It is found that small packets produce a severe performance penalty.

XPRS

The XPRS system [Stonebraker et al. 1988] under development at the University of California, Berkeley, is a high-performance multiprocessor database system project. The goal is to demonstrate that high performance for transaction processing, for complex ad hoc queries, and for managing large objects can be provided by a next-generation database system running on a general-purpose operating system. The XPRS system is using a shared memory architecture, in contrast to the shared-nothing systems previously mentioned. An objective is to provide inter-query as well as intra-query parallelism. Having a query optimizer that chooses a good access plan based on the available buffer space and available processors is one of its major concerns. In addition, the access plan generated by the query optimizer must be amenable to parallelization.

24.3 Parallel Relational Query Processing

In order to improve the response time for queries on very large databases, researchers have attempted to exploit parallelism. As such, a considerable amount of work is spent on developing strategies for the parallel execution of database operations [Bitton et al. 1983]. By employing a multiprocessor system, the performance of the database system can be improved by inter-query parallelism, or by intra-query parallelism, or by a combination of the two.

24.3.1 Inter- and Intra-Query Parallelism

With inter-query parallelism, multiple queries are executed independently and in parallel on multiple processors. With intra-query parallelism, independent parts of a single query are executed in parallel on multiple processors. Inter-query parallelism appears to be the easier approach to implement since parallelism within a query does not have to be exploited. An example of such an approach is running a conventional database management system on a shared-everything multiprocessor. Intra-query parallelism can be achieved, in a limited form, by simply partitioning the relations of the database across the disks and by performing the read and processing of each partition of a relation in parallel. The Gamma system [DeWitt et al. 1990] exemplifies this approach. An example of a commercial system that uses both types of parallelism (to a limited extent) is the DBC/1012 [Neches 1984]. The majority of research has been oriented towards intra-query parallelism—for example, performing the relational join operation for a single query in parallel.

24.3.2 Data Placement

Data placement or, more precisely, data partitioning, is an important issue in parallel database systems. By partitioning (also referred to as *declustering*) a relation across several disks, the database system can exploit the I/O bandwidth of the disks by reading and writing data to those disks in parallel. The three basic partitioning schemes that have emerged are round-robin, hash, and range partitioning [DeWitt and Gray 1992].

The round-robin partitioning scheme is the simplest. As the name suggests, tuples of a relation are placed on the disks in a circular fashion. With this scheme, the number of tuples for a relation on each disk will be the same—that is, if the total number of tuples in the relation is a multiple of the number of disks. This type of data placement balances the I/O load on each disk for queries that require a sequential scan of the entire relation.

However, if there is some search condition specified, as in the **Where** clause of an **SQL** query, it might be that only a small number of tuples satisfy the query. In fact, if the query is an exact match query, then only one tuple will satisfy it. So, even though the I/O load on each disk is balanced, more I/O is done than needed.

In the case of an exact match query, it is beneficial to direct the search to the disk that stores the desired tuple. This can be done in the case where the data is partitioned using hashing. The hash partitioning scheme places tuples on disks according to some hash function, which is then used to direct the retrieval to a specified disk. In this situation, other tasks—for example, tasks associated with other operators for the same query or tasks associated with operators of other queries—may take advantage of accessing the other disks.

The hash partitioning scheme is good for exact match type queries but suffers when range type queries are submitted. For this situation, range partitioning is the appropriate solution. Here, the tuples are allocated to the various disks based on some range function—for example, departments 1 through 10 are stored on disk 1, departments 11 through 20 are stored on disk 2, and so on. Hence, the search for tuples satisfying a range query may be directed to a subset of the disks (and processors). The problem that may be encountered with range partitioning is that a few disks (one or more) may have a much larger number of tuples allocated to it. This could possibly cause an I/O load imbalance.

In Ghandeharizadeh and DeWitt 1990a, a multiuser performance analysis of various declustering strategies is presented for Gamma. The authors examine the effect of the three declustering strategies on selection queries that use different access methods. The response time and throughput are used as the performance metrics. The results indicate that each partitioning scheme outperforms the others for certain query types. In Ghandeharizadeh and DeWitt 1990b, the authors introduce a new declustering strategy, called *hybrid-range partitioning*. This approach declusters a relation by analyzing the resource requirements of the queries accessing the relation, the processing capability of the processors, and the overhead of using additional processors to execute a query. This design provides effective support for small relations and for relations with a skewed distribution of values for the partitioning attribute.

For Bubba [Copeland et al. 1988], a partitioning scheme based on access frequency is employed in addition to the three standard schemes. The data is not simply allocated to disks so as to balance the amount of data stored at each disk but rather to balance the frequency with which each disk is accessed. It was shown from the experiments that as declustering increased, load balancing improved. However, carrying declustering too far resulted in decreased throughput for complex join queries due to various overhead. The heuristics used in Bubba provide a compromise between load balancing and overall load reduction.

24.3.3 Parallel Join Algorithms

The relational join operation has received the most attention since it is a commonly used and costly operation. The join operation involves two relations and thus is more expensive than other database operations that only involve a single relation. Consequently, a number of algorithms have been developed for implementing the join operation in parallel [Kitsuregawa et al. 1983; Schneider and DeWitt 1989; Wolf et al. 1991]. They include the nested-block method [DeWitt et al. 1993], the sort-merge method [Schneider and DeWitt 1989; Wolf et al. 1990] and the hash join method [DeWitt and Gerber 1985; Kitsuregawa et al. 1983]. The performance of the algorithms is usually predicted by analytical modeling or by simulation.

The (natural) join operator combines two relations on all their common attributes. The join of relations **R** and **S** is the set of tuples where each tuple is a combination of a tuple from **R** and a tuple from **S**, if these two tuples have the same value for the common attributes. In addition, only one copy of the joining attributes will appear in the tuples of the result. The simplest, although rarely the most efficient, approach is to compare each tuple from the **R** relation with each tuple from the **S** relation. This is what is done in the nested-block join method. The nested-block method is a variation of the original nested-loop approach, which takes into account the division of a relation into pages and thus reduces the I/O cost. The case when the nested-block method is efficient is when there is enough main memory available to store the smaller of the two relations.

The uniprocessor version of the nested-block join method consists of the following steps, which are repeated until the entire **R** relation has been read/processed. First, read as many pages of the **R** relation as can fit in main memory, leaving space for one page from the **S** relation. Next, read one page at a time from the **S** relation, and compare each **R** tuple, which resides in main memory, with each **S** tuple that resides in main memory. If there is a match on the joining attribute(s), then produce an output tuple. This inner loop is done until the entire **S** relation has been read and processed. For the multiprocessor version of the nested-block method, consider a shared-nothing system where both the **R** and **S** relations are fully declustered across all the nodes. A simple approach would have each processor broadcast its part of the **R** relation (i.e., the inner relation) to all the processors. So, each processor would have a complete copy of the **R** relation and could proceed with the nested-block algorithm using it and the part of the **S** relation that resides on its node.

A natural alternative to the nested-block method is to use sorting to collect tuples with the same joining value together. With the sort-merge method, both the **R** and **S** relations are sorted on the joining attribute(s). Next, the sorted **R** relation and the sorted **S** relation are merged together where tuples from the associated relations are concatenated, if they have the same join attribute(s) value. Generally, this method shows an improvement (i.e., less I/O) over the nested-block method since every tuple in the **R** relation does not have to be compared with every tuple from the **S** relation. Since the first phase of the sort-merge join method involves sorting the **R** and **S** relations, it is easily parallelized by employing a parallel sorting algorithm (e.g., an external merge-sort sorting algorithm) [DeWitt et al. 1992]. The second phase of the sort-merge join method is the merge phase, which can exploit a high degree of parallelism if the sorted relations can be partitioned across the nodes using the same range conditions.

A third approach for executing a join is by hashing. Hash-join algorithms [DeWitt and Gerber 1985; Kitsuregawa et al. 1983; Omiecinski and Tien 1989] partition the source relations **R** and **S** into disjoint subsets called *buckets*: $\mathbf{R}_0$, $\mathbf{R}_1$, ... , $\mathbf{R}_{n-1}$ and $\mathbf{S}_0$, $\mathbf{S}_1$, ... , $\mathbf{S}_{n-1}$. Tuples of a relation with the same join value will share the same bucket. Since the same partitioning scheme is used for both relations, tuples in bucket $\mathbf{R}_i$ will only have to be joined with tuples in bucket $\mathbf{S}_i$. Hence, a join of two large relations is reduced to separate joins of many smaller disjoint subsets of each relation. There are three hash-based join methods: simple hash-join, Grace hash-join, and Hybrid hash-join. Grace hash-join and Hybrid hash-join are the more efficient methods and hence have been used the most.

The uniprocessor version of Hybrid hash-join [Shapiro 1986] consists of two phases. In the first phase, both source relations, **R** and **S**, are partitioned one at a time into buckets: $\mathbf{R}_0$, $\mathbf{R}_1$, ... , $\mathbf{R}_{n-1}$ and $\mathbf{S}_0$, $\mathbf{S}_1$, ... , $\mathbf{S}_{n-1}$. While **R** is being partitioned, bucket $\mathbf{R}_0$ is actually used to build a hash table. Thus, when **S** is partitioned, tuples belonging to $\mathbf{S}_0$ can be used to probe the hash table immediately. In the second phase, the remaining n-1 corresponding buckets are processed. That is, tuples in bucket $\mathbf{R}_i$ are used to build a hash table and tuples in bucket $\mathbf{S}_i$ are used to probe the hash table. The main difference between Hybrid hash-join and Grace hash-join is that there is a complete separation between the building and probing phases in the Grace approach. That is, building and probing the hash table for $\mathbf{R}_0$ will be done after all the buckets of relation **S** have been fully constructed.

The basic idea in this multiprocessor version is to assign one bucket to each processor so that all the buckets can be processed in parallel. For a shared-nothing system, this can be accomplished by making a bucket/processor assignment, which is known to all processors. Hence, the buckets of the **R** and **S** relations that do not belong to a given processor are then sent to the appropriate processors. Once the buckets have been distributed, the building/probing phase can begin in parallel on all processors.

In recent work [Schneider and DeWitt 1989], the performances of four parallel join algorithms for Gamma are compared. The conclusion is that a hash-based join algorithm performs the best except when the join attributes are highly skewed. In that case, a non-hash-based algorithm such as sort-merge should be used over the standard hash-based method. We will examine the problem of data skew in the next section and will discuss particular algorithms that have been designed to handle data skew that are not considered in Schneider and DeWitt 1989.

Some work has appeared in the recent literature dealing with hash-join algorithms for a shared-everything architecture. In Lu et al. 1990, only hash-based join algorithms for a general-purpose shared memory multiprocessor are examined. The amount of available memory is assumed to be proportional to the number of processors. In this approach, a global hash table is built for each bucket. A locking mechanism provides exclusive access for a write to this hash table, although multiple reads may occur simultaneously. The authors provide an analytical model of the total processing time for their join algorithms. As in the previously mentioned work in this section, data skew is not considered.

The goal of Omiecinski and Lin 1989 is to compare the performance of different join algorithms on both cube and ring interconnections for multiprocessors and to investigate the effects of the number of processors and the type of interconnection on the performance. The Hybrid hash-join [Shapiro 1986] algorithm and the Join-index [Valduriez 1987] algorithm are parallelized for both cube and ring connected multiprocessors. The performances of these algorithms are then compared through analytical cost modeling. The results in Omiecinski and Lin 1989 show that the Join-index algorithm gives good performance only when the join selectivity is very small, and the Hybrid hash-join algorithm performs consistently well under most situations. The results also show that the cube topology yields better execution time than the same algorithm on the ring topology. Furthermore, increasing the number of processors has a more significant improvement on the execution time for the cube than the ring configuration.

24.3.4 Data Skew

As shown in the previous section, the basic idea behind parallelizing the join algorithms is to divide the problem, as well as the data, into independent pieces that can be processed in parallel. The performance of these algorithms depends in large part on how balanced the work is across the various processors. If the load is not very well balanced, for example, when one processor has to process a much larger number of tuples than the other processors, then that one processor becomes a bottleneck. The overall performance becomes dependent on that one processor. One factor that can cause a workload imbalance between the processors is data skew. *Data skew* refers to the situation in which certain values of a given attribute occur more frequently than other values. In a hash-based join approach, this implies that some buckets may contain many more tuples than other buckets, depending on the degree of data skew. Hence, the node that has to process the skewed data bucket(s) will become a bottleneck, if the skew is large. So, the problem is to design a join algorithm that is immune to data skew [Hua and

Lee 1991; Lakshmi and Yu 1988; Lu and Tan 1992; Wolf et al. 1991]—that is, where the load across the processors will be relatively balanced even when data skew occurs.

In Schneider and DeWitt 1989, the effect of limited data skew on four different join algorithms is examined. The authors conclude that the performance of the hash-based join algorithms degrades when the join values of the inner relation are highly skewed and that a non-hash-based algorithm should be used in those cases (e.g. sort-merge). However, the double skew case is not considered (i.e., when both relations are highly skewed).

In Wolf et al. 1990, the shared-nothing model of parallelism is assumed and a parallel join algorithm based on the sort-merge method is presented to handle data skew. The algorithm is based on the divide-and-conquer approach. It adds an extra scheduling phase to the usual sort, transfer, and join phases. During the scheduling phase, an optimization algorithm is used, which takes the output of the sort phase and determines how the join is to be divided into multiple tasks and how those tasks are to be assigned to processors so as to balance the load. The authors present an analytical model of their algorithm's performance and show that it achieves a good load balancing for the join processing phase in a CPU-bound environment.

In Kitsuregawa and Ogawa 1990, a robust hash-join based algorithm is devised for a specific parallel database computer architecture. This architecture is also based on a shared-nothing model. Instead of the previous approach of allocating buckets to processors, buckets are now dynamically allocated to processors so as to balance the load. The approach used is a bucket-spreading strategy that partitions buckets into fragments, and in a subsequent phase these fragments are assigned to processors. The bucket-spreading strategy is similar to the idea of disk striping. The method also makes use of a specific network structure (i.e., an omega network) to assist in the bucket-spreading strategy. A simulation model of their system is presented, and performance results show that their algorithm is not affected very much by the presence of data skew. The cost of writing the result of the join to a file and to disk is not considered.

In Omiecinski 1991, the author adapts the Grace hash-join method for a shared-everything environment and has designed and implemented a modified version that balances the load on the processors when the data are skewed. Cost models for the algorithms are developed, and experimental results show that the models accurately reflect the performance of the algorithms, under certain assumptions. The algorithms are run on a 10-node Sequent multiprocessor machine with the parallel I/O capability simulated. From the experiments, it was concluded that even single skew affects the performance of the basic hash-join approach for a shared-everything system. The performance degrades greatly when the result of the join is written to disk or when there is double skew. The load-balancing algorithm also shows a much better performance when compared with the basic method in all of those cases.

The goal of Omiecinski and Lin 1992 is to design efficient relational join algorithms for large databases on a hypercube multiprocessor in which data and processing power are distributed. The Cube Hybrid hash-join algorithm is shown to outperform other algorithms in the previous research [Omiecinski and Lin 1989]. Unfortunately, its performance greatly deteriorates when bucket overflow occurs in the inner relation of the join operation. In Omiecinski and Lin 1992, the authors present the cube adaptive hash-join algorithm, which is designed to combine the merits of nested-loop and hybrid hash algorithms. The performances of these algorithms are compared through analytical cost modeling. The nonuniform data value distribution of the inner relation is shown to have a greater impact than that of the outer relation. The cube adaptive hash-join algorithm outperforms the cube hybrid hash-join algorithm when bucket overflow occurs. In the worst case, this algorithm converges to the cube nested-loop hash-join algorithm. When there is no hash table overflow, the cube adaptive hash-join algorithm converges to the cube hybrid hash-join algorithm. Since the cube adaptive hash-join algorithm adapts itself depending on the characteristics of the relations, it is relatively immune to the data distribution. The conclusion is that the cube adaptive hash-join algorithm should be the algorithm of choice to perform the relational join operator for large databases on a hypercube multiprocessor.

24.3.5 Multijoin Query Execution

In section 24.3, several parallel algorithms are examined for executing a join operation. However, if several joins appear in the query (i.e., a multijoin query) other options are available. For example, consider the two query trees shown in Fig. 24–2, the bushy tree and the right-deep tree. With the bushy tree, the join of $\mathbf{R_1}$ with $\mathbf{R_2}$ and the join of $\mathbf{R_3}$ with $\mathbf{R_4}$ can be done in parallel using one of the join methods mentioned in section 24.3 for each. As an alternative, the joins in the right-deep tree can be executed in a pipelined manner. For example, if we assume that a hash-join method is being used for the joins, then a hash table can be built for relations $\mathbf{R_3}$, $\mathbf{R_2}$, and $\mathbf{R_1}$, as long as enough main memory is available. Once this is done, tuples from relation $\mathbf{R_4}$ can be used to probe the hash table for relation $\mathbf{R_3}$, and matching tuples can be used to probe the hash table for $\mathbf{R_2}$, and so forth.

In Schneider and DeWitt 1990, the processing of multijoin queries is discussed in the context of Gamma. The authors show how a different representation of a query tree can affect the degree of parallelism within a query and its performance. Specifically, a comparison of left-deep and right-deep tree representations is made. A left-deep tree is a plan that has at most

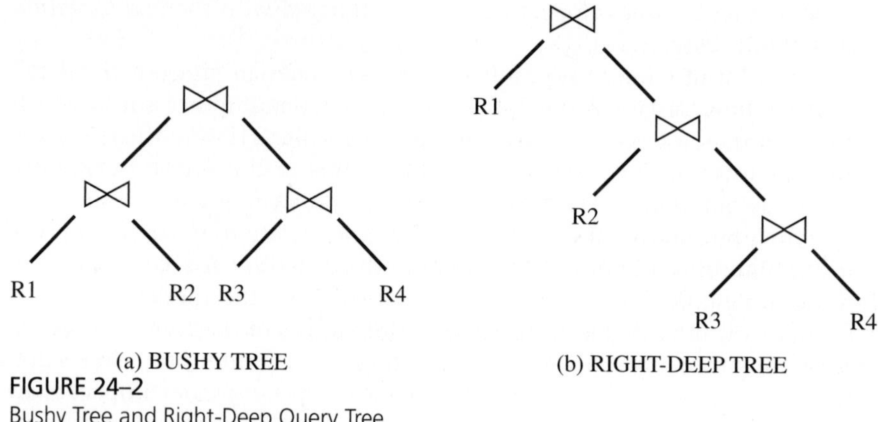

FIGURE 24–2
Bushy Tree and Right-Deep Query Tree

one operand as an intermediate result that is always used to build the hash table (the inner relation). Although similar to left-deep trees, in a right-deep tree the intermediate join result is always used to probe the hash table for the next join (the outer relation). Since the available main memory is a factor in pipelining, the right-deep trees are segmented such that the amount of memory needed for each segment does not exceed the total amount available. For example, in Fig. 24–2, the right-deep tree might be segmented such that the join involving $\mathbf{R_3}$ and the join involving $\mathbf{R_2}$ can be pipelined, but there may not be enough memory to accommodate a hash table for $\mathbf{R_1}$ as well. So, the pipeline is broken at that point and can be restarted for the upper part of the tree once the first segment has been completely processed. That is, the intermediate result of the first two joins would be written to disk, a hash table would be constructed for relation $\mathbf{R_1}$, and the intermediate result would be read back from disk and then used to probe the hash table. The conclusion from the simulation study shows that a right-deep query representation strategy can offer significant performance advantages in large multiprocessor database machines.

Other work has been done [Chen et al. 1992] that further improves the pipelined execution of multijoins. Heuristics are used in Chen et al. 1992 to generate segmented right-deep trees that can be executed efficiently. Pipelining is also exploited in the query trees constructed in Lu et al. 1991 and Srivastava and Elsesser 1993.

24.4 Future Work

Although a good deal of work has been done in the area of parallel relational database systems, there are still a number of important issues to be studied [DeWitt and Gray 1992].

One issue is that of parallel query optimization [Hong and Stonebraker 1992]. Even in a single-processor environment, the number of query plans (e.g., for multijoin queries) can be exponential. With a parallel database environment, even more options exist. This provides further complications for the query optimizer that is trying to determine the best plan for executing a query. The selection of good optimization objectives is important for the query optimizer, and in a parallel system, objectives may conflict [Srivastava and Elsesser 1993]. Dynamic query optimization will also play an important role in parallel database systems. Another issue is physical database design. There are many indexing and declustering strategies for a relation. Developing good strategies that take into account the expected workload will be a necessity. Since the workload is usually dynamic, these design strategies should be adaptive. Since databases are very large and the need for high availability is paramount, redesign (or reorganization) will have to be done incrementally as well as concurrently with user queries. Work on concurrent reorganization has already been done but within the context of a single-processor environment.

A third issue is executing long-running complex queries and short update queries together. The goal is to provide a suitable level of performance for both types of queries. In a single-processor environment, one approach would be to manage two distinct databases, one that is updated by the short queries and the other (slightly out of date) that is used for the retrieval of data by the complex queries. At some point the updated database will become the database to be used for the complex queries. With the use of parallel database systems, it might be possible to use only one database and still provide the needed performance and consistency levels.

24.5 Conclusion

The need, in the near future, to store terabytes of information will necessitate the use of parallel database systems to support the required high level of performance. In this chapter, we examined some of the important research issues for parallel relational database systems. They included system architecture, data placement, join processing, data skew, and multijoin query processing. We also presented a number of open problems that will provide a basis for further work in parallel database systems. It is expected that parallel database systems (both relational and nonrelational) will become commonplace in the near future.

REFERENCES

Bitton, D., Boral, H., DeWitt, D. J., and Wilkinson, W. K. 1983. Parallel Algorithms for the Execution of Relational Database Operations. *ACM Transactions on Database Systems*, Vol. 8, No. 3, 324–353.

Boral, H., Alexander, W., Clay, L., Copeland, G., Danforth, S., Franklin, M., Hart, B., Smith, M., and Valduriez, P. 1990. Prototyping Bubba, a Highly Parallel Database System. *IEEE Transactions on Knowledge and Data Engineering,* Vol. 2, No. 1, 4–24.

Chen, M. S., Lo, M. L., Yu, P. S., and Young, H. C. 1992. Using Segmented Right-Deep Trees for the Execution of Pipelined Hash Joins. *Proceedings of the Eighteenth International Conference on Very Large Databases,* 15–26.

Copeland, G., Alexander, W., Boughter, E., and Keller, T. 1988. Data Placement in Bubba. *Proceedings of the ACM-SIGMOD International Conference on Management of Data,* 99–108.

DeWitt, D. J., and Gerber, R. 1985. Multiprocessor Hash-Based Join Algorithms. *Proceedings of the Eleventh International Conference on Very Large Data Bases,* 151–164.

DeWitt, D. J., Ghandeharizadeh, S., Schneider, D. A., Bricker, A., Hsiao, H., and Rasmussen, R. 1990. The Gamma Database Machine Project. *IEEE Transactions on Knowledge and Data Engineering,* Vol. 2, No. 1, 44–62.

DeWitt, D., and Gray, J. 1992. Parallel Database Systems: The Future of High Performance Database Systems. *CACM,* Vol. 35, No. 6, 85–98.

DeWitt, D., Naughton, J., and Burger, J. 1993. Nested Loops Revisited. *Proceedings of the International Symposium on Parallel and Distributed Information Systems.*

DeWitt, D., Naughton, J., and Schneider, D. 1992. Parallel Sorting on a Shared-Nothing Architecture Using Probabilistic Splitting. *Proceedings of the International Symposium on Parallel and Distributed Information Systems,* 280–291.

Ghandeharizadeh, S., and DeWitt, D. J. 1990a. A Multiuser Performance Analysis of Alternative Declustering Strategies. *Proceedings of the Sixth International Conference on Data Engineering,* 466–475.

Ghandeharizadeh, S., and DeWitt, D. J. 1990b. Hybrid-Range Partitioning Strategy: A New Declustering Strategy for Multiprocessor Database Machines. *Proceedings of the Sixteenth International Conference on Very Large Databases,* 481–492.

Graefe, G. 1990. Encapsulation of Parallelism in the Volcano Query Processing System. *Proceedings of the ACM-SIGMOD International Conference on Management of Data,* 102–111.

Hong, W., and Stonebraker, M. 1992. Optimization of Parallel Query Execution Plans in XPRS. *Proceedings of the International Symposium on Parallel and Distributed Information Systems,* 218–225.

Hua, K. A., and Lee, C. 1991. Handling Data Skew in Multiprocessor Database Computers Using Partition Tuning. *Proceedings of the Seventeenth VLDB Conference,* 525–536.

Kitsuregawa, M., Nakano, M., and Takagi, M. 1989. Query Execution for Large Relations on Functional Disk System. *Proceedings of the IEEE Fifth International Conference on Data Engineering,* 159–167.

Kitsuregawa, M., and Ogawa, Y. A. 1990. Bucket Spreading Parallel Hash: A New Robust Join Method for Data Skew in Super Database Computer (SDC). *Proceedings of the Sixteenth International Conference on Very Large Data Bases,* 210–221.

Kitsuregawa, M., Tanaka, H., and Motooka, T. 1983. Application of Hash to Database Machine and its Architecture. *New Generation Computing,* Vol. 1, No. 1, 63–74.

Kitsuregawa, M., Tanaka, H., and Motooka, T. 1984. Architecture and Performance of Relational Algebra Machine GRACE. *International Conference on Parallel Processing Proceedings*, 241–250.

Lakshmi, M. S., and Yu, P. S. 1988. Effect of Skew on Join Performance in Parallel Architectures. *Proceedings of the International Symposium on Databases in Parallel and Distributed Systems*, 107–120.

Lu, H., Shan, M., and Tan, K. 1991. Optimization of Multi-Way Join Queries for Parallel Execution. *Proceedings of the 17th International Conference on Very Large Data Bases*, 549–560.

Lu, H., and Tan, K. 1992. Dynamic and Load-Balanced Task-Oriented Database Query Processing in Parallel Systems. *Proceedings of the Third International Conference on Extending Data Base Technology*.

Lu, H., Tan, K., and Shan, M. 1990. Hash-Based Join Algorithms for Multiprocessor Computers with Shared Memory. *Proceedings of the Sixteenth International Conference on Very Large Data Bases*, 198–209.

Neches, P. M. 1984. Hardware Support for Advanced Data Management Systems. *IEEE Computer*, Vol. 17, No. 11, 29–40.

Omiecinski, E. 1991. Performance Analysis of a Load Balancing Relational Hash Join Algorithm for a Shared-Memory Multiprocessor. *Proceedings of the Seventeenth VLDB Conference*, 375–386.

Omiecinski, E., and Lin, E. 1989. Hash-Based and Index-Based Join Algorithms for Cube and Ring Connected Multicomputers. *IEEE Transactions on Knowledge and Data Engineering*, Vol. 1, No. 3, 329–343.

Omiecinski, E., and Lin, E. 1992. The Adaptive-Hash Join Algorithm for a Hypercube Multicomputer. *IEEE Transactions on Parallel and Distributed Systems*, Vol. 3, No. 3, 334–349.

Omiecinski, E., and Tien, E. 1989. A Hash-Based Join Algorithm for a Cube-Connected Parallel Computer. *Information Processing Letters*, Vol. 30, No. 5, 269–275.

Schneider, D. A., and DeWitt, D. J. 1989. A Performance Evaluation of Four Parallel Join Algorithms in a Shared-Nothing Multiprocessor Environment. *Proceedings of the ACM-SIGMOD International Conference on Management of Data*, 110–121.

Schneider, D., and DeWitt, D. J. 1990. Tradeoffs in Processing Complex Join Queries via Hashing in Multiprocessor Database Machines. *Proceedings of the Sixteenth VLDB Conference*, 469–480.

Shapiro, L. 1986. Join Processing in Database Systems with Large Main Memories. *ACM Transactions on Database Systems*, Vol. 11, No. 3, 239–264.

Srivastava, J., and Elsesser, G. 1993. Optimizing Multi-Join Queries in Parallel Relational Databases. *Proceedings of the International Symposium on Parallel and Distributed Information Systems*.

Stonebraker, M. 1986. The Case for Shared Nothing. *Database Engineering*, Vol. 9, No. 1.

Stonebraker, M., Katz, R., Patterson, D., and Ousterhout, J. 1988. The Design of XPRS. *Proceedings of the Fourteenth VLDB Conference*, 318–330.

Teradata. 1985. *DBC/1012 Data Base Computer Concepts and Facilities*, 1.3 edition.

Valduriez, P. 1987. Join Indices. *ACM Transactions on Database Systems,* Vol. 12, No. 2, 218–246.

Wolf, J. L., Dias, D. M., and Yu, P. S. 1990. An Effective Algorithm for Parallelizing Sort-Merge Joins in the Presence of Data Skew. *Proceedings of the Second International Symposium on Databases in Parallel and Distributed Systems,* 103–115.

Wolf, J. L., Dias, D. M., Yu, P. S., and Turek, J. 1991. Comparative Performance of Parallel Join Algorithms. *Proceedings of the First International Conference on Parallel and Distributed Information Systems,* 78–88.

PART II

Technology for Interoperating Legacy Databases

25

Introduction to Part 2: Technology for Interoperating Legacy Databases

25.1 Overview

During the past three decades, file systems, navigational database systems (hierarchical and network systems), and relational database systems have been used as platforms for managing data for conventional transaction-oriented applications. The problems of developing applications that require access to heterogeneous data sources that are managed separately by different file systems and database systems have thus far been addressed in a few different ways.

One way has been to convert and migrate all data from one data management system to another. An installation may adopt this approach if it is sufficient to have data migrated from one system to another primarily to have the data read by the latter. An installation might also adopt this approach if it decides to replace its data management system (e.g., IMS or TOTAL) with a different data management system (e.g., DB2 or UniSQL/X). For example, the IMS EXTRACT facility is provided with IBM's relational database products, SQL/DS and DB2/MVS, to support conversion and migration of data from an IMS database to a relational database. There are potentially serious problems with this approach. First, if the purpose of conversion and migration of data from system A to system B is simply to make the data available for processing by B, reverse conversion and migration of the part of the data that is updated by B may be necessary from B to A. Second, if system A is to be discarded after mass conversion and migration of all data, there is still the issue of supporting the applications that may have been written in A. The applications may need to be converted to run in B, either manually or automatically; or an emulator of system A may need to be provided on top of system B to continue to run the applications. Supporting existing applications after a wholesale migration of data and data management system has proven to be a very difficult problem indeed.

Another solution that has been used, not very successfully, is the so-called gateways for specific pairs of data management system. For example, the INGRES line of database products includes gateways between the INGRES relational database system to the DEC RMS file system and between INGRES and PC-based dBASE systems. There are gateways (called *CONNECT) between the ORACLE relational database system and IMS and between ORACLE and RMS. A gateway between system A and system B translates a query in A's language into an equivalent query in B's language and submits the translated query to system B. The gateway solution has some serious limitations. First, the gateway approach does not support transaction management, even for a pair of systems. In other words, the gateway from system A to system B is merely a switch and query translator; system A does not coordinate concurrency control and recovery of transactions that involve updates to both systems' databases. Second, the gateway approach is only concerned with the problem of translating a query expressed in one language into an equivalent expression in another language. As such, it does not address the issues of homogenizing the structural and representational differences between different schemas.

Today, the database research community has concluded that the most viable and general solution to the problems of interoperating heterogeneous data systems is the federated multidatabase system. Simply put, a multidatabase system (MDBS) is a database system that resides unobtrusively on top of existing database and file systems (called *local database systems*) and presents a single database illusion to its users. In particular, an MDBS maintains a single global database schema against which its users will issue queries and updates; an MDBS maintains only the global schema, and the local database systems actually maintain all user data. The global schema is constructed by consolidating (integrating) the schemas of the local databases; the process of consolidating the local schemas in general requires neutralizing (homogenizing) the schematic differences (conflicts) among them. The MDBS translates the global queries and updates into queries and updates for dispatch to appropriate local database systems for actual processing, merges the results from them, and generates the final result for the user. Further, the MDBS coordinates the commit and abort of global transactions (queries and updates) by the local database systems that processed them to maintain consistency of data within the local databases. An MDBS actually controls multiple gateways (or drivers). It manages local databases through the gateways, one gateway for each local database.

25.1.1 MDBS Objectives

The following are the general objectives of an MDBS.

OBJECTIVE 1 It must obviate the need for a batch conversion and migration of data from one data source (e.g., an ORACLE database) to another (e.g., a Sybase database).

OBJECTIVE 2 It must require absolutely no changes to the local database system (LDBS) software; this preserves what is known as *design autonomy*. In other words, an MDBS must appear to any of the LDBSs as just another application or user.

OBJECTIVE 3 It must not prevent any of the LDBSs from being used in its native mode. In other words, users of an LDBS may continue to work with the system for transactions that require access only to data managed by the system, while users will use the MDBS to issue transactions that require access to more than one data source. In this way, applications written in any of the LDBSs are preserved, and new applications that require access to more than one data source may be developed using the MDBS.

OBJECTIVE 4 It must make it possible for users and applications to interact with it in one database language. In other words, the users and applications should not have to work with the different interface languages of the LDBSs.

OBJECTIVE 5 It must shield the users and applications from the heterogeneity of the operating environments of the LDBSs, including the computer, operating system, and network protocol.

OBJECTIVE 6 It, unlike most previous attempts at allowing the interoperability of heterogeneous database systems, must support distributed transactions involving both reads and updates against different databases.

OBJECTIVE 7 It must be a full-blown database system—that is, it must make available to users all the facilities provided by standard database systems, including schema definition, non-procedural queries, automatic query optimization, updates, transaction management, concurrency control and recovery, integrity control, access authorization, both interactive and host-language application support, graphics application development tools, and so forth.

OBJECTIVE 8 It must introduce virtually no changes to the operation and administration of any of the LDBSs.

OBJECTIVE 9 It must provide run-time performance that approaches that of a homogeneous distributed database system.

25.1.2 MDBS Architecture

An MDBS is a full-fledged database system. It provides data definition facilities so that the global database may be defined on the basis of the local databases. The data definition facilities include means to harmonize (homogenize) the different representations of the semantically equivalent data in different remote databases. An MDBS user may query the definition of the virtual database and query and update the virtual database (requiring query-optimization and query-processing mechanisms). Multiple MDBS users may simultaneously query, update, and even populate the virtual database (requiring concurrency control mechanisms); the users may submit a collection of queries and updates as a single transaction against the virtual database (requiring transaction management mechanisms); the users would grant and revoke authorizations on parts of the database to other users (requiring authorization mechanisms).

The architecture of an MDBS has a single MDBS site driving multiple local database sites. An MDBS is itself a client/server architecture; multiple MDBS clients interact with a single MDBS server. MDBS users may develop applications that access multiple local databases using a number of application development and database access tools that come with an MDBS. An MDBS manages all global database control information, including the global schema, and submits and manages transactions that invoke one or more local database systems. There is one driver for each local database system connected with an MDBS. The driver resides on the same site (computer) with the local database system. The MDBS and the drivers communicate via a communication subsystem (CSS). The architecture of an MDBS is completely nonintrusive to local database systems; as such, absolutely no changes are necessary to the local database systems, and applications and users may directly access their databases through their local database systems.

An MDBS maintains the global database as a collection of views defined over relations in local databases. MDBS global schema definition facilities allow mechanisms for neutralizing a full spectrum of schematic differences that may exist among heterogeneous local schema. Although an MDBS maintains the global schema, the user data of interest to MDBS users are all stored in local databases. Using the information in the directory, an MDBS translates the queries and updates to equivalent queries and updates for processing by local database systems that manage the data that the queries and updates need to access. The goal of MDBS query translation is to push as much processing as possible to local database systems. This means that as much of the WHERE clause of an MDBS query as possible is included in the query being dispatched to each local database system. In this way, an MDBS maximizes the selectivity of each query that is dispatched to a local database system; in other words, an MDBS minimizes the size of the query result that is returned from each local database system. The local database drivers pass the translated queries and updates to local database systems and pass the results to the MDBS for format translation, merging, and any necessary postprocessing (e.g., for processing the ORDER BY or GROUP BY clauses in a SQL query and also performing interdatabase joins).

An MDBS must support distributed transaction management over local databases, which means that all updates issued within one MDBS transaction, even when they result in updates to multiple local databases, are simultaneously committed or aborted. MDBS transaction management must preserve the traditional atomicity and serializability properties of transactions. This means not only that MDBS users are able to issue queries and updates against the LDBS but also that they will be able to group such queries and updates into transactions. An MDBS processes multiple concurrent global transactions by interleaving them to maximize transaction throughput and to protect each transaction from interferences from other transactions. Further, an MDBS guarantees that the effects of aborted global transactions are completely erased from the LDBS and the effects of committed global transactions are indeed committed in all LDBSs involved.

25.2 Organization of Part 2

The users of a multidatabase system need a single global schema that defines the global database across independently designed heterogeneous databases. Once a single global schema is defined, the users may issue queries and updates against the global database. The users also need to organize queries and updates into transactions for automatic enforcement of database integrity in the presence of crashes and simultaneous access to the global database by multiple users. This means that there are three key issues in multidatabase systems. The first is the construction of a global schema across independently designed heterogeneous databases. The basis of addressing this issue is a comprehensive taxonomy of schema differences that may exist among independently designed schemas and a technique for homogenizing each type of schema difference. The second issue is the processing of queries that the users will issue against the global database. Here the challenge is translating a global query into a set of subqueries to be dispatched by the LDBSs such that the total cost of processing the global query is minimized. The third issue is the management of transactions (i.e., reads and writes issued against the global database as an atomic unit) across heterogeneous databases. The problems to address include, as in transaction management in a single homogeneous database system, concurrency control, recovery, and deadlock detection and resolution.

Part 2 of this book consists of eight chapters (besides this introduction) organized around three subparts. The first two subparts, schema integration and architectural issues of query processing and transaction management, address the three key issues in the use and construction of multidatabase systems. The third subpart includes chapters that describe real multidatabase systems.

The first subpart is Chapter 26, titled "On Resolving Schematic Heterogeneity in Multidatabase Systems." The chapter provides a taxonomy of differences that may exist among schemas of independently designed databases, and offers techniques for resolving each type of difference. The framework includes schema differences between relational databases, between object-oriented databases, and between a relational and an object-oriented database.

The second subpart, Chapters 27 through 29, deals with key architectural issues in constructing a multidatabase system. Chapter 27, titled "Query Processing in Multidatabase Systems," discusses query translation, optimization, and processing issues. Chapter 28, titled "Transaction Management in Multidatabase Systems," summarizes issues in providing transaction management facilities over heterogeneous database systems. Chapter 29, titled "Specification and Execution of Transactional Workflows," presents a model and specification of workflows in a distributed heterogeneous database environment. A *workflow* is any task to be performed by any processing entity (a person, a software program, etc.) and may be specified by various means. The workflow model presented is a generalization of multidatabase transaction models.

The third subpart, Chapters 30 through 33, provides descriptions of real multidatabase systems. Chapter 30 gives an overview of the UniSQL/M commercial multidatabase system. In particular, it describes the schema construction and schema evolution aspects of UniSQL/M. UniSQL/M takes a unified relational and object-oriented data model for the construction of the global schema. It supports distributed transaction management, with simultaneous updates of the LDBSs, and supports a full object-oriented SQL for queries and updates. UniSQL/M may be connected to SQL-based relational database systems and even first-generation object-oriented database systems. Chapter 31 describes the Enterprise Data Access/SQL (EDA/SQL) multidatabase connectivity product from Information Builders, Inc. EDA/SQL provides connectivity to close to 50 database and file systems, including relational systems and hierarchical and network database systems. Chapter 32 describes the Pegasus research prototype multidatabase system at Hewlett-Packard. In particular, it describes the schema construction and query-processing aspects of Pegasus. Pegasus uses ObjectSQL and the unified relational and object-oriented model as the basis for the integration of heterogeneous database systems. Chapter 33 provides a description of the Amoco Distributed Database System (ADDS) prototype from Amoco Production. The ADDS prototype, which is not in use, used the relational model for the global schema and connected to IMS, DB2, and SQL/DS. ADDS also supported distributed transaction management.

I initially envisioned including papers on gateway products, database conversion and migration tools, and interoperability of applications in a distributed environment. However, I was unable to find any industry authors who could or would write on these topics.

26

On Resolving Schematic Heterogeneity in Multidatabase Systems

WON KIM
INJUN CHOI
SUNIT GALA
MARK SCHEEVEL

A schema contains a semantic description of the information in a given database. It is possible to define equivalent schemas in as many ways as there are data models. Further, the same (or similar) information can be represented in many ways in the same data model. Given such inter- and intra-model variability, it is a formidable task to integrate many schemas into a homogeneous schema. In this chapter, we first provide a general classification of schematic conflicts that may arise when integrating relational and object-oriented databases. We then give a comprehensive classification of conflict resolution techniques. We provide specific examples using the relational model and an object-oriented model.

26.1 Introduction

The proliferation of database systems based on different data models prevents the user from having uniform access to data from such heterogeneous sources. Recently, multidatabase systems (MDBs) have been proposed to provide a uniform environment in which the user can access data from heterogeneous component databases (CDBs) by using a single data definition and manipulation language [ACM Surveys 1990; Brill and Templeton 1984; Dayal and Hwang 1984; Landers and Rosenberg 1982; Litwin et al. 1990; Motro 1987]. An MDB is a federation of independently developed CDBs, and it provides a homogenizing layer on top of these CDBs to give the user an illusion of a homogeneous database system. An important element of the homogenizing layer is the MDB schema that integrates the schemas of component databases.

The schema integration process can be thought of as deriving a single schema from a set of schemas through a sequence of simpler functions, each of which addresses (resolves) a schematic discrepancy:

Reprinted with permission of Kluwer Academic Publishers, Norwell, Mass. Appeared in *Distributed and Parallel Databases, Volume 1, No. 3*, pp. 251–279, 1993.

$$\text{sch\_int\_proc: schema}_1 \times \text{schema}_2 \times \ldots \times \text{schema}_n \rightarrow \text{int\_schema}$$

Schema integration and related issues have been discussed in the literature [Batini et al. 1986; Kaul et al. 1990, Navathe et al. 1984, Sheth et al. 1993], typically in the context of the relational or the entity relationship model. However, to the best of our knowledge, there exists no general framework for the comprehensive enumeration and systematic classification of resolution techniques for schematic conflicts[1] that occur in an MDB context. Obviously, such a classification is important because homogenization can be realized only by resolving the various schematic conflicts arising from the heterogeneous CDBs.

A schema contains a semantic description of the information in a given database. It is possible to define equivalent schemas in as many ways as there are data models. Further, the same (or similar) information can be represented in many ways in the same data model. Given such inter- and intra-model variability, it is indeed a formidable task to integrate many schemas into a homogeneous schema. Of course, it is up to the user's discretion to decide how many schemas, and what portions of the relevant schemas, are to be merged.

In this chapter, we first provide a general classification of schematic conflicts that may arise when integrating relational and object-oriented databases (i.e, RDBs and OODBs, respectively). We then give a comprehensive classification of conflict resolution techniques. We provide specific examples in SQL (for RDBs) and SQL/X [UniSQL 1992], which is upward compatible with SQL (for OODBs). There are three basic possibilities when integrating a schema, which are listed below in increasing order of difficulty:

1. Integrating two RDBs.
2. Integrating an RDB and an OODB.
3. Integrating two OODBs.

While most of the schematic differences outlined in section 26.3 can occur in all three cases, some can occur only in the last two cases.

In section 26.2, we define CDB schemas that will be used in all examples throughout this chapter. In section 26.3, we extend the basic classification of schematic conflicts developed in Kim and Seo 1991 to include RDBs as well as OODBs. We then enumerate and classify various resolution techniques for each schematic conflict in section 26.4. For each kind of conflict, we first define it, state how it can be resolved, and then give an example. We discuss updatability criteria and null values in section 26.5.

1. Note that we limit our discussion to structural conflicts as opposed to semantic differences due to dynamic or temporal constraints.

Our conclusions are drawn in section 26.6. We use the term *entity* to collectively denote relational tables and object-oriented classes. Likewise, *attributes* denote columns in a table and elements in the signature of a class; *instances* denote tuples and objects.

26.2 Sample CDB Schemas

Throughout this chapter, we will use the following example involving universities. Faculty scholastic activities (teaching courses and advising theses) and students' performance at four universities (1, 2, 3, 4) are to be monitored. University 1 allows total autonomy to undergraduate and graduate student offices with their own DBs. At University 1, graduate students are considered as undergraduate students while they do their course work, and their records are turned over to the Graduate Study office only when they begin their thesis work. So, the Graduate Study office only maintains students' thesis information and grade point averages of their course work (the Undergraduate Study office calculates the gpa when a student's records are turned over to the Graduate Study office). Notice that the Graduate Study office of University 1 has only one table containing faculty information. So, the faculty information of University 1 is kept in two separate DBs (but some faculty members belong to only one DB). The schemas for Universities 1 and 2 are defined below.

```
ldb1: /* Undergraduate Study of University 1 */

Under_Grad(name CHAR(25), ssn INTEGER, major CHAR(20),
     address CHAR(50))
Faculty(name CHAR(25), ssn INTEGER, dept CHAR(20),
     rank CHAR(10))
Course(cname CHAR(30), cno INTEGER)
Restricted_course(cname CHAR(25), cno INTEGER,
     major CHAR(20))
Enroll(cno CHAR(7), fssn INTEGER, sssn INTEGER, grade REAL)
Employee(name CHAR(25), ssn INTEGER, position CHAR(25))
Emp_other(ssn INTEGER, age INTEGER, wt_in_lb INTEGER,
     ht_in_in INTEGER,
          salary INTEGER, bonus REAL, tax INTEGER,
               bracket INTEGER)

ldb2: /* Graduate Study of University 1 */

Grad_student(sname CHAR(25), sssn INTEGER, major
     CHAR(20), gpa REAL, fname CHAR(25),
             fssn INTEGER, frank CHAR(10),
                 thesis_title CHAR(50))

ldb3: /* University 2 */
```

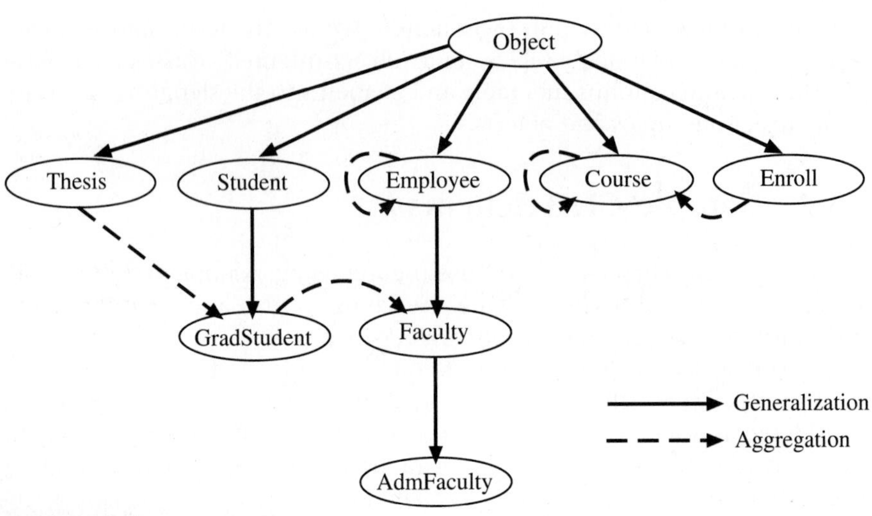

FIGURE 26–1
Schema Graph for University 3

```
Student(lastname CHAR(15), firstname CHAR(10), ssn INTEGER,
       type CHAR(1), major CHAR(20))
Graduate_info(ssn INTEGER, advisor_ssn INTEGER)
Faculty(lastname CHAR(15), firstname CHAR(10), ssn INTEGER,
       dept CHAR(20), rank CHAR(10))
Address(ssn INTEGER, street CHAR(25), city CHAR(20),
    zip CHAR(5))
Course(cname CHAR(30), cno CHAR(7))
Course_restriction(cno CHAR(7), major CHAR(20),
   prereq_cno CHAR(7))
Enroll(cno CHAR(7), fac_ssn INTEGER, stud_ssn INTEGER,
   grade REAL)
Thesis(title CHAR(50), ssn INTEGER, grade REAL)
Employee(name CHAR(25), ssn INTEGER, position CHAR(25))
Emp_personal(ssn INTEGER, age INTEGER, wt_in_kg
   INTEGER, ht_in_cm INTEGER)
Emp_tax(ssn INTEGER, salary INTEGER, bonus REAL,
       tax INTEGER, bracket CHAR(6))
```

Universities 3 and 4 currently use UniSQL/X [UniSQL 1992]. Shown in Fig. 26–1 is the schema graph for University 3. The `Student` class in Universities 3 and 4 OODB has the `gpa` method for computing students' grade point averages, whereas in other universities, separate queries have to be issued to compute the `gpa`. The schema graph for University 4, which is similar to that of University 3, is shown in Fig. 26–2. However, there are some interesting differences between the class definitions of `ldb4` and `ldb5`. The `ssn` attribute has different domains—namely, `INTEGER` and `CHAR(9)`. The advisor attribute has domains `SET_OF(Faculty)` and

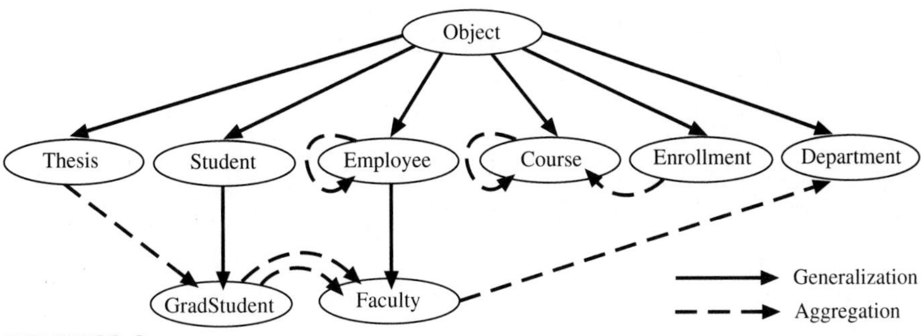

FIGURE 26–2
Schema Graph for University 4

Faculty, while GradStudent in ldb5 has an additional attribute committee. The attribute dept has domains CHAR(20) and Department. The monitoring project uses UniSQL/M, an extension to integrate SQL and UniSQL/X schemas, and the project team constructed an MDB schema over the participating universities' databases whose schemas are given below.

```
ldb4: /* University 3 */

CLASS Student
SIGNATURE name:CHAR(25), ssn:INTEGER, major:CHAR(20),
          gpa: REAL ...; /* methods */

CLASS Gradstudent
SUPERCLASS Student
SIGNATURE advisor:SET_OF(Faculty)

CLASS Employee
SIGNATURE name:CHAR(25), ssn:INTEGER, position:CHAR(25),
     supervisor:Employee

CLASS Faculty
SUPERCLASS Employee
SIGNATURE dept:CHAR(20), rank:CHAR(10)

CLASS Admfaculty
SUPERCLASS Faculty
SIGNATURE position:CHAR(15)

CLASS Course
SIGNATURE cname:CHAR(30), cno:CHAR(7), prereq:SET_OF(Course)

CLASS Enroll
SIGNATURE course:Course, fssn:INTEGER, sssn:INTEGER,
     grade:REAL

CLASS Thesis
SIGNATURE title:CHAR(50), author: Gradstudent, status:CHAR(10)

ldb5 /* University 4 */
```

```
CLASS Student
SIGNATURE fname:CHAR(15), lname:CHAR(15), ssn:CHAR(9),
     major:CHAR(20)
          gpa:REAL, ... /* methods */

CLASS GradStudent
SUPERCLASS Student
SIGNATURE advisor:Faculty, committee:SET_OF(Faculty)

CLASS Employee
SIGNATURE name:CHAR(30), ssn:CHAR(9), supervisor:Employee

CLASS Faculty
SUPERCLASS Employee
SIGNATURE dept:Department, rank:CHAR(10)

CLASS Course
SIGNATURE cname:CHAR(30), cno:CHAR(7), prereq:SET_OF(Course)

CLASS Enroll
SIGNATURE course:Course, fssn:CHAR(9), sssn:CHAR(9),
     grade:REAL

CLASS Thesis
SIGNATURE title:CHAR(50), author:GradStudent, status:CHAR(10)

CLASS Department
SIGNATURE name:CHAR(20), chairperson:CHAR(30)
```

Nota Bene: We shall adopt the following convention in all examples presented in this chapter. All class names begin with an upper-case letter. All attribute names begin with a lower-case letter. All reserved words are written in upper-case letters. Names of updatable virtual classes are prefixed with "U_"; names of nonupdatable virtual classes are prefixed with "N_"; and the names of multiviews are prefixed with "V_". Postfix letters like "_R" or "_OO" stand for *relational* and *object oriented,* respectively; and postfix numbers denote the CDB.

26.3 Schematic Conflicts in an MDB

As we can see in the sample CDB schemas above, a given concept may be expressed in different ways [Batini et al. 1986]. These differences may be in name, structure, data type, and the like. This makes it impossible to manipulate data in different CDBs using a traditional query language such as SQL, which is designed for use against a single, homogeneous database. Extensions to traditional DDLs and DMLs are necessary to define an MDB schema that will resolve various schematic conflicts in CDBs. This, in turn, will allow a user to formulate a single query against a federation of N databases instead of a sequence of N queries, one for each CDB.

1. Entity-vs-Entity
   (a) One-to-One Entity
      i. Entity Name
         - different names for equivalent entities
         - same name for different entities
      ii. Entity Structure
         - missing attributes
         - missing but implicit attributes
      iii. Entity Constraints
      iv. Entity Inclusion
   (b) Many-to-Many Entities
2. Attribute-vs-Attribute
   (a) One-to-One Attribute
      i. Attribute Name
         - different names for equivalent attributes
         - same name for different attributes
      ii. Attribute Constraints
         - integrity constraints
         - data type
         - composition
      iii. Default Values
      iv. Attribute Inclusion
      v. Methods
   (b) Many-to-Many Attributes
3. Entity-vs-Attribute
4. Different Representation for Equivalent Data
   (a) Different Expression denoting same Information
   (b) Different Units
   (c) Different Levels of Precision

FIGURE 26–3
A Classification and Enumeration for Structural Conflicts

In this chapter, we consider only those structural conflicts that arise within the context of integrating relational and object-oriented data models. In our framework, an object-oriented data model is one that supports generalization, aggregation, ability to define methods against classes, and the notion of unique identity for objects in the database. Our classification (shown in Fig. 26–3) is an extension of that proposed in the context of integrating only relational databases [Kim and Seo 1991] in which two basic causes of structural conflicts are identified. One class of conflicts arises when different CDB schemas use different structures to represent the same information, and the other class of conflicts arises when different CDB schemas use a similar structure but disparate specifications (such as different names or domains) to represent the same information.

Similarly, we extend this for the case of integrating RDBs and OODBs by noting that the only sources of additional types of conflicts are the introduction of generalization and aggregation (or composition) abstractions, as well as methods. Figure 26–3 includes five kinds of conflict in addition to those identified in Kim and Seo 1991. These are entity and attribute inclusion due to the generalization abstraction; data type and composition due to the aggregation abstraction; and methods. Just as the classification in Kim and Seo 1991 is complete within the context of integrating RDBs, the classification in Fig. 26–3 is complete within the context of integrating RDBs and OODBs. We now discuss only these in more detail since the others have already been discussed in Kim and Seo 1991.

26.3.1 Generalization Conflicts

Generalization is a key modeling abstraction in OODBs. Its inclusion in the integration process results in structural conflicts due to entity and attribute inclusion.

1. *Entity inclusion conflict*—an entity inclusion conflict arises when an entity in one CDB is logically included in another entity in another CDB. Consider two tables such as student and graduate student. These two tables can induce a natural inclusion relationship in an MDB schema. A more complex situation occurs when an inheritance hierarchy from one OODB is to be integrated with a related inheritance hierarchy from another OODB that has a different structure.
2. *Attribute inclusion conflict*—this conflict arises when an inclusion relationship exists between two or more attributes. For example, an attribute `son_name` can be regarded as being included in `child_name`. Clearly, this conflict falls into a category different from attributes with different names or data types. An inclusion relationship between two attributes may be used to induce a natural inheritance hierarchy among the corresponding entities in the MDB schema. These issues have been recently investigated in Effelsberg and Mannino 1984; Larson et al. 1989; and Sheth and Gala 1989.

26.3.2 Aggregation Conflicts

Structural conflicts due to the aggregation abstraction are caused by differences in the data type and composition of attributes.

1. *Data type conflict*—this conflict occurs when the domain or type of an attribute is different for semantically equivalent attributes. For example, the attribute `ssn` may have the type `CHAR(9)` in one CDB but `INTEGER` in another CDB. A more general conflict arises when integrating OODBs. The type of attribute `dept` in the class `Faculty` in `ldb4` is `CHAR(20)`, while the corresponding attribute in `ldb5` has the user-defined type `Department`.

2. *Attribute composition conflict*—this kind of conflict arises when similar concepts are represented in one data model as an *aggregation* or *composition* abstraction, while not in the other. In `ldb4`, consider the attribute `course` of the class `Enroll` with the domain `Course`, which in turn has an attribute `prereq` whose domain is `SET_OF (Course)`. Compare this with the corresponding tables in `ldb3`. Note that this type of conflict is different from the many-to-many entity conflict because it is not the difference in the number of entities involved; rather it arises because the relational model does not support the composition abstraction. However, conflicts between related composition hierarchies in more than one OODB can be thought of as a special case of the data type conflict mentioned above.

26.3.3 Conflicts Due to Methods

This conflict arises only when an OODB is integrated with an RDB or another OODB. Since a method declaration is part of the definition of an OODB class, a method can be treated just like an attribute. For example, when two entities E_1 and E_2 are identical except for a missing method, for our purposes, we may regard one entity as missing an attribute. Likewise, if two entities have methods with different names but equivalent semantics, the situation can be considered as identical to the attribute name conflict. When methods have arguments with different types, the two methods may be integrated by considering the data type conflicts between the corresponding arguments. In some sense, this situation may be seen as similar to an attribute composition conflict. When integrating an inheritance hierarchy, if a specializing method is defined in a subclass, the situation is analogous to an attribute inclusion conflict.

26.4 Conflict Resolution

As stated in section 26.3, the classification of conflicts in Fig. 26–3 is complete within the framework of integrating RDBs and OODBs. Since we define a resolution technique for each type of conflict listed in Fig. 26–3, our classification in Fig. 26–4 is also complete; that is, there is a correspondence between Fig. 26–3 and Fig. 26–4. For each type of conflict, the resolution technique can be modeled as a transformation from one or more entities defined in the CDB schemas to a single entity defined in the MDB schema. Whenever this transformation is isomorphic, the global entity is updatable.

We discuss each technique in detail using the CDB schemas defined in section 26.2. We shall use the syntax and semantics of SQL/M, a multidatabase language designed at UniSQL, Inc. It is an extension of SQL/X in which SQL and SQL/X-based CDBs can interoperate. In SQL/M, the user

1. Renaming Entities and Attributes
2. Homogenizing Representations
   (a) Expressions
   (b) Units
   (c) Precision
3. Homogenizing Attributes:
   (a) Type Coercion
   (b) Projection of a Composition Hierarchy
   (c) Default Values
   (d) Attribute Concatenation
4. Horizontal Joins:
   (a) Union Compatible:
      i. Simple Union Compatible Join
      ii. When Attribute is Missing
      iii. When Attribute is Missing but Value is Implicit
   (b) Extended Union Compatible:
      i. For Entity Inclusion
      ii. For Attribute Inclusion
5. Vertical Joins:
   (a) For Many-to-Many Entities
   (b) For Entity-versus Attributes
   (c) For Composition Hierarchies
6. Mixed Joins
7. Homogenizing Methods

FIGURE 26–4
A Classification and Enumeration of Resolution Techniques

can integrate one or more CDB entities into a virtual class. The definition of a virtual class has two components. The first component defines the signature of the virtual class by enumerating the attributes (and methods, if any) along with their domains. The second component defines how the virtual class is to be populated (materialized) with virtual instances from the CDBs. This is achieved by defining a set of queries, one for each CDB entity being integrated. The basic syntax[2] for the definition of a virtual class is shown in Fig. 26–5.

The *attr_def_list* consists of attributes and their domains, along with methods, if any. Each component query is separated by a comma. The *selection_list* is an extension to that of SQL — we shall discuss this in the following sections. The *entity_spec_list* determines the various entities (possibly from different CDBs) required to evaluate the query. The *search_conditions* are identical to those in SQL.

2. Terms in square brackets '[ ]' are optional, and those in curly braces '{ }' occur zero or more times. Further, we use a slightly modified syntax of SQL/M for clarity of exposition.

```
CREATE VCLASS  virtual_class_name
    SIGNATURE  attr_def_list
    AS SELECT  selection_list
         FROM  entity_spec_list
        WHERE  search_conditions,
             .
             .
             .
       SELECT  selection_list
         FROM  entity_spec_list
        WHERE  search_conditions
  entity_spec_list ::=cdb_entity_name [ variable ]
                      {, cdb_entity_name [ variable ] }
  cdb_entity_name ::= [cdb_name] entity_name
```

FIGURE 26–5
Syntax for Virtual Class Definition

26.4.1 Renaming Entities and Attributes

Conflict: Conflicts of type entity name and attribute name in Fig. 26–3 arise when concepts (entities or attributes) with similar meaning have different names or when different concepts bear the same name in the CDB schemas.

Resolution: A catalog is maintained in the MDB that captures the correspondence between MDB names and CDB names.

Examples: For example, the table `Under_Grad` in `ldb1` and `Student` in the remaining CDBs are similar concepts bearing different names. Similarly, the attributes `major` in `GradStudent` and `dept` in `Faculty` have the same meaning but different names.

26.4.2 Homogenizing Representations

Here we discuss homogenization of different expressions denoting the same information, different units, and different levels of precision. They correspond to the class of conflicts identified as "different representation for equivalent data" in Fig. 26–3. For each of these resolution techniques we shall use the following example. Consider the virtual class that integrates the employee information in `ldb1` and `ldb3`.

```
CREATE VCLASS N_All_Emp_Info_R
SIGNATURE name CHAR(25), ssn INTEGER, position CHAR(25),
          age INTEGER, wt_in_lb INTEGER, ht_in_in INTEGER,
          salary INTEGER, bonus INTEGER,
          tax INTEGER, bracket CHAR(6)
```

```
  AS SELECT name, ssn, position, age, wt_in_lb, ht_in_in,
            salary, bonus, tax, b.string
       FROM ldb1.Employee e, ldb1.Emp_other o,
            ldb1.bracket_codes b
       WHERE e.ssn = o.ssn AND
             o.bracket < b.ubound AND
             o.bracket > b.lbound
     SELECT name, ssn, position, age, 2.25*wt_in_kg,
         ht_in_cm/2.54,
            salary, bonus, tax, bracket
       FROM ldb3.Employee e, ldb3.Emp_tax t,
            ldb3.Emp_personal p
       WHERE e.ssn = t.ssn AND e.ssn = p.ssn
```

This class has a signature that contains all possible information about employees that is stored in `ldb1` and `ldb3`. It is materialized by evaluating two component queries and then taking the union of their results. The first component query denotes a join among the `Employee`, `Emp_other`, and `bracket_codes` tables in `ldb1`. The role of the `bracket_codes` table is explained on page 534. The second component query is a join among `Employee`, `Emp_tax`, and `Emp_personal` tables in `ldb3`. The expressions `2.25*wt_in_kg, ht_in_cm/2.54` are discussed on the next page.

Different Expressions Denoting the Same Information

Conflict: Conflicts of this type arise when different scalar values are used to represent the same data. Of particular interest are cases when different expressions describe the same piece of information and when different CDBs use separate codes to denote the same data.

Resolution: Since this type of conflict arises when different scalar values denote the same data, it is resolved by defining an isomorphism between different representations. This can be achieved either by creating a static lookup table that defines the isomorphism or by defining appropriate operators in the MDB query language.

Examples: For example, the position attribute of the class Faculty can equivalently have the value "asst. prof." or "assistant professor." It is possible to do some string matching with the LIKE operator. For example, the user can issue a query such as

```
SELECT *
FROM N_All_Emp_Info_R
WHERE position LIKE ass%t prof%
```

Similarly, different CDBs might use separate codes to denote distinct grades:

A Excellent 1
B Good 2

C Fair 3
D Poor 4
E Fail 5

Note that this is different from the situation in which the codes may have different levels of precision. Here, there is no difference in the precision level because there exists an isomorphism between the different kinds of codes. Therefore, it is possible to issue updates against a virtual class that homogenizes this conflict.

Different Units

Conflict: Conflicts of this type arise when numerical data denoting the same physical quantity are represented in different units across CDBs. Different units give different meanings to numeric data.

Resolution: This type of conflict is resolved by defining simple arithmetic expressions to convert a numeric value in one unit to another. However, there may be some loss of information due to lack of accuracy in these conversions. In general, arithmetic expressions are not isomorphic for two reasons:

1. Not all arithmetic operators are closed on numeric values (e.g., division is not closed for integers).
2. There are limitations of machine representations for real values.

Example: Since the information for weight and height is stored in different units in `ldb1` and `ldb3`, and the chosen units for integration in `N_All_Emp_Info_R` are pounds and inches respectively, we must make the appropriate conversions. These respective conversions are manifest in the query component for `ldb3` in the above virtual class in the expressions `2.25*wt_in_kg` and `ht_in_cm/2.54`. Note that there may be some loss of information due to lack of accuracy in these conversions. For example, if the user issues an insert command against this virtual class, the weight is specified in pounds, which must be converted to kilograms. This involves evaluating the expression `wt_in_lb/2.25`, which is inherently lossy due to the division operation. For most applications, this loss would be insignificant; however, for certain scientific applications or commercial applications that in-volve monetary conversions, the lack of accuracy may be significant.

Different Levels of Precision

Conflict: This type of conflict arises when semantically equivalent attributes draw values from domains with different cardinalities. This difference in cardinality results in different scales of precision for similar data.

Resolution: This type of conflict is resolved by defining a mapping between the domains of semantically equivalent attributes. Since the cardinalities of these domains are different, we define a many-to-one mapping for converting a value from a more precise domain to a value from a less precise domain.

Example: This problem arises with the `bracket` attribute in our example, which in `ldb1` has a string code and in `ldb3` has a numeric code. We can introduce a new table in `ldb1` as follows:

bracket_codes

string	lbound	ubound
upper	100000	1000000
middle	25000	99999
lower	0	24999

This table makes it possible for us to convert one code to another by computing a join as shown in the query component for `ldb1`. Note that there is loss of information here because we are converting from a more precise code (the numeric code in `ldb1`) to a less precise one. Thus, given a numeric value for bracket, it is possible to convert it to a string, but the reverse is not necessarily possible.

26.4.3 Homogenizing Attributes

An entity is a sequence of attributes; an attribute and its domain qualify an entity by defining membership criteria for instances to belong to that entity. Similarly, the signature of a virtual class qualifies it, and the query component determines how this virtual class is to be materialized. However, each component query must retrieve objects from the CDBs such that their attribute values conform to the signature of the virtual class. Thus, each corresponding attribute of the CDB entities being integrated must be redefined and appropriately transformed such that each attribute is compatible with that in the signature of the virtual class. We describe such transformations below.

Type Coercion

Conflict: Conflicts of type "attribute data type" in Fig. 26–3 arise when the domains (types) are different for semantically equivalent attributes.

Resolution: In many cases, it is possible to resolve this conflict by coercing the type of one attribute to another type, thus homogenizing the attributes in question. Shown in Table 26–1 are various meaningful type coercions. Most coercions are isomorphic. For example, it is always possible to convert an integer value from a CDB to a real in the

Table 26–1: Type Coercion Rules (Empty entries indicate that the virtual class creator must supply an explicit coercion.)

	CHAR(n_1)	SMALLINT	INTEGER	DECIMAL(p_1,s_1)	FLOAT
CHAR(n_2)	CHAR(max(n_1,n_2))				
SMALLINT		SMALLINT	INTEGER		FLOAT
INTEGER		INTEGER	INTEGER		FLOAT
DECIMAL(p_2,s_2)					FLOAT
FLOAT		FLOAT	FLOAT	FLOAT	FLOAT

MDB and back (which would be required for update purposes). However, it is likely that a real value from a CDB will be truncated (and, therefore, lose information) when converted to an integer in the MDB—note that there would be no loss of information in the reverse direction. In general, the syntax for type coercion is *attribute_name* AS *type*, and it can appear as an element of the *selection_list*.

Example: Consider the following virtual class definition for employees[3] in which the Employee entities from ldb1, ldb3, ldb4, and ldb5 are integrated:

```
CREATE VCLASS U_Employee
SIGNATURE name:CHAR(25), ssn:INTEGER, position:CHAR(25)
          supervisor:U_Employee
  AS SELECT name, ssn, position, NA
       FROM ldb1.Employee,
     SELECT name, ssn, position, NA
       FROM ldb3.Employee,
     SELECT name, ssn, position, supervisor
       FROM ldb4.Employee,
     SELECT name, ssn AS INTEGER, position, supervisor
       FROM ldb5.Employee,
```

Since the type of ssn in ldb5 is CHAR(9), while it is INTEGER in the other CDBs and in the virtual class, a coercion from CHAR(9) to INTEGER is required to achieve homogenization. The type is coerced by the AS INTEGER expression in the query component for ldb5 in the definition of U_Employee.

Projection of a Composition Hierarchy

Conflict: Composition hierarchies occur naturally in OODBs. Conflicts of type "attribute composition" in Fig. 26–3 arise when there are struc-

3. The symbol NA, which denotes the notion of "not applicable," will be discussed in section 26.5.1.

tural differences in related classes such that the domain of a semantically equivalent attribute in one is a user-defined class whereas that in another class is an atomic type. This situation occurs when integrating OODBs with RDBs or other OODBs.

Resolution: This conflict is resolved by projecting a *key* or *unique* attribute of the user-defined class, such that it is compatible with the other corresponding attributes. In certain cases, it may also be necessary to coerce the type of the projected attribute. In general, it is possible to combine the various conflict resolution operations.

Example: Consider the definition of the N_Faculty virtual class below. [4]

```
CREATE VCLASS N_Faculty
SIGNATURE name:CHAR(25), ssn:INTEGER, dept:CHAR(20),
          rank:CHAR(10)
  AS SELECT name, ssn, dept, rank
       FROM ldb1.Faculty,
     SELECT fname, fssn, major, frank
       FROM ldb2.Grad_student
       WHERE fssn NOT IN
             (SELECT ssn FROM ldb1.Faculty)
     SELECT [lastname, firstname], ssn, dept, rank
       FROM ldb3.Faculty,
     SELECT name, ssn, dept, rank
       FROM ldb4.Faculty,
     SELECT name, ssn AS INTEGER, dept.name, rank
       FROM ldb5.Faculty
```

The domain of dept in ldb5 is the class Department, whereas in other CDBs it is CHAR(20). In order to homogenize the respective Faculty entities, we must project the name of dept in ldb5.Faculty. This is effectively a join between Faculty and Department.

It is interesting to compare the supervisor attribute in U_Employee defined earlier and the dept attribute in N_Faculty. They are similar in that the domain of each attribute in question is a user-defined class in ldb4 and ldb5. However, we did not project the name of the supervisor in U_Employee. In contrast, we imposed the value NA (denoting "not applicable") on supervisors from ldb1 and ldb3, even though its domain is defined as U_Employee. When materializing this virtual class, the object identifiers (OIDS) returned by ldb4 and ldb5 as values for the supervisor attribute for the relevant objects. However, these OIDS are not unique in the MDB environment. Therefore, these OIDS are tagged with the CDB identifier from which they originated.

4. Here, we note that the faculty information is included in the Grad_student table in ldb2; thus, the faculty members in ldb2 whose records are also kept in the Faculty table of ldb1 are excluded in the WHERE clause.

Default Values

Conflict: Conflicts of this type (denoted by "default values" in Fig. 26–3) arise when the default values of semantically equivalent attributes in different CDBs are different. This conflict may manifest itself during an update against the MDB schema.

Resolution: This conflict is resolved in a manner similar to the case of missing but implicit attribute conflict.

Example: The `bonus` attribute in `ldb1` may have a default value of `10%`, whereas in `ldb3` the actual bonus value is expected to be provided when the tuple is inserted. Thus, if the `Employee` tables were to be integrated, choosing a default value would cause problems at update time.

Attribute Concatenation

Conflict: Information can be represented at different levels of detail, especially when represented as character strings. Thus, conflicts of type one-to-many attributes (which is a special case of the many-to-many attributes conflict in Fig. 26–3) arise if information captured by a single attribute in one CDB entity is equivalent to that in more than one attribute belonging to another CDB entity.

Resolution: This type of conflict is resolved by defining an operator for concatenating attributes whose domains are character strings. In general, we have *vc_attr_name* ≡ *[cdb_attr_name_list]* where *vc_attr_name* appears in the signature of the virtual class and *[cdb_attr_name_list]* appears in the selection list of a component query in the virtual class definition.

Example: In `ldb3`, the name of a person is broken into `firstname` and `lastname`, while it is simply `name` in other CDBs. We provide a means to resolve such differences by attribute concatenation, as shown in the query component for `ldb3` in the virtual class `N_Faculty` defined above.

26.4.4 Horizontal Joins

A horizontal join is a means to homogenize CDB entities by taking the union of all instances materialized from each CDB entity. There are two kinds of horizontal joins: union compatible and extended union compatible. The union compatible join allows the user to integrate entities across CDBs such that the resulting virtual class has a signature that is very similar to that of the CDB entities. The extended union compatible join extends this notion to provide a means to deal with inheritance hierarchies.

Union Compatible

Two entities are union compatible if and only if they have equivalent signatures. Note that the signatures need not be identical since simple transformations such as renaming or coercion may take place. Thus, two signatures are equivalent if and only if for each attribute in one there exists a corresponding attribute in the other signature such that the attribute is obtained after due transformation. There are three kinds of union compatible join:

1. *No structural conflicts.*

Conflict: Conflicts of type "one-to-one entity" in Fig. 26–3 arise when various CDB entities have similar or even identical definitions. In the simple case, there is no structural conflict, per se.

Resolution: The simple union compatible join operation provides us with a means to materialize an MDB entity—that is, a virtual class—by merely taking the union of the component queries corresponding to each CDB entity. It is usually employed in conjunction with other conflict resolution operations described in this chapter. A join is simple union compatible if the CDB attributes are transformed to be compatible with the signature of the virtual class such that virtual class is updatable.

Example: As an example, let us define a virtual class for courses as follows:

```
CREATE VCLASS U_Course
SIGNATURE cname:CHAR(30), cno:INTEGER
  AS SELECT cname, cno
       FROM ldb1.Course,
     SELECT cname, cno
       FROM ldb3.Course
       WHERE cno NOT IN
             (SELECT cno FROM ldb3.Course_restriction),
     SELECT cname, cno
       FROM ldb4.Course c
       WHERE NOT EXISTS c.prereq,
     SELECT cname, cno
       FROM ldb5.Course c
       WHERE NOT EXISTS c.prereq
```

U_Course is the simple union of all course objects without any restrictions and contains information about the cname and cno. Note that there is no WHERE clause in the query component for ldb1; that for ldb3, the inner SELECT clause eliminates courses with restrictions; and that for ldb4 and ldb5, the expression NOT EXISTS c.prereq eliminates courses with prerequisites.

2. *Missing attributes.*

Conflict: Conflicts of type "missing attribute" in the one-to-one entity case in Fig. 26–3 arise when the numbers of attributes in similar entities across CDBs are different.

Resolution: One way of resolving this problem is to coerce nonexistent attributes to NA (as we did in the definition of U_Employee above). Alternatively, we can resolve this by not including those extra attributes in the selection list of the component query for that CDB entity that has more attributes than other CDB entities with which it is being integrated. Another way of resolving this conflict is to view the entity with fewer attributes as the superclass of the others, provided that the entities in question induce a natural inclusion relationship.

Example: As an example of the last way of resolving this conflict, we define an inheritance hierarchy for graduate students in ldb4 and ldb5 as follows:

```
CREATE VCLASS N_GradStudent_OO_1
SUBCLASS OF Student
SIGNATURE advisor:SET_OF(N_Faculty_OO)
  AS SELECT name, ssn, major, gpa, advisor
       FROM ldb4.GradStudent,
     SELECT [lname, fname], ssn AS INTEGER,
            major, gpa, advisor
       FROM ldb5.GradStudent,
       WHERE NOT EXISTS committee

CREATE VCLASS N_GradStudent_OO_2
SUBCLASS OF N_GradStudent_OO_1
SIGNATURE committee:SET_OF(N_Faculty_OO)
  AS SELECT [lname, fname], ssn AS INTEGER,
            major, gpa, advisor, committee
       FROM ldb5.GradStudent,
       WHERE EXISTS committee
```

The class GradStudent in ldb4 does not have the attribute committee. So we integrate it with graduate students from ldb5 that have no committee. This is enforced by the clause WHERE NOT EXISTS committee in the definition of N_GradStudent_OO_1. Therefore, we define an inheritance hierarchy in which N_GradStudent_OO_2 is a subclass of N_GradStudent_OO_1. Note that ldb5.GradStudent is effectively horizontally partitioned into those that have a committee and those that do not.

3. *Missing attribute with implicit value.*

Conflict: Conflicts of type "missing but implicit attribute" in the one-to-one entity case in Fig. 26–3 arise when an attribute is missing (in the sense discussed above) but can be implicitly given a default value.

Resolution: In general, the syntax for resolving this kind of conflict is *cdb_attr_name = value*, where *cdb_attr_name* is the name of the attribute in the CDB entity that has a default value denoted by *value*. Further, the above expression must appear as an element of the *selection_list* of a component query.

Example: Suppose we modify the `Student` table in `ldb3` to have an attribute called `student_type` to denote whether a given student is an undergraduate or graduate student. But we know that the `Student` entity in other CDBs denotes only undergraduate students. Thus, one way of integrating these entities would be to think of the `Student` entities in all CDBs except `ldb3` as having an attribute `student_type` with a default value denoting undergraduate students.

Extended Union Compatible

The notion of union compatibility needs to be extended to deal with inheritance hierarchies. As one goes lower in such a hierarchy, classes tend to have more attributes defined in their respective signatures or to have attributes with more specialized domains. A class C_1 can be a subclass of C_2 if and only if the signature of C_2 subsumes that of C_1 and there exists an inclusion relationship between C_1 and C_2. This means that for each attribute of C_2, there is a corresponding attribute in C_1 such that its domain is union compatible (in the sense defined in the previous section) with that in C_2. An inheritance hierarchy also implies a set inclusion relationship between the instances of a class and its subclasses. Recall that a virtual class has a query component that determines how it is to be populated when materialized to evaluate an MDB query. We note that it is the responsibility of the designer of a virtual class hierarchy to ensure that the set inclusion semantics are not violated. Thus, when the signature of C_2 subsumes that of C_1, and the extent of C_1 is a subset of the extent of C_2, then C_1 and C_2 are said to be extended union compatible.

1. *Entity inclusion.*

Conflict: Conflicts of type "entity inclusion" in Fig. 26–3 arise when similarly related entities are distributed across more than one CDB. A more complex situation is when an inheritance hierarchy from one OODB is to be integrated with a related inheritance hierarchy from another OODB that has a different structure. Of course, this may manifest itself as a compound conflict, which can be resolved by decomposing it into the more primitive conflicts. Thus, when integrating two inheritance hierarchies, we must first integrate two CDB entities using other resolution techniques described in this chapter, such that the resulting MDB inheritance hierarchy reflects the inclusion relationships in the CDB hierarchies.

Resolution: We exploit the notion of an extended union compatible join to resolve entity inclusion conflicts. We do this by organizing a set of related CDB entities into a generalization hierarchy.

Example: As an example, we define a hierarchy of courses that existed in neither the RDBs nor the OODBs in our sample CDB schemas of section 26.2. Recall that U_Course was defined in a previous section. We now define its subclass N_Restricted_Course.

```
CREATE VCLASS N_Restricted_Course
SUBCLASS_OF U_Course
SIGNATURE major:CHAR(20), prereq:CHAR(30)
  AS SELECT cname, cno, major, NA
       FROM ldb1.Restricted_course,
     SELECT c.cname, c.cno, r.major, p.cname
       FROM ldb3.Course c, ldb3.Course p,
          ldb3.Course_restriction r
       WHERE c.cno=r.cno, r.prereq_cno=p.cno
     SELECT cname, cno, NA, c.prereq.cname
       FROM ldb4.Course c
       WHERE EXISTS c.prereq
     SELECT cname, cno, NA, c.prereq.cname
       FROM ldb5.Course c
       WHERE EXISTS c.prereq
```

Assume, for the sake of simplicity, that course numbers from different universities are distinct. Note that ldb1's Restricted_course table has major that restricts courses a student can take, whereas ldb4's Course class has prereq representing prerequisite courses of a course. The N_Restricted_course virtual class has both major and prereq attributes. Note that for the N_Restricted_course subclass we used NA for the value of the prereq attribute from ldb1 and for the value of the major attribute from ldb4. Also note that to simplify the class definition here, we defined the prereq attribute of the virtual class to have a course name rather than course (i.e., the attribute is not a nested one, whereas the corresponding attribute of ldb4 is nested).

Thus, courses are classified into those that have restrictions and those that do not. The intended semantics of ldb1.Restricted_course is that only those students with the same major as the department in which the course is being offered can enroll. The intended semantics of ldb3.Course_restriction is that only those students who satisfy the prerequisites may enroll for a given course. Another way of resolving the conflict would be to define two subclasses of U_Course called Course_with_restr_on_major and Course_with_restr_on_prereq.

2. *Attribute inclusion.*

Conflict: Conflicts of type "attribute inclusion" in Fig. 26–3 arise when there is an inclusion relationship between two or more attributes. This conflict falls into a category distinct from that in which attributes have different names or data types, as discussed above. An inclusion relationship between two attributes can be used to induce a natural inheritance hierarchy among the corresponding entities in the MDB schema.

Resolution: Attribute inclusion and entity inclusion are different kinds of conflicts. However, since an attribute inclusion relationship induces an entity inclusion relationship, both conflicts can be resolved using the extended union compatible join operation.

Example: For example, an attribute `son_name` can be regarded as being included in `child_name`, even if their domains are `CHAR(25)`. Consider two relations defined as follows:

```
ldb6: People(name, age, child_name)
ldb7: Person(name, age, son_name)
```

The inclusion relationship between `son_name` and `child_name` can induce a natural inclusion relationship between `People` and `Person` such that the former includes the latter. This information can be used to integrate the two relations as follows.

```
CREATE VCLASS U_Parents
SIGNATURE name CHAR(25), age INTEGER, child_name CHAR(25)
  AS SELECT * FROM ldb6.People

CREATE VCLASS U_Parents_of_Men
SUBCLASS OF U_Parents
SIGNATURE name CHAR(25), age INTEGER, son_name CHAR(25)
  AS SELECT * FROM ldb7.Person
```

26.4.5 Vertical Joins

A vertical join is used to integrate a number of entities or attributes across one or more CDBs into a single entity at the MDB level.

Many-to-Many Entities

Conflict: Entities in CDB schemas may be defined in different ways for various reasons, such as to remove redundant data or to reduce possibilities of inconsistency during updates or improve the efficiency of evaluating queries. This causes a given concept to be decomposed into a number of entities. Such decomposition is manifest in the process of normalizing an RDB schema. Thus, conflicts of type "many-to-many entities" in Fig. 26–3 arise when integrating related concepts that are normalized to different degrees in RDB schemas or when integrating a concept represented by many RDB tables with a single OODB class.

N_ALL_Emp_Info_R

ssn	name	position	age	wt_in_lb	ht_in_in	salary	bonus	tax
Employee			Emp_other					
ssn	name	position	age	wt_in_lb	ht_in_in	salary	bonus	tax
⋮ (tuples from ldbi)								
Employee			Emp_personal			Emp_tax		
ssn	name	position	age	wt_in_kg	ht_in_cm	salary	bonus	tax
⋮ (tuples from ldb3)								

FIGURE 26–6
Pictorial Representation of the `N_All_Emp_Info_R` Class

Resolution: We use the vertical join to integrate many CDB entities into one MDB entity (that is, virtual class). In order to integrate many CDB entities into many MDB entities, we employ a sequence of vertical joins; we consider the many-to-many entities conflict as a composite case of the many-to-one entity conflict.

Example: For example, reconsider the `N_All_Emp_Info_R` virtual class from section 26.4.2, which homogenizes the tables `Employee` and `Emp_ other` from `ldb1` and `Employee`, `Emp_tax`, and `Emp_personal` from `ldb3`. Since personal or tax information about employees is not available in `ldb4` and `ldb5`, `N_All_Emp_Info_R` only contains query components that effectively are vertical joins on `ldb1` and `ldb3`. Shown in Fig. 26–6 is a pictorial representation of the class `N_All_Emp_Info_R`.

Entity-Versus-Attributes

Conflict: Conflicts of type "entity-versus-attributes" in Fig. 26–3 arise when a concept (or part thereof) is represented as an entity in one CDB but as a set of attributes (belonging to a related entity) in another CDB.

Resolution: This kind of conflict can be resolved either by splitting an entity into two or more parts or by integrating two entities (or parts thereof) into one by performing a vertical join. Note that this is distinct from attribute concatenation because in that case, the domain of each attribute in question must be of type string; there are no such restrictions here.

Example: For example, in `ldb1`, the attribute `address` is used to represent the address of each undergraduate student, whereas the same information is represented by the table `Address` in `ldb3`. There are two ways of resolving this type of conflict. One way is to split the `Under_Grad` table in `ldb1`. The second predicate in the `WHERE` clause of

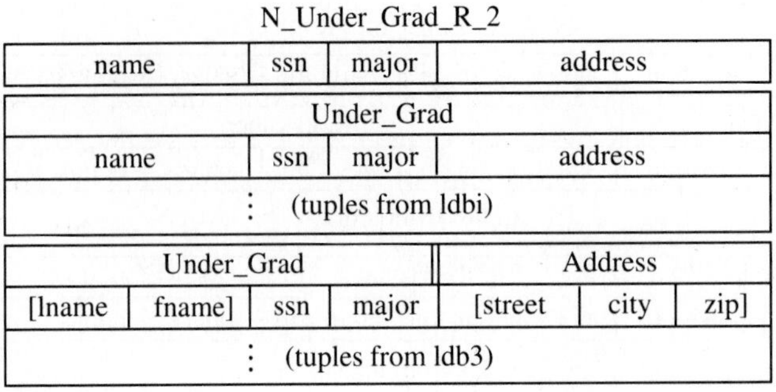

N_Under_Grad_R_2

name	ssn	major	address

Under_Grad			
name	ssn	major	address
⋮ (tuples from ldbi)			

Under_Grad				Address		
[lname	fname]	ssn	major	[street	city	zip]
⋮ (tuples from ldb3)						

FIGURE 26–7
Pictorial Representation of the N_Under_Grad_R_2 Class

N_Address_R removes redundant tuples since we are only interested in undergraduate students.

```
CREATE VCLASS U_Under_Grad_R_1
SIGNATURE name CHAR(25), ssn INTEGER, major CHAR(20)
  AS SELECT name, ssn, major
       FROM ldb1.Under_Grad
     SELECT [lastname, firstname], ssn, major
       FROM ldb3.Student
```

```
CREATE VCLASS N_Address_R
SIGNATURE ssn INTEGER, address CHAR(50)
  AS SELECT ssn, address
       FROM ldb1.Under_Grad
     SELECT a.ssn, [street, city, zip]
       FROM ldb3.Student s, ldb3.Address a
       WHERE s.ssn = a.ssn AND
             s.ssn NOT IN (SELECT ssn FROM ldb3.Graduate_Info)
```

The other way to resolve this type of conflict is to integrate the Address and Student tables in ldb3 into a single virtual class by performing a simple vertical join, also depicted in Fig. 26–7.

```
CREATE VCLASS N_Under_Grad_R_2
SIGNATURE name CHAR(25), ssn INTEGER, major CHAR(20), address
CHAR (50)
  AS SELECT *
       FROM ldb1.Under_Grad
     SELECT [lastname, firstname], ssn, major,
         [street, city, zip]
       FROM ldb3.Student s, ldb3.Address a
       WHERE s.ssn = a.ssn AND
             s.ssn NOT IN (SELECT ssn
       FROM ldb3.Graduate_Info)
```

Aggregation Hierarchy

Conflict: Conflicts of type "entity structure" and "attribute composition" in Fig. 26–3 in combination denote composition hierarchy conflicts. Thus, the conflicts arising when integrating RDBs and OODBs (since the former do not support the composition abstraction) or when integrating composition hierarchies in different OODBs that are similar but have different structures are said to be due to the composition hierarchy.

Resolution: This kind of conflict can be resolved by taking a vertical join of CDB entities that compose the virtual class being defined.

Example: As an example, let us define a virtual class called N_Advisement.

```
CREATE VCLASS N_Advisement
SIGNATURE advisor:CHAR(25), advisee:SET_OF(CHAR(25)), dept:
CHAR(20), thesis:CHAR(50)
  AS SELECT fname, sname, major, thesis_title
       FROM ldb2.Grad_student
     SELECT [f.lastname, f.firstname], [s.lastname,
         s.firstname], s.major, t.title
       FROM ldb3.Student s, ldb3.Graduate_info g,
            ldb3.Faculty f, ldb3.Thesis t
       WHERE s.ssn = g.ssn AND g.advisor_ssn = f.ssn
            AND s.ssn = t.ssn
     SELECT f.name, g.name, g.major, t.title
       FROM ldb4.Gradstudent g, ldb4.Faculty f,
            ldb4.Thesis t
       WHERE f IN g.advisor AND t.author = g
     SELECT f.name, g.name, g.major, t.title
       FROM ldb5.Gradstudent g, ldb5.Faculty f,
            ldb5.Thesis t
       WHERE f = g.advisor AND t.author = g
```

Note that the query component for ldb2 is a simple projection of attributes from one table—namely, Grad_Student. However, each remaining component query has join conditions defined in its WHERE clause, and attributes from different entities within the corresponding CDB are projected. Shown in Fig. 26–8 is a pictorial representation of the N_Advisement class.

26.4.6 Mixed Joins

A mixed join is a combination of vertical and horizontal joins. It is used to integrate arbitrary fragments of entities from one or more CDBs to define a virtual class. The above definition of N_Advisement can also be seen as a mixed join in which various fragments from different CDBs are joined. In

N_Advisement

advisor	advisee	dept	thesis

Grad_Student					
fname	sname	dept	thesis	···	—
⋮ (tuples from ldb2)					

Faculty			Student				Thesis		Grad_Info	
[lastname	firstname]	···	[lastname	firstname]	major	···	title	···	ssn	adv_ssn
⋮ (tuples from ldb3)										

Faculty		Grad_Student			Thesis		—
name	···	name	major	···	title	···	—
⋮ (tuples from ldb4)							

Faculty		Grad_Student				Thesis		—
name	···	[lastname	firstname]	major	···	title	···	—
⋮ (tuples from ldb5)								

FIGURE 26–8
Pictorial Representation of the `N_Advisement` Class

general, complex conflicts (i.e., conflicts that appear in combination) are resolved by a combination of the two join types and other simpler resolution operations.

26.4.7 Methods

Conflict: We have already discussed under what conditions methods give rise to conflicts and hinted at how they may be resolved in section 26.3.3.

Resolution: Although methods can be treated as attributes (see section 26.4.3), it is not possible in general to define methods in the signature of a virtual class that integrates RDBs and OODBs. However, under certain exceptionally favorable conditions, it is indeed possible to define methods when integrating RDBs and OODBs. In particular, an OODB method can be redefined in a virtual class if it is possible to represent that method as a derived attribute. There are two cases of interest: one in which the methods do not take arguments and the other in which they do take arguments.

Example: As an example of the first case, we define a virtual class `N_Student` as follows:

```
CREATE VCLASS N_Student
SIGNATURE name:CHAR(25), ssn:INTEGER, major:CHAR(20), gpa:REAL
  AS SELECT name, ssn, major, AVG(grade)
```

```
    FROM ldb1.Under_Grad, ldb1.Enroll
    GROUP BY ssn
    WHERE ssn=sssn,
  SELECT [lastname, firstname], ssn, major, AVG(grade)
    FROM ldb3.Student, ldb3.Enroll
    WHERE ssn NOT IN (SELECT ssn FROM ldb3.Grad_info)
    GROUP BY ssn,
  SELECT name, ssn, major, gpa
    FROM ldb4.Student;
  SELECT name, ssn, major, gpa
    FROM ldb5.Student;
```

It should be clear that N_Student is nonupdatable since its query components contain a GROUP BY clause and the aggregate function AVG; the FROM clause of ldb3 refers to two tables; gpa in ldb4 and ldb5 refer to a local method. But it offers the user more powerful query capabilities because now it is possible for the user to retrieve information about a student's gpa, which would not be possible with an updatable version of the student virtual class.

As an example of the second case (in which methods take arguments), we define the N_Enrollment and change the N_Student virtual classes as follows:

```
CREATE VCLASS N_Enrollment
SIGNATURE cno:INTEGER, fssn:INTEGER, sssn:INTEGER, grade:REAL
  AS SELECT * FROM ldb1.Enroll,
     SELECT * FROM ldb3.Enroll,
     SELECT course.cno, fssn, sssn, grade FROM ldb4.Enroll
     SELECT course.cno, fssn, sssn, grade FROM ldb5.Enroll

CREATE VCLASS N_Student_2
SIGNATURE name:CHAR(25), ssn:INTEGER, major:CHAR(20),
          grade_of(c:U_Course):REAL
METHOD s grade_of(c) /* s:N_Student, c:N_Course */
    =   SELECT e.grade
          FROM Enrollment e
          WHERE s.ssn = e.sssn AND c.cno = e.cno
  AS SELECT name, ssn, major
       FROM ldb1.Under_Grad s, ldb1.Enroll e
       WHERE s.ssn = e.sssn,
     SELECT name, ssn, major
       FROM ldb3.Student s, ldb3.Enroll e
       WHERE s.ssn = e.sssn
     SELECT name, ssn, major
       FROM ldb4.Student s, ldb4.Enroll e
       WHERE s.ssn = e.sssn;
     SELECT name, ssn, major
       FROM ldb5.Student s, ldb5.Enroll e
       WHERE s.ssn = e.sssn;
```

The METHOD clause indicates the definition of a method (with or without arguments) that can be applied to the instances of a virtual class. The attributes in the signature of a virtual class that are not defined in the METHOD clauses are those whose values are retrieved from component DBs. In the above definition of the grade_of method, s indicates the receiver and c the argument. Here, we used SQL as the pseudo-method definition language. In general, however, methods are defined as host language subroutines.

26.5 Conclusions

In this chapter, we presented a complete enumeration and classification of structural conflicts arising within the context of MDB schema integration. This classification of schema conflicts is derived from an examination of all possible structural discrepancies that may occur, such that intra- and intermodel variabilities are taken into account. While our framework is general enough to cover most data models, we claim completeness only within the context of integrating RDBs and OODBs.

We then presented a categorization and complete enumeration of various conflict resolution techniques. This categorization is derived on the basis of a primitive set of operations to resolve structural conflicts. For each operation, we first defined the conflict resolved, showed how it can be resolved, and then gave an example. These operations are captured as SQL/M statements in the examples presented. These operations may be combined in well-defined sequences to resolve complex conflicts.

We briefly summarize the main results of this chapter by correlating the resolution techniques (Fig. 26–4) to a corresponding structural conflict (Fig. 26–3). Renaming resolves the problems of having different names for equivalent entities or attributes or having the same name for different entities or attributes. Homogenizing representations resolves the problems of different expressions, units, or levels of precision denoting similar information. One-to-one attribute conflicts are resolved by type coercion, defining default values, concatenating attributes, and projecting parts of a composition hierarchy. The missing attribute conflicts for entities are resolved by the union compatible join. The entity and attribute inclusion conflicts are resolved by the extended union compatible join. The many-to-many entities and entity-versus-attributes conflicts are resolved by the vertical join. Complex conflicts (that is, conflicts that appear in combination) are resolved by the mixed join, which is a combination of the two join types and other simpler resolution operations. While methods are treated like attributes in general, we describe how they can be integrated under certain exceptional conditions. There are two main advantages to our approach:

1. It identifies a set of primitive operations that can be combined in well-defined ways to transform one or more CDB entities into a single MDB entity.

2. The operations form the basis of a multidatabase schema design methodology that distinguishes between updatable and nonupdatable entities. The MDB entity is updatable if a given sequence of transformations is isomorphic.

To the best of our knowledge, despite the extensive research done in heterogeneous databases and schema integration, there exists no comprehensive framework for resolving all possible conflicts in multidatabase systems. While we note that our particular categorization or nomenclature need not be unique, we believe it to be a prerequisite for defining an MDB data definition and manipulation language. It will also form the basis for designing and building tools for MDB schema designers to help them identify and resolve conflicts.

REFERENCES

ACM Surveys. 1990. Special issue on heterogeneous databases. *ACM Computing Surveys*, Vol. 22, No. 3.

American National Standards Institute. 1986. *Database Language SQL*, Document ANSI X3.135-1986. (Addendum 1: Document ANSI X3.135.1-1989.)

Batini, C., Lenzerini, M., and Navathe, S. B. 1986. A Comparative Analysis of Methodologies for Database Schema Integration. *ACM Computing Surveys*, Vol. 18, No. 4, 323–364.

Breitbart, Y., Olson, P. L., and Thompson, G. R. 1986. Database Integration in a Distributed Heterogeneous Database System. *Proceedings of the Second IEEE Conference on Data Engineering*, Los Angeles.

Brill, D., and Templeton, M. 1984. Distributed Query Processing Strategies in MERMAID: A Front-End to a Data Management System. *Proceedings of the IEEE Conference on Data Engineering*, Los Angeles.

Ceri, S., and Pelagatti, G. 1983. Correctness of Query Execution Strategies in Distributed Databases. *ACM Trans. on Database Systems (TODS)*, Vol. 8, No. 4.

Ceri, S., and Pelagatti, G. 1984. *Distributed Databases: Systems and Principles*, McGraw-Hill, New York.

Connors, T., and Lyngbaek, P. 1988. Providing Uniform Access to Heterogeneous Information Bases. In: *Advances in Object-Oriented Database Systems*. K. R. Dittrich, ed. LNCS 334, Springer-Verlag.

Dayal, U., and Bernstein, P. 1982. On the Correct Translation of Update Operations of on Relational Views. *ACM Trans. on Database Systems (TODS)*, Vol. 7. No. 3.

Dayal, U., and Hwang, H. 1984. View Definition and Generalization for Database Integration of a Multidatabase System. *IEEE Trans. on Software Eng.*, SE-10(11), 628–644.

Effelsberg, W., and Mannino, M. 1984. Attribute Equivalence in Global Schema Design for Heterogeneous Distributed Databases. *Information Systems,* Vol. 9, Nos. 3–4.

Kaul, M., Drosten, K., and Neuhold, E. J. 1990. ViewSystem: Integrating Heterogeneous Information Bases by Object-Oriented Views. *Proceedings of the Data Engineering Conference.*

Keller, A. M. 1985. Algorithms for Translating View Updates Involving Selections, Projections and Joins. *Proceedings of the Fourth ACM-SIGACT-SIGMOD Symposium on Principles of Database Systems.*

Kim, W. 1991. *Introduction to Object-Oriented Databases.* MIT Press, Cambridge, Mass.

Kim, W., and Seo, J. 1991. Classifying Schematic and Data Heterogeneity in Multidatabase Systems. *IEEE Computer,* December.

Landers, T. A. and Rosenberg, R. L. 1982. An Overview of Multibase—A Heterogeneous Database System. *Proceedings of the Second Symposium on Distributed Databases.* H-J. Schneider, ed. North-Holland.

Larson, J., Navathe, S., and Elmasri, R. 1989. A Theory of Attribute Equivalence in Databases with Applications to Schema Integration. *IEEE Trans. Software Eng.* Vol. 15, No. 4.

Litwin, W., Abdellatif, A., Nicolas, B., Vigier, P., and Zeroual, A. 1987. MSQL: A Multidatabase Language. *Information Sciences.*

Litwin, W., Mark, L., and Roussopoulos, N. 1990. Interoperability of Multiple Autonomous Databases. *ACM Computing Surveys,* Vol. 22, No. 3.

Motro, A. 1987. Superviews: Virtual Integration of Multiple Database. *IEEE Trans. on Software Eng.,* SE-13(7), 785–798.

Navathe, S., Shashidhar, T., and Elmasri, R. 1984. Relationship Merging in Schema Integration. *Proceedings of the International Conference on VLDB,* Singapore.

Sheth, A. P., and Gala, S. K. 1989. Attribute Relationships: An Impediment in Automating Schema Integration. *Proceedings of the NSF Workshop on Heterogeneous Database Systems,* Chicago.

Sheth, A. P., Gala, S. K., and Navathe, S. B. 1993. On Automatic Reasoning for Schema Integration. *Technical Report,* Bellcore, Piscataway, N.J. To appear in *IJICIS 1993.*

Spaccapietra, S., Parent, C., and Dupont, Y. 1991. Automating Heterogeneous Schema Integration. *Technical Report,* Ecole Polytechnique Federale, Lausanne, Switzerland, March.

UniSQL, Inc. 1992. *UniSQL/X Database User Manual,* Release 1.0, Austin, TX.

27

Query Processing in Multidatabase Systems

WEIYI MENG
CLEMENT YU

This chapter provides an overview of query processing in multidatabase systems. It includes *query decomposition*, *query translation*, and *global query optimization*. Some results are surveyed and remaining challenges are discussed.

27.1 Introduction

Various types of database systems are currently in use today. This is due to historical reasons and the fact that different applications can be better supported by different types of database systems. Since different types of database systems often use different data models and different query languages, their coexistence makes it difficult for users who are familiar with one system to access data stored in different systems. One solution is to construct a front-end system that supports a single common data model and a single global query language on top of different types of existing systems. The front-end system plus the underlying database systems is called a *multidatabase system*. The global schema of a multidatabase system, the schema used by the front-end system, is the result of a schema integration of the schemas exported from the underlying databases (i.e., local databases) [Heimbigner and McLeod 1985]. The export schemas are in the global data model employed by the front-end system. Each export schema is obtained by a schema transformation from the schema of a local database (local schema) [Sheth and Larson 1990]. The global query language can be used by users of the front-end system to specify queries against the global schema, which will be referenced as *global queries* hereafter. For example, if the global schema is in the relational data model, then SQL can be used as the query language of the global schema. Conceptually, a global query can be processed in three steps. First, it is decomposed into subqueries such that the data needed by each subquery are available from one local database. After the decomposition, subqueries are still in the global query language. Next, each subquery is translated to a query or queries of the corresponding local database system and sent to a local database system for execution. Third, the results returned by the subqueries are combined into the answer.

A different approach for extracting data from multiple databases is rather than constructing a global schema, to create a temporary view pertinent to a user query [Litwin 1984; Litwin et al. 1990]. In this approach, the multidatabase language must provide a means for defining a temporary view as well as the functions for querying multiple databases. It is the user's responsibility to create and maintain the view.

This chapter has two objectives. One is to provide a survey of the previous results in the areas of query decomposition, query translation, and global query optimization. Another is to provide a set of important issues that require further research and development. We assume a global schema for the multidatabase system.

The chapter is organized as follows. In section 27.2, we provide an overview of the major query-processing components in multidatabase systems. In section 27.3, we survey the previous results for each of the three major components—namely, query decomposition, query translation, and global query optimization. In section 27.4, we provide a list of problems that we think are important to enhance the query-processing capabilities of multidatabase systems.

27.2 An Overview

When a global query is submitted, it is first decomposed into two types of queries by the *query decomposer*. One is queries against individual export schemas. These types of queries will be called *export schema subqueries* or simply *subqueries* when there is no confusion. Another is queries that combine the results returned by subqueries to form the answer. These types of queries are called *postprocessing queries* [Dayal 1983]. Postprocessing queries may not be needed. A postprocessing query may be processed by the front end or by a local system designated by the front end system.

Query decomposition is usually accomplished in two steps. In the first step, the global query using global names is *modified* to queries using only names in export schemas [Chen 1990; Dayal and Hwang 1984; Stonebraker 1975]. Modified queries, though using only names in export schemas, may still reference data from more than one database. Therefore, in the second step, these queries are decomposed. Note that data transmission may be used to aid the decomposition. For example, consider the situation when a resulted query from query modification is nested. Such a query may be decomposed into two subqueries, one for the *inner query* and the second for the *outer query*. The result of the first subquery may need to be shipped to the database of the second subquery to make all data needed by the second subquery available. Since questions such as how much data should be shipped and what local processing should be performed before data transmission are related to the overall performance of the system, the second step in query decomposition is usually tightly coupled with global query optimization [Chen 1990; Dayal 1983]. All reported query decomposition algorithms in distributed multidatabase environments that we know allow data transmission.

After decomposition, each subquery needs data from only one database, and all subqueries are still in the global query language. If the global query language is different from the query language of a local database system, the corresponding export schema subquery must be translated to the local subquery by the *query translator*. For example, if the global query language is an OODB query language and a subquery is for a relational system using SQL, then this subquery needs to be translated to an SQL query. In order to translate different subqueries to different local database systems, different query translators are needed.

A given subquery may be translated to different sets of target queries and each set of target queries may be evaluated by the local system with different costs. Therefore, each query translator needs to consider not only the correctness, which ensures that the translated set of target queries is equivalent to the original query, but also the performance of the translated queries. Sometimes it is not possible to translate a query in one language to an equivalent set of queries in another language because certain operation in the source language may not be supported in the target language. For example, a relational query with a join predicate may have no equivalent queries in IMS. In that situation, the query is translated into a broader query (i.e., a superset of the desired result will be returned) such that the restriction (join, in the example) is handled by the postprocessing query. The *filter* component of MULTIBASE is used to identify those operations in the global query language that are not supported by local database systems [Landers and Rosenberg 1982].

Since the cost of evaluating an export schema subquery is related to the way in which the subquery is translated to the target queries and to the strategy by which each target query is executed by the corresponding local system, we need to coordinate query decomposer, global query optimizer, query translators, and local query optimizers to achieve optimal performance. The total cost of processing a global query is the sum of the costs of processing local queries, the costs of transmitting data across different databases, and the costs of the postprocessing queries.

Figure 27–1 illustrates the above description of query processing. In Fig. 27–1, SQ1, ..., SQn are subqueries and PQ1, ..., PQk are postprocessing

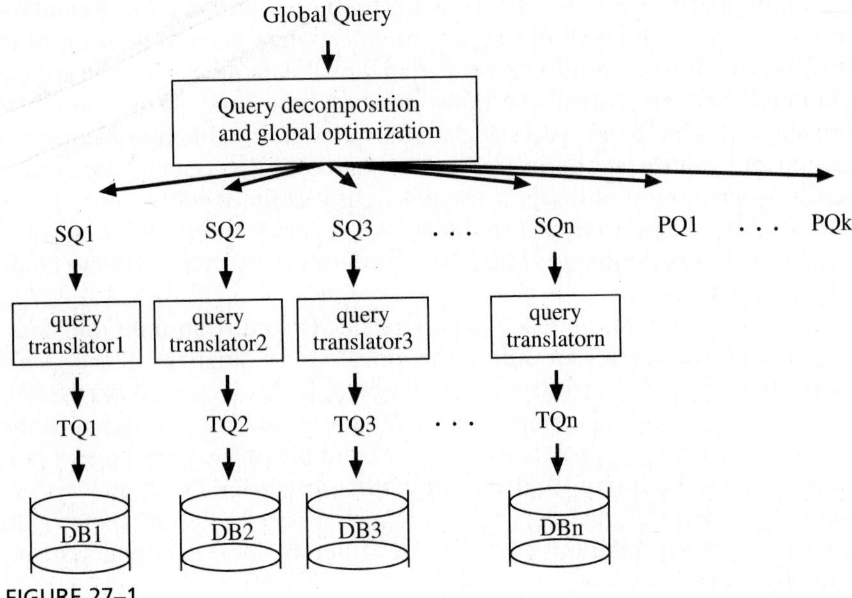

FIGURE 27–1
Outline of Query Processing

queries obtained by query decomposition and TQ1, ..., TQn are the corresponding target queries obtained by query translation. Each TQi may contain more than one query.

27.3 Query Processing

In this section, we provide a survey of the previous results in multidatabase query processing, query modification, query translations, and global query optimization.

27.3.1 Query modification

The following are some of the factors that affect the complexity of query modification.

1. The global query language and the global data model.
2. The method used for integrating export schemas. *Generalization* and *outerjoin* are probably the most widely used methods for schema integration [Breitbart et al. 1986; Chen 1990; Czejdo et al. 1987; Dayal and Hwang 1984; Kaul et al. 1990; Motro 1987]. Outerjoin is originally defined to be an operation between two relations [Codd 1979]. Informally, the outerjoin of

relation R1 and relation R2 is the union of three components: (a) the join of R1 and R2, (b) dangling tuples of R1 padded with null values, and (c) dangling tuples of R2 padded with null values.

3. Whether or not there is an overlap between different databases. This refers to the fact that some real-world objects are modeled by entities (records, objects) in two or more databases.

4. Whether or not there is *data inconsistency*. When a real-world object is represented by entities of different databases, data inconsistency may occur. For example, the same person may be represented in one database as `(Name=John, Age=25, Sex=M)` and in another database as `(Name=John, Age=26, Salary=30k)`. In this example, data inconsistency occurs on `Age`.

5. Other incompatibilities between local databases such as difference in naming conventions and scales.

Query modification when generalization is used for schema integration is discussed in Dayal and Hwang 1984, while query modification when outerjoin is used for schema integration is discussed in Chen 1990. The global data model and the query language used in Dayal and Hwang 1984 are the *functional data model* and DAPLEX [Shipman 1981], respectively. The global data model and the query language used in Chen 1990 are the *relational data model* and the relational algebra, respectively. Both allow overlapping data among different databases. Dayal and Hwang 1984 also discuss data inconsistency on nonidentifying attributes. Stonebraker 1975 studies query modification in the relational model in the context of modifying queries against a relational view to queries against base relations. Motro 1987 describes a formal method for schema integration based on a set of predefined operators. As such, a *superview* can be generated by a sequence of operators. A query against the superview can be decomposed and translated into local database queries by basically reversing the operators based on which the superview is defined. Data inconsistency is not discussed.

In this chapter, we use the object-oriented data model to present a query modification algorithm that is adapted from the algorithm presented in Dayal and Hwang 1984 with modifications to reflect properties of outerjoins. When there is no overlap between databases or when there is no data inconsistency, query modification can be accomplished relatively easily. The main idea is to represent each global name such as a class and an attribute in the global schema by names in the export schemas and then substitute these representations during query modification. If a class in the global schema is integrated from classes in the export schemas, then the global class is usually expressed as a query using class names in export schemas.

In the following, we discuss query modification in the presence of both overlap and data inconsistency. To simplify the discussion, we assume that there are only two export schemas, ES1 and ES2, and each schema contains only one class. Class C1 is in ES1 and class C2 is in ES2. Since there is overlap between the two databases, we need a means to determine when two instances from the two databases are for the same real-world object. For this, we assume that there is an identifying field, ID, in both classes such that an instance of C1 and an instance of C2 represent the same real-world object if and only if the two instances have the same ID value. The condition "C1.ID = C2.ID" will be called the *same-object condition*. Data inconsistency is not allowed in the ID field.

DEFINITION 1 **Given a class C, the *type* of C, denoted by type(C), is the set of attributes defined for C and their corresponding domains; the *extension* of C, denoted by extension(C), is the set of instances contained in C; the *world* of C, denoted by world(C), is the set of real-world objects described by C.**

When there is no data inconsistency, schema integration by outerjoin and generalization can be defined as follows:

DEFINITION 2 **Given two classes C1 and C2, their *outerjoin* is a new class C such that type(C) is the union of type(C1) and type(C2); extension(C) is the *equi-outerjoin* of C1 and C2 on attribute ID; and world(C) is the union of world(C1) and world(C2).**

DEFINITION 3 **Given two classes C1 and C2, their *generalization* is a new class C such that type(C) is the intersection of type(C1) and type(C2); extension(C) is the union of the instances in extension(C1) and the instances in extension(C2) projected on the attributes in type(C); and world(C) is the union of world(C1) and world(C2).**

If C is integrated by an outerjoin of C1 and C2, then C1 and C2 will not appear in the global schema since all information in C1 and C2 is retained in C. However, if C is integrated by generalization of C1 and C2, then C1 and C2 will also appear in the global schema since not all information in C1 and C2 is retained in C.

The above definitions are correct as long as there is no data inconsistency. If data inconsistency may exist, then *aggregate functions* [Dayal 1983] may be used to resolve the inconsistency. Consider Fig. 27–2. Assume that class `EmpG` is generalized from classes `Emp1` and `Emp2`. The first function in Fig. 27–2b says that for a real-world object in `world(Emp1)`, its name value is that used in `Emp1`, while for a real-world object in `world(Emp2)–world(Emp1)`, its name value is that used in `Emp2`. The function on `Salary` can be understood similarly.

Aggregate functions can also be used to denote the fact that some attribute in the global schema appears in only one export schema. For example, consider the integrated class `EmpO` from outerjoin (only one set of

```
Emp1: SSN      Emp2: SSN     EmpG: SSN      EmpO: SSN
      Name           Name          Name           Name
      Salary         Salary        Salary         Salary
      Age            Rank                         Age
                                                  Rank

           (a) Export schemas and integrated schemas
EmpG.Name     = Emp1.Name, if EmpG is in world(Emp1)
              = Emp2.Name, if EmpG is in world(Emp2) -
                     world(Emp1)
EmpG.Salary = Emp1.Salary, if EmpG is in world(Emp1) -
                     world(Emp2)
              = Emp2.Salary, if EmpG is in world(Emp2) -
                     world(Emp1)
              = sum(Emp1.Salary,Emp2.Salary),
                if EmpG is in world(Emp1) intersect
                     world(Emp2)
EmpO.Age      = Emp1.Age, if EmpO is in world(Emp1)
              = Null, if EmpO is in world(Emp2) -
                     world(Emp1)
EmpO.Rank     = Emp2.Rank, if EmpO is in world(Emp2)
              = Null, if EmpO is in world(Emp1) -
                     world(Emp2)
              (b) Sample aggregate functions
```

FIGURE 27–2
Handling Data Inconsistency

the common attributes of Emp1 and Emp2 is kept). The third function in Fig. 27–2b means that for a real-world object in world(Emp1), its age value is that used in Emp1, and for a real-world object in world(Emp2) - world(Emp1), its age value is Null. In general, every attribute in the global schema can be defined as an aggregate function of attributes in export schemas. More definitions of aggregate functions can be found in Dayal 1983.

With aggregate functions, the query modification with outerjoin for schema integration and the query modification with generalization for schema integration can be handled uniformly. Let C be a class in the global schema integrated from classes C1 and C2 in export schemas either by an outerjoin or by a generalization. By restricting C to be the only class referenced by the global query, with some modifications to the algorithm in Dayal and Hwang 1984, the following three-step query modification algorithm can be obtained:

1. For each attribute referenced in the global query, obtain a partition of world(C) based on the function used to resolve the data inconsistency on the attribute. For example, consider the class EmpG in Fig. 27–2a. If Name is

involved in the global query, then world(EmpG) is partitioned into two subsets: world(Emp1) and world(Emp2) – world(Emp1). If Salary is involved in the global query, then world(EmpG) is partitioned into three subsets: world(Emp1) – world(Emp2), world(Emp2) – world(Emp1), and world(Emp1) ∩ world(Emp2).

2. Identify the finest partition among all the partitions obtained in step 1. For example, if both Name and Salary are involved in the global query, then the desired partition is the one based on Salary. If there is no finest partition among the partitions obtained in step 1, then construct a partition such that it is at least as fine as any partition obtained in step 1. For example, if both Age and Rank are involved in the global query, then the desired partition is {world(Emp1) - world(Emp2), world(Emp2) - world (Emp1), world(Emp1) ∩ world(Emp2)}. For each class in the global schema, if it is integrated from two export classes, then the finest partition contains at most three subsets.

3. Obtain a query for each subset in the chosen partition. The query corresponding to a given subset can be obtained from the global query by replacing each global attribute by the corresponding export schema attribute associated with that subset. For example, for the subset world (Emp1) - world(Emp2), EmpG.Name is replaced by Emp1.Name. If the corresponding export schema attribute is defined to be Null and is a target, then it is removed. But if it involves a predicate, then the corresponding subquery will be discarded. For example, if a query with predicate "Emp2.Age = 20", then the query will be discarded since no object in world(Emp2) – world(Emp1) can satisfy the predicate.[1]

In addition, if the query is for the subset world(Emp1) - world (Emp2), then "AND Emp1.SSN NOT IN (Select Emp2.SSN > From Emp2)" is added to the Where-clause of the query. This is needed to ensure that only objects in world(Emp1) - world(Emp2) are considered.

Similarly, if the query is for the subset world(Emp2) - world (Emp1) then "AND Emp2.SSN NOT IN (Select Emp1.SSN > From Emp1)" is added to the Where-clause of the query.

If the query is for the subset world(Emp1) ∩ world(Emp2), then "Emp1.SSN = Emp2.SSN" is added to the Where-clause of the query. Condition "Emp1.SSN = Emp2.SSN" is needed to ensure that only real-world objects in world(Emp1) ∩ world(Emp2) are considered by the query.

EXAMPLE 1 Consider the global query against the class EmpO in Fig. 27–2b:

---

1. MAYBE_SELECT and MAYBE_JOIN as defined in Codd 1979 and Date 1982 are not used here.

```
Select EmpO.Name, EmpO.Rank
From EmpO
Where EmpO.Salary > 40000 AND EmpO.Age > 45
```

The finest partition is the one based on the attribute `Salary`. Since for `world(Emp2) – world(Emp1)`, `EmpO.Age` is `Null`, the query for this subset will be discarded. The other two queries using only names in the export schemas are:

For the subset `world(Emp1) – world(Emp2)`

```
Select Emp1.Name
From Emp1
Where Emp1.Salary > 40000 AND Emp1.Age > 45
        AND Emp1.SSN NOT IN (Select Emp2.SSN From Emp2)
```

For the subset `world(Emp1)` ∩ `world(Emp2)`

```
Select Emp1.Name, Emp2.Rank
From Emp1, Emp2
Where sum(Emp1.Salary,Emp2.Salary) > 40000 AND
    Emp1.Age > 45 AND Emp1.SSN = Emp2.SSN
```

A postprocessing query is needed to union the results returned by the queries obtained from the query modification. After the above query modification, some resulting query may still reference data from more than one database. These queries need to be further decomposed into subqueries and possibly also postprocessing queries. For example, consider the query Q for the subset `world(Emp1) – world(Emp2)`. This query still references data from two databases and may be further decomposed into two single database subqueries: One is "`Select Emp2.SSN >From Emp2`" and the other is the same as Q except "`Emp1.SSN NOT IN (Select Emp2.SSN From Emp2)`" is replaced by "`Emp1.SSN NOT IN X`", where `X` is the result of the first subquery. Clearly, with this decomposition, `X` needs to be shipped from the database containing `Emp2` to the database containing `Emp1`.

After query modification and further decomposition, several subqueries may be produced for the same database. It may be desirable to combine some of these subqueries into a smaller number of subqueries before query translation and local query processing so as to reduce the total query-processing cost [Meng, Liu, and Yu 1993].

27.3.2 Query Translation

When a query language of a local database is different from the global query language, each export schema subquery for the local database needs to be translated. The process and difficulty of the translation depend on the syntax and expressiveness of both the target query language and the source query language. If the source query language has a higher expressive power, then either some source queries cannot be translated or they must be translated using both the syntax of the target query language and some facilities of a high-level programming language (i.e., the host language of the target query language). For example, a recursive OODB query may not be translated to a relational query using SQL alone.

Correctness and performance are important issues in designing a query translator. Depending on whether a source query can be correctly translated to a single target query (or a set of target queries), different techniques can be used to achieve better performance as follows.

CASE 1: A single target query is generated.

If the target database system has a query optimizer (e.g., when a relational database is used as the target system), then the query optimizer can be used to optimize any correctly translated target query. If the target system has no query optimizer, then the query translator has to consider the performance of the translated query.

CASE 2: A set of target queries is needed.

Note that current query optimizers are designed to optimize individual queries. Therefore, they are not capable of optimizing a set of queries in terms of the total processing cost. Two stages of optimization may be possible to minimize the total cost of processing multiple queries during query translation, as follows.

Stage 1. Choose a good set of target queries that can guarantee correctness. By *good* we mean that the set of target queries should have certain features that are useful in reducing the total cost. For example, it might pay to have the minimum number of queries among all the correct sets. This minimizes the number of invocations of the target system, and it may also reduce the cost of combining the partial results returned by the queries to form the answer. This is important if each invocation of the target system is expensive. It is possible that there are several correct and different sets that contain the minimum number of target queries. Usually, each set corresponds to a different distribution of the target entities. One distribution may be better than others. As an example, suppose that the target system is hierarchical. Then it might be beneficial to put close-together target record types into the same target query. Sometimes it is possible to coordinate a set of target queries such that the results or intermediate results of the queries processed earlier can be used to reduce the cost of processing the remaining queries. Therefore, it might pay for a set to contain target queries that can be well coordinated.

Stage 2. Optimize individual queries. This is the same as Case 1.

Techniques for multiple-query optimization [Sellis 1988] can also be used to optimize the multiple target queries translated from the same source query.

Query translation between different query languages has been studied extensively by many researchers [Ahmed and Rafii 1990; Cardenas 1987; Chung 1990; Gray 1984; Larson 1983, 1990; Meng, Yu, and Kim 1994; Meng et al. 1993; Rosenthal and Reiner 1985] (see Hsiao and Kamel 1989 for more references). Most of the results provide the translation from relational queries to queries against hierarchical or network databases. Recently, as the object-oriented database systems have gained recognition, translations between relational queries and OODB queries have been proposed [Ahmed and Rafii 1990; Meng et al. 1993]. In the following two subsections, we provide a brief survey of some of the results.

Relational Queries to Hierarchical and Network Queries

In Rosenthal and Reiner 1985, an approach is provided to translate SQL queries into calls to the network access routines. The translation is accomplished in two steps. In the first step, an SQL query against the global schema is translated to another SQL query against the *access relation schema*. The access relational schema consists of access relations that are essentially CODASYL record types and link relations that correspond to the links in the CODASYL model. In the second step, the SQL query against the access relation schema is translated into calls to network access routines. Query optimization is considered during the translation in the second step, and optimization techniques similar to those used in relational systems are employed. For example, a traversal between the owner records and member records within a DBTG-set is considered as a join. [It is assumed that each record contains a system-generated tuple identifier (tid), and each member record has the tid of the owner and each owner has a repeating group of the member tids.] As a result, some techniques for optimizing join processing in relational systems, such as choosing the outer (inner) operand of the join and sort merge, can be applied.

The ASTRID system mentioned in Gray 1984 provides a translation from an extended relational algebra to CODASYL commands. The translation makes efficient use of CODASYL's links to improve performance.

Rather than directly translating relational queries to network or hierarchical queries, many proposals suggest the use of the Entity-Relationship query language [Atzeni and Chen 1981] as the bridge for the translation. The idea is that if we can provide a two-way translation between any database query language (i.e., SQL, DL/I, and CODASYL commands) and the E-R query language, then we can translate queries between any query languages. Some of the related work can be found in Cardenas 1987; Cardenas and Wang 1985; and Hwang and Dayal 1981.

In Meng, Yu, and Kim 1992; and Meng, Yu, and Kim, 1994, the principles of translating relational queries to generic hierarchical queries are studied. The study is based on a two-phase query-processing model for hierarchical systems. In the first phase, all qualified records of one record type are returned. In the second phase, the returned records from the first step are used to retrieve records of target record types. The provided algorithm guarantees that the minimum number of hierarchical queries will be obtained for any given relational query.

Commercial implementations of a relational interface on top of a CODASYL database are also available [Cullinet, Honeywell].

Between Relational Queries and OODB Queries

In Meng et al. 1993, an approach that translates relational queries to OODB queries is proposed. The objective is to form OODB predicates along *path expressions* [Kifer et al. 1992; Zaniolo 1983] from simple relational predicates involving selections and joins. A three-step mechanism is used to accomplish the translation. In the first step, a relational Where-clause is transformed to a *relational predicate graph* that retains all information of the relational Where-clause. In the second step, the relational predicate graph is transformed to an *OODB predicate graph.* In an OODB predicate graph, it is possible to have several vertices corresponding to different class instance variables of the same class. Therefore, an OODB predicate graph often contains more information than its corresponding *query graph* [Kim 1990] in which there is exactly one vertex for each class referenced in the query. In the third step, the OODB predicate graph is transformed to an OODB Where-clause.

EXAMPLE 2 Consider the OODB schema in Fig. 27–3a.

This OODB schema can be transformed to the following relational schema [Meng et al. 1993]:

```
Auto:   Auto-OID, Color, Company-OID
Company:  Company-OID, Name, Profit, Company-OID,
        People-OID
People: People-OID, Name, Age, City-OID, Auto-OID
City:   City-OID, Name, State, Population
```

Consider the query "Find all automobiles that are made by manufacturers whose presidents are 52 years old and own red automobiles, and the manufacturers' headquarters have the same name as that of the hometown of their presidents" against the transformed relational schema.

```
Select   Auto1.*
From     Auto Auto1, Auto Auto2, Company, People,
         City City1, City City2
Where    Auto1.Company-OID = Company.Company-OID
         and Company.People-OID = People.People-OID
         and People.Age = 52
         and People.Auto-OID = Auto2.Auto-OID
         and Auto2.Color = "red"
```

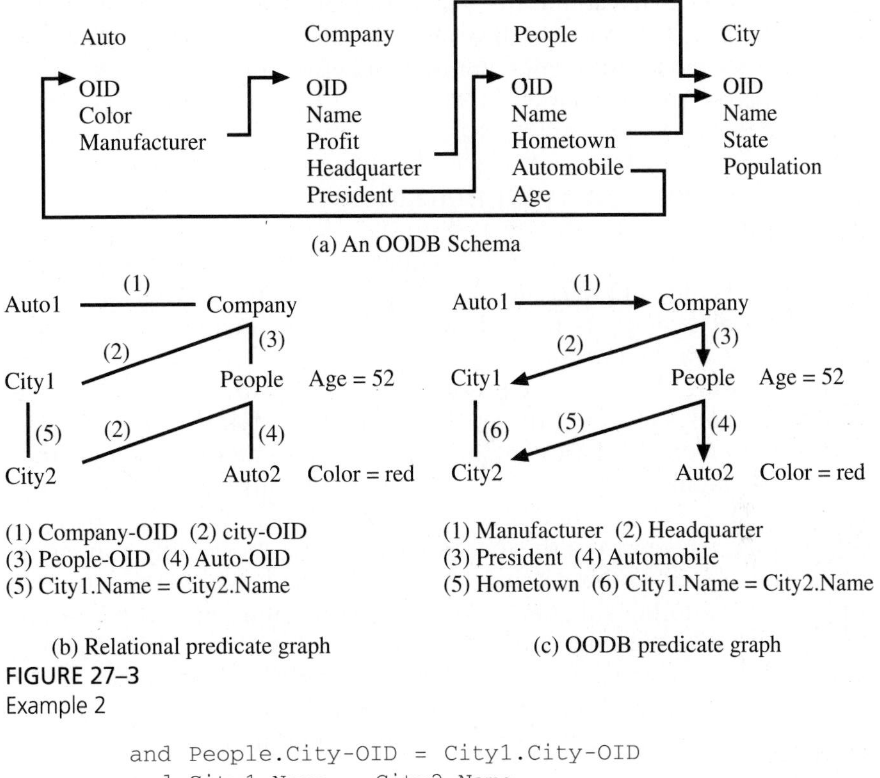

FIGURE 27–3
Example 2

```
and People.City-OID = City1.City-OID
and City1.Name = City2.Name
and Company.City-OID = City2.City-OID
```

Figure 27–3b is the predicate graph of the above relational query. A relational predicate graph is an annotated undirected graph whose vertices represent different relation tuple variables and whose edges represent join predicates. Each vertex is annotated with the selections associated with the tuple variable and each edge is annotated with a join predicate.

Figure 27–3c is the transformed OODB predicate graph. In an OODB predicate graph, each vertex represents a class instance variable, a directed edge from vertex v_1 to vertex v_2 with annotation ANNO indicates the need for a traversal between the complex attribute ANNO of the class corresponding to v_1 and the domain class of ANNO corresponding to v_2 (i.e., a directed edge represents an implicit join) and each undirected edge represents an explicit join.

The following OODB Where-clause can be obtained from the OODB predicate graph as shown in Fig. 27–3c. In the Where-clause, `X` and `Y` are reference variables [Kim 1990] and are defined by `"X Auto.Manufacturer"` and `"Y X.(President: Age = 52)"`.

```
Where   Y.Automobile.Color = red
        AND X.Headquarter.Name = Y.Hometown.Name
```

With some extension to the relational predicate graph and the OODB predicate graph, it is possible to reverse the above steps to translate relational queries to OODB queries. Translation between relational queries and OODB queries is also reported in Ahmed and Rafii 1990; and Keim et al. 1993.

27.3.3 Global Query Optimization

As we pointed out in section 27.3.1, a query obtained by the query modification process may still reference data from more than one database. Therefore, a global strategy is needed to process such queries. For example, consider the query for the subset `world(Emp1)` $\cap$ `world(Emp2)` in Example 1. This query may be processed in several ways: (1) the values of `SSN`, `Name`, and `Salary` of those `Emp1` objects satisfying `"Age > 45"` are retrieved from the database containing `Emp1` using a subquery and are then sent to the database containing `Emp2`, where the answer is formed using another subquery; (2) the values of `SSN`, `Salary`, and `Rank` of `Emp2` objects are retrieved from the database containing `Emp2` using a subquery and are then sent to the database containing `Emp1`, where the answer is formed using another subquery; (3) retrieve the values of `SSN`, `Name`, and `Salary` of those `Emp1` objects satisfying `"Age > 45"` from the database containing `Emp1` using a subquery, retrieve the values of `SSN`, `Salary`, and `Rank` of `Emp2` objects from the database containing `Emp2` using another subquery, and then send these results to the same site to form the answer using a postprocessing query.

Global query optimization in multidatabase systems is closely related to global query optimization in homogeneous distributed database systems. As a matter of fact, many distributed query processing algorithms have been directly used in the multidatabase environment [Bernstein et al. 1981; Chen et al. 1989; Templeton et al. 1987; Yu et al. 1985]. However, such direct application of the query-processing algorithms for conventional distributed database systems to the multidatabase environments is only possible under several hidden assumptions about the multidatabase environment that may not be true in general. These assumptions include (1) no data inconsistency, (2) transmittability of data between different local databases, (3) characteristics of local database systems, such as statistical information on cardinalities and selectivities, are available to the global query optimizer. More discussions of assumptions 2 and 3 will be provided in section 27.4.1.

Dayal 1983; and Meng, Yu, Guh, and Dao 1993 discuss some aspects of global query optimization when data inconsistency exists. Some of the main ideas are as follows.

With the existence of aggregated attributes, some operations that can be easily processed in conventional distributed database systems can no longer be easily processed. For example, consider a query with a simple select operation "$\sigma_{A\ op\ a}(C)$", where A is an attribute, op is a scale comparator and *a* is a constant. If { C1, C2 } is a horizontal partition of C in a conventional distributed database system or C is integrated from C1 and C2 with no data inconsistency on attribute A, then the select operation can be evaluated at each local database containing C1 or C2 independently. The answer to the query is the union of the results returned from the local databases. That is, we have

$$\sigma_{A\ op\ a}(C) = (\sigma_{A\ op\ a}(C1))\ iop\ (\sigma_{A\ op\ a}(C2))$$

where *iop* is an integration operator. However, if the integration operator is an outerjoin or a generalization and attribute A has data inconsistency, then the above equality may no longer hold. For example, consider the select operation "`Salary > 30000`" on the class `EmpG` in the global schema in Fig. 27–2. By retrieving only those local instances that satisfy "`Salary > 30000`", the query on the right-hand side of the above equation will not be able to retrieve employees who have two salaries such that neither is greater than 30000 but the sum is greater than 30000. In general, a selection on an aggregate attribute cannot be distributed over an outerjoin and a generalization. A general solution to this distribution problem is to express an outerjoin (or a generalization) as outer-unions as follows:

```
C1 OJ C2 = C1-O OU C2-O OU (C1-C J C2-C)(*)
```

where OU denotes an outerunion that is the same a regular union except that unmatched attributes will be padded with null values; C1-O denotes those tuples of C1 that have no matching tuples in C2; and C1-C denotes those tuples of C1 that have matching tuples in C2 (C1-O and C1-C are known as the *private part* and the *overlap part*, respectively, in Dayal 1983; C2-O and C2-C can be similarly understood); *J* is the join on the ID attribute and it inherits all the aggregate functions defined for the corresponding outerjoin. C1-O, C1-C, C2-O, and C2-C can be computed by exchanging their ID values using semijoin (i.e., semiouterjoin [Dayal 1983]). With the above partition, selections on the integrated class C can always be evaluated for C1-O and C2-O locally:

$$\sigma_{A\ op\ a}(\text{C1 OJ C2}) = \sigma_{A\ op\ a}(\text{C1-O})\ \text{OU}\ \sigma_{A\ op\ a}(\text{C2-O})\ \text{OU}\ \sigma_{A\ op\ a}(\text{C1-C J C2-C})$$

The distributability of selections over the operation *J* depends on the following three factors: (1) the domain of each argument attribute in the corresponding aggregate function *f*, (2) the type of the function, and (3) the operator associated with the function. When all argument attributes of *f* take non-negative values, the following four subcases can be identified [Meng, Yu, Guh, and Dao 1993].

1. f(A1,A2) op a ∫ A1 op a and A2 op a

An example of this case is "`max(Emp1-C.Salary, Emp2-C.Salary) < 10k ∫ Emp1-C.Salary < 10k AND Emp2-C.Salary < 10k`". In this case,

Table 27–1: Distribution rules for J

	>	≥	≤	<	=	≠	in	not in
sum(A1,A2)	4	4	2	2	3	4	4	4
avg(A1,A2)	4	4	2	2	3	4	4	4
max(A1,A2)	4	4	1	1	3	4	4	4
min(A1,A2)	1	1	4	4	3	4	4	4

the condition on C.A can be pushed down on C1-C.A1 and C2-C.A2. In addition, after the pushdown, the condition on A can be discarded. In other words, we have

$$\sigma_{A\ op\ a}(\text{C1–C J C2-C}) = \sigma_{A1\ op\ a}(\text{C1–C})\ \text{J}\ \sigma_{A2\ op\ a}(\text{C2–C})$$

2. f(A1,A2) op a ≡ f(A1 op a, A2 op a) op a

Here "A1 op a" inside f() means that only those tuples whose A1-values satisfying "A1 op a" will be returned from C1-C. An example of this case is when *f* is *sum* and *op* is <. In this case, the condition on C.A can be pushed down on C1-C.A1 and C2-C.A2. However, the condition on A must be retained. In other words, we have

$$\sigma_{A\ op\ a}(\text{C1–C J C2-C}) = \sigma_{A\ op\ a}(\sigma_{A1\ op\ a}(\text{C1–C})\ \text{J}\ \sigma_{A2\ op\ a}(\text{C2–C}))$$

3. f(A1,A2) op a ≡ f(A1 op1 a, A2 op1 a) op a

Similar as the second case except that the condition to be evaluated on C1-C and C2-C is different from the original condition (i.e., op1 vs. op, op1 is normally less restrictive than op). An example of this case is when *f* is *sum* and *op* is =. In this case, op1 is ≤ if both A1-values and A2-values are non-negative.

4. No improvement is possible without additional information. In this case, no condition on A can be pushed down. "`sum(Emp1.Salary, Emp2.Salary) > 10k`" offers such an example.

Table 27–1 summarizes the cases for different combinations of functions and operators when both A1 and A2 take nonnegative values. The number in a given row and a column indicates to which case the corresponding combination belongs. The reason that avg(A1, A2) and sum(A1, A2) have the same behavior is because predicate "avg(A1, A2) op c" is actually the same as predicate "sum(A1, A2) op 2c".

Chen 1990 studies outerjoin optimization in multidatabase systems. As indicated by the equation (*), an outerjoin of C1 and C2 can be expressed as the union of three components: (1) the join of C1 and C2, (2) the dangling tuples of C1 padded with null values; and (3) the dangling tuples of R2 padded with null values. If only the first two components are unioned, then the outerjoin becomes a left-outerjoin; if the first and third components are unioned, then the outerjoin becomes a right-outerjoin.

Left-outerjoin and right-outerjoin are called *one-side outerjoins*. If both the second and third components are empty, then the outerjoin becomes a regular join. Clearly, processing a join is cheaper than processing a one-side outerjoin, which in turn is cheaper than processing an outerjoin. Chen 1990 identifies the situations when an outerjoin can be reduced to a one-side outerjoin or even a regular join when there is no data inconsistency. Meng, Yu, Guh, and Dao 1993 extend the result to situations when data inconsistency exists.

Let C = C1 OJ C2. Under certain conditions, a global query referencing C can be satisfied without one of the two classes in the export schemas. The following property is discussed in Chen 1990 when there is no data inconsistency.

PROPERTY 1 A global query referencing C can be satisfied without class C1 if (1) no attribute of C1 involves any global predicate and (2) all target attributes can be found in C2.

By using the relational algebra, Chen 1990 provides detailed rules to modify global queries to local queries. Since the relational algebra is procedural, the queries from query modification imply a query-processing strategy. Therefore, query modification and query processing are tightly coupled. A necessary and sufficient condition for determining when one of two operands of an outerjoin will not be needed with data inconsistency is provided in Meng, Yu, Guh, and Dao 1993.

27.4 Future Research

Query processing in heterogeneous environments has been studied for more than 10 years. Although much has been accomplished, much work remains. In this section, we list a few research topics that we think are important and where more efforts are needed.

27.4.1 Global Query Optimization

Compared to the research that has been done on global query optimization in distributed relational database systems, little research has been done on global query optimization in multidatabase systems. This is partly due to the misconception that the query optimization techniques developed for distributed database systems [Yu and Chang 1984] are good enough and can be directly applied to multidatabase systems [Sheth and Larson 1990]. However, this is not quite correct, as pointed out in Litwin et al. 1990; and Lu et al. 1992, because of the autonomy and heterogeneity of local database systems.

The autonomy and heterogeneity of local database systems have the following implications for global query optimization in multidatabase systems.

1. Important information about local entity sets that is needed to determine global query processing plans may not be provided or only partially provided to the global query optimizer by local database systems. Such information may include cardinalities and the availability of fast access paths. This information is always assumed to be available and is critically important for the global query optimizer in traditional distributed database systems.
2. Different query processing algorithms and performance measurements may have been used in different local database systems. This makes cooperation across different systems and coordination between the global query optimizer and local query optimizers more difficult. As a result, the semijoin method may not be as effective in multidatabase systems as in conventional distributed database systems [Lu et al. 1992].
3. Data transmission between different local database systems may not be fully supported. For example, a local database system may only allow the retrieval of its data but not the insertion of any new data into its database. This simple restriction may make inapplicable many of the existing query-processing algorithms for traditional distributed database systems. Even if data transmission is allowed, it is far more complicated than in the case of distributed relational database systems. For example, certain format transformations may have to be performed before the data can be transmitted. In addition, preparing data for transmission in a multidatabase system may be much more expensive than that in a distributed relational database system. The reason is that in many nonrelational systems, such as hierarchical, network, and OODB systems, the instances of one entity set are more likely to be clustered with the instances of other entity sets. Such clustering makes it very expensive to extract data for one entity set.

To solve the first problem, sampling queries may be designed and issued to local databases to collect and update statistics about local databases, which, of course, adds more cost to global query optimization. Sampling techniques such as those proposed in Lipton et al. 1990 may be adapted for such purpose. Most recently, a calibrating technique is proposed in Du et al. 1992 to collect information from a local database system such that an approximate cost formula can be derived.

The first and the second problems may cause the estimated completion time of a global execution plan far from accurate. To remedy this, Lu et al. 1992 propose to create a *subquery execution monitoring* subsystem within the global query optimizer. The monitoring system collects the completion time for subqueries. The collected information can be used for two purposes: (1) for better estimation of the completion time of subsequent subqueries to the same underlying database system, and (2) to modify the original execution plan if necessary. For example, if the completion time of a subquery far exceeds the original estimation, the unexecuted parts of the subquery may be sent to another DBMS for execution. Whether or not this proposal is practically feasible remains to be investigated.

The third problem seems to prompt the need to develop more sophisticated decomposition algorithms that can take into consideration the new characteristics of data transmission in the multidatabase environment.

Dayal 1983 assumes that information about local entity sets and local systems such as speeds and capabilities is provided as parameters to the global query optimizer. Both Chen 1990 and Dayal 1983 assume that data can be transmitted between different local databases as desired. More research is needed to identify the unique characteristics of multidatabase systems and to develop new algorithms to accommodate the characteristics.

27.4.2 Inclusion of Nontraditional Database Systems

Traditional database systems manage structured data. However, structured data accounts for only a very small fraction of all data surrounding us. The majority of all data are not well structured and most are in the form of textual data, picture, image, and voice. To manage these nonstructured data, many specialized systems have been developed, such as the SMART system for textual data developed at Cornell University and the Cruiser system for multimedia developed by Bellcore [Fish 1989]. Clearly, the inclusion of textual data systems and multimedia systems as components of a multidatabase system will greatly enhance the usefulness of multidatabase systems.

The inclusion of specialized databases in a multidatabase system will have at least the following effects on query processing:

1. A new query language that can accommodate both structured data and nonstructured data needs to be developed. An SQL-based query language that can accommodate structured data and textual data has been proposed [Beech et al. 1992].
2. New algorithms for query optimization may need to be developed.

27.4.3 Query Decomposition

Earlier studies on query decomposition used relational query languages and the query language DAPLEX for the functional data model. As interest in an object-oriented data model as the global data model for multidatabase systems is increasing, using an object-oriented query language as the global query language may become a reality.

OODB queries are in general more complicated than relational queries and DAPLEX queries. Existing decomposition algorithms may not be sufficient for OODB queries. Therefore, new algorithms may need to be developed.

ACKNOWLEDGMENTS

This work is supported in part by NSF grants under IRI-9111988 and IRI-9309225 and by the Air Force under AFOSR 93-1-0059.

The authors would like to thank Won Kim for his valuable suggestions to an earlier manuscript of this chapter.

REFERENCES

Ahmed, R., and Rafii, A. 1990. Relational Schema Mapping and Query Translation in Pegasus. *Workshop on Multidatabases and Semantic Interoperability*, 22–25.

Atzeni, P., and Chen, P. 1981. Completeness of Query Languages for the Entity-Relationship Model. *Second International Conference on E-R Approach.*

Beech, D., Chellone, P., and Ellis, C. 1992. An ADT Approach to Full Text. *ISO/IEC JTC1/SC21/WG3 DBL CBR-57.*

Bernstein, P., et al. 1981. Query Processing in a System for Distributed Databases (SDD-1). *ACM Trans. on Database Systems*, 602–625.

Breitbart, Y., Olson, P., and Thompson, G. 1986. Database Integration in a Distributed Heterogeneous Database Systems. *IEEE International Conference on Data Engineering.*

Cardenas, A. 1987. Heterogeneous Distributed Database Management: The HD-DBMS. *Proceedings of IEEE*, May.

Cardenas, A., and Wang, G. 1985. Translation of SQL/DS Data Access/Update into Entity/Relationship Data Access/Update. *Fourth International Conference on the E-R Approach.*

Chen, A. 1990. Outerjoin Optimization in Multidatabase Systems. *Second International Symposium on Distributed and Parallel Database Systems*, 211–218.

Chen, A., Brill, D., Templeton, M., and Yu, C. 1989. Distributed Query Processing in a Multiple Database Systems. *IEEE Journal on Selected Areas in Communications*, 390–398.

Chung, C-W. 1990. DATAPLEX: An Access to Heterogeneous Distributed Databases. *Comm. of the ACM*, Vol. 33, No. 1, 70–80.

Codd, E. 1979. Extending the Relational Database Model to Capture More Meaning. *ACM Trans. on Database Systems*, December.

Cullinet Software Inc. *IDMS/R, Summary Description*. Westwood, Mass.

Czejdo, B., Rusinkiewicz, M., and Embley, D. 1987. An Approach to Schema Integration and Query Formulation in Federated Database Systems. *IEEE International Conference on Data Engineering.*

Date, C. 1982. Null Values in Database Management. *Second British National Conference on Database.*

Dayal, U. 1983. Processing Queries over Generalization Hierarchies in a Multidatabase System. *International Conference on Very Large Data Bases.*

Dayal, U., and Gouda, M. 1984. Using Semi-Outerjoins to Process Queries in Multidatabase Systems. *Proceedings of the ACM-SIGMOD Conference,* 153–162.

Dayal, U., and Hwang, H-Y. 1984. View Definition and Generalization for Database Integration in a Multidatabase System. *IEEE Trans. on Software Engineering,* 628–644.

Du, W., Krishnamurthy, R., and Shan, M-C. 1992. Query Optimization in Heterogeneous DBMS. *International Conference on Very Large Data Bases.*

Fish, R. 1989. Cruiser: A Multi-Media System for Social Browsing. *ACM-SIGGRAPH Video Review Supplement to Computer Graphics.*

Gray, P. 1984. *Logic, Algebra and Databases.* John Wiley & Sons, New York.

Heimbigner, D., and McLeod, D. 1985. A Federated Architecture for Information Management. *ACM Trans. on Office Information Systems,* July, 253–278.

Honeywell Information Systems. *Relational Query/Interactive Query Reference Manual.* Manual #DR52.

Hsiao, D., and Kamel, M. 1989. Heterogeneous Databases: Proliferations, Issues and Solutions. *IEEE Trans. on Knowledge and Data Engineering,* Vol. 1, No. 1.

Hwang, H.Y., and Dayal, U. 1981. Using the Entity-Relationship Model for Implementing Multi-Model Database Systems. *Second Conference on the E-R Approach,* 237–258.

Kaul, M., Drostern, K., and Neuhold, E. 1990. ViewSystem: Integrating Heterogeneous Information Bases by Object-Oriented Views. *Sixth IEEE International Conference on Data Engineering,* 2–10.

Keim, D., Kriegel, H., and Miethsam, A. 1993. Object-Oriented Querying of Existing Relational Databases. *Lecture Notes in Computer Science* 720 (DEXA'93).

Kifer, M., Kim, W., and Sagiv, Y. 1992. Querying Object-Oriented Databases. *Proceedings of the ACM-SIGMOD Conference.*

Kim, W. 1990. *Introduction to Object-Oriented Databases.* MIT Press, Cambridge, Mass.

Landers, T., and Rosenberg, R. 1982. An Overview of MULTIBASE. *Distributed Data Bases,* 153–184. H. J. Schneider, ed. North-Holland.

Larson, J. 1983. Bridging the Gap Between Network and Relational Database Management Systems. *Computer,* Vol. 16, No. 9.

Larson, P. 1990. *SQL-GATE: Providing SQL Access to Network and Hierarchical Databases.* Demonstration in ACM-SIGMOD Conference.

Lipton, R., Naughton, J., and Schneider, D. 1990. Practical Selectivity Estimation Through Adaptive Sampling. *Proceedings of the ACM-SIGMOD Conference,* 1–11.

Litwin, W. 1984. MALPHA: A Relational Multidatabase Manipulation Language. *IEEE International Conference on Data Engineering,* 86–93.

Litwin, W., Mark, L., Roussopoulis, N. 1990. Interoperability of Multiple Autonomous Databases. *ACM Computing Surveys,* Vol. 22, No. 3, 267–293.

Lu, H., Ooi, B., and Goh, C. 1992. On Global Multidatabase Query Optimization. *ACM-SIGMOD Record,* December.

Meng, W., Liu, K.L., and Yu, C. 1993. *Query Decomposition in Multidatabase Systems.* Techniques Report CS-TR-93-9, Dept. of CS, SUNY at Binghamton.

Meng, W., Yu, C., Guh, K.C., and Dao, S. 1993. *Processing Multidatabase Queries Using the Fragment and Replicate Strategy.* Techniques Report CS-TR-93-16, Dept. of CS, SUNY at Binghamton (also submitted for publication).

Meng, W., Yu, C., and Kim, W. 1992. Processing Hierarchical Queries in Heterogeneous Environment. *IEEE International Conference on Data Engineering,* 394–401.

Meng, W., Yu, C., and Kim, W. 1994. A Theory of Translation from Relational Queries to Hierarchical Queries. *IEEE Trans. on Knowledge and Data Engineering* (in press).

Meng, W., Yu, C., Kim, W., Wang, G., Pham, T., and Dao, S. 1993. Construction of Relational Front-End for Object-Oriented Database Systems. *IEEE International Conference on Data Engineering.*

Motro, A. 1987. Superview: Virtual Integration of Multiple Databases. *IEEE Trans. on Software Engineering,* 785–798.

Rosenthal, A., and Reiner, D. 1985. Querying Relational Views of Networks. *Query Processing in Database Systems.* W. Kim, D. S. Reiner, and D. S. Batory, eds. Springer-Verlag.

Sellis, T. 1988. Multiple-Query Optimization. *ACM Trans. on Database Systems,* March, 23–52.

Sheth, A., and Larson, L. 1990. Federated Database Systems for Managing Distributed, Heterogeneous, and Autonomous Databases. *ACM Computing Surveys,* Vol. 22, No. 3, 183–236.

Shipman, D. 1981. The Functional Data Model and the Data Language DAPLEX. *ACM Trans. on Database Systems,* March, 140–173.

Stonebraker, M. 1975. Implementation of Integrity Constraints and Views by Query Modification. *Proceedings of the ACM-SIGMOD Conference.*

Templeton, M. et al. 1987. Mermaid—A Front-End to Distributed Heterogeneous Databases. *Proceedings of the IEEE,* May.

Yu, C. et al. 1985. Query Processing in Fragmented Relational Distributed System: Mermaid. *IEEE Trans. on Software Engineering,* Vol. 11, No. 8, 795–810.

Yu, C., and Chang, C. 1984. Distributed Query Processing. *ACM Computing Surveys,* 399–433.

Yu, C., Guh, K-C., Brill, D., and Chen, A. 1989. Partition Strategy for Distributed Query Processing in Fast Local Networks. *IEEE Trans. on Software Engineering,* 780–793.

Zaniolo, C. 1983. The Database Language GEM. *ACM-SIGMOD Conference.*

28

Transaction Management in Multidatabase Systems

YURI BREITBART
HECTOR GARCIA-MOLINA
AVI SILBERSCHATZ

A multidatabase system (MDBS) is a facility that allows users to access and manipulate data located in a distributed heterogeneous database processing environment. Ensuring transaction consistency and atomicity in such systems is difficult since the participating local sites may be autonomous and the local transactions processed at these sites may not be executing under MDBS control. In this chapter we discuss the problems that arise and illustrate some of the possible solutions. Our intention here is to illustrate the key problems and solutions for the nonspecialist. However, we do assume basic knowledge of transaction processing concepts such as ACID properties, serializable schedules, two-phase locking, and two-phase commit protocols [Korth and Silberschatz 1991]. For more formal treatment of the problems discussed here, the reader is referred to Breitbart, Garcia-Molina, and Silberschatz 1992.

28.1 Introduction

A *multidatabase system* (MDBS) is a software system built on top of local DBMSs that facilitates access and manipulation of data from local data sources distributed among nodes of a computer network. A collection of local data sources that is accessible with MDBS is called a *multidatabase*. We assume that each local data source is independently managed by a local database management system (DBMS).

Access to data located in one or more local data sources is accomplished through *transactions*. A transaction results from the execution of a user program written in a high level programming language (e.g., C or PASCAL). A multidatabase environment supports two types of transactions:

- *Local transactions* that access data at a single site outside of the MDBS control. These transactions result from the execution of user programs submitted directly to a local DBMS.

- *Global transactions* that are executed under the MDBS control. These transactions result from the execution of user programs submitted to the MDBS. A global transaction consists of a number of subtransactions, each of which is an ordinary local transaction from the point of view of local DBMS where the subtransaction is executed.

Thus, there are two types of transactions executed at local systems: transactions that the MDBS system is not aware of (local transactions) and transactions that the MDBS has submitted to the local DBMS as a part of the execution of a global transaction (global subtransactions). Each local DBMS has its own concurrency control mechanism that ensures serializable and deadlock-free execution of local transactions and global subtransactions. The objective of MDBS transaction management is to ensure multidatabase consistency in the presence of local transactions.

A key issue in transaction management in an MDBS environment is *autonomy*—that is, how willing are the individual DBMSs to share their control information with the MDBS or to restrict access of local transactions to local data? Local site autonomy can be defined in many different ways. Defining local autonomy too broadly may lead to considerable difficulties in retaining global database consistency. On the other hand, defining local autonomy too narrowly would not satisfy the basic requirement that a local DBMS be largely independent from a centralized coordinator and thereby would make the multidatabase system unacceptable to users.

To date, researchers have identified three types of autonomy, each corresponding to a type of cooperation:

- *Design autonomy*—no changes can be made to the local DBMS software to accommodate the MDBS system. Making changes to existing DBMS software may not be even possible since source code might not be available. But even if source code is available, modifying it is expensive and creates a major software maintenance problem.
- *Execution autonomy*—each local DBMS retains complete control over the execution of transactions at its site. An implication of this constraint is that a local DBMS may abort a transaction executing at its site at any time during its execution, including the time when a global transaction is in the process of being committed by the MDBS.
- *Communication autonomy*—the local DBMSs integrated by the MDBS are not able to coordinate the actions of global transactions executing at several sites. This constraint implies that the local DBMSs do not share their control information with each other or with the MDBS system.

In this chapter we investigate the consequences of the *design, execution,* and *communication* autonomies on retaining global database consistency in a multidatabase environment. In general, the more autonomous the local sites are, the harder it is for the MDBS to guarantee global database consistency. Our goal in this chapter is to illustrate for the nonspecialist the difficulties that arise due to the desire to preserve the local autonomy of the various sites (section 28.2) and some of the solutions. Solutions for a no-failure environment are presented in sections 28.3 and 28.4, while a failure environment is covered in section 28.5. More formal treatment of multidatabase transaction management problems with a spectrum of solutions is given in Breitbart, Garcia-Molina, and Silberschatz 1992. We assume that the reader is familiar with elementary transaction concepts such as ACID properties, serializable schedules, two-phase locking, and two-phase commit protocols [Korth and Silberschatz 1991].

28.2 Multidatabase Transaction Processing

In this section we describe the major components of a multidatabase system and illustrate the types of difficulties that may arise in transaction processing.

A MDBS consists of a number of preexisting and autonomous local DBMSs located at sites s_1, s_2, ..., s_m, where $m \geq 2$. A transaction T_i is a sequence of *read* (denoted by *r*) and *write* (denoted by *w*) operations terminated by either *commit* (denoted by *c*) or *abort* (denoted by *a*). Each *read/write* operation is performed on a single database item (we denote database items with letters at the beginning of the alphabet).

The MDBS software that executes on top of the existing local DBMSs consists of a *global transaction manager* (GTM) and a set of *servers*, one associated with each local DBMS. (See Fig. 28–1.) Each global transaction submits to the GTM its *read/write* operations. For each submitted operation, the GTM determines whether to submit the operation to local sites, or to delay it, or to abort the transaction. If the operation is to be submitted, the GTM selects a local site (or a set of sites) where the operation should be executed.

The GTM submits global transaction operations to the local DBMSs through the server, which acts as the liaison between the GTM and the local DBMS. Operations belonging to a global subtransaction are submitted to the local DBMS by the server as a single local transaction.

The precise manner in which the server and the local DBMS interact depends on the *interface* exported by the DBMS. One possibility is for the DBMS to accept individual read and write operations. In this case, before the server initiates actions on behalf of a global subtransaction, it starts a new local transaction by issuing a *begin transaction* operation to the local DBMS. The DBMS returns a transaction identification that is used in subsequent actions of the subtransaction. After each read and write action is submitted, the DBMS acknowledges execution (and if the action was a read, includes the value read). When the GTM wishes to commit, it issues (via

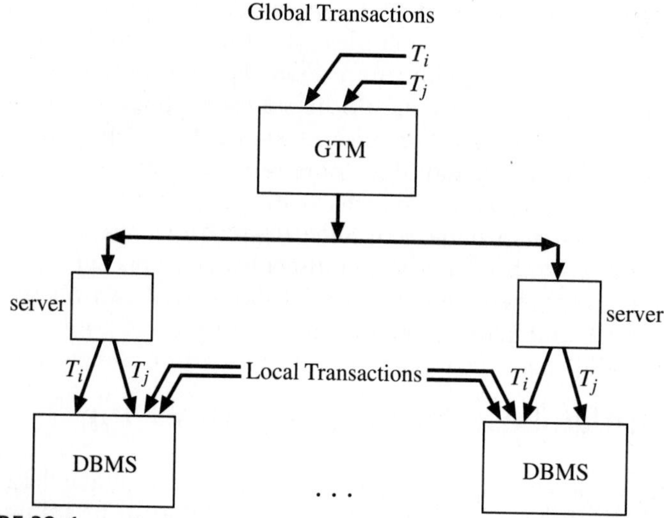

FIGURE 28–1
The MDBS Model

the server) a *commit* command. A different possibility altogether is for the DBMS to accept *service requests* such as "reserve a seat on flight *x*." In this case, the server can only call on a set of predefined services; each call represents an implicit local transaction.

A number of variations on the two basic interfaces described above have been discussed in the literature [Breitbart, Garcia-Molina, and Silberschatz 1992]. The most important variation deals with whether the local DBMS is willing to participate in a global commit protocol. Recall that for correctness, global transactions must be *atomic*—that is, either all their actions commit or they all abort. In a homogeneous distributed database system, atomicity of transactions is ensured by an *atomic commit protocol* [Bernstein et al. 1987] such as the two-phase commit (2PC) protocol. The 2PC protocol requires that the participating local sites provide a *prepare-to-commit* command in their interface. When the local DBMS receives and acknowledges a prepare-to-commit command, it makes a promise to the GTM that it will commit its work if so asked by the GTM in the future. If a DBMS exports a prepare-to-commit command, then it loses some of its execution autonomy since it is no longer free to make decisions regarding the resources held by the prepared transaction.

The GTM should guarantee (if possible) the ACID properties of global transactions, even in the presence of local transactions that the GTM is not aware of. In addition, the GTM should guarantee deadlock-free executions of global transactions and should provide means to recover from any type of system failure. In the next three subsections, we illustrate the difficulties that may arise.

28.2.1 Global Serializability Problem

Existing solutions for ensuring global serializability in a homogeneous distributed database assume that each site uses the same concurrency control scheme and shares its control information. The various local DBMSs integrated by the MDBS may use different concurrency control protocols [e.g., *two-phase-locking* (2PL), *timestamp ordering* (TO), *serialization graph testing* (SGT), etc.]. Hence existing solutions for a homogeneous distributed database system cannot be used in an MDBS environment.

Since local transactions execute outside the control of the GTM, the GTM can guarantee global serializability only through the control of the execution order of global transactions. However, in such an environment, even a serial execution of global transactions does not guarantee global serializability. The following example illustrates this fact.

EXAMPLE 1 Consider a multidatabase system located at two sites: s_1 with data items a and b and s_2 with data items c and d. Let T_1 and T_2 be two read-only global transactions defined as follows:

T_1: $r_1(a)$ $r_1(c)$
T_2: $r_2(b)$ $r_2(d)$

In addition, let T_3 and T_4 be two local transactions at sites s_1 and s_2, respectively, defined as follows:

T_3: $w_3(a)$ $w_3(b)$
T_4: $w_4(c)$ $w_4(d)$

Assume that transaction T_1 is executed and committed at both sites and after that transaction T_2 is executed and committed at both sites. Such execution may result in the following local schedules S_1 and S_2 generated at sites s_1 and s_2, respectively:

S_1: $r_1(a)$ c_1 $w_3(a)$ $w_3(b)$ c_3 $r_2(b)$ c_2
S_2: $w_4(c)$ $r_1(c)$ c_1 $r_2(d)$ c_2 $w_4(d)$ c_4

As far as the GTM is concerned, global transactions T_1 and T_2 are executed serially. At s_1, the resulting execution is also serial: T_1, T_3, T_2. At s_2 the execution is equivalent to serial execution T_2, T_4, T_1. Yet if we look at the global execution, it is nonserializable (to be serializable, T_1 should precede T_2 everywhere, or vice versa).

In Example 1, the problem arises because the local transactions create *indirect* conflicts between global transactions. Since the GTM is not aware of local transactions, it is also not aware of these indirect conflicts. This phenomenon is the cause of major difficulties in trying to ensure global serializability in a multidatabase environment.

28.2.2 Global Atomicity and Recovery Problems

If local sites wish to preserve their execution autonomy, then they may not export a prepare-to-commit command, as discussed earlier. In this case, a DBMS can unilaterally abort a subtransaction any time before its commit. This leads not only to global transactions that are not atomic, but to incorrect global schedules as well, as illustrated below.

EXAMPLE 2 Consider a global database consisting of two sites s_l with data item a and s_2 with data item c. Consider the following global transaction T_1:

T_1: $r_1(a)$ $w_1(a)$ $w_1(c)$

Suppose that T_1 has completed its read/write actions at both sites and the GTM sends commit requests to both sites. Site s_2 receives the commit and commits its subtransaction. However, site s_1 decides to abort its subtransaction before the commit arrives. Therefore, at site s_1 the local DBMS undoes the T_1 actions. After this is accomplished a local transaction T_2

T_2: $r_2(a)$ $w_2(a)$

is executed and committed at the site.

At this point, the resulting global schedule is incorrect as it only reflects the s_2 half of T_1. To correct the situation, say the GTM attempts to redo the missing actions by resubmitting to s_1 the missing write $w_1(a)$. The local DBMS, however, considers this operation as a new transaction T_2 that is not related to T_1. Thus, from the local DBMS viewpoint, what has transpired is

$r_2(a)$ $w_2(a)$ $w_3(a)$

However, T_3's write operation is the same as $w_1(a)$ as far as the MDBS is concerned. Thus, this execution results in the following nonserializable schedule S_1:

$r_1(a)$ $r_2(a)$ $w_2(a)$ $w_1(a)$

We note that if the local DBMSs provide a prepare-to-commit operation, and they participate in the execution of a global commit protocol, then the problems shown in Example 2 can be avoided. In particular, in that example, the GTM does not issue the commit actions for T_1 until both sites have acknowledged the prepare-to-commit. Because s_1 is prepared for T_1, it cannot abort it and the situation shown in Example 2 does not arise.

There is an ongoing debate as to whether sites in an MDBS should be required to provide prepare-to-commit operations and thereby give up their execution autonomy. One side argues that the two-phase commit protocol (with the prepare-to-commit operation) is becoming a standard, so that in the near future *all* databases will provide this service. The other side argues that there will always be autonomous sites that will want to preserve their execution autonomy and therefore will not want to export the prepare-to-commit operation, even if one is provided. This is because they do not want their site to hold resources (e.g., locks) on behalf of a remote transaction, which may be held for an indefinite amount of time. The first camp counterargues that with modern networks and computers, global transactions will be very fast, so the time a site needs to block its resources is minimal, and the site administrators will not mind allowing the prepare-to-commit. Furthermore, they claim, the operator at a site can always manually release a transaction that hangs for too long (e.g., break locks manually). So if a transaction ever waits too long in its prepare-to-commit state, it can be aborted. The second camp then counterargues that if the prepare-to-commit can be broken by the operator, then sites can unilaterally abort after all, so we are back at square one.

Without taking sides in the argument, we believe it is important to study both scenarios, with or without prepare-to-commit at the sites. However, since the case with prepare-to-commit is relatively easy, in this chapter we only review the no prepare-to-commit case, which arises when each local DBMS retains its execution autonomy.

28.2.3 Global Deadlock Problem

Consider a multidatabase system where each local DBMS uses a locking mechanism to ensure local serializability. We assume that each local DBMS has a mechanism to detect and recover from local deadlocks. However, in such systems there is a possibility of a global deadlock that cannot be detected by the GTM.

EXAMPLE 3 Consider a multidatabase system located at two sites: s_1 with data items a and b and s_2 with data items c and d. Local DBMSs at both sites use the two-phase locking protocols to guarantee local serializability. Let T_1 and T_2 be two global transactions defined as follows:

T_1: $r_1(a)$ $r_1(d)$
T_2: $r_2(c)$ $r_2(b)$

In addition, let T_3 and T_4 be two local transactions at sites s_1 and s_2, respectively, defined as follows:

T_3: $w_3(b)$ $w_3(a)$
T_4: $w_4(d)$ $w_4(c)$

Assume that T_1 has executed $r_1(a)$ and T_2 has executed $r_2(c)$. After that, at site s_1 local transaction executes $w_3(b)$, submits $w_3(a)$, and is forced to wait for a lock on a that is kept by T_1. At site s_2, transaction T_4 executes

$w_4(d)$, submits $w_4(c)$ and is forced to wait for a lock on c that is kept by T_2. Finally, transactions T_1 and T_2 submit their last operations and a global deadlock ensues.

Due to design autonomy, local DBMSs may not wish to exchange their control information and therefore will be unaware of the global deadlock. Similarly, the MDBS is not aware of local transactions and, therefore, will also be unaware of the deadlock. Due to space limitations, we will not discuss deadlocks further; see Breitbart, Garcia-Molina, and Silberschatz 1992 for a discussion of what a GTM can do to ensure deadlock freedom.

28.3 Global Serializability Schemes

In this section, we discuss techniques for ensuring global serializability in a failure-free environment where the local DBMSs cannot unilaterally abort transactions (e.g., due to a deadlock). This is clearly not a realistic scenario. However, studying this simplified scenario has yielded a formal understanding of the synchronization issues that arise in dealing with independent concurrency control mechanisms. Failures and aborts will be considered in section 28.5.

Example 1 illustrated the key problem for achieving globally serializable schedules: *Local transactions* (such as T_3) may generate indirect conflicts between global transactions that otherwise are not in conflict. In that example, T_3 creates the indirect conflict between T_1 and T_2 at site s_1 while T_4 creates the indirect conflict between T_2 and T_1 at site s_2. In this case, there is not much that can be done. The GTM completed T_1 and could be running T_2 an hour or 100 years later; yet it has no control over T_4 and the conflict it creates.

To ensure global serializability, the situation in Example 1 should not happen. This can be achieved by either (1) not allowing nonconflicting transactions like T_1 and T_2 to execute at the same local site, or (2) not allowing schedules like S_2, which although it is serializable, lacks some desirable properties. We now briefly discuss these two options.

28.3.1 Unknown DBMSs

Let us explore a scenario using the first approach. The idea is that the GTM will only run global transactions that conflict at every site where they execute together. If a pair of transactions does not naturally conflict, then the GTM modifies them so that they do. One way to do it is to define at each local site a special data item (called a *ticket)* and make nonconflicting global transactions conflict on the *ticket*. Only a single ticket is required for each local site, but tickets at different local sites are different data items. Only global transactions can access the ticket. Moreover, each global transaction executing at a site is required to read the ticket value, increment it, and write an incremented value into the database. Thus, the ticket value read indicates the serialization order of the global transactions at the site. This is in essence the method that was proposed in Georgakopolous et al. 1991.

For instance, in our example we can force T_1 to write some object at every site it accesses data and T_2 to read those objects. Thus, if the GTM executes T_2 after T_1 completes, then it ensures that conflicting operations of T_2 on the ticket is executed after the conflicting operation of T_1 on this ticket at both local sites. This guarantees that T_4 cannot cause an indirect conflict between T_2 and T_1 at s_2, as it would create a *local* cycle. (Remember: The local site generates locally serializable schedules.) In the example, when T_4 submits its $w_4(d)$ action at s_2, the local cycle would be detected at s_2 and T_4 would be aborted.

Several additional methods were described in Breitbart and Silberschatz 1988; Alonso et al. 1987; and Salem et al. 1989. One drawback of these methods, however, is that they generate either a large number of global transactions aborts or a low throughput for global transactions. In addition, all these methods generate a significant overhead on the part of the GTM, which also contributes to the low throughput of global transactions. This is a direct consequence of the generality of these methods.

28.3.2 Rigorous DBMSs

Consider a scenario where the GTM knows that all local DBMSs use the rigorous two-phase locking (R2PL) protocol (the read and write locks are held until the end of the transaction) as their concurrency control mechanism. (R2PL is one of the most popular types of mechanism used in practice.) In this environment, the undesirable schedule of Example 1 cannot occur. In particular, at site s_2, T_4 keeps a lock on c until it commits. Hence, T_1 cannot read c, and is delayed. If T_1 runs after T_4 at s_2, then the undesirable dependency $T_4 \rightarrow T_1$ does not happen.

With local R2PL, global serializability can be ensured as long as the GTM does not issue any commits for a transaction until all its actions have been completed. Notice that the GTM can only delay commits if the DBMS interface permits it. Specifically, with a service interface (see section 28.2), the GTM does not issue explicit commits and cannot control their timing. With a service interface, other techniques must be used to ensure serializability.

Note that R2PL is a particular example of what are called *rigorous* schedulers [Breitbart et al. 1991], and this is the key property in this case. That is, if local schedulers are restricted to be rigorous, and the GTM knows this (and delays commits as explained above), then global schedules will be serializable without need for a global concurrency control mechanism [Mehrotra et al. 1993]. This in turn allows increased throughput of global transactions. The drawback of the method, however, is that local DBMSs must keep local locks until the global transaction completes at all sites. Therefore, global transaction throughput may still suffer due to extended lock waits and increased deadlocks.

28.3.3 The Spectrum

In summary, a spectrum of scenarios exists [Breitbart, Garcia-Molina, and Silberschatz 1992], from one where local schedulers are not restricted (beyond guaranteeing serializability, section 28.3.1), to one where local schedulers are strongly serializable, to strongly recoverable, to rigorous (section 28.3.2). In general, the more restricted the local schedulers, the simpler and more efficient it becomes to guarantee global serializability.

28.4 Alternative Consistency Notions

As we have seen in sections 28.3.1 and 28.3.2, guaranteeing global serializability in a multidatabase environment carries a high price tag in terms of global transaction throughput. Moreover, as we shall see in section 28.5, it is very hard to obtain global serializability when failures occur. Thus, researchers have been asking the question: Is global serializability really needed in a heterogeneous MDBS?

The basic reason to ensure serializability is to guarantee both local and global database consistency. Database consistency is usually defined in terms of integrity constraints defined on the database items. A globally serializable schedule guarantees that all consistency constraints are preserved, even if transactions are executed concurrently [Bernstein et al. 1987]. (It is assumed that transactions executed serially always preserve consistency.) By *preserved* we mean that every transaction reads data that satisfied the constraints, and that if processing stops, the data are left consistent. We call such executions *strongly correct*. In this section we discuss multidatabase transaction management that guarantees strongly correct executions as opposed to serializable ones.

28.4.1 Local Serializability

In an MDBS, there are two types of constraints: *local* ones that involve data items located at a single site and *intersite* (global) ones that involve data items located at more than a single site.

In some MDBS applications there may be no global constraints because each database is quite independent from others and may wish to remain that way [Garcia-Molina 1991]. For instance, a bank is typically concerned about internal consistency ("our money should not be lost") but does not care if its money and others' money satisfies global properties (like $a_1 + a_2 = 100$, where a_1 is the balance of an account at one bank, and a_2 is a balance in the other bank).

When there are no global constraints to worry about, then there is no need for a global concurrency control mechanism. That is, *local serializability* is sufficient to ensure strong correctness of global executions (modulo proviso given below). A global schedule S is said to be locally serializable (LSR) if for every site the local schedule is serializable [Garcia-Molina and Kogan 1988; Korth and Silberschatz 1991]. If the MDBS runs an LSR schedule and excludes certain unusual transactions, then it can be shown [Breitbart, Garcia-Molina, and Silberschatz 1992] that all local consistency constraints are preserved. Intuitively, the unusual transactions are ones that can execute at a site, read data that is *locally* consistent, and still write locally inconsistent data. It is likely that such transactions do not arise in practice, but if they do, steps can be taken to protect against them and ensure that local consistency is preserved. It is also clear that read-only global transactions would not violate any local consistency constraints and hence are never unusual.

28.4.2 Handling Global Constraints

In some applications there may be global constraints that have to be preserved. However, it may still be possible to enforce them without the full generality of globally serializable schedules.

In one strategy, called *two-level serializability* [Mehrotra et al. 1991], the data that can be involved in global constraints are limited. To this end, two types of data are defined at each site: *local* and *global* data. Global constraints may only span global data. Furthermore, local transactions may not write global data. In a way, this limits the autonomy of a site: A site may no longer update some of its data (the ones we are calling global) on its own. (A site can, of course, submit a global transaction to the GTM so it modifies the global data, but now the update is in the hands of the GTM.)

Since the GTM controls writes to the global data, it is possible for it to ensure that those writes are executed in a serializable way. A global schedule is *two-level serializable* (2LSR) if it is LSR and its projection to the set of global transactions is serializable. If we again omit certain unusual transactions [Breitbart, Garcia-Molina, and Silberschatz 1992], it can be shown that both the global and the local constraints are preserved. If it is necessary to run some unusual transactions, other mechanisms can be used to still preserve the constraints [Breitbart, Garcia-Molina, and Silberschatz 1992], although some of these place further restrictions on what a local DBMS may do.

In LSR and 2LSR consistency criteria, we assumed that strong correctness is a sufficient criterion to guarantee global database consistency. It is indeed so, provided that all consistency constraints can be explicitly stated. However, for certain applications there are consistency constraints that are implicit. For example, consider a banking application that transfers money from one account to another one. The explicit consistency constraint for such an application is that each account should have a positive balance. An implicit constraint in this application is that a total of two accounts is the same before and after the application run. It is possible to have a strongly correct execution where the implicit constraint is violated [Mehrotra et al. 1992a]. Thus, LSR and 2LSR correctness criteria should be further refined by introducing special classes of transactions that are required to see the global database states that are consistent with respect to both explicit and implicit integrity constraints [Mehrotra et al. 1992a].

An alternative to 2LSR may be to enforce the global constraints via special-purpose mechanisms. It can be argued that global constraints, when they do occur, tend to be very simple and approximate, so that the GTM can enforce them in an efficient way. To illustrate, consider a copy constraint between item g_1 at site s_1 and g_2 at s_2 [Barbara and Garcia-Molina 1992]. (We assume that g_1 and g_1 are global data, not modified by local transactions.) Many applications, especially if they run on independent sites, can tolerate some divergence—for example, the copy constraint may be $|g_1 - g_2| \leq \varepsilon$, where ε is some application-dependent value. In this case, not every update to g_1 needs to be reproduced at s_2 and vice versa. The server at s_1 (see Fig. 28–1) can keep track of a window of allowable values for g_1, and while g_1 remains in this window, copies of the new values are not propagated to s_2. The advantages of this added flexibility will be more apparent when failures are considered in section 28.5.

28.4.3 Other Approaches

There is a large number of other alternatives to global serializability that have been studied in the literature; we refer the reader to Breitbart, Garcia-Molina, and Silberschatz 1992 for details. Here we only point out that the strategies we have discussed are constraint based. Another class of strategies attempts to extend the allowable schedules beyond global serializability without looking at what constraints may or may not hold. For example, in epsilon serializability [Pu and Leff 1991] a schedule is allowed a limited number of nonserializable conflicts. The larger the number, the wider the class of allowed schedules, but the greater the divergence from serializability. Another option is to define sets of compatible transactions representing transactions that are known to be interleavable [Garcia-Molina 1983]. A cycle in the serializable graph can be allowed if it involves compatible transactions only.

28.5 Atomicity and Durability

In the previous two sections, we considered a multidatabase transaction management problem in the absence of failures and global subtransaction aborts. We now assume that at any time processing of a global transaction may be aborted by one local DBMS (due to a site failure or due to a unilateral abort), while another DBMS continues processing. We consider such situations as failures and call them *global subtransaction* failure.

Since the recovery procedures at each local DBMS ensure atomicity and durability of local transactions and global subtransactions, the task of the GTM is to guarantee that global transactions either commit at all the sites or abort at all the sites.

If each local DBMS provides a prepare-to-commit operation, then the task of ensuring atomicity is relatively simple since an atomic commit protocol (e.g., 2PC protocol) can be used. However, if the local DBMSs do not support a prepare-to-commit operation, then it is possible that a global transaction commits at some sites and aborts at others. Three different mechanisms were proposed for dealing with this situation:

1. *Redo*—the writes of the failed subtransaction are installed by executing a *redo transaction* consisting of all the write operations executed by the subtransaction.
2. *Retry*—the entire aborted subtransaction, and not only its write operations, is run again.
3. *Compensate*—at each site where a subtransaction of a global transaction did commit, a compensating subtransaction is run to semantically undo the effects of the committed subtransaction.

We discuss these approaches in the following subsections.

28.5.1 The Redo Approach

Consider the situation in which the local DBMSs do not support a prepare-to-commit operation. In this case, to ensure global transaction atomicity, the GTM may still use the 2PC protocol, where the servers (see model definition in section 28.2) rather than the local DBMSs act as the participants. Since local DBMSs do not support a prepare-to-commit state, the global transaction may be aborted at the local DBMS at any time, even after the server has voted to commit the transaction. In such a case, the server at the site where the subtransaction aborted submits a *redo transaction* consisting of all the writes performed by the subtransaction to the local DBMSs for execution. Note that to be able to construct such a redo transaction, the server must maintain a *server log* in which it logs the updates of the global subtransactions. If the redo transaction fails, it is repeatedly resubmitted by the server until it commits. Since the redo transaction consists of only the write operations, it cannot logically fail.

In Example 2 we illustrated that in the presence of failures, the local schedule, while serializable from the point of view of local DBMS, may not be serializable from the GTM's viewpoint. We refer to the local schedule as being *m-serializable* [Breitbart, Silberschatz, and Thompson 1992; Mehrotra et al. 1992b] if it is serializable from the MDBS point of view. To ensure m-serializability of schedules produced by local DBMSs, some restrictions must be imposed on the data items accessed by local and global transactions.

Under the LSR and 2LSR consistency criteria, global consistency in the presence of failures is guaranteed, if each local DBMS is cascadeless [Bernstein et al. 1987] and if each local DBMS generates an m-serializable local schedule and, in addition, the GTM generates a rigorous schedule of global transaction's operations. On the other hand, the above result does not guarantee global serializability since it is possible that two global transactions that were not conflicting may indirectly conflict through local transactions due to the presence of failures. To ensure global serializability, one needs to use additional mechanisms to guarantee global serializability. Methods described in section 28.3 could be successfully used to deal with this problem.

The results we discussed so far indicate some weaknesses of the redo approach—namely, some restrictions need to be imposed on data access by local and global transactions, which may not be suitable for certain applications. It appears that these restrictions are unavoidable, if execution autonomy of the local DBMSs is to be preserved. One way of removing these restrictions, however, is to exploit the semantics of the transactions for the purpose of recovery. We discuss this issue in the following subsections.

28.5.2 The Retry Approach

Consider now the case in which local and global transaction may access any data items at local sites. Then, the *redo* approach discussed in the previous subsection would not work. To ensure the transaction atomicity in this case, we may attempt to *retry* the subtransaction that failed during the commit [Muth and Rakow 1991].

Consider a global transaction T_i that executes at two sites s_1 and s_2. Suppose that T_i successfully commits at s_1 and fails at s_2. Using the *retry* approach, the GTM should resubmit the failed subtransaction T_i^2 at s_2 as a completely new transaction T_3. This can only be done if the GTM saved the execution state of T_i, in particular, any values that were used as input by T_i^2. It is also important that the original database values read by T_i^2 were not communicated to other T_i subtransactions since those reads are now invalid. In other words, there should be no data dependencies between T_i^2 and any other subtransaction of T_i.

Further, it must be the case that subtransaction T_i^2 is *retriable* [Mehrotra et al. 1992b]; that is, if T_i^2 is retried a sufficient number of times (from any database state), it will eventually commit. This is important since before the subtransaction is retried the state of the local DBMS may be changed due to the execution of other local transactions. This should not result in the situation that the subtransaction cannot be committed.

It must be noted that not every transaction satisfies this property. Consider, for example, a subtransaction that is to debit money from a bank account. Such a transaction, if retried, depending upon the balance in the account, may not successfully complete. On the other hand, if a subtransaction is to credit money into a bank account, then we can safely assume that if it is retried a sufficient number of times it will eventually successfully complete. It is clear that due to these restrictions, the retry approach by itself is of limited applicability.

28.5.3 The Compensate Approach

Consider again the situation in the previous subsection in which a transaction T_i is committed at site s_1 and aborted at s_2. In contrast to the retry approach, another alternative is to *compensate* for the committed subtransaction T_i^1. This may be done by executing a *compensating transaction* CT_i^1 at site s_1 that undoes, from a semantic point of view, what T_i^1 did. For instance, if T_i^1 had reserved a seat for a given flight, CT_i^1 would cancel that reservation. Since the effects of the transaction have been externalized to other local transactions, the resulting state may not be the same as if T_i^1 had never executed but will be semantically equivalent to it.

To see this, consider for example that transaction T_i^1 had reserved the last available seat for the flight. In that case, another transaction, say T_j, that tries to reserve a seat will be refused a reservation since the flight is already full. Had T_i^1 not executed, T_j would have been able to obtain the reservation. Thus, the state that results after the execution of CT_i^1 differs from the state that would have resulted had T_i^1 not executed at all. This, as in the current flight reservation systems, is nevertheless quite acceptable. We stress that a compensating transaction for a committed global subtransaction is by itself a regular transaction and, thus, it must preserve database consistency.

Thus, executing compensating transactions does not result in the standard atomicity of transactions. The resulting notion of atomicity is referred to as *semantic atomicity*. Since the term *transaction* implies full atomicity, the term *saga* [Garcia-Molina and Salem 1987] has been used to refer to a collection of semantically atomic subtransactions. To ensure semantic atomicity, the GTM must keep a log or record of T_i subtransactions that have been committed.

In Levy, Korth, and Silberschatz 1991 and in Muth and Rakow 1991, an *optimistic two-phase commit (O2PC)* protocol is introduced to guarantee semantic atomicity. The protocol does not require that local DBMSs support a prepared state. The protocol works as follows. When a transaction completes, the GTM sends "prepare" messages to the servers at each site, as is done in the 2PC protocol. However, unlike the 2PC protocol, upon receiving the "prepare" message, the servers optimistically try to commit their subtransactions at that point. The result is reported to the GTM. If all subtransactions committed, then the transaction is declared committed. If not, the transaction is declared aborted, and compensating transactions are run for all the subtransactions that did commit. In the common case where subtransactions are successful, the O2PC lets sites commit sooner than in the 2PC protocol, leading to improved performance.

A compensating transaction *CT*, besides performing an inverse of the function performed by *T*, must also ensure that after it commits, the global constraints between different local sites where *T* executes hold. Note that even though the execution of compensating transaction *CT* will reestablish the consistency constraint violated due to the partial commitment of a global transaction, it will not prevent other global transactions that execute at these local sites before *CT* executes from seeing inconsistent data. In Levy, Korth, and Silberschatz 1991 and Mehrotra et al. 1992b, two different protocols were described that guarantee strong correctness of a combination of global and compensating transactions.

The design of compensating transactions has been discussed in the literature (e.g., Garcia-Molina 1983; Gray 1978). Note that some subtransaction may not have simple compensations. For example, say a subtransaction deposits funds in an account. By the time we wish to compensate, the funds may have been withdrawn by another transaction. So a compensation may involve charging the customer a penalty or sending a message to the legal department. Further certain transactions may not be compensatable (e.g., firing a missile).

28.6 Conclusions

Multidatabase transaction management is one of the very active areas of database research and is of crucial importance if one is to design an effective multidatabase system. Multidatabase transaction management research is still at a very early stage, and considerably more work needs to be done.

In this chapter we did not address an environment where some of the local systems do not support the notion of a transaction. Examples of such systems are file management systems, CAD systems, and information retrieval systems. A major challenge is to devise a transaction management scheme without reverting to the lowest common denominator—that is, without losing transactional capabilities altogether.

Another problem that we did not discuss is the performance implications of multidatabase transaction management. Most research to date has focused on *how* to run transactions in a heterogeneous environment, without paying much attention to the costs incurred in transaction processing. Clearly, such questions as how much more expensive will it be to run transactions when each local DBMS runs a different concurrency control protocol must eventually be answered!

Finally, full data consistency and serializability can only be achieved in a multidatabase system by imposing restrictions that many consider severe. Thus, there is a need to identify alternative forms of consistency and ways of restricting standard notions of consistency so that positive results can be stated, rather than impossibility results. The notions discussed in section 28.5 provide some guidance in this direction, but considerable more work is still needed.

ACKNOWLEDGMENTS

This material is based in part upon work supported by NSF Grant IRI-8904932 and by NSF Grants IRI-8805215, IRI-9003341 and IRI-9106450 and a grant from the IBM Corporation. Avi Silberschatz is on leave from the University of Texas at Austin, where this work was performed.

REFERENCES

Alonso, R., Garcia-Molina, H., and Salem, K. 1987. Concurrency Control and Recovery for Global Procedures in Federated Database Systems. *IEEE Data Engineering*.

Barbara, D., and Garcia-Molina, H. 1992. The Demarcation Protocol: A Technique for Maintaining Linear Arithmetic Constraints in Distributed Database Systems. *Extending Database Technology Conference*, Vienna.

Bernstein, P. A., Hadzilacos, V., and Goodman, N. 1987. *Concurrency Control and Recovery in Database Systems*. Addison-Wesley, Reading, Mass.

Breitbart, Y., Garcia-Molina, H., and Silberschatz, A. 1992. Overview of Multidatabase Transaction Management. *VLDB Journal*, Vol. 1, No. 2.

Breitbart, Y., Georgakopolous, D., Rusinkiewicz, M., and Silberschatz, A. 1991. On Rigorous Transaction Scheduling. *IEEE Transactions on Software Engineering*, Vol. 9.

Breitbart, Y., and Silberschatz, A. 1988. Multidatabase Update Issues. *Proceedings of ACM-SIGMOD 1988 International Conference on Management of Data*, Chicago, 135–141.

Breitbart, Y., Silberschatz, A., and Thompson, G. R. 1992. Transaction Management in a Failure-Prone Multidatabase Environment. *VLDB Journal,* Vol. 1, No. 1.

Garcia-Molina, H. 1991. Global Consistency Constraints Considered Harmful for Heterogeneous Database Systems (Position Paper). *Proceedings of the First International Workshop on Research Issues on Data Engineering,* Kyoto.

Garcia-Molina, H. 1993. Using Semantic Knowledge for Transaction Processing in a Distributed Database. *ACM Transactions on Database Systems,* Vol. 8, No. 2, 186–213.

Garcia-Molina, H., and Kogan, B. 1988. Achieving High Availability in Distributed Databases. *IEEE Transactions on Software Engineering,* Vol. 14, No. 7, 886–896.

Garcia-Molina, H., and Salem, K. 1987. Sagas. *Proceedings of ACM-SIGMOD 1987 International Conference on Management of Data,* San Francisco, 249–259.

Georgakopolous, D., Rusinkiewicz, M., and Sheth, A. 1991. On Serializability of Multidatabase Transactions Through Forced Local Conflicts. *Proceedings of the Seventh International Conference on Data Engineering,* Kobe, Japan.

Gray, J. N. 1978. Notes on Database Operating Systems. *Lecture Notes in Computer Science, Operating Systems: An Advanced Course,* Vol. 60, 393–481. Springer-Verlag, Berlin.

Korth, H. F., and Silberschatz, A. 1991. *Database Systems Concepts,* 2nd edition, McGraw-Hill, New York.

Korth, H. F., and Speegle, G. 1988. Formal Model of Correctness Without Serializability. *Proceedings of ACM-SIGMOD 1988 International Conference on Management of Data,* Chicago, 379–388.

Levy, E., Korth, H. F., and Silberschatz, A. 1991. A theory of relaxed atomicity. *Proceedings of the ACM-SIGACT-SIGOPS Symposium on Principles of Distributed Computing.*

Mehrotra, S., Rastogi, R., Breitbart, Y., Korth, H. F., and Silberschatz, A. 1992a. Ensuring Transaction Atomicity in Multidatabase Systems. *Proceedings of the Twelfth ACM-SIGACT-SIGMOD-SIGART Symposium on Principles of Database Systems,* San Diego.

Mehrotra, S., Rastogi, R., Breitbart, Y., Korth, H. F., and Silberschatz, A. 1993. Efficient Global Transaction Management in Multidatabase Systems. *Proceedings of International Conference on Advance Database Applications.*

Mehrotra, S., Rastogi, R., Korth, H. F., and Silberschatz, A. 1991. Nonserializable Executions in Heterogeneous Distributed Database Systems. *Proceedings of the First International Conference on Parallel and Distributed Information Systems,* Miami Beach.

Mehrotra, S., Rastogi, R., Korth, H. F., and Silberschatz, A. 1992b. Relaxing Serializability in Multidatabase Systems. *Second International Workshop on Research Issues on Data Engineering: Transaction and Query Processing,* Mission Palms, Arizona.

Mehrotra, S., Rastogi, R., Korth, H. F., and Silberschatz, A. 1992c. A Transaction Model for Multidatabase Systems. *Twelfth International Conference on Distributed Computing Systems,* Yokohama, Japan.

Muth, P., and Rakow, T. C. 1991. Atomic Commitment for Integrated Database Systems. *Proceedings of the Seventh International Conference on Data Engineering*, Kobe, Japan.

Pu, C., and Leff, A. 1991. Replica Control in Distributed Systems: An Asynchronous Approach. *Proceedings of ACM-SIGMOD International Conference on Management of Data*, Denver, 377–386.

Salem, K., Garcia-Molina, H., and Alonso, R. 1989. In: Altruistic Locking: A Strategy for Coping with Long Lived Transactions. In: *Lecture Notes in Computer Sciences, High Performance Transaction Systems*, Vol. 359, 175–199. D. Gawlick, M. Haynie, and A. Reuter, eds. Springer-Verlag.

29

Specification and Execution of Transactional Workflows

MAREK RUSINKIEWICZ
AMIT SHETH

The basic transaction model has evolved over time to incorporate more complex transaction structures and to selectively modify the atomicity and isolation properties. In this chapter we discuss the application of transaction concepts to activities that involve coordinated execution of multiple tasks (possibly of different types) over different processing entities. Such applications are referred to as *transactional workflows*. In this chapter we discuss the specification of such workflows and the issues involved in their execution.

29.1 What Is a Workflow?

Workflows are activities involving the coordinated execution of multiple tasks performed by different processing entities. A *task* defines some work to be done and can be specified in a number of ways, including a textual description in a file or an e-mail, a form, a message, or a computer program. A *processing entity* that performs the tasks may be a person or a software system (e.g., a mailer, an application program, a database management system). Specification of a workflow involves describing those aspects of its constituent tasks (and the processing entities that execute them) that are relevant to controlling and coordinating their execution. It also requires specification of the relationships among tasks and their execution requirements. These can be specified using a variety of software paradigms (e.g., rules, constraints, or programs). Execution of the multiple tasks by different processing entities may be controlled by a human coordinator or by a software system called a *workflow management system*. Table 29–1 gives several examples of workflows used in various (computing) environments. In our discussion we will concentrate on workflows involving processing entities that are DBMSs or software application systems.

Many enterprises use multiple information-processing systems that, in most cases, were developed independently to automate different functions. These systems are often independently managed, yet contain related and

Table 29–1: Example Workflows

Workflow Application	Typical Tasks	Typical Processing Entities
Mail routing in office computing	E-mail	Mailer
Loan processing in office computing [Dyson 1992]	Form processing	Humans, application software
Purchase order processing in office computing [Garcia-Molina et al. 1990]	Form processing	Humans, application software, DBMSs
Service order processing in telecommunications [Ansari et al. 1992a]	Transactions, contracts	Application systems, DBMSs
Product life-cycle management in systems manufacturing	Transactions	Application software, DBMSs

overlapping data. Certain activities require the participation of multiple application systems and databases. Such activities are characterized by three main components: tasks, processing entities, and the constraints and correctness criteria that are enforced by appropriately coordinating the execution of tasks. When used without additional qualifications, the term *workflow* will refer to such multitask activities. While such workflows can be developed using ad hoc methods, it is desirable that they maintain at least some of the safeguards of traditional transactions related to the correctness of computations and data integrity. A multidatabase transaction constitutes a special case of a workflow, in which the structuring, isolation, and atomicity properties are determined by the underlying transaction model. The term *multidatabase transaction* will be used to refer to specific types of workflows that operate on multiple database systems and have certain transactional characteristics.

The multisystem workflows considered here cannot be addressed in the context of transaction models developed for the distributed database management systems (DDBMSs). The main problem is the need to preserve the *autonomy* of participating systems. Since many systems used in multisystem workflows were designed for stand-alone operation, they normally do not provide the information and services that would be necessary to execute the distributed transactions while supporting the required transaction semantics. Furthermore, even if such facilities were made available, this could require a complete rewriting of the existing systems and extensive modifications in the applications software (hardly an attractive prospect considering the complexity and expense of such an activity, especially while supporting ongoing operations). It is necessary, therefore, to take advantage of the facilities that are provided by the component systems: Rather than developing new global mechanisms that duplicate the functionality of local systems, we should build a model for managing multisystem workflows that utilizes the known task structures, coordination requirements of a collection of tasks, and execution semantics of the systems that execute the tasks.

The remainder of this chapter is organized as follows. In the next section we briefly review related work in the area of multidatabase transaction and workflow models. Section 29.3 contains a discussion of the issues related to workflow specification. We show how an individual task can be specified and then review the problems of intertask dependencies, atomicity requirements, properties of the entities executing a task, and their impact on the execution. This section also includes an example illustrating how simple multidatabase workflows can be specified using multidatabase SQL. Section 29.4 discusses the execution of workflows. We review the possible approaches to workflow scheduling, including the problems of concurrent execution and recoverability.

29.2 Related Work

In this section we will briefly discuss the evolution of transaction models. The transaction models discussed in this section can be classified according to characteristics including transaction structure, intratransaction concurrency, execution dependencies, visibility, durability, isolation requirements, failure atomicity, and correctness criteria for concurrent execution. In the discussion below, we use the term *traditional transactions* to refer to transactions endowed with the atomicity, consistency, isolation, and durability (ACID) properties. *Extended transactions* permit grouping of their operations into hierarchical structures. The term *relaxed transactions* is used to indicate that a given transaction model relaxes (some of) the ACID requirements. We first discuss the relevant work in extended and relaxed transaction models [Elmagarmid 1992] and then the workflow models.

29.2.1 Extended and Relaxed Transaction Models

An important step in the evolution of a basic transaction model was the extension of the flat (single-level) transaction structure to multilevel structures. A *nested transaction* [Moss 1985] is a set of subtransactions that may recursively contain other subtransactions, thus forming a *transaction tree*. A child transaction may start after its parent has started and a parent transaction may terminate only after all its children terminate. If a parent transaction is aborted, all its children are aborted. Nested transactions provide full isolation on the global level, but they permit increased modularity, finer granularity of failure handling, and a higher degree of intratransaction concurrency than the traditional transactions. *Open nested transactions* [Weikum and Schek 1992] relax the isolation requirements by making the results of committed subtransactions visible to other concurrently executing nested transactions. They also permit one to model higher-level operations and to exploit their application-based semantics, especially the commutativity of operations.

In addition to the extension of internal transaction structure, relaxed transaction models focus on selective relaxation of atomicity or isolation and may not require serializability as a global correctness criterion. They frequently use intertransaction execution dependencies that constrain scheduling and execution of component transactions. Many of these models were motivated by specific application environments and attempt to exploit application semantics.

Most of the relaxed transaction models use some form of compensation. A subtransaction can commit and release the resources before the (global) transaction successfully completes and commits. If the global transaction later aborts, its failure atomicity may require that the effects of already committed subtransactions be undone by executing *compensating subtransactions*. Relaxing the isolation of multidatabase transactions may cause violation of global consistency (global serializability) since other transactions may observe the effects of subtransactions that will be compensated later [Garcia-Molina and Salem 1987; Korth et al. 1990]. The concept of a *horizon of compensation* in the context of multilevel activities has been proposed in Krychniak et al. 1992. Under this model, a child operation can be compensated only before its parent operation commits. Once the parent operation commits, the only way to undo the effects of a child operation is to compensate the entire parent operation.

The concept of a *Saga* was introduced in Garcia-Molina and Salem 1987 to deal with long-lived transactions. A saga consists of a set of ACID subtransactions $T_1, \ldots, T_n$ with a predefined order of execution and a set of compensating subtransactions $CT_1, \ldots, CT_{n-1}$ corresponding to $T_1, \ldots, T_{n-1}$. A saga completes successfully if the subtransactions $T_1, \ldots, T_n$ have committed. If one of the subtransactions, say T_k, fails, then committed subtransactions $T_1, \ldots, T_{k-1}$ are undone by executing compensating subtransactions $CT_{k-1}, \ldots, T_1$. Sagas relax the full isolation requirements and increase intertransaction concurrency. An extension allowing the nesting of sagas has been proposed in Garcia-Molina et al. 1991.

Split- and *join transactions* [Pu 1988] were designed for open-ended activities characterized by uncertain, but usually very long-duration, unpredictable development, and interaction with other activities. A transaction may split into two separate transactions (the resources are divided) and later join another transaction (the resources are merged). Split transactions provide a mechanism for direct resource transfer and provide adaptive recovery (a part of the work may be committed before completion of a transaction).

Flexible transactions [Rusinkiewicz et al. 1990a; Elmagarmid et al. 1990] have been proposed as a transaction model suitable for a multidatabase environment. A flexible transaction is a set of tasks with a set of functionally equivalent subtransactions for each and a set of execution dependencies on the subtransactions, including failure dependencies, success dependencies, or external dependencies. To relax the isolation requirements, flexible transactions use compensation and relax global atomicity requirements by allowing the transaction designer to specify acceptable states for termination of the flexible transaction, in which some subtransactions may be aborted. IPL [Chen et al. 1993] is a language proposed for the specification of flexible transactions with user-defined atomicity and isolation. It includes features of traditional programming languages such as type specification to support specific data formats that are accepted or produced by subtransactions executing on different software systems and preference descriptors with logical and algebraic formulae used for controlling commitments of transactions.

Polytransactions [Sheth et al. 1992] have been proposed as a mechanism to support maintenance of interdependent data in a multidatabase environment. It is assumed that interdatabase consistency requirements are specified as a collection of data dependency descriptors (D^3). Each D^3 contains a description of the relationships among data objects, together with consistency requirements and consistency restoration procedures. A polytransaction T^+ is a *transitive closure* of a transaction T with respect to all the D^3s. The main advantage of polytransactions is that they transfer the responsibility for preserving interdatabase consistency from an application programmer to the system.

Reasoning about various transaction models can be simplified using the *ACTA metamodel* [Chrysanthis and Ramamritham 1990, 1991]. ACTA captures some of the important characteristics of transaction models, and using it, one can decide whether a particular transaction execution history obeys a given set of dependencies. However, defining a transaction with a particular set of properties and ensuring that an execution history will preserve these properties remains a difficult problem.

29.2.2 Workflow Models

A fundamental problem with many transaction models that have been proposed is that they provide a predefined set of properties that may or may not be required by the semantics of a particular activity. Another problem with adopting these models for designing and implementing workflows is that the systems involved in the processing of a workflow (processing entities) may not provide support for facilities implied by a transaction model. Furthermore, the extended and relaxed transaction models are geared mainly toward processing entities that are DBMSs. The desire to overcome these limitations was a motivation for the development of workflow models.

The idea of a workflow can be traced to job control language (JCL) of batch operating systems, such as OS, which allowed the user to specify a job as a collection of steps. Each step was an invocation of a program, and the steps were executed in sequence. Some steps could be executed conditionally—for example, only if the previous step was successful or if it failed. This simple idea was subsequently expanded in many products and research prototypes, permitting structuring of the activity and providing control of concurrency and commitment. The extensions allow the designer to specify the data and control flow among tasks and to selectively choose transactional characteristics of the activity, based on its semantics.

ConTracts were proposed in Reuter 1989 as a mechanism for grouping transactions into a multitransaction activity. A ConTract consists of a set of predefined actions (with ACID properties), called *steps,* and an explicitly specified execution plan, called a *script.* An execution of a ConTract must be *forward recoverable*—that is, in the case of a failure, the state of the ConTract must be restored and its execution may continue. In addition to the relaxed isolation, ConTracts provide relaxed atomicity so that a ConTract may be interrupted and reinstantiated.

Some issues related to workflows were addressed in the work on *long-running activities* [Dayal et al. 1990, 1991]. A long-running activity is modeled as a set of execution units that may consist recursively of other activities or (top) transactions (i.e., transactions that may spawn nested transactions). Control flow and data flow of an activity may be specified statically in the activity's *script* or dynamically by event-condition-action (ECA) rules. This model includes compensation, communication between execution units, querying the status of an activity, and exception handling.

A recent proposal for a programmable transaction environment also contains several features of workflows, including support for a variety of processing entities and a variety of coordination and correctness requirements [Georgakopoulos et al. 1992].

Enforcement of intertask dependencies in workflows is discussed in Attie et al. 1993. Tasks are modeled by providing their states together with significant events corresponding to the state transitions (start, commit, rollback, etc.) that may be forcible, rejectable, or delayable. Intertask dependencies, such as the order dependencies $e_1 < e_2$ and existence dependencies $e_1 \rightarrow e_2$ between significant events of tasks are formally specified using computation tree logic (CTL) and have corresponding dependency automata that can be automatically generated. The dependencies may be enforced by checking relevant dependency automata.

Other terms used in the database and related literature to refer to workflows are *task flow, multisystem applications* [Ansari et al. 1992a], *application multiactivities* [Kalinichenko 1993], *networked applications* [Dyson 1992], and *long-running activities* [Dayal et al. 1991]. Related topics are also discussed in the context of cooperative activities [Lee et al. 1993] or cooperative problem solving [Chakravarthy et al. 1990].

29.3 Specification of Workflows

The following are key issues in specifying a workflow:

- *Task specification*—the execution structure of each task is defined by providing a set of externally observable execution states and a set of transitions between these states. In addition, those characteristics of processing entities that are relevant to the task-execution requirements may be defined.
- *Task coordination requirements*—coordination requirements are usually expressed as intertask-execution dependencies and data-flow dependencies, as well as the termination conditions of the workflow.
- *Execution (correctness) requirements*—execution requirements are defined to restrict the execution of the workflow(s) to meet application-specific correctness criteria. These include failure-atomicity requirements, execution-atomicity requirements (including the visibility rules indicating when the results of a committed task become visible to other concurrently executing workflows), as well as (inter-) workflow concurrency control and recovery requirements.

These issues will be discussed in the following subsections.

29.3.1 Specification of a Task in a Workflow

A task in a workflow is a unit of work that can be processed by a processing entity, such as an application system or a DBMS. A task can be specified independently of the processing entity that can execute it or by considering the capabilities and the behavior of the processing entity. In the latter case, the task is specified for execution by a specific entity or a specific type of processing entity. For example, a task specification may include a precommit state, and its execution may be limited to those processing entities that support such a state. We will limit our attention to the case where a task is defined for a specific type of processing entity.

Not all aspects of tasks need to be modeled for the purpose of workflow management. Let us take an example of a transaction executed by a DBMS. From the view point of a workflow, all details of the transaction that describe its sequential processing are unnecessary. Each task performs some operations on its underlying (database) system. Therefore, a task is a program (transaction) and it is very important that it be correct. However, as with the correctness of traditional transactions, on the workflow level we do not model the internal operation of the task—we deal only with those aspects of a task that are externally visible.

Hence, a task structure can be defined by providing

- a set of (externally) visible execution states of a task
- a set of (legal) transitions between these states
- the conditions that enable these transitions (the transition conditions can be used to specify intertask execution requirements)

An abstract model of a task is a state machine (automaton) whose behavior can be defined by providing its *state transition diagram.* In general, each task (and the corresponding automaton) can have a different internal structure resulting in a different state transition diagram. This depends, to a large extent, on the characteristics of the system on which the task is executed. Some of the properties of the processing entities responsible for the execution of a task, like presence or absence of the two-phase commitment interface, will directly affect the task structure and thus the definition of the workflow. Figure 29–1 shows the structure of some frequently encountered types of tasks.

Other characteristics of a system that executes a task may influence the properties of a task without affecting its structure. For example, a system executing a task may guarantee *analogous execution and serialization order* [Breitbart et al. 1991], which may allow the workflow scheduler to affect the local serialization order of the tasks by controlling their commitment (start, submission) order. Similarly, a system may guarantee *idempotency*[1], thus allowing safe repetition of a task, if a positive acknowledgment is missing or timed out.

Transitions between various states of a task may be affected by various scheduling events. Some of these transitions are controlled by the scheduler responsible for enforcing intertask dependencies. For example, a task can be submitted for execution, thus resulting in a state transition from "Initial" to "Executing." Other transitions are controlled by the local system responsible for the execution of the task. For example, an executing task may be unilaterally aborted by its system, thus resulting in the state transition from "Executing" to "Aborted." One or more states of a task may be designated as its termination states. When a task reaches such a state, no further state transitions are allowed. Finally, a task may have various isolation properties. For example, results of an incomplete task may be made visible to other concurrent tasks, or they may be deferred until task commitment. These and other

1. We say that a system is *idempotent* with respect to a task of type *T,* if the task can be executed one or more times without changing the result. Examples of idempotent tasks are: "set counter c to 0" or "allocate resource number x to the process number y" (but not "increment counter c" or "allocate an instance of resource of type X to process number y").

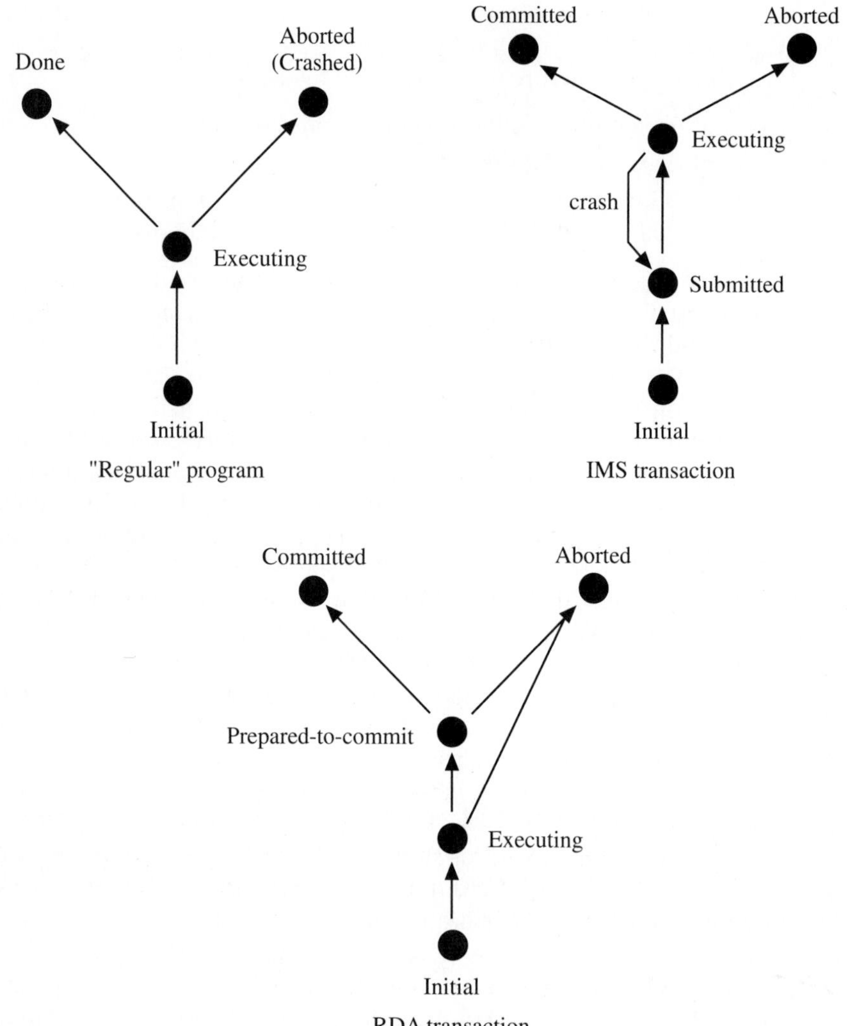

FIGURE 29–1
Examples of Task State Transition Diagrams

properties have an effect on the concurrency control and recovery mechanism that can be used by the scheduler.

A partial output of a task may be made available to other concurrently executing tasks, or a task may request input from other tasks. We assume that tasks of a workflow can communicate with each other through persistent variables, local to the workflow. These variables may hold parameters for the task program. Different initial parameters for the task may result in different executions of a task. The *data flow* between subtransactions is

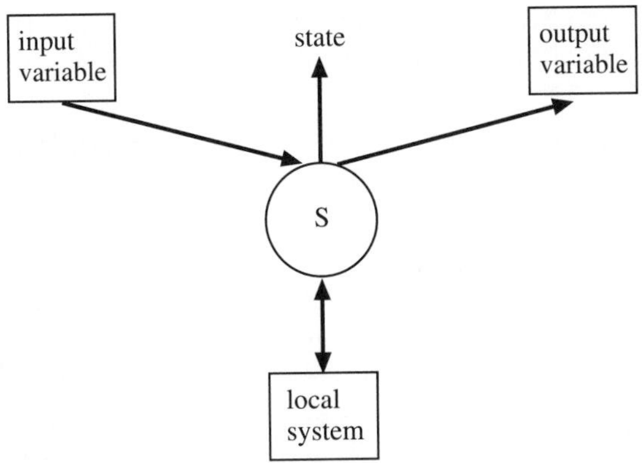

FIGURE 29–2
An Abstract View of a Task in a Workflow

determined by assigning values to their input and output variables. The execution of a subtransaction has effects on the state of a database and the value of its output variable.

Figure 29–2 depicts an abstract external view of a task. A task may use parameters stored in its input variable(s); it may retrieve and update data in the local system, store its results in its output variable(s), and be queried about its execution state.

At any time, the execution state of a workflow can be defined as a collection of states of its constituent tasks and the values of all variables (including temporal). The execution of a workflow begins in an *initial state*. The initial state of a workflow specifies its initialization parameters. Different initial states of a workflow may result in different executions.

29.3.2 Task Coordination Requirements

Once the tasks constituting a workflow are given, the internal structure of the workflow (or control flow) can be defined by specifying the task coordination requirements, usually as scheduling preconditions for each scheduler-controllable transition in a task. In general they can either be statically defined or determined dynamically during the task's execution.

- *Statically*—in this case, the tasks and dependencies among them are defined before the execution of the workflow starts. Some of the relaxed transactions (e.g. flexible transactions [Elmagarmid et al. 1990]) use this approach. A generalization of this strategy is to have a precondition for execution of each task in the workflow, so that all possible tasks in a workflow and their dependencies are known in advance, but only those tasks whose preconditions are satisfied are executed. Such an approach is reported in Ansari et al. 1992a. The preconditions may be defined through dependencies involving the following:

— *Execution states* of other tasks. For example, "task t_1 cannot start until task t_2 has ended" or "task t_1 must abort if task t_2 has committed."

— *Output values* of other tasks. For example "task t_1 can start if task t_2 returns a value greater than 25."

— *External variables* that are modified by external events that are not a part of the workflow (but may be related to the events of other tasks in the workflow or other workflows). Examples of such conditions are: "task t_1 cannot be started before 9AM GMT" or "task t_1 must be started within 24 hours of the completion of task t_2."

The terms *execution dependencies, data* or *value dependencies,* and *temporal dependencies* are used in the literature to refer to various scheduling preconditions. The dependencies can be combined using the regular logical connectors (OR, AND, NOT) to form complex scheduling preconditions.

ConTracts [Reuter 1989], multitransactions [Garcia-Molina et al. 1990], and multidatabase transactions [Rusinkiewicz et al. 1992] support a priori specification of dependencies.

- *Dynamically*—in this case, the task dependencies are created during the execution of a workflow, often by executing a set of rules. Examples are long-running activities [Dayal et al. 1991] and polytransactions [Sheth et al. 1992]. The events and conditions affecting the rule processing may change with changes in the execution environment and/or with earlier task executions.

29.3.3 Failure-Atomicity Requirements of a Workflow

Using the understanding of semantics of a workflow and of the multisystem consistency constraints, the workflow designer may specify the *failure atomicity* requirements of the workflow. The traditional notion of failure atomicity would require that a failure of any task results in the failure of the workflow. However, a workflow can, in many cases, survive the failure of one of its tasks—for example, by executing a functionally equivalent task at another site. Therefore, we should allow the designer to define failure-atomicity requirements of a workflow. The system must guarantee that every execution of a workflow will terminate in a state that satisfies the failure-atomicity requirements defined by the designer. We will call those states *acceptable termination states* of a workflow. All other execution states of a workflow constitute a set of *nonacceptable termination states,* in which the failure atomicity may be violated.

An acceptable termination state can be designated as committed or aborted. A *committed acceptable termination state* is an execution state in which the objectives of a workflow have been achieved. In contrast, an *aborted acceptable termination state* is a valid termination state in which a workflow has failed to achieve its objectives. If an aborted acceptable termination state has been reached, all undesirable effects of the partial execution of the workflow must be undone in accordance with its failure-atomicity requirements.

In general, a task can commit and release its resources before the workflow reaches a termination state. However, if the multitask transaction later aborts, its failure atomicity may require that the effects of already completed tasks (e.g., committed subtransactions) be undone by executing *compensating tasks (subtransactions)* [Gray 1981]. The notions of acceptable termination states and scheduling dependencies can be used to express the semantics of compensation without resorting to special constructs as required in other transaction models. The semantics of compensation requires that a compensating transaction eventually completes its execution successfully, possibly after a number of resubmissions. In the model described here, this property of compensating transactions can be defined by appropriately specifying their scheduling preconditions.

29.3.4 Execution Atomicity Requirements of a Workflow

Similarly to the failure-atomicity requirements, the designer can specify *execution-atomicity* requirements of a workflow. The traditional transaction model would require that a whole workflow constitute an execution-atomic unit. Therefore, an interleaved execution of workflows should have the same effects as if they were executed serially, in some order. Relaxing execution atomicity of transactions in centralized databases has been discussed in Lynch 1983. In Farrag and Özsu 1989, a transaction is divided into execution-atomic steps, and interleaving with other concurrent transactions is allowed only between these steps. In the workflow context, tasks are usually natural execution-atomic steps since they execute on separate processing entities.

However, sometimes the data integrity constraints span the boundaries of individual databases and, as a consequence, the tasks accessing interrelated data must constitute an execution atomic unit. For example, consider a workflow that transfers money between accounts in two different banks. To avoid inconsistent retrievals, tasks (subtransactions) accessing databases of those banks should constitute an execution-atomic unit with respect to other concurrent transactions.

29.3.5 Specification of Multidatabase Workflows in Extended SQL

Multidatabase SQL (MSQL) [Litwin 1990] is an extension of the SQL query language proposed as an access language for loosely coupled multidatabase systems. Since SQL is both an official and a de facto standard for relational databases, it is reasonable to think of MSQL as a testbed for a new emerging standard for multidatabase environments. The basic idea is that of providing SQL with new functions for non-procedural manipulation of data in different and mutually nonintegrated relational databases. In this subsection we will briefly discuss the recent extensions to MSQL proposed in Suardi et al. 1993 and show how they can be used to specify failure-atomicity requirements of multidatabase workflows.

MSQL allows the user to change the states of multiple databases. Therefore, the semantics of such multiple updates must be carefully defined. The following example helps in understanding the problems involved in the implementation of such updates in a loosely coupled environment. Let us consider a multidatabase system providing access to airline databases that store information about availability of seats on different flights and car rental company databases that store information about the availability of their cars. Let us suppose that we want to *raise the fares of flights from Houston to San Antonio on Continental, Delta, and United by 10 percent*. This update can be specified by the following MSQL statement:

```
USE       continental delta united
UPDATE    flights
SET       rate = rate * 1.1
WHERE     source = 'Houston' AND
          destination = 'San Antonio'
```

In the above example, the USE statement specifies the scope of the query or update identifying the databases to be accessed[2]. The multiple update is decomposed into three subtransactions to be executed by the three local database systems (LDBSs) of Continental, Delta, and United. We assume that the LDBSs are autonomous and heterogeneous; hence they may use different two-phase commitment (2PC) protocols; some may not support 2PC or may not provide a visible 2PC interface. Each system may be forced to abort its local subquery for reasons such as local conflicts, failure, or deadlock. The result of a multiple update may leave the multidatabase in a state that is inconsistent from the global user point of view. The only way to check if the multiple update was consistent would be to access each of the involved LDBSs and see what has happened. To address this problem,

2. Since naming and schema heterogeneities may exist in such an environment, MSQL provides mechanisms for their resolution [Litwin 1990].

the USE statement illustrated above has been extended to allow the user to specify the desired level of consistency for the execution of a particular multiple update. The multiple update shown above can be modified as follows:

```
USE      continental VITAL delta united VITAL
UPDATE   flights
SET      rate = rate * 1.1
WHERE    source = 'Houston' AND
         destination = 'San Antonio'
```

The semantics of VITAL designators are similar to those defined in Garcia-Molina et al. 1990 for subsagas. Databases in the query scope are designated as VITAL or NON VITAL (default). All VITAL subqueries must either commit or abort, so that the desired multidatabase consistency is maintained. A multiple query is successful when all VITAL subqueries commit. It fails when all VITAL subqueries are rolled back. The execution is considered incorrect if some VITAL subqueries are committed and some others are not. All NON VITAL subqueries can be executed in auto-commit mode, since their results have no effect on the success or failure of the global multiple query. If all subqueries are NON VITAL, the multiple query is always successful. The set of VITAL databases is called the *vital set*. Failure atomicity is enforced with respect to the vital set.

The described semantics of the VITAL designators are not applicable in cases in which the user wants to include in the vital set databases that do not support 2PC. If two or more such databases are VITAL, it is not possible to enforce failure atomicity with respect to the vital set. Nothing can be done if one of them commits and another aborts the related subquery, and global consistency is violated. A possible solution to this problem is the use of compensation. The extended MSQL allows the specification of compensating actions for individual data-manipulation statements. For each VITAL database in the scope of the query that does not support 2PC, the user must provide a COMP clause in which the needed compensating actions are specified. For example, assuming that the Continental database does not provide 2PC, the previous multiple update can be rewritten in the following way:

```
USE      continental VITAL delta united VITAL
UPDATE   flights
SET      rate = rate * 1.1
WHERE    source = 'Houston' AND
         destination = 'San Antonio'
COMP     continental
         UPDATE   flights
         SET      rate = rate / 1.1
         WHERE    source = 'Houston' AND
                  destination = 'San Antonio'
```

With the specification of the compensating action for the local update to the Continental database, the original semantics of the VITAL designator are preserved. If the Continental update is aborted, the United update can be rolled back. If the United update is aborted, the Continental update can be compensated.

The introduction of VITAL designators and compensation is a step in the direction of the specification of multidatabase transactions in relational environments. MSQL queries that specify VITAL subqueries and compensating actions constitute small transactional units. The natural next step is the specification of more complex transactions. In Suardi et al. 1993, we describe how multidatabase transactions can be specified in MSQL. The main idea is to expand the COMMIT statement to allow the specification of the failure-atomicity requirements of a transactions. For example, we can specify acceptable combination of commitment of tasks by using the following syntax:

```
COMMIT (when)
(Continental AND National) (or)
(Delta AND Avis)
```

In this example, the global transaction corresponding to the whole workflow will be committed only if either the transactions submitted to Continental and National databases commit or the transactions submitted to Delta and Avis databases commit. In all other cases, the global transaction will be aborted.

29.4 Execution of Workflows

A workflow-management system must permit specification and scheduling of intertask dependencies. In addition, concurrency and recovery may be supported, in which case it may be possible to integrate the scheduler enforcing intertask dependencies with a relaxed transaction management system.

A workflow management system consists of a scheduler and task agents. A task agent controls the execution of a task by a processing entity; there is one task agent per task. A scheduler is a program that processes workflows by submitting various tasks for execution, monitoring various events, and evaluating conditions related to intertask dependencies. A scheduler may submit a task for execution (to a task agent) or request that a previously submitted task be aborted. In the case of multidatabase transactions, the tasks are subtransactions and the processing entities are local DBMSs. In accordance with the workflow specifications, the scheduler enforces the scheduling dependencies and is responsible for ensuring that a task reaches an acceptable termination state.

There are three architectural approaches to the development of a workflow management system. A centralized approach has a single scheduler that schedules the tasks for all concurrently executing workflows. The partially distributed approach is to have one (instance of) a scheduler for each workflow. When the issues of concurrent execution can be separated from the scheduling function, the latter option is a natural choice. A fully distributed approach has no scheduler, but the task agents coordinate their execution by communicating with each other to satisfy task dependencies and other workflow execution requirements.

29.4.1 Scheduling of a Workflow

We first discuss the objectives of a scheduler and then review some approaches and prototypes.

The Objectives of a Scheduler

The main objectives of a scheduler are to ensure

- *Correctness of the scheduling*—the scheduling process cannot violate any of the dependencies provided in a workflow specification. Additionally, the scheduler is limited by constraints imposed by the global concurrency control, since uncontrolled interleaving of tasks belonging to different workflows may lead to incorrect results. Determining if the temporal scheduling dependencies can be satisfied is particularly difficult [Georgakopoulos et al. 1991]. The scheduler must be aware that in the presence of temporal dependencies the logical value of scheduling predicates can change dynamically, without any action of the system. At the same time, these dependencies limit the possible actions of the scheduler (e.g., by specifying that a task must not start before 10:00 a.m.).
- *Safety*—the scheduler must guarantee that a workflow will terminate in one of the specified acceptable termination states. Before attempting to execute a workflow, the scheduler should examine it to check whether it may terminate in a nonacceptable state. If the scheduler cannot guarantee that a workflow will terminate in an acceptable state, it must reject such specifications without attempting to execute the workflow.

  As an example, let us consider a workflow consisting of two tasks represented by subtransactions S_1 and S_2, and the usual failure-atomicity requirements indicating that either both subtransactions are committed or neither of them is. If we assume that S_1 and S_2 do not provide prepared-to-commit state and do not have compensating transactions, three execution strategies are possible: (1) execute S_1

first, and if S_1 commits, then submit S_2; (2) as in strategy 1, but try S_2 first and then S_1; or (3) try to execute both subtransactions concurrently.

In cases (1) and (2), if the second subtransaction aborts, the workflow is in a nonacceptable termination state. The same is true for (3) if one subtransaction commits and the other aborts. Therefore, such a workflow specification should be considered *unsafe* and rejected. Similarly, if in the course of processing a workflow the scheduler discovers that there is no safe continuation, the workflow should be immediately aborted.

- *Optimal scheduling policy*—a scheduler should achieve an acceptable termination state in the optimal way. However, the meaning of *optimal* can vary from application to application. One possibility is to define it as achieving the goal in the shortest possible time. Alternatively, we may associate a cost function with the execution of every task. The objective of a scheduler would then be to execute the entire workflow with the minimal possible cost. If the probabilities of tasks' commitment are known in advance, the scheduler can use them to find an execution strategy that yields the maximal probability of a global commit.
- *Handling of failures*—a scheduler should be able to reach an acceptable termination state even in the case of a failure. For example, the scheduler could continue processing after failure and recovery, as if nothing had happened, thus providing forward recoverability. Otherwise, the scheduler could abort the whole workflow (i.e., reach one of the global abort states). Both approaches require that state information be preserved in the case of a failure since even in the latter case some subtransactions may need to be committed or even submitted for execution (e.g., compensating subtransactions). Therefore, the scheduler should log on a secure storage all the information about its state that it would need to recover and proceed.

Scheduling Approaches

Several schedulers for multidatabase transactions are described in the literature. However, most of the proposed solutions address only some of the issues identified above. Therefore, they can be useful only in special, restricted cases. With the exception of Attie et al. 1993, all the schedulers were primarily developed for multidatabase transactions, a special type of workflow. Although the problem has attracted the attention of many researchers, no comprehensive and practical solution exists yet. We briefly review some of the prototypes and approaches below.

- *A scheduler based on the predicate petri nets model* [Elmagarmid et al. 1990]—this scheduler was written for flexible transactions. The scheduler uses predicate Petri nets to identify a set of subtransactions schedulable in a given state. The construction of the Petri net reflects in its structure the precedence predicates associated with subtransactions. However, this scheduler does not address safety or optimality issues. Therefore, it cannot guarantee that a multidatabase transaction will terminate in an acceptable termination state.

- *An executor for flexible transactions in a logically parallel language L.0* [Cameron et al. 1991; Ansari et al. 1992b]—this scheduler for flexible transactions achieves the maximal available parallelism among subtransactions; hence it can execute a transaction in the shortest time. However, the execution can be quite expensive (in a case when only one subtransaction out of N should be committed, the program will execute all N transactions and then compensate $N - 1$ of them). This method assumes that all subtransactions are compensable. If this assumption does not hold, the safety of scheduling is not guaranteed, and a transaction can stop in a nonacceptable termination state.
- *A scheduler as an interpreter of multidatabase transaction specification language*—the underlying idea is to map the transaction specifications into a set of production rules or logic clauses. Such a specification can then be interpreted as a pseudocode, to directly control processing of the multidatabase transaction. The responsibilities of the transaction designer are much broader in this case since the high-level transaction specifications must be translated into a logic program, which is a tedious and error-prone task.

  An example of such an approach for flexible transactions is described in Kuehn et al. 1991, where the Vienna Parallel Logic (VPL) language is used for multidatabase transaction specifications. A multidatabase transaction is specified as a set of executable VPL queries. The language is powerful enough to express both serial and parallel executions, explicit commitment, and to specify data exchange between subtransactions. As a Prolog-based language, VPL provides backtracking, which in this case means compensating and/or aborting subtransactions. The solution tree is searched until the terminating predicate is satisfied or the tree is traversed. Therefore, if a solution exists, it will be found, although no guarantees concerning its optimality can be given. The quality of the solution (including its correctness and safety of the execution strategy) depends to a large extent on the programmer who wrote the specifications.
- *A scheduler as an interpreter of event-condition-action (ECA) rules* [Dayal et al. 1990, 1991]—the authors describe the execution of long-running activities. The scheduler executes a script augmented by the actions that may be triggered as a result of ECA rules. A similar approach is discussed in Georgakopoulos et al. 1992, where the intertask dependencies in multidatabase transactions are implemented using ECA rules.

- *Scheduling as a game versus nature*—an approach under which the scheduling process is modeled as a game of the scheduler against its environment represented by the LDBSs is described in Rusinkiewicz et al. 1992. The LDBSs are considered to be nature, a stochastic, non-hostile player. A *move* in this game means changing the state of one or more subtransactions. Some changes can be done by the scheduler, while others depend on accessed LDBSs. For example, the scheduler can submit a subtransaction to execute, thus changing its state from *initial* to *executing*. The LDBS can abort an executing subtransaction, changing its state from *executing* to *aborted*. The scheduler wins when the multidatabase transaction reaches an acceptable termination state. This method exploits the maximal available parallelism and generally leads to the shortest execution time. The disadvantage of this approach is that it may lead to some transactions' being executed unnecessarily, to be compensated later.
- *Scheduler as a finite-state automaton* [Jin et al. 1993b]—in this model, the scheduler uses a finite-state automaton to analyze dependencies among subtransactions. The scheduler can use protocol analyzing tools to determine reachability of an acceptable state. This approach would guarantee a correct and safe processing strategy. If optimality criteria could be considered as yet another kind of dependency and implemented in the same way, it would also provide the optimal schedule. In the current state of development, this method suffers from high computational complexity due to the state explosion. Therefore, multidatabase transactions composed of a large number of subtransactions cannot be processed in this way. This scheduler has a partially distributed architecture.
- *Scheduling and enforcing intertask dependencies using temporal propositional logic* [Attie et al. 1993]—in the Carnot project, carried out at MCC in collaboration with Bellcore and the University of Houston, each task is modeled as a collection of significant events (start, commit, rollback, etc.) that may be forcible, rejectable, or delayable. Transaction semantics is defined using order dependencies $e_1 < e_2$ and existence dependencies $e_1 \rightarrow e_2$ between significant events of tasks. Intertask dependencies are specified as constraints on the occurrence and temporal order of significant events of the related tasks. A temporal propositional logic called computational tree logic (CTL) is used to specify dependencies discussed in Chrysanthis and Ramamritham 1991; and Klein 1991. This allows automatic generation of automata that enforce the dependencies. By accepting, rejecting, or delaying requests, the scheduler can enforce all dependencies. The scheduler is provably correct and safe. This scheduler has a centralized architecture and high computational cost. Hence it is not appropriate for managing many intertask dependencies without additional optimization.

29.4.2 Concurrent Execution of Workflows

We assume that each task of a workflow is executed under the control of an individual processing entity (e.g., a DBMS) that provides local concurrency control to the extent required by the semantics of each task. This guarantees that each processing system is left in a (locally) consistent state; however, it may not be sufficient to guarantee global correctness of concurrent and interleaved execution of workflows.

Assuming that each workflow is executed correctly, a concurrent execution of multiple workflows is correct if it is in some sense equivalent to running these workflows one at a time, without interference. In the absence of any additional information about the constraints that exist among the states of the multiple systems involved in the execution of a workflow and about the properties of the workflows, assuring such equivalence requires enforcement of global serializability and global commitment of workflows. If additional information (e.g., the failure- and isolation-atomicity requirements of each workflow) is available, weaker correctness criteria for concurrent execution of workflows may become applicable. In the discussion below, we first review basic concepts of multidatabase transaction management that are applicable in workflow management and then discuss the possible extensions. In Jin et al. 1993a, we discuss application and system semantics in a real-world environment that allows the use of simple and efficient concurrency control and recovery methods.

Global Serializability

Global serializability requires tasks belonging to different workflows to have the same relative serialization order at all sites on which they execute. To ensure that global serializability is not violated, local histories must be validated by the workflow-management system. The problems of determining local serialization order were discussed in the literature on multidatabase transactions [Breitbart and Silberschatz 1988]. The main difficulty is caused by the possibility of *indirect conflicts* that may be caused by the local tasks executed outside of global workflows. A possible mechanism for detection of inter-workflow conflicts may be based on the ticket concept proposed in Georgakopoulos et al. 1993.

Global Commitment

We say that a workflow can become *globally committed* when it reaches an acceptable termination state. To ensure failure atomicity of a workflow, recovery procedures must deal with problems caused by the autonomy of the systems involved in processing a workflow. The difficulties arise because the local systems cannot distinguish locally uncommitted tasks that belong to globally committed workflows from uncommitted local tasks. If a local system provides basic transaction management mechanisms, after a failure its local recovery procedures rollback all locally uncommitted tasks, even if they belong to globally committed workflows. In addition, workflows that have a locally committed task cannot be rolled back. Workflow-recovery actions at each local system constitute new transactions, which from the point of view of the local systems have no connection to the failed tasks they are supposed to complete.

These issues have been discussed in the context of multidatabase transactions and some solutions proposed in the literature [Wolski and Veijalainen 1990; Georgakopoulos 1991; Mehrotra et al. 1992] can be expanded to workflow management.

Relaxing Global Serializability Requirements

In the discussion below, we assume that the specifications of workflows provided by the designer and the initial parameters are correct—that is, a workflow executed in isolation does not violate consistency. The workflow scheduler guarantees that the execution of every workflow proceeds in accordance with its specification, and local concurrency controllers guarantee that interleaved execution of tasks preserves local consistency constraints. The workflow concurrency control mechanism has to guarantee that global histories are correct—that is, preserve *multisystem consistency constraints.* Below we define a class of global histories that are considered correct under the workflow model described above.

Tasks of various workflows issue operations that may locally conflict with operations of other workflows or local transactions. The execution order of committed conflicting operations of local transactions or tasks (in general transactions) results in the serialization precedence between transactions that have issued them (denoted by $<$). The serialization precedence relation between transactions is transitive and can be used to define *m-serializability,* a correctness criterion for concurrent execution of workflows.

Informally, a global history is m-serializable if every local history is serializable and no two workflows W_i and W_j have tasks T_{ik}, T_{il} belonging to the same execution-atomic unit of W_i and tasks T_{jk}, and T_{jl} belonging to the same execution-atomic unit of W_j, such that $T_{ik} < T_{jk}$ and $T_{jl} < T_{il}$.

Global serializability requires that the serialization order of workflows be *compatible* at all processing entities. That is, if a task T_i of W_i precedes task T_j of W_j at a processing entity, then at no other entities can a task of W_j precede a task of W_i. M-serializability requires only that tasks belonging to the same execution-atomic unit of a workflow have compatible serialization orders at all local sites they access. M-serializability allows some global histories that would be rejected under global serializability. This is because operations of a task T_i are not related to operations of tasks that belong to execution-atomic units other than that of T_i. Therefore, the serialization

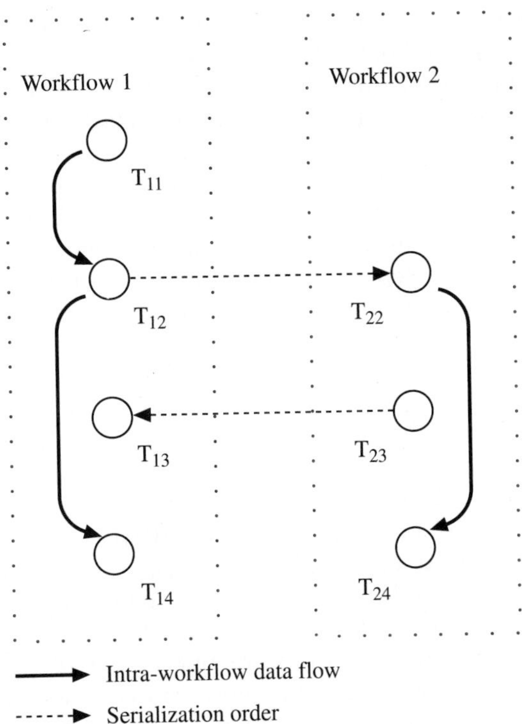

FIGURE 29–3
Example of M-Serializable Execution of Workflows

precedence of T_i imposes a serialization precedence only on tasks that belong to the same execution-atomic unit as T_i and not on all tasks of W_i, as in the case of global serializability.

As an example, consider the history in Fig. 29–3. Let us assume that workflow W_1 consists of two execution atomic units $\{T_{11}, T_{12}, T_{14}\}$ and $\{T_{13}\}$, while the execution atomic units of W_2 are $\{T_{22}, T_{24}\}$ and $\{T_{23}\}$. Then, the serialization precedence between T_{12} and T_{22} established at processing entity 2 has no effect on the serialization precedence at processing entity 3. On the other hand, if the tasks T_{14} and T_{24} were to conflict, T_{24} would have to be serialized after T_{14}. A formal definition of m-serializability and a mechanism to ensure it are presented in Rusinkiewicz et al. 1992.

29.4.3 Recovery of a Workflow

The objective of failure recovery in workflow management is to enforce the failure atomicity of workflows. The recovery procedures must make sure that if a failure occurs in any of the workflow-processing components (including the scheduler), the workflow eventually reaches an acceptable state—possibly using compensation. We may assume that the processing entities involved in the workflow have their own local recovery systems and handle their local failures. Therefore, we will discuss here only the handling of failures of the workflow execution controllers [scheduler(s) and the concurrency controller].

In order to recover the execution-environment context, the failure-recovery routines need to restore the state information at the time of failure, including the information about the execution states of each task and information about the scheduling dependencies of the concurrency controller. Therefore, the appropriate status information must be logged on stable storage [Jin et al. 1993a].

The failure of the concurrency controller may be detected using timeout mechanisms, and the status information can be reconstructed by scanning the logs. Assuming forward recoverability [Reuter 1989] and idempotency of the processing entities, the execution of the workflow may continue by resubmitting the tasks that were not completed.

We also need to consider the contents of the request queues. If a mechanism providing the functionality of persistent pipes is used (e.g., in DEC VMS system, the queues may be implemented using mailboxes—persistent message queues accessed as virtual I/O devices), the messages are stored in permanent storage and are not lost in case of failure. If the queues are in volatile storage (e.g., under UNIX the queues may be implemented using sockets), instead of recovering the contents of the queue, we let schedulers resend their requests.

29.5 Support for Workflow Execution

Three basic approaches to the implementation of a workflow-management system are: (1) an embedded approach that requires and exploits significant support from the processing entities for specification and enforcement dependencies—for example, an approach requiring processing entities to support some active data-management features; (2) a layering approach that implements workflow-control facilities on top of uniform application-level interfaces to entities by developing modules to support intertask dependencies and other workflow specifications; and (3) an approach that provides limited workflow-management facilities in an environment consisting of transaction monitors and event monitoring/synchronizing facilities (e.g., similar to those proposed in CORBA [Soley 1993]).

The first approach is aligned to the work reported in Dayal et al. 1991. Variants of the second approach are used in the Narada [Halabi et al. 1992], Interbase [Elmagarmid et al. 1994], and Carnot [Tomlinson et al. 1993] projects. The facilities provided by these projects may be used to implement relaxed transaction and workflow capabilities. GTE's Distributed Object

Management (DOM) project [Georgakopoulos et al. 1992] seems to follow a combination of the first two approaches by distinguishing between native DOM objects and data managed by non-DOM systems that support transactions (i.e., DBMSs) and do not support transactions (transactionless systems).

Work on execution of multisystem applications in a heterogeneous computing environment has been carried out in the Omnibase project since 1985 [Rusinkiewicz et al. 1988]. The basic contributions of this project to the workflow management were the development of a task specification language, DOL, and a distributed execution environment called Narada. The software architecture based on the concept of a task-specification language was later adapted and expanded in numerous projects, including ERNIE at Bellcore, Interbase at Purdue [Rusinkiewicz et al. 1990b], and Carnot at MCC [Woelk et al. 1993].

A DOL-based system consists of the *resource directory*, the *DOL engine* and a collection of *local access managers* (LAMs). The resource directory contains up-to-date information about all the services known to the DOL engine. The information includes physical addresses, communication protocols, login information, and data-transfer methods. The DOL engine is responsible for executing DOL programs by communicating with various services. It provides task activation, task synchronization, conditional execution, and data exchange between LAMs, as well as commitment control for local and global tasks. It is also responsible for opening and closing connections to the participating LAMs, setting up communication channels between them, sending them their local commands, and monitoring their execution status. A LAM acts as a proxy user for the processing entity it manages and provides an abstraction of the service it encompasses. LAMs preserve the autonomy of the processing entities. The DOL engine communicates with LAMs, which are responsible for executing the requested local commands.

DOL programs can be written directly by end users or can be automatically generated by another software system. The DOL engine receives a DOL program and produces an execution plan for it. It consults the resource directory to get relevant information about invocation of the corresponding LAMs. The DOL engine executes the DOL program by invoking the LAMs that support the corresponding services. These services can be database systems, knowledge-based systems, software packages, or other DOL engines. When each LAM executes its commands successfully, the output may be forwarded to another LAM. The DOL engine communicates with all LAMs using the same high-level communication protocol. This simplifies the architecture and allows addition of new services without modifying the other system modules.

The Interbase project extended the concept of LAM in DOL to what is called remote system interface (RSI). RSIs were developed for a variety of (heterogeneous) software systems to provide, in addition to the LAM functionalities, some of the novel features of IPL, such as more sophisticated format-translation and information-exchange facilities and coordination of concurrent workflows (termed *global applications* in [Elmagarmid et al. 1994]).

Carnot goes further in developing support for distributed services and applications, including relaxed transactions and workflows [Woelk et al. 1993, Tomlinson et al. 1993]. Its main component, called an extensible services switch (ESS), uses a language called Rosette based on an Actor model. Rosette supports interpretive control of distributed applications, high concurrency, and ultra-lightweight processes. Since control programs or scripts are interpreted, one site may send a script to another site to affect the local control of a distributed application. Furthermore, an ESS supports many distributed processing abstractions, such as ByteStreams and TreeSpaces, for easier development and efficient implementation of workflow and relaxed transaction management. ESSs that communicate with different communication resources (e.g., TCP/IP, SNA, X.25), information resources (e.g., commercial relational and object-oriented DBMSs), and application services (e.g., X.500, X.400) have been built.

29.6 Summary

Hierarchical structures of extended transaction models such as nested transactions [Moss 1985] and multilevel transactions [Weikum 1991] are often too rigid for workflow applications. A basic problem with the development of workflow management systems based on a particular transaction model is that a predefined set of properties provided by the model may or may not be required by the semantics of a workflow. For example, intertask dependencies required by the semantics of a workflow may be more complex than those supported by a given transaction model, or correctness guarantees (such as global serializability) that are provided may be stronger than are needed.

Another problem with adopting the extended transaction models for designing and implementing workflows is that the systems involved in the processing of a workflow (processing entities) may not provide support for facilities implied by a transaction model. For example, multidatabase transaction models are geared toward processing entities that are DBMSs; hence they are not applicable if the entities do not provide local transaction management facilities. While we may need to define workflows that also incorporate non-DBMS processing entities, it is clear that such workflow systems may not be able to provide global data consistency guaranteed by transactions.

The desire to overcome these limitations was a motivation for the development of workflow models. In our opinion, a comprehensive transactional workflow system should support multitask, multisystem activities where (1) different tasks may have different execution behavior and properties, (2) the tasks may be executed on different processing entities, (3) application- or user-defined coordination of the execution of different tasks, including data exchange, is provided, and (4) application- or user-defined failure and execution atomicity are supported.

A basic type of transactional workflow system uses transactions as the tasks and exploits support for transaction execution provided by systems (which is similar to extending a relaxed transaction model with intertask dependencies). The workflows may additionally require concurrency control to support execution atomicity and coordination requirements with respect to concurrent execution of multiple workflows. When the tasks are transactions and entities that execute them are DBMSs, it is possible and desirable to borrow from the extensive recent work on extended and relaxed transaction models. Further work is needed when the tasks are not transactions and/or the entities do not provide transaction execution support, but workflow failure- and execution-atomicity requirements exist.

While it may be possible to express some workflow correctness criteria as intertask dependencies, it may be desirable to incorporate them into a workflow model. In the future, we expect an evolution toward application development models that provide the extended transaction and workflow capabilities to suit the needs of complex applications accessing heterogeneous existing systems.

ACKNOWLEDGMENTS

This work was supported, in part, by the Texas Advanced Research Program Grant number 3652008. Some of the work was performed during the authors' short sabbatical at ETH, Zurich. We acknowledge our collaboration with the members of the Carnot Project at MCC (P. Attie, P. Cannata, M. Huhns, M. Singh, C. Tomlinson, D. Woelk) and discussions with N. Krishnakumar and L. Ness at Bellcore, G. Weikum and H-J. Schek at ETH-Zurich, and G. Karabatis and M. Bregolin at the University of Houston.

REFERENCES

Ansari, M., Ness, L., Rusinkiewicz, M., and Sheth, A. 1992a Using Flexible Transactions to Support Multi-System Telecommunication Applications. *Proceedings of the Eighteenth International Conference on Very Large Data Bases.*

Ansari, M., Rusinkiewicz, M., Ness, L., and Sheth, A. 1992b. Executing Multidatabase Transactions. *Proceedings of the Twenty-fifth International Conference on System Sciences,* Hawaii.

Attie, P., Singh, M., Sheth, A., and Rusinkiewicz, M. 1993. Specifying and Enforcing Intertask Dependencies. *Proceedings of the Nineteenth International Conference on Very Large Data Bases.*

Breitbart, Y., Georgakopoulos, D., Rusinkiewicz, M., and Silberschatz, A. 1991. On Rigorous Transaction Scheduling. *IEEE Transactions on Software Engineering*, Vol. 17.

Breitbart, Y., and Silberschatz, A. 1988. Multidatabase Update Issues. *Proceedings of ACM-SIGMOD International Conference on Management of Data.*

Cameron, E., Ness, L., and Sheth, A. 1991. An Executor for Multidatabase Transactions Which Achieves Maximal Parallelism. *Proceedings of the First International Workshop on Interoperability in Multidatabase Systems.*

Chakravarthy, S., Navathe, S., Karlapalem, K., and Tanaka, A. 1990. Meeting the Cooperative Problem Solving Challenge: A Database-Centered Approach. *Cooperating Knowledge Based Systems 1990*. S. M. Deen, ed. Springer-Verlag.

Chen, J., Bukhres, O. A., and Elmagarmid, A. K. 1993. IPL: A Multidatabase Transaction Specification Language. *Proceedings of the Thirteenth International Conference on Distributed Computing Systems*, Pittsburgh.

Chrysanthis, P., and Ramamritham, K. 1990. ACTA: A Framework for Specifying and Reasoning About Transaction Structure and Behavior. *Proceedings of ACM-SIGMOD Conference on Management of Data.*

Chrysanthis, P., and Ramamritham, K. 1991. A Formalism for Extended Transaction Model. *Proceedings of Seventeenth International Conference on Very Large Data Bases.*

Dayal, U., Hsu, M., and Ladin, R. 1990. Organizing Long-Running Activities with Triggers and Transactions. *Proceedings of ACM-SIGMOD Conference on Management of Data.*

Dayal, U., Hsu, M., and Ladin, R. 1991. A Transactional Model for Long-Running Activities. *Proceedings of the Seventeenth International Conference on Very Large Data Bases.*

Dyson, E. 1992. Workflow. *Forbes*, November, 192.

Elmagarmid, A., ed. 1992. *Transaction Models for Advanced Database Applications*. Morgan-Kaufmann, Los Altos, Cal.

Elmagarmid, A., Chen, J., and Bukhres, Ö. 1994. Remote System Interfaces: An Approach to Overcome Heterogeneous Barriers and Retain Local Autonomy in the Integration of Heterogeneous Systems. *International Journal on Intelligent and Cooperative Information Systems* (in press).

Elmagarmid, A.K., Leu, Y., Litwin, W., and Rusinkiewicz, M. 1990. A Multidatabase Transaction Model for InterBase. *Proceedings of the Sixteenth International Conference on Very Large Data Bases.*

Farrag, A., and Özsu, M. 1989. Using Semantic Knowledge of Transactions to Increase Concurrency. *ACM Transactions on Database Systems*, Vol. 14, No. 4, 503–525.

Garcia-Molina, H., Gawlick, D., Klein, J., Kleissner, K., and Salem, K. 1990. *Coordinating Multi-Transaction Activities*. Technical Report CS-TR-247-90, Princeton University.

Garcia-Molina, H., and Salem, K. 1987. SAGAS. *Proceedings of ACM-SIGMOD Conference on Management of Data.*

Garcia-Molina, H., Salem, K., Gawlick, D., Klein, J., and Kleissner, K. 1991. Modeling Long-Running Activities as Nested Sagas. *Data Engineering Bulletin*, Vol. 14, No. 1.

Georgakopoulos, D. 1991. Multidatabase Recoverability and Recovery. *Proceedings of the First International Workshop on Interoperability in Multidatabase Systems.*

Georgakopoulos, D., Hornick, M., and Krychniak, P. 1992. *An Environment for Specification and Management of Extended Transactions in DOMS.* Technical Report, GTE Laboratories Inc.

Georgakopoulos, D., Rusinkiewicz, M., and Litwin, W. 1991. *Chronological Scheduling of Transactions with Temporal Dependencies.* Technical Report UH-CS-91-03, Dept. of Computer Science, University of Houston.

Georgakopoulos, D., Rusinkiewicz, M., and Sheth, A. 1993. Using Ticket-Based Methods to Enforce the Serializability of Multidatabase Transactions. *IEEE Transactions on Knowledge and Data Engineering* (in press).

Gray, J. N. 1981. The Transaction Concept: Virtues and Limitations. *Proceedings of the Seventh International Conference on Very Large Data Bases.*

Halabi, Y., Ansari, M., Batra, R., Jin, W., Karabatis, G., Krychniak, P., Rusinkiewicz, M., and Suardi, L. 1992. Narada: An Environment for Specification and Execution of Multi-System Applications. *Proceedings of the Second International Conference on Systems Integration.*

Jin, W., Krishnakumar, N., Ness, L., Rusinkiewicz, M., and Sheth, A. 1993b. *Supporting Telecommunications Applications with Multidatabase Transactions.* Bellcore Technical Memorandum, submitted for publication.

Jin, W., Ness, L., Rusinkiewicz, M., Sheth, A. 1993a. Concurrency Control and Recovery of Multidatabase Work Flows in Telecommunication Applications. *Proceedings of the SIGMOD Conference.*

Kalinichenko, L. 1993. A Declarative Framework for Capturing Dynamic Behavior in Heterogeneous Interoperable Information Resource Environment. *Proceedings of the Third RIDE International Workshop on Interoperability in Multidatabase Systems.*

Klein, J. 1991. Advanced Rule Driven Transaction Management. *IEEE COMPCON.*

Korth, H. F., Levy, E., and Silberschatz, A. 1990. A Formal Approach to Recovery by Compensating Transactions. *Proceedings of the Sixteenth International Conference on Very Large Data Bases.*

Krychniak, P., Rusinkiewicz, M., Sheth, A., and Thomas, G. 1992. *Bounding the Effects of Compensation Under Relaxed Multi-Level Serializability.* Technical Report UH-CS-92-06, Dept. of Computer Science, University of Houston.

Kuehn, E., Puntigam, F., and Elmagarmid, A. 1991. Transaction Specification in Multidatabase Systems Based on Parallel Logic Programming. *Proceedings of the First International Workshop on Interoperability in Multidatabase Systems.*

Lee, K., Mansfield, W., and Sheth, A. 1993. A Framework for Controlling Cooperative Agents. In *IEEE Computer,* July.

Litwin, W. 1990. MSQL: A Multidatabase Language. *Information Sciences.*

Lynch, N. 1983. Multi-Level Atomicity—A New Correctness Criterion for Database Concurrency Control. *ACM Transactions on Database Systems,* Vol. 8, No. 4.

Mehrotra, S., Rastogi, R., Breitbart, Y., Korth, H., and Silberschatz, A. 1992. Ensuring Transaction Atomicity in Multidatabase Systems. *Proceedings of the Twelfth ACM-SIGACT-SIGMOD-SIGART Symposium on Principles of Database Systems.*

Moss, J. E. B. 1985. *Nested Transactions: An Approach to Reliable Distributed Computing.* Ph.D. thesis, MIT Press, Cambridge, Mass.

Pu, C. 1988. Superdatabases for Composition of Heterogeneous Databases. *IEEE Proceedings of the Fourth International Conference on Very Large Data Bases.*

Reuter, A. 1989. ConTracts: A Means for Extending Control Beyond Transaction Boundaries. *Proceedings of the Third International Workshop on High Performance Transaction Systems.*

Rusinkiewicz, M., et al. 1988. OMNIBASE: Design and Implementation of a Multidatabase System. *IEEE CS Distributed Processing Newsletter,* Vol. 10, No. 2.

Rusinkiewicz, M., Cichocki, A., and Krychniak, P. 1992. Towards a Model for Multidatabase Transactions. *International Journal of Intelligent and Cooperative Information Systems,* Vol. 1, No. 3.

Rusinkiewicz, M., Elmagarmid, A., Leu, Y., and Litwin, W. 1990a. Extending the Transaction Model to Capture More Meaning. *SIGMOD Record,* Vol. 19.

Rusinkiewicz, M., Osterman, S., Elmagarmid, A., and Loa, K. 1990b. The Distributed Operational Language for Specifying Multisystem Applications. *Proceedings of the First International Conference on Systems Integration.*

Sheth, A., and Kalinichenko, L. 1992. Information Modeling in Multidatabase Systems: Beyond Data Modeling. *Proceedings of the First International Conference on Information and Knowledge Management.*

Sheth, A., Rusinkiewicz, M., and Karabatis, G. 1992. Using Polytransactions to Manage Interdependent Data. In: *Transaction Models for Advanced Database Applications.* A. Elmagarmid, ed. Morgan-Kaufmann, Los Altos, Cal.

Soley, R. 1993. A Common Architecture for Integrating Distributed Applications. *Proceedings of the Second International Conference on Parallel and Distributed Information Systems.*

Suardi, L., Rusinkiewicz, M., and Litwin, W. 1993. Execution of Extended Multidatabase SQL. *Proceedings of the Ninth International Conference on Data Engineering.*

Tomlinson, C., Attie, P., Cannata, P., Meridith, G., Sheth, A., Singh, M., and Woelk, D. 1993. Workflow Support in Carnot. *Data Engineering Bulletin.*

Weikum, G. 1991. Principles and Realization Strategies of Multilevel Transaction Management. *ACM Trans. on Database Systems,* Vol. 16, No. 1.

Weikum, G., and Schek, H.-J. 1992. Concepts and Applications of Multilevel Transactions and Open Nested Transactions. In: *Transaction Models for Advanced Database Applications.* A. Elmagarmid, ed. Morgan-Kaufmann, Los Altos, Cal.

Woelk, D., Attie, P., Cannata, P., Meridith, G., Sheth, A., Singh, M., and Tomlinson, C. 1993. Task Scheduling Using Intertask Dependencies in Carnot. *Proceedings of the SIGMOD Conference.*

Wolski, A., and Veijalainen, J. 1990. 2PC Agent Method: Achieving Serializability in Presence of Failures in a Heterogeneous Multidatabase. *Proceedings of the PARBASE-90 Conference.*

30

Schema Architecture of the UniSQL/M Multidatabase System

WILLIAM KELLEY
SUNIT GALA
WON KIM
TOM REYES
BRUCE GRAHAM

We briefly introduce the schema architecture of UniSQL/M, a unified relational and object-oriented multidatabase system. Its data definition and manipulation language, SQL/M, provides various object-oriented abstraction facilities such as generalization, specialization, aggregation, and method specification and invocation. The multidatabase schema can change when there is either a change in user requirements or a change in the local database (LDB) schemas. Multidatabase schema changes are not hard changes for which the local database must be immediately reorganized, which introduces an additional dimension to the problem of schema change. The objectives of this chapter are to describe the schema architecture of UniSQL/M and to define a taxonomy of schema changes and their semantics in UniSQL/M.

30.1 Introduction

During the past three decades, file systems, navigational database systems (hierarchical and network), and relational database systems have been used as platforms for managing data for conventional transaction-oriented applications. This situation has prompted research into multidatabase systems (MDBSs). An MDBS is a federation of independently developed data systems that provides a homogenizing layer on top of such systems to give the illusion of a homogeneous database system to ordinary users.

This chapter briefly describes the schema architecture of UniSQL/M, a multidatabase system for managing a heterogeneous collection of relational database systems and UniSQL/X [Kim et al. 1992], a commercial unified relational and object-oriented database system. The main emphasis of this chapter is to describe the semantics for schema change operators in SQL/M,

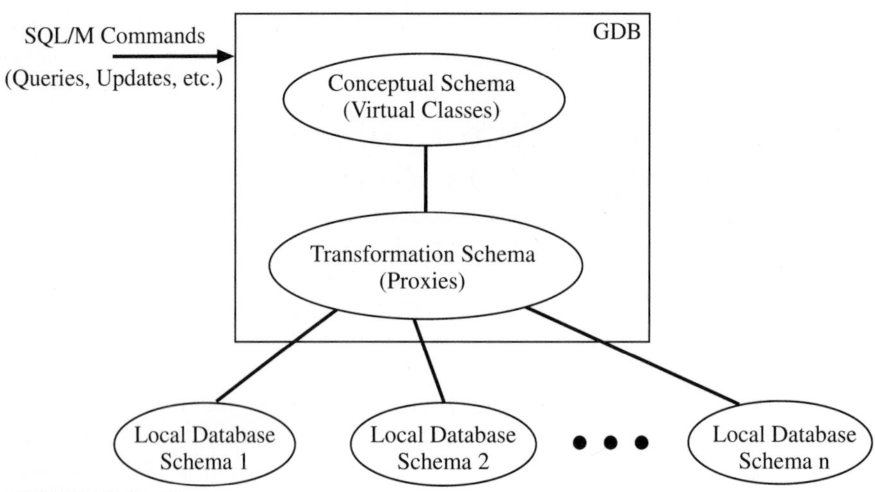

FIGURE 30–1
SQL/M Schema Architecture

which is the data definition and manipulation language [Kim et al. 1993b] of UniSQL/M. UniSQL/M extends the notion of relational views with various object-oriented abstraction facilities. The user defines global database (GDB) schemata to provide a uniform view of the local databases (LDBs).

A few specialized techniques have been employed in the past to integrate heterogeneous databases. These include manually integrating by writing application programs that access data from individual databases, physically migrating data from many databases into one single database, and building gateways. Each technique has serious limitations. They are expensive to implement and are not general solutions that can be extended to meet the changing needs of a user group. Two general techniques available are logical integration of multiple LDBs [Breitbart et al. 1986; Brill and Templeton 1984; Connors and Lyngbaek 1988; Heimbigner and Mcleod 1985; Landers and Rosenberg 1982], and interoperability of multiple DBs [Litwin et al. 1987]. UniSQL/M falls into the former category. There have been proposals for a formal framework and/or query language extensions for defining global database views through generalization/specialization of LDBs [Dayal and Hwang 1984; Motro 1987; Navathe et al. 1991]. Recent studies [Connors and Lyngbaek 1988; Kaul et al. 1990] have examined an object-oriented approach to integrating heterogeneous databases.

UniSQL/M has significant differences from other proposals. The GDB schema consists of two components: a transformation schema that consists of proxies and a conceptual schema that consists of virtual classes (views), as shown in Fig. 30–1. The attributes of a proxy form a 1–1 correspondence with those of a local entity (i.e., relation or class in a local database), which may also be renamed. Further, a proxy definition also contains a query specification that defines how it is to be populated from a given LDB entity. The primary role of a proxy is to aid in transforming a GDB command (query or update) into corresponding LDB commands. A virtual class is defined in terms of one or more proxies and is the union of virtual instances from LDBs.[1] It provides a higher level of abstraction. Both proxies and virtual classes can form an inheritance hierarchy that captures information about the relationship between classes and/or relations in the LDBs. However, a subclass relationship can be established between virtual classes independent of the relationship between classes and/or relations in LDBs.

The main contribution of this chapter is to lay a formal framework for enumerating various global schema change operators and describing their semantics. This is a continuation of our previous work, in which we describe the semantics of SQL/M schema architecture [Kim et al. 1993b] and prescribe a comprehensive scheme for schema conflict resolution [Kim et al. 1993a].

The rest of this chapter is organized as follows. In section 30.2, we provide sample local database schemas that we shall use throughout this chapter. In section 30.3, we describe the notions of proxies and virtual classes. In section 30.4, we discuss object-orientation in SQL/M, with emphasis on how it affects interoperability of relational LDBs. We break this discussion into three parts: inheritance hierarchies, composition hierarchies, and method definition and invocation. In section 30.5, we describe a taxonomy of schema changes and a set of DDL operators to implement each kind of schema change. Section 30.6 concludes the chapter.

30.2 Sample Local Database Schemas

Consider a U.S. company with branches in Great Britain and France. The British branch uses an Ingres database, denoted by rdb; the French branch uses a UniSQL/X, denoted by oodb. The headquarters in the United States wishes to integrate these two databases to facilitate preparing companywide reports.

```
/* oodb: UniSQL/X */
create class department
(
dept_no integer,
dept_name string,
address string
);
create class employee
(
emp_name string,
```

```
/* rdb: Ingres */
create table dept
(
dept_no integer,
dept_name char(15),
address char(30)
);
create table emp
(
e_name char(20),
```

1. If two LDBs each had Employee tables, then an Employee virtual class would be the union of the two corresponding proxies, which denote virtual instances of type Employee. We shall see detailed examples in section 30.3.

```
ssn integer,                              emp_id integer,
salary monetary, /* in francs */          sal money, /* in pounds */
dept department,                          d_no integer,
mgr manager                               mgr char(9)
);                                        );
create class manager                      create table mgr_emp
as subclass of employee                   (
(                                         mgr_ssn integer,
manages set_of(employee)                  emp_ssn integer
);                                        );
```

The above two schemas represent a simple parts-explosion scenario. Each LDB has an employee entity, which works in a department, for a given manager. Note that `salary` in `rdb` is in pounds sterling, while in `oodb`, `sal` is in French francs. Also, `oodb` has another class, `manager`, which is a subclass of `employee`. Corresponding information in `rdb` is captured by `mgr_emp`. This is because the relational model does not allow set-valued attributes.

Note: We shall adopt the following convention in all examples presented in this chapter. All class names begin with an upper-case letter. All attribute names begin with a lower-case letter. All reserved words are written in upper-case letters. Postfix letters like "`_R`" or "`_OO`" stand for *relational* and *object-oriented*, respectively.

30.3 Defining GDB Entities

The SQL/M schema architecture consists of the transformation and conceptual schemas. In this section, we show how to define proxies and virtual classes.

30.3.1 Proxies

The proxies, which comprise the transformation schema, have two components—namely, a signature and a query specification. The signature defines the attributes (and methods, if any) and their domains, and the query specification tells the system how to populate the proxy with instances (tuples and objects) from LDBs. The signature forms a 1–1 correspondence with the actual attributes defined in the LDB entity. The query specification is a SQL-like query, in which each item in the `select` clause defines a mapping (possibly as simple as renaming an attribute) between a value in the GDB and LDB. The transformation schema is similar to what has been called an *export schema* or *global catalog* in the literature [Heimbigner and Mcleod 1985]. The syntax[2] for defining a proxy is defined as follows:

2. Terms in square brackets '[ ]' are optional, and those in curly braces '{ }' occur zero or more times. Further, we use a slightly modified syntax of SQL/M for clarity of exposition.

```
CREATE VCLASS proxy_name ON LDB ldb_name
[ AS SUBCLASS OF super_proxy_name {, super_proxy_name } ]
'(' attr_def_list ')'
[ OBJECT_ID '(' attr_name ')' ]
AS SELECT select_expression_list
     FROM [user_id '.'] ldb_entity_name
  [ WHERE search_conditions ]
    [ order_by_clause ]
```

```
attr_def ::= attr_name data_type DEFAULT value
```

The subclause ON LDB *ldb_name* denotes the LDB in which *ldb_entity_name* is defined, and the location, host, database name, and other relevant information regarding the LDB is registered with the GDB. This ensures that the GDB knows from where to access data given a proxy reference. The *data_type* of an attribute can be any primitive type such as string or integer, or it can be another proxy. (This is allowed only when modeling a composition hierarchy—see section 30.4.2, in which we discuss the OBJECT_ID clause.) The query specification determines how the proxy is to be populated—the tuples or instances retrieved by this query are called the *virtual instances* of the proxy. This query is evaluated against the LDB and must thus be valid since errors will not be detected until run-time. The remaining constructs in the query are extensions to ANSI SQL. The order of attribute names in the *attr_def_list* corresponds to the order of expressions in the *select_expression_list*. We defer discussing the inheritance hierarchy of proxies (i.e., the SUBCLASS clause) to section 30.4.1.

We now give a few examples of proxies with respect to the sample schemas in section 30.2. Proxies for Employees can be defined as follows:

```
CREATE VCLASS Employee_R ON LDB rdb
(
name char(20),
ssn integer,
salary monetary, /* in U.S. dollars */
dept_no integer,
mgr char(9)
)
AS SELECT e_name, emp_id, 1.75*sal, d_no, mgr
     FROM emp;
```

```
CREATE VCLASS Employee_OO ON LDB oodb
(
name string,
ssn integer,
salary monetary, /* in U.S. dollars */
dept Department_OO,
mgr Manager_OO
)
```

```
AS SELECT name, ssn, 0.25*salary, dept, mgr
     FROM employee;
```

The first proxy is defined with respect to the emp table in rdb and the second one with respect to the employee class in oodb. In Employee_R, the LDB attributes emp_id and e_name are renamed to ssn and name, respectively. Salary denotes the expression 1.75*sal in U.S. dollars. In Employee_OO, the domains of the attributes dept and mgr are the proxies Department_OO and Manager_OO respectively. The proxy definitions below completely define the transformation schema for the example in section 30.2.

```
CREATE VCLASS Department_R ON LDB rdb
(
dept_no integer,
name char(20),
address char(30)
)
AS SELECT dept_no, dept_name, address
     FROM dept;

CREATE VCLASS Mgr_Emp_R ON LDB rdb
(
mgr integer,
emp integer
)
AS SELECT mgr_ssn, emp_ssn
     FROM mgr_emp;
```

Note the 1–1 correspondence of each proxy above with the corresponding table in rdb against which it is defined. Also, some attributes in Employee_R are renamed, some are scaled to match the GDB units, and some remain unchanged. All of these are reversible operations; thus, both proxies are updatable. In other words, an insert, delete, or update made by the user against a proxy will be appropriately translated by the SQL/M query processor into equivalent statements to be sent to the relevant LDB, in this case rdb. We define the proxies for oodb below.

```
CREATE VCLASS Department_OO ON LDB oodb
(
dept_no integer,
name string,
address string
)
AS SELECT dept_no, dept_name, address
     FROM department;

CREATE VCLASS Manager_OO ON LDB oodb
AS SUBCLASS OF Employee_OO
```

```
(
manages set_of(Employee_OO)
)
AS SELECT emp_name, ssn, 0.25*salary, dept, mgr, manages
    FROM manager;
```

As before, the attribute transformations are reversible. However, of particular interest is the `manages` attribute in the `Manager_OO` proxy, whose domain is `set_of (Employee_OO)`. SQL/M allows the user to mimic the composition hierarchy that is frequently found in OODBs. We shall see how to extend this composition hierarchy to RDBs in section 30.4. Also, note that `manager` was defined as a subclass of `employee` in `oodb`—we have reproduced this relationship here as well. The semantics of inheritance in SQL/M are discussed in more detail in section 30.4.

30.3.2 Virtual Classes

The conceptual schema provides the user with a unified perspective of the *stored* information in local databases. This is achieved by creating a homogenizing layer on top of the transformation schema. This layer allows the user to access data from the LDBs uniformly in one database language with location and replication transparency. There is often some loss of information in the process of homogenizing a set of proxies (which may represent relations or classes) into a virtual class. Thus, SQL/M allows the user to define two kinds of virtual classes—namely, those that are updatable and those that are not [Kim et al. 1993b].

A virtual class definition consists of two components. The first component is the signature and the second component consists of queries that tell the system how to populate the virtual class with instances from different but related proxies. Virtual classes thus provide location transparency to GDB users. Further, virtual classes can be organized into an inheritance hierarchy, thus capturing more information than is possible in the relational approach to global database management. SQL/M distinguishes between direct and indirect instances of a virtual class.

GDB users may wish to make global updates to the local databases through virtual classes. An update against a virtual class can be supported only if it is possible to generate a set of updates to be directly sent to the LDBs against the corresponding LDB entities. Clearly, this translation is possible if and only if the homogenization process of defining the virtual class in question is reversible—that is, if this homogenization process is reversible, the virtual class is said to be updatable. This means that the user can meaningfully issue updates and queries against updatable virtual classes and only queries against nonupdatable virtual classes. However, since there must not be any loss of information when integrating LDB entities into an updatable virtual class, it may not always be possible for such a virtual class to homogenize a large number of related LDB entities. Nonupdatable virtual classes may homogenize larger numbers of related entities. The user can then issue updates against the corresponding proxies of such nonupdatable virtual classes. The main difference between issuing an update to a virtual class and proxy is that the former can spawn a set of updates that are sent to many LDBs while the latter can result in exactly one update sent to the corresponding LDB entity.

The user can also define virtual classes against these virtual classes. This provides a mechanism whereby the user can reorganize the virtual class or proxy definitions into a perspective more suited to his or her needs. The terms *virtual class* and *view* are synonymous in SQL/M. The basic syntax for defining a virtual class is shown below:

```
CREATE VCLASS vclass_name
[ AS SUBCLASS OF super_vclass_name {, super_vclass_name } ]
'(' attr_def_list ')'
[ AS query {, query } ]

query ::= SELECT select_expression_list
            FROM from_list
          [ WHERE search_conditions ]
          [ group_by_clause [ having_clause ] ]
          [ order_by_clause ]
```

Since virtual classes and proxies share the same name space, `vclass_name` should be distinct from any other proxy, virtual class name, or data type name. The `data_type` of an attribute can be any primitive type such as strings and integers, or it can be another proxy or virtual class. (This is allowed only when modeling a composition hierarchy—see section 30.4.2.) Two queries in the query list are separated by a comma, which denotes the `UNION ALL` set operator in ANSI SQL. The virtual class forms a convenient means to unify or integrate related LDB entities. This is done by referencing the appropriate proxies and/or virtual classes for each corresponding LDB entity in the `FROM` clause of a query in the query list. That is, `from_list` can also contain other proxies or virtual classes, which means it is possible to have a query that performs cross-database joins. The attributes in the signature must correspond in type and number to the `select_expression_list` in each and every query of the query list.

As an example, we shall define a virtual class `Employee` to denote all the British and French employees but not managers.

```
CREATE VCLASS Employee
(
name string,
ssn integer,
salary monetary, /* in U.S. dollars */
```

```
dept string,
mgr string
)
AS SELECT name, ssn, salary, dept_no, mgr
     FROM Employee_R
     WHERE ssn NOT IN (SELECT mgr FROM Mgr_Emp_R),
   SELECT name, ssn, salary, dept.name, mgr.name
     FROM Employee_OO;
```

Note that the unit for `salary` is already in US dollars; hence there is no need for further conversion in the `SELECT` clause of each query. The `WHERE` clause above is required because there is no separate table for managers in `rdb` and we do not wish to include that information in `Employee`. The `SELECT` clause of the second query has path expressions to retrieve the department's and manager's names. This is an example of how SQL/M provides support in its query language to navigate composition hierarchies.

As another example, we define a virtual class for all departments.

```
CREATE VCLASS Department
(
dept_no integer,
name CHAR(15),
address string
)
AS SELECT dept_no, name, address
     FROM Department_R
   SELECT dept_no, name, address
     FROM Department_OO;
```

30.4 Object Orientation in SQL/M

We have so far seen how to define the transformation and conceptual schema by means of proxies and virtual classes, respectively. We now discuss the various extensions to these concepts that allow SQL/M to provide an object-based homogenizing layer while interoperating both RDBs and OODBs.

30.4.1 Inheritance Hierarchies

Proxies and virtual classes can be organized into an inheritance hierarchy; their semantics for inheritance are identical. In general, one class can be a subclass of another if they satisfy the following conditions:

1. Their signatures must be compatible—that is, the set of attributes (and methods) of a class must be a subset of the set of attributes (and methods) of its subclass.

2. Their (virtual) populations must satisfy the set inclusion property—that is, the instances belonging to the subclass must be a subset of the instances belonging to its superclass.

We distinguish between direct and indirect (virtual) instances that can belong to a (virtual) class. This is done to eliminate redundant results from a query against a virtual class hierarchy, thus providing replication transparency. Thus, to satisfy the second condition above, the materialized populations must be disjoint. For example, let `Parent` be the only subclass of `Person`, and let `Parent` have no other subclass. Also, let

I_1 = `SELECT * FROM ONLY Person`
I_2 = `SELECT * FROM ONLY Parent`
I_3 = `SELECT * FROM ALL Person`
I_4 = `SELECT * FROM ALL Parent`

Note the keyword `ONLY` implies that only the direct instances of the class referenced in the `FROM` clause will be considered, while the keyword `ALL` implies that all (direct) instances of the class referenced in the `FROM` clause along with (indirect) instances of each of its subclasses will be considered when evaluating the query. The following relationships must now hold: $I_1 \subset I_3$, $I_2 \subset I_3$, $I_1 \cap I_2 = \emptyset$, and $I_1 \cup I_2 = I_3$. Further, $I_2 = I_4$ since `Parent` has no other subclass. The system cannot enforce these conditions automatically. It is the GDB schema designer's responsibility to ensure that these relationships hold true when defining an inheritance hierarchy. The schema designer should verify that these relationships hold, for example, by evaluating queries against a newly defined virtual class hierarchy in the GDB schema.

For example, we define a virtual class for managers as a subclass of `Employee`, which was defined in section 30.3.2.

```
CREATE VCLASS Manager
AS SUBCLASS OF Employee
( manages set_of(integer) )
AS SELECT name, ssn, salary, dept_no, mgr,
          set(select emp FROM Mgr_Emp_R m WHERE
              e.ssn = m.emp)
     FROM Employee_R e
     WHERE e.ssn IN (SELECT mgr FROM Mgr_Emp_R),
   SELECT name, ssn, salary, dept.name, mgr.name
     FROM Employee_OO;
```

The subquery `select emp FROM Mgr_Emp_R m WHERE e.ssn = m.emp` returns the `ssn` of all employees who work for a given manager (which is correlated in its `WHERE` clause). The result of this subquery is then coerced into a `set`. This is an example of our extensions to derived tables in SQL-92. Recall that the direct virtual instances of `Employee` and `Manager` are disjoint. This is because:

1. The WHERE clause above is a negation of the corresponding WHERE clause in Employee.
2. The instances of employee and manager classes in oodb are disjoint, which also implies that the virtual instances of Employee_OO and Manager_OO are disjoint.

Therefore, all the conditions stipulated above concerning the relationship between the instances of a virtual class are satisfied.

30.4.2 Composition Hierarchies

SQL/M allows the user to define a composition hierarchy in the proxy or virtual class definitions when integrating RDBs with RDBs. This is made possible by allowing one virtual class (or proxy) to have an attribute whose domain is another virtual class (proxy). We note that in previous proposals for multidabatase systems based on the relational model, this is not possible. There are two fundamental reasons for it:

1. There is no notion of a unique identifier for tuples in the relational model.
2. The domain of a relational attribute cannot be another relation.

We now illustrate extensions in SQL/M that allow us to define an object view on top of RDBs. This fundamentally affects the users' perception of how RDBs interoperate with OODBs or even other RDBs. For example, let us redefine proxies in rdb as follows:

```
CREATE VCLASS Department_R ON LDB rdb
(
dept_no integer,
name char(20),
address char(30)
)
OBJECT_ID(dept_no)
AS SELECT dept_no, dept_name, address
     FROM dept;

CREATE VCLASS Employee_R ON LDB rdb
(
name char(20),
ssn char(9),
salary monetary, /* in U.S. dollars */
dept Department_R
)
OBJECT_ID(ssn)
AS SELECT e_name, emp_id, 1.75*sal, d_no
     FROM emp;
```

The attribute dept_no plays the role of a foreign key in the emp table. Note that the organization of data is parallel to that of oodb. The OBJECT_ID clause in a proxy denotes the primary key[3] of the LDB entity that proxy is modeling. As a simple example, the attribute dept_no gives us a unique handle on each tuple of the LDB table dept and, therefore, OBJECT_ID(dept_no) gives us a unique handle on each virtual instance of Department_R; similarly, OBJECT_ID(ssn) gives us a unique handle on each virtual instance of Employee_R.[4] As an example of a composition hierarchy for relational proxies, in Employee_R above, the domain of dept is the proxy Department_R, and its corresponding SELECT item is dept_no, which is of type integer in the LDB table emp. The semantic analyzer will recognize this as correctly typed because the OBJECT_ID of Department_R is dept_no, which is also of type integer in the LDB table dept. By similar reasoning, we find that the attribute ssn in the Employee_R proxy provides a unique handle for each of its virtual instances. Also, as we shall see in section 30.4.3, a method can operate on a virtual instance only if it has a unique identifier: For RDBs, the OBJECT_ID clause provides this.

Thus, the OBJECT_ID clause allows us to exploit the object orientation of SQL/M to the fullest extent and still be able to define updatable virtual classes. We show this by redefining the virtual classes for this segment of the original LDB schemas.

```
CREATE VCLASS Department
(
dept_no integer,
name string,
address string
)
AS SELECT dept_no, name, address
      FROM Department_R
   SELECT dept_no, name, address
      FROM Department_OO;

CREATE VCLASS Employee
(
name string,
ssn integer,
salary monetary, /* in U.S. dollars */
dept Department
)
```

3. It is the designer's responsibility to ensure that the argument is indeed the primary key of the local table or at least is unique.

4. We are ignoring manager information for clarity of exposition.

```
AS SELECT name, ssn, salary, dept
     FROM Employee_R,
   SELECT name, ssn, salary, dept
     FROM Employee_OO;
```

The above definitions were made possible by the OBJECT_ID clause, which lets the RDB proxies mimic those of the OODB. The user can issue updates and queries against this schema and also treat the RDB as if it were object oriented. This is possible because SQL/M will appropriately translate queries and updates to send to the RDB. For example, the query

```
SELECT dept.name, dept.address, name
  FROM Employee
  WHERE salary > 100000;
```

is translated to the following two queries to be sent to rdb and oodb respectively:

```
rdb:  SELECT dept.name, dept.address, emp.name
        FROM dept, emp
        WHERE salary > 100000/1.75
AND dept.dept_no = emp.dept_no;

oodb: SELECT dept.name, dept.address, name
        FROM employee
        WHERE salary > 100000/.25;
```

30.4.3 Methods

Methods are essentially programs written outside of SQL/M that can manipulate virtual instances and can be written against both proxies and virtual classes. The syntax for declaring methods is as follows:

```
CREATE VCLASS gdb_entity_name [ ON LDB ldb_name ]
  .
  .
  .
[ METHOD method_definition {, method_definition }]
[ FILE path_name {, path_name }]
  .
  .
  .
method_definition ::= [CLASS] method_name '('[arg_data_type
                                         {, arg_data_type }]')'
                                         [':' result_data_type]
                      FUNCTION function_name
```

The proxy or virtual class name is denoted by *gdb_entity_name*. To define a method against GDB entities, the user must supply the *method_name* and a list of zero or more argument data types; optionally, a return type can also be specified. If the return type is left out, the system assumes that no value is returned by the method. The FUNCTION specifies the name of a C function that implements the method. The FILE path name locates the object file that contains the implementation of the method function; by default, the system will look for the file in the current working directory. The semantics for inheritance of methods is the same as that for attributes.

A method is invoked in SQL/M via the CALL command, or it can appear as an expression in the SELECT clause. A method defined in an LDB cannot be directly invoked from SQL/M—to do so, it must first be redefined in the appropriate proxy and/or virtual class and then be invoked as a SQL/M method. An important caveat for a method to operate on virtual instances materialized from an RDB is that the OBJECT_ID clause must be specified in the corresponding proxy.

As an example, let us define a method called compute_tax against the virtual class Employee, which evaluates the annual tax owed by each employee. We redefine the virtual class as follows:

```
CREATE VCLASS Employee
(
name string,
ssn integer,
salary monetary, /* in U.S. dollars */
dept string,
mgr string
)
METHOD compute_tax() : monetary
FUNCTION compute_tax
FILE 'compute_tax.o'
AS SELECT name, ssn, salary, dept_no, mgr
     FROM Employee_R
     WHERE ssn NOT IN (SELECT mgr FROM Mgr_Emp_R),
   SELECT name, ssn, salary, dept.name, mgr.name
     FROM Employee_OO;
```

Note that there is no change in the definition of Employee except for the additional method-related information. We have defined a method called compute_tax() with no arguments and a return value of type monetary. Its implementation is a C function called compute_tax, and the corresponding object file is compute_tax.o. The queries in the above virtual class refer to proxies that access both LDBs rdb and oodb. The proxy Employee_R must include the OBJECT_ID clause in its definition, as we saw in section 30.4.2 above. This allows the method total_cost to operate on emp data from rdb. No further identification is required for instances from oodb since object identifiers (OIDs) are automatically assigned based on OIDs already existing in oodb. So there must be OIDs associated with every virtual instance that is manipulated. This method can now be executed in the SQL/M interpreter as follows:

```
SELECT Employee TO :i
  FROM Employee
  WHERE ssn = 123123123;

CALL compute_tax() ON :i;
```

The above commands compute the tax of the employee (who may exist in either rdb or oodb) whose ssn is 123123123. The virtual instance that is to be manipulated by the method compute_tax must be identified by an OID. We get a handle on this OID by the above query;[5] this handle is denoted by the variable :i. If the WHERE clause results in selecting more than one object, the system will return a run-time error. However, this will not be the case here since ssn is unique. Once we have a handle on the object, we also know what (virtual) class it belongs to, Employee in this case. Thus, when evaluating the CALL statement, the system knows that compute_tax is a method defined on the virtual class Employee and that :i denotes an object of this class, so it is legal to execute the method on this object.

Alternately, to compute the tax of each employee in both LDBs, the user can issue the following command:

```
SELECT name, ssn, salary, compute_tax() on e
  FROM Employee e;
```

This query will print the name, ssn, salary, and tax for each employee in the GDB.

30.5 Schema Changes

There are two main reasons for the GDB schema designer to change the GDB schema:

1. A change in user requirements can prompt the designer to reorganize the GDB schema.
2. A change in one of the LDB schemas that needs to be reflected in the GDB schema can also prompt the designer to appropriately modify the GDB schema.

An important capability of a multidatabase language is to support schema changes, especially in connection with LDB schema changes. There

5. In SQL/M, a query of the form SELECT foo FROM foo returns a set of OIDs belonging to the proxy or virtual class foo.

are two aspects to LDB/GDB schema changes. First, there is usually more than one way to reflect an LDB schema change in the GDB schema. Therefore, we cannot fully automate GDB schema changes. Second, the GDB schema consists of proxies and virtual classes. In other words, schema changes are not hard changes for which the database must be immediately reorganized [Kim 1991]. Hence, in principle we may just edit proxy and virtual class definitions. The purpose of SQL/M schema change commands in this regard is, therefore, to change only the part of the GDB schema affected by LDB schema (or user requirement) changes.

The semantics of a schema change command in the single database context needs to be modified [Banerjee et al. 1987]. We thus consider extensions and modifications to the semantics of schema change commands in the single database context and define additional commands to facilitate GDB schema changes. We also describe the relevant portions of the DDL for schema changes and illustrate them with examples.

30.5.1 A Taxonomy of LDB Schema Changes

The LDB schema change taxonomy presented in this section is a subset of that described in Kim 1991. We use the term *entity* to collectively denote relational tables and object-oriented classes. Likewise, *attributes* denote columns in a table and elements in a class signature. Further, *instances* denote tuples and objects.

1. Changes to schema structure
   a. creation of a new entity
   b. deletion of an entity
   c. addition of a superclass to a class
   d. removal of a superclass from a class
   e. renaming a class
2. Changes to an entity
   a. creation of a new attribute
   b. deletion of an attribute
   c. renaming an attribute
   d. changing the domain of an attribute
   e. changing the defaults of an attribute

The reason we do not consider schema changes involving methods (of local OODBs) is that they basically have similar effects as changes to attributes.

A change to a local entity requires a change in the corresponding proxy and virtual class. The changes required in both cases are similar.

Since a proxy mirrors a local entity, any local change is also mirrored exactly so. Thus the creation of a new local entity may require the creation of a new proxy. Changes required to a virtual class are more subtle, and we shall examine these in more detail. For example, the creation of a new local entity need not result in the creation of a new virtual class but more likely will result in the addition of a new query in its query list.

Below is the syntax of DDL commands in SQL/M for schema changes:

```
alter_stmt ::=     ALTER VCLASS vclass_name alter_clause |
                   RENAME VCLASS vclass_name AS vclass_name

alter_clause ::=ADD alter_add |
                   CHANGE alter_change |
                   DROP alter_drop |
                   INHERIT resolution_list |
                   RENAME alter_rename

alter_add ::=      ATTRIBUTE attr_def_list |
                   METHOD method_def_list |
                   QUERY query |
                   SUPERCLASS class_name_list

alter_change ::= METHOD method_def_list |
                   QUERY [unsigned_int] query |
                   ATTRIBUTE attr_name data_type |
                   ATTRIBUTE attr_name DEFAULT value

alter_drop ::=     [ ATTRIBUTE | METHOD ] attr_mthd_name_list |
                   QUERY [unsigned_int] |
                   SUPERCLASS class_name_list

alter_rename ::=[ ATTRIBUTE | METHOD ] attr_mthd_name
                        AS attr_mthd_name
```

One or more of these commands can be used to change the GDB schema. We now show how these commands are used to effect changes in the GDB schema caused by changes in the LDB schema.

30.5.2 Mapping of LDB Schema Changes onto the GDB Schema

In this section, we describe changes to virtual class definitions in a GDB schema that must be made in response to each category of the above LDB schema change taxonomy.

Entity Creation

When an entity is created in an LDB and is to be included in a virtual class definition, there are three cases to consider. For each case, one must first define the corresponding proxy (see section 30.3.1) before modifying or creating new virtual classes. First, if there is a virtual class with an identical set of attributes, each of which corresponds to an attribute of the created entity, then we can simply extend the query component in the definition of the virtual class to include a query against the created entity (to be more precise, its proxy). To facilitate this kind of GDB schema change, we provide the following GDB schema change command that adds a query part to a virtual class definition:

```
ALTER VCLASS vclass ADD QUERY query
```

If there were n queries in the query part of the virtual class `vclass`, then `query` would be inserted as the $(n + 1)^{th}$ query. The SQL/M semantic analyzer automatically checks if the `SELECT` clause of `query` is compatible with the signature of `vclass`.

Second, if there are only virtual classes with fewer attributes than the corresponding attributes of the created entity, then there are two alternatives:

1. If the created entity is related to existing virtual classes in the GDB schema by the *IS-A* relationship, then a virtual class corresponding to the new entity can be created such that it is a subclass of the other related virtual classes; if such a virtual class contains the keyword `ALL` in the query part involving a superclass of this new entity (note that this case is meaningful only in the case of an object-oriented database), then the new entity is automatically included in the scope of the query's result.
2. Add a query corresponding to the created entity to the query component of one such virtual class (ignoring the additional attributes of the created entity).

A special case is when there is no appropriate existing virtual class that can be used as a superclass of the created entity. In this case, a new virtual class subhierarchy (i.e., put it as an immediate descendant of the root) can be defined.

As an example, let us assume that a class called `engineer` is created in oodb, and its definition is as follows:

```
CREATE CLASS engineer
AS SUBCLASS OF employee
 (major CHAR(40));
```

The GDB schema designer can define an LDB virtual class `U_ Engineer_OO` as a subclass of `U_Employee_OO` and a virtual class `U_Engineer` as a subclass of `U_Employee`.

```
CREATE VCLASS Engineer_OO ON LDB oodb
AS SUBCLASS OF Employee_OO
   (major CHAR(40))
AS
  SELECT ssn, name, 0.25*salary, dept_no, mgr, major
    FROM engineer;
```

```
CREATE VCLASS Engineer
AS SUBCLASS OF Employee
   (major CHAR(40))
AS
  SELECT ssn, name, 0.25*salary, dept_no, mgr, major
    FROM Engineer_OO;
```

Third, if there are only virtual classes with more attributes than the corresponding attributes of the created entity, then a superclass of such virtual classes may be defined if there exists an *IS-A* relationship between them. This can be achieved by defining a new virtual class for the created entity and making the existing virtual classes subclasses of the new virtual class by using the command

```
ALTER VCLASS vclass ADD SUPERCLASS superclass
```

This will make `vclass` a subclass of `superclass` (the new virtual class). Note that the `INHERIT resolution_list` clause is needed to inherit attributes from `superclass`, as well as to resolve conflicts in `vclass`, if any. Another alternative to handle this case is to add a query against the created entity to the query part of one of the virtual classes using the `NA` (i.e., "Not Applicable") value for attributes that are not in the created table.

Entity Deletion

If an entity participating in a virtual class definition is deleted from an LDB, there are two cases to consider:

1. The query part of the affected virtual class has more than one query component.
2. It has only one query component.

In the first case, the component query referencing the deleted entity must be removed from the query part of the virtual class definition. This is achieved by the following schema change command:

```
ALTER VCLASS vclass DROP QUERY n
```

After the command is executed, the $(n + i)^{th}$ query of the query part of `vclass` will become the $(n + i - 1)^{th}$ query, where $n, i > 0$. As an example, if the table `emp` is deleted from `rdb`, the virtual class `Employee` is modified as follows:

```
ALTER VCLASS Employee DROP QUERY 1
```

Recall that the first query in the query part of the definition of `Employee` pertains to `rdb`. Further, the proxy `Employee_R` also is deleted.

In the second case, the virtual class must be deleted. Further, the attributes of the virtual class may need to be moved to its direct subclasses if the virtual class has subclasses. This involves attribute addition. If the deleted virtual class has no superclass, then the direct subclasses must include the attributes of the virtual class in their signatures. Otherwise, the subclasses must have the superclass of the virtual class as their direct superclass and include the attributes of the deleted virtual class in their signatures. Of course, this action is based on the assumption that the subclasses need those attributes because there are other LDB entities with the corresponding attributes. The same argument applies for proxies. In SQL/M, the `DROP VCLASS` command

```
DROP VCLASS vclass
```

will remove the definition of the *`vclass`* virtual class and delete *`vclass`* from the `SUBCLASS OF` clauses of its direct subclasses. The GDB schema designer is now forced to add each attribute of *`vclass`* using the `ADD ATTRIBUTE` subclause. As an example, if the table `Engineer` is now deleted from `rdb`, then the virtual class `Engineer` also is deleted by issuing the following command:

```
DROP VCLASS Engineer
```

To illustrate the modification of the signature of a subclass when a virtual class is deleted, consider the following command:

```
DROP VCLASS Employee
```

Since the subclass of `Employee` is `Manager`, it is modified; we show the changes required for `Manager` below:

```
CREATE VCLASS Manager
(
name string,
ssn integer,
salary monetary, /* in U.S. dollars */
dept string,
mgr string,
manages set_of(string)
)
AS SELECT name, ssn, salary, dept_no, mgr,
          set(select emp FROM Mgr_Emp_R m WHERE e.name = m.emp)
     FROM Employee_R e
     WHERE e.name IN (SELECT mgr FROM Mgr_Emp_R),
   SELECT name, ssn, salary, dept.name, mgr.name
     FROM Employee_OO;
```

The signature of `Manager` now includes the `name`, `ssn`, `salary`, and `mgr` attributes in addition to `manages`. There is no change in the query component.

An entire virtual class subhierarchy can be deleted by issuing the command

```
DROP VCLASS ALL vclass_name
```

which will delete each subclass of *vclass_name*.

Addition of a Superclass to a Class

As seen, whenever a new LDB entity is created that must participate in the GDB, a corresponding proxy is first created, followed by a virtual class that refers to this proxy. If the LDB entity is related to existing proxies or virtual classes by the *IS-A* relationship, then these existing proxies (or virtual classes) are made a subclass of the newly created proxy (or virtual class) by the ALTER ... ADD SUPERCLASS clause.

For example, suppose we create a table called person in rdb as follows:

```
CREATE TABLE person
  (name CHAR(40), ssn integer);
```

The GDB schema designer can extend the GDB schema by defining a proxy Person_R and a virtual class Person.

```
CREATE VCLASS Person_R on LDB rdb
  (name CHAR(40), ssn integer)
AS
  SELECT name, ssn FROM person;

ALTER VCLASS Employee_R ADD SUPERCLASS Person_R;

CREATE VCLASS Person
  (name CHAR(40), ssn integer)
AS
  SELECT name, ssn FROM Person;

ALTER VCLASS Employee ADD SUPERCLASS U_Person;
```

Removal of a Superclass from a Class

When an LDB entity that has a proxy that is the superclass of another proxy is deleted, one must delete the superclass proxy and also modify the other proxy by removing the deleted proxy from its superclass list. For example, if we dropped person in rdb, the following changes would have to be made to the GDB schema:

```
DROP VCLASS Person_R;

ALTER VCLASS Employee_R DROP SUPERCLASS Person_R;

DROP VCLASS Person;

ALTER VCLASS Employee DROP SUPERCLASS Person;
```

Renaming a Class

If an LDB entity is renamed, one can modify the query of the corresponding proxy. However, to rename the proxy in keeping with the LDB entity's name, one uses the RENAME clause:

```
RENAME VCLASS vclass_name AS new_vclass_name;
```

All virtual classes that refer to this proxy must have the corresponding query parts modified to reflect this name change. Further, all proxies and virtual classes that have attributes whose domain is a renamed entity must have their domains changed to reflect the new name.

Creation of a New Attribute

If a new attribute is added to an LDB entity and the new attribute is to participate in a proxy, it must be added to the corresponding proxy's definition. If this new attribute is to participate in a virtual class definition, there are two ways to change its definition:

1. The first way is to simply add an attribute (corresponding to the new attribute of the LDB entity) to the affected virtual class. Since the addition of an attribute is propagated to the subclasses as in SQL/X, this type of schema change is possible only if all other LDB entities participating in the definition of the virtual class and its subclasses (via the corresponding proxies) have that corresponding attribute; such compatibility can also be achieved by coercing the attribute to NA in each affected query of the virtual class.
2. The second way is to remove the query against the changed local entity from the affected virtual class and add a new query (which includes the new attribute) to a subclass of the virtual class. There may already exist a proper subclass in which the new query can be added, or a new subclass may have to be created.

Adding a new attribute to a proxy or virtual class can be performed by the following command:

```
ALTER VCLASS vclass ADD ATTRIBUTE attribute_name data_type
```

which will change the definition of *vclass* by adding the *attribute_name data_type* to its signature. It is the GDB schema designer's responsibility to ensure that each component in the query part of *vclass* is appropriately modified such that the new attribute either appears in the SELECT clause or is coerced to NA.

As an example, let us add the attribute budget to the department class in oodb. The GDB schema designer can modify the definition of Department_OO such that the extra attribute is included in the signature. This is done by adding an attribute as follows:

```
ALTER Department_OO ADD ATTRIBUTE budget monetary;
```

The query specification of Department_OO is modified as follows:

```
ALTER VCLASS Department_OO CHANGE QUERY
      SELECT dept_no, dept_name, address, budget
        FROM department;
```

Alternately, the GDB schema designer must make the following changes to the query in the virtual class Department:

```
ALTER VCLASS Department ADD ATTRIBUTE budget monetary;

ALTER VCLASS Department CHANGE QUERY 1
      SELECT dept_no, dept_name, address, NA
        FROM Department_R;

ALTER VCLASS Department CHANGE QUERY 2
      SELECT dept_no, dept_name, address, budget
        FROM Department_OO;
```

Deletion of an Attribute

When an attribute is deleted from an entity in an LDB, it must first be deleted from its proxy and then from each virtual class that refers to this attribute. In both cases, their queries will have to be modified to reflect the deletion of an attribute. For a proxy, the attribute is deleted from its signature, and its query is modified such that the deleted attribute is no longer in the SELECT list. For a virtual class, this change may be effected in one of two ways:

1. The corresponding attribute may be dropped from the virtual class as well as the corresponding attribute name from the SELECT clause of the relevant query components of the virtual class. The following command achieves this:

```
ALTER VCLASS vclass DROP ATTRIBUTE attribute
```

This will not automatically delete the corresponding attribute in the SELECT clause of each query component in *vclass*. Therefore, the user must appropriately modify the query with the CHANGE QUERY subclause.

2. The query component in the affected virtual class corresponding to the modified entity can be deleted, and a superclass (if it does not already exist) of that virtual class with a query against the modified entity is created with the remaining attributes of the entity.

As an example, if the attribute salary is deleted from the table emp in rdb, the proxy Employee_R is modified, and a virtual class named Emp_No_Sal can be created as follows:

```
ALTER VCLASS Employee_R DROP ATTRIBUTE salary, CHANGE QUERY
      SELECT e_name, emp_id, d_no, mgr
        FROM emp;

CREATE VCLASS Emp_No_Sal
(
name char(20),
ssn integer,
dept_no integer,
mgr char(9)
)
AS
  SELECT name, ssn, dept_no, mgr
    FROM Employee_R,
  SELECT ssn, name, dept_no, mgr
    FROM Employee_OO
   WHERE salary IS NULL;
```

Further, the virtual class U_Employee is modified as follows:

```
ALTER VCLASS Employee ADD SUPERCLASS Emp_No_Sal,
     CHANGE QUERY 2
       SELECT ssn, name, dept_no, salary, mgr.name
         FROM U_Employee_OO
        WHERE salary IS NOT NULL;
```

If the deleted attribute appears in the selection condition or some other option such as GROUP BY, the entire query part (and hence the virtual class definition) needs to be invalidated. Further, application programs and methods involving a virtual class with a deleted attribute may no longer be used. If they do not have references to the deleted attribute, however, they may continue to be used without recompilation.

In SQL/M, a change in an attribute of an LDB entity does not require GDB schema changes if the attribute does not participate in a virtual class definition. This is another advantage of SQL/M over other approaches in which a GDB schema created by generalization or specialization directly over local entities may need to be changed every time an attribute is added or deleted.

Renaming an Attribute

If an attribute in an LDB entity is renamed, the query of the corresponding proxy must be modified. However, if the attribute of this proxy is also to be renamed, then the change must be reflected in each query of each virtual class that refers to this proxy. For example, if emp_id in the rdb table emp is renamed to emp_num, the proxy Employee_R is modified as follows:

```
ALTER VCLASS Employee_R CHANGE QUERY
      SELECT emp_num, e_name, dept_no, 1.75*sal, weight
        FROM emp;
```

If we also decide to rename the attribute in the proxy (or virtual class), we can do so as follows:

```
ALTER VCLASS Employee_R RENAME ATTRIBUTE ssn AS soc_sec_num;

ALTER VCLASS Employee CHANGE QUERY 1
      SELECT soc_sec_num, name, dept_no, salary, location, weight
        FROM Employee_R;
```

Changing the Domain of an LDB Attribute

The change in the domain of an attribute belonging to an LDB entity may require a change in the domain of the corresponding attribute in each proxy or virtual class that has a query component that refers to this LDB entity. Alternately, a change may be required in the SELECT clause of the corresponding query component of the affected virtual class. As an example of this latter case, consider changing the domain of the emp_id attribute of the emp table in rdb from integer to char(9). This requires a modification in the query specification of the proxy employee_R such that emp_id is coerced to an integer and thus will be compatible with the signature of the vclass Employee. This operation can be performed as follows:

```
ALTER VCLASS Employee_R CHANGE QUERY
      SELECT e_name, itoa(emp_id), 1.75*sal, d_no, mgr
        FROM emp;
```

The conversion function itoa is specific to the LDB rdb (for instance, this is a valid query in Ingres). SQL/M currently does not support such conversion functions but allows the user to exploit such functions as may be available in the specific LDB. Also, using the itoa function renders the proxy nonupdatable since the GDB schema has no information about its inverse function, which would be required for updates. The way out of this is to define the ssn attribute of Employee_R with domain CHAR(9), add a method to convert a string to an integer, and modify the corresponding query in the Employee virtual class. This can be done as follows:

```
ALTER VCLASS Employee_R DROP ATTRIBUTE ssn;

ALTER VCLASS Employee_R
      ADD ATTRIBUTE ssn char(9),
      ADD METHOD cnv_atoi(string) : integer
          FUNCTION cnv_atoi
          FILE 'cnv_atoi.o';
```

```
ALTER VCLASS Employee_R
      CHANGE QUERY
      SELECT e_name, 1.75*sal, d_no, mgr, emp_id
        FROM emp;

ALTER VCLASS Employee CHANGE QUERY 1
      SELECT name, cnv_atoi(ssn) on e, salary, dept_no, mgr
        FROM Employee_R e
       WHERE ssn NOT IN (SELECT mgr FROM Mgr_Emp_R)
```

The first ALTER command drops the attribute ssn from Employee_R; the second one adds it back with the changed domain—namely, char(9). The second ALTER command also declares a new method cnv_atoi, which will convert a character string to an integer.[6] The third ALTER command changes the query because the order in which attributes are defined has changed. Whenever a new attribute is added to a proxy or virtual class, it is positioned at the end. Finally, recall that the domain of ssn in the virtual class Employee is integer. Therefore, the value of ssn retrieved from Employee_R is converted into an integer by exploiting the cnv_atoi method. This is done in the expression cnv_atoi(ssn) on e.

If the common supertype of the corresponding attributes in LDB entities is to be used as the domain of attributes in a proxy or virtual class, the GDB schema may need to be changed. For example, if the domain of the dept_name attribute of the dept table of rdb is changed to CHAR(20), the domain of the name attribute of the proxy Department_R and the virtual class Department needs to be changed from CHAR(15) to CHAR(20) as well.

Changing the Defaults of an Attribute

A change in the default of an attribute of an LDB entity must also be reflected in the corresponding proxy to avoid run-time errors. For example, suppose that the default value for sal in the table emp in rdb is changed from NULL to 0. This change is reflected in Employee_R as follows:

```
ALTER VCLASS Employee_R CHANGE ATTRIBUTE salary DEFAULT 0;
```

30.6 Conclusions

We discussed the schema architecture of UniSQL/M, a unified relational and object-oriented multidatabase system, which is commercially available from UniSQL, Inc. UniSQL/M provides various object-oriented abstraction

6. We assume that Employee_R already contains an OBJECT_ID clause—see section 4.

facilities such as generalization, specialization, aggregation, and methods. We described the notion of *proxies*, against which are defined *virtual classes*. A GDB schema consists of proxy definitions (transformation schema) and virtual class definitions (conceptual schema). This schema architecture provides the user with location and replication transparency. Thus the user can easily issue queries as well as updates.

Changes in user requirements or an LDB schema prompt changes in the GDB schema. Since proxies are defined against LDB entities, and virtual classes are defined against proxies, any change in the LDB schema needs to be reflected in both kinds of GDB entities. We defined a set of schema change operations with respect to a taxonomy of LDB schema changes. This taxonomy is categorized based on changes to the schema structure and changes to the entity itself. Changes to the schema structure include the creation or deletion of a new entity, addition or removal of a superclass, and renaming an entity. Changes to the entity include the creation or deletion of an attribute, renaming an attribute, and changing the domain or default of an attribute. The corresponding changes to the GDB schema are effected by various clauses of the `ALTER` statement in conjunction with the `DROP` and `CREATE` statement. We described how the user can employ these statements to maintain the GDB schema in a consistent state.

REFERENCES

Abiteboul, S., and Bonner, A. 1991. Objects and Views. *Proceedings of the ACM-SIGMOD*, Toronto.

Ahmed, R., et al. 1991. The Pegasus Heterogeneous Multidatabase System. *IEEE Computer.*

Banerjee, J., Kim, W., Kim, H. J., and Korth, H. F. 1987. Semantics and Implementation of Schema Evolution in Object-Oriented Databases. *Proceedings of the ACM-SIGMOD International Conference on Management of Data*, San Francisco.

Batini, C., Lenzerini, M., and Navathe, S. B. 1986. A Comparative Analysis of Methodologies for Database Schema Integration. *ACM Computing Surveys*, Vol. 18, No. 4, 323–364.

Breitbart, Y., Olson, P. L., and Thompson, G. R. 1986. Database Integration in a Distributed Heterogeneous Database System. *Proceedings of the Second IEEE Conference on Data Engineering*, Los Angeles.

Brill, D., and Templeton, M. 1984. Distributed Query Processing Strategies in MERMAID: A Front-End to a Data Management System. *Proceedings of the IEEE Conference on Data Engineering*, Los Angeles.

Ceri, S., and Pelagatti, G. 1984. *Distributed Databases: Systems and Principles*. McGraw-Hill, New York.

Connors, T. and Lyngbaek, P. 1988. Providing Uniform Access to Heterogeneous Information Bases. In: *Advances in Object-Oriented Database Systems*. K. R. Dittrich, ed. *LNCS* 334, Springer-Verlag.

Dayal, U., and Hwang, H. 1984. View Definition and Generalization for Database Integration of a Multidatabase System. *IEEE Trans. on Software Eng.*, SE-10(11), 628–644.

Heimbigner D., and Mcleod D. 1985. A Federated Architecture for Information Management. *ACM, TOOIS*, Vol. 3, No. 3.

Kaul, M., Dorsten, K., and Neuhold, E. J. 1990. ViewSystem: Integrating Heterogeneous Information Bases by Object-Oriented Views. *Proceedings of the Data Engineering Conference.*

Kim, W. 1991. *Introduction to Object-Oriented Databases.* MIT Press, Cambridge, Mass.

Kim, W., Choi, I., Gala, S., and Scheevel, M. 1993. On Resolving Schematic Heterogeneity in Multidatabase Systems. *Journal of Distributed and Parallel Databases,* Vol. 1, No. 3.

Kim, W., Kelley W., Gala, S. and Choi, I. 1993b. SQL/M: A Unified Relational and Object-Oriented Multidatabase Language. *Journal of Computer and Software Engineering* (in press).

Kim, W., Kifer, M., and Sagiv, Y. 1992. Querying Object-Oriented Databases. *Proceedings of the ACM-SIGMOD,* San Diego.

Landers, T. A., and Rosenberg, R. L. 1982. An Overview of Multibase—A Heterogeneous Database System. *Proceedings of the Second Symposium on Distributed Databases,* H. J. Schneider, ed. North-Holland.

Litwin, W., Abdellatif, A., Nicolas, B., Vigier, P., and Zeroual, A. 1987. MSQL: A Multidatabase Language. *Information Sciences.*

Motro, A. 1987. Superviews: Virtual Integration of Multiple Database. *IEEE Trans. on Software Eng.,* SE-13(7), 785–798.

Navathe, S. B., Gala, S. K., and Geum, S. 1991. Application of the CANDIDE Semantic Data Model for Federation of Information Bases. Invited paper, *Proceedings of the Conference on Management of Data (COMAD'91),* Bombay.

Scheevel, M., Gala, S., and Kim, W. 1991. Decomposition and Recombination of Queries in the SQL/M Multidatabase Language. Technical Report, UniSQL, Austin.

Templeton, M., Brill, D., Dao, S., Lund, E., Ward, P., Chen, A., and McGregor, R. 1987. MERMAID: A Front End to Distributed Heterogeneous Databases. *Proceedings of the IEEE,* Vol. 75, No. 5, 695–708.

31

EDA/SQL

RALPH L. STOUT

This chapter describes the salient features of EDA/SQL, the purpose of which is to mine information from arbitrary, distributed, heterogeneous collections of files and databases and deliver it to the desktop. The system is noteworthy not simply because it can process more than 50 file and database types in combination but because it is able to provide a uniform, relational view of diverse data to its end users.

31.1 Introduction

EDA/SQL fits comfortably into the client-server paradigm. Part of it always resides on client platforms, typically personal computers or workstations, and part of it always resides on machines running multiaccess database management systems. Application programs invoke its services by issuing function calls. These are interpreted locally by call-level interface modules, which route database requests and procedure calls to remote servers for processing. Servers honor such requests by returning zero, one, or more annotated answer sets to the client. The system employs a proprietary protocol designed to carry requests from client to server and answer sets from server to client.

EDA/SQL is a software hybrid consisting in part of components drawn from FOCUS, a software system with very different goals and capabilities. System development began in the summer of 1990 and, following a protracted period of beta testing, EDA/SQL made its debut in the fall of 1992. Over 400 servers are currently in use worldwide.

31.2 A Brief History

EDA/SQL came into being because of the inability of large organizations to provide convenient and timely access to information. Although by 1990 attractive end user tools—spreadsheets, query processors, executive information systems, generalized data management packages, and the like—had become commonplace, the software industry had been singularly unsuccessful in its attempts to connect them to live data. The problem: Information was being held hostage by structures dating from an era when database systems and access methods were built without reference to any theoretic framework. That these arcane structures proved to be impenetrable to modern (e.g., relationally based) tools surprised no one. First-generation DBMSs had been a source of frustration and irritation for years. What was surprising, though, was the degree to which large enterprises had become dependent on so-called legacy data. At the time, studies showed that barely 10 percent of all enterprise information was stored in relational form [Gartner Group 1992]. Overreliance on legacy data would never have become a problem worthy of note had the application systems manipulating it been more amenable to change. But rewriting old application systems to work in a relational setting was too slow, too costly, and too disruptive an activity to be countenanced by many organizations. Under pressure to deliver timely information to the desktop and either unable or unwilling to take more direct action, MIS managers scrambled to find a respectable compromise between wholesale redevelopment and making do without. Many elected to pull information from their central repository, using whatever off-the-shelf software could be pressed into service, and to distribute extract files to their users frequently enough to keep them satisfied. One package that was used extensively for this purpose was the FOCUS report generator [Information Builders 1992a] from Information Builders, Inc. (IBI).

FOCUS was never intended to be used in this way, but it proved to be an effective data-extraction tool. Supplied with suitably encoded data descriptions (called *master file definitions*) and set membership conditions (expressed as TABLE requests), FOCUS could access information from virtually any source, manipulate it powerfully, and generate two-dimensional tabular reports. Most tools that mattered could import suitably formatted FOCUS reports without much difficulty.

Software vendors tend to be alert to unplanned uses of their systems—and IBI was quick to realize that it had a marketable legacy data-access solution within its grasp. IBI had accumulated 50 or more database-specific drivers over a period of 15 years; it had the venerable FOCUS data engine, which by 1990 had evolved into a capable query processor[1]; and it had recently completed a client-server architecture designed to tie PC FOCUS to mainframe databases. What was missing was an effective way to link FOCUS servers seamlessly to other desktop tools, nearly all of which seemed to depend on an SQL view of the world. Because considerable glue—not to mention some new and significant system components—

1. FOCUS, at this stage in its development, was prerelational in the sense that, while it had grown to support most of the classical relational operations, its TABLE language retained its own distinctly pragmatic 4GL personality.

would be required to give shape to this collection, the new product idea was nothing if not controversial. Large project proposals generally are—but this particular project, involving organizational as well as technical challenges (IBI, long a one-product company, was flirting here with an entirely new line of business) generated more debate than it probably deserved. Development did not begin, in fact, until a large client committed resources to a special project designed to enable a UNIX-based general-purpose natural language processor with an SQL orientation to access hierarchical MVS-based M204 files.

FOCUS components, it turned out, could be reused, though not without exquisite care. The database interface modules alone comprised several hundred thousand lines of code written by programmers following a variety of styles, standards, and beliefs. While some interfaces were of a recent vintage and, presumably, well understood, many had not been touched for years. In self-defense, developers adopted strict rules regarding the encapsulation and reuse of code. They treated existing FOCUS modules, for example, as black boxes and rejected most proposals to change them out of hand. With strict project controls and guidelines in place, work went more smoothly than many had anticipated, and it was not long before many of the promised capabilities were demonstrable.

EDA/SQL development commenced in the summer of 1990 and the system, following a protracted period of beta testing, made its official debut in the fall of 1992. Since then, over 400 EDA/SQL servers have been installed. What follows is a snapshot of the system as it was constituted in early 1994.

31.3 Operational Overview of EDA/SQL

EDA/SQL creates a relational view of heterogeneous, distributed data by translating ANSI SQL requests into commands that can be handled by other database management systems. Because it mediates between users and DBMSs, it is in an ideal position to create the illusion that fragmented, distributed, heterogeneous collections of data are coherent relational databases. When an EDA/SQL server receives an SQL request, R, it reduces it to a structure known (internally at IBI) as a J-tree. Providing R conforms to normal SQL syntactic and semantic standards, the translator generates a strategy for processing it. If, for example, R were framed entirely in terms of tables managed by a single local relational DBMS, it would be passed relatively unchanged[2] to that DBMS for processing. If R were heterogeneous, or if it addressed legacy data, it would be converted into an internal represen-

2. Some minor changes are often required. The translator accepts ISO SQL and emits DBMS-specific SQL dialects.

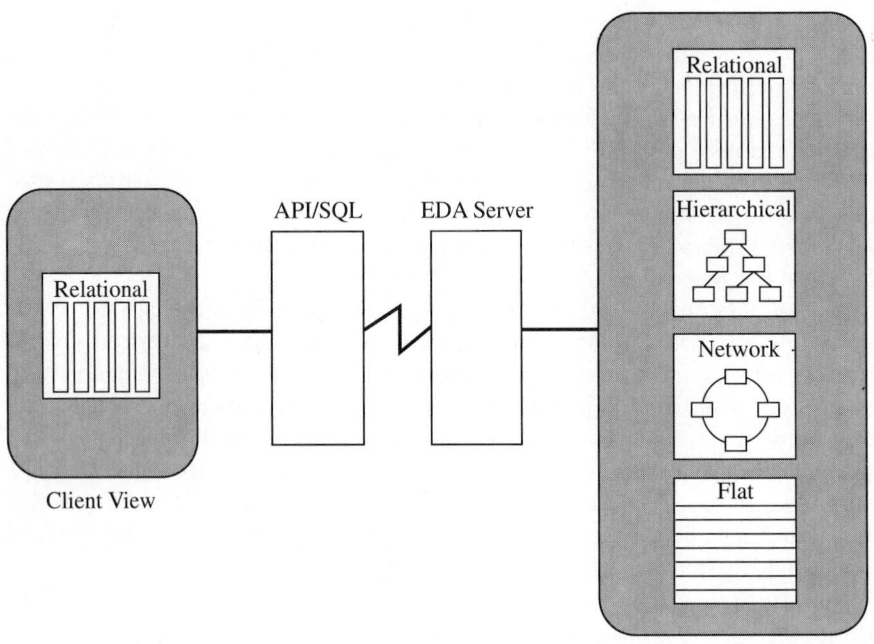

FIGURE 31–1
Client View

tation (iSQL) understood by the EDA/SQL data engine. If R addressed tables situated on some remote server, it would be passed unchanged to that server for processing. Finally, if R were a distributed remote request, the translator would factor it and distribute work requests, expressed in SQL, to other servers. In short, the EDA/SQL Universal SQL translator formulates a plan, expresses it in SQL, iSQL, or some combination thereof, and depends on other components of the system to carry it out.

The EDA/SQL database engine, the iSQL interpreter, contributes plans of its own. When a request is heterogeneous, a local VSAM to IMS join, for example, the database engine also distributes work to other system components. Query splitting at this level, however, applies to iSQL commands, not SQL statements, and the other components in question are resident DBMS interface driver modules, not remote EDA/SQL servers.

The basic operation of an EDA/SQL server can be summarized succinctly: (1) the server unpacks client requests and directs them to the translator; (2) the translator rejects all invalid requests; (3) the translator detects homogeneous relational requests and relays them to native relational DBMSs for pass-through processing; (4) the translator formulates plans for all other requests and expresses them in an internal language known as iSQL; (5) the EDA/SQL database engine refines and interprets iSQL; (6) the DBMS interface modules convert iSQL strings into command streams to be

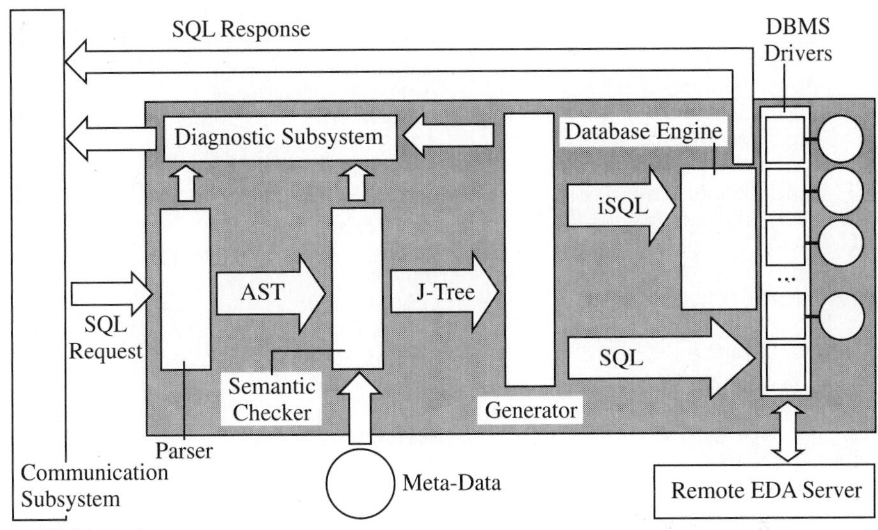

FIGURE 31–2
SQL Translator

processed by supported DBMSs; (7) the interface modules return their results to the database engine; (8) the database engine performs whatever postprocessing (joining, sorting, merging, aggregating, etc.) is required and formats answer sets; (9) EDA/Link, the communications module, returns answer sets to clients.

Application programs invoke EDA/SQL services by executing subroutine calls. The primary low-level programming interface modules, API/SQL and EDA/CLI, which offer similar capabilities[3], reside, along with an EDA/Link component, on the client side of the client-server equation. Other programming interfaces, called *extenders*, layered on top of these basic components, accommodate popular desktop tools. The objective of the extenders is to make selected software packages work without reprogramming them. As of March 1993, no fewer than 86 desktop tools (see Fig. 31–2) had been enabled for use with EDA/SQL [Information Builders 1992b].

31.4 System Architecture

An EDA/SQL distributed system comprises servers, translators, routers, data drivers, communication subsystems, APIs (or CLIs if you prefer), and additional client-based programming interface layers. What follows is a brief functional overview of each significant component of the system.

3. API/SQL was there first. EDA/CLI was added later to accommodate programs written to the X/Open Call-level specification.

Tools Enabled via API/SQL	Tools Enabled via Extenders
ACCESSWORKS (DEC)	AMIPRO (Lotus)
ADW (KnowledgeWare)	Approach (Approach)
Approach (Approach)	AS (IBM)
Argus (Munro Engineering)	ATLASPRO (Strategic Mapping)
AXSYS (Info Advantage)	Command Center (Pilot)
BOTH (Connectivite)	Cross Target (Dimensional Inst.)
Business Objects (Business Obj.)	Data Pivot (Brio)
CAINET (Century Analysis)	DIS (IBM)
ClearAccess (ClearAccess)	DXT (IBM)
DataLens (Lotus)	Excel (Microsoft)
DATAPRISM (Brio)	Executive Decisions (IBM)
EASEL Workbench (Easel)	EXPRESS (IRI)
EDA/Compose (IBI)	Geoquery (Geoquery)
EIS Builder (Lex Software)	HyperCard (Apple)
ENFIN (Easel)	IFPS (COMSHARE)
EXPRESS (IRI)	Language Access (IBM)
F3Forms (Bloc)	Lightship (Pilot)
FOCUS (IBI)	Lotus 1-2-3 (Lotus)
Forest & Trees (Trinzic)	MS-Access (Microsoft)
GQL (Andyne)	Muse (OCCAM)
Guideware (Guideware)	ODBCPACK (Pioneer Software)
InfoPump (Trinzic)	OracleLink (Oracle)
LEVEL5 OBJECT (IBI)	PageAhead (InfoPublisher)
Lightship (Pilot)	PageMaker (Aldus)
MicroFocus (COBOL Workbench)	PowerBuilder (Powersoft)
Mozart Workbench (Mozart Sys.)	QMF (ROCKET)
NetWare SQL (Novell)	QMF (IBM)
NEWWAVE ACCESS (HP)	QQF (Platinum)
OBJECTVIEW (KnowledgeWare)	Spinnaker Plus (Spinnaker)
ODBC (Microsoft)	Spreadbase (Objective Software)
Office Automation (Third Wave)	SQL Windows (GUPTA)
OMNIS7 (Blyth)	Superbase (SPC)
Open ODB (HP)	Toolbook (Asymetrics)
OPENBOOK (OPENBOOK)	SYSTEM W (COMSHARE)
Paradox (Borland)	Visual Basic (Microsoft)
PC EXPRESS (DataEase)	Wingz (Informix)
PC/FOCUS (IBI)	Word (Microsoft)
Q + E (Pioneer Software)	WordPerfect (WordPerfect)
Skipper (Flower)	
Snap (Temple Software)	
SQL Assist (Software Interface)	
SQL NLMExtender (Novell)	
Startrieve (SelectStar Inc.)	
SUPERNOVA (FOURSEASONS)	
TableBase (Data Kinetics)	
TACTITIAN (TACTICS)	
Visual Planner (ViSolutions)	
Visual Works (Parc Place)	

FIGURE 31–3
Client Tools

31.4.1 EDA/SQL Servers

EDA/SQL servers are self-contained, scaleable systems capable of processing a mix of SQL requests and remote procedure calls simultaneously. Servers manage data flow and perform accounting, security, and other administrative functions. Most importantly, from an external viewpoint, they convert SQL requests into answer sets.

Servers process requests in three ways: by translating SQL statements into nonrelational command sequences, by passing SQL requests through to native relational DBMSs (including remote EDA/SQL Servers), and by executing remote procedures (which may issue SQL queries of their own).

Some servers act as request routers, receiving and analyzing SQL requests before distributing work to other nodes in the network. Although any full-function EDA/SQL server can do this, scaled-down servers known as routers and distributors can be used for this purpose. *Routers* can only route requests to local relational DBMSs and remote servers; a *distributor* is a router that can handle distributed requests. Because they must assemble partial results into answer sets, Distributors are able to merge, sort, and perform SQL aggregations. Note that routers and distributors, since they never use local databases, require no data drivers.

EDA/SQL servers are modular: The *scheduler/initiator* manages tasks and threads of execution and, under duress, initiates recovery procedures; the *communication subsystem* manages client-server and server-server information flow via EDA/Link using a variety of communication protocols; the *security interface module* employs local operating system security mechanisms to control access to database objects and other system resources; the *universal SQL translator* maps SQL requests into iSQL command streams; the *data access engine* interprets iSQL and calls on data drivers to produce answer sets and intermediate results; *data drivers* map iSQL into navigational commands and route the results of their efforts to the data access engine; and the *administrative subsystem* provides tracing and accounting functions.

31.4.2 The Scheduler/Initiator Subsystem

The scheduler/initiator subsystem manages the resources consumed by client-based application programs. Multithreaded EDA/SQL servers, like those provided for MVS and UNIX, may be configured as a mixture of public server subtasks (which share resources among several users) and private server subtasks (which dedicate all resources to a single user). One can balance resource consumption by varying the public-private mix to suit individual needs and priorities.

Public and private server subtasks differ in that the former queue requests and the latter do not. But public or private, all servers behave in the same way. Resource consumption and speed of execution are the only perceivable differences between them.

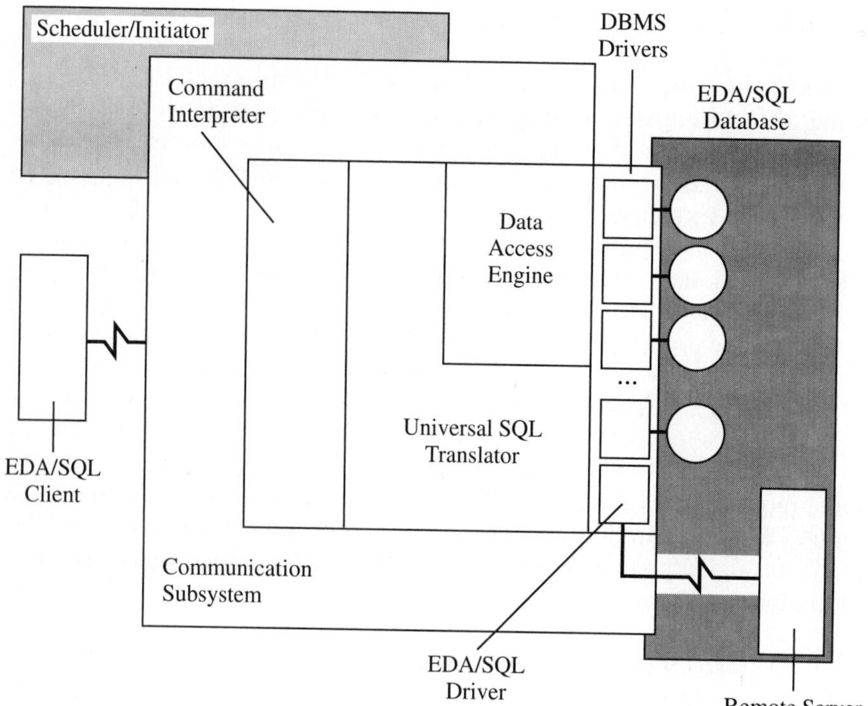

FIGURE 31–4
EDA/SQL Server Architecture

31.4.3 The Security Interface Subsystem

EDA/SQL complements and extends security measures that are already in place. It can exploit IBM's system authorization facility (SAF) [IBM 1988] together with RACF, for example. It can also invoke CA-ACF2 [Computer Associates 1992a] or CA-TOP SECRET [Computer Associates 1992b] to authenticate users. EDA/SQL has been designed to function securely no matter what software local administrators select.

EDA/SQL employs operating system security either via already verified connection processing (AVP) [Information Builders 1992c], via explicit verification processing (EVP) [Information Builders 1992d] or via a generalized security exit. AVP relies on the host operating system and EVP on the server for user authentication. A user exit makes customized solutions possible.

EDA/SQL also adapts to other security mechanisms. API/SQL and EDA/CLI permit application programs to supply passwords for the row or field-level security checks required by some DBMSs and allow users to invoke additional security features by means of remote procedure calls. An application program addressing an Oracle DBMS on a VAX, for example, can invoke the Oracle-specific SET USER directive by issuing a remote procedure call.

31.4.4 The Universal SQL Translator

The Universal SQL translator can either convert dynamic SQL statements into iSQL and pass them unchanged to a relational engine or factor them into parts and execute them elsewhere. The translator parses statements and, with the help of meta-data obtained from the catalog, checks their semantics. Having established that a request makes sense, the translator recasts it in terms of base tables (this step is crucial in a distributed environment because the location of an SQL view need not coincide with the tables referenced in its definition). Once it has removed view references, the translator decides whether it should distribute work to other servers, pass the request through to a local RDBMS, or generate iSQL. In its code-generation phase, the translator converts its plan, encoded as a J-tree, into iSQL streams. Although the primary function of the translator is to process well-formed SQL requests, it also produces meaningful diagnostic and warning messages.

The translator normally processes all the SQL requests the server receives. But it can be bypassed. Strictly speaking, translation need only occur when the target database or file is nonrelational or when the SQL statement in question addresses a heterogeneous mix of files or tables. If these circumstances never arise, the client can invoke a DBMS-specific passthrough mode of operation. When passthrough mode is in effect, the server hands requests directly to a designated relational DBMS interface module for processing. Passthrough mode was first conceived as a way to eliminate translator overhead. Users rarely require it for this purpose because the translator now detects homogeneous relational requests and passes them to an appropriate DBMS driver without user intervention. But passthrough mode has another important use: Because it bypasses the translator, it makes it possible to employ a nonstandard SQL dialect naturally—without resorting to awkward escape sequences.

The universal SQL translator supports standard ANSI X3.135-1989 syntax [ANSI 1989]. This aspect of EDA/SQL enables administrators to enforce standard SQL usage in circumstances that might otherwise encourage the uncontrolled exercise of nonstandard SQL statements and features. Because only native relational, VSAM, and FOCUS databases can be updated within a transaction, the solution provided by the translator is not fully compliant to the standard. Ultimately, characteristics of the targeted DBMS dictate whether correctly formed UPDATE, INSERT, or DELETE operations can be honored. Consequently, many consider EDA/SQL a read-mostly database system. This is a fair characterization when EDA/SQL is applied to heterogeneous or legacy data. But when users apply it to a relational database, as they frequently do, the system supports updating as a matter of course.

31.4.5 The Data Access Engine

The purpose of the data access engine is to turn iSQL request descriptions into SQL answer sets. The engine employs navigational or relational drivers to get to raw data, which it then transforms into result sets. This can entail grouping, aggregation, sorting, and merging as well as the classic operations of set theory. The presence of a fully capable data access engine determines whether a server is a router or a distributor.

31.4.6 EDA/Data Drivers

Collectively, EDA/SQL data drivers provide access to information recorded in over 50 different formats. Each driver is responsible for mapping iSQL statements into navigational procedures. A specialized data driver, sensitive to language syntax, schema content, data types, object naming conventions, and data representation is provided for every supported DBMS. Data drivers are like building blocks. Users choose which ones they require when they configure their servers.

31.4.7 EDA/Link

EDA/Link implements a proprietary protocol layer (eSQL) designed to carry requests from client to server and answer sets from server to client. Its responsibilities include password authentication, data conversion, encryption and compression, error detection, and message routing. EDA/Link is independent of the underlying communications protocol(s) in use at a given installation. It can employ LU 0, LU 2 (3270 Datastream), LU 6.2 (APPC and CPI-C), TCP/IP, HLLAPI, DECnet, Named Pipes, and NetWare for SAA. It even allows servers to mix communications protocols. EDA/Link comprises a *communications kernel*, a *client-side session layer*, a *server-side session layer* and several *protocol-specific interface modules*.

31.5 The EDA/SQL Catalog

The kernel of the EDA/SQL catalog describes databases and files accessible via the EDA/SQL universal translator. It is patterned on the DB2 catalog schema.

The EDA/SQL catalog contains more than SQL meta-data; at connect time, for example, API/SQL obtains the characteristics of the referenced server from the catalog and alters its behavior accordingly. The catalog contains SQL meta-data, system capabilities information, and remote procedure call definitions. Every EDA/SQL server comes with a set of interactive catalog creation and maintenance utilities.

It would not have been possible to approach the goal of universal data access without a serviceable catalog. Most generalized desktop data manipulation tools rely on three things: a suitable application programming interface, an SQL view of data, and information describing tables and columns accessible to end users. The third leg of this triad is crucial because, without it, the tools would be unable even to display lists of available tables and their columns.

31.6 Client-Server Operation

EDA/SQL fits comfortably into the client-server paradigm. Part of it resides on client machines, frequently but not necessarily personal computers or workstations, and part of it resides on machines running multiaccess database management systems. The issuance of a dynamic database request (R) via an EDA call-level interface triggers a typical client-server exchange: The interface layer packages R and hands it off to a local EDA/Link module; EDA/Link delivers R to a server; the server processes R and returns zero, one, or more answer sets and (possibly) diagnostic information to the client.

Originally, EDA/SQL offered a single native application programming interface: API/SQL. Typically supplied as a dynamically linked library (DLL), it offers a compact repertoire of functions for manipulating databases, invoking remote procedures, and processing answer sets. API/SQL is available on several platforms including DOS, MS Windows, OS/2, Macintosh, UNIX Workstations, VAX, AS400, and IBM mainframe computers. Information Builders will add an alternative interface, EDA/CLI, and a proprietary driver manager component to its complement of client-side EDA/SQL software in 1994 to bring applications conforming to the X/Open SQL call-level interface standard into the fold. The driver manager, which will support ODBC as well as X/Open applications and drivers, will be available on a variety of client platforms, including OS/2 and UNIX. Figure 31–5 depicts the relationships among the various components of this architecture.

Also available in EDA/SQL are several additional programming interfaces called *extenders*. Extenders make it possible for existing application programs to run unchanged as EDA/SQL clients. These shells, built around an API/SQL core, are available for programs employing ODBC (Microsoft Windows), DB2 (IBM MVS), SQL/DS (IBM VM), OS2 Database Manager (IBM PC), DDE (Microsoft Windows), HyperCard (Apple Macintosh), Data Lens (LOTUS), SQL Base (Gupta), Data Prism (Brio), and Page Ahead (Info-Publisher).

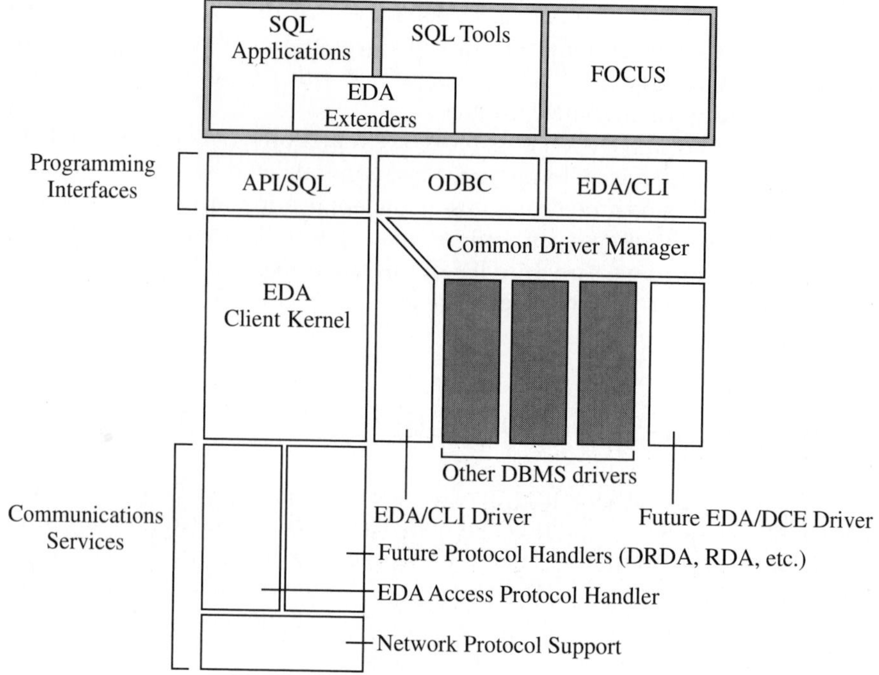

FIGURE 31–5
EDA/SQL Client Architecture

Although the technology underlying EDA/SQL is enormously complex, the view API/SQL provides to the application programmer (and by implication the end user) is simple. Programmers need not be aware, for example, of table location, EDA/Link, communications protocols, SQL translation, data drivers, the behavior of legacy DBMSs, how hierarchical and network structures are made to look relational, answer set and message queue representations, data conversion and compression, or record locking and database recovery mechanisms. Such detail is hidden from view by a model that nevertheless encompasses administrative matters (program initialization and termination, the maintenance of internal variables, asynchronous operation, tracing and debugging, version control), server interaction (connecting to and disconnecting from the system), and database management concerns (executing SQL requests and remote procedure calls). The API/SQL command repertoire (outlined below) reflects the three major aspects of the model.

- Administrative

EDAINIT	Initialize the application
EDATERM	Terminate the application
EDASET	Set an internal API/SQL variable

EDAINSPECT	Access an internal API/SQL variable
EDALOG	Write a record to the default tracing log

- Communication

EDACONNECT	Connect to a server
EDAXCONNECT	Disconnect from a server
EDASERVERS	Obtain a list of available servers
EDAWAIT	Wait for server request completion
EDATEST	Test for server request completion
EDAACCEPT	Access a message from a message queue
EDAREPLY	Reply to a server-generated prompt

- Database

EDASQL	Execute an SQL request
EDAINFO	Describe a given column in an answer set
EDABIND	Bind a column of values to a variable
EDASETPARAM	Bind a variable to a SQL parameter
EDAFETCH	Retrieve the next row of an answer set
EDANEXT	Activate the next row of an answer set
EDAFIELD	Access a value from an answer set
EDAPREPARE	Prepare an SQL statement for execution
EDAUSING	Initialize a parameter value
EDAEXECUTE	Execute a prepared SQL request
EDACOMMIT	Commit or rollback a transaction
EDARPC	Invoke a remote procedure call
EDADESCRIBE	Describe the format of a table
EDAQUIT	Release the current answer set; make the next answer set (if one exists) current
EDANULL	Test for a NULL value in an answer set

Once initialized, an application program must establish at least one server connection before addressing the database. Client-server relationships are created via EDACONNECT and purged by means of EDAXCONNECT. EDA/SQL permits users to maintain multiple server connections. This capability is required by the system (servers processing distributed queries must act as clients to multiple servers simultaneously). Version 3.0 of EDA/SQL, scheduled to appear early in 1994, will encourage users to connect associatively to hub servers, which will automatically route requests to the data server that can process them most efficiently. The hub server concept is expected to reduce end user reliance on multiple server connections considerably.

Most application programs are bracketed in time, on the outside by EDAINIT and EDACONNECT and then by EDAXCONNECT and EDATERM. Having initialized and connected to a server, the user may manipulate the database. API/SQL provides two types of database commands. One initiates requests and the other accesses results. Asynchronous operation begins with the execution of a request operation (EDASQL, EDAEXECUTE, EDARPC, EDADESCRIBE, EDAPREPARE). While the server processes the request, the application program is free to do anything at all—even issue a new request over another connection. Resynchronization occurs when an application program explicitly tests for command completion or attempts to fetch data from an answer set.

31.7 The Future

EDA/SQL 1.0 represented a serviceable solution to a long-standing problem, but it had SQL limitations and other rough edges that could not be sustained for long in a competitive marketplace. It was superseded several months later by release 2.0. The 2.0 server provided better SQL support and, on the client side, a new suite of extender packages made it possible to accommodate an impressively broad class of GUI-based desktop tools.

Release 2.0 and its immediate successors, designated 2.1 and 2.2, respectively, achieved nearly everything the EDA/SQL planners had set out to accomplish in the first place. It could read almost any kind of data, process cross-DBMS joins, service every targeted client-based decision support tool—and it was nicely produced (among other things, the 2.x series of products provided automatic tracing, an accounting subsystem, and a full complement of software development tools and conveniences). Left to their own devices, the EDA software developers would probably have been content to declare the system a success and move on to some new project.

But while EDA/SQL 2.2 was taking shape, the market for which it was intended shifted, significantly enough to prompt yet another round of improvements. In effect, customers had raised the technological ante—by demanding more flexible data distribution capabilities, location-transparent access to data, legacy-to-relational (and frequently object-oriented) migration tools, high-performance transaction processing support, a scaleable architecture, foolproof system installation procedures, and rigorous adherence to international standards. Information Builders' response to this broad new set of requirements, EDA/SQL 3.0, took over a year to prepare.

Though the 3.0 release with its modular composition, distributed database orientation, high-performance connectivity architecture, and relative SQL sophistication exceeds the original system blueprint, there is still ample room left for improvement. The 3.0 transaction-processing model, for example, is inadequate (transactions are not permitted to cross DBMS boundaries), and the distributed query optimizer is incomplete. Data type support should be generalized and expanded. Any number of SQL/92 features merit inclusion. And, despite the presence of an effective copy management subsystem, the issue of data replication has not yet been addressed. One could go on in this vein, however, cataloging missing features and technical deficiencies, without shedding much light on the future of EDA/SQL. If experience is any guide, the stimulus for the next wave of changes will not come from such an assessment.

The first three major releases of EDA/SQL represent straightforward responses to what a small, fairly insular committee of individuals perceived as the needs of the marketplace. The next is likely to reflect a less provincial attitude. Middleware vendors are loath to provide services formerly associated only with full-scale DBMSs—the cost of developing them, for one thing, tends to be prohibitive—but their customers are demanding that they do exactly that. Database vendors find themselves in a similar bind. They lack the time and resources to build a universal data access capability of their own—yet that is clearly what their customers would like them to do. With DBMS and middleware vendors encroaching more and more on one another's turf, without accomplishing the degree of generality people actually require, the pressure to produce confederated systems is mounting.

For middleware and DBMS vendors, this could signal a shift in emphasis—away from what some would call a features war to a more sedate form of competition. If it does, the next release of EDA/SQL is more likely to stress interoperability and conformance to industry standards than anything else.

REFERENCES

American National Standards Institute (ANSI). 1989. Document ANSI X3.135-1989.

Computer Associates. 1992a. CA-ACF2 Administrative Guide. Document no. R002J160AGE.

Computer Associates. 1992b. CA-TOP-SECRET MVS Release 4.3 Auditor's Guide. Document no. R20243AUE.

Gartner Group. 1992. SMS: K-110-1205. September 21.

IBM. 1988. MVS/SA System Programming Library: Application Development Guide. Document no. GC28-1852-0.

Information Builders. 1992a. EDA/SQL Server for MVS Installation Guide. DN3500004.0792.

Information Builders. 1992b. FOCUS for IBM Mainframe. User's Manual Release 6.5. DN1000903.0492.

Information Builders. 1992c. EDA Enabled Vendor's Guide. Product Brochure. DN3600119.0093.

Information Builders. 1992d. EDA/SQL Server for MVS Installation Guide. DN3500004.0792.

32

Pegasus: A Heterogeneous Information Management System

MING-CHIEN SHAN
RAFI AHMED
JIM DAVIS
WEIMIN DU
WILLIAM KENT

Pegasus is a heterogeneous multidatabase management system being developed at Hewlett-Packard Laboratories. Its goal is to provide an open and integrated information environment to support the database and service interoperability for diverse applications in the 1990s. Pegasus defines an object-oriented model for unifying the data models of the external systems and supports transparent access to the multiple, autonomous, heterogeneous, distributed external information systems through a uniform interface.

32.1 Introduction

The pressure of increasing competition is forcing major corporations to reengineer their business organizations. The major factor driving this restructuring is a focus on the improvement of product/service delivery and quality and the reduction of cost. Access to data is a *critical process* for most of such tasks, as it is fundamental to maintaining productivity and quality.

One objective of this business restructuring is looking for opportunities to utilize new information technology to support the business organization more effectively. The strategic goal of most of these efforts is to develop enterprisewide solutions that tie together information systems across business units within an organization. This corporatewide information architecture defines a comprehensive framework within which a unified information environment for the entire enterprise can be built.

Due to the heterogeneous nature of such an environment and the increasing maturity of open systems technology, people are pursuing solutions that utilize open system components. Recent advances in standards have created a plausible illusion of interoperability. Practitioners once believed that the availability of communications and OS standards (e.g., ISO/OSI, OSF/DCE, and IEEE/POSIX) would make interoperability a reality. Now people realize that interoperability does not stop at the operating systems or the communication infrastructure. It extends to every facet of the information environment.

Between the end-user/application layer and the operating system/ communication layer of today's computing enterprise lies what many developers consider a no-man's land: middleware. The information management system is at the heart of this middleware [Wagner 1992].

Any leading-edge applications of the 1990s —those likely to have the greatest strategic impact on large enterprises—will require such a new information environment. Typical applications include telephone service handling, computer integrated manufacturing processes, financial decision making, automated warehouses, and travel reservations.

To meet this requirement, our goal is to provide an open and integrated information environment, allowing users to access up-to-date information using a single unified interface. This offers a much more powerful information environment than the information warehouse approach [IBM 1992], which basically provides periodic data extracting service.

Based on the object-oriented technology, the Pegasus project at Hewlett-Packard Laboratories is developing a heterogeneous multidatabase management system, with the view to facilitating the access and manipulation of multiple, autonomous, heterogeneous, distributed information management systems through a uniform interface. Pegasus is envisioned as a complete database management system that integrates *native* and *external* databases. A native database is created in Pegasus and both its schema and data are managed by Pegasus. External databases are accessible through Pegasus but are managed by various external data resource managers (EDRMs), which can have different data models (e.g., object oriented, relational, network, hierarchical, etc.), different query languages, and different world views. These EDRMs are autonomous and grant varying degrees of access privileges to Pegasus, ranging from simple retrieval to both retrieval and update of data and schema. Currently, we are focusing on the integration of conventional database management systems (e.g., DB2, Oracle, Informix, Allbase, OpenODB, and IMS), multimedia systems, and legacy applications.

An external database is represented in Pegasus by its *imported* schema. Pegasus's data definition language provides mapping facilities for generating an imported schema for each external database schema. Once imported, these schemas can be further integrated to support the needed views for different applications.

32.2 The Pegasus Data Model and Language

Pegasus provides an object-oriented model as the framework for uniform interoperation of multiple data sources with different information management systems.

The Pegasus model, which is based on the HP OpenODB's functional object model [Hewlett-Packard 1992] contains three basic constructs: *types, functions*, and *objects*.

A type has a unique name and represents a collection of objects that share common characteristics. Types are organized in a directed acyclic graph that supports generalization and specialization with multiple inheritance. A type may be declared to be a subtype of other types. Objects that are instances of a type are also instances of its supertypes.

Objects, which represent real-world concepts, are instances of one or more types. Objects are uniquely identified by their object identifiers (OIDs). Some objects, such as integers, are self-identifying. Objects may gain and lose types dynamically.

Properties of, relationships among, and computations on objects are expressed through functions. Function arguments/results are defined on a list of types. A function defined on a given type is inherited by all of its subtypes.

Data definition and data manipulation in Pegasus are performed with the language HOSQL (Heterogeneous Object SQL), which is an extension of OSQL, the DDL/DML of OpenODB. It is a functional and object-oriented language, that provides declarative statements to manipulate multiple heterogeneous databases.

An HOSQL query is expressed using a *select*, a *foreach*, and an optional *where* clause. The select clause contains a list of variable names or function calls. The foreach clause contains the names and types of variables used in the select clause and the where clause. The where clause contains a predicate expression that may involve (nested) functions, variables, constants, or nested subqueries.

A simple personnel database can be established by issuing the following HOSQL statements, which create two new types with their associated attributes and two instances of each type:

```
CREATE TYPE Department
       FUNCTIONS (Deptno INTEGER, Location CHAR);

CREATE TYPE Employee SUBTYPE OF Person
       FUNCTIONS (Name Char, Age INTEGER, Dept Department,
           Salary INTEGER);
CREATE OBJECT AS Department (Deptno, Location)
       :sale_dept (11, 'S.F.'),
       :support_dept (22, 'L.A.');
```

```
CREATE OBJECT AS Employee (Name, Age, Dept, Salary)
      :john ('John Smith', 53, :sale_dept, 40000),
      :bob ('Bob Hanson', 28, :support_dept, 20000);
```

To retrieve the information of all employees located in San Francisco, the request can be formulated in an HOSQL query as follows:

```
SELECT Name(e), Age(e), Deptno(d), Salary(e)
FOREACH Employee e, Department d
WHERE Dept(e) = d AND Location(d) = 'S.F.';
```

32.3 Pegasus Architecture Overview

32.3.1 Pegasus Functional Architecture

There are four major functional layers in the Pegasus information environment as depicted in Fig. 32–1. Pegasus aims at providing the middleware service between individual information systems and end users/applications. Therefore, Pegasus focuses on the development of the middle two layers [Shan 1993].

The basic integrated information service layer provides such application-neutral services as schema mapping and integration, distributed query processing, business operation flow management, directory management, and network/external information systems access.

The domain-specific information service layer deals with special needs for different application domains. This includes the information mining and query-formulation capabilities for the mobile computing devices application, and effective presentation and specific business modeling capabilities for interactive applications, and data caching and versioning capabilities for transaction applications.

32.3.2 Pegasus System Structure

Figure 32–2 illustrates the major components of the Pegasus system.

A request is submitted to Pegasus in the form of an HOSQL statement. After parsing, the executive module routes it to the appropriate managers: the schema and object manager, the query manager, and the operation flow manager.

The schema and object manager implements data definition operations and catalog management, including EDRM registration, schema importation, and integration. The query manager generates efficient execution plans and coordinates the execution of the plans. It consists of the global optimizer, query decomposer, query evaluator, and a number of query translators, one for each kind of EDRM. The operation flow manager [Dayal

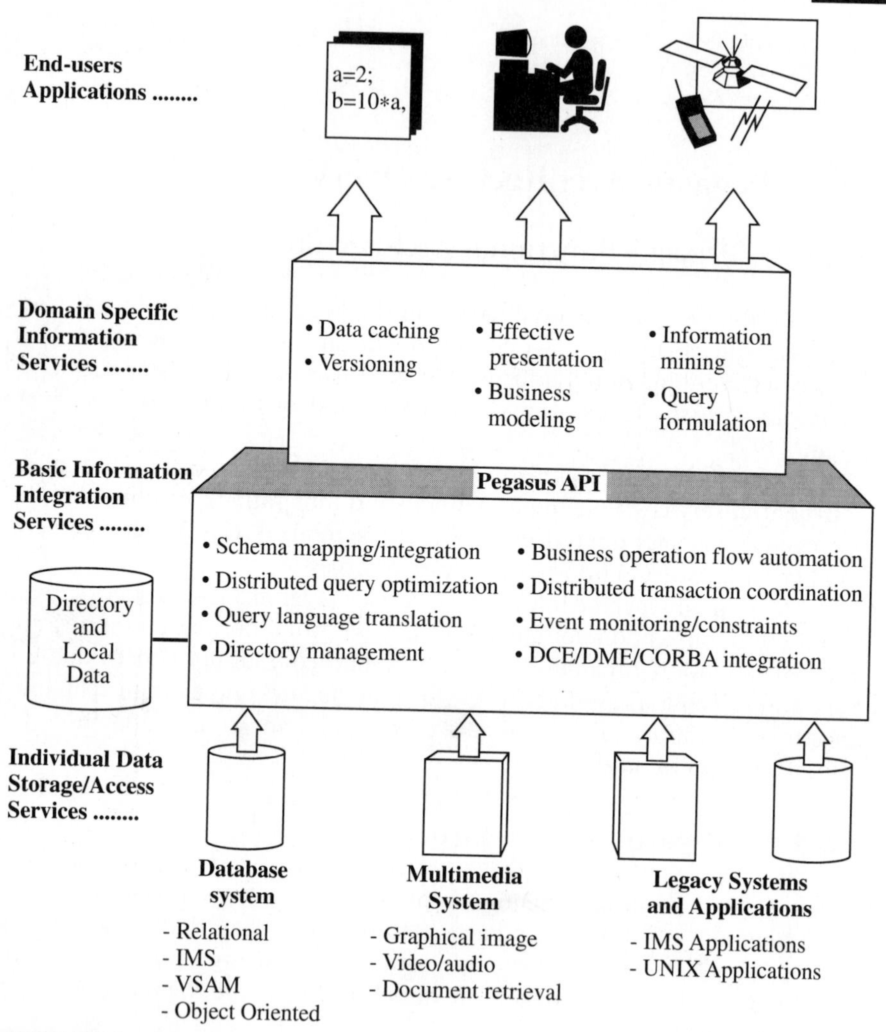

FIGURE 32–1
Pegasus Functional Architecture

and Shan 1993] schedules and controls the flow of processes supporting complex work. It also coordinates the interaction with a distributed transaction manager (e.g., Transarc/Encina [Transarc 1991] or MIA [Nippon

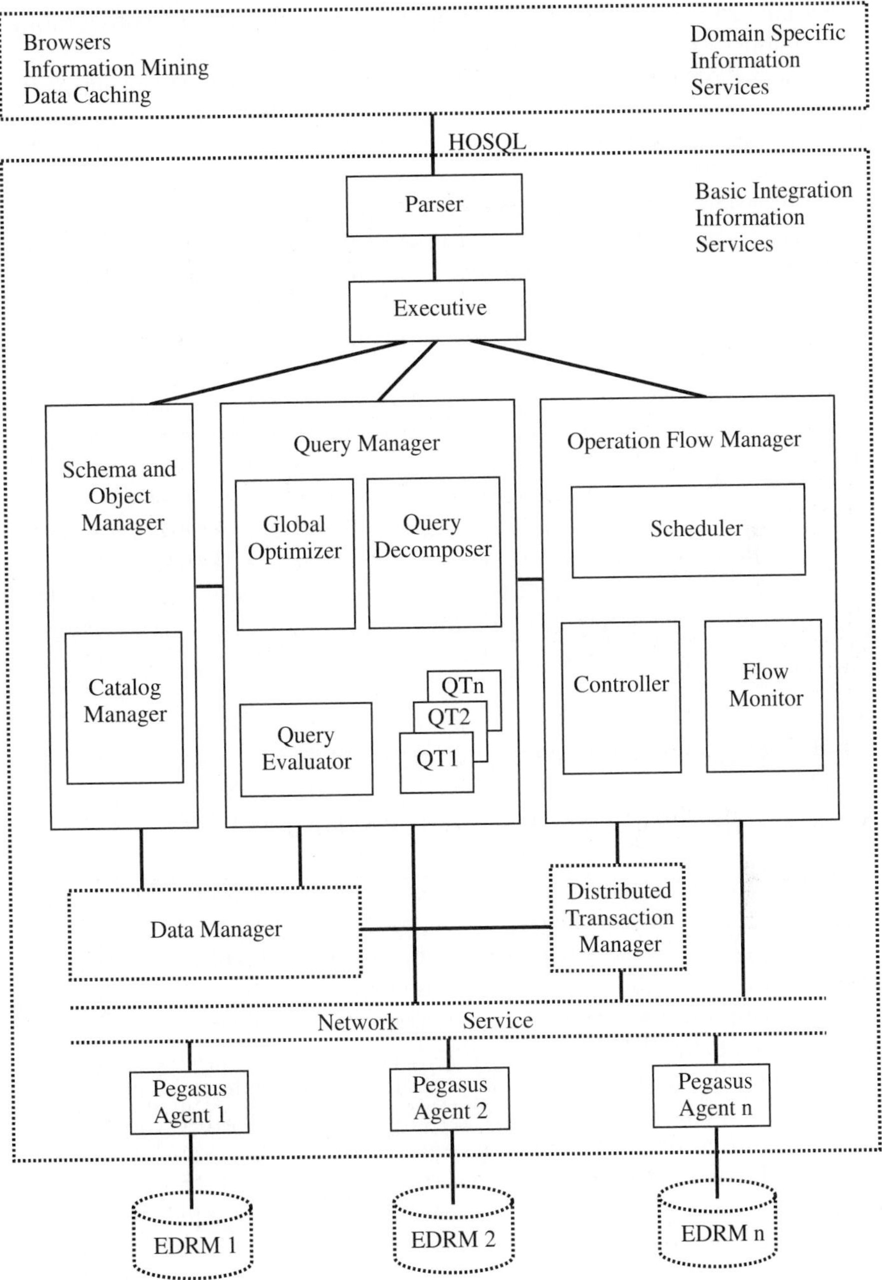

FIGURE 32–2
Pegasus Component Structure

Telegraph and Telephone Corporation 1991]) to support conventional transactions.

Meta-data and local user data are kept in a local data manager, which can be any standard relational system (e.g., HP/Allbase or Sybase) or even a low level storage manager (e.g., System R/RSS [Astrahan et al. 1980] or WiSS [Chou et al. 1985]).

The interaction with various EDRMs is implemented via a number of Pegasus agents. A Pegasus agent is a process that runs in the same machine as an EDRM. Its role is to perform the needed functions on behalf of Pegasus at the external site. It provides the services of EDRM invocation, network communication, data routing and buffering, data format exchange, and flow management related tasks.

Currently, we are focused on the development of a single Pegasus server. The design principles of major functional components are detailed in Shan 1993. We plan to extend Pegasus into a distributed system, as shown in Fig. 32–3.

We are also investigating the relationship and integration of the OMG/CORBA (Common Object Request Broker Architecture) technology [Object Management Group 1991] and Pegasus technology to support the needs of information/service access in many diverse distributed computing environments.

32.4 Importation of External Data

32.4.1 External Data Resource Registration

To make an external data resource known to and accessible from Pegasus, it must be registered with Pegasus using the HOSQL *register* statement.

We will use the following example (Fig. 32–4) involving three external databases throughout the rest of this chapter. DB1 is an IBM/DB2 database consisting of two tables—`Programmer` and `Language_Skill`. Each programmer has a `name`, `programmer_id`, `social security number`, and `salary`. Each programmer may master in one or more languages and the information is stored in the `Language_Skill` table. DB2 is an Oracle database consisting of three tables—`Engineer`, `Project`, and `Assignment`. Each engineer has a `name`, `engineer_id`, `social security number`, and `salary`. Each project has a `project_id` and the `budget` allocated to the project. The `Assignment` table describes the assignment relationship between projects and engineers and the starting date of the assignment. DB3 contains people's social security numbers and their home street maps stored in a graphical image system.

The data resources can be registered via the following HOSQL statements:

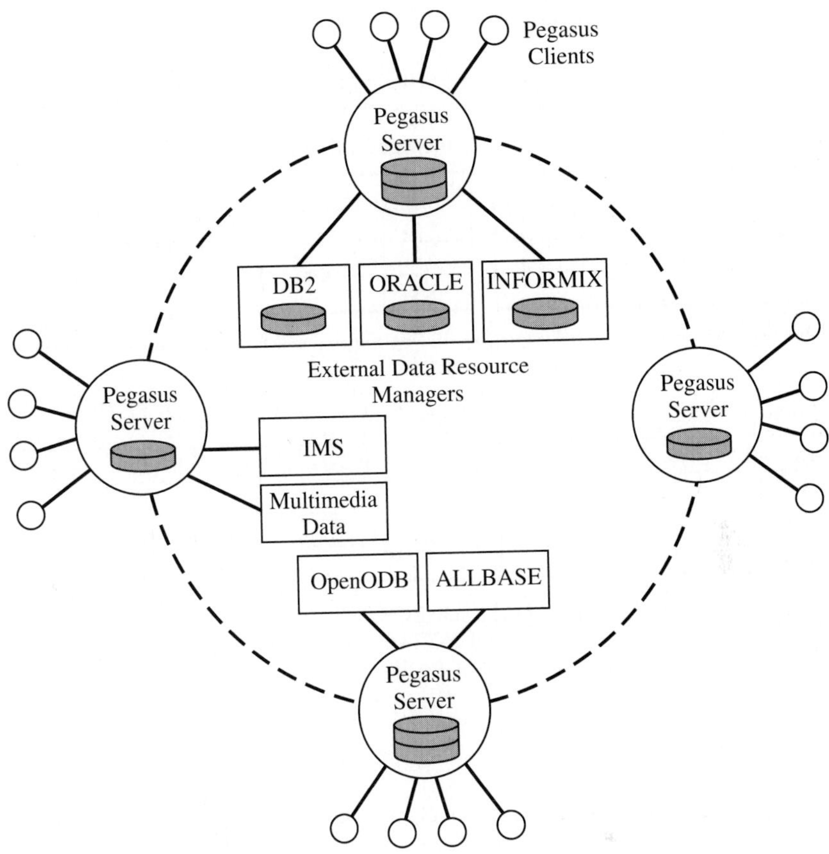

FIGURE 32–3
Pegasus Distributed System

```
REGISTER Relational IBM/DB2 DATASOURCE DB1 'Smith@host1'
     AS Pdb;
REGISTER Relational Oracle DATASOURCE DB2 'Fisher@host2'
     AS Edb;
REGISTER Multimedia Gis DATASOURCE DB3 'Victor@host3'
     AS Hdb;
```

These HOSQL statements provide information such as the external data system type, data resource name, external host system, and login id.

32.4.2 Schema Importation

Once an external data resource is registered, its data can be selectively made accessible from Pegasus by importing its schema into Pegasus. The import process generates a Pegasus schema that captures the semantics of the schema of the external data being made accessible. Pegasus can import

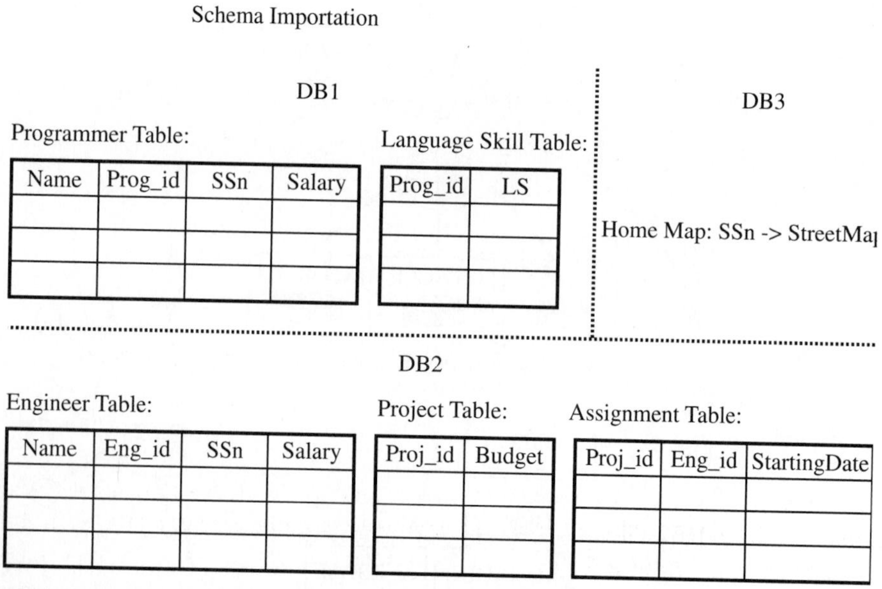

Schema Importation

DB1

Programmer Table:

Name	Prog_id	SSn	Salary

Language Skill Table:

Prog_id	LS

DB3

Home Map: SSn -> StreetMa

DB2

Engineer Table:

Name	Eng_id	SSn	Salary

Project Table:

Proj_id	Budget

Assignment Table:

Proj_id	Eng_id	StartingDate

REGISTER Relational IBM/DB2 DATASOURCE DB1 'Smith@host1' AS Pdb;
REGISTER Relational Oracle DATASOURCE DB2 'Fisher@host2' AS Edb;
REGISTER Multimedia Gis DATASOURCE DB3 'Victor@host3' AS Hdb;

FIGURE 32–4
Example Databases

external schemas defined in various data models. An imported schema contains constructs with definitions of derived data, much like relational views, but defining constructs in the Pegasus model whose extensions are derived from the external data.

Pegasus provides two data-definition facilities to construct imported schemas: *imported types* and *imported functions*. An imported type defines the existence of its instances according to a rule, the *producing expression*, based on some literal-valued property. The producing expression is evaluated whenever instances of the imported type need to be determined. An imported type generates objects corresponding to values currently existing in an external data source.

The attribute and relationship information of objects are imported via imported functions, which define the mapping onto the data stored in external data sources.

The following example illustrates the use of HOSQL statements for type and function importation of DB1 and DB3:

```
CREATE TYPE Programmer AS
IMPORTED FROM Relational DATASOURCE Pdb RELATION Programmer
PRODUCING BY (Prog_id)
```

```
FUNCTIONS (Programmerid INTEGER UNIQUE AS MATCHING Prog_id;
          Ssno INTEGER UNIQUE AS MATCHING SSn;
          Name CHAR AS MATCHING Name;
          Salary INTEGER AS MATCHING Salary);

CREATE FUNCTION Lskill (Programmer p) -> SETTYPE (CHAR y)
AS IMPORTED FROM Relational DATASOURCE Pdb RELATION
    Language_Skill
(Programmerid(p) AS MATCHING Prog_id;
 y AS MATCHING LS);

CREATE TYPE HomeMap
AS IMPORTED FROM Multimedia DATASOURCE Hdb FILE hmapfile
PRODUCING BY (SSn)
FUNCTIONS (Ssno INTEGER UNIQUE AS MATCHING SSn;
          Streetmap GRAPHICS AS MATCHING StreetMap);
```

Similarly, we can create two imported types (i.e., `Engineer` and `Project`) on DB2. The relationship between engineers and projects can be imported as a function defined below:

```
CREATE FUNCTION WorksOn (Engineer e) -> SETTYPE (Project p)
AS IMPORTED FROM Relational DATASOURCE Edb RELATION
    Assignment
(Engineerid(e) AS MATCHING Eng_id;
 Projectid(p) AS MATCHING Proj_id);
```

There will be one instance of an imported type for each distinct value in the set determined by its producing expression. The current implementation of Pegasus supports only the specification of a candidate key of the corresponding external data in the producing expression. In the future, it will be extended to support a query specification returning distinct values.

Object identifiers (OIDs) are generated for instances of imported types. In current implementation, they are constructed using a *prefix* associated with the imported type and a *suffix* from the value set of its producing expression.

In Pegasus, imported types are assumed to be disjoint on instances, unless it is declared explicitly via an HOSQL OVERLAP statement or implied by the supertype/subtype relationship. Pegasus will assign the same prefix to nondisjoint types, and therefore the same instance will have exactly the same OID within each type it belongs to.

Ideally, a Pegasus import schema should capture as much of the semantics of the imported data as possible in Pegasus constructs. This facilitates subsequent integration with other schemas, as well as enriching the model for the user.

One design objective of the Pegasus import facility is to develop efficient algorithms for automatic generation of Pegasus schemas that capture the useful semantics of a schema being imported. An importation utility has been implemented to convert relational schema into Pegasus schema. In addition to the SQL DDL statements, additional information regarding foreign keys and referential integrity constraints can be provided by users to facilitate the Pegasus schema generation. Details are described in Albert et al. 1993.

While such an automatically generated schema can serve as the default one, a user can explicitly use the HOSQL data definition facilities to create or modify any desired import schema.

32.5 Integration of Data

32.5.1 Object Equivalence

Even without an overlapping or supertype/subtype relationship declared, instances of two imported types may semantically represent the same object in the real world. A language facility is provided in Pegasus to support the equivalence specification of objects among multiple types. For example, from an application point of view, it may be desirable to treat a programmer from DB1 and an engineer from DB2 as the same person if they hold the same social security number. This can be done via the following HOSQL statement:

```
DEFINE OBJECT IDENTITY ON (Programmer p | Engineer e)
BY Programmer.Ssno(e) = Engineer.Ssno(p);
```

Current implementation supports the conjunctive form of multiple equality predicates in the BY clause of the object equivalence specification.

Note that circularly declared object equivalence relationships may lead to the equivalence of objects in the same type. This could complicate the process of determining object equivalence and seriously affect the run-time performance. Therefore, intratype equivalence is prohibited in Pegasus and an efficient algorithm has been developed to detect intratype equivalence specification [Ahmed 1993].

32.5.2 Function Value Reconciliation

Imported functions resulting from the import process faithfully reflect the external data sources, including any discrepancies in information values. A major task of data integration is the reconciliation of disparate information, such as a given person (as a programmer and an engineer) having inconsistent salaries or names stored in different databases (DB1 and DB2). In Pegasus, a reconciling facility is provided to resolve this type of inconsistency. For example, for a person with more than one income, it may be desirable to return the sum of his salaries from different sources. A reconciler can be defined via the following HOSQL statement:

```
DEFINERECONCILINGFUNCTIONSalary(Programmer|Engineer) ->REAL
DISAMBIGUATEDISAMB_SUM;
```

Similarly, a reconciler can be defined for Name function to return either all names associated with a person or the one recorded in the DB2 first.

```
DEFINE RECONCILING FUNCTION Name (Programmer | Engineer) ->
    BAGTYPE(CHAR)
DISAMBIGUATE DISAMB_ALL;
```

or

```
DEFINE RECONCILING FUNCTION Name (Programmer | Engineer) -> CHAR
DISAMBIGUATE DISAMB_BEST(Engineer);
```

Currently, Pegasus supports the following built-in disambiguators: DISAMB_ANY, DISAMB_ALL, DISAMB_AVG, DISAMB_MED, DISAMB_MODE, DISAMB_SUM, DISAMB_MAX, DISAMB_MIN, and DISAMB_BEST. User-supplied reconciler routines are planned to be supported in the future.

32.5.3 Schema Integration

To provide a unified view of related data, a mechanism is needed to collect the instances of several imported types into a single type. A *covering* supertype is introduced to serve this purpose. For example, a simple view consisting of a single type (e.g., Employee) for referencing all workers (e.g., engineers and programmers) in a company can be established by the following HOSQL statement.

```
CREATE TYPE Employee
AS COVERING SUPERTYPE OF Programmer, Engineer;
```

A covering supertype is a special kind of type having no immediate instances of its own. All its instances are instances of its subtypes. Only derived functions are allowed to be defined on a covering supertype. In particular, null-valued dummy functions can be defined. Note that, since all instances of a covering supertype are instances of one of its subtypes, all references to null-valued functions will be resolved onto references of functions defined on its subtypes, based on the function overloading mechanism, assuming appropriate reconciling functions are defined on the subtypes for value inconsistency resolution.

```
CREATE FUNCTION Salary (Employee e) -> REAL AS NULL;
CREATE FUNCTION Estreetmap (Employee e) -> GRAPHICS g
AS HOSQL
```

```
SELECT g FOR EACH Homemap m
WHERE Ssno(e) = Ssno(m) and g = Streetmap(m);
```

This completes the integration process in Pegasus.

It is worth mentioning that a function renaming mechanism is also used in Pegasus to facilitate the integration process in two ways: (1) for imported functions with different names that should be logically the same, renaming using the same name will ease the integration process; (2) for imported functions with different semantics but accidentally the same name, renaming will eliminate unnecessary conflicts.

32.6 Query Processing

Pegasus has the capability of a general purpose database management system. It provides a uniform schema and the appearance of a single system, enabling the user to retrieve information from multiple external data sources through a query expressed in HOSQL.

The component structure of query manager is shown in Fig. 32–2. During query processing, an HOSQL query is first parsed and converted into an internal form, called the F-tree, which contains references to Pegasus objects, types, and functions. Query manager takes the F-tree as input and, after going through several phases, converts it into an optimized execution plan, called the E-tree, which contains a set of subqueries and operations to be performed on their results. The E-tree is then interpreted by the query evaluator to assemble the final answer of the query. The intermediate phases involve the following.

The query manager performs the usual catalog lookup and view resolution first. It converts the F-tree into a B-tree (i.e., Binding-tree), which represents the query in an extended relational algebra form. The type and function names referenced in the F-tree are converted into names of imported types or functions that correspond to data stored in EDRMs.

Complex queries containing unions, derived functions, and subqueries are simplified. In addition, semantic rules are applied to convert full outerjoins into one-sided outerjoins and merge outerjoins and joins into joins [Du and Shan 1993].

If the data referenced in the B-tree resides in a single EDRM, no global query optimization is needed; otherwise, depending upon the availability of statistical information, either a cost-based or a heuristic-based query optimization is performed. In either case, the optimized tree, called O-tree, is then processed wherein each largest subtree processable by a single EDRM is converted into a single VT (virtual table) node representing the work to be handed to that EDRM. The resulting execution plan is specified as an E-tree.

The VT nodes in the E-tree define the sets of data retrieved from each EDRM. The appropriate query translators are called to translate the subqueries, constituting the data set of the VT nodes, into the native query languages of the involved EDRMs. This completes the E-tree generation.

32.6.1 Cost-Based Query Optimization

The process of cost-based query optimization is modeled by three characteristics: an execution space, a cost model, and a search strategy. For a heterogeneous DBMS environment, one main issue is the autonomy of EDRMs. This implies the lack of knowledge of the EDRM local query optimizer and control of the choice of execution plans for subqueries to be executed by each ERDM. The challenge is to design cost models for different EDRMs such that they can be used by the Pegasus query optimizer.

EDRM Calibration and Subquery Cost Estimation

In our approach, the external EDRMs are classified, in relationship to Pegasus, into three categories: proprietary, conforming, and nonconforming. An EDRM is called *proprietary* if its cost functions and database statistics are known to Pegasus; it is called *conforming* if its database statistics but not its cost functions are available to Pegasus; it is called *nonconforming* if neither its statistics nor its cost functions are fully available to Pegasus.

Instead of using cost formulae based on physical parameters such as page I/O and CPU time, we developed a set of cost formulae based on logical parameters such as data cardinality and selectivity. We believe that this is the only practical way to cope with the cost model issue in a heterogeneous system environment since the autonomy of an external EDRM prevents Pegasus from utilizing any internal system information in cost computation.

To facilitate the cost estimation of subquery execution, a set of calibrating databases and queries is designed to estimate the values of the coefficients in the cost formulae [Du et al. 1992]. These values are calculated to reflect most system-dependent factors such as hardware speed, operating system, and EDRM configurations. We also include a system weight factor in the cost formulae, which is adjustable by the DBA to reflect different EDRMs' accounting/work-load characteristics.

The data in the calibrating database is produced deterministically by a set of procedures. Each data set holds specific characteristics so that a specific set of queries can be used to compute a particular coefficient for each EDRM.

So far, we have calibrated four commercial relational systems: Allbase, DB2, Informix, and Oracle. The results of the experiments show that in all cases, the estimated costs-based calibrated data and the actual costs measured at run-time are within 10 percent. We are extrapolating our approach for nonconforming systems such as IMS and multimedia systems.

Our goal is to develop a unified mechanism to optimize queries referencing data stored in any kind of EDRM and develop a single general method to model the execution and cost of all EDRMs.

Outerjoins

In Pegasus, outerjoin is often needed to support the materialization of an integrated view (e.g., supertype and associated functions). Queries referencing an integrated schema (e.g., the `Employee` type mentioned in section 32.5.3) are usually translated into outerjoins of underlying schemas (e.g., the `Programmer` and `Engineer` tables). Outerjoins are expensive operators and usually hold no associative or commutative properties. However, the outerjoins introduced in Pegasus are often performed on unique attributes (e.g., ssn). By taking advantage of this property, several identities can be developed below:[1]

- $T1 \bowtie (T1 \Leftrightarrow T2) = T1 \Rightarrow T2.$
- $T1 \bowtie (T1 \Rightarrow T2) = T1 \bowtie T2.$
- $(T1 \Rightarrow T2) \bowtie T2 = T1 \bowtie T2.$

We are exploring additional identities and conditions under which the commutative and associative laws hold to facilitate query optimization.

Example

Consider the following query based on the schema developed in section 32.5.3:

```
SELECT Ssno(e), Name(e), Salary(e), Streetmap(e)
FOR EACH Employee e, Project p
WHERE p IN WorkOn(e) and Projectid(p) = 66;
```

Figure 32–5 shows the O-tree of the query after catalog lookup and regular steps of optimization. Each node in the O-tree is denoted by a node type corresponding to either an extended relational operation (e.g., the join operation) or a data source [e.g., the Data Source (DS) node]. A few new node types have been added to support schema integration (e.g., the reconciliation node).

In Pegasus, we conduct semantic analysis and convert operators to cheaper ones. In this example, the full outerjoin can be converted to left outerjoin since project information is available only on engineers, so a programmer who is not an engineer will not be qualified for the answer. We also explore the possibility of moving all joins and outerjoins into the same level by moving up reconciler operators. This will provide the optimizer

1. $\bowtie$ denotes join. $\Leftrightarrow$ denotes full outerjoin. $\Leftarrow$ denotes left outerjoin. $\Rightarrow$ denotes right outerjoin.

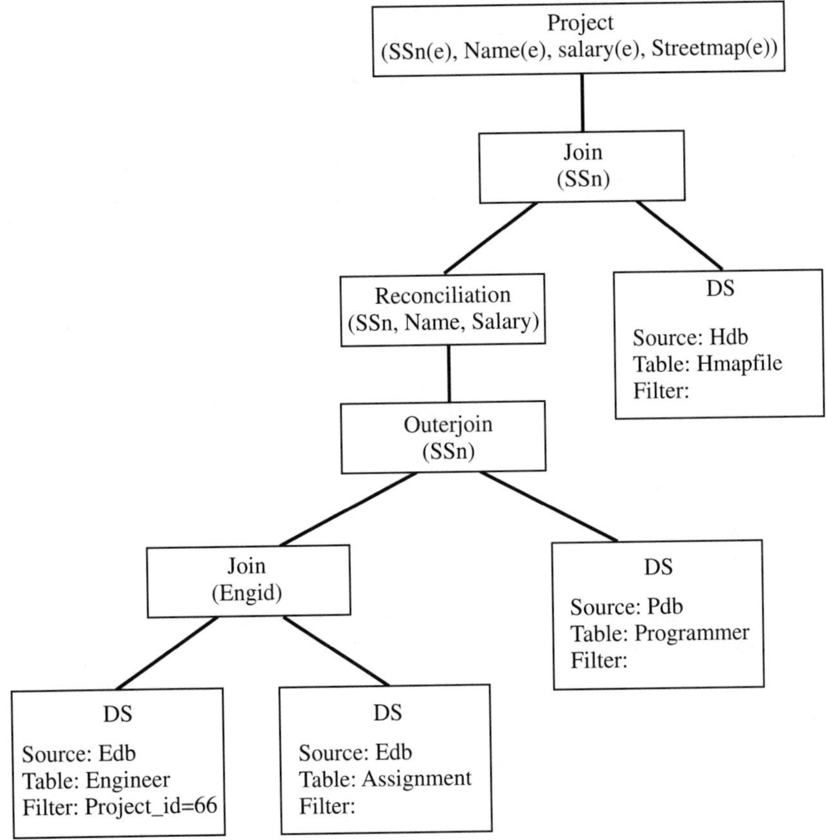

FIGURE 32–5
Preliminary Optimized Tree

more freedom for join/outerjoin order selection. Again, in this example, since both the left outerjoin and the join are performed on the same unique attribute (i.e., ssn), the following identity holds. This provides the query optimizer with two choices on the order of performing the join and left outerjoin.

$$(VT1 \Leftarrow VT2) \bowtie VT3 = (VT1 \bowtie VT3) \Leftarrow VT2$$

After the execution plan has been computed, the nodes in a subtree corresponding to data residing in one EDRM are merged into a VT node. The appropriate query translator is then called to formulate a query in the native language of the underlying EDRM for each VT node. This completes the query compilation. The final E-tree is shown in Fig. 32–6.

Once we complete our current prototype, we plan to pursue related areas to improve performance, such as data caching, collection of run-time statistical data, and a postoptimization process that analyzes the execution

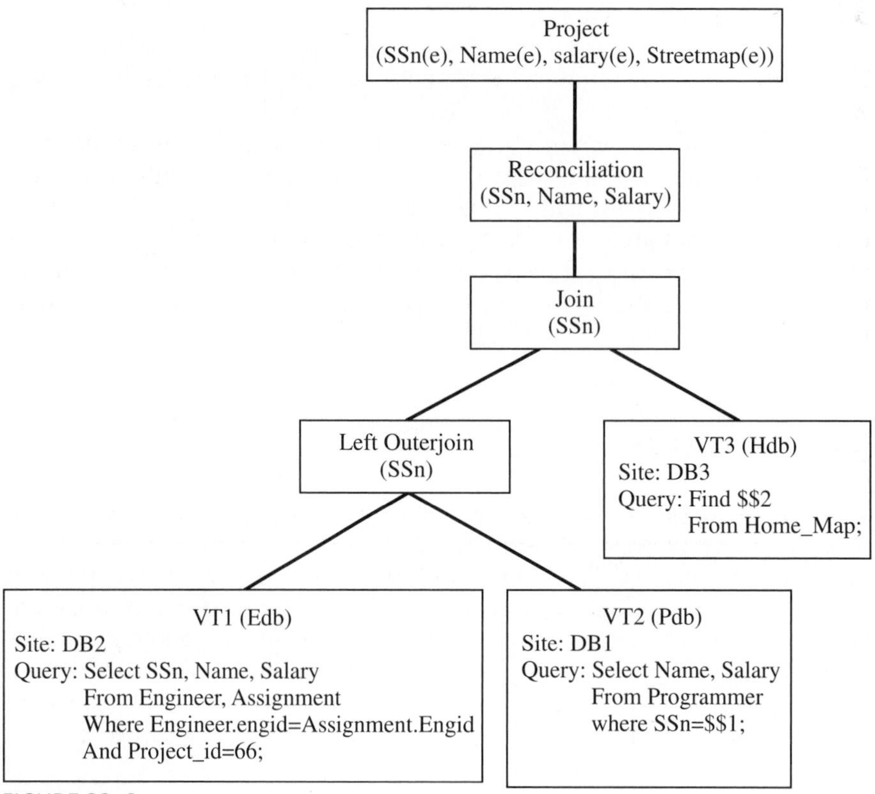

FIGURE 32–6
Execution Tree

plan and converts it into a cost-equivalent plan with faster response time by introducing more parallel executions among tasks.

32.6.2 Heuristic-Based Query Optimization

If a given query references external databases that do not provide adequate information for cost-based query optimization, or if an ad hoc query is executed only once and cost-based optimization would be expensive, a set of heuristic rules, called the *decomposition algorithm* [Ahmed et al. 1991], is used to generate an execution plan.

It analyzes the interdependencies between functions within a given query and groups the related functions belonging to the same database in a single subquery. This minimizes invocations of EDRMs since a single subquery, instead of multiple imported function evaluation, is sent to each EDRM. This also allows each EDRM to compute the optimal execution plan for the subquery, assuming the best utilization of its storage-access mechanisms.

32.6.3 Query Evaluation

The E-tree is executed concurrently by Pegasus and various Pegasus agents, with synchronization on required data.

The non-leaf nodes of an E-tree perform sorting, joins, outer joins, GROUP BY, subqueries, aggregate and simple functions. Only leaf nodes (i.e., VT nodes) are evaluated by a Pegasus agent at the location of their data. Other nodes are evaluated by Pegasus at the Pegasus site. This avoids excessive data movement, keeps the Pegasus agent code simple, and allows for extensibility in the set of reconcilers and computed and aggregate functions available to the DBA and end user.

32.7 Conclusions

The Pegasus project is investigating and prototyping a heterogeneous information management system to facilitate enterprise information access and operation management. Our first prototype was completed in November 1991 and demonstrated the integration of two HP/Allbase relational systems and a GIS system. Currently, we are working on our second prototype, supporting all functionalities described in this chapter. The first phase of this prototype is scheduled to be completed by December 1993. We expect to continue the research and prototype effort until a product is released.

REFERENCES

Ahmed, R. 1993. Detection of Intra-Type Equivalence—A Simplified Approach. Hewlett Packard Technical Report, June.

Ahmed, R., Rafii, A., Du, W., DeSmedt, P., and Shan M. 1991. Multidatabase Query Processing in Pegasus. Technical Report.

Albert, J., Ahmed, R., Ketabchi, M., Kent, W., and Shan M. 1993. Automatic Importation of Relational Schema in Pegasus. *Proceedings of the Third International Workshop on Research Issues in Data Engineering: Interoperability in Multidatabase Systems,* Vienna.

Astrahan, M., et al. 1980. System R: A Relational Approach to Database Management. *ACM Transaction on Database Systems,* Vol. 5, No. 4.

Bernstein, P., Hsu, M., and Mann, B. 1990. Implementing Recoverable Requests Using Queues. *Proceedings of the ACM-SIGMOD International Conference on Management of Data,* Atlantic City.

Chou, H., Dewitt, D., Katz, R., and Klug, A. 1985. Design and Implementation of the Wisconsin Storage System. *Software—Practice and Experience,* Vol. 15, No. 10.

Dayal U., Garcia-Molina, H., Hsu, M., Kao, B., and Shan, M. 1993. Database Challenges: Third Generation TP Monitors. *Proceedings of the ACM-SIGMOD International Conference on Management of Data,* Washington, D.C.

Dayal, U., Hsu, M., and Ladin, R. 1991. A Transactional Model for Long-Running Activities. *Proceedings of the Seventeenth International Conference on Very Large Data Bases*, Barcelona.

Dayal, U., and Shan, M. 1993. Operation Flow Management for Long-Running Activities. *Data Engineering Bulletin*, June.

Du, W., Krishnamurthy, R., and Shan, M. 1992. Query Optimization in a Heterogeneous DBMS. *Proceedings of the Eighteenth International Conference on Very Large Data Bases*, Vancouver.

Du, W., and Shan, M. 1993. Critical Issues of Query Optimization in Heterogeneous Databases. *Proceedings of the Fifth International Workshop on Foundations of Models and Languages for Data and Objects Databases: Optimization in Databases*, Aigen, Austria.

Elmagarmid, A. 1992. *Database Transaction Models for Advanced Applications*. Morgan Kaufmann, San Mateo, Cal.

Fishman, D., et al. 1987. Iris: An Object-Oriented Database Management System. *ACM TOOIS*, Vol. 5, No. 1.

Hewlett-Packard. 1992. *OpenODB Reference Document*. Part No. B2470A- 90001.

IBM. 1992. *Information Warehouse: An Introduction*. Publication No. GC26-4876.

Kent, W. 1991. Solving Domain Mismatch and Schema Mismatch Problems with an Object-Oriented Database Programming Language. *Proceedings of the Seventeenth International Conference on Very Large Data Bases*, Barcelona.

Krishnamurthy, R., Litwin, W., and Kent, W. 1991. Language Features for Interoperability of Databases with Schematic Discrepancies. *Proceedings of the ACM-SIGMOD International Conference on Management of Data*, Denver.

Lu, H., and Shan, M. 1992. Global Query Optimization in Multidatabase Systems. *Proceedings of the NFS Workshop on Heterogeneous Databases and Semantic Interoperability*, Boulder.

Nippon Telegraph and Telephone Corporation. 1991. *Multivendor Integration Architecture*, January.

Object Management Group. 1991. The Common Object Request Broker: Architecture and Specification. OMG Document no. 91.12.1.

Shan, M. 1993. Pegasus Architecture and Design Principles. *Proceedings of the ACM-SIGMOD International Conference on Management of Data*, Washington, D.C.

Sheth, A., and Kalinichenko, L. 1992. Information Modeling in Multidatabase Systems: Beyond Data Modeling. *Proceedings of the First Conference on Information and Knowledge Management*.

Transarc. 1991. *Encina Toolkits Administration: Programmer's Guide and Reference*.

Wagner, M. 1992. A New Class of Software. *Open System Today*, No. 113.

33

Overview of the ADDS System

YURI BREITBART
TOM REYES

Amoco Distributed Database System (*ADDS*) is a multidatabase system that allows users to retrieve and update semantically related data from multiple database sources located in a distributed heterogeneous hardware and software environment. ADDS does not require any changes in preexisting applications or in local DBMS software. It shields users from a need to know either the location or the internal structure of local DBMS data or details of local systems in accessing the local data. ADDS guarantees a consistent and efficient as well as a quick and dirty access to the data. This chapter describes the ADDS data integration model, the ADDS system architecture, and ADDS query optimization. The system has been designed and implemented at Amoco Production Research and was used there on an experimental basis.

33.1 Introduction

The present data processing situation is characterized by the growing number of applications that require accessing and manipulating data from various *preexisting* and *autonomous* data sources located in *heterogeneous* hardware and software environments distributed among nodes of the computer network.

The data sources are *preexisting* in the sense that they were created independently, in an uncoordinated way without a consideration that one day they might need to be integrated. The DBMSs involved are *heterogeneous* in the sense that they may use different underlying data models and different data definition and data manipulation facilities and may operate in different operating environments. Semantically identical data contained in heterogeneous data sources may have different physical and logical data representation and even different data values. The data sources are *autonomous* in the sense that they are managed by different software and management policies, neither of which should be required to change in order to facilitate the data integration process.

If an application needs the data located in heterogeneous data sources, it needs to know for each data source physical data location, data item names for the data at the local site, data formats for required data items, and local query language used at the data location. Users should be able to prepare transactions to access data at each data source or use vendor's tools for data access. Furthermore, users should prepare programs to manipulate and merge data retrieved from various sources. An attractive alternative to a development of such applications is to provide users with tools to access and manipulate data from different data sources. Such tools are called *multidatabase systems* [Sheth and Larson 1990].

Amoco Distributed Database System (*ADDS*) [Breitbart and Tieman 1984] is a multidatabase system that allows users to retrieve and update semantically related data from multiple data sources distributed among nodes of a computer network. ADDS does not require any changes in preexisting users' applications or in local DBMS software. ADDS supports data access to hierarchical, network, and relational databases as well as to ordinary users' files.

The ADDS project was undertaken at Amoco Production Research in the mid-1980s. The ADDS project had the following goals:

1. Provide an SQL-compatible, easy-to-use query and data manipulation language as a part of the ADDS user interface.
2. Ensure global and local consistency of the integrated data sources in the presence of failures.
3. Ensure that preexisting applications at each local site remain operational in the integrated environment.
4. Minimize the ADDS system response time as well as the overhead incurred.

These goals were achieved in ADDS under the following constraints:

1. Each local data source retains complete autonomy in its management policies. A local DBMS has complete authority over a local data source. The ADDS system is not aware of local applications that are not under its control. It is not provided with any local DBMS control information (such as wait-for-graph, local DBMS transaction log, local schedule, etc.). No changes can be made to the local DBMS software to accommodate the ADDS system. A local DBMS is not able to distinguish between ADDS applications (called *global*) and local applications (i. e., applications executing at a local site outside of the ADDS control). A local DBMS at one site is not able to communicate directly with local DBMSs at other sites to synchronize an execution of a global application that is executing at several sites.
2. Data security constraints that are imposed on local sites should be maintained regardless of the ADDS system.

3. Each local DBMS integrated by the ADDS system should use the strict two-phase locking protocol (i.e., transaction locks are released only after the transaction aborts or commits) [Bernstein et al. 1987]. The local DBMS ensures freedom from a local deadlock.

4. No changes are required in preexisting local applications to make them compatible with ADDS applications.

The ADDS approach is to provide tools for a logical integration of the data needed by an application into one logical database [called *composite database* (*CDB*)]. Such integration creates the illusion of a single database system and hides from users the intricacies of different DBMSs and access methods. It shields users from a need to know either the location or the internal structure of local DBMS data, or details of local systems in accessing the local data. ADDS guarantees a consistent and efficient as well as a quick and dirty access to the data. ADDS users are provided with a relational interface to integrated data sources and are presented with a relational view of the data.

The integrated database permits users to retrieve and manipulate data simultaneously from several data sources using the ADDS query and data manipulation languages without knowing the specifics of the underlying data source's management programs. ADDS provides two relationally complete query languages: one based on an extended relational algebra [Codd 1979] and another an SQL-based query language [Corfman 1988].

ADDS design guarantees that the system is capable of integrating any new data source (under different DBMS) with minimal effort. Furthermore, the system is compatible with a variety of users' operating environments. It is achieved by separating a data source access module (called *server*) into two major parts: non-data source specific and data source specific. The data source specific access part should be written for each new DBMS being integrated into ADDS, while the non-data source specific part is common to all servers. The data source specific part of the server does not require extensive programming and thus any new DBMS can easily be integrated into ADDS.

ADDS concurrency control and recovery features ensure that ADDS data manipulation is consistent in a failure-prone database environment. It ensures local data source autonomy along with the coordination of execution of a user request at different local sites.

The ADDS system was designed and developed primarily in an IBM operating environment. Users access the system from either VM or MVS operating environments. The current version of ADDS, however, allows users to access data from UNIX workstations and PCs that use the DOS operating system. ADDS proved to be useful especially for engineering and scientific applications that need both business-oriented data located on mainframes and scientific data located on either workstations or supercomputer platforms.

The problems of heterogeneous database management systems were extensively addressed in the literature [Sheth and Larson 1990]. The first designed and implemented multidatabase system prototype was Multibase [Landers and Rosenberg 1982]. Multibase provides a uniform integrated interface for retrieving data from preexisting heterogeneous distributed databases. It uses a global schema to create an integrated view of the data. Multibase uses a functional data model and functional language, DAPLEX [Shipman 1981], to generate a global data model and to retrieve data from the integrated data sources, respectively. Multibase is strictly a retrieval system without any transaction management features. Several additional prototype systems are described in Thomas et al. 1990.

The remainder of this chapter describes the ADDS system. In the next section we describe the ADDS Schema integration model. Section 33.3 describes the ADDS system architecture and its major components. Section 33.4 describes ADDS query optimization. Section 33.5 concludes the chapter.

33.2 ADDS Schema Architecture

To insulate users from the data location and from local schema and system details, ADDS provides users with a relational definition of the integrated data sources expressed in the ADDS data definition language. This is achieved by defining a composite database as a set of preexisting data sources where each data source is described as a set of relations in the ADDS SQL-compatible data definition language. All data incompatibilities and/or inconsistencies are resolved by ADDS using information from definitions of physical data sources and their representations as ADDS relations.

In Breitbart et al. 1986, we described in detail our approach to defining a global database and resolving semantic inconsistencies that such integration may create. Here we review an integration process illustrating it with the following example. Consider an oil engineer who needs results of tests conducted on samples taken from oil wells at a certain depth. The test results are distributed among three databases each located at a different company location. One data source is a hierarchical database containing information about oil permeability, porosity, and oil saturation tests performed on samples taken from a well at the indicated depth. Another data source is again a hierarchical database containing oil well number, well name, well owner, and state where the well is located. For each well, the database contains a list of geological formations that the well is drilled through, and for each geological formation, the database contains compressibility test results conducted on samples taken from the indicated well. The third data source is a relational database that contains porosity and grain density test results performed on samples taken from the indicated well at the indicated depth. The three databases were developed by three

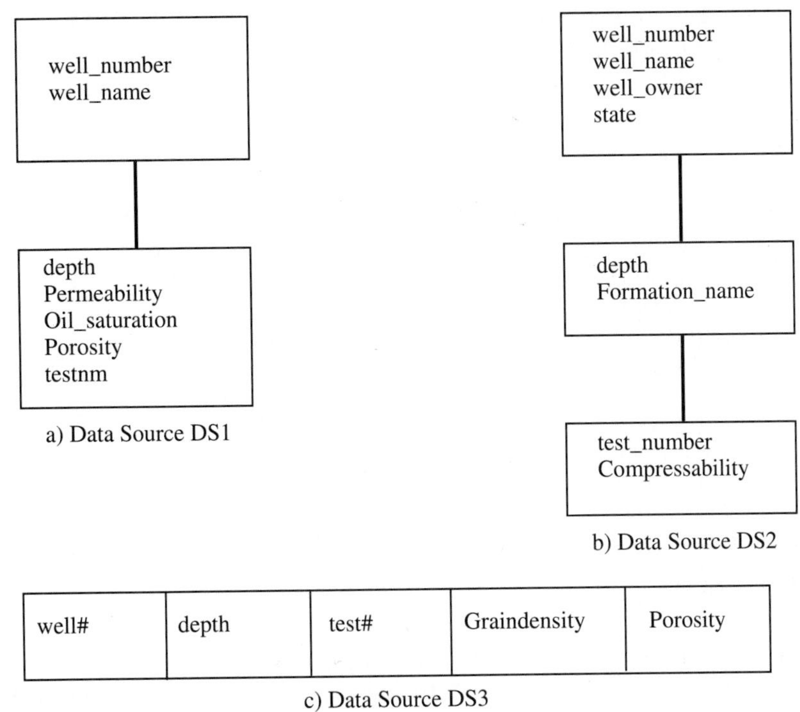

FIGURE 33–1
Example of Data Sources Integrated with ADDS System

independent user groups. Figure 33–1 depicts the data sources from which the information is being sought.

Each local data source, along with its network address and the DBMS used by the source, is called *a logical database (LDB)*. To access the information from these three sources, the user should define a composite database (CDB) using the ADDS data definition language. A CDB in ADDS is defined from two viewpoints. On one hand, a CDB is a set of logical databases that constitutes a single database as far as the user is concerned. On the other hand, a CDB is also seen as a set of relations defined on a set of logical data fields.

A CDB is designed from preexisting data sources and uniquely named by the CDB designer using the data definition DEFINE CDB statement. A CDB definition for our example is shown in Fig. 33–2. The first line of the definition contains the name under which the CDB will be registered in the ADDS directory. The next several lines define logical data fields and their attributes. Each logical data field (LF) is obtained as a generalization of the semantically related data fields of the physical data sources being integrated. The CDB designer makes a determination of whether two physical data fields from two different data sources are semantically related and, if they are, what logical attributes should be assigned to the logical data field into

```
DEFINE CDB TEST-DATA
    (WELLNUM       char (10)    key    nonull,
     WELNAME       char (20)                 ,
     DEPTH         float                     ,
     PERMEABILITY  float                     ,
     SATURATION    float                     ,
     POROSITY      float                     ,
     WELLOWN       char (10)                 ,
     STATE         char (2)                  ,
     FORMATION     char (30)                 ,
     TESTNUM       integer                   ,
     COMPRESS      float                     ,
     GAINDENSITY   float                     )
LDB
    (DS1   IMS    mycity.mycompany.com,
     DS2   IMS    city1.mycompany.com,
     DS3   SQL    city2.mycompany.com);
```

FIGURE 33–2
ADDS Definition of the TEST-DATA CDB

which they are mapped. Each LF is characterized by name, length, and data attribute (integer, character, etc.). In addition, for each logical data field, the CDB designer provides an indication whether the field can serve as a key for any CDB relation as well as whether it can contain non-null values. The LF name is unique within a CDB.

The LF list is followed in the CDB definition with a list of LDB definitions comprising the CDB. For each LDB, the definition contains the LDB name (assigned by the CDB designer), the name of the DBMS with which the physical data source associated with the LDB is managed, and the network address of the local data source associated with the LDB. Each LDB name is also unique within a CDB definition. In our example, the *TEST-DATA* CDB contains three LDBs and twelve logical data fields.

Recall that each LDB in ADDS is associated with a unique physical data source. ADDS requires that the fragment of a physical data source that is used by the application be defined as a part of a composite database. Each such fragment, called a physical database (PDB), is fully characterized in ADDS by the physical database name under which it is registered in a local DBMS and the local DBMS-dependent information that uniquely identifies the physical database within the DBMS. A PDB definition also includes information on how to access the data as well as physical data fields and their characteristics.

Each physical data field is mapped to one of the logical data fields defined in the `DEFINE CDB` statement. For example, the data field *`WELL-NUMBER`* from the first IMS data source is mapped to the logical data field *`WELLNUM`*. If attributes of a physical data field *X* are different from those of a

```
DEFINE PDB DATABASE1 ACCESS-PROG-1
    (WELL-NUMBER  char (10)   key  nonull  as   WELLNUM,
     WELL-NAME    char (15)                as   WELNAME,
     DEPTH        float                    as   DEPTH,
     PERMEABILITY float                    as   PERMEABILITY,
     SATURATION   float                    as   SATURATION,
     POROSITY     float                    as   POROSITY,
     TESTNUM      integer                  as   TESTNUM )
 FOR CDB TEST-DATA
 FOR LDB DS1
```

FIGURE 33–3
ADDS Definition of One of the PDBs for TEST-DATA

logical data field *Y* to which *X* is mapped, then ADDS performs a data transformation to comply with the logical data field definition. Figure 33–3 illustrates a PDB definition for the first IMS data source in the *TEST-DATA* CDB. In the example, the PDB shown in Fig. 33–3 defines the IMS data source as a set of physical fields with a logical data field it is mapped to. In effect, each PDB can be considered as a universal relation defined on a physical data source.

The first line of the definition indicates that the data source is known to IMS as *DATABASE1* and it can be accessed by a local application program *ACCESS-PROGRAM-1*. The next several lines define physical data fields of the IMS database that can be accessed by the user of the *TEST-DATA* CDB. Each data field is identified by its local name along with its attributes as they are defined in the local database. The last two lines of the PDB definition identify the CDB and LDB to which the PDB belongs.

The set of all PDBs comprises ADDS data items. Each data item in ADDS is assigned a unique data item identification by the ADDS system. Every data item in ADDS is either updatable by ADDS transactions or can be updated only outside of the ADDS system by local transactions. In the latter case, such data item is called *locally updatable*, while in the former, *globally updatable*. No ADDS data item can be both locally and globally updatable. This is one of the major restrictions of the ADDS system. The restriction is adopted to guarantee global atomicity and global serializability in a failure-prone multidatabase environment [Breitbart et al. 1992]. On the other hand, if each local DBMS implements the two-phase commit protocol, then the above restriction is not required. In this case, however, each local database administrator must abide by the rules of the two-phase commit protocol, and as a result no global transaction in the prepared state can be aborted by the local database administrator.

The user views a CDB as a collection of relations defined on the set of the CDB's logical data fields. Relations are defined by the CDB designer in such a way that no relation can span PDB boundaries. A PDB, in turn, is semantically equivalent to a natural join of relations defined for the PDB.

```
DEFINE RELATION SR1  (WELLNUM key nonull, WELNAME, DEPTH,
                      TESTNUM, PERMEABILITY, POROSITY,
                      SATURATION)
FOR CDB TEST-DATA
FOR LDB DS1
FOR PDB DATABASE1

DEFINE RELATION SR2  (WELLNUM key nonull, WELNAME, STATE,
                      WELLOWN, DEPTH, FORMATION, TESTNUM)
FOR CDB TEST-DATA
FOR LDB DS2
FOR PDB DATABASE2

DEFINE RELATION SR3  (WELLNUM key nonull, DEPTH, TESTNUM,
                      GRAINDENSITY, POROSITY)
FOR CDB TEST-DATA
FOR LDB DS3
FOR PDB DATABASE3
```

FIGURE 33–4
ADDS Definition of Relations for TEST-DATA CDB

Each CDB's relation is defined uniquely for a single PDB within a CDB. Figure 33–4 illustrates ADDS relation definitions for the *TEST-DATA* CDB.

ADDS provides users with view capabilities. Users can define a view on a CDB by means of either an extended relational algebra [Codd 1979] or SQL language expressions. If, for example, a user of TEST-DATA uses only data on oil wells owned by his or her company, then the following view MYWELLS can be defined:

```
DEFINE VIEW MYWELLS
AS
Select *
From SR1, SR2, SR3
Where WELLOWN = "My-Company" and
SR1.WELLNUM = SR2.WELLNUM and
SR1.WELLNUM = SR3.WELLNUM
```

The information from the ADDS application schema definition (CDB, PDB, Relations, and View statements) is stored in the ADDS directory. The ADDS directory contains six basic tables shown along with the directory structure in Fig. 33–5. The composite database table contains the names of CDBs and their descriptions. In addition, it contains the name of the user who designed the CDB and the numbers of LDBs, PDBs, relations, and physical and logical data fields that the CDB consists of.

The logical data fields table contains descriptions of all logical data fields along with their attributes for all CDBs defined in ADDS. In addition,

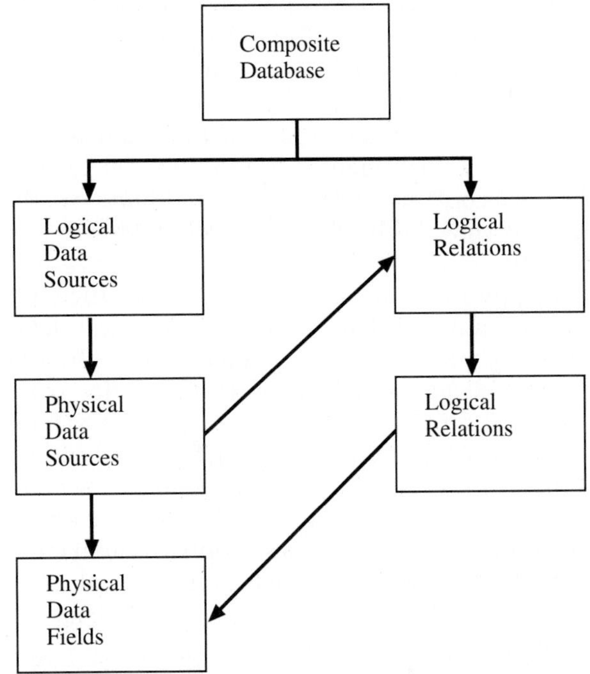

FIGURE 33–5
ADDS Directory Structures

it contains information about the number of different values of the field for a specified CDB and the maximum and minimum values of the field in the CDB.

The logical data sources table contains the names and descriptions of LDBs for all ADDS CDBs. For each LDB, the table also contains the name of the LDB's DBMS as well as the LDB network address. In addition, for each LDB in the table, a parameter is defined that indicates the relative difficulty of the DBMS in working with the data. The parameter is used by the optimizer to make a decision about the access strategy. The DBMSs with lesser difficulty are accessed before DBMSs with greater values for this parameter. The value of the parameter is assigned by the CDB designer based on available information about local data processing performance patterns. For example, assume that the company has two data sources: One is under IMS DBMS and another is under the Oracle DBMS. If a CDB designer has information that the data source under IMS is large and that the physical data source of interest to a user does not have any indexes, he or she may choose to assign a higher level of difficulty to the IMS data source. In doing so, the CDB designer adopts an access strategy that requires one first to access the Oracle data source and use the data obtained from the Oracle data source to reduce the search in the IMS data source. The relative difficulty parameter is highly subjective and can be changed by the database administrator as more information is received about data sources comprising the CDB as well as the access patterns of users' queries.

Information about CDB's relations are stored in the logical relations table. For each relation, the table contains a tuple defining a relation name, its creator, and its description. CDB views are also recorded in the table. Thus each entry in the table contains a relation type indicating whether it is a logical relation or a CDB view. Each relation is associated with a unique PDB name for a given CDB.

Information about physical data sources (PDBs) and their physical data fields is stored in the physical data sources and physical data fields tables, respectively. For each PDB, there is a tuple in the physical data source table that contains all physical database names under which the source is known at the local site. It also contains statistics on the approximate size of the PDB in the CDB for which it is defined. All information required by the local DBMS to access the PDB is also stored in the table.

The physical data fields table contains information about each physical data field that is defined for a given CDB. It also contains the name of the logical data field on which the physical data field is mapped. If a local site contains an index for the physical data field at the site, then the name of the index is also stored for that physical data field.

The ADDS directory also contains information about all users authorized to use ADDS, and for each authorized ADDS user the ADDS directory contains a list of all CDBs and views the user is authorized to access. The ADDS directory is used to resolve various data incompatibilities and/or inconsistencies between data located at different local sites. This is done by invoking conversion routines to convert data retrieved from local sites. Local data values of the physical data field are converted to comply with the attributes of the logical data field to which the physical data field is mapped.

33.3 ADDS System Architecture

The ADDS system consists of a user interface, a compiler, an optimizer, a transaction manager (sometimes called a taskmaster or *TM* in this chapter), a data manager, and a set of servers, as shown in Fig. 33–6.

We illustrate the functioning of ADDS by following a user's request through the system. Imagine that the user wants to retrieve oil well names and test results conducted on samples taken from wells owned by the user's company at a depth between 1500 and 1550 feet from the `TEST-DATA` CDB. Using the ADDS user interface, the user prepares the following query in the ADDS query language:

```
Select WELNAME, DEPTH, TESTNUM, POROSITY, PERMEABILITY,
SATURATION, GRAINDENSITY, COMPRESS
```

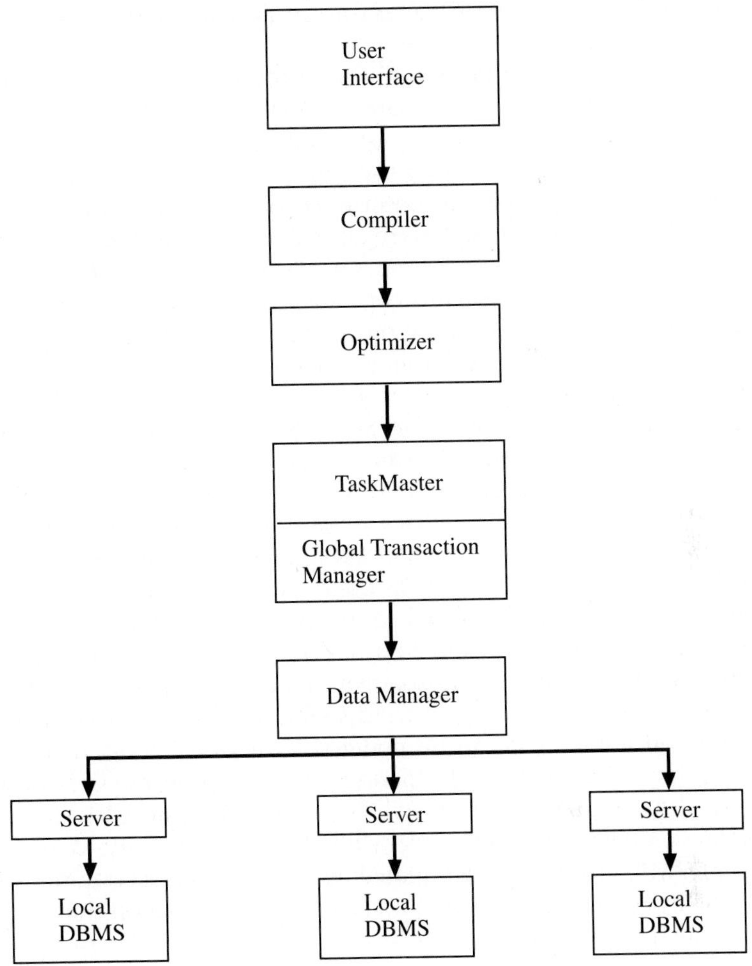

FIGURE 33–6
ADDS Component Architecture

```
From SR1, SR2, SR3
Where WELLOWN = "MYCOMPANY" and SR1.DEPTH ≤ 1550 and
SR1.DEPTH ≥ 1500 and SR1.WELLNUM = SR2.WELLNUM and
SR1.WELLNUM = SR3.WELLNUM and SR1.DEPTH = SR2.DEPTH
and SR1.DEPTH = SR3.DEPTH and SR1.TESTNUM = SR2.TESTNUM
and SR1.TESTNUM = SR3.TESTNUM.
```

After the user's request (called a *global transaction)* is received, it is submitted to the ADDS user interface module. The *user interface* first verifies whether the user is authorized to use ADDS, and if he or she is authorized, it verifies the user's authority to access and maintain the data that the user specified in the ADDS transaction. In our example, the user interface verifies whether the user is allowed to access `TEST-DATA` CDB and whether within that CDB the user is allowed to access the physical databases on which SR1, SR2, and SR3 are defined.

In addition to the verification function, the ADDS *user interface* permits users to inquire about operating characteristics of the system. For example, the user may request to select the list of all CDBs for which he or she is authorized. The *user interface* allows users to inquire about the current user's transaction status and execution information at each local site where the transaction is being executed. A user can submit a transaction and disconnect from the system. In such a case the user's transaction is executed in the background, enabling the user to continue with other work in the foreground. Periodically, the user may reconnect back to the transaction running in the background to check the transaction status.

The results of a transaction can be stored and/or directly loaded into predefined relations (say under the SQL/DS system). For frequently run queries and updates, the user can store the transaction in the ADDS transaction catalog for a further reuse.

If the user successfully passes an authorization check, the user's request is sent to the ADDS compiler. After receiving a user's request formulated as a statement in the ADDS query language, the ADDS compiler, using information in the ADDS directory, checks the syntactic correctness of the statement (that is considered as a transaction) and generates a tree of transaction operations. If a transaction operation requires an update of some ADDS relation, the compiler checks whether the relation is updatable in general and whether it can be updated by a global transaction. Some ADDS relations cannot be updated since they describe physical database entities of a local DBMS that are views as far as the local DBMS is concerned. Some other ADDS relations, while describing the physical database of a local DBMS, may still be designated by the local database administrator as only locally updatable. In such a case, any user transaction that attempts to update such relations is aborted.

For each ADDS statement in a user transaction, the compiler decomposes the ADDS statement into a set of single-site subtransactions that are passed to the ADDS query optimizer. The optimizer analyzes the parse tree along with the set of single-site subtransactions generated by the compiler and generates a set of temporary relations required to store intermediate transaction results. In our example, the set of subtransactions includes three SELECT statements — one for each site — with results stored in three temporary relations. To obtain the final result required by the user, two join operations on temporary relations must be performed. The optimizer determines a strategy to execute these retrieval and join operations to minimize both local processing and communication costs. In the next section, we describe the optimizer in more detail.

The set of subtransactions along with the transaction parse tree is sent to the taskmaster/transaction manager (*TM*). TM schedules each subtransaction that guarantees consistency of the integrated data sources. It allocates a server to the transaction in the site at which the subtransaction should be executed, provided that the transaction does not yet have a server at the site, and passes the subtransaction to the data manager to monitor the operation execution at the site.

One of the transaction manager's functions is to monitor execution of the transaction at local sites. In the case of read-only transactions, the transaction manager also performs a restart of the failed query at a local site. This is done as follows. After the transaction manager receives the information that a site has failed, it continues to process the query at other sites. After the site becomes operational, the query at that site is restarted at the point of failure. Thus ADDS achieves a minimal loss of information due to site failures. It should be noted, however, that query restart does not guarantee the same result as that which would have been obtained without the site failure. However, in many practical situations, query restart proved to be valuable and did not violate local database consistency.

The data manager sends the subtransaction to the transaction's server at a local site for execution and awaits results from the operation. If the operation fails for whatever reason, the data manager takes corrective actions to recover from the failure or aborts the transaction. Upon completion, the transaction results are passed to the user interface for display or loading in the user's work space.

The ADDS data manager is also responsible for managing all temporary relations that are required to store intermediate results obtained from local sites. The data manager is in fact a full-fledged relational data manager. It is capable of performing a wide variety of relational algebra operations to obtain the final result of a user's request. The data manager expands local systems with relational capabilities. For example, if a local system is not capable of performing a join operation between two relations, then the ADDS data manager performs the join after the local system retrieves data from the relations.

Each server is responsible for interactions with a local DBMS at the local site on behalf of a transaction. The server translates a subtransaction in the ADDS query language into the language of the local DBMS and submits the subtransaction to the local DBMS. In some cases, however, the server may find that the received subtransaction cannot be translated into the language of the local system due to the local system limitations. In such a case, the server splits the subtransaction into smaller pieces such that each piece can be handled by the local system and sends them back to the transaction manager for rescheduling.

The local DBMS considers a server as a separate transaction and does not know that it is a part of a global transaction. The server reports the results of the operation to the data manager. The server also keeps a server log of all update operations submitted to the local data source and data received from the local data source. After the transaction has completed, the server of each local subtransaction disconnects from the local DBMS.

33.4 ADDS Query Optimizer

Query optimization in a heterogeneous distributed database environment is a complicated problem. The complexity of the problem stems from the unavailability of local information that could be useful in deciding what strategy should be used for the query execution, the geographical distribution of local databases, and performance differences among different local systems. Nevertheless, the query optimization problem must be solved in order to make the system applicable in practical database environments. In this section, we describe the optimization strategy used in ADDS.

The main cost factors of concern in a heterogeneous database environment are local processing costs and communication costs involved in shipping local query results to another site for further processing (e.g., to join the data from two local sites). ADDS optimizes communication costs by using semijoins to minimize data transfer, and local costs are optimized by performing equivalent transformations to reduce the amount of local data to be retrieved from the local site.

The ADDS query optimizer does not try to improve or replace any optimization capabilities of the local DBMS and leaves all storage access path optimizations to the local DMBSs. Instead, ADDS concentrates on generating an efficient sequence of single-site subqueries that can be handled by the servers interfacing with the local DBMSs.

Recall that for each relational query submitted to ADDS, the ADDS compiler translates the query into an internal tree representation and passes it to the ADDS optimizer. The ultimate goal of the optimizer is to minimize query response time. To achieve this, the optimizer uses a variety of strategies described below:

1. A disjunctive query is transformed into a cardinality preserving `UNION` of subqueries.

   This transformation eliminates `OR` conditions in the `WHERE` clause and increases the number of selection conditions that can be pushed down the subquery trees. This transformation is not always desirable. For example, if the entire query can be executed by one local DBMS, then the transformation is not performed and optimization is left to the local system. Thus, the transformation is applied only if the query spans more than one local DBMS.

2. A query containing a sequence of associative and commutative binary relational operations is collapsed into an n-ary query tree. For example,

the join sequence `(JOIN r1 (JOIN r2 r3))` is collapsed into `(JOIN r1 r2 r3)`. This transformation provides the optimizer with a freedom to decide on the most efficient evaluation order for these n-ary operations.

3. Selection conditions are pushed up the query tree to allow the creation of new selection conditions. For example, the query

```
JOIN * (r1; SELECT * FROM r2 WHERE r2.x > 0)
WHERE r1.x = r2.x
```

may be transformed into

```
JOIN * (r1; r2) WHERE r2.x > 0 AND r1.x = r2.x AND r1.x > 0
```

The selection condition "r1.x > 0" is derived from the other two predicates. The reason to push selection conditions up is that it allows further distribution of these conditions among other parts of the query.

4. Selection conditions (supplied by the user and also derived using the previous rule) are pushed down the query tree. For example, the query

```
JOIN * (r1; r2) WHERE r2.x > 0 AND r1.x = r2.x AND r1.x > 0
```

may be transformed into

```
JOIN * (SELECT * FROM r1 WHERE r1.x > 0; SELECT * FROM r2
WHERE r2.x > 0) WHERE r1.x = r2.x
```

5. N-ary operations are transformed into a tree of binary operations. N-ary UNIONs are transformed into a complete binary tree of UNIONs to maximize parallelism. Finding the most desirable evaluation order for n-ary JOINs is a difficult problem. The ADDS query optimizer uses a simple heuristic to arrive at a desirable solution quickly. Given a list of candidate join operands, it repeatedly applies the following strategy to pick out two join operands whose result is then added to the candidate list until only two candidates are left:

a. Select an equi-join on two attributes that have local indexes on them.
b. In the absence of equi-join with two attributes with local indexes, select an equi-join on an attribute that has a local index on it.
c. If there are no equi-joins with attributes that have local indexes, select an equi-join that is amenable to semijoin optimization (i.e., at least one of the join operands is a SELECT subquery that retrieves data from one of the local databases).
d. If there are no equi-joins satisfying a or b or c, select any equi-join.
e. In the absence of equi-joins, select any join.
f. Cartesian products are executed only as a last resort.

6. An equi-join involving at least one SELECT subquery undergoes through a semijoin optimization. Semijoin optimization determines the most desirable equi-join condition and the semijoin direction. This determination is performed by the optimizer based on the statistical information collected by the optimizer and stored in the ADDS directory. For example, given the query

```
JOIN * (r1; r2)
WHERE r1.x = r2.x AND r1.y = r2.y
```

the semijoin optimizer determines whether to use "r1.x = r2.x" or "r1.y = r2.y" as the semijoin condition, based on the information from the directory on how many different data values data attributes *x* and *y* contain. In addition, it determines whether r1 or r2 will have its subquery search condition augmented by a semijoin predicate. If the chosen condition is "r1.x = r2.x" and its direction is toward r2, the following actions will be taken at query execution time:

a. The data manager will eliminate null and duplicate values on the joining column (r1.x) or r1's subquery result and make this set of semijoin values available to the server assigned to execute the r2 subquery.
b. The server for r2 uses the data manager supplied semi-join values for r1.x to modify r2's subquery predicate into

```
SELECT * FROM r2 WHERE r2.x IN (value1, value2, ...).
```

The semijoin optimizer applies a cost estimation strategy to try to pick a semijoin condition and direction that would yield the greatest data reduction. Semijoin optimization finds its greatest use in reducing the amount of data retrieved from huge IMS databases.

7. The partially optimized binary query tree is placed in a canonical order form to facilitate the detection of common subqueries. This transformation imposes a uniform ordering on commutative operations. For example, the query "UNION * (JOIN * (r2; r1); DIFF * (r4; 43))" and the query "UNION * (DIFF * (r4; r3); JOIN * (r2; r1))" can both be transformed into their equivalent canonical order form of "UNION * (DIFF * (r4; r3); JOIN * (r1; r2))".

8. Redundant subqueries are detected, eliminated, and replaced with references to their previously computed subqueries. Two subqueries are considered equal if and only if their query predicates, including any semijoin predicates, projected fields, and sort specifications, are equal, and their subquery operands or source relations are equal.

Under the equality conditions, the names of column references need not match, provided the same name is not bound to two different relation names in the resulting optimized query. Moreover, a subquery S1 whose projected fields are a subset of the projected fields of another subquery S2 is still considered equal to S2 if both S1 and S2 do not require elimination of duplicate tuples.

A bottom-up traversal of the query tree examines each node, testing it for equality against nodes that have traversed before. Projected fields of new nodes are expanded to increase the chances of future matches and are entered into a table of pairwise different subqueries for a given query.

9. Projections are pushed down the query tree to further reduce the amount of retrieved data and shrink the temporarily expanded list of projected fields in the surviving common subquery nodes.

10. Finally, the optimized query graph is broken up into schedulable single-site subqueries. This decomposition step decides where JOINs and other relational operations are done. In the simplest case, where all the leaf nodes in the query graph belong to one site, the entire query graph is packaged as one query for that site. At the other extreme is the case where each leaf node belongs to a different site and each node, whether a leaf or an internal node, becomes a schedulable subquery. In the current ADDS system, all schedulable internal nodes representing relational operations are done at the original query submission site.

This decomposition strategy deliberately makes the false assumption that all target DBMSs at all sites can handle all relational query operations. This strategy allows ADDS to exploit the optimization capabilities of highly optimized target DBMSs such as DB2 and SQL/DS by sending them maximal size subqueries. The servers that access less optimized DBMSs understand this strategy and will break up a complex query into a set of simpler subqueries. After decomposing a complex query, the server sends the set of simpler subqueries back to the taskmaster for rescheduling. Eventually, a complex query is broken up into

- retrieval subqueries that can be handled even by target DBMSs with no optimization capabilities
- relational operation subqueries that can be handled by the ADDS relational servers

The optimization algorithm implemented in the ADDS system has proven to be effective. For example, in a simple ADDS query that included the joining of two relations retrieved from two different local sites, the algorithm using strategy ten in the above description was able to reduce the response time by a factor of 2. We also conducted experiments with real user queries that included more than 10 common subqueries and retrieved data from three local sites with their subsequent join. In these cases applying strategies 8 and 10 of the algorithm we were able to reduce the query response times by a factor of 3.

33.5 Conclusions

This chapter presented an overview of the ADDS system developed at Amoco Production Research Center in the mid-1980s. The system provides a uniform relational access and manipulation of the data stored in heterogeneous database sources. We described here the ADDS approach to data integration, the ADDS system architecture, and the ADDS query optimization strategy. ADDS is designed to be easily extendable to integrate additional DBMSs by creating an additional server process. ADDS capabilities include the following:

- ADDS data definition language to define an integrated view of the data
- Relationally complete SQL-like query language to uniformly access and manipulate data from integrated heterogeneous data sources
- ADDS application program interface that allows users to access integrated data sources from application programs
- Ability to update data in heterogeneous data sources that ensures local and global data consistency

ADDS has been tested with a variety of *live* users applications and has gained wide acceptance by the user community within Amoco. It was used at at least four Amoco locations to retrieve data from several databases distributed among various company locations. At least one of these databases was a fairly large IMS database that contained several gigabytes of company data.

ACKNOWLEDGMENTS

This material is based in part upon work sponsored by the Center for Manufacturing and Robotics of the University of Kentucky, the National Science Foundation under grants No. IRI-8904932 and IRI-9221301, and a grant from Hewlett-Packard Corporation.

REFERENCES

Bernstein, P. A., Hadzilacos, V., and Goodman, N. 1987. *Concurrency Control and Recovery in Database Systems*. Addison-Wesley, Reading, Mass.

Breitbart, Y., Olson, P., and Thompson, G. 1986. Database Integration in a Distributed Heterogeneous Database System. *Proceedings of the International Conference on Data Engineering*, Los Angeles.

Breitbart, Y., Silberschatz, A., and Thompson, G. 1992. An Approach to Recovery Management in a Multidatabase System. *VLDB Journal*, Vol .1, No. 1.

Breitbart, Y., and Tieman, L. 1984. ADDS—Heterogeneous Distributed Database System. In: *Distributed Data Sharing Systems*. F. Schreiber and W. Litwin, eds. North Holland.

Codd, E. F. 1979. Extending the Database Relational Model to Capture More Meaning. *ACM Transaction on Database Systems,* Vol. 4, No. 4.

Corfman, M. 1988. Open SQL—ISO OSI Remote Database Access Standards. *Fourteenth International Conference on Very Large Data Bases,* Long Beach.

Landers, T., and Rosenberg, R. 1982. An Overview of Multibase. In: *Distributed Databases*. H. J. Schneider, ed. North-Holland.

Sheth, A., and Larson, J. A. 1990. Federated Databases: Attributes and Integration. *ACM Computing Surveys,* Vol. 22, No. 3.

Shipman, D. 1981. The Functional Data Model and the Data Language DAPLEX. *ACM Transaction on Database Systems,* Vol. 6, No. 1.

Thomas, G., Thompson, G., Chung, C. W., Barkmeyer, E., Carter, F., Templeton, M., Fox, S., and Hartman, B. 1990. Heterogeneous Distributed Database Systems for Production Use. *ACM Computing Surveys,* Vol. 22, No. 3.

Index